EUROPEAN DIARY
1977–1981

EUROPEAN DIARY

1977–1981

ROY JENKINS

COLLINS
8 Grafton Street, London W1
1989

William Collins Sons & Co. Ltd
London · Glasgow · Sydney
Auckland · Toronto · Johannesburg

BRITISH LIBRARY CATALOGUING IN PUBLICATION DATA

Jenkins, Roy *1920–*
European Diary, 1977–1981
1. Western Europe. Political events, 1970–
1989
I. Title
940.55'7

ISBN 0-00-217976-8

First published by William Collins 1989
Copyright © Roy Jenkins 1989

Set in Linotron Meridien by
Rowland Phototypesetting Ltd
Bury St Edmunds, Suffolk
Printed and bound in Great Britain by
Butler & Tanner Ltd, Frome and London

CONTENTS

LIST OF ILLUSTRATIONS

Between pages 78 and 79

Arriving at the Berlaymont in a winter dawn
Taking over from Ortoli
The new Commission at its first session
Addressing the European Parliament, January 1977
With Jennifer, Georges Spénale and Ludwig Fellermaier, January 1977
Greeting President Mobutu of Zaïre, January 1977
A European Council in London, June 1977 (*The Times*)
With Davignon, 1977
With Gundelach, 1979
Natali, Tugendhat, Giolitti and Vredeling, 1978

Between pages 238 and 239

Anthony Crosland in December 1976 (*Popperfoto*)
Jennifer with Secretary of State Vance, April 1977
President Carter visits Brussels, January 1978
With Chancellor Schmidt in Bonn, February 1978 (*Bundesbildstelle, Bonn*)
With President Giscard d'Estaing, June 1979 (*Jean Guyaux, Brussels*)
François Mitterrand on his Commission visit in May 1977
The King of the Belgians at the Berlaymont, 1977
Exchanging gifts with Prime Minister Fukuda, July 1978
The drawing room at rue de Praetère (*Christian Lambiotte, Brussels*)
East Hendred (*Joe Partridge*)

Between pages 438 and 439

Prime Minister Mário Soares in Brussels, March 1977
With Pierre Trudeau in Ottawa, March 1978
With the King of Spain in Madrid, April 1977 (*Juan Bautista de Toledo, Madrid*)
Willy Brandt in the Berlaymont, July 1978
A European Council in Brussels, December 1978 (*Bundesbildstelle, Bonn*)
At the Temple of Heaven, Peking, March 1979

Most of the unattributed photographs were provided by the Photo Library of the European Commission in Brussels to which the author and publishers are grateful.

PREFACE

The four years covered by this book are the only period of my life for which I have kept a narrative diary. I have fairly careful engagement diaries for the past forty years and from 1964 substantial chunks of unworked memoir raw material, dictated close to the event. But I had never previously (nor have I since) attempted a descriptive outline of each day in the calendar. However I decided that the Brussels years were likely to be a sharply isolated segment of my life, and that I might mark them by attempting this new exercise.

I found it fairly burdensome, for I am naturally a slow (and I like to think meticulous) manuscript writer and not a fluent dictater; and a slowly written manuscript diary was clearly not compatible with the scale of the task and the pattern of life which I was recording. However, I kept it up to the end, but was glad when it was done.

I dictated to a machine, sometimes within forty-eight hours of the events, but more typically a week or so later. When there was this sort of gap I worked from a detailed schedule of engagements. The tapes were then typed up and corrected by me during my next period of semi-leisure.

The result was a typescript of six hundred thousand words. About a quarter of these owed their existence to nothing more than the periphrasis of dictated work, and required pruning for any purpose. That left a total still more than twice as long as was convenient for one-volume publication. So I undertook a further two stages of stripping away. First I cut what was of least interest to me. And then, a more painful process, I cut what seemed to me and others to be of least interest to the likely reader.

The second stage involved sacrificing the principle of a separate entry for each day of the year and this to some extent diminished the 'pattern of life' aspect of the picture. Nevertheless, I have retained a good deal of material which is of interest for illustrating this rather than because the incident itself was in any way crucial; and I have also kept in mind my own tendency when reading other people's diaries to find that it is often the trivial which is most interesting.

If there has been a bias in the cutting it has been against the minutiae of Commission business and in favour of the broader issues of Europe, of clashes with or between governments, and, in 1979 and 1980, of political developments in Britain. As a result, although the book is bounded by my Brussels years, it would be wrong to describe it as a *Brussels Diary*. A good two-thirds of the action takes place outside that city.

There remains the question of cuts that I have made for reasons other than those of space. I have exercised some but not much censorship. I have cut out a number of unfriendly comments about individuals of relatively little note. If the degree of pain caused to the person concerned was likely to exceed the interest aroused in others that seemed to me a good reason for excision. The more important the person, the less discreet I have been. Thus Giscard and Schmidt are almost entirely unprotected by any afterthoughts. I took the view that they, and others near to their eminence, could look after themselves.

So it could be argued that to be the subject of sharp comment is a tribute. I hope that some of those involved will recognize the compliment to their self-confidence, or will at least look at the picture of themselves in the round. In a four-year relationship even with fundamentally respected collaborators, there are bound to be moments of irritation, and any accurate moving picture of events is bound to reflect them. I have also cut some comments recorded from the mouths of others, particularly where I thought the remarks might cause them embarrassment in offices they continue to hold.

So for a variety of reasons I have greatly shortened the text, and any shortening of course is bound to be selective. But have I doctored it? I obviously do not think so. I have tidied up a good deal, but I have never consciously changed the sense, I have resisted (with some difficulty) *esprit d'escalier*, and where I have added, mainly but not exclusively in footnotes, it has been for purposes of clarity. The only exception has been where, seeking economy in words, I have suddenly seen that a new linking sentence could get one from A to B in fifteen words rather than five hundred.

I do not therefore claim complete textual integrity, as opposed to integrity of substance. But the original text exists, can be published in due course if anyone so desires, and is available in the meantime for inspection by anyone who feels they might have been maligned by *ex post* judgements.

My last comment is that editing a volume of diaries has proved an immensely more time-consuming process than writing an original book. It is the equivalent of altering an existing house as opposed to building a new one, and causes a good deal more trouble to the neighbours as well.

The long-suffering neighbours in this case have been Diana Fortescue, my research assistant, who, with the help of the libraries of Chatham House, the French, German, Italian, American, Japanese, Greek and Belgian embassies, as well as those of the House of Lords and House of Commons, has done an immense work on footnotes and references, and Lord Bonham-Carter and Miss Alison Wade, my Collins editors. Sir Crispin Tickell and Mr Hayden Phillips provided a perspective on Brussels, and Sir Christopher Audland and Mr Michael Emerson assisted on several more recondite points of Community lore. The original texts were typed by Mrs Bess Church and Miss Patricia Smallbone, the reduced version (with great speed) by Miss Monica Harkin and the footnotes by Mrs Xandra O'Bryan Tear.

ROY JENKINS

East Hendred, April 1988

SKETCHMAP OF BRUSSELS

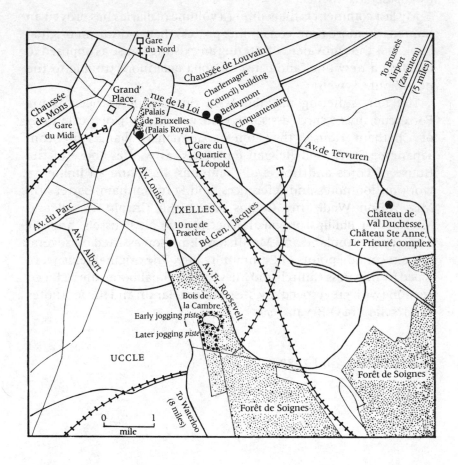

Gare du Nord

Chaussée de Louvain

Charlemagne (Council) building

Grand' Place

rue de la Loi

Berlaymont

Cinquantenaire

Chaussée de Mons

Palais de Bruxelles (Palais Royal)

Gare du Midi

To Brussels Airport (Zaventem) (5 miles)

Gare du Quartier Léopold

Av. de Tervuren

Av. Louise

IXELLES

Bd Gen. Jacques

Château de Val Duchesse, Château Ste Anne, Le Prieuré complex

Av. du Parc

10 rue de Praetère

Av. Albert

Av. Fr. Roosevelt

Bois de la Cambre

Early jogging *piste*

Later jogging *piste*

UCCLE

Forêt de Soignes

Forêt de Soignes

To Waterloo (8 miles)

0   1
mile

THE COMMISSION

The membership of the Commission of the European Community which held office from 6 January 1977 to 4 January 1981 was as follows.

PRESIDENT

Roy Jenkins

VICE-PRESIDENTS

François-Xavier (Francis) Ortoli, b. 1925, was first encountered by me when he was French Minister of Finance in November 1968. He had been sent by General de Gaulle to Bonn to arrange an agreed devaluation of the French franc in a meeting of the (IMF) Group of Ten. He began by asking me if I could provide a fig leaf by taking the pound down a little way with the franc. I had to refuse. He nonetheless doggedly and successfully negotiated a 11 per cent depreciation over twenty hours of wearing talks. When he got back to Paris the General called the devaluation off, which made Ortoli look rather exposed and the rest of us feel unnecessarily exhausted.

Despite this inauspicious beginning, and the fact that he as an ex-President of the Commission was serving under me, I like to think that we got on well. He was probably the nicest of all my colleagues. He could occasionally be prickly about his public position, but prickliness usually dissolved quickly in the warmth of his friendliness. He had a very high sense of public duty which made him feel that he was only properly occupied when holding high office in the service of the French state. But I am not sure how much he enjoyed his public service, for he was of a nervous disposition. What he enjoyed was intellectual conversation on aesthetic subjects, about which he was very well informed.

His Commission experience began in 1958–61 as its youngest Director-General. He returned as President in 1973 and stayed, for the last eight years as a Vice-President, until 1985. He is now head of the Compagnie Française des Pétroles. His portfolio in my Commission was Economic and Monetary Affairs.

Wilhelm Haferkamp, b. 1923, was a German trades unionist of generous instincts and indulgent tastes who possessed most of the attributes of a good Commissioner except for that of application. He was experienced (a member of the Commission since 1971), of broad internationalist outlook, and an engaging personality. If he did not take his job too seriously, he at least had the advantage of not taking himself so either. He was never pompous. He was sometimes a little difficult to find. He reminded me in this respect only of a now dead friend of mine who was briefly a not very diligent Member of Parliament and replied to a message of rebuke and recall from his Chief Whip by telegraphing from the Ritz Hotel, Madrid: 'You must take me as you find me – if you can find me.'

Haferkamp's penchant for caravanserai of this sort led to a great deal of difficulty in 1979, but I nonetheless recall 'the old Willi', as his Director-General (Sir Roy Denman) constantly referred to him, with considerable affection.

Finn-Olav Gundelach, 1925–81, shared with Davignon in the Commission the quality of being *papabile*, that is they were seen by both themselves and others as possible future Presidents. He was a Danish public servant who had previously been their Permanent Representative to the Community as well as deputy Director-General of the GATT and a member of the Ortoli Commission with the portfolio of the Internal Market. In my Commission he held the vital Agricultural portfolio.

On balance I do not think he was quite as effective as Davignon, although his set-piece exposés before both the Commission and the Council of Ministers were more brilliant. The reason why the balance was just against him may have been that his life was bleaker (his wife was a Danish preacher who never appeared in Brussels) and that he was always working at or beyond the edge of his capacity, while Davignon always kept his reserves. Partly as a result Gundelach was more brooding and more tricky. But he was of very high quality. Unfortunately his overwork killed him. He was reappointed to the 1981 Commission but died suddenly in Strasbourg in its first month.

He was pretty detached from Denmark, visited it little more frequently than I did, and rarely used its language. Yet his English while wholly efficacious was less authentic than that of Davignon or Cheysson or Brunner. He really spoke 'Gundelachese', a powerful agricultural vernacular which owed something to Old Norse but more to Monetary Compensatory Amounts in which he dealt with equal facility with Green Pounds and breeding 'soes' (as he always pronounced those porcine animals).

Lorenzo Natali, b. 1922, was an excellent nominee of Italian Christian Democracy, encapsulating most of its virtues and just enough of its vices to make him a true representative, although not a delegate. He was an Abruzzan from the left of that broad-based party, who had a good Resistance record at the end of the war, who had been Minister, at different times between 1966 and 1973, of the Merchant Marine, Public Works, and Agriculture. He took a little time to settle into the life of Brussels and the Commission, mainly because his very agreeable wife did not at first come and because he spoke no English and very little French. Later, with the arrival both of his wife and of adequate French, he became the *homme moyen sensuel* of the Commission, respected for his amiability and shrewdness. He remained a Commissioner until 1989.

In my Commission his portfolio comprised the rather mixed bag of the Enlargement negotiations, the Environment, and, from 1979, relations with the Parliament. He was the only Commissioner in whose home (at Rocca di Mezzo, near L'Aquila) we ever stayed.

Henk Vredeling, b. 1924, had been Dutch Socialist Minister of Defence for the four years before he came to the Commission. He had arrived at the pre-Christmas Ditchley weekend full of enthusiastic but slightly truculent left-wing European ideas and accompanied by a uniformed *aide-de-camp* with whom he proceeded to carouse for most of the night. He remained fairly true to these contradictions throughout his four years in the Commission, although his self-confidence took a sad plunge in 1979. He was not considered a Commission success and there was no question of his being reappointed for 1981. But he was a man of warmth and courage, and as a result of the Vredeling Directive he imprinted his name on the history of the European Community in the late 1970s much more than did the rest of us. The portfolio he held was that of Social Affairs and relations with 'the Social Partners', i.e. employers and trade unions. He has since played little part in public affairs.

COMMISSIONERS

Vicomte Etienne (Stevy) Davignon, b. 1932, taken in the round was the best member of my Commission. He was a Belgian career diplomat, whose grandfather had done well out of the Congo and been ennobled by King Leopold II. Stevy Davignon, although a Christian Democrat, had first come into prominence as a collaborator of Paul-Henri Spaak (Socialist). Before coming to the Commission he had been *Directeur Politique* in the Belgian Foreign Ministry and was the author of the Davignon Report on Political Cooperation. He knew the workings of Europe and of the whole Atlantic world inside out.

He spoke French with a determined Belgian accent, and English with a fluency which owed its little words to the nursery and its big ones to the ante-rooms of many a NATO, GATT, OECD or UN conference. He was very self-confident and moved easily in all Belgian (and wider) circles without being bounded by any of them. I would not however describe him as a *grand seigneur*. He was too active a fixer for that. He worked very long hours, rarely I think got nearer to exercise than Sunday lunch at the Ravenstein Royal Golf Club, liked social life but never entertained. He had a very pretty wife who asserted her independence by declining to speak English.

Davignon's *forte* was ingenuity. As a result he fell into the small and splendid category of those who prefer finding solutions to complaining about the difficulties. He ought to have become President when I left. Instead he stayed on as a Vice-President and dominated the Thorn Commission. He is now a leading Belgian banker, but I suspect would respond to a twitch upon the thread which led him back to international public service.

Claude Cheysson, b. 1920, was a French career diplomat (Ambassador in Indonesia 1966–9) who took to Socialist politics a little too late in life. As a result they went slightly to his head. But he was a man of high intelligence, warm, with an exceptional knowledge of and authority in Africa, lacking sometimes in judgement. He held the Development Aid portfolio in the Ortoli Commission as in mine, and liked visiting his African Empire. 'What is the difference between God and Cheysson?' had become an old Brussels joke/ riddle before I arrived. The answer was, 'Le Bon Dieu est partout, et Claude Cheysson également, sauf à Bruxelles.'

He was a Commissioner until 1989, sixteen years after his arrival, although he had a period away including three years (1981–4) as French Foreign Minister. In my *cabinet* we occasionally referred to him as the electric mouse, which was a tribute to his energy, although as he expended so much of it away from Brussels he was a little peripheral to the central work of the Commission. He was an engaging companion who spoke almost perfect English.

Antonio Giolitti, b. 1915, was the oldest and the most *racé* member of the Commission. He was a Piedmontese, who made me constantly aware that Turin is as far from Naples as London is from Marseille. He was the grandson of Giovanni Giolitti, who was five times Prime Minister of Italy between 1892 and 1921. He was himself a Socialist (his grandfather had been a non-party, left-of-centre figure) who had been an (Italian) Communist 1943–57 and joined their list again in 1987 to be re-elected to the Italian Parliament. He had been Minister of the Budget and Economic Planning on several occasions between 1964 and 1974. He held the Regional portfolio in my Commission. In 1978 he was nearly snatched away from us to become President of the Italian Republic.

He was as elegant and nervous as a finely bred racehorse. To begin with he thought he ought to speak French at Commission meetings, which made him take his fences rather slowly. One summer, when Commissioners were asked to give their holiday addresses, he submitted a quiet *pensione* in Venice for ten days plus

Villa Giolitti, via Giolitti, Cuneo, for the rest of the time. That perfectly summed up his mixture of modesty and hereditary slightly other-worldly authority. His wife had translated Proust into Italian.

Guido Brunner, b. 1930, was a German professional diplomat (Ambassador in Madrid since 1982) who had become a Free Democrat nominee to the Commission on the resignation of Ralf Dahrendorf in 1974. By 1977 he thought that he was entitled to the External Affairs portfolio, but I did not consider that he had enough weight. He had a Spanish mother and was an excellent conversationalist, able to adjust to his interlocutor's interests with equal ease in German, Spanish, English and French. He sometimes engaged less robustly with his Commission responsibilities, which were Energy and Science. He resigned in November 1980 when he was elected a member of the Bundestag, but he did not long remain a legislator.

Raymond Vouël, 1923–88, was a Luxembourger Socialist who had served in the Ortoli Commission for its last six months. Despite this short head-start over a half of us and the centrality of his country to the Community, he was never much at home in the Commission. Taciturn and suspicious, although honest and determined, he was I fear always ill at ease with me, and frequently locked in conflicts with Davignon (their portfolios were adjacent), who danced around him like a hare with a tortoise, except that the tortoise did not win in the end. He was in charge of Competition policy. He was not reappointed in 1981, and although only fifty-seven went home to retirement.

Richard Burke, b. 1932, was a devout and provincial Irish-Catholic who came from the same party, Fine Gael, as Garret Fitzgerald but did not share many of his liberal views. He had been a minister and was a man of dignity and of a certain shy charm. I rather liked him, but did not often succeed in handling him well. His portfolio in my Commission, arrived at with considerable difficulty (see pages 666–8), comprised Transport, Taxation, Consumer Affairs, and Relations with Parliament. This last item (the most interesting one) he voluntarily surrendered in June 1979. He was not reappointed in 1981, but came back to Brussels in 1983 for the last two years of the Thorn Commission.

Christopher Tugendhat, b. 1938, was the only Commissioner under forty. He had been Conservative Member of Parliament for the Cities of London and Westminster since 1970. He was very much my personal choice as second British Commissioner. Mrs Thatcher looked in another direction, but James Callaghan was pleased to be able to throw a bone to me and irritate her at one go. I never regretted the choice. Tugendhat was a very good Commissioner. What particularly impressed me was that, starting as he did beholden to me, he never allowed this to affect our relations. He was neither subservient, nor (a more likely reaction) tiresomely contrary or overassertive. He was a pillar of support on the EMS and staunchly committed on all European issues. His father was a distinguished Austrian refugee who rejected his homeland to the extent of not bringing up his son to speak German, which was a pity as it meant that Christopher Tugendhat arrived in Brussels almost monolingual. His portfolio comprised the Budget, Personnel, and Financial Services. It was a mixed bag in which the first item assumed an importance in the affairs of the Community greater than was thought likely when he was appointed. Tugendhat continued in Brussels until 1985, and is now Chairman of the Civil Aviation Authority.

SECRETARY-GENERAL

Emile Noël, b. 1922, was Secretary-General from the creation (1958) to 1987. He was French in nationality and style, but the epitome of a European who transcended nationalism in motive and performance. He conducted most of his business in a series of elegantly phrased memoranda, heavily dependent upon a very precise use of the subjunctive. Yet he rarely allowed this precision to lead him into negativism. He was capable of major constructive swoops. His personality was at once warm and elusive. He had been the *Chef de Cabinet* to Guy Mollet when the latter was Prime Minister of France at the time of Suez. He may well know more about the hidden mysteries of that affair than anyone else now alive. Since 1987 he has been Rector of the European University Institute in Florence.

THE *CABINET*

My Brussels *cabinet* or, in the by no means exact English equivalent, Private Office:

Chef de Cabinet

(Sir) *Crispin Tickell*, b. 1930, later Ambassador to Mexico, Permanent Secretary, Ministry of Overseas Development, and now Permanent Representative to the United Nations, New York.

Senior Adviser

Michael Jenkins, b. 1936, having been *Chef de Cabinet* to George Thomson in the Ortoli Commission, stayed on for my first seven months as a supernumerary but valuable member of my *cabinet*. In the autumn of 1978 he returned to Brussels as a member of the Secretariat-General (later Deputy Secretary-General) and in this capacity worked closely with me, particularly on the British budgetary question. Now British Ambassador in The Hague.

Chef Adjoint

Hayden Phillips, b. 1943. (Until January 1979.) Formerly my Home Office Private Secretary 1974–6, now a Deputy Secretary, HM Treasury.

Nick Stuart, b. 1942. (From January 1979.) Now a Deputy Secretary, Department of Education and Science.

Senior Counsellors (Grade A3)

Michael Emerson, b. 1940. Dealt primarily with economic and monetary affairs until the end of 1977 when he became a Director (A2) in the Directorate-General dealing with these matters (DG2) where he still is. He continued to work closely with me on monetary matters, but was replaced in the *cabinet* by:

Michel Vanden Abeele, b. 1942, Belgian, for the remaining three years. He is now Head of Division in DG8 (Development) in charge of relations with UNCTAD and primary products.

Graham Avery, b. 1943, who dealt primarily with agriculture and enlargement. He had come from the Ministry of Agriculture to the Soames *cabinet* but in 1981 entered the *services* of the Commission and is now a Director (A2) in the agricultural Directorate-General.

Spokesman

Roger Beetham, b. 1937. He was attached to the Spokesman's Group in DG10 rather than in the *cabinet* itself, but he worked closely with it. A member of the Diplomatic Service, he was Counsellor in Delhi, 1981–5, and is now in the FCO.

More junior members

Klaus Ebermann, b. 1945. German. Dealt with industrial affairs and overseas development. Now in the external affairs Directorate of the Commission.

Etienne Reuter, b. 1944. Luxembourgeois. Dealt, under Crispin Tickell, with relations with countries outside the Community. Now in the Spokesman's Group of the Commission.

Laura Grenfell, b. 1950. (Until June 1979.) She dealt, under the *Chef Adjoint*, primarily with parliamentary affairs. Now Mrs Hayden Phillips.

Penelope Duckham, b. 1952. (From June 1979.) Later parliamentary adviser to the Consumers' Association. Now Mrs Matthew Hill.

Secretaries

Celia Beale. Inherited from the Thomson *cabinet*. Stayed with me throughout and for three subsequent years in London. Now Mrs Graham Cotton.

Susan Besford. Inherited from the Soames *cabinet*. Went to Tokyo in early 1979 and was replaced by:

Patricia Smallbone (now Mrs James Marshall) who stayed until December 1979 (but see under London Secretary) and was then replaced by:

Sara Keays who stayed until the end.

Secretary (London)

Bess Church who had worked for me since 1957 and who stayed until the spring of 1980, when she was replaced by Patricia Smallbone.

Drivers

Peter Halsey, who had worked for me during both my periods as Home Secretary and who continued to drive me in London until 1982. He died in 1988.

Ron Argent, expatriate English, inherited from the Soames *cabinet*, now retired to Spain, until mid-1977, when he was replaced by:

Michael O'Connor (Irish) who stayed with me to the end of my Brussels time.

Introduction

From the late 1950s onwards a commitment to European unity, and to Britain's participation in it, became my most dominating political purpose. It provoked my first withdrawal from the Opposition front bench in 1962, although from a post so minor that hardly anyone noticed, and my only political quarrel with Hugh Gaitskell in that same last year of his life.

In 1964–70 I was much occupied with the day-to-day business of being a minister, but I think that from Aviation to the Home Office to the Treasury I managed to remain reasonably faithful to Europe within my own Departments as well as, of course, enthusiastically supporting Harold Wilson's conversion and the consequent lodging of Britain's second application to join the European Economic Community in 1967.

When the exigencies of the party game led him to change his position again in 1971 I considered this second switch to be neither good politics nor good sense and had no hesitation in leading sixty-eight Labour MPs into the 'yes' lobby on the principle of joining. And six months later, when it had become clear that the majority of the Labour leadership attached more importance to the short-term embarrassment of the Government than to either the long-term orientation of Britain or to their own reputation for consistency, I resigned again from the Opposition front bench. This time I at least attracted more notice, for I had progressed from being number three spokesman on economic affairs to being deputy leader of the party and shadow Chancellor.

I did not see this resignation at the time as a decisive separation. I thought that I would probably be back in full communion within a few years. In retrospect however these 1971–2 events obviously marked the beginning not merely of my separation from the Labour Party but also of a disenchantment with the mould which two-party politics had assumed by the early 1970s. I reluctantly went back into government in 1974, but nothing fully engaged my general political enthusiasm until the European referendum of the spring of 1975. In that campaign I was President of the Britain in Europe organization, with Willie Whitelaw and Jo Grimond as the principal vice-presidents, and achieved the most satisfactory national election result in which I have ever significantly participated.

By early 1976, when the question of my becoming President of the European Commission first arose, it could therefore be said that my general European credentials were fairly good. But they were very general. My conviction was complete, but my experience was negligible. The only ministerial portfolio which I held after Britain's entry in 1973 was that of the Home Department, which, as its name implied and its ethos confirmed, was about as far removed from the business of the Community as any within the compass of the British Government.

I participated in no Councils of Ministers. I liked to say, only half as a joke, that I kept my European faith burning bright by never visiting Brussels. And this was almost startlingly true. France, Italy, Germany I knew fairly well. But the embryonic capital of Europe I had visited on only four occasions between 1945 and the date of my appointment as the head of its administration. I was an enthusiast for the *grandes lignes* of Europe but an amateur within the complexities of its signalling system.

Until January 1976 I had no thought of penetrating these complexities. I regarded myself as a buttress rather than a pillar of the church of European unity. I would support it passionately from the outside when called upon to do so. But the *rouages* were not for me. I remembered my dismay one evening in the spring of 1972 when George Thomson told me that he had accepted an invitation to go to Brussels as a Commissioner in the following January. I thought our joint role was to save the Labour Party from extremism and Britain from insularity. But we should accomplish these tasks without getting mixed up in issuing directives or administering regulations. Success in domestic politics was the way to achieve international goals.

By early 1976, however, this devotion to national politics had considerably but surreptitiously eroded itself. The pleasures of membership of a Government with the general outlook and policy of which I was fairly steadily out of sympathy were distinctly limited. The Home Office was perhaps the best department from which to be the licensed leader of an internal opposition, and my prerogatives there as a senior minister were not infringed upon by the easy-going regime of the second Wilson premiership. But it was a job which I had done before when I was forty-five not fifty-five, and a *réchauffé* helping did not keep the blood racing. Furthermore, I was increasingly interested in foreign rather than domestic issues (which made the Home Office a bit of a cage), and increasingly impatient of Britain's addiction to believing it always knew best even though its recipes ended only too frequently in it doing worst.

This was the background against which I went to see the Prime Minister for an hour's routine *tour d'horizon* in the early evening of Thursday, 22 January. The position was complicated, although not on the surface, by the facts that he had come to a settled resolve to remain in office for only another two months, and that I had been given the strongest possible 'tip-off' of this, from an impeccable source, on the day after Christmas. But he was not I think aware of my knowledge which, despite the quality of the source, was well short of amounting to a certainty in my mind, and the subject was not open to discussion between us.

In the course of the discussion Harold Wilson raised, but not very strenuously, the future presidency of the European Commission, in which a change was due at the beginning of 1977. There was a predisposition in favour of a British candidate, he said, but it was not sufficiently strong that the British Government could nominate whomever they liked. Giscard d'Estaing and Schmidt had apparently reacted unfavourably for some reason or other to the suggestion of Christopher Soames, who was currently one of the five vice-presidents of the Commission. They had more or less said, half paraphrasing Henry Ford, that the British could confidently put forward any candidate they liked, provided it was Heath or Jenkins. I am not sure whether or not Wilson consulted Heath. In any event, he offered the job to me, saying that I ought certainly to have the refusal, but that he rather assumed that I would not want to go, and indeed hoped that this would be so.

I reacted at the time in accordance both with his expectation and with the settled groove of my thought over the past several years. I thanked him, but reached for an old gramophone record and said that I was resolved to remain in British politics. Over the next few days I became increasingly doubtful of the wisdom of this reply. Brussels would certainly be an escape from the nutshell of British politics. It would be an opportunity to do something quite new for me and in which I believed much more strongly than in the economic policy of Mr Healey, the trade union policy of Mr Foot, or even the foreign policy of Mr Callaghan. There might also be the chance to help Europe regain the momentum which it had signally lost since the oil shock at the end of 1973.

There was however one major complication. If Harold Wilson was to resign in March there would obviously follow an election for the leadership of the Labour Party and the Prime Ministership. Contrary to the position from, say, 1968 to 1971, it had become rather unlikely that I could win. There was still a clear moderate majority in the parliamentary Labour Party (then the sole electing body), but too many of the cautious members of it had come to feel that I would be insufficiently compromising and might provoke a split. I had certainly not gone out of my way to respect Labour Party shibboleths.

On the other hand, I still had a substantial, gallant and militant body of troops behind me. They had been in training for this battle for years. Probably most of them had come to realize that the time for victory was past. But they nonetheless wished to fight. To have avoided the engagement by slipping off to Brussels would have been intolerable.

I therefore had not to dissimulate but to procrastinate. There was no need for dissimulation because my order of preference was clear. I would have preferred to be Prime Minister of Britain than President of the European Commission. Who would not? As the argument which was supposed to have decided Melbourne was put: 'It is a damned fine thing to have been, even if it only lasts for two months. It is a thing no Greek or Roman ever was.' And this was a view of which there was no need to be ashamed in Europe (apart perhaps from the insular irrelevance of the addendum), for in view of the uncertain powers of the Commission President it would have been taken by every French, German and Italian politician, and probably by Dutch, Belgian, Danish and Irish ones as well.

I was however equally clear that if a change of leadership closed up the succession and left me with no domestic opportunity but to soldier on where I was, I would be both more usefully and more interestingly employed in Brussels. I therefore wrote to Harold Wilson four days after our conversation, withdrawing my dismissal of the proposition and endeavouring to preserve my options for as long as possible.

Such attempts to have the best of both worlds are liable to leave one without much of either. However I was lucky in that the strength of my position, such as it was, did not stem primarily from being the candidate of the British Government. In late February I went to Paris for forty-eight hours, nominally for a bilateral visit to Michel Poniatowski, then Minister of the Interior, but in fact at the wish of the President of the Republic, Valéry Giscard d'Estaing. In the course of a long interview in the Elysée, Giscard strongly urged me, saying he was speaking on behalf of Helmut Schmidt, the German Chancellor, as well as of himself, to become President of the Commission. I tried to preserve my room for manoeuvre by saying elliptically that there was an election I had to get out of the way first. At first he thought I was telling him of an imminent British general election, but when I steered him away from this he did not press either for clarity or for an immediate decision. One advantage of Harold Wilson's apparent but deceptive dedication to office was that, even with a hint, no one could conceive of his resigning.

The next day I lunched with Jean Monnet, the founding father of the Community, at Montfort L'Amoury, thirty miles from Paris. He also strongly pressed me to accept the Commission position. Insofar as I was still doubtful, the net could be perceived as closing in oppressively. Insofar as I was increasingly tempted, I was exhilarated by being blessed by the spiritual as well as the temporal authorities of Europe.

Three weeks after that Harold Wilson resigned and the contest began. Nine days later the result of the first ballot was announced. It was broadly as I had expected, although the gap between James Callaghan and me – 84 to 56 – was worse than I had hoped for. Michael Foot led with 90 votes, but this was not of the first relevance because he could manifestly be overhauled by whoever qualified for a run-off against him. The determining factor was therefore the relative positions of Callaghan and myself. The other three candidates – Healey, Benn and Crosland – were all well behind. The last two were compulsorily eliminated, but Healey with 37 votes fought on with characteristic pugnacity for another round, though without improving his position. I could see no point in prolonging the contest into a third (maybe a fourth) slow round. The country needed a new Prime Minister, and from 56 votes it was clearly not going to be me. The barrier between failure and success was not vast. A direct swing of 15 votes from Callaghan to me would have given me the premiership. But it was nevertheless decisive. I withdrew and turned my thoughts, which was not difficult – perhaps too many of them had been there already – to Europe.

There were two hiccups. I had decided following the Giscard meeting that my order of preference was clear. First was to be Prime Minister, provided I did not have to do too much stooping to conquer. Second was to become President of the Commission. Third, but not all that far behind, was to become Foreign Secretary. And a bad fourth was to remain where I was. In drawing up this list I think that I had rather complacently assumed that James Callaghan, both on grounds of seniority and out of gratitude for the early release to him of my 56 votes, would be happy to offer me the Foreign Office.

I was wrong, as clearly emerged when I saw him on 6 April. He was evasive at the time, but his memoirs* put his position with convincing frankness: 'The post of Foreign Secretary had to be filled and in other times Roy Jenkins would have been a natural successor. . . . But the wounds had not healed since his resignation as deputy leader during the European Community battles, and as he had been the leading protagonist on one side, every action he would have taken as Foreign Secretary would have been regarded with deep suspicion by the anti-Marketeers on our benches. . . . In any case there was another suitable candidate, in the person of Tony Crosland.'

This had the perverse effect of temporarily upsetting my preference between courses two and three. That however was both short-lived and irrelevant, as the new Prime Minister knew his mind on this issue. His alternative offer of a reversion to the Chancellorship of the Exchequer after 'six months or so' did not

* *Time and Chance* (1987), p. 399.

tempt me. It was, to mix the metaphor, the offer of another *réchauffé* helping which remained very much in the bush.

In late April the bird in the hand also showed some faint signs of fluttering. Giscard indicated that he was against any early announcement of my presidency. His mind was firm on the substance, he said, but there must be no premature publicity: it might prejudice the position of François-Xavier Ortoli, the incumbent French President. This was strange, in view both of Giscard's urgent pressure of February and of the fact that he had never previously shown much consideration for Ortoli – nor did he subsequently. It was balanced however by enthusiastic support given publicly from the Italian Government and more privately by Chancellor Schmidt, who did not wish to seem publicly out of step with President Giscard. Thus I had an early taste of a pattern of European attitudes which was to become only too familiar to me over the next few years.

The explanation of Giscard's wobble, I retrospectively think, is that my candidature, launched by him and Schmidt, was being too enthusiastically received by the small countries of the Community. This was because they wanted a politician and not a bureaucrat and found a Briton with European conviction a heady combination. When I visited two or three of them that spring I was treated very much as a President-elect. Giscard's response was not to change his mind but to try to demonstrate that I was becoming President not by the acclaim of the little ones but by the nomination of France. Up to a point he succeeded.

The issue was however safely out of the way by the end of June, when the European Council, meeting in Luxembourg, conveyed to me an informal (legal formality followed only in December) but public and unanimous invitation to assume the presidency at the beginning of January. Thereafter the majority of my time and the overwhelming part of my interest was devoted to the affairs of Europe. I remained Home Secretary until 10 September, when I left a British Government for the last time, but this was only because it suited the Prime Minister better that way, and a large part of this twilight period was in any event taken up by holiday.

During July a number of Commissioners who were candidates for staying on came to see me in London, and I also began a series of visits to the governments of the member states. Rightly or wrongly,

I kept away from Brussels. I decided that if I was to make any impact both upon the bureaucracy (which I thought of as being dedicated but rigid) and upon the tone of Europe, I must arrive only with full powers and not become a familiar figure hanging about in the corridors in the preceding months. I went there only once, in mid-November, mainly to see the house which we had taken, and to visit the Belgian Prime Minister, although we were in no dispute about the excellent Commissioner, Etienne Davignon, whom the Belgians had chosen in consultation with me. This abstinence from Belgium may or may not have given drama to my arrival, but it certainly had the effect, when I eventually plunged into the murk of a Brabant January, of making the ambience of the Berlaymont (the Community office building), the ways of those who lived in and around it, and indeed the whole atmosphere of Brussels, seem almost gothically strange to me.

It was only Belgium as the areopagitica of the Community (and Luxembourg, its subsidiary in this respect) that I eschewed. The other six countries I went to frequently. Over the summer and autumn of 1976 I made twenty visits to their capitals. I also went twice to the United States, mainly on preparatory Community business. And there was a fairly constant procession of visitors – future Commissioners, senior officials, politicians – to see me in London. After I left the Home Office I was established in a modest suite of rooms in the Cabinet Office. Crispin Tickell, whom I chose from a list of strong candidates, came to me as *Chef de Cabinet* from the Foreign Office in October. Hayden Phillips left the Home Office with me to become *Chef Adjoint* but disappeared fairly soon on a month's 'immersion' language course in the South of France. I devoted a good deal of time, both over the summer holidays and during the autumn, to improving my French by less baptismal methods. I also spent many hours on the history of the Community and on the structure of the Commission, playing with a variety of plans for its improvement.

The main purpose of my European visits was to discuss who would be my future Commission colleagues with the nominating heads of government. The Tindemans Report on European Union, drawn up by the Belgian Prime Minister at the request of the other governments in 1975, had suggested, *inter alia*, that the incoming President of the Commission should have a considerable voice in this. Many of the Tindemans proposals wasted on the desert air, but it was difficult for the heads of government to deny this one so quickly after it had been put forward; no firm precedent was established, however, for I believe that neither of my successors, Gaston Thorn and Jacques Delors, has attempted to play much part in this process.

Nor did the relative enthusiasm with which different governments embraced this obligation follow any predictable pattern. The three governments in the Community most opposed to supranationalism were the British, the French and the Danish. With the small one of these three there was no issue. The Danish Government and I were both equally eager to renew the appointment of Finn-Olav Gundelach, and quite right we were from every point of view except that of his own health – he died in early 1981. He was one of my two best Commissioners. The British Government was equally but more controversially (with Mrs Thatcher) willing for me to nominate Christopher Tugendhat as the second and Conservative British Commissioner. He turned out to be a very good choice.

What was most surprising was the willingness of the French Government to parley at considerable length and the highest level about their choice. I had two long Elysée meetings with President Giscard, as well as several exchanges of messages, about the issue, which in the French case was tangled. At that stage I was determined to keep Claude Cheysson, the existing and Socialist Development Aid Commissioner, in that portfolio. The French were determined to keep the portfolio but would have preferred it to go to some other Frenchman, perhaps to Ortoli, the retiring President. I was for a time uncertain whether I wanted my predecessor in my Commission. Conventional wisdom advised against. Nor was Ortoli pressing his claims. He was as uncertain as I was. But if he was to be there, I wanted him to have Economic and Monetary Affairs, as did he. So Giscard and I danced around, he occasionally concentrating my mind by suggesting a highly unacceptable candidate, but always stressing that he would not impose Ortoli upon me. Eventually we settled for Ortoli.

By contrast, the governments of the Little Five, other than Denmark, were traditionally the most in favour of supranationalism and the powers of the Commission. Belgium I have already dealt with. Luxembourg was in a special position in that they had appointed a new Commissioner, Raymond Vouël, to fill a vacancy only a few months previously. He would not have been my choice, but they wanted him to stay on, which he did. There was no argument. Both the Dutch and Irish engaged in lengthy and agreeable discussion and ended up by nominating Commissioners who, while they both had considerable qualities, were not by any stretch of imagination my choice. Nor were their Commission careers entirely successful.

That left the two big traditionally 'federalist' European countries, Italy and Germany. The Italian Government was immensely forthcoming. They wanted two new Commissioners, as did I. They wanted them to strike a political balance, one Christian Democrat and one Socialist, and they therefore steered me gently away from one or two non-politicians I had in mind. Eventually they appointed the two they had probably wanted from the beginning, but not before they had brought me also to feel that they were the best choices. And in the course of leading me to their conclusion they gave me a very good familiarization course in Italian politics, encouraging me to discussions with all political parties, Communists included. It was a very elegant performance, and in my view not at all cynical.

The Germans handled matters less happily. It is one of the paradoxes of Europe that while the Federal Republic has always been a massive and crucial supporter of the European ideal, and indeed of the policies necessary to achieve it, it has never since the end of Hallstein's day adequately sustained the European institutions. This has shown itself in two ways: first in a German governmental habit, epitomized by Chancellor Schmidt towards the end of the Ortoli presidency, of complaining at large about the Commission; and second, insofar as there was any force in the first point, doing their best to prevent its being corrected by resolutely refusing to appoint first-rate people to Brussels. This applied not merely to their Commissioners (although Ralf Dahrendorf, 1970–4, had been an exception) but also to their Permanent Representatives to the Community. In my experience Germany never exercised an intellectual weight in COREPER (the Committee of Permanent Representatives of the member states) commensurate with either its pre-eminent economic position or with that of the lesser economies of France, Britain or Italy. Nor was its position in the Commission any better.

In part, but only in part, this stemmed from the deep-seated reluctance of post-1945 Germany to play a strong political hand. Much of the stage of modern Europe has been occupied with, on one side, the British and the French, each in their different way, trying to exercise a power somewhat beyond their capacity, and on the other, the Germans trying to push it away like a magnet trying to reject metal. On the reverse side of this coin were the strenuous but unavailing attempts of the Bundesbank to prevent the D-mark becoming a reserve currency – in complete contrast with the British clinging on to the Sterling Area into the 1960s.

Nevertheless there was something more to this German attitude than a simple *nolo episcopari*. There was an unease with, leading to a certain distaste for, the complicated dance of international *hauts fonctionnaires*. It was utterly unlike the French attitude, close though the Franco-German partnership was becoming in those years. Whatever its causes, however, this almost shoulder-shrugging indifference on the part of the Germans created a weakening semi-vacuum in the heart of Europe.

It exhibited itself strongly during my consultations with the Bonn Government, and marked the first real setback of that autumn of preparation. This must be seen against the background of my very high expectations of the Germans. I regarded Schmidt (as indeed I still do) as the most constructive statesman of that period, and the one with whom I had the easiest personal relations. I regarded their Government as a model of centre-left internationalist good sense, and likely to be my strongest champions in any battles that lay ahead.

As late as 2 November I was still being encouraged by Schmidt to seek two new German Commissioners. I should have noticed on that visit that a very much more reserved attitude was being taken by other ministers, most notably by Hans-Dietrich Genscher, the Foreign Minister and leader of the Free Democrats.

I overestimated the power of the Chancellor. As soon afterwards as 15 November he told me that he could not do it. The political pressures were too great. The FDP insisted on their existing Commissioner being renominated and the trade unions were equally adamant about the long-serving SPD one from their ranks. It was an early lesson to me of the dangers of putting too much 'trust in princes', i.e. leaders of governments faced with domestic political difficulties. It was also a classic example of how to get the worst of both worlds. The two German Commissioners (both of whom had considerable and engaging qualities, although the one in my view did not have energy and the other did not have weight) knew that I had tried to replace them and had failed.

Furthermore, it presented me with a severe practical problem. It was my firm view that, with Ortoli in Economic and Monetary Affairs, the Germans must have the other obviously major portfolio of External Relations. This was so both for reasons of balance and because a German was more likely than most to conduct relations with the Americans and the Japanese on the liberal lines which I desired. But I did not believe either of them to be up to the job which Christopher Soames had done with conspicuous success in the Ortoli Commission. I was therefore faced with the dismal prospect that the new Commission, so far from having a new authority with which to relaunch Europe, would look less convincing to the outside world than the previous one had done.

This produced a sharp change of mood six weeks before I was due to go to Brussels. During the preceding four or five months I had been in a higher state of morale than at any time since 1971, if not earlier. Once the decision to go to Brussels had been finally made, I felt both liberated and exhilarated. I realized how ill the shoe of British politics had been fitting me for some years past. I also exaggerated, encouraged by the enthusiasm with which they had greeted my appointment, the extent to which I could persuade the governments to do what I wanted. During the summer and the first half of the autumn most things seemed possible and difficult decisions did not oppress.

No doubt the period of semi-euphoria would in any event have corrected itself as the happy prospect of preparing for an exciting new job gave way to the harsher reality of having within a few weeks to plunge into the complexities of actually doing it. The German experience therefore probably did little more than tear along a perforation which was already there. But that it certainly did. I remember that on 11 November, my birthday as it happened, the Prime Minister, walking through the division lobby with me, had lightly enquired (but not I think as a birthday greeting) whether I was still available to be Chancellor of the Exchequer. Sterling was crashing, the Government's economic policy appeared in disarray, and there was a good deal of press and parliamentary speculation about a change from Denis Healey. I would at least have been buying at the bottom of the market. However my mind was fixed on Brussels and I took Callaghan's suggestion even less seriously than he had made it. The following week after my next visit to Bonn, I might have been tempted to give him a more forthcoming reply.

In reality, of course, I could not possibly have changed direction at that stage. The juddering would have been appalling: my assembled *cabinet* to be stood down, the Brussels house to be unrented, my constituency farewells to be unsaid, not to mention the governments of Europe whose every suspicion about the insularity of the British would be confirmed. So I settled down to the last stages of preparation, and in particular to the untying of the knot of portfolio allocation. But it was never quite 'glad confident morning again'.

The portfolio issue was perplexing. It was crucial to the effective functioning and repute of the new Commission. It also involved relations with twelve individuals, several of them of potential prickliness, with whom I was going to have to spend the next four years; and with the governments of the nine member states, without considerable goodwill from which nothing could be done. Obviously some governments were more important than others, as were some portfolios, of which in any event there were not enough satisfactorily to occupy twelve Commissioners (other than the President). And I did not have anything approaching prime ministerial powers: once appointed, Commissioners had to be lived with as though they were members of a college of cardinals. They certainly could not be sacked by the President. Nor could solutions be imposed upon one without the almost unanimous support of all the others. In practice dispositions had to be negotiated.

The central difficulty was that I could not put Ortoli into Economic and Monetary Affairs unless I could first get Wilhelm Haferkamp out of this portfolio which he held in the existing Commission. And if I could not put Ortoli there, where could I put him? Nowhere to his pleasure, except perhaps for External Affairs (and I did not think he was the right man or the right nationality for

relations with the Americans), and nowhere at all of any significance except at the price of disrupting one of my other cherished
plans: Gundelach for Agriculture, Davignon for Industry and the
Internal Market, Cheysson to stay with Development Aid.

Haferkamp was stubbornly resistant to going to Social Affairs. I
did not see how I could possibly impose this upon him as the senior
Commissioner of the most important country without at least
acceding to the wish of the German Government that his junior,
Guido Brunner, should have External Affairs. But I thought (and
several of those who had been in the Ortoli Commission agreed
with me) that Haferkamp was the bigger man of the two. I therefore
decided that the only thing to do was a sudden switch of expectation: take the risk of putting Haferkamp into External Affairs,
which was only a risk that he would not do much, and all the other
major dispositions would fall into place.

This was the position when I assembled the new Commission for
twenty-four hours of familiarization and discussion at Ditchley
Park in north Oxfordshire on 22 and 23 December. I am not sure
that excursion was a total success. It was inconveniently close to
Christmas, but there was no other time we could find. It was a
summoning of the metropolitan Europeans to the periphery of the
empire. The weather was raw and misty, and some at least of the
visitors were more struck by the coldness of the bathrooms than by
the splendours of Ditchley. Perhaps the most memorable outcome
was a *Financial Times* fantasy by David Watt in which a murder *à la*
Christie (*Orient Express*) was apparently committed: all twelve had
separate but convergent motives for committing the crime. The
victim was obviously me.

However there was some useful discussion and considerable but
not complete progress was made with portfolios. Haferkamp
embraced the prospect of External Affairs with enthusiasm. Ortoli,
Gundelach and Davignon were also settled. But quite a lot of loose
ends remained to tie up. My fellow Commissioners (all of whom
I had met individually before, but never collectively) were a
variegated lot (as they should have been), not only as to nationality
but also as to background, knowledge and ability. Insofar as there
was any obvious division of category between them, it was between
the five who had substantial experience of a previous Commission
plus Davignon (who knew just as much from his Belgian Foreign

Ministry experience) on the one hand, and the seven tyros on the other. The seven of course included the President, of which fact the first six occasionally let it slip that they were fully aware.

Ditchley therefore had the effect of slightly heightening the atmosphere of apprehensive anticipation in which the Christmas holidays would in any event have been passed. The fourth of January, the date of departure, drew inexorably nearer.

1977

The first month or so of 1977 was taken up with initial dispositions – first of Commission portfolios and then of Directors-General, the rough equivalent of Whitehall permanent secretaries – and with the semi-formal establishment of relations with the other Community institutions: the Court of Justice, the Parliament (then nominated from the Parliaments of the member states and not directly elected), the Council of Ministers and its Brussels-resident shadow, the Committee of Permanent Representatives (COREPER).

The allocation of Commission portfolios was much the most difficult of these tasks. Despite the efforts at Ditchley before Christmas there was substantial work on the fitting of pegs into holes still to be done when I arrived in Brussels on 4 January. It was made more difficult by the fact that the rules (two Commissioners for a big country, one for a small one) created more Commissioners than there were proper jobs for them to do. And it had to be completed, unless the new Commission was to start very much on the wrong foot, by the night of 6/7 January.

This led to the first days in Brussels being dominated by bilateral negotiations with individual Commissioners. The story has a certain retrospective interest, but not I think sufficiently so for the reader to be thrown into a long account of these proceedings. I have therefore abstracted it and put it in an appendix which appears at the end of the book. This abstraction may have the effect of making the first days seem undercharged, rather than overcharged as in reality they were.

In mid-February I began a customary round of inaugural visits to the governments of the member states. Such visits typically lasted a day and a half, and I did them over five months in the not entirely haphazard order of Italy, France, Netherlands, Luxembourg,

Germany, Ireland, Denmark and Britain. The Belgian Government received a non-travelling visit in September.

On the second of these visits – the Paris one – a tiresome and in some ways ludicrous issue of form and prestige which was to dominate much of that spring (and to continue with diminishing reverberations throughout the rest of my presidency) erupted to the surface. In November 1975 President Giscard had inaugurated a series of 'intimate' meetings between the leaders of the Western world. He had brought together at Rambouillet the heads of government of the United States, Germany, Britain and Japan, with Italy somewhat reluctantly added almost at the last moment. In June 1976 President Ford had responded almost too quickly by organizing a meeting at Puerto Rico. On this occasion Canada had been added at the request of the Americans. There had also been some movement away from the genuine informality of a country house gathering at Rambouillet towards the international circus trappings of more recent Western Economic Summits.

There was considerable feeling amongst the Little Five of the European Community that Ortoli, my predecessor as President, ought to have been present at Puerto Rico. The gatherings were specifically 'economic' and not political or military in their intent. The countries of Western Europe had charged the Community with a significant part of the responsibility for conducting and coordinating their economic policies, particularly but not only in the field of trade relations. In these circumstances it appeared both perverse and divisive for four of them to go off and try to settle matters with the Americans and the Japanese, leaving the coordinating body in the dark and five of the member states of the Community unrepresented.

There had been some suggestion that Ortoli ought simply to have packed his bags and arrived forcefully even if uninvited at the Summit. However no invitation was forthcoming and Ortoli, wisely I think, did not attempt to gate-crash. This issue was left unresolved but with a settled determination on the part of the Little Five, supported with enthusiasm by Italy and with moderate enthusiasm by Germany, that there should be no repetition of the crime.

A repetition of the Summit itself was however by then inevitable, and by the time that I took office one had been firmly arranged for

London in May 1977. The only question at issue was therefore whether or not I would be present. Ortoli's absence had unfairly been seen as a blow to his prestige and to that of the Commission. Part of the role I was expected to perform was to restore this prestige. My credibility as an effective new President was therefore somewhat at stake.

But there was more to it than the questions of pride or position. The Little Five regarded my own determination to get there as an essential test of whether I was to be a true spokesman of the Community as a whole or a lackey of the big countries, from one of which I came and by another of which my appointment had been initiated. Almost independently of my own views, I therefore had no choice but to fight for a place at the London meeting. And when Giscard at the conclusion of our Elysée discussion on 28 February announced with silken politeness that he was equally resolved the other way, a battle between us became unavoidable. While it was being fought it was, like most battles, disagreeable. The outcome however was reasonably satisfactory, particularly as the ground gained was never subsequently lost. But the price paid was a long-term deterioration in the relationship between Giscard and me (interrupted only by a brief and cautious second honeymoon in the summer of 1978), which probably mattered more to me than it did to him.

At the time I could see no merit in his position. At best it could be explained, but not excused, by political difficulties with the Gaullist wing of his coalition. In retrospect however I can see a little more in his case. He had successfully initiated a new forum for Western leaders to talk to each other in semi-spontaneous intimacy. It was a formula which he and his friend Schmidt particularly liked, because they were the best at it. Already he had been forced to admit first Italy and then Canada. Now there was me. Furthermore the Americans, with their need for back-up, were already making the meetings more bureaucratic, and the Commission was famous for bureaucracy. Where was it going to stop? The Australians were already knocking at the door; and was the Prime Minister of one of the Little Five, when his country held the presidency of the European Council, also to be admitted?

However Giscard's status-conscious and schematic mind did not see things in these quantitative and practical terms, which might have appealed to Schmidt. Instead he raised theoretical issues in a *de haut en bas* way. In his long letter to me of 22 March (see page 74 *infra*) he based his attitude on the syllogism that the Summit was a meeting of sovereign governments, and that as the Commission was not a sovereign government it manifestly could not participate. This had the advantage of appealing to the British, who react to the word 'sovereignty' with all the predictability of one of Pavlov's dogs, but the disadvantage (from his point of view) of repelling the others, including the Germans, because it struck at the heart of Community doctrine.

Despite my partial Summit victory (but with the circumstances of the Downing Street meetings on 6–8 May hardly enabling me to feel that I was taking part in a triumphal parade), the summer of 1977 was for me a period of low morale. Apart from anything else the Belgian weather that year did not lift the spirits. One of the advantages of my large room at the top of the Berlaymont was that a great deal of sky was visible from its windows. One of the disadvantages of that Brussels summer was that the sky was hardly ever even partially blue. There were seventeen consecutive days in June during which the sun never appeared.

At a more serious level I did not feel that I had so far found a theme around which I could hope to move Europe forward. My first European Council in Rome in March had been dominated by the peripheral issue of representation at the Summit. My second European Council in London in late June was perhaps the most negative of the twelve that I attended. Schmidt and Giscard were firmly in control of Europe, but for the moment had no direction in which they wished to take it. They were rather hostile to Callaghan, whom they saw as semi-detached towards Europe, too attached to the unesteemed President Carter, and running an ineffective economy to boot. Towards Italy and the Little Five they were in a rather sullen phase. The Franco-German axis was working internally well, but, temporarily, it was doing no good for Europe.

In these circumstances, which were also unfavourable to Commission initiatives, I cast around for ideas and pondered the advice which Jean Monnet had given, both publicly and privately. On at least two occasions his ideas had been spectacularly successful in gaining the initiative, and on the second occasion he had done it by rebounding from setback and switching from one blocked avenue to another which was more open. The successful inauguration of the Coal and Steel Community in 1951 had been followed by the juddering halt to the plan for a European Defence Community in 1954. By the following year the Messina Conference was meeting to plan the Economic Community and by 1957 the Treaty of Rome was signed. The lesson he taught me was always to advance along the line of least resistance provided that it led in approximately the right direction.

It was against this background that, during July, I came firmly to the view that the best axis of advance for the Community in the circumstances of 1977 lay in re-proclaiming the goal of monetary union. This was a bold but not an original step. At least since the Werner Report of 1971 (named after the Prime Minister of Luxembourg) 'economic and monetary union' had been a proclaimed early objective of the Community. But no obvious progress towards it had been made, and in a curious way the Janus-like title had the effect of making rapid advance seem less likely. If economic convergence and monetary integration were never to move more than a short step ahead of each other, there was no place for three-league boots.

I decided that there was a better chance of advance by qualitative leap than by cautious shuffle. And such a leap was desirable both to get the blood of the Community coursing again after the relative stagnation of the mid-1970s and on its own merits – because it could move Europe to a more favourable bank of the stream. The era of violent currency fluctuations, which had set in with the effective end of the Bretton Woods system in 1971, had coincided with the worsening of Europe's relative economic performance. In the 1960s, with fixed rates, the Europe of the Six had performed excellently, at least as well as America or Japan. In the mid-1970s, with oscillating exchange rates, it had performed dismally. Nor was this surprising. For the other two main economies the fluctuations had been external, affecting only trading relationships across oceans. For the Community they had been viscerally internal, with the French franc and the D-mark diverging from each other at least as much as either had done from the dollar or the yen.

The key dates for the promulgation of the ideas were: 2 August, when I discussed them at a day-long meeting of my *cabinet*, held at my house at East Hendred; 17–18 September, when I discussed them at a Commission strategy weekend held at an hotel in the Ardennes; 8–9 October, when I presented them to the regular six-monthly meeting of Foreign Ministers, at another hotel in the Belgian countryside; 27 October, when I launched them on the public in a Monnet Memorial Lecture to the European University Institute in Florence; 5–6 December, when I expounded them to the heads of government at a European Council in Brussels; and 8 December, when I chose Bonn as the most appropriate capital in which to try to refute such sceptical comment as had been forthcoming.

I did not end the year with any lively expectation that early 1978 was going to see the governments launching themselves on the qualitative leap. But the sustained advocacy of it had given my presidency a theme and a focus which had been lacking before the summer holidays.

There was one other feature of that autumn which is perhaps worth recalling by way of background. From early September to mid-November the German Government was thrown into a state of total disarray and semi-paralysis by terrorist attacks within the country.

TUESDAY, 4 JANUARY 1977. *London and Brussels.*

The long-awaited day of departure for Brussels: awaited recently more with trepidation than with eager anticipation. Jennifer and I were met at Zaventem airport by the Chiefs of Protocol of the Commission and of the Belgian Government, as well as by my *cabinet* and a lot of photographers. Drove to the house we had rented, 10 rue de Praetère. It looked better than I had expected, although a bit dark, and had made vast progress since I had seen it in November. At 1.30 I gave a lunch in the Auberge Fleurie, a little restaurant near the Berlaymont, for my *cabinet* and other members of the staff. I think we had a total of thirteen – one being missing – which seemed at first sight unfortunate, but I then recalled that the Commission in any case was thirteen, and met on the thirteenth floor, so that one had better get used to that number.

After lunch I went briefly to my temporary, unattractive office in the rue de la Loi and then back to the house to begin a series of 'portfolio' interviews.

WEDNESDAY, 5 JANUARY. *Brussels*.

George Thomson* to lunch, whom as always it was a pleasure to see. He seemed to me in surprisingly good form. It was his last day in Brussels; he would like to have stayed; and he did not know what he was going to do when he got back to London. But he was pleased with his peerage and I think was boat-happy. The prospect of freedom in England was outweighing any Brussels tugs at his heart strings.

THURSDAY, 6 JANUARY. *Brussels*.

The cliff-face day. The day of inauguration, the first day in the Berlaymont, the first day as President. A day to some extent of ceremonial speeches, of public appearances, but also a day in which I had to get the portfolios disposed of, unless we were to start with a major setback.

A semi-ceremonial arrival at 9.45, greeted by the Chief of Protocol and a vast horde of photographers and conducted up to my room where Ortoli was waiting officially to hand over. Again a great series of photographs.

After lunch I went straight into the formal proceedings. After recording for television a ninety-second extract from my opening statement I went into the Commission meeting room to preside for the first time. My first impression was of an agreeable enough room, a round table, with fourteen places around it, one for each of the Commissioners and for Noël, the Secretary-General, room perhaps for about another twenty people to sit behind, and then at either end the glass windows of the interpretation facilities, which are superb in the Commission.

First, I had to walk round the table shaking hands with every Commissioner, and giving television cameras of their various

*George Thomson, b. 1921, cr. Lord Thomson of Monifieth 1977, KT, was a Commissioner 1973–7, having previously occupied three Labour Cabinet offices. Chairman of the Independent Broadcasting Authority 1981–8.

nationalities time to take shots. The cameras then withdrew and I made a twelve-minute exhortatory statement to the Commission. After that we disposed without difficulty of some fairly formal business and then came on to the question of the allocation of portfolios. Apart from saying that I much hoped to be able to find adequate jobs for everyone and that it was vital that we reached decisions that day, I did not attempt to go into any detail and merely suggested, as was expected, an adjournment which I hoped might not be for more than a few hours for bilateral consultations. The Secretary-General announced that he had arranged for a buffet supper, and I said that no doubt was reasonably encouraging but I very much hoped that he had not also thought it necessary to provide for a buffet breakfast, a remark which would have seemed a little too near the bone to be even mildly amusing ten or twelve hours later.

We eventually got an agreed, unanimous, though painfully arrived at solution by just before 5.30 in the morning. I then went down and met the press: a packed press conference of I should think two hundred, which lasted from 5.40 to 6.10. The atmosphere when we came into the room was a mixture of the fetid and the sullen. The press had been kept waiting all night without a great deal of information, though most of them knew the main cause of our hold-up. The bar had apparently been shut since about 2.30, so they were not so much drunk, as I had been warned they would be by Cheysson, as rather hung-over and bad-tempered, which was worse. However, during the half-hour's conference, the atmosphere improved quite a bit. That over, I went back to the thirteenth floor and did five television interviews for a variety of European networks.

FRIDAY, 7 JANUARY. *Brussels.*

Crispin, Michael Jenkins, Celia Beale and I went to the Amigo Hotel for a large bacon and eggs breakfast between 7.00 and 8.00. That was undoubtedly by far the best hour which I had had in Brussels so far. Then home to rue de Praetère, tolerably satisfied. And the satisfaction proved not altogether misplaced, for the fact of having got agreement far outweighed any illogicalities and loose ends, and the press generally, despite some sour briefing from Brunner and Burke, was not unsatisfactory.

I slept for half the morning and then went to lunch with Jennifer at a small restaurant at Uccle.

MONDAY, 10 JANUARY. *Brussels and Luxembourg.*

This was essentially a day for the final preparation of my speech to the Parliament at Luxembourg; the speech had been basically written out by me over Christmas at East Hendred, but it needed titillating in the context of the moment. Received the Papal Nuncio, Archbishop Cardinale, as *doyen* of the Diplomatic Corps, and then had an hour's meeting with the Directors-General we had inherited from the old Commission. 4.27 TEE (Trans European Express) from the Gare du Quartier Léopold to Luxembourg.

On the journey the weather for the first time since our arrival began to improve. As we pulled out of Brussels there was a clear sky with some snow on the ground, and we travelled, working hard on the speech the whole way, through a dramatic sunset and then up through the Ardennes with heavy snow and to Luxembourg just after 6.30. I had the speech complete by the time we arrived and went straight to the unsatisfactory Aerogolf Hotel; unsatisfactory because the food was indifferent, the service slow, and the windows would not open, a typical new hotel.

TUESDAY, 11 JANUARY. *Luxembourg.*

An agreeable morning with deep and hard freezing snow and a good light, but the Aerogolf managed to destroy the effect of the light by having tinted windows. At 10.45 I went to the European Parliament building to call on Georges Spénale, the French Socialist deputy for the Tarn* and President of the Parliament. Then I made a courtesy call on Kutscher,† the President of the European Court, before the formal ceremony of taking the oath of office at 11.30. During this call he gave me his speech which was a speech of

---

* And, as such, the successor at several removes of Jean Jaurès.
† Dr Hans Kutscher, b. 1911, was a Judge of the German Federal Constitutional Court 1955–70, a Judge of the Court of Justice of the European Communities 1970–6, and its President 1976–80.

substance with happily a reference to President Madison which I was able to use as a peg to work in the rather good quotations from Chief Justice Marshall with which Anthony Lester* had provided me.

The Justices and I all assembled in an ante-room where they put on their impressive purple robes, which are a mixture of those used by the Hague Court and those used by the German Federal Court at Karlsruhe. A few moments later we went into the main building before an audience of about two hundred people. Kutscher, an agreeable and impressive man, made his speech seated from the bench and I then made a response of about eight minutes, and the content, particularly the Lester parts, was clearly welcome to the Justices who responded appropriately.

We then took the oaths of office. I saw in some newspaper a criticism that I had read mine in English and not in French. As, however, it was presented to me in English, as I would have wished, I had little choice, and I do not think that I could have been unduly faulted on grounds of insularity as Burke chose to read his in Erse, and Vredeling in Dutch. Kutscher then gave us a very good lunch, though I was not greatly able to appreciate it owing to my concentration on the speech for the afternoon to the European Parliament.

The Parliament met remarkably punctually by European standards and I was on my feet at six minutes past three. The speech lasted exactly thirty-two minutes, only two minutes longer than I had been advised was the optimum. I had put a lot of effort into it and it went reasonably well. At the end there was a good deal of applause, though not I thought overwhelming, but I was told subsequently by Noël that the Parliament was not much given to applause and that I could regard the speech as *une grande réussite*, which was at least polite. The press was also satisfactory. Later that evening I had a thirty-five-minute television panel interview with six journalists from a variety of European countries and which was sent out by a television network in each of the member countries. I was exhausted by this time, and even the English words were not coming easily to me, let alone the French ones at the end.

---

* Anthony Lester, QC, b. 1936, had worked as a special adviser to me in the Home Office, 1974–6.

WEDNESDAY, 12 JANUARY. *Luxembourg and Brussels.*
We had a fairly formal meeting of the Commission in the Kirchberg (Commission office in Luxembourg) at 9.00 before the sitting of Parliament at 10.00.

In the Parliament there were questions to the Council of Ministers* which were answered very well by Crosland† and then questions to the Commission, one of which was for me. I then listened to Crosland's speech, which was too long – forty-five minutes – cautious in tone, but extremely interesting in analysis and on the whole well received, though not exactly with positive enthusiasm. Then a lunch in honour of the Commission given by the President of the European Parliament. I was sitting opposite Spénale across a narrow table. He had Crosland on one side of him, Ortoli on the other side, and I had Kutscher on my left-hand side so that we were four Presidents *carrés*. It was a beautiful day, with a sparkling view to the wide horizons of the surrounding snow-covered countryside. Not much political conversation: it was mostly a mixture of geography and culture, with Ortoli becoming tremendously animated, agreeable and informed about the monuments of south-west France and indeed of Italy. Brief speeches at the end of the lunch.

Seven o'clock reception for me given by the Socialist Group under the presidency of Fellermaier.‡ TEE to Brussels, dining in the Swiss restaurant car which had started from Zurich. Home at 10.45, back out of the snow and glittering sun of Luxembourg into the murk of Brussels.

---

*The Council of Ministers is under the Treaty of Rome the legislature of the Community. The Commission proposes, it disposes. As its name implies, it is made up of ministers from all the member states. The Foreign Affairs (or General Affairs) Council, which I always attended, is the central council. But it has subdivided itself into a number of specialized councils of which the Economic and Finance Council (Ecofin) and the Agricultural Council are the most important. The Council of Ministers is not to be confused with the more recently created European Council, made up of heads of government and their Foreign Ministers, which met three times (now twice) a year as opposed to once a month. The presidency of all these councils rotates between member states every six months (see page 673).

†Anthony Crosland, 1918–77, was British Foreign Secretary from April 1976 until his sudden illness and death in February 1977. As such the six-monthly rotating arrangement made him President of the Council of Ministers from 1 January.

‡Ludwig Fellermaier, b. 1930, was an SPD Deputy for Bavaria 1965–80, and leader of the Socialist Group in the European Parliament 1968–79.

THURSDAY, 13 JANUARY. *Brussels*.

Lunch at the adjacent Charlemagne (Council of Ministers) building with the members of COREPER (the ambassadors or permanent representatives of the member countries). I made a few introductory remarks. The discussion was a good tutorial for me which lasted until well after 3 o'clock.

By that afternoon, back at the office, I was applying myself determinedly to the allocations of director-generalships. These have to be balanced almost as carefully as Commission portfolios.

FRIDAY, 14 JANUARY. *Brussels*.

A series of meetings with Commissioners during the morning, culminating with Ortoli from 12.00. A very typical Ortoli interview. I went to see him rather than vice versa, because I had been told that his room had much the best furniture in the building, and for redoing mine I wanted to see it. He was pleased with this, so we started well. I then asked him his general views about economic and monetary policy and he replied characteristically, requiring a little time to get going and then speaking with great lucidity and analytical precision, but the analysis leading to no remedies. There is a certain French intellectual view that once you have analysed a problem you have done as much as anyone can expect you to do about it.

Commission meeting for two and a half hours in the afternoon. We disposed of a good deal of business, including some reports from Haferkamp on the external scene and on the prospects for Vice-President Mondale's* visit. Then we dealt with Gundelach's fish, on which he made a very good presentation, and there was no great difficulty in getting it through as he wished.

Then Cheysson to see me to describe the meeting which he had had with Giscard† that morning at the Elysée. Giscard, he said, had not been in a very good mood, not surprisingly in view of his press

---

*Walter ('Fritz') Mondale, b. 1928, had been Senator for Minnesota for twelve years before becoming Carter's Vice-President 1977–81. He was the unsuccessful Democratic candidate for the presidency in 1984.
†Valéry Giscard d'Estaing, b. 1926, was President of the French Republic 1974–81, having been Minister of Finance 1962–6 and 1969–74.

conference (difficult because of the Daoud* affair) looming up for Monday. Nonetheless Cheysson said he had two pieces of rather good news from him, though they cannot have been very good for I forget what they were.

They were outweighed by his piece of bad news, which was that the French Government would oppose Commission representation at the Carter-convened Summit, whenever that took place. He said that Giscard himself was rather in favour of such representation, but that Barre[†] was firmly against, not on personal but on institutional grounds, and that Giscard, being now in a weak position and also, he added, rather a weak man, whereas Barre was a stronger man, would probably give way to him, though whether Giscard would hold this position would depend upon how strongly the other members of the Community made contrary representations.

Cheyssons and Tinés[‡] and Roger Beetham and Laura to dine, rue de Praetère.

SATURDAY, 15 JANUARY. *Brussels.*

Three hours of solid paper work until 1 o'clock. We had intended to lunch in the country, but the weather was so awful that there seemed no point in driving through the sodden suburban battlegrounds of Brussels. So we went to Bernard, a fish restaurant above a serious fish shop near the Porte de Namur. A cinema in the afternoon, for the first time for several years.

MONDAY, 17 JANUARY. *Brussels.*

Jennifer and I had Garret Fitzgerald,[§] the Irish Foreign Minister, to dinner. The main object was to repair relations which might have

*Abu Daoud, 'Black September' terrorist, had been arrested in France in connection with the murder of Israeli athletes at the Munich Olympics in 1972. In spite of extradition demands from the German and Israeli Governments, the French Government, provoking scathing criticism from both the French and foreign press, had released him.
†Raymond Barre, b. 1924, a Vice-President of the European Commission 1967–73, was Independent UDF Prime Minister of France 1976–81, candidate for President of the Republic 1988.
‡Jacques Tiné, b. 1914, was French Ambassador to NATO, 1975–9. We had known him and his wife, Helena, since 1955.
§Dr Garret Fitzgerald, b. 1926, son of the first Minister of External Affairs of the Irish Free State, was Irish Foreign Minister 1973–7, and Taoiseach 1981–2 and 1982–7.

been breached by the trouble in the Irish press about Burke's portfolio, though Fitzgerald is no great partisan of Burke's, and also to discuss the Irish director-generalship. No problem about relations.

TUESDAY, 18 JANUARY. *Brussels.*

Suddenly a fine, cold winter's day. My first meeting of the Council of Ministers at 10.15. A rather good discussion on the accession of Portugal. Then back to the Berlaymont for a meeting of eight Commissioners in preparation for Mondale's visit. Fairly satisfactory, brisk going over of the brief. Then to the Château de Val Duchesse* for a luncheon given by the Council for the signature of the agreement with the Mashrek countries, Egypt, Syria and Jordan. Sat in the Council for Gundelach's excellent opening of the Fish discussion. Crosland a pretty effective chairman. David Owen,† though going on about one obscure point of very doubtful validity, also made a good impression around the table.

WEDNESDAY, 19 JANUARY. *Brussels.*

A Commission meeting which was due to start at 10.00 and which I was able to get started, by an effort, by 10.10. A totally punctual start is a Brussels impossibility. We spent the morning on a variety of business, by far the most important aspects of which were dominated by Gundelach. He reported on the Fish Council and then went on to outline in a masterly half-hour *exposé* his thoughts about the agricultural price-fixing, and indeed about medium-term agricultural questions. Then we went into restricted session on the wretched subject of the disposition of director-generalships, and I circulated my proposals. We lunched together, unusually, in the Commission dining room, and had some fairly relaxed conversation there until we reassembled at 3.40 and came down to the real hard knots about directorates-general. However, we had untied

---

*A little nineteenth-century château in a *petit parc* about three miles from the Berlaymont which the Belgian Government had given to the Community for entertainment purposes. The Château Ste Anne (20 January) was a subsidiary establishment in the same complex.

†David Owen, b. 1938, was Minister of State at the Foreign Office until he became Foreign Secretary at the end of February 1977.

quite a lot of them by about 6.30. One of our rue de Praetère dinner parties mainly for Commissioners plus wives, with the Haferkamps and the Giolittis.

THURSDAY, 20 JANUARY. *Brussels.*

A special Commission meeting for an informal *tour d'horizon* in the Château Ste Anne. I said we would start on internal Community matters as we had discussed these less than external ones in the Commission, and got Ortoli to open; strong on logical analysis as usual but not much suggestion of a way forward. We then went round the room with nine speakers before lunch. So far as intellectual content was concerned, Ortoli was probably the best, Davignon the second, and Tugendhat the third best.

We then had an enormously long speech from Natali about direct elections and enlargement. Cheysson then spoke quite well and much shorter, and Haferkamp (surprisingly) very well and for a still briefer time. I summed up, saying that enlargement could be a disaster unless we quickly worked out a programme for handling it in the Commission.

FRIDAY, 21 JANUARY. *Brussels.*

An official visit from President Mobutu of Zaïre. Cheysson and I went down to meet him at the front door and conducted him up in due state to my room, where we had a twenty-minute talk before going to join what was nominally the full Commission but was in fact five members plus a number of Directors-General brought in to fill up the table. The talk with him went only moderately well. He handled himself quite impressively, but not friendlily. He spoke no English and his Belgian French was not very easy to dance in step with because he was completely unforgiving of all mistakes and hesitations made by others, particularly no doubt white others. We then went to the Commission room, where I made a six- or seven-minute speech of welcome to him. Mobutu then responded for about fifteen minutes, and talked well. He made more sense than he had done in my room, where he had launched a pretty lunatic idea, calling for the immediate mounting of a European expeditionary force to deal with Rhodesia, under British command he implied, but possibly supported by a few *francs-tireurs* which he would be glad to supply. An hour's discussion with him and I then went off to the Château de Val Duchesse to greet him on his arrival for the official luncheon.

This was a peculiarly disagreeable occasion. I really disliked sitting next to him more than to almost anyone else I have recently encountered. Fortunately on the other side of me I had the thoroughly agreeable Ambassador from Trinidad and Tobago, but on the other side of Mobutu there was a silent and austere-looking Fleming (a Vice-President of the European Investment Bank). Mobutu gave practically nothing at lunch. I tried almost every subject under the sun. I must have opened about twenty with him – and got nowhere of any interest on any of them, and began to feel, which is not always the case, that my French was more and more inadequate.

Perhaps his ill-humour was partly due to the fact that in helping myself to the fish course I had managed to get a large unfilleted sole to come apart on the plate with a splash of sauce over one of his holy hands. As he apparently regards himself as a near God-like figure and appears on television in Zaïre coming out of the clouds, no doubt this was almost sacrilege. However, the impression I had towards the end of lunch was that he was a man of a certain effectiveness, considerable disagreeableness, with no general interests at all, certainly not in anything historical, geographical, not really much in what was going on in Europe or the rest of the world, not even interested in his own life, since most of the early parts of it were not glorious enough for him to wish to recall them.

At the end of lunch I made a two-minute speech and then, to the great dismay of Cheysson, Mobutu did what apparently he is quite inclined to do, which was not to respond to it himself but to get his Foreign Minister* to do so. I did not mind this alleged slight nearly as much as others appeared to – what I minded was having an extremely boring hour and a half at the table with Mobutu – after which I conducted him downstairs fairly chillily, delivered him to his press conference and escaped as quickly as I could.

*Karl-i-Bond Nguga, b. 1938, was seven months later arrested and condemned to death by the regime although his sentence was subsequently commuted to life imprisonment by Mobutu.

Back at the Berlaymont I saw the New Zealand Ambassador (Ian Stewart), a nice, very pro-European Community man who was about to leave reluctantly and go back to live in New Zealand for the first time in ten years. I never expected to be so pro-'white Commonwealth'.

SATURDAY, 22 JANUARY. *Brussels.*

Woke feeling more buoyant than at any time since arrival. Two hours' French before breakfast, two hours on Commission papers after breakfast, before leaving with Jennifer at 11.45 to drive ourselves to Namur, my first substantial drive in Belgium. Drove up most of the way to the Citadel, a fine dominating complex with a lot of fortifications by Vauban above the junction of the Sambre and the Meuse. There we walked for three miles before descending to the town for lunch. Afterwards a quick walk round the *centre ville*, which has a few attractive things in it, but the whole badly spoiled by redevelopment. The general atmosphere was slightly reminiscent of Aylesbury, or Gloucester without the cathedral.

SUNDAY, 23 JANUARY. *Brussels.*

Bill Rodgers* arrived to spend twenty-four hours. Took him to lunch at Groenendaal, which was good in a heavy Flemish way, immensely slow, with very serious eating going on all around us. At 4 o'clock we were almost the first people to leave. Bill was enjoyable, not obsessed by English politics, but giving me a good insight into what was going on, as usual perhaps a little more optimistic than circumstances warranted, but not ludicrously so. He was not enchanted by the Cabinet, but enjoying the Ministry of Transport. It was a satisfactory talk, no chasm created by the separation of our paths. We had the Tugendhats to dinner with him, plus Laura (Grenfell). Both the Tugendhats very nice; he in my view is turning out to be an excellent Commissioner.

---

*W. T. Rodgers, b. 1928, had become Secretary of State for Transport in 1976, after occupying junior and intermediate posts in the Foreign Office, Treasury and other departments.

MONDAY, 24 JANUARY. *Brussels.*

An audience with the King of the Belgians at 10 o'clock. It was in the Palais de Bruxelles in the city, which he uses entirely for business purposes, living all the time at Laeken, five miles away. The Palais de Bruxelles is almost on the scale of Buckingham Palace, built I suppose at about the same time (1840). Grand rooms, rather sparsely furnished, no ornaments or signs of life about it. I was conducted in to him and found an agreeable-looking, shy, young middle-aged man, whose whole manner was quite unlike that of any member of the British Royal Family, less 'royal' I suppose is the simplest description. Talking to him was remarkably like talking to David Astor;* one had the same feeling of intelligent involvement, sense of worry and concern with 'the world on his shoulders', interest in a wide range of subjects and anxious in a slightly unchannelled way to do something about them.

We had fifty minutes' conversation, mostly in English though he occasionally lapsed into French. He asked a great deal about the work of the Commission, the new Commissioners, how I saw the future of Europe, and did it out of apparent deep interest. He has a strong commitment to the idea of Europe and cannot understand why governments are so foolish as not to move it forward further. At the end he said he would very much like to come to the Berlaymont, and 'assist' (in the French sense) at a meeting of the Commission. I said that we would be delighted to arrange this, thinking that if we could arrange a special meeting for Mobutu we could certainly do one for the King of the Belgians, and asked him to lunch afterwards. He expressed pleasure at all this and saw me off very graciously, conducting me out to my car, which again is very different from Buckingham Palace protocol.

In the afternoon we had a visit from Vice-President Mondale, which wasn't bad going on the fifth day in office of the new administration. I received him at the front door at 3 o'clock. We then had an hour's discussion with five people on each side. The conversation covered an obvious range of subjects and was not particularly deep, but was friendly with a fair mutuality of

---

* David Astor, b. 1912, the second son of Waldorf (2nd Viscount) and Nancy Astor, was editor and proprietor of the *Observer* 1948–75.

approach, particularly about a timetable for various meetings, the Summit, the resumption of the North/South dialogue* etc., and was generally thought by those on our side – perhaps to a greater extent than by me – to have been very satisfactory and worthwhile. I thought we only skimmed the surface of issues, but that was clearly all that he wanted to do at that stage and indeed all that he was briefed to do. But within the limits which he wanted to explore he was well-informed and spoke fluently and confidently without any significant reference to notes.

He made it clear, to our pleasure, that he was strongly in favour of Community representation at the Summit, and also at the end delivered to me an invitation to go to Washington on an official visit to the President at some reasonably early date. He presented me with an embossed and personally signed copy of Carter's inaugural address, the oratorical quality of which, such as it was, seemed to me to be somewhat diluted by ending up 'Thank you very much', which is not exactly how I think the Gettysburg Address concluded.

We then proceeded to the Commission room, I introduced him before cameras to all the other Commissioners, and we settled down for a rather formal twenty-five minutes, with expressions of greeting and exchange of views. Haferkamp and I saw him off downstairs, with great mutual expressions of goodwill.

TUESDAY, 25 JANUARY. *Brussels.*

Left home just after 10.00 for my second visit in two days to the Palais de Bruxelles, this time for the diplomatic reception given by the King and Queen for the Commission and for the ambassadors accredited to the Community. On going in I noticed that the Commissioners who were before or round about me walking up the stairs all seemed rather more formally dressed than I was, i.e. wearing black suits, white shirts and dark ties, whereas I was wearing a striped shirt, having been firmly told that dress was informal. However, I need not have worried, for Davignon, who was presumably the most at home in those surroundings of any Commissioner, had also omitted to reduce himself to white, and

* Jargon of the time for the Conference on International Economic Cooperation (CIEC) between nineteen developing countries and seventeen industrial ones which met intermittently between 1975 and 1977.

indeed more significantly the King, when we were taken in to see him, was wearing brown shoes with a very light blue suit!

George Ball* and Fernand Spaak (our Ambassador in Washington) to lunch, rue de Praetère.

In the evening we gave the first of our obligatory Val Duchesse dinners for the Permanent Representatives, other Commissioners etc. to mark the change of Council presidency, i.e. from Dutch to British. A party of fifty.

WEDNESDAY, 26 JANUARY. *Brussels.*

Our longest ordinary Commission session yet: 10.05 to 1.05, and 3.20 to 6.30. It is exhausting presiding for this length of time. The degree of strain is quite different from that of participating as a non-presiding member in the British Cabinet. Apart from the fact that they go on longer in total, being in the chair imposes a different degree of effort, for one is not able to have those agreeable half-hours or so in which to abstract one's mind from the boredom of the colleagues by doing some forward diary planning or concentrating on some similar matter. That is nearly impossible in the chair, though I noticed that Davignon – not of course in the chair – was wisely doing precisely this at one stage.

We had Gundelach's fish issue, then the so-called Complementary Memorandum† which has to be put before the Luxembourg Parliament at the same time as my Programme speech, and then an interesting but rather sombre debate, so intractable are the difficulties in this field, about the accession of Portugal. During the afternoon we then had about an hour's discussion on an exposé of Gundelach's thoughts on agricultural price-fixing. Although the two Frenchmen gave notice that they were not going to give up the tax on vegetable-oil margarine without a fight, he on the whole got a pretty fair wind behind him.

Towards the end I rather galloped them through a résumé of my speech for Luxembourg; the subsequent discussion politely warned me not to be too encouraging or optimistic. Ortoli and Brunner rather predictably did this, so to some extent did Davignon, and so

---

* George W. Ball, b. 1909, was US Under-Secretary of State, 1961–6.
† A detailed written schedule of proposals which has to supplement the Programme speech.

more surprisingly did Vredeling. He seems to have been converted to pessimistic conservatism fairly early in his Commission career compared with his ebullience of two and a half weeks ago, when he gave the impression that he was going to solve the unemployment problem of Europe at the stroke of a pen.

Dined with Léon Lambert* in his large, strikingly furnished apartment above the Banque Lambert. Very good books, beautifully arranged, also five or six good paintings and some remarkable Eastern *objets* as well. This was my first foray into Brussels society, but, perhaps because he is of *le grand juiverie*, it was not that of the moneyed cousinage of La Hulpe. The inevitable but agreeable Davignons were there, also Fernand Spaak and his sister Antoinette (the younger Paul-Henri Spaak† daughter, Marie Palliser's sister) whom I had not previously met; also a couple of bankers and their wives. Lambert himself was intelligent and friendly.

FRIDAY, 28 JANUARY. *Brussels, Strasbourg and East Hendred.*

The day of my first return to England, but by the rather roundabout route of Strasbourg, for the opening of the new Council of Europe building, which the European Parliament will also use. 10.30 meeting with the Japanese Ambassador, and then an avion taxi to Strasbourg. We drove in to the elegant Hôtel de Ville, where Mayor Pflimlin gave a lunch for about eighty, mainly from the Council of Europe. I had on one side the Turkish Foreign Minister, whose identity I took a little time to discover and who spoke a curious old-fashioned but efficacious French. 'Plait-il?' was his favourite phrase but that may have been more a commentary on my French than on his.

On my other side was Michael Yeats, the son of the poet, candidate for the presidency of the European Parliament, Irish senator, and member of the Fianna Fáil Party. I had a rewarding conversation with him about the difference between Fianna Fáil

---

*Baron Léon Lambert, 1928–87, was President of the Banque Lambert de Bruxelles.
†Paul-Henri Spaak, 1899–1972, Prime Minister and/or Foreign Minister of Belgium intermittently between 1936 and 1957, and Secretary-General of NATO 1957–61, had three children: Fernand, a senior Commission official; Antoinette, a member of the European Parliament; and Marie, the wife of Sir Michael Palliser (see page 130).

and Fine Gael of which he gave a convincing historical explanation; and also about why Fianna Fáil was linked up with the Gaullists. Partly accident, he said, and partly because they were both nationalist parties, but both believing in Europe and both dedicated to the Common Agricultural Policy.

Pflimlin made a gracious but too long speech after lunch and was replied to by Garret Fitzgerald, as the chairman of the Council of Europe Council of Ministers, speaking very good French. Then to the new Palais de l'Europe, where we assembled to greet Giscard at 3.30. He did not seem on very buoyant form, though he was perfectly gracious in the few words which I had with him, and made a show of interest as we went round the building. The so-called *hémicycle* or chamber was rather good; the rest of it, and particularly the exterior, was not inspiring. Six preliminary speeches, including mine which came third. It was at least shorter than most of the others, who all, except for Garret Fitzgerald who was under time, overran their time by 100 per cent or more. Spénale, the French President of the Parliament, made a considerable oration in the old Herriot style. Giscard spoke rather elegantly for half an hour, giving the impression that he was always about to say something of importance, but never did so.

Avion taxi to Northolt at about 7.00. I gave David Owen, who was deputizing for Crosland, a lift back. In the midst of more agreeable bits of intelligence he told me that he thought I would have difficulty with Callaghan about the presence of the Commission at the Summit. East Hendred at 9.20. The strangeness of being back after a fairly long and traumatic period was not as great as I would have expected. It all seemed rather normal.

MONDAY, 31 JANUARY. *London*.

Ladbroke Square* at 10.30. Harold Evans of the *Sunday Times* came. On the way out it became clear that he was in a great state of tension and pressure. The *Sunday Times* didn't seem to be doing very well, the top management regime was more difficult since Roy Thomson's death and there was obviously a tendency to blame

---

*Ladbroke Square was where we lived in London until the late summer of 1977 when we moved across the square to a flat in Kensington Park Gardens.

Evans for the troubles. They had also become rather frightened of the competition from the new *Observer*.

To Lancaster House at 3.00 for my first Political Cooperation meeting.* I had been told that it was much more intimate than the Council of Ministers and so I suppose in a relative sense it was: in other words there were only about one hundred people in the room as opposed to the two hundred-plus that one has for a Council of Ministers. Nonetheless the table was large enough and the crowd was great enough for it to be a fairly formal session. It was well conducted by Crosland and we almost galloped through the business, dealing, rather superficially, with about six items between 3.15 and 6.15. The main dispute was as to whether we should issue a statement on the Middle East. The American Government, though not at an enormously high level, were firmly against our publishing a statement at all. With Genscher's† rather skilful help they got their way.

After the meeting I took Garret Fitzgerald with Crispin for a drink at Brooks's. This proved a well-spent half hour, for in the course of it we evolved a successful idea for lancing the Irish grievance that they had lost their one Director-General by creating a new one for fish.

We then returned to Lancaster House for the dinner and post-dinner discussions. This was devoted to a substantial discussion about the admission of Portugal. I opened saying that we recognized the political imperative but that we were determined that the real economic difficulty should not be glossed over, as it had been with Greece.

The discussion afterwards was inconclusive and interesting mainly from the personality point of view. Genscher was good and weighty, though perhaps not tremendously constructive; Thorn‡

---

* 'Political Cooperation' between the member states was established outside the Treaty of Rome following the Luxembourg Report of 1970. As its name implies, its object is coordination of foreign policy. Because it is alongside but outside the Community as such it follows somewhat different procedures from the Council of Ministers. The Commission participates but less centrally. Different officials of member states (the Political Directors) are involved, but the same Foreign Ministers.
† Hans-Dietrich Genscher, b. 1927, German Free Democratic leader, Minister of the Interior 1969–74, and of Foreign Affairs from 1974.
‡ Gaston Thorn, b. 1928, was Foreign Minister of Luxembourg 1969–80, and Prime Minister (as well) 1974–9. He became my successor as President of the European Commission 1981–5.

and Fitzgerald described rather good circles in the sky but it was not clear what they amounted to; Guiringaud* was half difficult though personally agreeable, and intervened rather skilfully at the end to make sure that the conclusion did not go any further than he wanted; Forlani† was opaque; Van Elslande‡ talked too much and made a lot of jokes in rather bad French, but didn't get anywhere. Crosland, who had been very good in the afternoon, I thought jollied them along slightly too much as though they were members of the Grimsby Labour Party General Management Committee, but maybe that is what they like. However, he seemed in perfectly good control.

THURSDAY, 3 FEBRUARY. *Brussels.*

Dinner at a very good fish restaurant enlivened, if that is the word, on the way out by sensing a slight feeling of embarrassment amongst the staff, which was indeed well founded, as we saw on the ground floor – we had been eating on the first floor – the upturned soles of a Japanese who seemed at least unconscious and possibly dead. When we got outside an ambulance drew up and a stretcher was rushed in. We asked Ron Argent, our inimitable driver, whether he knew what was happening. He said: 'Oh, yes, certainly, oyster poisoning. Quite often happens, but the restaurant is insured against it, so there is no need to worry.'

FRIDAY, 4 FEBRUARY. *Brussels.*

A deputation from the European trade unions at 10.45. About twelve people, in some ways a strong deputation. Vetter, the principal German trade unionist, in the chair, flanked by Jack Jones§ and various others. Jones in the most agreeable, butter-wouldn't-melt-in-his-mouth mood. Vetter was difficult to form a

---

*Louis de Guiringaud, 1911–82, was a professional diplomat who was French Foreign Minister 1976–8.
†Arnaldo Forlani, b. 1925, Italian (Christian Democrat) Foreign Minister 1976–9, Prime Minister 1980–1.
‡Renaat Van Elslande, b. 1916, was Belgian Foreign Minister 1974–7, and Minister of Justice 1977–80.
§Jack Jones, b. 1913, General Secretary of the Transport and General Workers' Union 1968–78, then the most powerful British union leader.

view about – courteous, slightly withdrawn, giving the impression, of which indeed I had read, of deteriorating relations with the German Government. A matching deputation in the afternoon from UNICE, the employers' body; less strongly represented as only three of their presidents out of the nine turned up and I was able to get through the meeting in about an hour or so. Though a nominally less strong deputation, some of their points were harder. At 5 o'clock I saw Douglas Hurd* about direct elections.

During the course of dinner, I had what might be described as my first Brussels emergency telephone call. Noël rang up to say that there had been a tremendous snarl-up in the junior COREPER (not ambassadors but their number twos) because during the meeting in the afternoon all the Nine had agreed to something which was unacceptable to the Commission as it did not meet our prerogatives under the Treaty in the arrangements for negotiating with the Russians. He wanted to have a Commission meeting the next morning. I resisted this on the grounds that a formal Commission meeting, even if it could be arranged, would inevitably attract publicity and a heightening of the atmosphere, and said it was much better to have an informal meeting in my own room at 11 o'clock for which he could get as many of the Commissioners as seemed relevant.

SATURDAY, 5 FEBRUARY. *Brussels.*

Into the office about 10.30. Talked to Crispin, read a slightly legalistic paper from Noël, and started the meeting at 11.00. Only two Commissioners arrived – Gundelach, whom I had seen on the way in and who implied that a nonsense had been made and that we could sort it out, and Davignon. Haferkamp's *Chef de Cabinet* said he had been unable to find Haferkamp in the previous sixteen hours. The meeting was slightly confused, partly because Gundelach was slightly confused, giving at different times differing impressions. Davignon saw it in very good proportion, saying that this was a typical bit of nonsense, but that although it was nonsense it was important to get it right. But he had seen so many similar nonsenses from his position in the Belgian Foreign Ministry on the

*Douglas Hurd, b. 1930, a Conservative MP since 1974, was then Opposition spokesman on European affairs and since 1986 has been Home Secretary.

other side of the table that he was a connoisseur of them, although this on the whole was one of the more nonsensical snarl-ups.

After about an hour's rather rambling meeting we managed to get a line and agreed that Gundelach should immediately summon Maitland,* the British Permanent Representative (Chairman of COREPER) and put a new formula to him. It was typical of the sort of problem which arises in the Commission. In a sensible national government no one would dream of summoning the Foreign Minister for a Saturday morning meeting on such a relatively minor issue, though it probably wasn't a bad idea for me to have to deal with a problem typical of one aspect of the Community's convoluted life.

MONDAY, 7 FEBRUARY. *Brussels.*

Received credentials from the Kenyan and Costa Rican Ambassadors in the morning. The main point of interest the latter produced was that Costa Rica with a population of just under two million had no fewer than forty-five missions abroad, although only about thirty of them, he assured me, were headed by ambassadors. Nonetheless it was an extraordinary figure and, given the fact that their income per head is $750, must mean on a quite conservative estimate of the cost of a mission that 3 to 4 per cent of their national income goes on diplomatic representation abroad – God knows why!

At 4.30 I had the Israeli Foreign Minister, Yigal Allon. He complained about the Community being too friendly to the Arabs and our agreement with the Israelis not being good enough, etc. I then asked him if he would like to stay alone for ten minutes, feeling that I slightly owed him this in view of the day he had given us on his kibbutz fifteen months or so ago, and he then talked with some interest about the Israeli internal position. He thought that Rabin would maintain his position as leader of the Labour Party and therefore probably as Prime Minister after the elections, in spite of a fairly strong challenge from Peres. He himself was strongly in favour of Rabin, who he thought was a much wiser man, even though a less superficially attractive personality or good talker.

* Sir Donald Maitland, b. 1922, Permanent Representative to the UN 1973–4, to the EC 1975–9 and Permanent Under-Secretary for Energy 1980–2.

Of the forthcoming visits to the Middle East, he said he was awaiting Vance's with interest. He would also be glad to see Genscher. He thought that Waldheim's was a waste of time, and that on the following day he might well have to advise Guiringaud to put his off for a few weeks, as the atmosphere might be too hostile. (On the following day, however, he did no such thing, but patched up a truce with Guiringaud and said that he would be very welcome.) Allon said that the fact that the Israeli elections were impending did not mean that there could be no progress on a Middle Eastern settlement at the moment; he would be perfectly prepared to go to a reconvened Geneva conference before 17 May, provided that he was not expected to agree in advance what the results of the conference would be. I stressed that it was very important that he did not lose what might well be an opportunity during the next few months which would not recur.

TUESDAY, 8 FEBRUARY. *Brussels and Luxembourg.*

Foreign Affairs Council which concerned itself almost exclusively with Portugal until I left just before noon. No real debate of substance, although the underlying tone implied that a good deal had been learned from our discussion over dinner in London the week before. Haferkamp did rather well for us, and intervened forcefully. The issue was unresolved when I left, but was finally concluded, at about 7.00 that evening, when Crosland, Guiringaud and Haferkamp worked out a compromise draft.

Genscher behaved characteristically during the morning. He appeared suddenly, spoke to Dohnanyi* and left after about seven minutes, not having said a word to the meeting. The purpose of his journey from Bonn was not altogether clear, but when I asked Thorn of Luxembourg about this later he said it was to be explained by the fact that Genscher has television obsession. He therefore comes for these very brief visits in order to get televised walking in and then goes off and gives television interviews to as many German chains as he can find and hopes to get televised again on the way out.

*Klaus von Dohnanyi, b. 1928, German Social Democratic Minister of State responsible for European business 1976–81, Governing Mayor of Hamburg 1981–7.

Then a very rough flight to Luxembourg. Hayden was nearly sick, but recovered fairly rapidly after we got on the ground and was reassuringly able to eat a perfectly hearty lunch. In the afternoon I delivered my so-called 'Programme speech' to the Parliament. It took fifty-four minutes, to a house which was about three-quarters full and moderately responsive. Getting this speech over was a great relief. A Programme speech, at any rate at this stage in the life of the Commission, really is an appalling task as it is impossible to work out and get together firm hard proposals, and therefore the whole thing has to be a sleight of hand in which you are pretending to be more specific and interesting than can in fact be the case. Thanks to a great deal of work, mainly by Hayden, we escaped without disaster, got a reasonably favourable press, although some complaints from members that it had been vague, unspecific and bland.

The Conservative Group had me to dinner at the dreaded Aerogolf. This Group is in reality a purely British concern, although they manage to find one Dane who will affiliate to them. As a result they count as a Group, as opposed to a collection of individuals, and are able to get all the finances and secretarial services which go with being a transnational group. They were thoroughly agreeable. Peter Kirk,* who was in the chair, was as always a highly intelligent neighbour, and we then had an interesting general discussion.

THURSDAY, 10 FEBRUARY. *Luxembourg and Brussels.*

All-day discussion on my Programme speech. I replied for thirty-five minutes in an unprepared debating speech. In the luncheon interval I entertained Thorn at the Restaurant St Michel. Prime Ministers of little countries do not mind eating in public in their own capitals. Those of big ones do.

Back to Brussels by the evening TEE.

FRIDAY, 11 FEBRUARY. *Brussels.*

A special Commission meeting from 11.00 to 1.00 and again from 3.15 until 5.45, to deal with Gundelach's agricultural price package. He presented it very well. As a result no really solid pro-farm lobby

* Sir Peter Kirk, 1928–77, was Conservative MP for Gravesend 1955–64, and for Saffron Walden 1965–77. He was a dedicated European of high intellectual quality.

opposition built up. I lunched with Gundelach in my dining room and had an agreeable talk with him. We were able to get through remarkably early. A successful day.

SUNDAY, 13 FEBRUARY. *Brussels.*

Jennifer and I drove to Antwerp where we had an hour's look round and then drove on across the Dutch frontier (which indeed is so little of a frontier there that we never noticed when we were passing it), first to Goes and then to Middelburg in the centre of the Walcheren peninsula, where we lunched. Middelburg seemed curiously dead on a Sunday compared with the Belgian towns. To Vlissingen to take the ferry back to the other side of an arm of the Scheldt, and thus within a few miles we got back into Belgium, with a very noticeable change of countryside. Holland looks much neater than Belgium; the roads and the houses are somewhat better. That bit of Belgium has a dark and dejected air which would make it natural suddenly to see King Albert leading a defeated troop of 1914 soldiers down the side of the road. We drove through Ghent which was a surprisingly large, very splendid town, and got home at about 6.00.

MONDAY, 14 FEBRUARY. *Brussels.*

Denis Healey* to see me between 11.00 and 12.00. It was during this meeting that we first heard the news of Tony Crosland's illness the previous day. It was difficult to tell how severe this was, though there was clearly some risk of it being very serious indeed. Denis and I contemplated, not I think his death, but the possibility that he might be out of action as chairman of the Council of Ministers for some time to come.

I had asked Denis what were his own intentions about the future, slightly independently of this, and he said that he intended to stay at the Treasury at least until after the Budget, that a move then had been seriously discussed, but in his view it was not definitely a switch with Crosland, and that in any event his (Healey's) mind

*Denis Healey, b. 1917, Defence Secretary 1964–70, Chancellor of the Exchequer 1974–9, deputy leader of the Labour Party 1980–3.

was moving towards staying at the Treasury for a substantially longer time. This was based on a typically complacent view by Denis, who although he knew he had very bad trade figures that afternoon told me nothing about these and indeed spoke in terms of the utmost euphoria about every aspect of the situation.

I then lunched with the Economic Council. Healey there was in a way quite good, though as insufferably know-all as ever, lecturing everyone about every detail of the new American administration, which he said, manifestly untruly, was going to have all its policies absolutely cut and dried by the end of February, and interrupting everybody a good deal. When I complained, Apel* said, 'Oh, we are used to that; we all have to put up with that.' I said, 'I am used to it too, but that is no reason for not complaining.'

I then went to the Agricultural Council for one and a half hours, and watched Silkin† get into a mess about the agenda (but I am told he did rather well later in the evening on fish), and heard Gundelach present his price proposals for the first time, and listened to the reactions: the Belgians – not very good, but to be expected; the Danes – pretty good; the Germans – huffing a bit but fundamentally friendly; and the French surprisingly friendly. Dinner at home with Jennifer, much disturbed by the appalling bulletins coming in about Tony.

TUESDAY, 15 FEBRUARY. *Brussels.*

Lunch with Henri Simonet,‡ the Belgian ex-Commissioner, at a restaurant near the Basilique. Back for a series of meetings during the afternoon: first a delegation from the Spanish Socialists, headed by Felipe Gonzales,§ an extremely effective, impressive young man, aged only about thirty-four, of humble origin in the south of Spain, and certainly one of the most impressive – though a little frighteningly tough – young leaders whom I had met for some time; then Klaus von Dohnanyi, the excellent European Minister in the

*Hans Apel, b. 1932, German Minister of Finance 1974–8, and of Defence 1978–82, a former Commission official.
†John Silkin, 1923–87, British Minister of Agriculture 1976–9.
‡Henri Simonet, b. 1931, Belgian (Walloon Socialist) Economics Minister 1972–3, a Vice-President of the European Commission 1973–7, Foreign Minister 1977–80.
§Prime Minister of Spain since 1983.

German Foreign Office. Dinner party at home, composed of Dohnanyis, Ruggieros,* Natali and Laura.

WEDNESDAY, 16 FEBRUARY. *Brussels.*

Commission day, but a remarkably easy one. Thirteen or fourteen routine items, but I got them all through in two hours. Lunch at home for Duncan Sandys† and then back to the office to see David Owen, who had been in Brussels to open the fishery negotiations with the Russians and from whom I particularly wanted to hear just how awful the news was from London. He said he regarded Tony as already morally and mentally dead; it was settled; there was no question; he would probably live only about forty-eight hours; he might live longer but there could be no possibility of recovery. He clearly did not think that he was at all likely to get the Foreign Secretaryship himself, although I would not say that he ruled it out completely.

FRIDAY, 18 FEBRUARY. *Brussels and Rome.*

A frenzied morning in the office trying to patch together a statement for the routine general press conference which I had rashly arranged for that day at noon. Rashly because I agreed to do it simply because six weeks had gone by since the previous press conference, and the whole Brussels press corps is addicted to press conferences. The result however was undesirable as I had very little to say, hence the difficulty of preparing a statement. Left for Rome via Geneva at 3.50. Dinner with Crispin and Jennifer when Crispin told us he was going to be married again.

SATURDAY, 19 FEBRUARY. *Rome and the Abruzzi.*

I awoke about 6.30, having had a vivid dream about Tony being present and his saying in an absolutely unmistakable, clear, rather

*Renato Ruggiero, b. 1930, Italian Minister of Foreign Trade since 1987, was then head of the 'Spokesman's Group' and subsequently Italian Permanent Representative to the Community and Secretary-General of the Foreign Ministry.
†Lord Duncan-Sandys, 1908–87, as well as being a minister for most of the time between 1941 and 1964, had been an early pillar of the European Movement and was the founder of the Civic Trust in Britain and of the wider Europa Nostra.

calm voice, 'No, I'm perfectly all right. I am going to die, but I'm perfectly all right.' Then at about 8 o'clock we had a telephone call from the BBC saying that he had died that morning, curiously enough at almost exactly the same moment that I awoke from my dream about him. I pulled myself together with some difficulty and after about half an hour did a brief recording over the telephone to the BBC in London, which they used for the 8 o'clock news, it then being 8.50 in Rome.

After speaking to Hayden in Brussels, I decided that I ought to write a *Sunday Times* piece. We therefore slightly postponed our departure with Natali so that I got it going and made the telephone arrangements in the hotel. I then wrote the greater part of its 650 words in the hour or so's drive between Rome and L'Aquila. It was a difficult feat of concentration. I had very little idea of what I was going to say when I started and the effect of writing about Tony was to bring the immense closeness of our earlier relationship flooding back into my mind, much more than had hitherto been the case, so that during the rest of that day in the Abruzzi, and indeed during the whole Roman trip and beyond, I found I was much more affected than I had been during the previous week, even though I had already realized that he was dying.

Official lunch in L'Aquila with the prefect, the mayor, the chairman of the regional council, etc. and then to Rocca di Mezzo where Natali lives in a modest but agreeably furnished house about a mile from the centre of this fairly small, almost ski-resort-like town. A large dinner party. Conversation in a mixture of French, English, Italian; certain difficulties of comprehension but not insurmountable. Natali's French is improving a good deal; his wife seems to understand a certain amount of it, and his Roman surgeon brother-in-law, who devoted himself to a lot of highly cynical remarks about Natali's politics and Christian Democratic politics in general, but in a thoroughly agreeable way, spoke very good English. Bed at about 11.30 for what should have been a good night's sleep, but very typically was considerably interrupted by the noise of the police cars changing over outside. Policemen up in the middle of the night to provide guards for politicians behave equally noisily over the whole of Europe. They do not see why others should sleep if they are awake.

MONDAY, 21 FEBRUARY. *Rome.*

Horrible humid, soggy morning. It felt like Lagos or some tropical capital rather than Rome in the winter. Crispin and I went to the Vatican for a Papal audience, which went on much longer than we expected. At first they had said a quarter of an hour or twenty minutes, but in fact it took forty or forty-five minutes. The Pope (Paul VI) was too frail happily to talk French, so he talked in Italian and I replied mostly in English. Unfortunately, this was pretty badly interpreted by a young monsignor from California. It was very much more informal than I had remembered when I previously had an audience with Pius XII over twenty years ago.

The Pope switched about in a rather bewildering way between matters of high generality like his support for the European family of nations to those of almost overprecise detail, like asking me why the Nine at its Political Cooperation meeting in London had decided not to issue the statement on the Middle East, and also implying rather worryingly that he would like to get into several negotiating acts in relation to the Middle East generally and the Palestinian position in particular, and indeed also in relation to the Lebanon. He said that if I ever felt that he could do anything useful would I merely let him know by telephone and he would be prepared to proceed immediately! It was not quite clear in which direction he was prepared to proceed, but clearly the intention was good, and the general impression he made was friendly and agreeable.

He then gave us medals, we had photographs taken, and were conducted out. The ceremonies going in and out are rather splendid, with the Swiss Guards and the Papal Chamberlain still fully in operation. A group of about thirty Mezzogiorno bishops were waiting outside. It was not obvious to me (I had never thought about it previously) what to do when passing through an assembled group of bishops in this way. The best thing seemed to incline one's head gravely first in one direction and then in the other. The impressiveness of my departure was however somewhat reduced when one of them was heard to say in a strong stage whisper, 'è Callaghan'.

We were conducted round the Sistine Chapel and other bits of the old Papal apartments and then drove to the house of the President of the Senate, where I had a twenty-minute conversation with Fanfani,* who told me that Soares,† whom he had been seeing the day before, thought that Portugal could be in the Community and participating in direct elections by 1978, which was a fairly surprising and disturbing piece of information, but one not subsequently confirmed by anyone else.

Then on, with Fanfani, to a lunch for various Senate figures of note, but mainly the chairmen of the different specialist commissions who between them added up to a good Italian political cross-section, Christian Democrat, Communist and Socialist. At the end of lunch we had about an hour's general discussion which I had to lead and reply to. Then to see Marcora,‡ the Minister of Agriculture. He launched off into a great diatribe against Gundelach's price proposals and the unfair treatment which Italian agriculture had received, but when pressed became a little more reasonable, in particular saying that in Gundelach's position he would not have done anything very different himself.

Next to the Commission's Rome office where I did a short television performance and went round meeting the staff; then across to the Farnesina, the new Foreign Ministry at the bottom of Monte Mario, for, first, a private meeting with Forlani, the Foreign Minister, and then a rather pointless, wider meeting, with about eight of us sitting lined up on either side of a great table, with blotting pads and pencils as though we were about to negotiate a treaty. However, Forlani is a nice man and the informal meeting went thoroughly well, he giving a very firm assurance of Italian support in relation to the Commission's presence at the Summit.

Then back to the Hassler for a hurried change, a ten-minute programme on the main TV chain on the way to dinner, which was a large mixed affair at the Villa Madama, with speeches at the end. In the course of dinner we received from Italian sources the news of David Owen's appointment as Foreign Secretary, which surprised and greatly pleased us. Hotel by about 11.00 having got through quite a heavy day.

*Amintore Fanfani, b. 1908, was three times Italian Prime Minister 1954–68, and President of the Senate from 1968.

†Mário Soares, b. 1924, Portuguese Socialist leader, was Foreign Minister 1974–5, Prime Minister 1976–8 and 1983–5, and has been President of Portugal since 1986.

‡Giovanni Marcora, 1922–83, was Italian Minister of Agriculture 1974–80, and of Industry 1981–2.

TUESDAY, 22 FEBRUARY. *Rome and Brussels.*

Jennifer to London, and I went at 10 o'clock to the Palazzo Chigi for an hour's meeting with Andreotti,* the Prime Minister, whom I always like. He is quick, intelligent, and has a curious air of engaging shiftiness. He looks like an intelligent and quite attractive tortoise. He is very agreeable to talk to, he knows what he wants to talk about, takes the points quickly, easily, in good, well-arranged order. Difficult to say whether he is gloomy or optimistic about the situation. He is so used to living on the edge of a political and economic precipice that he tends to discount gloom, though it doesn't lead him into Healey-like complacency.

Then on to a three-quarters-of-an-hour meeting in the Palazzo Montecitorio, the Parliament building, with Stammati,† the rather elderly Finance Minister. But this unfortunately made me late for the press conference which followed in the Commission's Rome office and was packed, though partly I think with the Commission staff. It looked as though it was going to be a rather formidable occasion but turned out better than might have been expected and we got quite a good press out of it.

Then on to the Quirinale for a 12.45 interview with Leone,‡ the pocket-sized President of the Republic, conducted in quite a stately form as had been the case in August, in other words a gathering of about sixteen or eighteen people sitting round and he and I talking in periods. He is an agreeable, cultivated Neapolitan lawyer, said to be benignly corrupt. Then a very splendid lunch given at the top of the Quirinale with a magnificent view from the sea to the Apennines including the whole of the city of Rome. It was apparently the old games or sports room of the immensely tall Quirinale guards. What they now do for exercise was not clear.

What, however, was remarkable about the lunch was that it was clearly intended to be a great Italian mark of respect for the Commission, for no fewer than eleven ministers turned up, including Andreotti, Forlani, Stammati, Marcora, almost everyone one

*Giulio Andreotti, b. 1919, was Italian Prime Minister 1972–3 and 1976–9, and has been Foreign Minister since 1982.
†Gaetano Stammati, b. 1908, was Italian Foreign Minister 1976–8, and subsequently Minister of Public Works and Foreign Trade until 1980.
‡Giovanni Leone, b. 1908, was twice briefly Prime Minister in the 1960s and then President of the Italian Republic 1971–8.

could think of, plus a number of other state dignitaries like the President of the Constitutional Court (Rossi). There was supposed to be no speeches other than informal toasts, but when we arrived there was a three-and-a-half-page, foolscap, English translation of Leone's speech, so Crispin had to work hard during lunch in order to patch together something for me, upon which I improvised and made what turned out to be a successful fifteen-minute speech.

Straight from there to the airport, Brussels at 6.30, and into the office for a preparatory meeting for the next day's Commission.

WEDNESDAY, 23 FEBRUARY. *Brussels*.

I lunched at Comme Chez Soi, the first time since 1962 when Eric Roll* took me there with Jean-François Deniau,† and found it just as good as I had remembered, although the size of the bill had increased about tenfold.

FRIDAY, 25 FEBRUARY. *Brussels*.

Presided over a lunch at Val Duchesse for about forty or fifty principal information officers in the member governments. Then an interview with the *Figaro*. Then a series of discussions, including one by telephone with Gundelach in Washington about suspending the export subsidy on cheap butter sales to third countries, which had caused a considerable press outcry that morning.

Then to Liège, where I had arranged to have dinner alone with Willy Brandt.‡ Consultation between our offices led us to believe that he was going to be in Aachen. I therefore said that I would happily come down, but that it would be easier for me, as I had not paid my official visit to Germany, if he could possibly come over the frontier and meet me just in Belgium. He was twenty-five minutes

---

* Sir Eric Roll, b. 1907, was cr. Lord Roll of Ipsden later in 1977. In 1962 he had been one of the 'flying knights' who had conducted the negotiations for Britain's first attempt to join the European Community. Since 1974 Chairman of S. G. Warburg.
†Jean-François Deniau, b. 1928, French Commissioner 1969–73, French Minister of Overseas Commerce 1977–81.
‡Willy Brandt, b. 1913, having been Federal Chancellor 1969–74, was at this time Chairman of the SPD and President of the Socialist International. Later in 1977 he became Chairman of the international committee which produced the Brandt Report in 1979.

late and came in very apologetically, saying that he had got lost on
the way in. I said, 'It is very good of you to have come from Aachen
at all.' 'Aachen?' he said. 'I haven't been to Aachen for years.'
'Where have you come from then?' I asked. 'Bonn,' he said, which
made it even more agreeable of him to have come.

He was more relaxed and talked better, I think, than I had ever
heard him: a good deal about the European Parliament, of which he
still intends to be a member, although seeing some conflict with his
presidency of the Socialist International, a good deal about German
politics, on which he was surprisingly loyal to Schmidt, although
with a modicum of criticism. He believed the Bonn Coalition would
hold. Also a certain amount about Europe, though I had the
impression that he was getting more interested in Third World
issues.

SATURDAY, 26 FEBRUARY. *Brussels and Paris.*

A quick visit to Crispin, who was in hospital, then to the Gare du
Midi for the 11.43 TEE to Paris. From the Gare du Nord to the
Embassy, where David Owen was staying, though just about to
leave, and from 3.00 to 4.00 I had a talk in the little upstairs sitting
room with him and Debbie. There was undoubtedly a slight problem of adjustment, perhaps more on my part than on theirs. When
somebody has been a loyal, young, junior supporter for a long time,
it is a little difficult to get used to his suddenly being Foreign
Secretary. He had made a very good impression in Paris. He was
forthcoming and friendly and I think the meeting went well. Not
unnaturally he was very pleased with himself, very full of himself,
so was Debbie, because he had after all just had a most remarkable
political breakthrough.

He talked sensibly about the position of the Government, though
he told Nicko Henderson* on the way to the airport that he saw
himself as standing in the centre of the Labour Party, neither on one
wing nor the other; but maybe that is a sensible thing for him to *say*.

---

* Sir Nicholas Henderson, b. 1919, was British Ambassador to Paris 1976–9, having been
Ambassador to Warsaw 1970–3 and to Bonn 1973–6. From 1979–82 he was Ambassador in Washington. He has been a friend of mine for fifty years. Mary Henderson is his
wife.

SUNDAY, 27 FEBRUARY. *Paris.*

Drove with Nicko and Mary to lunch with the Ganays* at the Château de Courances near Fontainebleau. Very handsome 1630 house, with a horse-shoe perron, a copy of that at Fontainebleau, added a great deal later. Moved in the evening for reasons of protocol from the Embassy to the Crillon for the beginning of my official visit to the French Government. Installed by them in a magnificent suite, looking over the Place de la Concorde. Rather typically, they paid for this for one night only, though I clearly had to stay there for two!

MONDAY, 28 FEBRUARY. *Paris.*

Another most beautiful day. My first appointment was with Giscard at the Elysée. I walked there, which rather confused protocol arrangements, and indeed made it mildly difficult for me, for there was a guard of honour, to my surprise, lined up in the courtyard, and I was not quite clear whether I ought to walk over to them and see if their hair was short enough, etc. or just walk straight to the steps where people were waiting to receive me. Michael Jenkins firmly and rightly advised doing the latter, saying that had we come by car we would have just swept up and there would have been no question.

I saw Giscard absolutely on the dot, and had eighty minutes with him. On this occasion, unlike the last two on which I had seen him, he spoke English, and spoke it very well. The only crunch was relating to my presence at the Western Summit meeting. He raised it himself, in a glancing way, saying that as I might be aware, the French Government were not in favour of this, not of course at all for personal reasons, etc. but because in their view the Summit should be a meeting of sovereign governments. I hope I left him in no doubt about the strength of my contrary view. I avoided getting substantially drawn into detailed arguments and merely said that I thought it was an enormous waste of time to cause difficulties about this issue, rather than the substance of the European line at the Summit. He took this reasonably well.

At the end, when I was about to leave, I said, 'Thank you very

*The Marquis and Marquise Philippe de Ganay were very anglophile (and anglophone) members of the *'gratin'*.

much. It has been a great pleasure to talk to you and I much look forward to seeing you again in Rome, and after that in London.'*
'Don't say it,' he said, 'don't say it. Just say, "Certainly on many occasions after that".' So on this reasonably agreeable but inconclusive note, we parted, and I drove across to Hôtel Matignon for lunch and subsequent talks with Barre.

After lunch I had about twenty minutes alone with Barre in which we discussed the Summit. I forget who raised it, probably me, for he immediately said: Oh, yes, he had had a telephone call from Giscard after my meeting there informing him about this. He then put his case, which was a remarkably weak one, as I made fairly clear to him. One advantage or disadvantage of both Barre and Giscard is that their lucidity is such that it becomes a positive disadvantage when they have to put a very bad case, and Barre I think at least had the grace to recognize that his case was bad. Then nearly an hour's good conversation with him with others present, mainly about the state of the French economy, but also international monetary affairs.

A series of meetings in the afternoon, and then a Quai d'Orsay dinner of about fifty, with speeches, in a very grand upstairs room.

TUESDAY, 1 MARCH. *Paris and Brussels.*

Rue de Varenne for a meeting with Lecanuet.† I had met him once before, as he recalled, in London, in about 1968. Then he seemed much younger and was regarded at the time of his presidential candidature as a sort of French Kennedy. He still has a faintly American look about him, though he now reminds me more of Nelson Rockefeller, despite the fact that he speaks no English; very agreeable smile, but in a curious way rather difficult to talk to, so that we had some difficulty in spinning out the conversation for forty-five minutes. It was mainly about regional policy, in which he seemed to announce a complete change of French line. Previously they had been against the Regional Fund.‡ He now expressed great

* Rome for the European Council in March and London for the contentious Summit.
† Jean Lecanuet, b. 1920, was in 1977 French Minister of Planning and Development, having been a centrist presidential candidate in 1965.
‡ The European Regional Development Fund (ERDF) had been established in 1975. The Fund was originally all allocated to member countries on a fixed but periodically adjusted quota basis. A small 'non quota' section for specific Community projects was established under my presidency.

interest in it, said that the French very much wanted to participate in it, but wanted a much larger quota for themselves; a move, in other words, from being indifferent to being slightly grasping.

After that, I moved across the road for a meeting with Christian Bonnet,* the Minister of Agriculture. This went much more fluently, as he poured out words almost on the scale of Marcora, his Italian *vis-à-vis*. This quality seems to be a feature of European Ministers of Agriculture. However, perfectly friendly conversation in which rather notably he did not mention the butter sales problem, though saying a great deal about a range of other issues, including their dispute with the Italians about wine. After this, on to the offices of the Commission, just off the Avenue Foch, for a very crowded press conference.

Lunch Au Petit Riche, a nice old-style Paris restaurant which seemed hardly to have changed since Alexander Werth was constantly writing about it in the thirties. 3.20 train to Brussels in pouring rain, across the sodden Somme countryside. I also have the impression it has hardly stopped raining on these battlefields since 1916.

WEDNESDAY, 2 MARCH. *Brussels.*

A meeting with Gundelach at 9.30. Difficulties clearly blowing up about the handling of butter sales to Russia. Our statement suspending so-called prefixation had been welcomed by the British press, though with a good deal of implication that we were closing the stable door after the horse had gone (though as only one horse had gone, while there were several still there, this was not wholly valid). However, this had been followed by much contrary criticism, building up in the early part of the week, from the French press in particular, but to some extent in one or two other countries too. *Le Monde* had distinguished itself by a violent attack on me for interfering with the working of the agricultural *acquis*, which had come out on the Tuesday evening. Gundelach at first seemed to be weakening, but on investigation it appeared that what he was proposing was thoroughly sensible. Into the Commission at 10.00

---

*Christian Bonnet, b. 1921, was French Minister of Agriculture 1974–7, and of the Interior 1978–81.

and disposed of this item without too much difficulty, within about half an hour. The Commission until 1.00 and then again for two hours in the afternoon.

THURSDAY, 3 MARCH. *Brussels.*

Berlaymont fairly early for a meeting with Ruggiero, concerned both with a briefing on the previous day's Commission and with the general press blow-up, particularly in *Le Monde*, about our butter activities. Special Commission meeting from 10.00 to 12.30 on Ortoli's general economic papers, which were fairly negative and into which I tried hard to inject a strategy for mobilizing all the borrowing funds that we could, as an alternative to a rather tiresome and probably ineffective line about the Germans reflating, in the hope that this would give us some room for manoeuvre and for coordination on the whole complex of Regional Fund, Social Fund, Sectional Intervention, FEOGA Guidance etc. Only about four Commissioners understood the significance of this; one or two of whom – Davignon, Tugendhat – liked it, and one or two others – Ortoli at any rate – probably did not, though he did not react violently against it.

Then across to the Charlemagne building for a brief meeting with COREPER before lunching with them. I was amazed to discover that they met in the great 'football pitch' of a room which the Council of Ministers use, and find it difficult to understand how in these circumstances they can get any intimate discussion. We then adjourned for lunch, which was long and interesting; two hours with a lot of discussion about the Rome European Council. The Belgians put round a letter which they had addressed to everybody, taking a very strong line in favour of Commission representation at the Western Economic Summit, but, partly because I did not wish it to be done, it was not discussed at lunch.

Later to the Cinquantenaire for our rather belated New Year reception for the diplomatic corps. As we have approximately 110 ambassadors accredited, and as they nearly all turned up, there was a considerable receiving-line job to do, in which Haferkamp assisted manfully.

FRIDAY, 4 MARCH. *Brussels and East Hendred.*

9.35 plane to London. Read in the *Figaro* that the Gaullist/Fianna Fáil Group in the Parliament had decided to put down a vote of censure on the Commission about the butter affair, but hoped that this need not be too serious. It is very difficult to see who they can get to coalesce with them on their criticism of what we have done. Plenty of other people would be willing to join in criticism, but it would be from the opposite direction.

MONDAY, 7 MARCH. *East Hendred, London and Brussels.*

Motored from East Hendred to London with Jennifer for Tony's memorial service in Westminster Abbey. Sat in the front row of the north transept, surrounded by Foreign Ministers and other European representatives. The Cabinet and the ambassadors were in the choir stalls and Susan and her daughters opposite us and a little nearer to the altar. The service, which was a mixture of a traditional Westminster Abbey 'Church and State' occasion and some unorthodox, more personal elements, was on the whole successful and moving. Jack Donaldson's address was excellent, assisted by some obvious Frankie touches.* Derek Gladwin[†] read the lesson well. Dick Leonard's[‡] reading from *The Future of Socialism*, although in my view not at all badly done by him, did not quite come off, and at the end the Welsh Male Voice Choir from Caerphilly, who had been specially brought and performed from high up in the roof between the choir and the nave, seemed to me to get slightly lost in the rafters and not to produce as emotionally swelling a rendering of 'Cwm Rhondda' and one other Welsh hymn as I would have expected. But it was an impressive and harrowing occasion.

After the service, I walked across towards 10 Downing Street, where Callaghan had a lunch for the four Foreign Ministers who had come − Forlani of Italy, Andersen[§] of Denmark, Thorn of

*Lord Donaldson of Kingsbridge, b. 1907, was Minister for the Arts 1976−9; 'Frankie' is Frances Donaldson, his wife and distinguished historical writer.
†Derek Gladwin, b. 1930, comes from Grimsby (Crosland's constituency) and is an official of what was then the General and Municipal Workers' Union.
‡Dick Leonard, b. 1930, Labour MP for Romford 1970−4, and Parliamentary Private Secretary to Crosland 1980−5. *Economist* correspondent in Brussels.
§K. B. Andersen, 1914−84, was Danish Foreign Minister 1971−3 and 1975−8, and subsequently President of the Folketing (Parliament).

Luxembourg, and van der Stoel* of Holland – as well as for Maurice Schumann representing Guiringaud, and David Owen and me. The conversation was fairly stilted, I thought, with Callaghan rather ill at ease trying to lead the assembled people through a mixture of international gossip and semi-serious points. What did they want him to put to Carter? What did they think of Carter's views about dissidents? he asked, and nobody seemed to have anything very much to say. Then at the end he did a rather deliberate and calculated rehearsal of his difficulties about getting through the legislation for direct elections, while saying that he would of course do his best.

After lunch I had twenty minutes' official bilateral talk with him, and then we leant over the banisters at the top of the staircase at Number 10 for some time and talked more widely. He told me that he would not have appointed Tony Chancellor, even had Denis moved and even had Tony lived, because he had decided that his health was not good enough, which if true obviously showed considerable foresight. I asked him who then he would have appointed and he said he didn't know, and talked rather vaguely about splitting up the Treasury. At no time, though he was perfectly civil, did he express any regret that he had let me go.

3.55 plane to Brussels. Back in the Berlaymont more or less on time, we started rather long consultations with Gundelach about how to handle the European Parliament vote of censure. We eventually decided without too much difficulty, though with the consumption of a good deal of time as consultations with Tugendhat and Burke were also involved, that we would take the initiative in forcing a debate before the vote of censure itself could be taken, at which Gundelach would open and I would wind up.

TUESDAY, 8 MARCH. *Brussels and Strasbourg.*

Foreign Affairs Council. Routine business until just after 12.00, with David Owen proving a good and effective, self-confident but not aggressive chairman. Then a restricted session to discuss primarily the matter of Community, i.e. my, presence at the Western

---

*Max van der Stoel, b. 1924, was Dutch Foreign Minister 1973–7 and 1981–2, and Permanent Representative to the UN 1983–6.

Economic Summit. David Owen threw it to the meeting without a
lead, Guiringaud immediately spoke, but in a rather unengaged
manner, slightly shame-facedly, saying the French Government
were against. Almost immediately afterwards he left the room,
leaving poor Nanteuil* to hold the fort. Van Elslande and van der
Stoel then spoke in strong opposition to the French.

I followed, making a statement for about ten minutes, knowing
the Belgians and others wanted something pretty strong from me,
stating that our position was clearly and firmly in favour of being
there, arguing the case in relation to the items under discussion and
saying that it clearly would be absolutely ridiculous if we wasted
our time at the Rome European Council, as we would have to
unless Community presence was agreed to, debating this procedural question, rather than what at this moment of economic
crisis we should say when we actually got to the Summit. The Irish
State Secretary, Fitzgerald being away, supported this view, as did
Forlani, as did Thorn, though rather tortuously.

David then said that regrettably there was not a consensus in
favour and therefore – I think this was in accordance with his brief –
the decision was that we should not be invited. He had first asked
Nanteuil if the French wished to change their position. Nanteuil,
who looked rather like an apprehensive goat tethered to his post,
wishing he could go away and certainly not wanting to be called
upon to say anything, produced a monosyllabic 'non'. Genscher
then came in rather reluctantly. He had been leaning back throughout the discussion. He said the Germans had not changed their
position; they were in favour of Community participation; that
would continue to be their view, but they did not want to have any
great rows with anybody.

I then contested David's summing up, saying the fact that there
was not unanimous agreement certainly did not mean that a
decision had been taken against; there were still two months to go
and clearly the matter would have to be raised at Rome apart from
anything else. This was strongly supported by a number of other
delegations and agreed to. We then went down to lunch. I reluctantly had to sit next to Guiringaud. We had some perfectly polite

*Vicomte Luc de La Barre de Nanteuil, b. 1925, was French Ambassador in The Hague
1976–7, Permanent Representative to the European Community 1977–81 and 1984–6,
and to the UN 1981–4. Since 1986 he has been French Ambassador in London.

general conversation until near the end, when I told him that I had not been very pleased with what he had said, which would not surprise him, and that I wondered how much give there was in the French position. He implied that he thought there was some, without entering into any very definite commitment.

We then went upstairs, when curiously enough he twice came running up to me to make some little point: Giscard hoped very much I would do some work on the institutional implications of enlargement; and that nothing was to be taken personally. Rather surprisingly overforthcoming for the French.

Back to the Council for three hours. Then to Strasbourg by avion taxi. Dinner with Gundelach. Then half an hour's walk round the cathedral.

WEDNESDAY, 9 MARCH. *Strasbourg.*

To the new Parliament building at 8.30. The building, the *hémicycle* apart, is ghastly and inconvenient, as generally irritating and unattractive as I had feared at the opening ceremony it would be. Routine Commission meeting for an hour in a room about seventeen times too big, in which we sat as though we were on the platform of the Birmingham Town Hall with nobody in the audience. I spent most of the morning working on my fairly short speech on butter for the afternoon, its shortness being balanced by my relative ignorance of the subject.

The speech did not satisfy me, and whether it satisfied anyone else I could not quite tell, but perhaps it more or less did. The Parliament is not really a rewarding body to which to speak. There is of course the linguistic difficulty and the fact that the Chamber is often pretty empty (not that it is different from the House of Commons in that respect, but it is bigger), and these difficulties are compounded by the extraordinary proliferation of the photographic industry in Strasbourg, so that not only are you liable to have moving television cameras producing film which is hardly ever used, but you also have flashlight photographers who come and photograph you the whole time you are on your feet – and even when you are not.

FRIDAY, 11 MARCH. *Brussels.*

Commission meeting from 11.00 to 1.15 involving Davignon on steel, which he did excellently. One of the best discussions on a specific issue which we had had in the Commission. Lunch in my dining room in the Berlaymont, with Jennifer, who had arrived in Brussels for the first time for nearly three weeks, and George Thomson, who was in Brussels, plus one or two *cabinet* members. Then back for another two hours' Commission meeting, this time mainly on North/South questions.

Soares, the Prime Minister of Portugal, arrived at 6.00 and Haferkamp and I went down to meet him at the front door. I then saw him alone for forty minutes. He speaks good French but no English at all. Agreeable, friendly, quite impressive man, who seemed rather tired, as well he might be after his tour round Europe. He talked reasonably interestingly but not fascinatingly. I asked him had he found much difference in the approaches to Portuguese admission as he went round the capitals, and he said yes, the Benelux countries were mildly *réticent* and the French were difficult, but the main thing the French wanted was that Portugal should pay a price and buy their colour television system. I said, 'What – you mean that even Giscard raised this with you? The great head of this great Government, confronted with this great issue, is acting as a television salesman?' 'Yes, indeed,' he said, 'Giscard pressed it more than anybody else.'

We then went into the special Commission meeting which lasted just over an hour. Soares did most of the talking: long, not bad, introductory statement, rather less good, slightly rambling reply to some general questions. We then adjourned until the dinner at the Château Ste Anne at 9.15. Relations became still warmer after my speech there, which the Portuguese were particularly pleased with, and which indeed did sound rather good. I had done very little of it myself; it was a considerable achievement of Michael Jenkins. Unfortunately the young woman interpreter was so moved that she fainted about three-quarters of the way through. Soares was a little slow to go – he seemed particularly interested in talking to Nanteuil, I think about general French cultural matters rather than about politics – and we did not get home until 12.30.

SATURDAY, 12 MARCH. *Brussels*.

Into the Berlaymont just before 10.30 in order to receive Soares again. He was very late, so we gave up the attempt to receive him at the front door and retreated to the top of the lift, where Davignon said, 'For every minute he is late, put an extra year on the transition period.' Soares's great concern was against 'globalization', in other words the Portuguese application being treated as part of a package with Greece and Spain. He was quite realistic economically. He left us at 12.00 for a press conference.

MONDAY, 14 MARCH. *Brussels*.

Lunch with the Ecofin (Finance Ministers) Council. Sat between Apel and De Clercq,* with Denis Healey opposite. Considerable row at the end about representation at the Summit, Duisenberg[†] being very effectively aggressive and saying that if we were treated like this the Dutch would not lend any money to the British, or for that matter the French, in the future. A good sledge-hammer technique for dealing with Denis's thick skin, and I think it was moderately effective. De Clercq said he wasn't sure the Commission was strong enough on the need for representation and I assured him he was quite wrong and did a ten-minute piece.

WEDNESDAY, 16 MARCH. *Brussels*.

A ghastly day. Two hours' work at home in the early morning because the Commission papers did not arrive until ridiculously late the night before, a rather bad-tempered briefing meeting in the office at 9.30, then into the Commission at 10.00. Commission business not perhaps too difficult during the morning. We disposed of a good many routine items and began Vredeling's major paper on the Social Fund.[‡]

Commission farewell lunch for Lebsanft (German Ambassador),

*Willy De Clercq, b. 1927, Belgian Minister of Finance 1973–7 and 1981–5. Member of European Commission 1985–9.
†Wilhelm Duisenberg, b. 1935, Dutch Minister of Finance 1973–7.
‡The Social Fund, established 1974, can finance 50 per cent of member states' projects to deal with redundancy, training, resettlement, help for migrant workers etc.

at which I had to make a short speech, and then a resumed Commission at 3.30, which, alas, went on until 9.50. The main subject of contention was one aspect of Vredeling's Social Fund proposals, in which the 'regionalists', Giolitti and Natali, were against the 'sectoralists', who were primarily Ortoli and Davignon. At one stage we had an adjournment for redrafting. Then Giolitti and Natali said they would vote against. I thought this unfortunate. A minority of two is one thing. But a minority of both the Italians on regional policy is another. So we went on and on, trying to find a compromise and eventually put it to a *Chefs de Cabinet* meeting for an hour, who did then produce an acceptable draft, a rather good piece of work by the *Chefs*, with Michael Emerson in the chair. But it was all very time-consuming and I doubt if I ought ever again to allow a Commission meeting to go on as long as this.*

In addition to the Social Fund problem we had the very difficult issue of certain personnel appointments, including that of Christopher Audland† as deputy Secretary-General, David Marquand‡ as head of the special new Parliamentary and Social Partners Group, and my proposal to set up a Central Planning Unit with a German at its head. A good deal of opposition on all grounds. Davignon was against Audland, supported by Haferkamp and Giolitti. I then thought I ought to give Ortoli a chance to support Audland, which he had said he would do, but in fact didn't and merely went off into a typical 'defend-the-old' attack on the Central Planning Group. A bit of general muttering against that, and I had to say that I would provide them with a more clear outline of its role. But I hope that will go through eventually. David Marquand's job – though not for the moment his appointment – I got through by a small sleight of hand. Tugendhat was not very effective at this meeting, which was important for him as Personnel Commissioner and which is unusual with him. But I suspect everybody was tired and rather bad-tempered. I went home at 10.30, too exhausted to eat.

---

*I never did.
† (Sir) Christopher Audland, b. 1926, was deputy Secretary-General of the Commission until he became Director-General for Energy 1981–6.
‡ David Marquand, b. 1934, who had been Labour MP for Ashfield 1966–77, came with me to Brussels. Now Professor of Politics and Contemporary History at the University of Salford.

FRIDAY, 18 MARCH. *Brussels, Bonn and East Hendred.*

Crispin and I set off by car for Bonn just after 12 o'clock. Rather cold, standing-up picnic lunch by the side of the autoroute just short of the German frontier. Into Bonn shortly before 3.00 for my meeting with Schmidt.*

It was a bad day for him, as is now often the case, for the telephone bugging row which had been simmering away in Germany for some time had suddenly blown up to a new dimension. As a result he was half an hour late, although full of apologies. I then had a one-and-a-quarter-hour meeting with him, talked a little about the Commission, and secondly about representation at the Western Economic Summit, which was the main purpose of my visit. Here he opened hard, aggressive/defensive: he wasn't going to quarrel with his 'friend Valéry'; he was the only real friend he had; he was the only person who supported him, while others were yapping away at him to reflate the whole time, etc.

I argued the case in a variety of ways. The point he was keenest on was when I told him I wasn't going to preach reflation at him, which indeed I did not think was very sensible. The point that at first he seemed less keen on was any argument about the Americans being eager that we should be there, which provoked a good number of anti-Carter complaints, and I wondered whether my having slipped in that Carter was inviting me to an early visit to Washington was wise, as Schmidt obviously was not tremendously pleased to hear this. However, later aspects of the conversation made me slightly change my mind about this. He dismissed the Dutch – 'The trouble is that the Dutch ought to be 60 million and the Germans 12 million; it would no doubt be better for the world, but God had decided otherwise.'

Towards the end I made it clear I was not asking him to have a major row with Giscard, but that I did not think the French position was as hard as it was thought to be, and that if he used some gentle influence it could be quite effective. 'Why doesn't Callaghan do it?' he said. 'Well, I don't know,' I said, 'but in any event you have more influence with Giscard.' 'That's true,' he said contentedly. Then he

---

*Helmut Schmidt, b. 1918, was Chancellor of the Federal Republic of Germany 1974–82, having been Minister of Defence 1969–72 and Minister of Finance 1972–4.

said, 'Well, I think probably that it will work itself out at Rome so that you will be there.'

We next discussed direct elections, my encouraging him to put some beneficial pressure on Callaghan. I then expounded to him my ideas for a very substantial increase in the Communities' borrowing role, in order to lend money not just for balance-of-payments reasons, but for infrastructure and 'sectoral' improvements in the weaker economies, although accompanying these by firm measures of macroeconomic 'conditionality', as it is called; in other words a requirement upon the receiving Government to accept effective disciplines. He was rather favourable, warmed to the idea a good deal, even suggested that there might be some German money available for borrowing from their large reserve funds. A successful conversation on this, although necessarily vague at this stage.

It was then 4.15, I had been with him three-quarters of an hour, and I thought he was showing signs of wishing to bring the interview to an end, which indeed would have been totally reasonable, as he wanted to go to Hamburg for the weekend. However, he then began one of his cosmic gloom conversations. How long did I think he should stay in the job? 'As long as you think you can do it better than anyone else,' was my opening bid (which would have given him substantial tenure). We then talked about who could succeed him if he went. 'Apel is the only person within the Government,' he said. 'It may be a break-up of the Coalition.' 'Would Willy Brandt be brought back?' I asked. 'Ah, a lot of people would like that,' he said, 'but I don't know that Willy would really want to come back in the present extremely difficult circumstances. What he probably most wants is to feel that people would like him to come back, without his having actually to return and do the job.' We then gossiped a little about our respective experiences in German and English politics.

He then got on to his relations with America and it became clear that he was deeply offended at not having been invited by Carter, and although superficially very irritated with the American administration – particularly over the Brazilian nuclear deal – was also profoundly concerned at a deterioration of German/American relations to 'a worse point than they had been in for at least ten years'. He brooded on this for some time saying, 'I am very pro-American. I am much more pro-American than I am pro-British, and I have never really been pro-French. But Valéry is my only real friend.' Then a certain amount of: 'Well, I have done what I can. I sent my Foreign Minister to see Carter. Genscher was rather impressed by him. I sent Brandt, the leader of my party, to see Carter; he was impressed by him too. But I can't go myself unless I am asked, and in present circumstances, even if asked, I do not think I could easily respond very quickly.'

Then, very surprisingly, he said, 'I suppose you see a lot of Americans and have a lot of American contacts, do you? This is the reason why I have been exposing to you my mind about this.' So I said that I would certainly do anything I could to ease this extremely delicate and dangerous problem and I was glad he had raised it. He showed no sign of wishing to bring the conversation to an end until a protocol man came in to say that as (to Schmidt's surprise) I had no special plane (a good mark for the Commission's sense of economy, which I hope was noted), I would have to leave if I was to catch my commercial flight. So I left with a warm farewell, was just in time for a good punctual flight, and got to East Hendred at 7.15 feeling much better than for several days. It is part of Schmidt's quality that his gloom has an inspiriting effect.

SUNDAY, 20 MARCH. *East Hendred*.

Beaumarchais',* Rodgers' and Leslie Bonham Carter† to lunch. Bill on surprisingly good form. Rather wanted a pact with the Liberals, but ready if necessary to face an election, and thought the Labour Party might even win it. Surprisingly pro-Callaghan, rather more settled in the Cabinet than a few weeks ago. No sign of jealousy of David Owen.

MONDAY, 21 MARCH. *East Hendred and The Hague*.

10.15 plane to Amsterdam and to the Hôtel des Indes at The Hague, a wonderful re-creation with infinite pains of the nineteenth-century atmosphere of Jakarta, built about 1840. Then to the

---

*Jacques de Beaumarchais, 1913–79, was French Ambassador in London 1972–7. We had known him and his wife, Marie-Alice, since 1953.
† See note on page 108.

Catshuis, for half an hour's talk with Joop den Uyl,* the Dutch Prime Minister, before the lunch he was giving for me. He was extremely interested, despite the fact that he was in the midst of a major Cabinet crisis, in what Schmidt had said to me on Friday (about the Summit, not about the Dutch, which I did not repeat), very firm and keen about Community representation there. A very informal atmosphere, as seems usual in The Hague. Den Uyl himself opens the front door and then towards the end of the conversation ministers who have been asked to lunch drift in. There were about eight at lunch: Max van der Stoel, the Foreign Minister, van der Stee,† the Agricultural Minister, plus Ruud Lubbers,‡ the Economics Minister, and Duisenberg, the Finance Minister, with both of whom I am increasingly impressed. Extremely agreeable and interesting lunch, with a good half-hour's discussion about the Summit.

Then we adjourned to the Cabinet Room next door and settled down for two and a half hours' discussion on a whole range of issues, agriculture, enlargement, North/South dialogue, economic and monetary policy, Social Fund, regional policy, agenda for the Summit, etc. Fairly exhausting, but well worthwhile. They fielded a team of about five ministers, who changed from time to time, whereas I had to deal with the whole thing myself.

Then to the Parliament building for a public session on direct elections of the Second House's (the principal chamber in Holland) Foreign Affairs Committee. I spoke for about ten minutes and then answered questions for another quarter of an hour. Before that a television interview, after that a press conference for twenty-five minutes and a radio interview. Then a pause. Then an official dinner in a restaurant almost alongside the hotel. I got the news during the day that Carter was definitely inviting me to Washington and was offering the dates we had suggested. Good news this; important to decide how to handle the announcement of it in relation to the Rome European Council. A good day in The Hague too. It is a pleasure to talk to the Dutch Government because of their

* Joop den Uyl, 1919–87, leader of the Dutch Labour Party, was Prime Minister 1973–7, and Minister of Social Affairs and deputy Prime Minister 1981–2.
† Alfons van der Stee, b. 1928, was Dutch Minister of Agriculture 1973–80, and of Finance 1980–2.
‡ Ruud Lubbers, b. 1939, was Minister of Economic Affairs 1973–7, and has been Prime Minister of the Netherlands since 1982.

commitment to the Community and the common premises from
which we start a discussion.

TUESDAY, 22 MARCH. *The Hague and Brussels.*

Drove to Soestdijk to see Queen Juliana. Arrived there in time for
an 11.15 audience. An agreeable palace in a belt of woodland, built I
think about 1690 or 1700, but with I would guess a good number of
subsequent additions. Rather pretty, light style of architecture. The
amenities somewhat diminished, however, by there being a six-
lane highway literally within 250 yards of the front entrance.

As with the King of the Belgians, the proceedings were immensely informal by British court standards. I was met by a sort of
Wren officer who took me upstairs to the first floor, where we
waited for a moment and then Queen Juliana appeared from an
unexpected door, looking remarkably healthy after a holiday in
Austria. She began by saying she had heard that unfortunately I
had to leave for Brussels at noon. Could I not postpone this
departure and stay for lunch at Soestdijk? I explained why my 4
o'clock meeting made this impossible. We then went into an
upstairs sitting room, which was full of agreeable *bric-à-brac* and
might easily have been the sitting room of any elderly publicly
involved well-off lady of the previous generation, Violet Bonham
Carter or Stella Reading, say, except for there being two rather
official-looking telephones on the desk. She poured coffee, rather
incongruously from under a tea-cosy, saying, 'I am sure you would
like elevenses.'

I then had a talk of nearly an hour with her. I found her
interesting, extremely easy to talk to and with a fairly wide range of
knowledge and considerable interest about European questions.
Rather anti-German. Nothing of great profundity emerged in the
conversation, but it was worth doing. Then at the end she said,
'Now, I think we ought to go downstairs, because people want to
take photographs of us.' So we went down to the front hall, where I
presented Michael Jenkins and had the photographs taken and
then went off, she standing waving from the top of the perron as I
left in my car. The slight problem then was what you do in these
circumstances. Do you try to bow inside the car or do you wave
back? I forget how I answered the problem.

WEDNESDAY, 23 MARCH. *Brussels, Luxembourg and Brussels.*

Early start by avion taxi for Luxembourg. This was an unexpected visit to deal with the vote of censure on butter sales to Eastern Europe, which we had been confidently informed would not be taken. But this had proved (as so often with Parliament intelligence) to be quite mistaken. I arrived at the Parliament building just in time for a few quick words with Gundelach before the debate began at 10.00. Cointat, French Gaullist ex-Minister of Agriculture, opened, a Dane spoke for a minute and I then replied for about twenty minutes. After that there were four or five speeches from the members of the other groups and the whole thing was over, except for the vote, by just after 11.15.

The atmosphere was quite calm and the proceedings fairly satisfactory. Cointat's speech was not particularly effective, mine seemed to go fairly well. Broadly the line-up in favour of the censure was almost entirely French, plus a few Irish. Bordu,* nominally on behalf of the whole Communist Group, announced they were going to support the vote of censure, but the Italian Communists quickly repudiated him. The vote did not take place until 1 o'clock, when I had gone back to Brussels, but then produced the very good result of 95 votes to 15 against the censure.

A Commission meeting from 3.30 to 7.15. Fairly routine business. High morale afterwards as a result of having got a number of things out of the way.

THURSDAY, 24 MARCH. *Brussels and Rome.*

Plane to Rome. Hassler Hotel by about 4.15. Stayed in the hotel from then until about 8.30, working hard on papers for the next day's European Council. Then with Ruggiero and Crispin to dine with my predecessor Malfatti† at his flat in the old part of Rome. He had invited five or six of the editors of the main Italian papers.

---

* Gérard Bordu, b. 1928, was a French Communist Deputy for Seine et Marne, Member of the European Parliament 1974–9, and one of its Vice-Presidents 1977–9.
† Franco Malfatti, b. 1927, was President of the European Commission 1970–2, when he resigned to return to Italian politics; Minister of Finance 1978–9 and of Foreign Affairs 1979–80.

FRIDAY, 25 MARCH. *Rome.*

Up early on a most beautiful morning. (The weather throughout this Rome visit, in contrast to the one of a month ago, could not have been better: continuous clear sky, temperature nearly 70° during the day but down to about 40° at night.) I worked over breakfast for about an hour and a half and then had a 9.30 briefing meeting with Ortoli and the four or five Directors-General we had with us.

Left at 11.30 to drive to the Campidoglio for the ceremony of the twentieth anniversary of the Treaty of Rome. We milled about for some time with the heads of government and Foreign Ministers, and then proceeded to the main, rather grand room, for the ceremony itself, which was quick, as there were speeches only from Leone, the President of the Republic, and a strikingly good one from the Communist Mayor of Rome. Then off to the Quirinale and the grand presidential luncheon. During the milling about there was a great deal of conversation on arrangements for the Summit. Giscard said nothing to me at this stage, but Schmidt implied that things were going to be all right for a compromise, and there was a good deal of muttering from den Uyl, Max van der Stoel, the Belgians, Thorn, Garret Fitzgerald, the Danes, all very excited about the issue, and feeling no certainty about the outcome.

The luncheon was a big affair for about one hundred and fifty. The heads of government and I were conducted into an inner room and then from there we were led out to shake hands with all the assembled, mainly Italian, guests. Rather to my surprise, Berlinguer* was there, in the middle of a row, and was routinely introduced to me. As a result of all this, we did not get into lunch until 1.45 and it looked as though everything was set for a major Italian cock-up, with the Council itself starting hours late. This could not have been more wrong. The lunch, which was very good for a banquet of this size, was served, four courses, in forty-five minutes flat, and this included brief speeches from Leone and from Callaghan (as President-in-office of the European Council). The whole thing was over by 2.30. This result was achieved by having a fleet of waiters – there must have been about a hundred – who

---

*Enrico Berlinguer, 1922–84, was the Italian Communist leader, and a dominating although far from extreme figure in Italian political life.

advanced into the room like a swarm of bees as soon as each course was released.

Afterwards to the Palazzo Barberini for the Council itself. Great chaos in all the ante-rooms; difficulty in assembling my papers, though I was more successful than Schmidt, who didn't find his at all until the meeting had been going for some time. But he doesn't care much about briefs. On the way in, Giscard came up to me, full of apparent charm, calling me rather unusually for him by my Christian name, and asking had I got his letter, the four-and-a-half-page document which he thought it wise, most extraordinarily, to write me on the Wednesday, to which I replied rather coldly, 'Yes.' He then said, 'I do not understand why you are making such a fuss about presence at the Summit, my dear Roy. Your position in Europe is such that I would have thought this was a matter of complete unimportance to you.' I said it was a matter of very great importance, not personally but from the point of view of the Community. In any case, whatever my views, at least five countries felt very strongly about it. He then made an even more curious remark, saying, 'I never believe in arguing about matters which are unimportant, but when I see something as a matter of principle, then I never bend.'* He was friendly, I was chilly throughout, and we then separated and moved in.

The European Council itself is in form a surprisingly satisfactory body, mainly because it is intimate. There were only twenty-five people in the room and we sat round a relatively small table, looking at most beautiful cartoons on the walls and ceiling. The twenty-five were made up of the nine heads of government, plus their Foreign Ministers, plus Ortoli and me from the Commission, plus four staff from the presidency – British Foreign Office staff, on this occasion, who were there for note-taking purposes – plus one *huissier*, who can be sent out with messages. This was a vast improvement on the huge gatherings which characterize the Council of Ministers, with up to three hundred people present in the huge room, talking from one end of the table to the other as though across an empty football pitch.

We met from 3.30 until 7.30 and talked mainly about the general economic position and then about the North/South dialogue. No

---

*Curious, because this was exactly what he was about to do.

Foreign Minister spoke throughout, nor did Ortoli. I intervened two or three times, fortunately being called by Callaghan to speak second, after den Uyl had spoken first on the general economic prospect, and therefore got into the water fairly quickly and easily. There was little discussion on the Summit issue, because although this was raised with a hint of menace by den Uyl, and supported by all the other five, it was agreed that it should be settled at dinner.

The meetings of the European Council, although intimate and restricted, are not at all secret. There are few in the room, but everybody goes out and tells great numbers of people exactly what they think has happened, and amongst their staffs there are those who in the course of duty immediately go and tell the press. It is a restricted meeting with full subsequent publicity, which is perhaps not a bad formula. At 7.30 I did a short debriefing session with my staff, who cluster around like a group on a rugby field when a player is changing his shorts.

To the Hassler about 7.45 for a very quick change (not of shorts) and then back to the Barberini for the official dinner an hour later. The dining arrangements were rather like those of a feudal court. Dinner, although of the same quality, I think, was provided for everybody, but in a series of rooms of declining hierarchical order. The nine heads of government and I dined in the inner one, then the Foreign Ministers and Ortoli, then the various officials present in a series of about three subsequent rooms. I sat at dinner between Andreotti and Cosgrave,* the Irish Prime Minister. Cosgrave distinguished himself by eating more than almost any man I have ever seen, although his figure shows less sign than mine of this being his habit. The main course was *pièce de boeuf rôti*, over which I hesitated between taking one or two pieces, and took one, without a second helping. He took four for a first helping and three for a second helping, and followed this by two enormous helpings of ice-cream *gâteau* and then went to sleep for most of the rest of the evening!

Talk at dinner was broadly divided into two halves. Giscard, who was sitting opposite Callaghan, mostly led the conversation down our side of the table, mainly in French with Tindemans† and

---

*Liam Cosgrave, b. 1920, Irish Fine Gael Foreign Minister 1954–7, and Prime Minister 1973–7.
†Leo Tindemans, b. 1922, Belgian Prime Minister 1974–8 and Foreign Minister since 1981.

Andreotti and me, with Cosgrave concentrating on his food and talking no French at all. Schmidt, Callaghan, den Uyl, Thorn and Jørgensen* were mostly talking together at the other end in English. After dinner, I suppose about 10.15, we got down to discussing the dreaded Summit. Den Uyl opened, speaking much worse English than usual for some reason or other. It was late in the evening and perhaps he was getting tired. Indeed at times it was difficult to tell whether he was speaking English or Dutch. Then, after one or two other interventions, Giscard spoke, handling himself rather well but making a highly contradictory statement, explaining why on no possible ground – this being supported by a whole series of specious arguments – could the French Government agree to the Commission being present, and then ending up by saying, which was no doubt what Schmidt had got out of him on the telephone, that he would agree to my being present for a session dealing with matters of Community competence. There was considerable argument around this, and it was made clear that it must be sessions and not a session.

I spoke only once for about five or seven minutes, and others chimed in in varying ways. Schmidt was not very strong, although he claimed to me afterwards that this was his deliberate tactic. He was trying to make it easier for Giscard, he said, having done his real work on the telephone, which was indeed I think true. Callaghan was not very strong either, but not too bad, and on one or two points slightly helped my position. The Little Five plus Italy were disappointing. Andreotti, who suffers grave linguistic disadvantage on these occasions – everyone else spoke in English at this stage of the discussion – said practically nothing. Tindemans was probably the best of the others. Thorn as usual was slightly irrelevant, and then he and Jørgensen left the room for quite a long time, going off I think to look for a loo, which was indeed extremely difficult to find without a walk of about three hundred yards in the Barberini, which was throughout its main disadvantage.

We went on round and round the subject in varying ways, but eventually arrived at the compromise solution, put forward in these terms: 'Present for discussions within Community competence at session or sessions'. It was made clear that there would be no

*Anker Jørgensen, b. 1922, Danish Social Democrat Prime Minister 1972–3 and 1975–82.

question (1) of this being restricted just to one session, or (2) of my being asked to go out of the room at times and wait in the corridor outside.

Towards the end David Owen came in and said that the Foreign Ministers were bored and in a state of revolt outside, could they go to bed? They were told 'Yes', but in fact when we came out most of them were hanging about having last drinks. I then did a debriefing exercise and the press were informed indirectly of what had taken place. I returned to the Hassler reasonably satisfied. The outcome was certainly better than most people had expected and made it peculiarly difficult to see why Giscard had got himself into such a complicated position and why in particular he had taken the trouble to write me an elaborately drafted letter into which many hours of Elysée or Quai d'Orsay talent had clearly been poured such a short time ago.

SATURDAY, 26 MARCH. *Rome and Brussels.*

Up early to another beautiful morning, but in a more relaxed mood than on the previous day. Some work over breakfast, a short briefing meeting, and then to the Barberini for the resumption of the Council at 10.00. Photographs outside on the terrace before we resumed, during which time the Dutch and the Belgians began to get very excited, saying that they were very worried that there had been a long meeting between Callaghan and Giscard that morning and they thought that the French were going to rat, with some degree of British connivance, on the agreement arrived at the night before. They proved to be wrong, but I awaited the acceptance of the agreed statement with some trepidation. But at this stage at any rate such concern proved unnecessary. The Council met from 10.00 until 12.15 and got through a good deal of business fairly expeditiously. Statements were approved on a Common Fund,* North/South dialogue, the economic position, the Summit, Japanese trading relations, and we had a somewhat more substantial debate on steel. Callaghan was a good and efficient chairman.

One of the more extraordinary features of the morning was

---

* 'The Common Fund' referred to an industrialized countries' impending offer in the Conference on International Economic Cooperation (see page 85 *infra*) to allow *virement* between the different funds available for Third World commodity stabilization.

Genscher's behaviour. As, like other Foreign Ministers, he was not encouraged to speak, he spent the whole of the session engrossed in reading newspapers. He must have read every word in two days' issues of *Die Welt*, as well as getting on to several others. Quite frequently also he read them, not looking down at them on the table in front of him, but holding them up open before him, as though he were sitting at his own breakfast table. His performance reached a crescendo during a longish intervention of Schmidt — when Schmidt was arguing powerfully some point which he clearly regarded as of importance. Genscher was engrossed in his newspaper throughout, and then at a more than usually crucial point in Schmidt's discourse, decided to turn over the page, as a result of which Schmidt was practically enveloped in the folds of the *Frankfurter Algemeine* and was trying to address the Council through newsprint.

Schmidt showed remarkably little irritation at this, but it certainly did not point to very good Schmidt/Genscher relationships, the more so as Genscher, during Schmidt's next intervention, got up and walked heavily and slowly, as is his way, out of the room. However, the Council survived these various vicissitudes and got through fairly satisfactorily. We then hung about for some time, debriefing and preparing for a press conference which I was to give jointly with Callaghan at 1.00. This was a relatively easy and short performance.

While I was sitting in my car in the courtyard of the Barberini waiting to leave, Nanteuil, the French Permanent Representative, approached the car, half-laughing in a slightly embarrassed way. I had my window about a third down and went to unwind it right down, but by some misfortune (it might easily have created a major diplomatic incident) succeeded in winding it bang up in his face. However, he surmounted this and said: 'I am afraid this is rather a farce, but I have to ask you whether you still want the original of that letter which the President of the Republic wrote to you on Wednesday. It is rather out of date now, so perhaps you don't want it.' I said, 'Mais, si. C'est un document historique.'

We both laughed a certain amount over this, and I give Nanteuil rather good marks for his handling of the embarrassment. Then, poor man, he had to put his attaché case on the back of the car and try, as is always difficult in such circumstances, to find this heavily

The first day: arriving at the Berlaymont in a winter dawn.

Taking over from Ortoli.

The new Commission at its first session. From my right the order is Haferkamp, Vredeling, Giolitti, Davignon, Vouël, Natali, Ortoli, Gundelach, Cheysson, Burke, Tugendhat, Brunner, Noël. Behind me is Crispin Tickell. Beneath the interpreters' boxes are Hayden Phillips (far left) and Michael Jenkins (second from the right).

Addressing the European Parliament in Luxembourg, January 1977.

With Jennifer, Georges Spénale (President of the Parliament) and Ludwig
Fellermaier (leader of the Socialist Group), Luxembourg, January 1977.

Greeting President Mobutu of Zaïre, my first African visitor and my third
week. His hat and my tie matched better than our conversation at lunch
(see 21 January 1977).

A European Council in London, June 1977. Left to right: Callaghan, Thorn,
Cosgrave (hidden), Schmidt, Giscard, Jenkins, Jørgensen.

With Davignon, 1977.

With Gundelach, 1979.

A day in the country for Commissioners. Left to right: Natali, Tugendhat, Giolitti and Vredeling, September 1978.

embossed document and hand it over to me. Fortified by this, we set off for a celebratory lunch at Passetto until we left to drive at great speed to the airport. We were in the air barely thirty minutes after leaving the restaurant. Why we wanted to get back so early I cannot think, for it was a perfect day in Rome and a horrible evening in Brussels.

TUESDAY, 29 MARCH. *Brussels.*

Into the office fairly early, to be photographed beside the Rover, which was in a state of almost total collapse and was about to go back to England for various major overhauls.* Nonetheless, ironically, British Leyland thought it was a good thing to have me photographed outside the Berlaymont with it. It had to be pushed into position!

FRIDAY, 1 APRIL. *Brussels.*

Commission meeting at 10.00 on Mediterranean agriculture. It opened in an extremely disagreeable atmosphere with the French in particular, but also to some extent Davignon and the Italians – Giolitti more than Natali – complaining of the statement (about a new aspect of the old butter exports row) which had been put out in the name of myself and Gundelach. Gundelach gave an explanation which improved things a good deal, and then he went off and did a reasonably satisfactory press conference. But it looked at one time as though we were set right back into the middle of another major row which was going to be quite as difficult as the February one. This did not, however, materialize despite the fact that at the end of the Commission meeting I had Nanteuil muttering dark threats from Paris down the telephone. I did not take these too seriously but I was depressed by the Commission meeting, both because of the disagreeable atmosphere at the beginning and also because of a very unsatisfactory discussion of Mediterranean agriculture.

---

*We had two official cars in Brussels, one English and one German. Equality of numbers was not, alas, matched by equality of performance.

MONDAY, 4 APRIL. *Brussels.*

A meeting with Bob McNamara,* accompanied by William Clark,†
at 12.30, and took them home to lunch. Apart from Jennifer and
Thea Elliott‡ (staying), we had a Commission lunch for him,
including Ortoli, Davignon and Cheysson. McNamara as always
was both nice and impressive. He spoke very well across the table
after lunch and made a considerable impression on both Ortoli and
Davignon. Cheysson already knew him well.

THURSDAY, 7 APRIL. *London.*

Went with Jennifer to see a rather pretty little house in Addison
Avenue as a possible alternative to Ladbroke Square. Then to the
British Council to look at some good pictures which they were
offering to lend me for my room in Brussels. We got a Sutherland, a
Matthew Smith, a Sickert and also one or two possible large
abstracts.

Then to Downing Street for three-quarters of an hour with
Callaghan, who was in what I would describe as his bluff bullying
mood. We talked perfectly friendlily for some time. Then I spoke to
him about the need to unravel the really very tight knots tied by the
breakdown of the Agricultural Council, particularly if Britain
wanted JET,§ or indeed if he wanted to have any success during the
remaining three months of the British presidency of the Council of
Ministers. He then raised without warning some new difficulties
about the Summit, on which the French were going on being
endlessly tiresome, and suggesting a rather unsatisfactory arrangement by which I did not go to the first dinner, did not go to the
Saturday session, and went only to the large Buckingham Palace
dinner on Saturday night and to the Sunday sessions. Apparently
the French with almost unbelievable impertinence were trying to

*Robert S. McNamara, b. 1916, was US Secretary of Defense 1961–8, and President of
the World Bank 1968–81.
†The career of William Clark, 1916–85, ranged from being diplomatic correspondent of
the *Observer* 1950–5, to a vice-presidency of the World Bank 1974–81.
‡Thea Elliott, widow of Anthony Elliott, 1921–76, British Ambassador in Finland and
then Israel and a close friend from Oxford days.
§Joint European Torus, a major research undertaking into the possibility of producing
nuclear power by fusion rather than fission, which was likely to be sited either at
Garching in Bavaria or Culham in Oxfordshire.

say that the British must exclude me from lunch on the Sunday. Callaghan, I thought, was pretty weak in dealing with all this, and it wasn't a very satisfactory conclusion to the interview.

SATURDAY, 9 APRIL. *East Hendred.*

Large lunch party with, amongst others, Nicko Henderson. Nicko told me that François-Poncet,* Secretary-General at the Elysée, had been on to him on either Tuesday or Wednesday about the vital issue of my non-presence at the preliminary dinner for the Summit on the Friday evening, and also the Saturday sessions, Giscard still fighting a hard rearguard action. He also said that throughout the British had been basically just as difficult as the French and that he was amazed that, given this essential weakness of position, I had got as far as I had at Rome.

SUNDAY, 10 APRIL. *East Hendred.*

Easter church from 10.15 to 11.15, then croquet with Edward.† Family lunch, followed by a visit from the David Owens from 2.15 to 4.15. It was very good of them to have come, because it could hardly have been convenient, for they had driven up from Plymouth that morning and David was seeing Nkomo at 5.30 before preparing to fly to Africa that evening. I had a good talk with him, although in a way it does now remind me slightly of talking to Tony (Crosland) in the last four or five years. There is a certain reticence on both sides. We got on to the subject of the Summit towards the end, where he was rather anxious to justify himself and to say that he had done the best that he possibly could, although explaining that Giscard was making a lot of new difficulties. He also said that Callaghan, who had started by being very bad on this point, as bad as Schmidt and Giscard – I said, 'Not fair to say that Schmidt was as bad as the other two' – was in his view becoming steadily better. However, it was quite a useful conversation, although I hate being a *demandeur* with David.

---

*Jean François-Poncet, b. 1928, was Secretary-General at the Elysée 1976–8, and French Foreign Minister 1978–81.
†Edward Jenkins, b. 1954, is our younger son, now a barrister.

SUNDAY, 17 APRIL. *East Hendred and Washington.*

1.05 Pan-American plane to Washington, which, amazingly, was in the air at 1.15. Quick and agreeable flight. Slightly irritating not to be able to go by Concorde, a plane which never seems to go from the right place at the right time. I was considerably amused to discover on the plane a large party of British MPs, about ten in all, led by Nicholas Ridley and Brian Sedgemore, travelling first-class of course, who, when asked what they were doing, said they were members of the House of Commons Public Expenditure Committee who were going to Washington to study methods of effective control and saving. I hope they don't spend as much as they save.

We were met by Fernand Spaak, our Ambassador, Peter Ramsbotham, the British Ambassador, and American protocol people. We drove into Washington on a most beautiful spring afternoon, temperature about 75°, sky cloudless, all the trees out and the atmosphere still and fresh. We were installed in Blair House, which I had only visited once before when Joe Fowler* gave me a dinner there in 1968. It is splendidly furnished with a lot of good early American furniture, as well as mementoes of Presidents. We had a huge suite with a library, a drawing room, two bedrooms and, strangely, three bathrooms. My bedroom was a sort of Eisenhower memorial room. However, in a curious way, the practical amenities were by no means up to the splendour. The main disadvantage was that no window could be opened, for security reasons I suppose.† As a result we were unable to establish contact with the sparkling atmosphere outside and had throughout rather stuffy airconditioning. My bathroom also was remarkably inconvenient and I never managed to get any hot water to come out of the bath taps. Equally, the rather beautiful quite large paved garden at the back was ruined as a place to sit or even walk in by the sound of one of the noisiest air-conditioning machines ever heard. It was like being in a small forge.

*Henry H. (Joe) Fowler, b. 1908, was in 1968 US Secretary of the Treasury.
†I now realize, which I did not then, that it was almost certainly the room to the window of which President Truman rashly rushed on 1 November 1950, when the Puerto Rican assassination attempt on him led to two deaths in the street outside.

MONDAY, 18 APRIL. *Washington.*

This was the crucial central day of the visit. I awoke inevitably very early, and did a good deal of further work on briefs between 6.10 and 9.30. A most beautiful morning again and Jennifer and I walked for a mile. Then left at 11.25 in a cavalcade of cars for the one-minute drive to the White House. Into the Cabinet Room, where we were greeted by Mondale and Vance,* as well as Brzezinski* and one or two other people. Then I was taken into the Oval Room for a private talk with Carter. He and I stood with our backs to the fireplace for photographs, while the following extraordinary exchange took place:

He said, 'I expect you know this room well. Have you been here often before?' I said, 'Yes, I think I have seen four of your predecessors here.' He very quickly said, 'That means you start with Kennedy, does it?' So I said, 'Yes, though I also met both Truman and Eisenhower, though neither when they were in office and therefore not in this room.' I then added, conversationally, 'But, to my great regret, I never set eyes upon Roosevelt. Did you, Mr President, by chance see him when you were a boy?'

'See him,' said Carter incredulously. 'I have never seen *any* Democratic President. I *never* saw Kennedy. I *never* saw Lyndon Johnson [astonishing]. I *saw* Nixon, and I both saw and talked to Ford of course, and that's all. You see I am very new to this scene of Washington politics.' This he said without prickliness or chippiness or bitterness, simply as a matter of fact of which he was half but not excessively proud. It was quite different from the aggressive/ defensive way in which Lyndon Johnson would have reacted had one got on to an analogous conversation with him about the Kennedy years.

After this we sat down as I had said that I wanted to have a word or two alone with him, discussed how he would like to take the agenda in the formal meeting, and told him that I was concerned about relations between Germany and America, giving him a very brief description of my conversation with Schmidt, and said that I was sure Schmidt would like to improve relations and that I

* Cyrus R. Vance, b. 1917, was US Secretary of State from 1977 to the summer of 1980, when he resigned. Zbigniew Brzezinski, b. 1928, was National Security Adviser at the White House throughout the Carter administration. He and Vance did not get on very well together. I preferred Vance.

thought this could be one very useful outcome of the Summit. Carter responded easily, with interest and warmth.

We then proceeded to the Cabinet Room and settled down for our meeting across the table. There was a total of fifteen or sixteen people in the room, a few more on their side than ours, but not many. Carter conducted the meeting well. It lasted about fifty minutes and I do not suppose that he spoke for more than ten minutes of the time himself. I must have spoken for a total of thirty minutes at least, mainly because I was the only person who spoke on our side and also because a lot of questions were put to me. On their side interventions were made by Vance and, once, by Brzezinski, and too frequently by Henry Owen,* the loquacious Brookings Institute man, who is now in charge of the preparatory work for the Summit.

The atmosphere was very friendly, the Americans making it absolutely clear how keen they were to work closely with us and what nonsense they thought it that we were being excluded from the preparatory meetings for the Summit. Carter gave the impression of being well structured both physically and mentally. He has a neat body, in spite of his odd face, holds himself well, moves compactly, and conducted a tight meeting.

After it was over we went to the State Department, I riding with Vance in his car, and discussing on the way a mixture of gossipy items and subjects of real importance. Lunch, again about eight a side. Blumenthal, Strauss and Cooper† were there, the first two not having been present at the White House. Quite a good, general discussion at lunch. After lunch half an hour's talk with Vance alone in his room. I decided to repeat to him what I had said to the President about Schmidt. I think that he is fairly cool about the French, although he is anxious to have tolerable relations.

He expressed great admiration and affection for David Owen, said that he got on very well with Genscher, but found Guiringaud by comparison stiff, rigid and very unwilling to go in any way

---

*Henry Owen, b. 1920, formerly of the Brookings Institute, was the American 'sherpa' (as they came to be called) for ascents to and descents from the Western Economic Summits, and as such the opposite number of Crispin Tickell, the British Cabinet Secretary (Sir John Hunt), the Governor of the Bank of France (Bernard Clappier) etc.
†Michael Blumenthal was then US Secretary of the Treasury, Robert Strauss was Special Trade Representative, and Richard Cooper was Under-Secretary for Economic Affairs at the State Department.

outside his instructions or to engage in a relaxed conversation. I said he was lucky not to have had to deal with Sauvagnargues.* He also agreed that Carter and Schmidt, certainly if they set themselves to it, would get on thoroughly well together, but that relations between Carter and Giscard were likely to be a good deal more difficult. Vance also told me, almost with incredulity, although I heard it with no such incredulity, that they had had semi-official protests from the French Government about having very briefly received Michel Rocard, the number two man in the French Socialist Party, at the State Department.

After this meeting Vance escorted me down to the front of the State Department and I returned to Blair House for a brief pause before a meeting at 3.30 with Robert Strauss, the new Special Trade Representative, who called upon me there. Quite a good meeting with him. He, as at lunch, was very anxious to recall our previous encounters and to establish a relationship of personal friendship, and, although obviously a political 'pro', should be more than tolerable to deal with on the personal level. He does not know much about Multinational Trade Negotiations† yet (nor do I) but he has people who do and will probably pick the subject up quite quickly. He is clearly determined to make a personal impact in this field, which means pushing the MTNs to a successful conclusion. He took the Trade job rather reluctantly but having done so will want to make the most of it.

I then set off for a more formal meeting, with more people present, with Blumenthal at the Treasury. Blumenthal was accompanied by his Under-Secretaries, Solomon and Bergsten, and chose to talk a lot about North/South CIEC (Conference for International Economic Cooperation) matters. Despite their choice of subject they were not wholly well-informed, certainly not Blumenthal, who had not much applied his mind to these matters, and nor on one point was Solomon, who had. They both, however, gave the impression of being quite impressive intellectually, and Blumenthal was very good on trade matters, though knowing less about monetary affairs.

* Jean Sauvagnargues, b. 1915, a career diplomat, was French Foreign Minister 1974–6, and Ambassador to London 1977–81.
† MTNs: negotiations for the implementation of the so-called 'Tokyo Round' of tariff reductions in the GATT, which was the main formal business between the Commission and the US Government.

Back at Blair House I had an hour's visit from Teddy Kennedy which was partly politics and partly gossip. He looked very well and seemed perfectly reconciled to his new role of being a major senator, but not a figure with any likely immediate presidential prospect. I asked him if he still managed to find time for instance to do much speaking around the country, and he said, 'No, there isn't much point, and as a matter of fact I don't now get many invitations.' He was reasonably friendly towards Carter, not overboard about him, but not bitterly, irresistibly critical like George McGovern.

That evening we gave our dinner party for about forty at Blair House. The Vances came, and also the Charles Schultzes (Chairman of the Council of Economic Advisers), as well as some other Government figures, Richard Cooper, etc. It was difficult, however, to get people from Congress and of the three or four legislative notables whom we asked, I think that only Rhodes, the Republican Leader in the House, turned up. However, a lot of old friends, like Harrimans,* Bruces,† McNamaras, Arthur Schlesingers,‡ came with apparent alacrity. The food was not very good and the drink (provided by the house) entirely American. David Bruce, when we lunched with him the next day, retaliated by giving us Haut-Brion 1945!

TUESDAY, 19 APRIL. *Washington and Chicago.*

A walk from 7.15 to 8.00. Then back to Blair House for a Voice of America programme followed by a meeting with Henry Owen on the preparatory work for the Summit. Then a press conference at 11.30, followed by one or two individual interviews and the Bruces' lunch with Joe Alsop§ and Ben Bradlee (editor of the *Washington Post*) at 1.15.

*Averell Harriman, 1891–1986, former US Secretary of Commerce, Ambassador to Moscow and London, and Governor of New York, had married Pamela Digby, formerly Mrs Randolph Churchill, in 1971.
†David Bruce, 1898–1977, who had married Evangeline Bell in 1945, was the most distinguished American diplomat during the plenitude of his country's power. He was Ambassador to Paris 1949–52, Bonn 1957–9, London 1961–9, and NATO 1974–6, the intervals being filled with major *ad hoc* appointments.
‡Arthur M. Schlesinger, Jr, b. 1917, historian of the ages of Jackson, Roosevelt and Kennedy, was married to Alexandra Emmet.
§Joseph W. Alsop, b. 1910, wrote for thirty years a famous political column, at first with his brother Stewart Alsop and then alone, until he tired of politics and turned in 1974 to old furniture and the history of art.

At 2.30 I went to see Tip O'Neill, Speaker of the House, who in some ways is a caricature of a Boston Democratic politician, but at the same time quite different from his equally Bostonian predecessor, McCormack. He was for instance extremely impressed when he discovered that I had a Harvard honorary degree – it must be said that his constituency embraces Cambridge – whereas McCormack would have been totally unmoved by that and thought it a typical bit of eastern establishment international frippery.

Then a good meeting with a selection from the Senate Foreign Affairs and Finance Committees. About twelve senators present, mostly important ones. Hubert Humphrey presided, his appearance having changed most dramatically since his illness. He now looks like a death head mask, shrunken, but at the same time seemed for the moment fit and vigorous. Also Russell Long, Frank Church, Abe Ribicoff, Jack Javits, George McGovern and a number of others I knew less well. We talked around for about an hour or so. Then from there to the British Embassy where I did a debriefing with the ambassadors of the Nine, and direct from there to the 7.30 plane to Chicago, arriving in a thunderstorm, with a slow drive in from O'Hare to the Whitehall Hotel, the Drake being full.

WEDNESDAY, 20 APRIL. *Chicago and New York.*

Lunch speech to the Council on Foreign Relations. Only about a hundred people, almost entirely male and business, but a fairly receptive audience who produced a very good question session afterwards. The speech itself was rather long, about thirty-five to forty minutes, but also went quite well despite (1) my cold and (2) a curious indifference on the part of those present to my reference to Adlai Stevenson, who had been chairman of the Council for six years in the thirties. Afterwards a quick visit to the Art Institute opposite, which was as spectacular as I had remembered it, then back to the hotel, followed by a tedious one-and-a-quarter-hour drive to O'Hare. This, however, was nothing compared with the tedium at O'Hare itself, which really is the major disadvantage of the otherwise splendid city of Chicago. We moved off from the terminal about forty minutes late and then proceeded to sit on the ground for another one and three-quarter hours, so that when we got to New York we were two and a half hours late. To the Plaza Hotel.

THURSDAY, 21 APRIL. *New York.*

Recorded an ABC breakfast programme with John Lindsay,* whom I was pleased to see again. A call on Waldheim at the UN at noon. Having heard very little in his favour, I found him somewhat more impressive than I had expected. He was not very interested in or knowledgeable about economic affairs, which he left to his French deputy who was present, but he talked well about political issues like Cyprus, Southern Africa and the Middle East.

Lunch with *Newsweek* at the Century Club, typical of all these American editorial luncheons, in that six or seven people do nothing but ask questions and therefore do not, I think, get nearly as much out of one as they might do if they contributed rather more to the conversation themselves. Afterwards to the office of the Communities' Mission to the UN for a debriefing of the ambassadors of the Nine to the UN. Then our dinner which Arthur Schlesinger had organized in the new Windows on the World restaurant on the 107th floor of the equally new Trade Building. The Mac Bundys† and Betty (Lauren) Bacall epitomized the guests.

FRIDAY, 22 APRIL. *New York and East Hendred.*

Day plane to London, and East Hendred by 11 p.m.

WEDNESDAY, 27 APRIL. *Brussels.*

Commission for five and a quarter hours. Quite long, a lot of business transacted but all rather easy, a gentle stream meandering in an agreeable way through a rather flat landscape. Lunch in the middle for Mountbatten,‡ with Tindemans and Simonet as Belgian guests, Plaja,§ the Italian Permanent Representative, and Michael Jenkins. Mountbatten talked well in set pieces. He had to leave at half past two and I then stayed another half hour or so listening to Tindemans and Simonet warily purring at each other. It was a

*John Lindsay, b. 1921, Mayor of New York 1965–73. Much discussed as a possible Democratic presidential candidate (even though he had been elected as a Republican) for 1972.

†McGeorge Bundy, b. 1919, was National Security Adviser to Presidents Kennedy and Johnson 1961–6, and head of the Ford Foundation 1966–79.

‡ Lord Mountbatten was in Brussels partly to lobby me in favour of his Atlantic College at St Donat's in the Vale of Glamorgan.

§Eugenio Plaja, b. 1914, was Italian Permanent Representative to the UN 1973–5, and to the European Community 1976–80.

crucial day for the formation of the new Belgian Government. Tindemans very much wanted the Socialists, and particularly Simonet, in the Government, and Simonet himself very much wanted to be in the Government. The points at issue were that Tindemans wanted Simonet to be Minister of Finance, while Simonet wanted to be Foreign Minister, and that Tindemans wanted the Socialists and the Liberals to come into a grand coalition and the Socialists wanted to keep the Liberals out and have the Communal parties in their place.

THURSDAY, 28 APRIL. *Brussels.*

At 12.45 to the COREPER meeting in the Charlemagne building where we marched in and sat down facing the chairman, flanked by the other ambassadors, as is the routine, and Donald Maitland read out their report on the agenda for the next meeting of the Council. I deliberately made practically no comment on this and then said to him afterwards that, while I valued the luncheons and his calls upon me, I thought that these meetings were absolutely useless and I proposed not to go to them in future. He said he quite agreed, although he hoped very much that the luncheons would go on. This one was enjoyable, as I gave them at their request a Washington briefing and was able to have quite a good tease of both Maitland and Nanteuil about the ploys of their respective governments in trying to keep us out of the Summit preparatory meetings and trying to keep away from us documents which the Americans had been only too pleased to show us.

FRIDAY, 29 APRIL. *Brussels.*

I received the King of the Belgians for his somewhat postponed visit to the Commission at 11.30. We had a Commission meeting with him for about one and a quarter hours, in which I introduced all the Commissioners to him, described what they each did and said a few words of welcome. I then asked first Haferkamp and then Cheysson to introduce a slightly but not excessively artificial discussion about North/South relations, followed by Davignon on the problems of the steel industry. After Davignon, Vouël, Tugendhat and Giolitti spoke. Everybody did rather well; perhaps particularly the King who asked some very sensible questions in his diffident way and seemed thoroughly interested. Then a lunch, at which I talked half to him bilaterally and then widened the discussion for a further talk about a whole range of Community issues. We broke up at about 3.00 after a surprisingly successful and worthwhile occasion.

At 4.30, Hallstein,* the *doyen* of ex-Presidents, came in for an hour. I went down to meet him at the front door. He was physically feeble, so that it took about five minutes to walk from the top of the lift to my room, and even longer for me to walk with him at the end from my room to Emile Noël's room. But he seemed thoroughly bright and alive in mind and was friendly and informative to talk to. I tried to discover how different things were in his day and got some impression. The Commission was a smaller, more intimate, tauter body. He was in the habit, he said, of addressing all the staff from the level of A2 (Director) and above after each important event, which might be two or three times a year. The Council obviously worked somewhat better and more intimately. The Parliament, he claimed, played almost as great a part in the life of the Commission as is the case now, although I remain sceptical about this. He never worked in the Berlaymont and clearly and rightly hated it as a building.

SATURDAY, 30 APRIL. *Brussels.*

Perhaps the first real spring day. Drove via Ghent to Breskens where we took the ferry across to Vlissingen and through Middelburg to Veere, where we lunched sitting at the window in an old tower looking at an inlet of the sea speckled with sailing boats on very sparkling water. Then another walk along the dikes after lunch and then back by a different, further inland ferry and through St Niklaas and into Brussels by 6.30.

MONDAY, 2 MAY. *Brussels.*

A Mitterrand† visit at 11.30. Cheysson had approached me four or five weeks earlier and said that Mitterrand would like to visit the

---

* Walter Hallstein, 1901–82, former German State Secretary, had been President of the Commission 1958–67, and was 'the Pope' to de Gaulle's 'Emperor' during the 1960s disputes between supranationalism and sovereignty.

† François Mitterrand, b. 1916, was then preparing to lead the Socialist challenge to President Giscard's majority in the National Assembly at the French legislative elections due in ten months' time. He had been unsuccessful candidate for the presidency of France in 1965 and 1974. He was elected President of the Republic in 1981 and re-elected in 1988.

Commission with one or two of his Socialist collaborators; would this be agreeable to me, and would I give him lunch? I said, 'Yes, certainly, I would be thoroughly glad to see him, just as I would be to see Mrs Thatcher or Kohl.' Cheysson then asked me to keep the matter confidential until he had taken further soundings with Mitterrand, and I did not therefore speak to Ortoli or anyone else. But while I was away over Easter and in the United States, the Cheysson *cabinet*, merely discovering from my office that I would be in Brussels and free, and without consulting me, arranged the date of 2 May.

When we were informed of this in the United States I immediately sent Michael Jenkins to inform Ortoli, whose reaction was not enthusiastic but not violently hostile either. I then saw Ortoli when I got back and explained the position to him. He was still rather reserved about it but said it was much too late to put it off; he did not think it would do great damage (in Paris); we should try to play it in as low a key as possible. This indeed was what I endeavoured to do without erring on the side of discourtesy. I did not give Mitterrand anything like head of government treatment. I did not go down and meet him. I received him in what is normally my dining room, and did not invite photographs, although he came accompanied by a great barrage of press and television cameras. I then had an hour and a quarter's meeting with him at which Natali, Haferkamp and Cheysson were present throughout, with Davignon and Gundelach joining us in the course of the meeting. I had been particularly anxious that there should be a political balance of Commissioners and had therefore swollen the numbers by inviting Natali and Davignon as Christian Democrats. Gundelach was not on the original list, but Cheysson had particularly asked for him to come.

The meeting started slightly stickily – Mitterrand is not the easiest man to deal with – but improved as it went along. He made a good, clear statement about the French Socialists' commitment to direct elections and their opposition to the Gaullist/Communist view that these should be accompanied by a commitment to no further extension of the powers of the Parliament. On other matters, however, he appeared fairly unsatisfactory. He was very reserved about enlargement, accepting without enthusiasm the Portuguese application, was firmly opposed to Spain, and disinclined to accept that we were irreversibly down the road with Greece. He made a lot of anti-American and protectionist remarks, and generally gave the impression of a complete Gaullist of the Left. He did, however, express himself firmly in favour, no doubt partly on anti-Giscard grounds, of the Community's presence at all parts of the Summit.

At lunch afterwards nearly all the other Commissioners turned up − I couldn't easily prevent their doing so as they all wished to meet Mitterrand. Ortoli, who had hovered and havered, eventually decided to turn up, and behaved thoroughly graciously. At the meal there was partly bilateral conversation between Mitterrand and me, during which I found him more easy and agreeable than during any previous encounter. He talked frankly and sensibly about his own position, saying two things in particular. (1) He thought that short of some international upheaval, i.e. some uprising in Eastern Europe or some great Yugoslav crisis, it was as certain as could be that the Left would win in France next spring and that he would then have to be asked to and would form a government under Giscard. (2) So far as 1981 was concerned, he expressed the view, rather to my surprise, that he might well be too old and it would therefore be a mistake to assume that the 1981 presidential election would take the form of a contest between him and Chirac.* At the end of lunch I avoided speeches by turning the conversation into a general discussion. He left soon after 3.00 and I said goodbye to him at the top of the lift shaft.†

*Jacques Chirac, b. 1931, Prime Minister of France 1974−6 and 1986−8. Mayor of Paris since 1977. Unsuccessful candidate for the presidency 1974 and 1988.
†The reason for my uneasiness about this visit was that I knew the French Government were watching like hawks to make sure that Mitterrand received no treatment above what they regarded as his status or which he could exploit for political purposes. (God knows how; I would not have thought a Berlaymont visit would swing many votes in Château-Chinon or anywhere else.) I wrote a few weeks later: 'Although there was a great deal of French press comment and some suggestion that this visit had been a considerable additional factor in provoking Giscard to a still harder position over the Summit, I myself doubt whether it was in any way decisive. I had read in the papers on the morning of the visit that Giscard was not coming to the dinner on Friday evening, probably because of my presence, but we had heard hints earlier that he was thinking of not attending this occasion for at least a few weeks beforehand and that in any event it was intended as a slight mark of his displeasure with the British Government over excessive Atlanticism, rather than being exclusively directed towards me.

'Ortoli's subsequent view, which he relayed to me three or four days later, was that it was a pity that Mitterrand had been allowed to have a joint meeting with several Commissioners, instead of having to go round and see them all individually in their offices (which seemed to me rather foolish) but that in any event the matter was not of great significance; and that this was his view after subsequent contacts with the French Government. Only the French Government, of course, would have reacted at all. That was the point of my remark about Kohl and Mrs Thatcher.'

TUESDAY, 3 MAY. *Brussels*.

Foreign Affairs Council with a special restricted session on the Summit. David Owen told me privately beforehand that the final proposition from London was that I should be excluded from all the Saturday sessions which would deal with the general economic matters in the morning and then with non-proliferation in the afternoon. This was not satisfactory, but not a great surprise. When it was announced, all the Little Five expressed themselves very strongly against the arrangement. The Italians and the Germans said nothing and Guiringaud kept his head down. I argued the complete illogicality of the division. This part of the meeting was fairly but not very bad-tempered. David summed up in an embarrassed way saying that while it was a compromise it was bound, like all compromises, to be slightly untidy, and somewhat self-pityingly complained that others did not show sufficient sympathy for the extremely difficult position in which the British presidency had been placed.

I was besieged by British pressmen on the way out, who regarded this as a setback from the Rome position. But it was not really much worse than I had expected and I therefore tried to play it fairly cool. Then to a state dinner given by the King of the Belgians in the Palais de Bruxelles for Houphouët-Boigny (President of Côte d'Ivoire). The dinner itself, for about two hundred people, was very grand, in a splendid room, with all the style of Buckingham Palace. I sat between Tindemans, with whom I had an extremely interesting and agreeable general conversation, and Madame De Clercq, the wife of the Finance Minister, herself a fairly leading lawyer in Ghent.

WEDNESDAY, 4 MAY. *Brussels and Luxembourg*.

Lunch at home for Emanuele Gazzo, the remarkable and wise editor of *Agence Europe*, a cyclostyled sheet which comes out every day in four languages and contains a great deal of detail about what goes on in the Commission, as well as some very sensible leading articles, and has considerable influence in Brussels.

Then by train to Luxembourg for the fourth of my inaugural visits. An hour with Thorn in his office before dinner. He had expressed himself very strongly at the Council the day before and repeated this to the press, coining a good phrase on my Saturday exclusion. 'The Community isn't only a Community for Sundays,' he announced. Privately, however, his view was that we had not done too badly even though he held the position of the French and the British to be fairly intolerable.

I asked him about the British presidency and Britain's general standing in Europe. He said the presidency was going fairly badly and that the sense of disillusion was considerable. Perhaps unfairly, they put up with things from the French they wouldn't put up with from the British because they were used to the French and they were used to playing a tiresome game with them, and they could have one country doing this but they could not have two. Furthermore they had thought that when the British came in, while we would not bring great economic strength or wealth – but this they did not mind; indeed to some extent, in comparison with the past when we were much the richest country in Europe, they rather liked it – they had thought that we would bring a democratic infusion, and therefore our hesitancy over direct elections was a mystifying disappointment. And they had also thought that we would bring not so much a sense of efficiency, but a sense of fair play to our chairing of the various Councils, and therefore our handling of the Agricultural Council and of the Research Council had also been damaging.

THURSDAY, 5 MAY. *Luxembourg and Brussels.*

I awoke with some sort of allergy, producing monstrous weals. There was no particular evidence that I felt unwell, although obviously rather apprehensive (what a farce if I could not go to the Summit after all!). I rang (Dr) Ann Phillips in Brussels and consulted her, she taking a reasonably reassuring view, and also made tentative soundings with Antony and Anne Acland,* with whom we were due to have a drink at 12.30, about the possibility of getting a doctor. One and a half hours' meeting with about half the Luxembourg Government, and then to the Grand Ducal Palace for an audience with the Grand Duke and the Grand Duchess.

* (Sir) Antony Acland, b. 1930, then British Ambassador in Luxembourg, is now Ambassador in Washington, having in the meantime been Ambassador in Madrid and Permanent Under-Secretary at the Foreign Office. Anne Acland died in 1984.

They were thoroughly agreeable – he charming, she sharper, sister of the King of the Belgians, but very unlike Baudouin – despite the fact that I had refused their invitation to dinner that evening on the thoroughly good grounds, which they appeared completely to understand, that I had to get back to Brussels and prepare for the Summit. The conversation essentially took the form of their asking me what I had thought of Carter and my describing this rather anecdotally, and then going on to the same thing at their prompting about Mitterrand, and to some sort of general discussion about Euro-Communism and the difference between the position and attitude of the Communist Party in France and Italy. The atmosphere of the Court was, curiously, slightly more formal and more like our own than the monarchies of Belgium and Holland.

Lunch with Thorn and a large collection of Luxembourgeois notables – at a late nineteenth-century château (Senningen) in rather pretty woods about five miles out. During lunch it became pretty obvious to me that the improvement of my allergy was not being sustained. Nevertheless to a press conference with Thorn, a briefing of the ambassadors of the Nine and then to the new Jean Monnet building for an opening ceremony with the Grand Duke and Duchess and speeches from Thorn, the Chairman of the Comité des Anciens, i.e. those who had been there with Monnet from the beginning, and me.

Then at 7.15 to see Dr Schau, who was said to be the best doctor in Luxembourg. He was agreeable, competent and not at all reassuring. He said it was a very bad allergy and he was by no means sure I would be all right for the Summit, which was of course beginning to obsess me. It would be a superb piece of irony, and indeed bathos, if, after all the fuss, I were ill and unable to be present for that reason. He then gave me two injections and suggested I take anti-histamine tablets as well. Michael Jenkins and I then drove to Brussels, where things seemed worse again and I went to bed in great gloom.

FRIDAY, 6 MAY. *Brussels and London.*

I woke to find that a miracle had occurred and that there was not a single trace left of the tribulations of yesterday. Received Houphouët-Boigny at 11.30 and into the Commission for one of our routine formal meetings, before taking him for a quick lunch at

Val Duchesse. Speeches on both occasions. He is an agreeable, able, moderate, little man, much more so than Mobutu, but at the same time not easy to do a French conversational dance with. He was reasonably forthcoming, with none of Mobutu's pretence of being a demi-god, but showed a curious self-centredness, a lack of interest in anything to do with one's own life, a complete absence of conversational initiative.

Plane to London and via Ladbroke Square to the Downing Street dinner, at which we had been requested to arrive at 7.48 (!) and which we did exactly punctually, although it seemed a little ludicrous.

I was received by Callaghan and then went upstairs to find David Owen and Denis Healey. I was of course asked to be the first – as the most junior – of the delegations to arrive. The others then came in fairly thick and fast and I was greeted extremely warmly by Carter and Vance and Blumenthal; by Trudeau,* whom I had not seen for about eight years; by Schmidt; by Andreotti; by the Japanese – I had forgotten that Fukuda, the Prime Minister, had been Finance Minister when I was his opposite number in the late sixties; and indeed perfectly courteously by Guiringaud, who was the only French representative present.

On arrival, however, I had been far from pleased to be told that there were three tables and that I was to sit, not at the heads of delegation table, not indeed even at the Foreign Ministers' table (although this perhaps did not matter), but at the Finance Ministers' table. This was a gratuitous piece of nonsense by Callaghan. Having lost Giscard for his dinner – and Giscard, incidentally, that morning had told Le Monde that it was my presence which was preventing him from coming – the least he could have done was to play the thing with some style.

SATURDAY, 7 MAY. London.

Inevitably a frustrating day of waiting, heel-kicking and over-febrile preparation at home in Ladbroke Square. At about 12.00 Marie-Alice de Beaumarchais arrived, mainly I think as an expression of anti-Giscard solidarity. I shuffled her out of the drawing

* Pierre Elliott Trudeau, b. 1919, was Prime Minister of Canada 1968–79 and 1980–4.

room and downstairs into the dining room and garden with Jennifer, because Crispin, Ruggiero and Hijzen, the Dutch Director-General of External Affairs, were due and I thought her French diplomatic presence might appear rather confusing, perhaps not to Crispin, but certainly to the other two!

The Buckingham Palace dinner was, in the circumstances, a surprisingly agreeable occasion. The Royal Family plus courtiers were extremely nice and forthcoming to me; so indeed – no reason at all why they should not be – were the Owens, and even the Healeys. However, I had no contact with Callaghan at all, which was probably as well. Jennifer sat at dinner between Barre and Martin Charteris.* I sat between Mrs Macdonald, the wife of the Canadian Finance Minister, and Forlani, the Italian Foreign Minister. But I certainly could not complain about *placement* as I was next but one to Callaghan. Standing about before dinner, Giscard, who with Carter, as heads of state, had been allowed to arrive after the rest of us, suddenly emerged from behind my shoulder, swept up, seizing me by the hand, saying, 'Ah, mon ami Jenkins, bon soir. Comment allez-vous?' 'Bon soir, Monsieur le Président de la République,' I replied fairly, but not excessively, coolly. He then seized Jennifer's hand and kissed it, and swept on.

I had another encounter with him a little later, when we were standing talking – Jennifer and I and Carter, and he and Martin Charteris – and Princess Margaret came up and said, 'Ah, two Presidents together.' 'No, no,' said Giscard. 'We are three Presidents. Monsieur Jenkins is President of the Commission.' So I said, 'We are all Presidents, except Sir Martin Charteris, and he is going to be a Provost, which is even better.' Slightly edged raillery was the keynote.

After dinner, Barre, having talked to Jennifer throughout dinner in French, made a point of having a long and friendly conversation with me in English, and when we said goodbye to him he insisted on inviting us to come and see him at Matignon whenever we were in Paris. I found myself at one stage having a conversation with the Queen in French, which was mainly because Barre was also there and Trudeau had come and joined us and she started very politely

---

* Sir Martin Charteris, b. 1913, Private Secretary to the Queen 1972–7, became Lord Charteris of Amisfield and Provost of Eton College later in 1978.

to talk to Barre in French, but he and Trudeau remained rather silent so one had the slightly ludicrous spectacle of the Queen and me going on exchanging conversation in French for about ten minutes. Her French is better than mine.

Foreign dignitaries treat the Royal Family differently from the way in which they are used to being treated in England. However they rolled quite well with this punch. Schmidt was smoking before the main course at dinner (an activity in which he was quickly joined by Princess Margaret) and stubbing the ends out on very high quality plate. And at the end, instead of the Royal Family withdrawing, as is normally the case, and everybody then shuffling off when they wanted to, people began to go on their own, coming up to them, saying, 'Thank you very much, it has been a very nice party but we must now get off and do some work.' But the Queen sensibly accepted this and stayed until the end so that everyone went up and thanked her on the way out and said goodbye in exactly the same way as one would do at a normal, non-royal, party.

SUNDAY, 8 MAY. *London and East Hendred.*

Downing Street at 10.30. We spent the morning on two main subjects: first, North/South, which Giscard was asked to introduce and did very well. I intervened about fourth and then several times subsequently. We then went on to MTNs, which I think Carter introduced but said little about, and which therefore in effect I introduced with the second speech. The discussions were both quite good without being sensationally so. Probably, I regret to say, Giscard performed the best, looked the most 'statesmanlike' figure, all done in a very head-of-state way. Callaghan was a pretty good chairman, adopting the attitude of a bluff common-sense man, although once on the Special Action Fund he made a major tactical error and put the British in a very difficult position for some time, from which Denis Healey half extracted him. Fukuda of Japan spoke surprisingly effectively through the linguistic barrier, and the others listened to him attentively. Andreotti did not make much impact.

Trudeau did a sort of strip-tease. He had been wearing a velvet suit on the Friday evening, but on this occasion he was wearing a slightly trendy pin-stripe, of which he proceeded to divest himself during the morning. First his coat came off, then his waistcoat, then his tie was loosened. Somewhere in the course of the proceedings, the yellow rose which he wears most of the time was put into a glass of water in front of him. He occasionally intervened, not powerfully but pertinently. Schmidt talked powerfully, confidently, in English as he usually does, but rather too much and in a sense rather too much of a gramophone record. A great number of the phrases and arguments we had heard at Rome came out a second time. Carter did not speak much and adopted a modest, anxious-to-learn attitude, which was quite effective. What is difficult to evaluate is how much this effectiveness was due to his being President of the United States, with a national income of rather over 40 per cent of the total of those seated round the table. If he had been a new Prime Minister of Canada, or of Italy, would he have been regarded as a rather marginal contributor? Probably.

Lunch at Carlton Gardens with the Foreign Ministers, which was solely occupied with a drafting session on the communiqué. David Owen (who was not very effective throughout the whole Summit, acting too much as Callaghan's office boy) was less good at the English redrafting than I had expected, so that Vance and I did most of it. We then had another two and a half hours on the communiqué in full Downing Street session.

Then to the press conference in the Banqueting House. I sat at the end of the front row without, as was subsequently widely reported, a microphone, although I was not aware of this. I knew that I was not going to be allowed to speak, as the elaborate compromise which had been worked out was that I should sit in the front row (I had declined to sit anywhere else, saying that I was either the head of a delegation or nothing) but had been forced to accept the mute role. The press conference was interminable. After Callaghan as chairman had spoken, the others were supposed to make statements of two or three minutes; in fact most of them spoke for more like twelve or fifteen minutes, and as there had to be subsequent translation, the whole thing lasted until 7.45. The best statements were made by Fukuda and by Carter.

This over, I went to the Stafford Hotel where I did three or four television interviews and held my own press conference in which I tried to strike a balanced and fairly up-beat note, although I am not sure how much this came through. Drove down to East Hendred for the night.

My thoughts at the end of the Summit were (1) immense relief at it being over, (2) almost equal relief at having got rid of the beastly allergy, (3) embarrassment at the extreme and constant awkwardness of the position, (4) a mounting resentment against Callaghan, and a greater but slightly diminishing resentment against Giscard, and (5) a hope that on the Sunday at any rate I had played a tolerably useful part.

MONDAY, 9 MAY. *London.*

Lunch with David Steel* in an attempt to stiffen him in his pressure on the Government about direct elections. He was agreeable, but certainly needed this stiffening. Speech to a European Movement dinner – a discreet fund-raising affair – at the Reform Club, which was attended by about sixty or seventy people, and was a remarkable roll call of the great and the good, insofar as they exist, of British business.

TUESDAY, 10 MAY. *London and Strasbourg.*

Breakfast with David Owen at Carlton Gardens for the Foreign Ministers of the Little Five, nominally in order to debrief them on the Summit. Some discussion after two opening statements by David and me, in which K. B. Andersen asked the only interesting question, which was whether I thought that the arrangements in London had been compatible with the Rome compromise. I said 'No', but I nevertheless thought it had been worthwhile that we were there.

Left Carlton Gardens at 9.30 and was in the hotel in Strasbourg only two hours and five minutes later. Answered questions in the Parliament after lunch. Gave a dinner for Colombo† as President of the Parliament. An enjoyable discussion during which my morale improved, partly because I suddenly realized that I had made a

---

*David Steel, b. 1938, had become leader of the Liberal Party in 1976.
†Emilio Colombo, b. 1920, Italian Minister of the Treasury 1967–70 and 1974–6, Prime Minister 1970–2, Foreign Minister 1980–3; President of the European Parliament 1977–9.

French breakthrough. During my first three months in Brussels I thought it had definitely retrogressed, and even after that had not improved, but it has now jerked forward and I suddenly felt much more fluent and had no difficulty in leading the whole two-hour discussion in French.

WEDNESDAY, 11 MAY. *Strasbourg and Bonn.*

Very good early Commission meeting, 8.30–11.00. We dealt with several issues of difficulty and substance, such as the internal fishing régime, Brunner's weak proposals for mixed teams between the Vienna Agency and Euratom,* on which we turned him down. Then into the Chamber ready to make my statement on the Summit, which lasted ten minutes and went quite smoothly. Then by car and train to Bonn for the fifth of my inaugural visits, arriving just after 9 p.m.

For the first time this year it was almost a summer evening. Drove about forty miles to Schloss Gymnich, the German Government hospitality château. Huge rooms, bedroom, sitting room. The château itself very agreeable and the outlook from the windows attractive, but furnished so as to create a special mixture of modernity and inconvenience.

THURSDAY, 12 MAY. *Bonn.*

An early start to a long and over-busy day. By helicopter to breakfast with Genscher in the Auswärtiges Amt at 8.00. I had a fairly good talk with him, partly on a number of detailed issues which he wished to raise, partly on post-Summit views, partly on the institutional consequences of enlargement raised by me, and the dangers of a split on the issue between the small existing members of the Community and the big ones, and the importance of the Germans as having a key role to play resisting this. Genscher is an odd man. Despite our *malentendu* over German Com-

---

* Euratom was the European Atomic Energy Community, one of the three Communities (the others being the EEC and the Coal and Steel Community) which merged in 1967 to form the European Community. The Vienna Agency was the International Atomic Energy Agency, based in the Austrian capital. The issue was that some Community Governments wished to deal too directly with Vienna, thereby leap-frogging Community competence in civil nuclear power.

missioners in early November, I found him thoroughly agreeable, perfectly easy, and yet difficult to get alongside, despite the lubricating pleasures of his huge breakfast.

At 9.00 to the Bundestag to be ceremonially introduced by the President. This meant standing up in the gallery and being quite loudly applauded by the two hundred or so members present. Then listened to Schmidt's statement on the Summit which lasted over forty minutes, much more of an argumentative speech than is the British habit on these occasions. It contained one important passage from the Commission point of view, referring to his satisfaction that I had been present and hoping that this provided a good basis on which to build for the future. This was enthusiastically received. Then I listened to about half of Franz Josef Strauss's* rather good debating speech, before leaving for a meeting with Friderichs,† Minister for Economic Affairs. Then back to the Auswärtiges Amt for a meeting with Dohnanyi and a lot of officials. Then to the Chancellery for a half-hour with Schmidt alone. We had agreed in London that this was not to be a serious business talk, but it was quite interesting to hear that (1) he was firmly resolved to be the host for the next Summit which he thought might take place in January or February 1978, (2) he regarded free trade and therefore progress in the MTNs as being almost the single most crucial German national interest, and (3) his slight defeatism about the prospect of making real reforms in the CAP, despite his desire to do so.

Then we walked across to the old Chancellery for a luncheon of about sixty people. After lunch Schmidt made a long, rambling but quite interesting speech. He had thrown away his text at my invitation before we left his office, saying it looked much too long, and then proceeded to speak for at least twice as long as the text would have taken. However, amongst the things he said was that he and Giscard had decided that it was very desirable that I should become President of the Commission because they wanted a politician of standing who might have become Prime Minister of his

*Franz Josef Strauss, 1915–88, was President of the Christian Social Union 1961–88 and Minister-President of Bavaria 1978–88; Federal Minister of Defence 1956–62, and of Finance 1966–9.
†Hans Friderichs, b. 1931, was German Economics Minister 1972–7, and then head of the Dresdner Bank until 1985.

own country, and that he himself had complete faith in my ability to do a very good job in this capacity. My only trouble, he said, was that I had wanted to have twelve other potential Prime Ministers supporting me in the Commission, a very rash wish. He would never do that in his own Government. It made things very uncomfortable. It was much better to be surrounded by people who could never be Prime Ministers. It was a friendly but not very European speech, in which he said that Germany did not want to be in the front row. In reply, I said that Germany was inevitably in the front row, the question was in which direction they pushed. But the whole occasion passed off thoroughly pleasantly.

In the afternoon I saw first Frau Schlei, the rather arch Minister of Development, and then Willy Brandt, accompanied by Horst Ehmke, in the SPD headquarters. Willy was extremely friendly, very hospitably relaxed and treated me as an old friend, as indeed I treated him. We mostly talked about his projected chairmanship of the committee on the Third World. In putting this together he is doing exactly what Schmidt had described me as wanting to – assembling a group of Prime Ministers or equivalents. He thought he had got Kissinger, he preferred Heath rather than Home from England, Mendès-France from France might be very good but was a little old, Palme from Sweden would come along, etc.

Then at 5.15, flagging distinctly by this stage, an hour with Hans Apel, at the Ministry of Finance, followed by a meeting with Matthöfer, Minister for Research and Technology, in which he broadly invited me to find some way in which the British could assemble a majority to vote down the Germans and get the JET project for Culham as opposed to the Garching site. It is remarkable the mess that has been made of this. In the car from there Crispin gave me the extraordinary news that Peter Jay* had been appointed Ambassador to Washington. Dinner in the Steigenberger Hotel, presided over by Anna-Maria Renger, ex-President of the Bundestag, and a very nice woman. Back at Schloss Gymnich by about 11.15, exhausted by ten meetings on the run.

---

*Peter Jay was then the forty-year-old economics editor of *The Times* and the son-in-law of the Prime Minister.

FRIDAY, 13 MAY. *Bonn and East Hendred.*

10 o'clock meeting in the Bundestag with Kohl, accompanied by Narjes. Kohl, as had been my impression when I had previously met him in July 1976 in London, is a considerable man. Schmidt does not think so, but he is wrong. We exchanged views on a number of issues and found a close identity of European view with, I hope, a considerable continuing Christian Democratic commitment to the Community. In the latter part of the interview Kohl expounded why this was particularly important for Germany in view of their divided position, their historical rootlessness, all done in a mixture of practical and philosophical terms which was effective. Then to the Commission office for a pointless but not testing debriefing of the ambassadors of the Nine, and then a long press conference.

Lunch at the Redout presided over by Dohnanyi. Then to the Villa Hammerstein, the presidential residence, for a meeting with Walter Scheel.* This was impaired by the Germans having far too many people present, sitting round like crows on a branch. I had taken only Crispin, but they had at least twelve in the room. I find a large, silent audience of this sort particularly inhibiting, especially as I wished to raise points of substance with the Federal President. Scheel, however, is a nice man who has grown a lot and I think is now a major figure. He has some unrealistic ideas about the reform of the Council of Ministers, but he is generally firmly on the right side.

Plane to London, and East Hendred by just after 8.00, very glad to be back after a fairly exhausting three weeks, morale a good deal up in the last two to three days.

MONDAY, 16 MAY. *East Hendred and Brussels.*

Back to Brussels by noon. I gave lunch to the Council of British Shipping, which was all right apart from the fact that my left-hand neighbour, who was otherwise an engaging companion, choked on a piece of meat and nearly died during lunch. However, he revived afterwards under the care of the *service médicale*.

---

*Walter Scheel, b. 1919, was leader of the FDP before Genscher, Foreign Minister 1969–74, and President of the Federal Republic 1974–9.

THURSDAY, 19 MAY. *Brussels, London and Dublin.*

To London for Peter Kirk's memorial service at St Margaret's. Then with Jennifer to Dublin for our official visit. Met by Garret Fitzgerald and conducted in with, as usual in Ireland these days, a heavy security guard, endless police cars, motorbikes, screaming sirens, etc. To the Hibernian Hotel, just off St Stephen's Green. A Prime Minister's (or Taoiseach's) dinner at Iveagh House, with a big turn-up of most Irish notables, including about half the Government, the leader of the Opposition (Lynch), and various other figures. I liked Cosgrave at dinner; although a quiet and reticent man, he was nice to talk to, as was his wife, and made a good, prepared, pro-European speech after dinner, to which I responded.

FRIDAY, 20 MAY. *Dublin and London.*

Thirty-minute visit to the Commission office, a rather splendid Georgian house in Merrion Square, then to the Taoiseach's office for an hour's conversation alone with him, apart from Crispin and one on his side, in which I mainly gave him a debriefing on the Summit. Again impressed by him; he listens well, is serious and takes in what is said. Following that, a large governmental meeting at Iveagh House, presided over by Garret Fitzgerald, with six other ministers. These meetings with groups of ministers are quite a strain as I have to conduct all the talk on our side and we range over a lot of subjects, whereas they have a revolving cast. After that, to a nominally but not very working lunch in the other part of Iveagh House, with Garret Fitzgerald presiding over a table of about twenty.

Then out to Phoenix Park to call on the President – Patrick Hillery, a previous Vice-President of the Commission – at the old Vice-Regal Lodge, now called Áras an Uachtaráin. A beautiful afternoon with sparkling, very clear Dublin light, and I was much reminded of Dilke's description of a drive from there on the occasion of his only visit to Ireland at almost exactly the same time of year, ninety-two years before, when he had been struck by the view to the Wicklow mountains and the number of people riding out on 'cars' to the strawberry gardens but all of them refusing even to acknowledge the Viceroy (Spencer, I suppose). Hillery and I spent half the time walking in the gardens. Then back to the Dail for a call on Jack Lynch.* It was the beginning of the election campaign. He was friendly and modest but gave me the impression that he had very little chance.† After that a press conference and to the airport, again under screaming escort, for the 5.55 for London. A beautiful flight on the way back until we got to about Henley-on-Thames. A spectacular early summer evening, particularly over Monmouthshire and Herefordshire.

SATURDAY, 21 MAY. *London and Leeds Castle.*

With Crispin to Leeds Castle for the Foreign Ministers' 'Schloss Gymnich'-type meeting, which Tony Crosland had been particularly keen to arrange there, thinking that it would be a striking and agreeable place. So indeed it was. A remarkable house, or rather castle, of which I had never before had more than a distant glimpse, very well furnished and with a most unusual arrangement of views. However, the weekend was not a total success. People had come slightly too far at too great an inconvenience, despite the helicopters which had been assembled to transport them from various airports, and David Owen, with his many qualities, is not a naturally gracious host; he is not keen enough on surroundings or food or drink to enjoy providing them for others.

However, all the Nine Foreign Ministers turned up and the discussion, desultory over lunch and then for about three and a quarter hours after lunch on enlargement, was worthwhile. Towards the end we had an awkward passage about the representation of the Community at the Belgrade follow-up meetings to the Helsinki Conference on Security and Cooperation in Europe. We nearly got a very satisfactory agreement and then it was torn apart. It nominally turned on what the *pancarte* in front of our delegation should say, but the real issue was the independent position of the Commission as opposed to its subordination to member state governments. We had thought the French would be the most difficult but in fact the most trouble came from the Danes followed by the British. Despite the splendour of my room, I slept badly.

*Jack Lynch, leader of Fianna Fáil 1966–79, was Irish Prime Minister (Taoiseach) 1966–73 and 1977–9.
†In fact he won handsomely.

SUNDAY, 22 MAY. *Leeds Castle and London.*

Morning session of about the same quality as the previous afternoon. Then Geoffrey Lloyd and Peter Wilson* for a drink at about noon – some ministers were going by that time – in their capacity as trustees for the Leeds Castle Foundation, and then a lunch at which about half the Foreign Ministers were present, just before which I had a better conversation with David (Owen) than any since he has become Foreign Secretary. London at 3.30.

WEDNESDAY, 25 MAY. *Brussels.*

Six and a half hours of Commission meetings, the afternoon almost entirely taken up with the first major bite at the budget. Tugendhat definitely performing well; also an extremely skilful performance by Davignon, who managed to get away with a certain amount of murder in his field by (1) arguing his individual case well and effectively, and (2) being helpful to everybody else, particularly me, on all other issues. Budget discussions in the Commission are remarkably reminiscent of a public expenditure exercise in the British Cabinet.

THURSDAY, 26 MAY. *Brussels.*

Commission from 9.30 to 1.05, by the end of which, after ten hours on two days, we had completed the budget. There was difficulty during the morning, but only about overseas representation, a rather silly issue, in which Cheysson and Haferkamp (through his representative; he, typically, was not present) were both over-demanding. We settled the Regional Fund fairly quickly at 750 million units of account, and then had a difficult issue on the Social Fund at the end, where we weren't prepared to allow very much increase in the credit voted, although owing to the speed-up of payments there would be a very considerable increase in operations on the ground. Vredeling, discontented and unhappy, voted sullenly against, but did not actually throw a tremendous scene, and clearly was in no resignation mood. Ortoli intervened rather helpfully and persuasively at the end, urging him to accept the decision and make the best he could of it, which I think he is doing.

* Respectively a former Conservative Minister and the Chairman of Sotheby's.

Then to lunch with the Trilateral Commission* who were having an all-day meeting in Brussels with sessions with various Commissioners. I spoke and answered questions for an hour.

Back to the Berlaymont to see Giolitti, who was very pleased with the outcome in the morning and has really got much better and crisper and came with two very sensible further points about national quotas within the Fund and the proportion which should be quota-free. Rue de Praetère dinner party for Brunners, Ersbølls (Danish Permanent Representative), Ronald McIntosh† and Tickells. Mrs Brunner, who is General Speidel's daughter, was very interesting at dinner. I also had a good talk with Ersbøll afterwards, whom I like, and found very sensible on a broad range of European issues.

FRIDAY, 27 MAY. *Brussels and Sussex.*

Plane to Gatwick and drove with Jennifer to the Bonham Carters‡ at Ripe.

Before dinner I drove with Leslie and Jennifer up to Firle Beacon on a most memorable evening,§ not outstandingly clear in the far distance, but with the countryside a gleaming green, and a perfect light over Newhaven Harbour and in the other direction up the valley of the Ouse towards Lewes and the Weald.

SUNDAY, 29 MAY. *Sussex and Paris.*

Weather still perfect and I felt a good deal less exhausted than for the past ten days. Early morning expedition to Lewes for the newspapers and back over Glyndebourne. Tennis with the Annans¶

*A well-financed, unofficial but high-level body designed to familiarize Americans, Japanese and Europeans with each other's problems.
†Sir Ronald McIntosh, b. 1919, former civil servant and Director-General of NEDO, latterly a company chairman, has been a friend since we went to Balliol on the same day in 1938.
‡Mark (Lord cr. 1986) Bonham Carter, b. 1922, has been a friend for forty-five years and my publisher (on and off) for thirty years. His wife, Leslie (daughter of Condé Nast who founded *Vogue*), is the mother (by a previous marriage) of Laura Grenfell (now Phillips) who came to Brussels in my *cabinet*.
§As Keynes had done thirty-one years before on the last evening of his life; he walked down, which we did not.
¶Noël (Lord cr. 1965) Annan, b. 1916, Provost of King's College, Cambridge, 1956–66, and of University College London 1966–78, Vice-Chancellor of University of London 1978–81. Married to Gabriele Annan, book reviewer of note.

who came to lunch. Spent the afternoon in the garden before departing at 7.00 for Paris and the CIEC North/South Conference. I was met by Michael Jenkins and drove to the Ritz Hotel.

MONDAY, 30 MAY. *Paris.*

Drove on a perfect morning through the empty streets of Paris – it being a public holiday – with an unnecessary motorcycle escort to the conference in the old Hotel Majestic (British peace treaty negotiating HQ in 1919, Gestapo HQ from 1940, now the Palais Kléber).

First a meeting with Cyrus Vance, who had not moved much on most of the issues of substance – the Common Fund, Special Action,* Official Development Aid, etc., though he was I think anxious to be reasonably forthcoming within the limitations of the American Treasury view. But he had done a sudden switch on the question of a possible continuation of CIEC. In response, apparently, to some suggestion of the Saudis (who would give in return consultation on oil prices) Vance was prepared to contemplate this and to say so in his opening speech.

This led immediately, just before the opening of the conference itself, to a rather tetchy row between him and David Owen, who was strongly opposed to the idea. David was apparently in a generally bad temper, so the Foreign Office officials said, although this did not show itself in his relations with me during the week. However, it was silly of him to have this rather unnecessary row with Vance for I managed immediately afterwards (and fairly easily) to get the most objected-to passage out of Vance's speech. It is also a pity he has got on such generally bad terms with the Foreign Office.

The conference began with formal statements: Guiringaud for the host country, then Waldheim of the UN, then the two co-chairmen (MacEachen of Canada for the Group of Eight, or G8, and Pérez-Guerrero of Venezuela for the Group of Nineteen, or G19). Then, rather to our surprise, we discovered that the two chairmen wished to go further in the morning, and so David Owen and I both

---

*Special Action was jargon for a crash programme to help peculiarly low-income countries with identifiable development needs.

spoke on behalf of the Community; rather flat speeches both of them I thought. Then I walked the one and a half miles or so to near the Rond Point for a slightly pointless lunch given by the Canadians. Then we had a strategy meeting of G8, in which MacEachen outlined his scheme for dividing into four Commissions for detailed negotiating, with about three representatives of our side facing about five of G19 across each table, and a rule that only heads of delegations should do the actual negotiating. This was a dangerous procedure so far as anyone's ability to keep overall control of the conference was concerned. However, it was a good and interesting experience to have to do for once the detailed negotiating which is normally done by officials. The Community was to be on three out of four groups, which meant that David Owen had to take one, I another and Cheysson the third. I did the so-called 'Development' one, including Special Action, Indebtedness and Official Development Aid.

Then I saw the new Indian Foreign Minister for about half an hour. He talked little, but K. B. Lall, their extremely experienced Ambassador to the Community, talked a good deal and gave us fairly clear information that G19 were in a reasonably moderate mood and anxious for a tolerable outcome of the conference.

TUESDAY, 31 MAY. *Paris.*

An early meeting of the G8 representatives on my negotiating group. It soon became clear that they were pretty useless. There was the Canadian Minister of Mines and Industry, Gillespie, who looked and indeed was a nice man, in appearance a curious cross between Giscard and Senator McGovern, but who appeared to know little about the subjects, and was fairly slow at picking them up. The third representative, the Swedish Foreign Minister, Mrs Karin Söder, was terrified. There had been a suggestion that she should be the moderator of the group, but she had backed away from this with enormous energy, and it was quite clear that I had to do it.

Lunch at the British Embassy, where there seemed to be some uneasy ambiguity as to whether Nicko or David Owen was host to about eight Foreign Ministers. Then back to the Kléber for a five-hour negotiating session of my group. My principal interlocutor was Bouteflika, the Foreign Minister of Algeria, clever, reputedly difficult, but in my view quite engaging to deal with on a basis of reasonably good-tempered verbal sparring. There was also the Finance Minister of the Cameroons who negotiated a bit about agricultural aid, briefly, effectively and helpfully, and also a Pakistani gentleman who was a slight caricature of a Pakistani, began all statements with a very loud 'Sir', and was also fortunately a tremendous literary snob, who claimed to have read all my books, and kept on saying he would not engage in stylistic arguments with such a distinguished author, etc. The negotiations were enjoyable and went rather well, but were exhausting as nobody else spoke from our side.

Then instead of going to Guiringaud's dinner at the Quai d'Orsay – I had had enough official meals and felt under no obligation to accept a French invitation – Michael and I gave dinner to the Hendersons in the very pretty ambience of the Grand Véfour looking out over the garden of the Palais Royal. Nicko told me that at a dinner the week before, Giscard had sent for him to pass on a message that he hoped that I had not taken personal offence over his behaviour in London. It was not his whim, it was French official policy, and what he had done was not much, if any, worse than Callaghan or Schmidt. This message neither greatly surprised nor excited me. On the whole I prefer that Giscard should take this view rather than the opposite one, but a half-apology in private after offence in public is, I fear, rather typical of him.

Back to the Kléber at 11.00. Gillespie was deeply involved in trying to negotiate the industrialization and transfer of technology passages and was without question making a good old cock-up of it, although it was a fairly complicated and unrewarding subject. I therefore stayed until we adjourned at 1 o'clock.

WEDNESDAY, 1 JUNE. *Paris and Brussels.*

I had hoped to go to Brussels in the morning, but this became impossible. Gillespie had gone home to Canada after his not very good performance the night before and the Swedish lady was still incapable of speech. As the hours went on some progress, notably on the passage about Official Development Aid which, with great difficulty, we managed to get agreed. The Americans, by late in the afternoon, were getting into what I thought was a rather ill-judged confrontation mood and Ryan, their principal operating man in my Commission (although mysteriously both Senator Javits and ex-Governor Gilligan of Ohio spent most of the time sitting in). Ryan kept coming up to me and saying, 'Tell them if they won't accept this, the whole thing's off. We are withdrawing everything else we have agreed.' But I was certainly not prepared to go back on agreements which, apart from anything else, had been so laboriously hammered out, and firmly declined to go along with him.

As a result we managed by about 8 o'clock to complete the work, leaving a number of things disagreed, but with substantial accomplishment nonetheless. The rest of the conference was still grinding on, but I decided there was nothing more I could do and therefore rushed down to the Gare du Nord and just caught the 8.30 TEE. A nice journey across northern France on a perfect June evening.

THURSDAY, 2 JUNE. *Brussels.*

Kenneth Kaunda of Zambia at 11.45, first for a short private talk, then for a formal Commission meeting, and then for lunch at Val Duchesse. Kaunda is a nice, honest and quite interesting man, certainly the best of the African heads of state that I have so far entertained at the Commission, although he harangued us unnecessarily aggressively about Rhodesia.

Dinner with Luns, the NATO Secretary-General, who was in his usual large canine mood. I was struck by how incomparably grander a house the Secretary-General of NATO has than the President of the Commission could possibly afford out of his allegedly so large salary. (The difference of course is that the NATO house is provided and staffed officially.) A male dinner: Haferkamp who arrived late and said practically nothing; Davignon who talked a good deal very sensibly; André de Staercke (famous Belgian ex-diplomat), whom I had not seen since Grimaud, behind St Tropez, in 1966; Pansa Cedronio, the Italian deputy Secretary-General; and Killick, the British Ambassador to NATO. Killick talked a good deal too much in his usual RASC colonel manner and ended up with a spirited defence of South Africa. Stevy Davignon carved him up over this, but at least the fact that he (Killick) did it showed a certain bloody-minded independence.

FRIDAY, 3 JUNE. *Brussels, Bonn and East Hendred.*

Motored to Bonn to deliver the first in a series of German Marshall Fund Lectures to mark the thirtieth anniversary of Marshall's Harvard speech. An audience of about two hundred, a lot of ambassadors, a lot of Americans who had come over, Carstens,* Dohnanyi and a moderately distinguished German gathering. I talked about enlargement and North/South relations. Plane from Düsseldorf to England.

MONDAY, 6 JUNE. *East Hendred.*

To the Berlins'† at Headington for a rather grand but highly enjoyable lunch party. Apart from the Berlins and us, the Beaumarchais', the Asa Briggs',‡ Arnold Goodman§ and Ann Fleming,¶ Michael and Pam Hartwell,‖ Nin Ryan** and Joe Alsop.

WEDNESDAY, 8 JUNE. *Brussels.*

Commission all day, but now working quite well and no immense difficulties. The main subject in the morning was Gundelach's attempt to impose Monetary Compensatory Amounts (MCAs) upon durum wheat (essential for pasta) which provoked a lot of Italian opposition, both Giolitti and Natali speaking with great passion. It was the first time Gundelach had failed to carry the Commission with him when he had been deploying an issue with full force directly within his own field. Following this his extremely

---

*Karl Carstens, b. 1914, was then President of the Bundestag and became President of the Federal Republic 1979–84.

†Sir Isaiah Berlin, OM, b. 1909, the *doyen* of Oxford intellectual and social life.

‡Lord Briggs, b. 1921, Provost of Worcester College, Oxford, since 1976, was Vice-Chancellor of the University of Sussex 1967–76.

§Lord Goodman, b. 1913, a solicitor of unusual influence, was Chairman of the Arts Council 1965–72, and Master of University College, Oxford, 1976–86.

¶Ann Fleming, 1913–81, was married to the 3rd Lord O'Neill 1932–44 (when he was killed in action), the 2nd Viscount Rothermere 1945–52 (when they were divorced), and Ian Fleming, the creator of James Bond, 1952–64 (when he died). She was a great friend and fairly close country neighbour in the years of these diaries.

‖Lord Hartwell (formerly Michael Berry), b. 1911, was for many years principal proprietor and editor-in-chief of the *Daily* and *Sunday Telegraph*. His wife was a daughter of F. E. Smith, 1st Earl of Birkenhead.

**Mrs John Barry Ryan, anglophile New Yorker, is the daughter of financier Otto Kahn and the mother of the Countess of Airlie.

ingenious solution for the British pig problem went through, as Asquith would have said 'on oiled castors' with merely a little grumble from Vredeling and one or two others, mainly because the Commission could not possibly turn Gundelach down on two agricultural issues running.

Anthony Lewis* of the *New York Times* and Crispin and Hayden to an enjoyable lunch, rue de Praetère. After the Commission I saw Davignon for a general round-up, although his preoccupation was his complaints about the laziness of Haferkamp, fully justified but not for the moment at any rate leading to anything very much. Haferkamp is, I fear, without doubt a disappointment and I may have made a mistake in giving him the big external job, although I still do not see a better realistic alternative. Gundelach or Davignon would of course have been individually better, but this would have left the Germans without a major portfolio.

THURSDAY, 9 JUNE. *Brussels and Copenhagen.*
Philippe Le Mâitre of *Le Monde* for half an hour to see if I could delicately improve relations with him and therefore *Le Monde*'s reporting of the Commission, with which we could most certainly do.

To Copenhagen, where we were met on the tarmac by K. B. Andersen, the Foreign Minister, and pouring rain. Drove to the Hôtel d'Angleterre, a nice turn-of-the-century hotel, where I had rather magnificent rooms, though no luggage until after midnight owing to a cock-up, and did a little work there before going to the Prime Minister's dinner of about fifty. I sat between him (Anker Jørgensen) and K. B. Andersen. Jørgensen neither speaks nor understands English perfectly by any means; he is however an agreeable man with a great deal of sense, pro-Community, and with a strong position in the country; and as one gets to know him better it is not difficult to see why. Speeches, in English, about a quarter of an hour each; fortunately I managed to think up a *Hamlet* quotation to match his prepared one, but was quite unable to match his Hans Christian Andersen one.

* Anthony Lewis, b. 1927, chief London correspondent of the *New York Times* 1965–72, subsequently a Boston-based columnist.

FRIDAY, 10 JUNE. *Copenhagen and East Hendred.*

A three-mile walk confirmed my view that Copenhagen is both agreeable and handsome. Then a short talk with Jørgensen alone, during which I told him of the plans for the Bonn Summit in the early months of 1978, i.e. during the Danish presidency, but added that I thought it likely that this would in fact have to be postponed because of the imminence of the French elections. I suggested that Jørgensen did not raise the issue of double Community representation, i.e. his possible presence as President of the European Council, as well as mine, for a few months, and he seemed to agree.

Following this there were two large meetings (both in length and size of attendance), the first with the Prime Minister in the chair, and the second under the Foreign Minister. We covered agriculture, with particular reference to MCAs, economic and monetary union, the Snake,* Tripartite Conference, direct elections and the remote but delicate issue of Greenland's relations with the Community. The veteran (but not old) Per Haekkerup spoke remarkably well on a whole range of issues.

Then we drove about twenty miles to Fredensborg for the royal lunch with Queen Margrethe. Fredensborg is a large, quite impressive early eighteenth-century palace, with a park on one side, a small town very close to its gates on the other, slightly in this way like a very miniature Versailles. Lunch for about two dozen: the Prime Minister and the Foreign Minister – I drove out with Anker Jørgensen and drove back with K. B. Andersen – plus a few other politicians, also the Prince of Denmark (the Queen's young French Consort who was in the embassy in London) and Queen Ingrid. They had very decently asked to lunch all the people of my party, including my secretary.

I sat between the two Queens and got on fairly well with both of them. A perfect though remarkably different English from each of them; Queen Margrethe's more 'educated', no doubt the result of Girton, and Queen Ingrid's more in a traditional upper-class English female mould. Rather curiously there was no politics, not even in the broadest European sense, at lunch, and the conver-

*The countries adhering to the pre-EMS 'Snake' or D-mark bloc were Benelux, Denmark, Norway, Sweden and, obviously, Germany. Italy had been a member but had left in 1973. France had twice been a member but had last left in 1976.

sation was purely social throughout, which was not wholly to the taste of the Danish politicians and a contrast with my visits with Queen Juliana, the King of the Belgians, or the Grand Duke of Luxembourg.

By the end of lunch there had been a remarkable change in the weather. A hazy sun had come out and it had become immensely hot and humid. My crowded press conference at the Community office in Copenhagen was one of the most drenching Turkish baths I had ever been in. Then another talk of nearly an hour and a half with K. B. Andersen. There was one point on which we could not get agreement. We wanted the Danes to hold up their ratification of the Baltic Convention in order that the Community should try and be a party to it. The Germans, who are also a party, are willing to do this, but not the Danes. I found it difficult to know whether my Commission brief was excessively legalistic or not. However, we managed to avoid this degenerating into a nasty argument, and finished up and parted with expressions of goodwill at about 6.30.

This Danish expedition was one of the best of the opening official visits to the capitals; both the two major ministers and several others were well worth talking to; difficulties were not glossed over, and high consideration for the Commission was shown by both the Danish State and the Danish Government.

SUNDAY, 12 JUNE. *East Hendred and London.*

To Oxford to lunch in Univ. with Arnold Goodman. Only Arnold and the now very old Goodharts* – the former Master of Univ. They were thoroughly agreeable but a bit out of touch with reality. At one stage Arthur Goodhart asked me if I had ever been to America, which left me slightly breathless. Arnold presided benignly, talking rather well on a number of subjects. One of his advantages is that he is largely audience-insensitive; he talks almost as well whether he has got a sympathetic, comprehending audience or not. Spent another sodden afternoon sitting in front of the East Hendred fire. Drove to Isleworth and dined with the Gilmours,† plus

---

* Arthur Goodhart, 1891–1978, was an American citizen who had mostly lived in England since 1919 and was Master of University College, Oxford, 1951–63.
† Sir Ian Gilmour, b. 1926, a Conservative MP from 1962, a minister throughout the Heath Government ending as Secretary of State for Defence, became Chancellor of the Duchy of Lancaster (with much European responsibility) 1979–81. He and his wife, (Lady) Caroline Gilmour, appear in a variety of places throughout the diary.

Anthony Lewis', Beaumarchais', Rees-Moggs,* Robert Blakes[†] and Carringtons.[‡] Enjoyable and interesting dinner.

MONDAY, 13 JUNE. *London and Brussels.*

Rue de Praetère dinner for the Gough Whitlams (former Labour Prime Minister of Australia). A surprisingly agreeable dinner after a slightly sticky start. Whitlam is most engaging and so is the mammoth Mrs Whitlam. The conversation became general halfway through dinner and he began to talk with extraordinary knowledge and interest about the genealogy of European nineteenth-century royal houses. He is a great expert on who exactly was every Hapsburg relation of the Emperor Maximilian of Mexico. No detailed discussion about current issues, but brief exchanges of view, with Mrs Whitlam mainly, on Fraser[§] whom she was against – not surprisingly – and Peacock,[¶] to whom she was much more favourable.

TUESDAY, 14 JUNE. *Strasbourg.*

Dinner for the *bureau* of the Socialist Group with an unsatisfactory conversation led by Fellermaier; they are not an inspiring group and most of the conversation was about some incredibly detailed, pointless, trivial matters of relationship between the Commission and the Parliament. The only man who tried to raise the level a bit, and up to a point succeeded, was John Prescott.[‖]

*William (Lord cr. 1988) Rees-Mogg, b. 1928, was editor of *The Times* 1967–81, and has subsequently been Vice-Chairman of the BBC and Chairman of the Arts Council.

†Lord Blake, b. 1916, historian and biographer, was Provost of Queen's College, Oxford, 1968–87. He was to be one of my rivals for the Chancellorship of Oxford.

‡Peter, 6th Lord Carrington KG, b. 1919, succ. 1938, had been Defence Secretary 1970–4 and was to be Foreign Secretary 1979–82, and Secretary-General of NATO 1984–8. In the summer of 1976 I tried to get him to come to Brussels as the second British Commissioner and was surprisingly close to succeeding.

§Malcolm Fraser, b. 1930, succeeded Gough Whitlam as Prime Minister of Australia in 1975 and held the office until 1983.

¶Andrew Peacock, b. 1939, was Australian Foreign Minister 1975–80 and leader of the Liberal Party 1980–5.

‖John Prescott, b. 1938, has been Labour MP for Kingston-upon-Hull since 1970, leader of the British Labour Group in the European Parliament 1976–9.

WEDNESDAY, 15 JUNE. *Strasbourg*.

Horrible morning as so often this summer. Lunch for a group of
Labour stalwarts and possible candidates brought by Jim Cattermole.* This was a surprisingly successful occasion. They were lively
and good, temporarily raised my spirits and, as David Marquand
said afterwards, made one realize what a lot of nice people there still
are in the Labour Party.

THURSDAY, 16 JUNE. *Strasbourg and Brussels*.

Jennifer rang to say that Ladbroke Square had been sold within two
hours of being put on the market. Mixed feelings, both because it is
one thing putting a house on the market and another to realize that
(after twenty-three years) it has gone; and also because its going so
quickly makes one think we sold it too cheap.†

FRIDAY, 17 JUNE. *Brussels and Bernkastel*.

A meeting, followed by lunch, with Malcolm Fraser, the Prime
Minister of Australia. He is a rather surly fellow who looks a
mixture of the self-confident and the suspicious. What in fact he
most reminds me of is a fast bowler on an off day, tall, quite strong,
but looking as though throughout a hot afternoon he had been
taking very long runs to the wicket and bouncing them down short
without getting any result; shirt out, trousers slightly coming
down. He was anxious to be awkward and I had to respond once or
twice. He came out with a ludicrous theory that we had all been
beastly to the Japanese and that, as a result of his talks with Fukuda,
he thought that Japan, unless allowed much better access to
markets than at present – surely a work of supererogation – would
go back to its policies of the thirties, i.e. reversal of alliances, no
support for the Western world, possibly moving into the Soviet
sphere. I, and I think everybody else, had interpreted Fukuda's
remarks – particularly about the thirties – in London in a totally
different sense.

*Jim Cattermole, b. 1910, had been my agent when I was adopted as candidate for
Solihull in 1945. Subsequently a Labour Party regional organizer and then the organ-
izational linchpin of all pro-European activity within the Labour Party.
†We did.

We then moved to lunch and I found Fraser slightly more agreeable. It emerged, most extraordinarily, that although I had begun by saying, 'I don't think we have ever met,' and his agreeing, except to say, 'Maybe we shook hands,' it then transpired in the course of lunch, fortunately coming to us both almost simultaneously, that I had in fact been to his house in the country in western Victoria in 1965 when I had been there on my visit as Minister of Aviation. I was driven over for a drink before lunch on the Sunday. Fortunately, as the occasion had been equally non-memorable for both of us, there was no great embarrassment about this. We then moved into a fairly rough discussion round the table which ran until 4 o'clock. An awkward, aggressive man, who does not put his best face forward. His attitudes obviously caused considerable embarrassment both to Peacock, his Foreign Minister, a much smoother man, and to his Ambassador (Sir James Plimsoll and not smooth), but perhaps ambassadors always dislike abrasiveness.

Motored to Bernkastel to join Jennifer and the Annans, who had gone that morning. After dinner at the Hotel zum Post we went to a café where impromptu singing broke out, and I wondered how different it had all been forty-three years before when Noël had first been there. He thought not immensely, apart from more people now – it was a German holiday weekend. The Annans have an extraordinary attachment to Germany, rather surprising in Gaby's case as she was brought up as a small child in grand Jewish circles in Berlin and left sometime in the 1930s. Noël likes the *lederhosen* aspect, and had indeed been on a walking tour there in 1934.

SATURDAY, 18 JUNE. *Bernkastel.*

To the Prüms at Wehlen at 11.00. He is both a substantial wine grower and a substantial wine merchant: a young man, who is a doctor of something or other, aged about forty, living with his mother. He gave us an extraordinarily good selection of Mosel wines to drink throughout the day, ranging from a 1921, through one of the wartime years, to the great 1949, and a whole variety of more recent ones. It taught me a lot about Mosel. It is remarkably unintoxicating because the alcoholic content, which I had long suspected, turned out on investigation to be not more than about 7 per cent. The Prüms live in an oppressive Wilhelmine house, built about 1902, of dark red, sombre appearance – all our wine tasting was done in a very heavy *salon* and the lunch, rather good, was in a hermetically sealed dining room. His mother, an opera-loving widow, was present at lunch but at nothing else. Then he drove us up to a hill on top of one of his Wehlen vineyards, where we had yet more tasting.

SUNDAY, 19 JUNE. *Bernkastel and Brussels.*

Motored to Trier (good cathedral and Marx's birthplace) which we looked round briefly and agreeably; and then on into northern Luxembourg where we had a picnic just on the edge of the rain. In the evening we had a dinner party rue de Praetère for the Annans, with the Tindemans amongst others. After dinner I arranged with Tindemans that he would be glad to attempt a JET mediatory job. He would endeavour to see both Schmidt and Callaghan during the early part of the following week.

MONDAY, 20 JUNE. *Brussels.*

Received and had a short talk with Seretse Khama,* President of Botswana, before taking him in for a *pro forma* Commission meeting. I had previously suggested that our Wednesday dinner for him ought, if his wife were in Brussels, to be a mixed one, contrary to our normal pattern, but this had been resisted by the Protocol Department on the ground that it had not been done for other African heads of state; and I had not persisted, partly because Ruth Khama is an Englishwoman. On the way down in the lift, however, I said to Seretse that I understood his wife was in Brussels and I was sorry that the dinner was not a mixed one. 'Oh, don't worry in the least,' he replied, 'she is used to being treated like that in Arab countries.' The point was sufficiently well made that I insisted that we changed our arrangements immediately, particularly as Jennifer was in Brussels that week.

*Sir Seretse Khama, 1921–80, was an hereditary tribal ruler who became the first President of the newly independent Botswana in 1966. His 1948 marriage to Ruth Williams of Croydon plunged him into racial controversy and made him a temporary hero of the left in Britain.

To the house of the American Ambassador to the Community, Deane Hinton, deep set in rhododendrons, for lunch with General Haig,* Nixon's old White House aide and now Supreme Allied Commander. He turned up in full uniform. He was, however, an agreeable and interesting man, maybe, as some people say, rather a politicians' general, but so for that matter was Eisenhower.

Then in the evening I addressed a dinner for the Advisory Council of the Ford Motor Company – a rather grand body presided over by Henry Ford himself and containing about ten of their world managers but also a lot of notable outside figures, like Edwin Plowden,† Karl Schiller‡ of Germany, whom I had hardly seen since the Bonn monetary conference of 1968, and Guido Carli§ of Italy. I rather liked Henry Ford, and did not find the whole dinner nearly as much of a chore as I had expected.

WEDNESDAY, 22 JUNE. *Brussels.*

Our dinner for Sir Seretse and indeed Lady Khama at Val Duchesse, with a more or less adequate complement of about 25 per cent women. I found Ruth Khama thoroughly agreeable, although a curiously uncoordinated mixture of south London secretary and Botswana duchess, rather reminiscent of old Mrs Philips Price,¶ who was a still more uncoordinated mixture of Berlin proletarian (Philips Price did indeed literally pick her up in the gutter after she had been clubbed in a 1919 Rosa Luxemburg/Spartacist riot) and Gloucestershire châtelaine. I made a brief speech, Seretse a rather longer one. He is a man of interest and distinction, though seems fairly ill.

---

*Alexander Haig, b. 1924, was Chief of the White House Staff 1973–4, Supreme Allied Commander Europe 1974–9, and US Secretary of State 1981–2.
†Lord Plowden, b. 1907, had been Chief Planner at the Treasury under Cripps, Gaitskell and Butler, Chairman of the Atomic Energy Authority 1954–9, and Chairman of Tube Investments Ltd 1963–76.
‡Professor Dr Karl Schiller, b. 1911, had been Minister of Economics in the Federal German Government 1966–72.
§Guido Carli, b. 1914, had been Governor of the Bank of Italy 1961–76.
¶Morgan Philips Price, 1885–1973, was a fox-hunting squire who, after being *Manchester Guardian* and *Daily Herald* correspondent in Russia and later Berlin 1914–23, became a Labour MP 1929–31 and 1935–59.

THURSDAY, 23 JUNE. *Brussels.*

Our six-monthly dinner for COREPER to mark the change of presidency, which I had decided against all precedent to give, not at Val Duchesse because we were so fed up with it, but in a restaurant, the Barbizon, in the splendidly named suburb of Jezus-Eik. By some miraculous chance the weather changed and the sun came out for the first time for weeks in Brussels. Speeches from me, Donald Maitland as the retiring President of COREPER, and Van der Meulen,* the incoming President, the last partly in English, partly in French, partly in Dutch, and embellished by two Latin quotations.

TUESDAY, 28 JUNE. *Brussels, Keele and London.*

Breakfast with Tindemans in the rue Ducale, finding him rather depressed about the collapse of his efforts to solve the JET problem. He had telephoned Schmidt and found him in a very disagreeable, hard, anti-British mood, saying that it was no good at all Tindemans coming to see him. However, it was quite useful intelligence before the London European Council to know Schmidt's state of mind.

Short Commission meeting at 9.45, then by plane to Birmingham and through pouring rain to lunch at Keele University with Princess Margaret before the degree ceremony. She was in quite a good temper considering she had just got her feet wet planting a tree. Professor Paul Rollo delivered a very warm encomium of me in his honorary degree presentation speech.

WEDNESDAY, 29 JUNE. *London.*

The first day of the two-day London European Council meeting. Downing Street luncheon. Most people had arrived when I got there and were assembled in the garden, Schmidt looking in a heavily black and gloomy mood. The luncheon conversation was fairly desultory to begin with; I sat between Cosgrave and Andreotti. Cosgrave was particularly agreeable and I am sorry that he is going. Towards the end of lunch when we began to get on to

---

*Josef Van der Meulen, 1914–84, was Belgian Permanent Representative to the European Community 1959–79.

some more general discussion, Giscard, supported by several others, said that he thought it would be useful to go on in this way for some time, and we therefore decided to put back the formal meeting in Lancaster House for two hours and adjourned to one of the drawing rooms in Downing Street. During this move I talked to Schmidt for about five minutes, trying to see if there was any 'give' from him so far as JET was concerned, but found him very complaining about the British attitude, particularly in relation to the budgetary contribution, and disinclined to move except as part of some broad overall settlement.

In the general discussion Giscard opened with an account of his talks with Brezhnev, saying broadly that Brezhnev found Carter very difficult to deal with, alleging that his amateurish foreign policy was endangering *détente*; French sympathy, Giscard said, was much on the Russian side. Schmidt supported this strongly, making it clear that his relations with Carter had gone back to their pre-Summit nadir. Indeed, Schmidt and Giscard supported each other on every point which came up during this European Council. This axis is always very powerful when working smoothly, and can sometimes be advantageous, but on this occasion was the reverse as they were both in a negative mood.

Schmidt and Giscard also worked themselves into a fine old anti-American mood, which Callaghan, supported by me, tried to resist. We then had some discussion about JET without getting anywhere much, though with various people, notably den Uyl, suggesting that the Commission ought to produce a solution for the next meeting and Schmidt suggesting openly the possibility of a package arrangement. Callaghan was definitely in a corner, both on this and on direct elections, but handling himself well, as he often does in such circumstances.

At 5.00 we moved to Lancaster House and a more formal meeting. There we began with our Commission loans proposal,* which I introduced briefly and not very well and then handed over to Ortoli. The discussion on this and some other matters went on until about 7 o'clock with a general *tour de table*, most people speaking and supporting us, including, surprisingly strongly,

*This was the proposal which I had tentatively outlined to Schmidt on 18 March (see page 68 *supra*) and which we eventually achieved under the name of 'the Ortoli facility' (he administered the loans).

Callaghan, as did Jørgensen, Cosgrave and den Uyl. But Schmidt and Giscard were both depressingly negative. Schmidt's view was to be expected but we were not quite prepared for Giscard's wet blanket, particularly as he argued rather more powerfully than did Schmidt.

Another Buckingham Palace dinner at 8.15. The Queen, to whom as usual these days I found myself speaking French, this time because of the presence of Guiringaud, was in a much better mood than Schmidt or Giscard. After dinner we went on to the balcony to watch Beating the Retreat, which seemed rather an appropriate ceremony in view of the general mood in the Council, but was very well done and worth watching. Afterwards I raised with Martin Charteris the possibility of the Queen paying a visit to the Commission in Brussels, to which he was very favourable but said it would have to depend upon advice from the British Government. We agreed that I should say to the Government that I had discussed it informally with the Palace who were sympathetically inclined.

THURSDAY, 30 JUNE. *London.*

A morning session for two and a half hours which was not much better than the day before, except that, after Andreotti and Tindemans had spoken favourably on the loans proposals, I made a reply which was more effective than my opening the previous evening and ended the discussion in a reasonably up-beat way. However this relative optimism did not allow for the impact of what would emerge from Schmidt's press conference afterwards. There was then a long discussion about the communiqué, with Giscard making a strong attempt, surprisingly not opposed by Schmidt, to get in a protectionist note. Callaghan and I then did a press conference, which he handled much better than I did.

FRIDAY, 1 JULY. *London, Glasgow and East Hendred.*

10.10 shuttle to Glasgow for the Collins factory opening at Bishopbriggs and for my long-prepared anti-Benn* speech. I was feeling

* Anthony Wedgwood Benn, b. 1925, the foremost advocate of the 1975 referendum 'to settle the issue', was then mounting a campaign to ignore that decision and bring Britain out of Europe.

rather gloomy on the way up to Glasgow, mainly as a result of the generally depressing atmosphere of the European Council, but rather improved on arriving there. It was a grey day but the views, as is often the case in the Clyde valley, were nonetheless quite wide under a sort of tent of cloud. The factory was impressive both in lay-out and its atmosphere of apparent efficiency. The lunch was in a marquee for about four hundred people, including staff, Collins authors, local notabilities, etc., and the speech, which had been widely put out beforehand and was as a result well-publicized, was well received by at least 90 per cent of the audience. After lunch I went into Glasgow and did a Scottish Television interview and showed the city to two members of my *cabinet*. East Hendred for dinner.

MONDAY, 4 JULY. *East Hendred and Brussels.*

Plane to Brussels. With Crispin to lunch with the Rumanian Ambassador who, without notice, produced his Minister of Foreign Trade, who wished to turn things into a very serious discussion about our trade negotiations with them which are due at the end of the month, and said what great importance he and President Ceausescu attached to these as a test of our relations. I decided to play it rather hard and said that we had indeed recognized for a long time that the Rumanians had a rather special pro-Community position amongst the East European countries, and were therefore the more amazed to know that they had been in the lead at Belgrade in trying to exclude Community representation (from the Conference on Security and Cooperation in Europe) and that whereas we would of course conduct commercial negotiations on a commercial basis at the end of July in any event, if they wanted any oil of goodwill they had better have another look at this policy. They seemed rather taken aback by this but I hope and believe it did no harm.

A very late dinner in the garden of the Chalet de la Forêt. The disadvantage of these immensely light (double summer-time) Brussels evenings, with almost full sunlight at 10.00, is that it is easy to slip into Spanish hours, as indeed we did on this occasion, dining from about 10.15 until 12.45.

TUESDAY, 5 JULY. *Brussels and Luxembourg.*

Avion taxi to Luxembourg at 11.00. Meeting of four Commissioners on MTNs. This was the first meeting at which Roy Denman,* as the new British Director-General of DG1, had appeared,
and a very good performance he put up. Lunch with Colombo, the
President of the Parliament. Dinner for the Christian Democratic
Group, a very agreeable lot of people, apart from Scelba, who must
have been better in 1947.†

WEDNESDAY, 6 JULY. *Luxembourg and Brussels.*

The fifth day of cloudless skies, good for the wide Luxembourg
views. Into the Chamber to listen to Simonet's report on the
London European Council, and then made my own; it went better
than I had feared. In the early evening Simonet and I each wound
up for about ten minutes. Simonet, who had been answering
Council questions in the morning, and doing it extremely well, is
not quite as good as a speaker. However, he is a most agreeable man
to get on with and it is a pleasure, so far at any rate, to have the
Belgians in the presidency of the Council.

MONDAY, 11 JULY. *Brussels.*

A noon meeting with Bob Strauss, the American Special Trade
Representative. Since I had seen him in Washington he did not
seem to have learnt a great deal more about the details of MTNs, but
this did not impair his strategic determination. He wanted to push
ahead and, indeed, laid down a timetable for work in the autumn
which seemed to us reasonable and to which we wanted to give a
positive response.

In the afternoon I saw Peter Jay who was on a Brussels briefing
visit. He was anxious to be friendly, and made rather a good
impression on me, but we soon got locked into a reasonably
good-tempered argument about economic and monetary union.

---

*Sir Roy Denman, b. 1924, had previously been a Second Permanent Secretary in the
British Cabinet Office. Head of the Commission delegation in Washington since 1982.
†In 1947 Scelba was Italian Minister for the Interior and played a notable role in
narrowly averting a Communist takeover following a collapse into strike-induced chaos.

TUESDAY, 12 JULY. *Brussels, Luxembourg and Brussels.*

Plane to Luxembourg, accompanied by Davignon, for my address to the Coal and Steel Community Consultative Council under the chairmanship of Joe Gormley.* A beautiful morning (although nonetheless the usual bumping over Bastogne) with Luxembourg under baking heat which rather suited it. Back to Brussels for the lunch for the Political Cooperation meeting of Foreign Ministers in the Palais d'Egmont. The protocol arrangements are notably better with the Belgian than the British presidency; no question of being anywhere but firmly on Simonet's right. In the afternoon a long and extremely hot meeting of the Political Affairs Committee of the European Parliament. Dinner early with Hayden and Ann Phillips at the Chalet de la Forêt, where we sat outside until 10.15 when the great heat came to an end in a most violent storm.

WEDNESDAY, 13 JULY. *Brussels.*

Historic Houses luncheon rue de Praetère with Edward Montagu,† George Howard,‡ the Prince de Ligne and Lord O'Hagan,§ but ironically without Jennifer. Caroline and her daughter Jane Gilmour to stay. Took them for a drive round Waterloo and part of the centre of Brussels.

SATURDAY, 16 JULY. *Brussels.*

Nicko and Mary Henderson arrived from Paris, complete with Rolls-Royce, at about 5.00. I drove them (plus Gilmours) on a great Brussels tour and then back for a somewhat ingrowing dinner party, in other words no non-English. Nicko was seized by a great desire about 11.30 to go on some huge fairground wheel which he had seen on our expedition during the afternoon. However, he retracted from this as he became sleepier.

---

*Joe (cr. Lord 1982) Gormley, b. 1917, President of the National Union of Mineworkers 1971–82.
†Lord Montagu of Beaulieu, b. 1926, now Chairman of English Heritage.
‡George Howard, 1920–84, was a Balliol contemporary, lord of Castle Howard and later Chairman of the BBC.
§Lord O'Hagan, b. 1945. He became a Conservative Member of the European Parliament in 1979.

SUNDAY, 17 JULY. *Brussels.*

The others went off to Ghent at about 11.00 in the Rolls, leaving Nicko and me to follow. Nicko said he had some work to do, but in fact spent the morning reading H. Nicolson's *Some People,* for about the seventh time I would guess. He and I left at noon and, partly because we were deep in conversation, got lost and went round and round Brussels. We had planned to have a picnic but Jennifer and I both became rather despairing about a site. The essential difficulty with Belgium is that either you go south for countryside or you go north for towns, and if you go north for towns there is no country-side except cabbage patches between bungalows, gasometers and chemical works in which to picnic. So we had a drink in a café on the Quai des Herbes with a pretty view and then decided the only thing to do was to stay and picnic there, even though it did not look at all the sort of café which would welcome one's own food. However, by sending Nicko to negotiate with the management and getting the Rolls-Royce to bring up the picnic basket we managed to achieve our objective, and had a very satisfactory lunch there until the Hendersons left for Paris.

THURSDAY, 21 JULY. *Brussels, Birmingham and London.*

To Birmingham for an Aston University honorary degree cer-emony. Then train to Euston and to Downing Street under motor-cycle escort by precisely 7.30 for my talk with Callaghan at the beginning of my official visit to London.

He greeted me at the front door and throughout the meeting, which lasted until nearly 9.00, was remarkably agreeable and forthcoming. He even sounded rather pro-Europe. David Owen was unexpectedly present but this on the whole helped. We discussed JET for a long time, in which he was encouraged, perhaps overencouraged, by what I had to say; and Article 131* for a considerable time too, on which he was not totally rigid; and a range of other issues. It was certainly by far the most agreeable talk I had had with him, not merely since I had left the Government, but

---

* Article 131 was the provision in the accession arrangements for Britain, Denmark and Ireland allowing a strictly limited adjustment if the budgetary burden upon one country became manifestly excessive.

since he had become Prime Minister. At some stages he was sufficiently forthcoming that I began to think he must have had some news which I had not heard, saying that all North Sea oil was turning out to be salt water, and that they needed the Community more than I thought!

FRIDAY, 22 JULY. *London and East Hendred.*

To see Mrs Thatcher in her new and rather lavish accommodation in the House of Commons, which was the Serjeant at Arms's old suite and which is incomparably better than anything any leader of the Opposition has had before. It was the first time I had been in the Palace of Westminster since leaving, but the return occasioned little in the way of upsetting twitches upon the thread. Mrs Thatcher I found agreeable, and more pro-European than when I last talked to her, although she reverted a bit towards the end of the conversation to a few routine and tedious complaints. But the success of her recent European speech in Rome had obviously, as I had rather expected, helped to commit her to the cause and she was definitely forthcoming. However, the conversation with her about the legislation for direct elections, as with everybody else, was like ten angels dancing on a pin, or whatever the phrase is. The more people you talk to, the more you go round and round as to how the guillotine will or will not work, will it come after Clause 1 or after Clause 3. It was all rather reminiscent of Chesterton's 'Chuck it, Smith':

> Where the Breton boat-fleet tosses,
> Do they, fasting, trembling, bleeding,
> Wait the news from this our city?
> Groaning, 'That's the Second Reading!',
> Hissing, 'There is still Committee!'

John Davies* joined us about half-way through and was surprisingly good and robust. I think I have undoubtedly underjudged him. He seems a very effective man at the present time. This does

*John Davies, 1916–79. Having been Director-General of the CBI 1965–9, he was a minister throughout the Heath Government and shadow foreign affairs spokesman 1976–8. Mrs Thatcher tried to nominate him as the second British Commissioner in 1976, but I successfully preferred Christopher Tugendhat.

not mean that I wish he had come to Brussels as a Commissioner, because I do not think he is quite right for that, but by any standard he is a first-class man with a good, wide-ranging mind, and treats Mrs Thatcher very firmly.

Then to the Secretary of State's room in the Foreign Office. Again, it was the first time I had been in that room for some time, almost since I frequently called on George Brown there nearly ten years ago. The room despite the splendour of its outlook is in a curious way slightly tatty and there is a good deal of rather second-rate c. 1910 furniture. Curzon ought to have complained about more than his ink-stand.

It was not a good meeting, not disagreeable but desultory, partly due to the fact that David Owen began by asking me to read the overnight telegrams from Bonn, which showed that JET, to which I am getting rather emotionally attached, has taken a considerable setback, but also because he conducted it in a rather desultory way, and Michael Palliser,* in contrast with what I think would have been the position a year ago, was less firm or able to pull the meeting together. I wasn't on particularly striking form either.

I left the Foreign Office at about 12 o'clock and drove to Buckingham Palace to see the Queen alone for half an hour. She was friendly and forthcoming in spite of the protocol which makes it a much more formal occasion than in any other royal house in Europe. Her Europeanism did not extend to an uncritical acceptance of the major European leaders. She got Giscard right, but underestimated Schmidt, perhaps too influenced by his having stubbed out his cigarettes all over the Buckingham Palace plates. Nonetheless her European commitment seemed very strong and when I broached the question of her paying a visit to the Commission she was positively enthusiastic, and said that something in the New Year ought to be possible.

Then a Carlton Gardens lunch for about thirty people which David Owen gave for me. I sat between him and Geoffrey Rippon† and had rather a good talk with David, although he was extremely

---

* Sir Michael Palliser, b. 1922, was Permanent Under-Secretary at the Foreign Office 1975–82.
† Geoffrey Rippon, b. 1924, cr. Lord Rippon 1987. Edward Heath's chief negotiator for Britain's entry to Europe, 1970–2. Secretary of State for the Environment 1972–4. Leader of the Conservative Group in the European Parliament 1977–9.

unconvincing on why he had removed Peter Ramsbotham* from Washington. He had previously implied that there was something terrible which Ramsbotham had done, which he would tell me about some day, but all this appeared to amount to was that he had discovered that Ramsbotham was not taken tremendously seriously by Callaghan, which left me with a slight sense of bathos. Otherwise, he was very agreeable and forthcoming and made a nice attractive speech – saying with remarkable frankness that he had been much in favour of my going to Europe, which, as he was clearly the greatest beneficiary from it, he might have been slightly reticent about at this stage. I made an unprepared reply.

After lunch to the Board of Trade for a slightly heavy conversation with Edmund Dell,† a good, worthy but not sparkling man, who was flanked by my old friend Leo Pliatzky.‡ It was mainly about Multinational Trade Negotiations, not perhaps a very sparkling subject. Then on to the Department of Energy on Millbank to find Master Benn waiting alone, unattended, upon the pavement for me, a very typical and courteous Benn gesture. We then went up to his room. Because I had Crispin with me, he introduced a pudding of a woman whom I had met before, called Ms Frances Morrell,§ who sat morosely throughout the interview, saying nothing and rather weighing upon everybody. However, Benn talked very well, did not spend much time on energy, although we discussed one or two subjects in this field, one of which, a relatively minor one, I gather he has since cleared in response to my request. But his main interest was in trying to raise some general hares and ask my views about the future of the Community (probably to take it down in evidence against me), which I gave him along economic and monetary union lines.

From there – with Benn, again with his great energy, coming down on his own and seeing me off from the pavement into my car (perfectly agreeable yet a constant sense that everything is

*Sir Peter Ramsbotham, b. 1919, was Ambassador to Teheran 1971–4, and to Washington 1974–7. Subsequently Governor of Bermuda.
†Edmund Dell, b. 1921, Labour MP for Birkenhead 1964–79, was Secretary of State for Trade 1976–8, when he left the Government and became Chairman of Guinness Peat and subsequently of Channel Four TV.
‡Sir Leo Pliatzky, b. 1919, was an Oxford contemporary who was a Treasury official 1950–77, and Permanent Secretary, Department of Trade, 1977–9.
§Frances Morrell, b. 1937, became Chairman of the Inner London Education Authority 1983–7.

calculated, no effort is too much, but the eye is never taken away from the ball of the main political purpose) – to the Charing Cross Hotel for a press conference. From there to East Hendred. It is an unusual experience to be able to pay an official visit to one's own country and to look at familiar scenes, persons and institutions from outside.

TUESDAY, 26 JULY. *Brussels.*

Foreign Affairs Council all day. At the lunch JET was discussed, the vote not having come out very well: Culham had received four votes, Britain, Denmark, Ireland and Belgium; Garching had received two, Germany and Luxembourg. Three had abstained, including two big countries, France, who were abstaining because they had gone slightly cool on the whole project, and Italy and Holland, who were both more capable, if only the British would play their hand well, of being swung pro-Culham. I tried hard and successfully to get Genscher to accept a moral commitment to take a firm positive decision at the next Council.

David Owen, I thought, was being rather obtuse about this and making things more difficult for himself, but then everybody can be obtuse from time to time. Back for a rather desultory early afternoon in the Council. Both Brunner and I, I thought, dealt rather badly with Commission representation at INFCEP (International Nuclear Fuel Cycle Evaluation Programme), when we should have roughed up Guiringaud, who was talking absolute nonsense, much more than we did. Maybe it is not a good idea to have great rows at the end of the summer when everyone is tired. However, I went home slightly discontented and displeased with myself, as is so often the case after the Council of Ministers.

WEDNESDAY, 27 JULY. *Brussels and London.*

Awoke on a dark July morning typical of nearly the whole of this summer: at 8 o'clock I had to have the light on. The last Commission meeting before the holidays. Oreja,* the Spanish Foreign Minister, to lunch, preparatory to the official presentation of their

* Marcelino Oreja Aguirre, b. 1935, was Spanish Foreign Minister 1976–80, and has been Secretary-General of the Council of Europe at Strasbourg since 1984.

application the following day. A small, bright, highly intelligent youngish career diplomat. I very much enjoyed seeing him and, indeed, the whole of his party, who struck me as very good indeed.

At 4.45 I adjourned the Commission with a few brief words, wishing people good holidays, to which Ortoli responded with particular warmth (he is a very nice man) saying how well I had run the Commission. There was then, to my surprise, a round of applause around the table, so perhaps the six months haven't been as bad as they have sometimes seemed. Rather encouraged by this, I had the *cabinet* for a glass of champagne at 5.30 and caught the 6.25 plane to London.

Ann Fleming gave a restaurant dinner party with Bonham Carters, Jo Grimond,* David Carritt,† Garrett Drogheda,‡ Evangeline Bruce and Diana Phipps.§ And then on to the Beaumarchais' for a remarkable farewell party of nearly three hundred. It was very carefully chosen, and there is I think no English couple who could have brought together such a collection of people from so many strands of English life. At about 12.30, Jennifer and I walked home. Rather the end of an epoch, having known that embassy so well for so long, to some extent under the Chauvels, then very well under the Courcels, and even better under the Beaumarchais'. I doubt if we will ever go there much in the future, and the sense of the end of an epoch was greatly accentuated by walking back to Ladbroke Square to spend almost our last night there.

THURSDAY, 28 JULY. *London.*

Threw away a lot of old clothes. I dislike both the decision of throwing things away and the sense of dismantling one's past life. Lunch in Albany with the Walston group.¶ About a dozen people turned up, including to my surprise David Owen. Having been told

*Jo Grimond, b. 1913, cr. Lord Grimond 1983, leader of the Liberal Party 1956–67.
†David Carritt, 1927–81. Highly talented in the attribution of Renaissance paintings.
‡11th Earl of Drogheda, b. 1910. Managing Director of the *Financial Times* 1945–70, and Chairman of the Royal Opera House, Covent Garden, 1956–74.
§Diana Phipps, b. 1937, the daughter of a Bohemian family with land in Czechoslovakia (see her mother's book, *The Journey*, by Cecilia Sternberg, 1982), married the scion of a well-known New York family who died young, and was settled in England, mainly at Buscot Parsonage, during the period of this diary.
*So called because it normally met in the Albany apartment of Harry Walston, b. 1912, cr. Lord Walston 1961. It was composed of embryonic members of the SDP who were strongly pro-European and had supported me for the Labour Party leadership in 1976.

the night before by Bill Rodgers that David had circulated a Cabinet paper arguing in favour of an extremely loose, confederal, non-dynamic, semi-free trade area EEC, I had decided rather deliberately to refute this, but was not expecting to do it in his presence. However, it was better that he was there, and we had a perfectly good-tempered argument. Bill strongly joined in on my side. Some of the others were rather mixed in their views. John Harris,* coming in late, was struck by the extent to which, on arrival, David looked defensive, with his eyes on the ground. I was not aware of this. However, it was good of him to have come.

Back to Ladbroke Square and saw Edward off in his one smart suit and bands, carrying his gown, about to pick up his wig, to be called to the Bar. Edward going off in this way heightened the sense of the end of a long chapter, as the first time I remember being in Ladbroke Square, particularly alone in the afternoon, was when he was being born twenty-three years ago and we had just moved in and Jennifer was in hospital.

FRIDAY, 29 JULY. *London and East Hendred.*

Finally left Ladbroke Square at 10.00, and drove to East Hendred. To Crowmarsh Gifford to a seventy-third birthday party of dear old Selwyn Lloyd's.† He told me on the way out that he was going to write about Suez, to which I said that my Secretary-General, Emile Noël, probably knew as much about it as anyone else, having been Mollet's *Chef de Cabinet*, to which Selwyn agreed that Noël probably knew more than he did as there were certain things about collusion which were known, he thought, to Mollet and Eden but were kept from him.

SUNDAY, 31 JULY. *East Hendred.*

Wrigglesworths to lunch. Ian Wrigglesworth‡ is a remarkable young man, with great sense and energy and buoyancy. I was extremely lucky to have him as my PPS.

*John Harris, b. 1930, cr. Lord Harris of Greenwich 1974, Minister of State at the Home Office 1974–9, has been closely associated with me since 1965.
†Selwyn Lloyd, 1904–78, cr. Lord Selwyn-Lloyd 1976, Foreign Secretary at the time of Suez and until 1960, then Chancellor of the Exchequer 1960–2, and Speaker of the House of Commons 1971–6.
‡Ian Wrigglesworth, b. 1939, a Teesside MP, first Labour and then SDP, 1974–87. Now President of the Social and Liberal Democrats.

TUESDAY, 2 AUGUST. *East Hendred.*

The *cabinet* plus one or two others arrived at about 11.00 for a day's strategy meeting. We were in the garden, and after three-quarters of an hour Renato Ruggiero began to complain about the heat. He was sitting in full sunlight which Italians quite rightly cannot stand. So we had to have a short adjournment to move up into the shade. Otherwise I feared that Renato's Neapolitan blood would soon liquefy. Apart from or perhaps in addition to this, Renato put up a very impressive performance, indeed nearly everybody did rather well and we had a very useful morning's discussion on relations with the different member governments and how this affected our attitude to monetary union and enlargement in particular. In the afternoon we talked mainly about agricultural policy, the Mediterranean, and monetary union again. Graham Avery was extremely good on agriculture. Michael Emerson opened crucially on monetary union.

I did a general summing-up, of which the main import was that as the harsh reality was that none of the three main governments, France, Germany or Britain, was prepared to support a major Commission initiative, we, combined with trying to get certain urgent, practical things through, had to be prepared to go against them and to blaze a trail to a greater extent than we had done previously, however much this offended people, and that the obvious direction for this was towards monetary union.

THURSDAY, 4 AUGUST. *East Hendred.*

Another perfect day; up early and had an eight-mile walk from 7.30. Too long. Exhaustion set in during the morning. Beaumarchais' to stay for the final visit of their London life. They were in a good and easy mood despite their extreme irritation of the early summer at the abruptness of their removal.* Their final period had been such a success that this had put them back in a fairly sunny condition.

---

*Giscard suddenly decided that he wanted the job for his ineffective ex-Foreign Minister, Jean Sauvagnargues.

SUNDAY, 7 AUGUST. *East Hendred and Ripe.*

Took the Beaumarchais' to near Basingstoke to lunch with Christopher Soames,* who had two of his children there, Nicholas, a nice, intelligent boy in spite of his size, and Emma; but not Mary. A very good lunch, as one would expect at the Soames', a fine *gigot*, good wine. There was a mild political row between Jacques and Christopher after lunch, and then Christopher and I went off and talked for a bit in his new library, during which he was remarkably friendly and uncritical about my Brussels régime, considering how tempting it would be for him to take a different attitude. I am not sure that he had much positive advice, except that I ought to go and visit the Berlaymont telephone exchange. Then motored on through Surrey and Sussex to Ripe (Bonham Carters') for the last time, as that house too is being abandoned.

WEDNESDAY, 10 AUGUST. *Ripe.*

In the afternoon we drove via Cuckmere Haven and Birling Gap to Beachy Head, where we walked to the edge and lay looking out over the cliffs. There was a perfectly calm sea and the towering chalk cliffs made it, although there were too many people about, a rather memorable day. It was the first time that I had spent a summer afternoon looking out from those cliffs towards France since July 1943 when I lay there all day on an army exercise and the French shore seemed more forbidding.

THURSDAY, 11 AUGUST. *Ripe, London and East Hendred.*

Left just before 3 o'clock, feeling sentimental about leaving Ripe for the last time. However the best corrective for feeling sentimental about Ripe is to drive from it to London, as it is the most appalling route with the most appalling traffic. Went to the new flat for the first time. It is rather splendid and removes part of my regrets about Ladbroke Square. The Rodgers' came to dinner. They were particularly nice; an immense pleasure seeing them. East Hendred at 11.30.

* Christopher Soames, 1920–87, cr. Lord Soames 1978, had been Ambassador to Paris 1968–72, and a Vice-President of the European Commission 1973–7. He was married to Mary Churchill.

FRIDAY, 19 AUGUST. *East Hendred.*

Eric and Frieda Roll brought Robert Marjolin* to lunch. Marjolin sympathetic and interesting as always, depressing about the future of Europe, thought the essential task was to hold what we had achieved. When I pointed out that this was hardly inspiring, he agreed and said, 'Yes, maybe we have to move forward,' but he was sceptical about my ideas on monetary union. Said that he could not vote for Mitterrand, which was rather surprising for a Socialist candidate of the 1960s. He would vote for Mitterrand on his own but not for Mitterrand plus Marchais.† Therefore he would vote for the 'majority' whether the candidate was Giscard or even Chirac. He might vote for a Lecanuet-like figure. We had quite a good talk after lunch, which was rather mind-clearing from my point of view, about the general European position and Schmidt/Giscard relations. When I said that Schmidt insisted that he had to work closely with Giscard because 'Valéry is my only friend', Marjolin said, 'Well, he must be a very lonely man indeed if Valéry is his only friend, because Valéry is nobody's friend but his own.' It was a day of indescribable awfulness: almost continuous rain, low cloud, very dark, very cold.

MONDAY, 22 AUGUST. *East Hendred and Lucca.*

Flew to Pisa at 8.00, arriving, as quite often, in extremely disagreeable weather. Drove to the Gilmours' house, La Pianella, up its dreadful drive from Torcigliano, eight miles north-west of Lucca. The weather had apparently been pretty filthy for at least five days past though having, as is so often the case, been good during the first part of August. The Italian weather always breaks at Feragosto: sometimes it comes back quickly and sometimes it doesn't, but this is such a reliable rule that one is lunatic not to take notice of it.

TUESDAY, 30 AUGUST. *Lucca and Portofino.*

To the Berlins' near Portofino. Despite the rain, the Gilmour visit was enjoyable, and we had at least had three (out of eight) good

*Robert Marjolin, 1911–86. Secretary-General of OEEC 1948–55, and a Vice-President of the European Commission 1958–67.
†Georges Marchais, b. 1920, has been Secretary-General of the French Communist Party since 1972.

days of weather, which was a higher proportion than most people in England or Italy had had during the previous fortnight. I had written the introduction to the English edition of Monnet's memoirs, read in proof Ian's new book, as well as the new volume of Virginia Woolf's diaries, a life of E. M. Forster, and finished a Simenon.

Arrived at Parragi, a mile or so short of Portofino, where we met the Berlins and the Donaldsons at the bottom of their great hill. During lunch, to our amazement, there came a real clearance, blue sky and full sunshine. A beautiful evening and this bit of coast, with the Berlins' villa perched 500 steps above the little bay, still more attractive than I had remembered it six years before. There is one great advantage to the old Riviera, whether French or Italian, but particularly Italian: if one has to be in a fairly built-up area, as is now almost inevitable in the western Mediterranean, it is much better that it should have been built up sixty, seventy or a hundred years ago, because it was then done with much less violence to the landscape, much more spaciously, much better set in the trees, much better building indeed, than where the development has just been done.

MONDAY, 5 SEPTEMBER. *East Hendred and Brussels.*

To Brussels via Antwerp, as the interminable semi-strike seemed to have disorganized the direct service. It was by no means wholly disagreeable being back, particularly as the weather in Belgium, in contrast with that on most of our holiday, seemed rather good. The holiday has been too long; forty days in a row, although in itself agreeable, is not the right balance. It is so long away that after the half-way mark there is a greater feeling of apprehension about the return than of enjoyment of the actuality. It would be better to have only four weeks without Commission meetings, as indeed I told them at the first meeting, with two other weeks of break.

TUESDAY, 6 SEPTEMBER. *Brussels.*

During the morning I saw Signora Allende, widow of the assassinated Chilean leader, of whom I did not think much. She had actually played no part in politics while her husband was alive and is a rather stupid and slightly hysterical woman, who has become very much a professional political widow. There was a faint touch of Jennie Lee,* but I don't think she has ever done anything nearly as effective as Jennie Lee did for the arts.

THURSDAY, 8 SEPTEMBER. *Brussels.*

Simonet to lunch. He, as usual, was on good and buoyant form though, less usually, was neither eating nor drinking much. He was gloomy about being able to settle JET because of the obsession of the German Government with its kidnapping problems and his consequent inability to see Schmidt, as well as the failure of the bilateral visit of Callaghan to Schmidt to take place. Full of some good plans for the autumn including, which is of interest and value to us, a seriously focused discussion about the longer-term economic position, which would give me a chance to try and deploy my monetary union ideas at the European Council on 5/6 December.

I asked Simonet why the so-called 'Rubens Summit', which had been proposed by Giscard in London and set up for Wednesday, 21 September, in Antwerp, had been unexpectedly cancelled. He said because Giscard had gone completely cold on it and when he had gone to see him in Paris had claimed not to be able to remember having heard of it, still less having suggested it. 'Ah, yes,' he said, 'an interesting idea, but what purpose would it serve?' Giscard had obviously been very much on this lofty form throughout Simonet's visit. On Giscard's general attitude to him and Belgium, he said: 'He treated me like a farmer, a quite substantial farmer, who had come to pay the rent and should be allowed to have a sort of annual visit with some conversation, and even refreshment, but not lunch, in the course of doing so.'

FRIDAY, 9 SEPTEMBER. *Brussels.*

A serious meeting at 11.45 with Gundelach with whom for more than an hour I went through all our commitments and his agricultural plans for the autumn and winter. He looked greatly revived

---

*Lady Lee of Asheridge since 1970, widow of Aneurin Bevan, Labour MP 1929–31 and 1945–70. Minister of the Arts (under various titles) 1964–70.

by the holiday, and the meeting was both useful and agreeable. He I think was a little oppressed at the fact that I had learnt a good deal about the CAP and the details of his portfolio during the summer. Stevy Davignon to lunch, and I expounded to him my plans for the autumn.

George Thomson came to dine and stay the night. He is sensible and wise about nearly all the issues and had obviously found, *mutatis mutandis*, much the same difficulties in Brussels that I have. In particular he said that, having always previously had very good and easy press relations, he found the Brussels press corps an absolute nightmare. Our only disagreement was that he was cautious and sceptical about the wisdom of my determination to relaunch monetary union.

TUESDAY, 13 SEPTEMBER. *Brussels and Luxembourg.*

Left for Luxembourg by car about 7.40. The first perfect autumn morning; mist in the valley of the Meuse at Namur, but brilliant sunshine most of the way. Budget debate all day in the Parliament. After the speech of Eyskens, the Belgian Budget Minister, which was competent and wisely low key, Tugendhat spoke extremely effectively, staking out our strong line of conflict with the Council, and was very well received by the Parliament.

I took Ted Heath, who was paying a visit to prepare for his great Europe lecture at the Conservative Conference, to lunch at a restaurant about four miles out and found him on quite good form, very willing to listen and inform himself, and favourably disposed towards monetary union. Then back for the continuation of the debate. I spoke for about twenty-five minutes, and this again, like Tugendhat's speech, was regarded as effective. Eyskens wound up in a slightly battered but skilful way at the end. I gave a dinner for the Liberal Group.

WEDNESDAY, 14 SEPTEMBER. *Luxembourg and Brussels.*

Breakfast with Simonet and Colombo at the curiously Washington-style house of the Belgian Ambassador to Luxembourg. This was exclusively concerned with the boring old issue of the Parliament's new offices in Brussels, a subject in which I am determined to avoid the Commission getting deeply involved. Back to Brussels by TEE over lunch.

Dined with General Haig and a largish party at Mons. The party was principally for the new US Ambassador to NATO, Tapley Bennett, whose wife I sat next to and found intelligent and agreeable. I was not quite so sure about him. He made a markedly bad speech in reply to the General's almost equally bad one after dinner. It is curious that Americans should be so addicted to these little after-dinner speeches mentioning and welcoming all the guests when they are so bad at it. However, my impression of Haig as being an effective man with a modest manner even if vaulting ambitions, remained unimpaired by the evening.

THURSDAY, 15 SEPTEMBER. *Brussels.*

Lunched with COREPER. A slightly awkward issue surfaced: whether the Council presidency (i.e. for the moment the Belgians, next the Danes) should be represented as well as us at the official follow-up talks to the London Summit which Crispin attends for us. There also sadly emerged the certainty that we cannot take JET at the September Council owing to the post-kidnapping paralysis of the German Government. I spoke to Dohnanyi on the telephone in Bonn and got him to promise that the matter would be dealt with at the Belgian 'Schloss Gymnich'-type meeting in early October, or, at the very latest, at the October Council itself.

Speech in the evening to the British Labour Group in Brussels. It was the sort of semi-informal speech to a Fabian group or a Labour Party dinner or a university Labour Club, which I had done constantly over thirty years, but at which I have got rather out of practice in the last year. I found it highly enjoyable and rather stimulating. It was a pleasure to speak leaning against a table and without a text, rather than to make the much more formal statements with translation, to which I have recently become used.

FRIDAY, 16 SEPTEMBER. *Brussels and La Roche-en-Ardennes.*

The day of my ninth and last official introductory visit, but as it was to Belgium not much travel was involved. We began with a Laeken luncheon with the King and Queen, also the Tindemans', the Simonets, various Court officials, etc. The lunch enjoyable, the King as nice as ever, and the Queen, whom I had hardly previously talked to and between whom and Mme Simonet I sat, was also agreeable: rather good-looking in a sad sort of way, quite interesting, even better English than the King, who goes off into French fairly quickly, which she doesn't.

Then a fairly serious discussion for almost two hours in Tindemans's office which was constructive, except getting rather snarled up at the end on the question of (Council) presidency representation at the Summit follow-up official meeting. Simonet was being rather wild, in favour of rushing at this in an ill-considered manner, and was supported by Van der Meulen, but Tindemans in the middle was a great deal more sensible and balanced, and saw possible consequences far more clearly. Eventually Tindemans got his (and our) way on this.* Finally a reception in the Parliament building given by the Presidents of the two Chambers. Then drove to the Hôtel-Restaurant de l'Air Pur a few miles beyond La Roche-en-Ardennes, for our Commission strategy weekend.

SATURDAY, 17 SEPTEMBER. *La Roche-en-Ardennes.*

Morning session on the institutional aspects of enlargement. First, the question of how we would deal with a member state, old or new, in which democracy was overthrown (this issue is clearly made much more actual by the three applicant members, none of whom only five years ago was under any sort of democratic régime). Then there was a good deal of discussion about the size and shape of the Commission itself, most but not all thinking that seventeen would be far too large.

Afternoon session on Mediterranean problems, with particular reference to enlargement. Gundelach very good indeed; Natali not at all bad. After them the discussion began to get all over the place. However, we managed to steer well away from illusions about massive industrialization of the Mediterranean or any commitment

---

*I.e. that we should not press for a representative of the country holding the presidency of the Community (then Belgium) to accompany Crispin Tickell to meetings of Summit 'sherpas'.

to deal with its agricultural problems by price support. It is vital not to transpose the price support system, with all the excesses which flow from it in northern agriculture, into the Mediterranean.

Very enjoyable dinner talk with Brunner, who can be an extremely engaging conversationalist; he has a remarkable range of knowledge about English politicians, both of the present day and the late nineteenth century. He is much better on such subjects than when dealing with energy. Perhaps I ought to find another portfolio for him.

SUNDAY, 18 SEPTEMBER. *La Roche-en-Ardennes and Brussels.*

The morning session was extremely important for me as it would determine whether I could carry the Commission with me on monetary union. Ortoli opened in a slightly worried, defensive mood, because of my having put round my paper on the need for an urgent re-launch of the idea of monetary union; I thought he was more worried than offended, but you can never be quite sure. I then spoke for about twenty minutes, and we had a good discussion which came to a fairly natural end about lunchtime, there being general support, with the exception only I think of Haferkamp, who is by far the most conservative member of the Commission, and of Burke who, for some extraordinary reason, got excited about the difficulty of countries giving up monetary sovereignty, which is an odd view for an Irishman, as of course they have never had it, always being tins on the tail of the Bank of England.* But apart from those two, and Ortoli moving slowly and reluctantly, but moving, there was strong general support for our launching the wider idea and proclaiming the need for an early leap forward. Davignon and Gundelach and, indeed, Brunner and Vredeling were all I thought particularly good in the discussion. So was Tugendhat, as he had been throughout the two days. At the end we all thought we had had a good weekend, and broke up buoyantly with agreeable drinks outside in strong sunshine.

* No longer so. One result of the British decision to stay out of full EMS participation has been to cut the special monetary links between Dublin and London.

TUESDAY, 20 SEPTEMBER. *Brussels*.

Foreign Affairs Council at 10 o'clock. A good discussion on the Spanish application, with the French bewilderingly having decided to withdraw the reservation they were going to put up. However, they were awkward about Commission representation on INFCEP. Guiringaud was not there, but a rather tawdry-looking champagne merchant called Taittinger, who is Under-Secretary at the Quai, put up French objections unsustained by any possible argument. I spoke, I hoped and thought, rather firmly – and this matter ended up by Taittinger saying he would have to get further instructions, which by the afternoon he got and more or less withdrew.

At the ministers' lunch I gave a long *exposé* of what we had done at La Roche, and they seemed quite interested. Then the French rounded off their bad day by coming under powerful gunfire from Gundelach and Cheysson, both of whom spoke extremely well, over our negotiating position in the International Sugar Conference.* They were completely isolated.

WEDNESDAY, 21 SEPTEMBER. *Brussels*.

Jennifer went to Bremen to launch a huge ship. Commission meeting all day, adjourning at 6.15. This gave me time to give a little further thought to our 7 o'clock meeting with Bob Strauss, the US Special Trade Representative. The meeting, however, did not demand much thought for Strauss was still at a high level of generality, agreeable as usual, full of bantering conversation, telling us a bit about what was going on in Washington, how anxious he was to make some progress, to produce something he could sell to the public, but showing no desire to get down to any details, or indeed to be awkward, as we thought at this stage he might be.

THURSDAY, 22 SEPTEMBER. *Brussels*.

Commission lunch for Strauss and his party, who had been meeting with Haferkamp, Gundelach and Davignon during the morning. Over lunch there was general conversation followed by a brief

*The French wanted to take a very hard line against the Third World cane sugar producers in order to protect the beet sugar farmers of Picardy and Champagne.

exchange of complimentary speeches. Strauss was interesting on a number of points. He had spent most of the night on the telephone to Washington resisting becoming Director of the Budget in succession to Lance, who had just resigned. Who were the important senators? Russell Long (Mississippi) he placed almost at the top of the list. How were the various Cabinet officers doing? Blumenthal not very well, though an able man. Then the draft communiqué was brought in and we worked on this for a short time and got agreement without too much difficulty on the basis of the so-called Swiss formula, with a tacit understanding that we should try and go for tariff cuts of about 40 per cent, minus perhaps 5 per cent, worked out on the basis of this formula – but the understanding not at this stage to be published.

MONDAY, 26 SEPTEMBER. *London.*

Dinner at the Annans, with only the Rothschilds* there besides us. An extremely agreeable evening; a great bashing around with Victor, a mixture of literary, political, gossipy conversation.

TUESDAY, 27 SEPTEMBER. *London and Brussels.*

At 6.30 I saw Howard,† the new Australian Minister of External Trade, who was perfectly nice but inexperienced. He had clearly been sent by the egregious Fraser with an extremely rough but foolish negotiating brief. It meant that they were trying to go back on the plan we had laboriously agreed to in June for having a general review of trading matters at official level, but *not* ministerial talks and not with a view to the conclusion of a bilateral agreement at this stage. As a result of this he had stubbornly refused the evening before to allow talks to take place between officials on the agreed basis. The object of my meeting was to get him to change his mind on this, which I did, but not without the chilliness and roughness which seems, far more than with any other government, to be involved in dealing with the Australians at the present time.

*Victor (3rd Lord) Rothschild, b. 1910, had, amongst other notable accomplishments, set up the Central Policy Review Staff ('Think Tank') in the Cabinet Office, 1971–4.
†John Howard, b. 1939, in 1985 replaced Andrew Peacock, who had replaced Malcolm Fraser, as leader of the Opposition in Australia.

WEDNESDAY, 28 SEPTEMBER. *Brussels.*

Leo Pliatzky, now Permanent Secretary to the Department of Trade, to lunch rue de Praetère. A little preliminary conversation about trade matters, and then a fascinating conversation about the past with him. He had been a close friend, not so much at Oxford as in post-Oxford days, in the late forties and early fifties, but I had seen him hardly at all since I left the Treasury. He had quite a lot of interesting things to say. He was deeply critical of almost everybody within sight, or indeed out of sight: Douglas Allen,* who had lost his cutting edge since he went to the non-job of being head of the Civil Service; Denis Healey, who had certainly been a very bad Chancellor of the Exchequer in the early days and was not all that good now; Joel Barnett,† who was ineffective as a Chief Secretary, etc. However, Leo's mixture of prickly charm and angular honesty meant that this did not create a disobliging atmosphere.

Clearly Leo himself, though fighting through great vicissitudes of ill-health, motor-car accidents, losing an eye, having lost his wife, God knows what else, had played a decisive part in getting control over public expenditure when he was Second Permanent Secretary in the Treasury charged with this side of things. He had relied not so much on cash limits, though he thought these were important, but even more on a formula which he had evolved with John Hunt,‡ by which in Cabinet committees Treasury ministers should not be allowed to be overruled, whatever the majority, without an obligation to go to Cabinet resting upon the minister who wanted to spend, not upon the Treasury; and that if there was no agreement, this immediately unlatched a process by which the exact state of the contingency reserve had to be reviewed and placed before the Cabinet. This he thought made a great difference.

He was also interesting, though unforgiving even in retrospect, about Tony Crosland, who had at times been a still closer friend of Leo's than I was. He had known him very well up to some time in the early 1960s. But, like a lot of people, Leo had been deeply

---

*Sir Douglas Allen, b. 1917, cr. Lord Croham 1978, was Permanent Secretary of the Treasury when I was Chancellor.
†Joel Barnett, b. 1923, cr. Lord Barnett 1983, was Chief Secretary of the Treasury 1974–9, and is now deputy Chairman of the BBC.
‡Sir John Hunt, b. 1919, then Secretary of the Cabinet, is now Lord Hunt of Tanworth, and Chairman of the Prudential Assurance Company.

offended by Tony on a personal basis, and then subsequently, perhaps partly because of this but I don't think principally so, thought that Tony had an appalling responsibility for public expenditure accelerating out of control during the early days of the 1974 Labour Government, mainly because he had always provided the most sophisticated arguments in favour of an open hand at the till. It was in his view a real example of *trahison des clercs*. Leo is still as always very much his own man, rather like a senior Graham Avery, with great intellectual self-confidence, in some ways also not unlike the maligned Douglas Allen, but with substantial differences too.

THURSDAY, 29 SEPTEMBER. *Brussels*.

Worked at home on the highly complicated subject of the effect on agriculture of the transfer to the European unit of account, preliminary to an hour-long meeting with Gundelach, in which he explained to me why he did not want to make a move on this for several months. Quite a convincing explanation: the intellectual case was overwhelmingly against him and he had the good sense to admit this and said his reluctance was based purely on a judgement of how the various personalities would react; a good example of how to present a difficult case, and he moved my mind somewhat.

I had Sigrist,* the German Permanent Representative, to lunch, partly because I felt a little out of touch with the German scene. Good, rather serious, conversation. First, without great shafts of penetrating light, but highly intelligently, he described why the Germans reacted so much to the terrorist threat and the effect on various German alignments and the position of the different parties at this stage. Then a routine exchange about JET and Article 131, and then at the end my expounding to him some of my ideas on economic and monetary union. I wonder how he will report back.

FRIDAY, 30 SEPTEMBER. *Brussels*.

A visit from Bill Rodgers, who gave me an advance copy of the public letter which Callaghan had written to the Labour Party on

*Helmut Sigrist, b. 1919, German Permanent Representative to the European Community 1977–9, Ambassador to Greece 1979–84.

the eve of its annual conference. On balance quite a good letter, very firm on rejecting any possibility of British withdrawal from the Community and recognizing how damaging the continuing speculation about this was both to the Labour Party and Britain's position in Europe; presenting some good arguments against this, but also concentrating far too much on wanting a loose Community with an absolute ceiling to any significant powers for the Parliament, and welcoming, as it is right to welcome for *other* reasons, the prospect of enlargement on the basis that it would make a loose Community more certain – a very silly view indeed, this. Not too unreasonable a slant on reform of the Common Agricultural Policy, and quite constructive, though very vague, about energy policy.

I saw an agitated Tugendhat at 4.30, who was greatly upset, and with some reason, to discover that, without consultation with him, Gundelach had apparently announced that export sales of Community butter, with restitution, i.e. with huge budgetary costs and the likelihood of extremely adverse public reaction, in Britain at any rate, were likely to be 150,000 tons for the year, not 105,000 tons as had previously been thought. Gundelach was in Paris so there was nothing to do except await his explanations.

MONDAY, 3 OCTOBER. *Brussels.*

Mário Soares, Prime Minister of Portugal, from 11.00 until 12.00. Soares on this occasion more realistic, more self-confident, more impressive than when I had seen him in March. A quite good conversation (in French) with him. He seemed reasonably satisfied with the way the application was being handled and gave a mixed picture of the Portuguese economy.

I pointed out to him the difficulty raised by the Callaghan letter, in which Callaghan got very close to saying that one of the great advantages of enlargement was that it would inevitably mean a looser, less effective, less supranational Community; and that Soares ought to be aware of this because if he aligned himself with this it would inevitably cause an ideological split amongst those who wanted his accession to the Community. He reacted immediately, saying it certainly was not his view at all; the last thing he wanted was to dilute the Community by coming in. He convinced me that he was not just talking for the book by coining the good aphorism that he was not going to take the trouble of resigning from EFTA (the European Free Trade Association) in order to join what was no more than a glorified EFTA. What he wanted to join was a real political Community with a momentum towards economic and political union.

Crispin back from Washington with the news that the next Summit is not to be until after the Danish presidency is out of the way, and therefore under the German presidency. Thus the big countries will rather skilfully obviate the problem of what they would do with a small country holding the presidency. He also reported on Strauss's feeling following his visit to us, which apparently amounted to his thinking that we had slightly taken the pants off him and that he had given us more than we had given him; but this may be a ploy.

WEDNESDAY, 5 OCTOBER. *Brussels.*

Commission meeting, disrupted but agreeably so by the visit of Queen Juliana and Prince Bernhard. Out to the airport to meet them at 10.15. It was a surprisingly cold morning, and I stood rather chillily on the tarmac although they arrived on time, she dressed in her typical comfortable Dutch way, he, stripped of his uniforms by Vredeling (although I do not suppose he would have come in one in any event), dressed in one of his rather flash pepper and salt suits. However, he is an intelligent and, I find, likeable man in spite of the Lockheed affair.* Drove in with both of them to the Berlaymont, it having been made clear by the Dutch authorities that the Prince did not wish, which was the previous plan, to drive with Vredeling and therefore he sat in the front of the car, and the Queen and I sat in the back.

Both of them were very anxious to be agreeable, which I think comes naturally to them. At the Berlaymont they were greeted with flowers for her and a good cheering crowd, mainly of Dutch. They then came up to my room where they expressed great interest in the view, the pictures, everything; the only hiccup being when Umberto, my anglophone Italian *huissier*, brought the coffee in and

---

*In 1976 Prince Bernhard had been touched by a Lockheed bribery scandal relating to the sale of military aircraft. Vredeling, who was then Dutch Minister of Defence, presided over the subsequent surrender by the Prince of his military rank, and hence his uniforms.

she, who hadn't spoken a word of this language to anyone else, suddenly addressed him in Dutch, and asked for some hot water with the coffee. 'Warm wasser,' she said, or some such words. Poor Umberto was absolutely flummoxed. She presumably assumed that all people in subordinate positions in Belgium were Dutch-speaking. However, when I told her that he was an anglophone Italian she apologized profusely.

In the Commission meeting various members gave *exposés*, including notably Ortoli, who was not on the list but spoke with great passion and enthusiasm, and much impressed the Queen. She was slow to get going and ask questions and Prince Bernhard performed a very useful role in being ready with one or two quite shrewd ones. Then lunch, lasting until nearly 3.30, with nearly all the members of the Commission and turning towards the end into a rather good general discussion: the Queen, idealistic, perhaps a little naïve, but genuinely interested and enquiring; Prince Bernhard quick and intelligent and very agreeable to talk to on a personal plane; and at the end, when I thanked him warmly and privately for having come and said how much he had contributed to the visit, I found him rather moved.

For this successful visit we paid the mild price of not being able to start proper Commission business until 3.30, which meant a wearing five-hour meeting until 8.30. Ortoli was overcome by his oratorical triumph in the morning and indeed another good and striking performance at lunch. On the way back up in the lift, he told me, 'Elle est une dame très distinguée,' which is not exactly the obvious phrase to use about Queen Juliana. Then when I saw him for an hour the next day and said how splendidly he had spoken the day before and how much he had impressed the Queen, he said sadly, 'Ah, yes, but that was yesterday. I am on much less good form today.'

FRIDAY, 7 OCTOBER. *Brussels.*

A meeting with four or five Commissioners about the enlargement paper we had promised to the Council. Contrary to my hopes and expectations after La Roche, the draft before us was almost useless, with all the edge of the two previous papers taken away. I recalled across forty years a remark of G. D. H. Cole, who, when somebody had said that a book was very bad, replied that it was not quite as bad as it seemed at first sight; if you only read every other sentence, the text made reasonable sense. This was the case here. However, what the sense was depended whether you started with an even or odd sentence. I announced that Kergorlay* was to rewrite the whole thing, so that it could at least have the coherence of single authorship, as near as possible to the La Roche form, and try to get it through a special Commission on Tuesday, although I alas would be in Japan.

SATURDAY, 8 OCTOBER. *Brussels and Villers-le-Temple.*

Breakfast rue de Praetère for James Schlesinger, the United States Energy Secretary, with a great party of officials. A rather sticky occasion – I hate working breakfasts in any case – and I didn't take greatly to Schlesinger. No doubt he is an able man, but I rather dislike his habit of carrying on a conversation by a series of laconic, not very funny, wisecracks, with too much straining after epigram. It was rather like talking to a less witty Ken Galbraith[†] whom one did not know.

To Villiers-le-Temple for the Belgian 'Schloss Gymnich' weekend. This wasn't quite Leeds Castle but it took place at a rather attractive hotel called La Commanderie, converted out of a sort of mixture of priory and barracks for Knights Templars. Everyone, except Guiringaud, was there for lunch. David Owen was asked to begin by giving an account of the British position after the Labour Party Conference, which he did in somewhat complacent terms. I then said I thought the Callaghan letter did mark a step forward, although I could not entirely agree with David's view that it had buried the issue in the Labour Party for ever; it had probably buried it for this Parliament, and possibly the next if the Labour Party won, but by no means necessarily with the Labour Party in opposition.

I also thought there were grave dangers in at least one sentence of the letter, that which expressed the view that enlargement was to be welcomed as an almost inevitable weakening of the Community. This provoked others, particularly Genscher and Thorn, to

---

*Roland de Kergorlay, b. 1926, was the chief official dealing with enlargement. From 1980 to 1982 he was head of the Commission delegation in Washington.
†John Kenneth Galbraith, b. 1908, Harvard professor since 1949 and US Ambassador to India 1961–3.

complain slightly more strongly along the same lines; Genscher said it was very nice of the British not to ask for another renegotiation, implying strongly that if we had that would have been the end; but also committing himself, which was satisfactory, to a view that on the contrary enlargement must mean a strengthening of the Community. However, there was not tremendous pressure upon David.

There was some complaint about Crispin not having distributed to the Little Five the text of the communiqué which had been agreed upon, though not for publication, at the Washington meeting of Summit 'sherpas', and I defended him vigorously on this, saying that he could not possibly stand out against the unanimous view of the others that there was to be no communication of this, except to the heads of governments represented at the Summit. Inevitably a slightly difficult issue as we are in a way there as the representative of the Little Five, though also, of course, nominally as that of the other four, and if they give us no support for action helpful to the Little Five, it is very difficult for us to know how to strike the balance.

Then a four-hour, more formal session in the afternoon. We opened with an institutional discussion on enlargement, and then I did about a twenty-minute *exposé* on monetary union. This was not at all badly received round the table, notably (as one would expect) by Ireland, Italy, Belgium, Luxembourg, but also by Denmark, Holland and even Genscher for Germany. David Owen was sceptical, but not particularly hostile or indeed particularly informed.

There was a curious flare-up at dinner. We got on to Summitry and the question of future representation, Guiringaud playing this in a relaxed way and also Dohnanyi who had by this time replaced Genscher, partly of course because they knew, as most of the Little Five were beginning to find out, that there was not going to be a Summit during the Danish presidency, but only during the German presidency. This made the question of the representation of the presidency, as opposed to the Commission, fairly academic. On Commission representation, the strong impression which emerged from Guiringaud was that we would not have the same trouble from Giscard next time round. Giscard, he implied, had had enough of the issue.

Then Guiringaud, supported by Dohnanyi, with Forlani giving silent acquiescence, said that he had no objection at all to the communiqué of the Washington official meeting being distributed to the governments of the Little Five. So I said, 'Excellent.' Whereupon David got into a most excited state and said he couldn't possibly agree without, as he foolishly put it, the explicit approval of his Prime Minister who took a great interest in these matters. I said that there was no need for anybody to get excited because I only had one copy with me and therefore could not distribute it immediately; and if David wanted to speak to his Prime Minister, that was clearly a matter for him, though if by chance his Prime Minister wished to stop the distribution, it would then be for me to act on my own judgement and responsibility, which indeed I would do. This was what the Little Five wanted to hear, so it somewhat calmed them down.

I then asked the Five, and particularly Andersen, who had been making a great fuss, to note that Her Majesty's Principal Secretary of State for Foreign Affairs felt unable to take a decision without consulting his Prime Minister, and would they therefore stop blaming my official, even if a peculiarly self-reliant and fairly senior one, for not having taken a decision in Washington on his own to go against the otherwise unanimous view of the meeting. I am not quite sure how much David liked this slight teasing, but he had behaved foolishly. He showed no sign of bad temper towards me, indeed specifically asking for a long talk for the next morning.

SUNDAY, 9 OCTOBER. *Villers-le-Temple and Brussels.*

After the short morning meeting I had an hour's talk with David Owen. We started with the news of Prentice's* switch to the Conservative Party in the *Observer*, which had just arrived. But David did not know him as I did. The trouble with Reg is that, while he has many admirable and rare qualities, he is a heavy-footed elephant crashing through the jungle. He is in a curious way an extremist, not a moderate at all, and he is inconsiderate of other people, which makes him difficult to work with. Still, this is better than being hopelessly trimming as so many people are; but I feel

*(Sir) Reg Prentice, b. 1923, was Secretary of State for Education and Minister of Overseas Development 1974–6. He was MP for Newham, where his left-wing local party tried to disown him. Shirley Williams and I spoke for and with him at a very riotous meeting in the local Town Hall in September 1975. After he joined the Conservative Party he became MP for Daventry 1979–87, and a middle-rank minister 1979–81.

sorry for people who supported him closely, like Shirley (Williams), and who are still in British politics. David was cheerful but not intolerably euphoric after the Labour Party Conference. He was rather agitated by news of the strongly anti-British briefing on the Callaghan letter which Genscher appeared to have done on leaving the meeting the previous evening.

MONDAY, 10 OCTOBER. *Brussels.*

The day of departure for Japan. 11.43 TEE from the Gare du Midi to Paris. Dismal day, raining as usual at Mons and across the Somme and indeed into Paris. Took off from Charles de Gaulle at 4 o'clock on a remarkable and indeed memorable flight. During the first three and a half hours, when I worked extremely hard on the Japanese briefs, flying on a more easterly route than usual we went over Norway and Finland. Meanwhile it got dark, but with a red rim remaining on the south-western horizon. During dinner it began to get light, on the same day, of course. We had turned westward and were galloping through the time zones in that latitude. By the end of dinner we had got into a cold grey winter dawn light, a little brighter to the left of the aeroplane, while to the right, over the North Pole, about four hundred miles away, we could see the night sitting like a patch on an eye. We flew in that unchanging dawn for three or four hours, with no cloud, so that we could see a sort of packed ice which looked like ranges of low hills down below us in this curious, haunting, endless half-light.

After a short sleep I awoke to full light, all still the same day, with strong sunshine on the massive snow-capped mountains of western Alaska. Then we came into horrible Anchorage in a much less good light. Very soon after take-off from there, the most ghastly shuddering began, and went on for over ten minutes. From the agitated tone of his voice, curiously instructing us not to smoke, I don't think the Air France pilot liked it at all. However, it eventually died away.

TUESDAY, 11 OCTOBER. *Tokyo.*

Tokyo just before 6.30 p.m. A great line-up on the tarmac of the ambassadors of the Nine, plus representatives of the Japanese

Government. Some of the Nine had apparently been reluctant to come – the French and, more surprisingly, the Italians – but they had been brought into line by the Belgian presidency. Drove to the Imperial Hotel with Nishibori, the Japanese Ambassador in Brussels, who had come over the day before and accompanied me throughout the visit. I came to find him a nice, increasingly helpful man.

The old Imperial in which I had stayed twelve years ago has completely gone. The Frank Lloyd Wright honeycomb has apparently been moved to some sort of Japanese Williamsburg about a hundred miles away, and in its place there is a new, anonymous, but well-appointed building in which we all had rooms surrounded by security guards on the sixteenth floor.

WEDNESDAY, 12 OCTOBER. *Tokyo.*

Sunny, temperature moving up to about 70°. At 8.45 the Foreign Minister came to call on me in the hotel; very considerate on his part to have suggested this in view of the heaviness of my pro- gramme, and we had about forty minutes' general exchange of views. I then saw George Howard, who was staying in the hotel, for five minutes, before going to the Imperial Palace for an audience with the Emperor at 11 o'clock. I had been warned that these audiences tended to be sticky as he is difficult to talk to unless one is a great expert on marine biology. I did not find this. The audience went along reasonably smoothly, just the Emperor, an interpreter, me obviously, a sort of Court Chamberlain, who had been Ambassador in London, and one other Court official.

A slightly stilted conversation inevitably, the Emperor having fairly carefully rehearsed his subjects – general welcome, import- ance of Japanese/European relations, some request for information about how the Community operated; then a reference to my books, with my responding with a reference to his and saying I understood that he had published fourteen. 'Oh, no, no,' he said. 'I had a certain small hand in them, but I am afraid I don't really write myself; I engage scholars to do it for me.'

Then, ludicrously, about seven minutes on croquet, about which he knew practically nothing, but of which he had been told I was a keen player and about which he therefore politely spoke with a show of interest. I left him about 11.40. He seemed an agreeable, serious-minded man, looking remarkably fit for his seventy-eight years. The palace is modern, built about 1968, but the park and the views on to it from the large windows are rather splendid.

Then to the Foreign Correspondents' Club for an early lunch and a prepared speech to an audience of about three hundred, mainly Americans, Australians and Europeans, but about a third Japanese as well. The speech went fairly well, I thought, questions rather less so.

In the afternoon I went to the Parliament building, and started with an interview with the President and his deputy, whom I think I persuaded that their principal European relations should be with the European Parliament rather than with the loose Council of Europe.

The building is in fact 1936, but looks like an earlier example of Pullman-style comfort. I watched a Budget Committee, attended by *all* the members of the Government who have to sit there *all* day for about nine hours and make constant replies to a whole range of questions which can be brought up without notice. We heard Prime Minister Fukuda, the Secretary of the Cabinet who is a politician, and also the Foreign Minister within a very brief space. They have no desks in front of them, are completely exposed, and therefore have no opportunity to get on with any work of their own: a most extraordinary arrangement.

At 7 o'clock to the Prime Minister's residence for the central talk of the visit (one and a half hours) and his subsequent dinner. We were about eight strong, the Japanese about ten, including the Foreign Minister and one or two others, plus officials. It was all done through interpretation, of course.

Fukuda began with a welcome, then went into a description of what had happened in the Japanese economy and how he saw the economies of others since the Downing Street Summit, skilfully though perfectly pleasantly putting us on the defensive for having failed to attain our growth targets, whereas the Japanese claimed to have done so, and allowed that the Americans were not too bad either. I then did quite a long response, partly with the object of getting out of this defensive corner and partly to raise for their own sake some wider issues about the Third World, about the equal need for a stimulus to the developed economies, and about the change in relationship between employment and the business cycle. What became clear to me was that I could not stop without raising our bilateral complaints, otherwise there might be great difficulty in ever coming to them. This meant that I made about half an hour's statement including the pauses for interpretation, but I think that Fukuda was pleased with the wide-ranging approach, and probably took the particular bilateral points better in this context.

The point which he seemed to take in, allegedly for the first time, was that our problem with deep Japanese penetration of particular markets was not so much a balance-of-payments problem as an employment problem. On the opening of their market he was reasonably sympathetic, and in particular gave a fairly good response to my suggestion that they should buy the European Airbus,* which would have a psychological impact, as well as a quantitative impact, on the level of trade.

There were then about fifty guests to a very good dinner with French food and wine. Short speeches afterwards from Fukuda and me; I spoke unprepared and I think this went better as a result. After dinner we were intended to go fairly quickly, but Fukuda kept me talking over the coffee, raising new subjects, Euro-Communism, the rigidity of political systems, and his reminiscences of 1930s Europe until about 10.45. The Prime Minister's residence, incidentally, is also a Frank Lloyd Wright building, but again in danger of being pulled down because they do not think it large enough.

THURSDAY, 13 OCTOBER. *Tokyo.*

I had a pointless early talk with Bo, the ineffective Finance Minister. He seemed ill-informed about international monetary affairs and indeed one of his Under-Secretaries there was manifestly more on the ball. Bo had indicated that they were not worried about the depreciation of the dollar and the appreciation of the yen, whereas this clearly in fact is not the case. Then, for an hour, a rather important meeting with Tanaka, the Minister for International

*They did not.

Trade and Industry, at which we went into more detail on bilateral questions.

Then at 11.00 to the Keidanren, the powerful employers' association. A long and reasonably useful meeting with them, with a venerable figure, Doko, aged eighty-two, in the chair. Then a rather less useful lunch (still with them) when it was not quite clear whether there was intended to be continuous working discussion or not. Afternoon press conference of about eighty people, which went not badly, I thought. I was interested to note that the Japanese woman interpreter (we kept on changing interpreters, whose quality varied – this one was extremely good) quite regularly took one-third longer than I had taken to translate my replies to questions, despite the fact that she spoke much more quickly than I did, and required no pauses for thought. Japanese must be a prolix language.

At 6.15 to the offices of the EEC Mission for our reception. Great excitement amongst our officials, ambassadors, etc., because Fukuda decided with some difficulty to get the Diet Committee adjourned and to attend himself for half an hour, bringing half his Cabinet with him. This slightly Soviet-leadership-like gesture was obviously intended to be a mark of signal favour and friendliness and was certainly forthcoming on his part.

FRIDAY, 14 OCTOBER. *Tokyo, Moscow and Brussels.*

Our solitary piece of sight-seeing was a drive of about five miles to a shrine, which I had been to in 1965, but is in a nice park. My impression driving round Tokyo was that it appeared much more Westernized that I had remembered it twelve years ago, and also more agreeable, mainly because pollution has completely disappeared. I was struck, not surprisingly, by the sense of prosperity, but also by the American nature of the scene. This cannot be entirely a result of the occupation and subsequent imitation for there are quite a lot of buildings along the main boulevard facing the Imperial Palace of the twenties and thirties, which look very similar to the American buildings of that epoch. But it is not only a question of buildings, it is also a question of general atmosphere – a lot of lean, eager young men, in good, thin, dark business suits, swinging their despatch cases as they hurry to their offices, the traffic also looking American, although no American cars of course; the whole atmosphere not like New York, but more like either Washington or Chicago.

I then briefed the ambassadors of the Nine at the hotel and left for the airport in the first rain since our arrival. This time the ambassadors attended at the airport less complainingly, the visit having been thought to go well, the Frenchman particularly going out of his way to be agreeable.

We took off just after 1 o'clock, went northwards across the Sea of Japan, missing China easily, and over the mountains north of Vladivostok. Agreeable lunch, feeling the mission had been accomplished; bad film, some sleep, then across the plains of Siberia as the afternoon wore on: endless flying hour after hour after hour across Siberian wastes, a good deal of cloud but we could occasionally see down to the ground, which was always frozen, for five hundred mile after five hundred mile. When we got west of the Urals, which one hardly noticed because they are pretty low hills, we got into rather worse weather and came into Moscow on a filthy afternoon, landing there after ten hours in the air. A thoroughly disagreeable approach to a disagreeable airport in very low cloud and driving rain which quickly turned into sleet as the temperature was about 30°F.

A slight contretemps at Moscow as Crispin had rightly decided that the Russians should be informed that we were passing through. They riposted by insisting on sending COMECON to greet us, and COMECON in the shape of three fairly unprepossessing-looking gentlemen – one of whom was known to Denman through trade discussions – insisted on conducting us (although inefficiently in a cold and windy airport bus) to a huge meal which they had prepared in a rather gloomy basement. We were in a bad temper, partly no doubt due to the long flight but also because we do not regard COMECON as our *interlocuteur valable*, only toyed with the five-course meal – and also made it clear that we were not prepared to engage in any trade discussions of substance. We were therefore reduced to talking about Siberian geography and climatology, and Crispin did particularly well on this.

We were nervous of being left behind when the plane went, as we didn't trust the competence of our hosts, and the organization of Moscow Airport is well known to be chaotic. So when we had been on the ground for one and a half hours we said firmly that we wished to get back on the plane. This they reluctantly accepted, pooh-poohing our bad nerves. Air France greeted us by saying that they had already held the plane for quarter of an hour and could not have done so for more than another five minutes. My impression of Moscow Airport was not favourable. Beautiful clear night over Western Europe, every light from Amsterdam to Paris sparkling beneath us. Charles de Gaulle at 8.35. We had been around the world in exactly 100 hours and 25 minutes. Brussels by midnight.

SUNDAY, 16 OCTOBER. *Brussels.*

Early evening meeting with Crispin, Hayden and Christopher Audland, and became rather gloomily aware that a great cock-up had been made about the enlargement paper in my absence, with Natali in a sullen minority of one, and the rest of them deciding to put in nothing worthwhile to the Council at all, which had been very badly received by COREPER, probably accurately foreshadowing their governments.

MONDAY, 17 OCTOBER. *Brussels and Luxembourg.*

Lee Kuan Yew, Prime Minister of Singapore, and his wife to lunch alone with Jennifer and me. He was mainly concerned to know what the future trade orientation of the Community, protectionist or otherwise, was going to be, and how he should adjust to this. He did not much mind provided he knew, he said. I said I did not see much future for Singapore selling textiles to the Community. He said fine, he would get as fast as he could into financial services and micro-chips. He was very bright and quick as usual; we did not get on to any difficult internal Singapore affairs.

At 2.30 I motored to Luxembourg through a totally splendiferous autumn afternoon and into a joint meeting of the Foreign Affairs Council and the Economic and Financial Council, to deal with two complicated little financial issues. In the intervals of these I did some work with Crispin on the draft statement which had been prepared for me to make in the Council the following morning as a supplement to the enlargement paper and which was clearly of considerable inportance in view of the bad atmosphere which was prevailing and the criticism which had already appeared in *Le*

Monde and one or two other papers about the inadequacy of the Commission contribution. I became gradually aware that the statement as it stood was totally miscast and would do more harm than good. I therefore decided at about 7 o'clock that it had to be rewritten completely, which task, as I had no time, fell on Crispin, who did it brilliantly.

A formal dinner with the Greek negotiators, which happily did not last very long. At 11.00 Crispin produced the redrafted statement, which I worked on until 1.00.

TUESDAY, 18 OCTOBER. *Luxembourg and Brussels.*

Up at 7.00 for another two hours' work on the redrafted statement, which I delivered as soon as the Council, punctually for once, assembled at 9.15. It lasted seventeen minutes and, thanks largely to Crispin, went incomparably better than could have been expected. It rather took the wind out of the French and Italian sails, and was supported by nearly everybody else. We were warmly thanked for having made this constructive, clear contribution. It was a very difficult corner happily turned.

A Council working lunch at 1.45, after a restricted working session downstairs in which we tried to deal with JET. No news at that stage, but on the way up to the dining room news came through from Bonn that a settlement (in favour of Culham) had in fact been arrived at between Schmidt and Callaghan which could be endorsed by the Research Council.

Drove back to Brussels and went to a mysterious, hidden-away clinic to see an alleged orthopaedic expert about my ankle which had been revolting against my running habits for about the past ten days. The visit had been arranged through the *service médicale* of the Commission. It was one of the most ludicrous medical encounters I have ever had in my life. Dr Frère* was an immensely old man, with a little white hat on his head, who greeted me upstairs in an extremely old-fashioned clinic, accompanied by two other doctors, one, his principal assistant, a fairly old-looking sixty — Frère himself must have been at least eighty-five — and the other, a rather young-looking twenty-five. The consultations took fifty minutes

* An altered name.

and led to no result at all, except that Frère managed to make me feel that I must be gravely ill with a mildly sprained ankle, arising from a very obvious cause (jogging).

They made detailed measurements of both ankles, had X-rays taken in incredibly awkward positions. At this stage, with the three doctors peering over me, it was like the scene in Rembrandt's 'Operation', except that happily they did not use any of the rather rusty-looking instruments hanging on the walls. Then they disappeared to consult the photographs, coming back saying that they needed some more X-rays, then coming and saying that there was little to be seen, then Frère saying what he was rather worried about was that the pain didn't seem sufficient for the swelling! Then a suggestion that I must have a whole series of blood tests, urine tests, kidney tests, everything else you could think of and come back in a week. It was a farcical example of the combination of lack of common sense and slight racketeering of expensive Belgian medicine. After this ludicrous performance I decided to sign off from them and have it fixed if I could in London or at Wantage. Home to rue de Praetère, where Ann Fleming had arrived to stay.

THURSDAY, 20 OCTOBER. *Brussels and Belfast.*

Avion taxi to Belfast. The beautiful October disappeared on the way. Drove to Hillsborough, the old Governor-General's residence, and now the Government guest house, lunched with Concannon, Minister of State, Mason* being kept in London for a Cabinet meeting, and a rather good gathering of twenty-four official and unofficial Northern Irishmen. Then helicopted, in great discomfort, to Stormont. Then to a rather rundown hotel near at hand, where I did three television interviews, one radio interview and a press conference. Dinner speech to a British Institute of Management gathering.

FRIDAY, 21 OCTOBER. *Belfast, Birmingham and East Hendred.*

To Birmingham and the Midland Hotel, where I gave a sort of civic lunch – both Vice-Chancellors, the Deputy Mayor (the Lord Mayor

* Roy Mason, b. 1924, cr. Lord Mason 1987, was Labour MP for Barnsley 1953–87, and Secretary of State for Northern Ireland 1976–9.

being away), the Anglican Bishop, the Roman Catholic Archbishop, the editor of one newspaper and the deputy editor of the other, George Canning,* a trade unionist, two industrialists. At 6.00 I delivered the Baggs Memorial Lecture at the university on 'Happiness' (of all subjects), which I interpreted as the quest for national satisfaction; audience of 650, who applauded at the end I thought rather more appreciatively than the lecture deserved.

SATURDAY, 22 OCTOBER. *East Hendred.*

Went to Oxford with the Bonham Carters (who were staying) and did one or two touristic things I had never done before, like climbing to the top of the Sheldonian, which has a splendid view. Then to see Dr Loudon at Wantage about my ankle, who took only ten minutes to deal with the matter and suggested an elastic bandage, which seemed to work rather well.

TUESDAY, 25 OCTOBER. *Brussels, Luxembourg and Brussels.*

To Luxembourg in Simonet's plane for the Research and Energy Council which dealt finally with JET. At last this wretched dispute has been satisfactorily settled.

Then a meeting with Bordu, the French Communist Vice-President of the Parliament. He talked mildly interestingly about the general European situation in a moderate and indeed platitudinous way. I told him that I proposed to follow the same rules for the Communists as I had for the other groups and invite them to a dinner at Strasbourg. He seemed pleased but not excessively so. The main burden of what he really had to say was contained in his last few sentences, when he announced that Marchais would very much like to see me and asked whether I would receive him. I said I would reflect upon that grave matter. (My first reflection was that I had already had enough trouble over Mitterrand.)

Then some sustained work on my speech for Florence, which was in a fairly advanced state of preparation but not sufficiently so. Dinner for the Gaullist Group, which, rather like the Conservative

---

*Councillor George Canning, 1925–1981, who became Lord Mayor of Birmingham 1979–80, had been my Stechford agent, and later chairman, for many years. He was a man on whose opinions I placed great reliance.

Group, is mainly made up of one party, i.e. the French Gaullists, buttressed by the now Irish majority party, Fianna Fáil, and the one statutory and inevitable Dane. Brussels through fog at 12.40 a.m.

THURSDAY, 27 OCTOBER. *Brussels and Florence.*

Avion taxi to Pisa for Florence, the first time I had been over the Alps in a tiny plane. Excelsior Hotel, Florence, at about 4.30. Delivered the Monnet Lecture at the European University Institute in a fine old gothic chapel, with a good audience of about seven hundred, and a friendly pro-European money demonstration outside. The lecture took almost exactly an hour, sounded rather better than I feared it would, and was certainly well received.

At dinner at Max Kohnstamm's* splendid villa I sat next to a rather fascinating elderly lady who had just become French Consul-General in Florence. She had gone to London with De Gaulle in 1940 and had personally typed the *Appel aux Français* there issued. Then she had gone to Canada for about two years as representative of the Free French. She spoke with great contempt of the Québécois: 'Vichyites to a man and absolutely intolerable to deal with.' The Canadian Government was much better, though the American Government at that stage was very hostile; they simply hated the Free French, she claimed. She had been *Porte-parole Adjoint* to De Gaulle during his 1945/6 period of government, and said that at that time he was remarkably bad with the press, having no idea of how to communicate with or through them. His mastery over this medium developed only after his return to power in 1958.

FRIDAY, 28 OCTOBER. *Florence and Rome.*

Flew to Rome, and drove immediately to the Confindustria building in EUR for my meeting with the so-called Groupe des Présidents. Rather an impressive group of about eight people: Agnelli†‡ in the chair, Plowden from Britain, the head of Rhône-Poulenc from France, the younger Boël from Belgium, Wagner of Royal

---

*Max Kohnstamm (Dutch), b. 1914, an adjutant of Monnet's in the later fifties, sixties and early seventies, was Rector of the European University Institute in Florence 1975–81.
†Giovanni Agnelli, b. 1921, Chairman of Fiat since 1966.

Dutch Shell from Holland, etc. No Germans had come because they were too frightened to travel, so I was told. Lunch and discussion on monetary union; they thought it desirable, but were sceptical as to whether the politicians would ever agree to do anything about it.

Palazzo Chigi at 3.15 for a meeting with Andreotti and Forlani. Andreotti was courteous and agreeable as always, but seemed to me not on good form, or on good terms with Forlani. However, he gave an absolutely firm assurance that he would support my monetary union proposal. 'Certamente,' he said. Then to the Hassler, with a sense of having got a difficult week over.

SATURDAY, 29 OCTOBER. *Rome and Avallon.*

9.30 plane to Paris. Jennifer arrived just after me from London. While waiting for her at Charles de Gaulle I read the *Economist* leader on my Florence speech entitled 'A Bridge Too Far'. Avallon at 6.00.

SUNDAY, 30 OCTOBER. *Avallon and Vézelay.*

Drove to Vézelay where we paid our first visit since 1957 to Ste Madeleine, which despite restoration is a magnificent and striking church, and then went for (probably) the last picnic of this magnificent autumn. Installed ourselves at Hôtel l'Espérance at St Père.

MONDAY, 31 OCTOBER. *Vézelay.*

Jacques and Marie-Alice de Beaumarchais arrived for lunch (and to stay). To Avallon in the afternoon and visited by accident on the way back a little château inhabited by an ex-Deputy called Max Broussé who talked without ceasing (and pretty good nonsense at that).

TUESDAY, 1 NOVEMBER. *Vézelay.*

To lunch with Jacques Franck at Châtel-Censoir. Franck, a Paris interior designer, was flanked by his elderly American companion, a great cook as well as a second cousin of Adlai Stevenson; another strange little Parisian gentleman; and a lady of unprepossessing appearance with a Dutch name but a great deal of blue French blood. A very pretty house, but I thought a purposeless lunch, with a slightly uneasy atmosphere, curiously reminiscent of Buscot Park in the old days.

WEDNESDAY, 2 NOVEMBER. *Vézelay.*

To Autun where I had never been: a sombre town, built round a sombre but nonetheless splendid cathedral. Did Talleyrand* like it? Or did he never visit it? Then back over the high plateau of the Morvan in mist, which added to the striking atmosphere of remoteness and lack of habitation. This part of Burgundy is much less agriculturally rich than I had imagined; it looks rather like Breconshire.

THURSDAY, 3 NOVEMBER. *Vézelay and Brussels.*

A long (350 mile) drive back to Brussels. The end of this *Toussaints* holiday suggests a few reflections on this autumn. It has been much better, more enjoyable, I hope more successful, than the period before the summer. I then often deeply regretted my decision to come to Brussels. Since returning in September I have felt much more buoyant, and I think this has reflected itself in my general grip on the work, which has in many (although not all) ways gone successfully. I have got more used to the pattern of living here, find the house more agreeable, and can have relaxed periods without having to rush back to England.

Balancing all this, however, has been a certain continuing regret at the severance from British politics. Was I wise? Who can possibly tell? Clearly had I taken Callaghan up on his offer (in April 1976) to stay as Home Secretary and then become Chancellor again in six or so months' time, this would, in retrospect, have been a more enticing prospect than it looked at that stage. Would he have stuck to the bargain? I don't know. But had I been there in the Government and available it might have been very difficult for him, under pressure, not to have moved Healey and put me in the Treasury when everything seemed to be collapsing in November last year,

---

*Talleyrand was Bishop of Autun from 1788 to 1791.

and clearly that would have been very much buying at the bottom of the market with, fortuitously and no doubt undeservedly, a considerable reputation developing over the next six to nine months for having put things right a second time. But that would have been no more than chance, and I suppose one should not regret missing undeserved bonuses. In any case, my mind had become sufficiently detached from the general current of opinion in the Government that it was better that I should leave.

FRIDAY, 4 NOVEMBER. *Brussels.*

A visit from the Spanish Prime Minister, Suárez,* and Oreja, his Foreign Minister: a very impressive couple, probably the best pair that any European country could produce. Suárez at forty-three is a good-looking, sharply cut man, who can speak nothing but Spanish. But we nonetheless had a good talk with him before, during and after lunch. Spain has had a remarkable evolution, though they face a pile of almost insurmountable economic difficulties.

In the afternoon I addressed the European Federalists' Conference, with an enthusiastic reception, due no doubt to Florence. Then saw Cheysson, who told me of conversations with Barre and Giscard. Barre very friendly, Giscard less so – doesn't like the Commission, Cheysson said, but added surprisingly that Giscard's complaint about the Commission now was that we didn't put forward enough positive proposals. 'In previous years we needed the Commission just to manage things; now the state of Europe is such that we need them to do more: Jenkins has put forward his monetary union hobby horse. That is all right in theory. I am not sure it is practical, but it is a good thing he should have said it. However, I would like more proposals, more plans, of this sort to be forthcoming.' I have my doubts about the reliability of Cheysson's reporting, but at any rate this was mildly interesting.

MONDAY, 7 NOVEMBER. *Brussels.*

To dinner at Belœil, the very grand mansion beyond Mons and close to the French frontier where the Prince de Ligne holds court in

*Adolfo Suárez, b. 1932, was Spanish Prime Minister 1976–81.

considerable style. Great flag-flying, illuminated facade, men in swallow-tail coats and knee-breeches bearing flaming torches on the way in, etc. The house unfortunately was mostly burnt down, in I think 1901, and therefore the main part is an Edwardian rebuild. There are, however, some eighteenth-century pavilions left and some fairly good contents. But the point is more the scale and style than any outstanding furniture or architectural glory.

The Princesse de Ligne, sister of the Grand Duke of Luxembourg, has the appearance of a neat, agreeable-looking schoolmistress. Also present were the Archduke Rudolf of Austria, plus his second and younger wife, who is a sister of Antoine de Ligne – all very *Almanach de Gotha*, but broadly speaking (apart from the English element, which included the Dunrossils,* as well as General Tuzo† and wife) representing what one might call the King Baudouin side of Belgium society, more serious-minded and less money-oriented than the *demi-gratin* of La Hulpe.

TUESDAY, 8 NOVEMBER. *Brussels.*

Lunch for Reuters who brought over an impressive group of newspaper publishers – Garrett Drogheda (*Financial Times*), Vere Harmsworth (*Daily Mail*), Barnetson as Chairman of Reuters, and Denis Hamilton. I had Barnetson on one side of me and Denis Hamilton on the other at lunch and heard a lot of good, interesting *Observer* gossip into one ear and *Sunday Times* gossip into the other.

Evening meeting with Ortoli about how we handle the preparation of the paper on economic and monetary union for the European Council. He wants to go along the traditional lines of a catalogue of minor economic measures and avoid any dramatic leap. It will be quite difficult to work out a sensible compromise.

THURSDAY, 10 NOVEMBER. *Brussels, Bonn and Lisbon.*

Avion taxi to Bonn, and lunch with Schmidt. The Chancellery was ringed with tanks, and Schmidt was still suffering from the after-

---

*Viscount Dunrossil, b. 1926, the son of Mr Speaker W. S. Morrison, was then Counsellor at the British Embassy to Belgium. Later Governor of Bermuda.
†General Sir Harry Tuzo, b. 1917, was then deputy Supreme Allied Commander, Europe.

math of the Lufthansa hijacking and the Schleyer murder. We talked for the first hour about terrorist matters, including our Irish experiences, and I explained to him some of the SAS methods. He was interested and ill-informed about our siege techniques.

Then on to a run-up to the European Council. He was mostly in a negative mood, which is not unusual, but he at least recognizes that there are a lot of questions to which he doesn't know the answers. He is not unnaturally proud of the way in which he has run the German economy – 'kept the garden tidy' is the phrase which I think I used, and he agreed with, but he also feels that it is a walled garden the way out of which he doesn't see. The room for initiative is very limited, the German economy is materially sated; people don't want to consume more, so he says; if you pump more money in it goes into savings rather than into consumption, and the only way you can stimulate investment is in export-directed invest-ment, and this makes the balance-of-payments position still more favourably unbalanced. Therefore a very boxed-in position and a pessimistic view on his part about the future German competitive position and the world economic situation generally.

He was full of his normal German neuroses: the world needed a lead, but he couldn't give it; Germany was at once too big and too small to do that; it aroused too much antipathy, too much jealousy. A small country might. . . . I said, 'Which small country?' He said, rather dismissively: 'I don't know; maybe Holland, maybe Belgium, but they are not big enough. The United States almost effortlessly could, but Carter shows no signs of doing so.' Less so than on previous occasions, however, he was not obsessed by complaints against Carter. Nor was he full of praise for any of his European colleagues. There was noticeably throughout the whole long conversation no mention at all of 'my friend Valéry'. There was a good deal of complaint about the attitude of the French (and Italian) press towards the Germans. There was also complaint that he had been accused of being a new Hitler, I am not quite sure by whom. The Swedes, he mentioned darkly, had been particularly unhelpful.

The London press, he allowed, had not been similarly difficult, although he had begun the general conversation by saying that he was pretty fed up with the British. He had done a great deal to bring them into the Community, and now he was blamed by other people and given the responsibility for their generally unhelpful attitude. I asked him of what exactly this consisted, but he was vague, muttering something about direct elections and agricultural policy, but not taking a strong or precise line.

He ended by agreeing that he didn't know the way out, perhaps nobody did, but accepting my remark that, this being so, he should not be too sceptical, or slap down attempts like my monetary union plan to get some movement. He said he was in favour in principle of monetary union, but against it if it meant German inflation going to 8 per cent. I said I would be too; the great thing was that the best part of German policy should be accepted by other countries; and what was absolutely essential was that both the strong and the weak economies should feel that they had something to gain. He expressed himself with remarkable enthusiasm about enlargement and said that it was a central duty of the Community; he was totally dedicated to assisting the Greeks, Spaniards and Portuguese in this way.

I am not sure how much this long discussion advanced things, but it was a good free-ranging talk with an easy atmosphere, and we both came out looking quite pleased. I flew for a short hour to Geneva, and then on to Lisbon. A most beautiful day all across Europe, particularly at Geneva, where the Alps in the fading light were suffused in a rose-coloured glow. Met at Lisbon airport by the Prime Minister (Soares) and various other dignitaries and drove to the Ritz Hotel, a twenty-year-old building filled with typical mock-Empire Ritz-style furniture. Restaurant dinner given by the deputy Foreign Minister (there being no Foreign Minister, Soares holding the portfolio himself); amiable but not pointful discussion.

FRIDAY, 11 NOVEMBER. *Lisbon.*

My fifty-seventh birthday, not greeted with great pleasure, particularly as no celebrations were scheduled during the extremely hard day ahead. I began with Constâncio,* an effective young man about thirty-five, who is in charge of the Portuguese negotiating team and seems to be the most sensible economics man in the Government. Then back to the hotel for an hour to receive the leaders of the five

---

* Victor Constâncio, b. 1943. Recently leader of the Portuguese Socialist Party, having been Governor of the Bank of Portugal before that.

political parties in quick succession, followed by a deputation of industrialists. Cunhal, the hardline Stalinist Communist leader, was the most interesting, and not ostensibly particularly hardline. He was against Portugal's entry more on economic than on political grounds, which is not entirely without sense, and he was in favour of loans from outside, but not primarily from Germany or America. He thought from Britain and Italy, with a rather touching faith in the ability of these countries to have any money to lend.

Then to see Soares: eighty minutes of French exposition from him, with a few questions from me. He gave a lucid analysis of the political situation in Portugal and how he hoped to deal with it by forming a common platform to get the hard budget through, but not by a coalition which would be either impossible or undesirable. He has a good logical mind on political questions, and drew a very effective little socio-political map of Portugal, on which he pointed out the various groupings on the ground of the party forces in a way that I found easy to follow and helpful. On economics he is much less sure; he knows he has got to be fairly tough, though he is complaining a good deal, as all the Portuguese are, about the IMF terms.* I told him fairly bluntly that in my view they had little alternative but to accept them, though I thought that the IMF after their return from Washington would be a little more reasonable, as was their habit. The Portuguese must get the IMF money and, indeed, in the position they were, it was no good saying that this might prevent sustained expansion, since a policy of *reculer pour mieux sauter* was inevitable.

Then a 2.30 luncheon (though the Portuguese don't in general keep Spanish time), presided over by Constâncio, at the Port Wine Institute. Next to the Parliament to address the Foreign Affairs Commission and answer questions. Then to the Belgian Embassy residence for the ambassadors of the Nine. Then a press conference at the Ministry of Foreign Affairs presided over by Soares.

Next out quite a long way to the presidential palace to call on General Eanes,† the head of state. Crispin thought he was very nervous of me. I don't think this terribly likely. Once again the interpretation was bad. (We must take our own interpreter on

---

* Portugal was in a great balance-of-payments mess, and the IMF, as is their wont, were demanding stringent deflation as a condition of further credits.
† General António Eanes, b. 1935, was President of Portugal 1976–86.

these trips in future.) Eanes is a youngish man, in his forties, hard, rather limited in intellect, but plunged straight into the main issues and gave his explanation of what he thought might or might not happen. Some parts of it, in translation, came through rather horrifyingly, as when he said that the General in the North, whom everybody knew had been recalled because he had been plotting with the doubtfully named Social Democrats and generally making too political an impact, had been recalled to 'pursue his military studies at a higher level', which had a splendid ring of Nigeria, if not of Eastern Europe. However, Soares had assured me that Eanes was a good democrat and he said nothing else that contradicted this. He was obviously working very closely with Soares, though he complained even more strongly about the IMF terms than the Prime Minister had done. He showed no desire to take over full power himself and hoped that Soares should be able to steer through and carry on.

Then a long drive out to Cintra of Peninsular War Convention fame, where Soares gave a state dinner of 150 in an old castle with a splendid ceiling. I sat between the Minister of State in the Government, who is a sort of deputy Prime Minister, and the Speaker of the Assembly. Both spoke fairly good French. Indeed Lisbon as a whole was remarkably francophone, and amongst the middle-aged and older generation almost equally non-anglophone. Speeches after dinner, then a television interview, and back in thickening mist to Lisbon.

It had been too heavy a day, but worthwhile for getting an impression of the government and the atmosphere in the country. Lisbon has great charm. It is curiously unlike a Mediterranean city. Geographically and almost climatically it is more like a poor San Francisco. It is southern and oceanic, which I suppose is what one would expect it to be. The country is in a mess economically, and there are some elements of post-revolution chaos, but there does seem to be a genuine attachment to democratic and constitutional processes. The Portuguese are a non-violent people and their dedication to coming into the Community also seems pretty strong.

SATURDAY, 12 NOVEMBER. *Lisbon and Cascais.*

To the Jeronimus church with its splendid cloisters and magnificent nave: a late fifteenth-century product of the first flood of Portuguese trading wealth, in an architectural style which is quite separate from that of most of Western Europe. Then on to Cascais to the Tinés' flat by lunch. A great sight-seeing tour in the afternoon, round the coast to Cintra, back to Lisbon, and south over the new (still generally called Salazar) bridge with the object of getting on the return the remarkable view of the setting sun on the roofs of Lisbon as they tumble down to the sea. Then around the Alfama part of the old town, which has great attraction and interest. I was very struck by Lisbon and its surroundings. At dinner at a rather smart restaurant I was amazed by the cheapness of the bill, and at first thought there must be a nought missing. It was less than £4 a head, which is unknown elsewhere in Western Europe.

SUNDAY, 13 NOVEMBER. *Lisbon and Brussels.*

Back to Brussels after an immense detour over the Atlantic owing to a Spanish air controllers' strike. We were greeted at Zaventem by Michael Emerson who had got locked into a great dispute with Ortoli's *cabinet* about the draft of our monetary union paper.*

MONDAY, 14 NOVEMBER. *Brussels.*

A rather *pénible* one and a half hours with Ortoli at 9.30, not making much progress. Lunch for John Davies and Donald Maitland, which for some reason or other was conversationally draining.

Ortoli again at 6.00, still making no real progress and parting in an *impasse*, but on reasonably good terms, with my saying: 'The trouble is, Francis, that you and I have very different approaches. You are much more cautious and you don't believe you can move people's minds by shocking them. I do, sometimes.' I didn't add: 'You believe in boring them rather than shocking them,' but this was the thought in my mind about his style of presentation. A short meeting with Davignon after that who indicated that while friendlily disposed he thought I should find a solution with Ortoli rather than have a head-on challenge.

* Essentially the dispute was between my desire for a leap forward and his determination to stick to the traditional step-by-step approach.

TUESDAY, 15 NOVEMBER. *Brussels and Strasbourg.*

Avion taxi to Strasbourg. A conference at the airport with Michael Emerson, Crispin and Hayden before taking off, when we decided, rightly or wrongly, that we had better try to come to some arrangement with Ortoli rather than presenting two different texts for the Commission to decide between on the following day, as this would have considerable disadvantages. I would have a clear majority in the Commission, none of us was in any doubt about that; but the fact that we were split would leak, leaving Ortoli bruised and having to present to the Economic and Financial Council on the following Monday a paper which had been imposed upon him. Therefore Crispin was instructed to try and arrive at a last-minute compromise which was compatible with my Florence lecture but did not hammer the points too hard. A bridging passage was to be inserted in order to show the semi-real compatibility between my more adventurous approach and Ortoli's more cautious, pragmatic and, to judge from past experience, ineffective approach to EMU.

To the Parliament a little late after yet another nasty flight over the Ardennes/Vosges complex, but this did not matter as Simonet had been so shaken by his much worse flight that he had had to ask for a suspension of the session before he could address them. Took George Brown* to lunch. I had not seen him for a year. He was a good deal changed: old, white, walking with a stick, but, at the same time, curiously sprightly in mind and, to some extent, in body. He had completely given up drink and cigars; he ate a great deal and, despite his unwonted teetotalism, was an immensely stimulating companion. It is curious how very good he can be: he was greatly enthused with the prospect of standing as an independent candidate under direct elections and drafting a great personal manifesto. He left me inspirited by seeing him.

Walked back from the Parliament to the Sofitel by the cathedral: a cold, early winter evening with a pre-Christmas atmosphere in Strasbourg already. Then a large dinner for the Conservative Group, which is almost entirely British. An excellent interchange afterwards. They are a pretty good group. Most of them even wrote appreciative letters.

*George Brown, 1914–85, cr. Lord George-Brown 1970, was deputy leader of the Labour Party 1960–70, First Secretary 1964–6, and Foreign Secretary 1966–8.

WEDNESDAY, 16 NOVEMBER. *Strasbourg and Brussels.*

A special but flat Commission meeting on the EMU paper over lunch. Ortoli opened at some length, and I then endeavoured to go round the table. But Cheysson, typically and mischievously, but maybe legitimately, said that what they all wanted to know was my opinion. So I, having done my deal with Ortoli, had to give a muffled reply, which took the heat but also the interest out of the discussion. There was undoubtedly a sense of let-down that there was no great gladiatorial contest between Ortoli and me, with blood on the sand. This would have exacted too heavy a price, but it is never satisfying to produce an anti-climax.

6.07 TEE back to Brussels. Gautier-Sauvagnac, Ortoli's *Chef de Cabinet* (who always looks as though he were playing Saint-Loup at Doncières), joined us in the restaurant car in too jaunty a mood. Rue de Praetère at 10.30, and there had a rather dismal discussion with Hayden who was obviously worried about the result of the Commission, though he had been in favour of what we had done.

THURSDAY, 17 NOVEMBER. *Brussels.*

To the Palais de Bruxelles for half an hour's audience with the King of Spain: a very engaging young man. Even the Spaniards are now immensely less formal than the British Royal Family. At the end of the interview he discovered that there was a crush of cameramen outside the room, and that he had forgotten we were supposed to have photographs taken. Whereupon we went out and stood around shaking hands and talking while the photographs were taken. In the audience he spoke well, but not quite as authoritatively as I would have expected. His Foreign Minister, Oreja, whom I like, was with him and the King left him to do much of the exposition, although never looking bored, being extremely friendly and pressing me hard to go to Madrid.

Dinner party at home for the Nanteuils, Robert Armstrong,* who was staying with us for the night, Léon Lambert, etc. Luc de Nanteuil held forth to me for some time after dinner, urging me not

---

* Sir Robert (cr. Lord 1988) Armstrong, b. 1927, was then Permanent Under-Secretary at the Home Office. He had been my Private Secretary in 1968; Secretary of the Cabinet 1979–87.

to get too bogged down in detail and to be as controversial a figure as possible, as that in his view was the way to play the hand of a President of the Commission.

FRIDAY, 18 NOVEMBER. *Brussels*.

I gave a lunch for British Liberals, Thorpe,* Steel and Gladwyn.†
Poor Jeremy was looking appallingly haggard, like Soames Forsyte in the last episode of *The Forsyte Saga*. But this did not affect the flow of his conversation. Even Gladwyn could hardly get a word in, partly because he has got rather deaf and hardly heard what was going on. David Steel was nice but silent.

SATURDAY, 19 NOVEMBER. *Brussels and Paris*.

Motored to Paris on a beautiful morning. One and a half hours with Barre, most of the time on economic and monetary union, where we managed to achieve a considerable identity of view. He is a sensible, lucid man and I think if he has anything to do with it we should have a reasonably successful European Council. Alas, of course, he will not be there, but he said he would try to get a reasonably fair though not committing wind for my ideas on EMU.

I asked him whether he thought I should try and see Giscard in the next week or so. He wasn't sure, maybe Giscard would like to see me. 'He has a very high opinion of you,' he added encouragingly but implausibly in view of the rows of last summer.

MONDAY, 21 NOVEMBER. *Brussels*.

In a Foreign Affairs Council we had a long wrangle over Article 131. It was a typical example of being unable to contain at the same time the British and the French. It is like that pocket game in which you have to get little balls into holes. As you try to put the second in, the first comes out. The British, represented by Joel Barnett, were towards the end being quite good; if they had been good earlier I think we might have got a solution which would have been accepted by everybody and would have been rather favourable

---

*Jeremy Thorpe, b. 1929, was leader of the Liberal Party 1967–76.
†Lord Gladwyn, b. 1900, had as Sir Gladwyn Jebb been Ambassador to the United Nations and to Paris 1950–60. Deputy leader of the Liberal Party in the House of Lords since 1965.

from the British point of view. But by the time they had come round to it, the French had got difficult in a different way. The Council can deal with one recalcitrant major member, but not two.

TUESDAY, 22 NOVEMBER. *Brussels.*

A rather good session of the Council before lunch, in which, amazingly, we disposed quickly and without difficulty of the question of Community representation at future Summits. It was agreed, without the French dissenting, that the Rome agreement on the Community being represented by the Commission and the presidency should apply indefinitely in the future. Thereby a difficult corner was turned.

THURSDAY, 24 NOVEMBER. *Brussels, Strasbourg and London.*

A bumpy flight to Strasbourg for the twice-yearly meeting of the Committee of Ministers of the Council of Europe, which I had been under great pressure to attend. Formal speeches by Forlani, Oreja and me. Simonet failed to turn up. He is suffering from 'Eurofever' to which it is almost impossible not to succumb at a certain stage in view of our mad *calendriers*.

In the air again at 1.00, and set myself on the bumpy journey to try to get the last part of the Israel Sieff Memorial Lecture which I was due to deliver in London at 6.00 into some sort of shape. The lecture was at the Royal Institution in Albemarle Street in a nice little theatre, with an audience of about 120. Harold Wilson, whom I had certainly not expected, sat huddled in the corner of a row, listening, applauding at the end though my lecture certainly contained no words of comfort for him, and then coming up very agreeably afterwards, saying he had agreed with parts of it. Eric Roll was in the chair.

FRIDAY, 25 NOVEMBER. *London.*

One and a half hours' Downing Street meeting with Callaghan. He was extremely genial, as he had been on the previous occasion, but quite different from his attitude in the spring, and on a number of issues not bad. Fairly confident, though not foolishly so, both about the economy and the next election. On the way out I said, 'What worries me is that if you win the next election, what do you do after that? How do you control the Labour Party?' He said, 'Well, it worries me a bit too, but I think I've got some thoughts as to how to deal with that.' Whatever they were, he did not disclose them.

The only issue on which we got near to a snarl-up was direct elections, on which he fairly quickly gets emotional; starts thumping away about his difficulties and how he has done as much as he possibly can and how he is much more interested in British elections, etc. But on other issues, even the CAP, certainly 131, certainly regional policy, even EMU, certainly Community loans, he was reasonably forthcoming and helpful.

MONDAY, 28 NOVEMBER. *London.*

Michael Palliser to lunch at Brooks's. While not on as good a form as he was when dealing so self-confidently and reliably with the problems of my transition to Europe in the summer of 1976, he was more buoyant than when I had last seen him in July. He said that he was undoubtedly getting on better than at the beginning with David Owen; he thought that Owen's relations with the office still had room for improvement but had picked up somewhat. He complained about his unnecessary rudeness and, probably in response to a suggestion of mine, gave enthusiastic endorsement of the view that David ought now to lengthen his pace a little, as his whole prospect was different from that during his first six months when he might soon have been out of the Foreign Office and even the House of Commons. He said that, while meetings with David were often very difficult, he rarely, in his (Palliser's) view, failed to come out with a sensible policy decision at the end of them.

In the afternoon I went to see Harold Macmillan to fulfil an undertaking I had made to the Liberals to try to get him to use what influence he had in favour of a proportional list (for European elections). He did not seem to have aged a great deal, was friendly and relaxed, a little difficult to get to focus upon the point, as it were playing himself in with a lot of high generalizations which, for once, were not particularly well directed. However, when we got on to the point he was quite good. He was not enthusiastic for proportional representation, though not strongly against it either, open-minded so far as the effect on Britain was concerned. He was therefore quite disposed to go along with it for Europe and maybe to lobby a little in its favour. He put his finger rather well on the weakness of the regional list system, which was that it gave excessive power to the party machines. 'I am not sure', he said, 'that under such a system I would have been elected for Stockton in the thirties.'

THURSDAY, 1 DECEMBER. *Brussels*.

Gundelach at 10.45. I tried to persuade him to go for a 1 per cent rather than a 2 per cent Common Agricultural price increase, but did not feel I was making much progress, not because there is a great gulf between us, but because his judgement is that 2 per cent might stick and 1 per cent certainly won't. He may easily be right and, in any case, the general thrust of our policies march alongside each other fairly closely. In spite of some attempts to stir up suspicion against him, I think he is a nice, effective, overworked, somewhat 'flying by the seat of his pants' man, whom I enjoy talking with and whom I think is reasonably straightforward.

At 6.30 to the little prime ministerial *hôtel particulier* for a meeting with Tindemans. After half an hour he arrived rather flustered and was as usual not only late but extremely nice and agreeable. However, his mind did not appear to have focused very sharply upon the European Council, and he was very open to every possible piece of advice.

FRIDAY, 2 DECEMBER. *Brussels*.

At 12 o'clock Mrs Thatcher arrived on a visit. I received her at the top of the lift shaft, Tugendhat having met her at the front door, which it is protocol for me to do only for heads of state or government, of which grave issue Mitterrand's visit made me aware. (I have in fact made exceptions for Mondale and Hallstein.)

She brought with her Douglas Hurd, John Davies and a PPS called Stanley. We began in a small meeting in my room with these plus Crispin and Tugendhat. She was anxious to be pleasant and the conversation ran into no great snags over the next hour. I spent a good part of it explaining how the different Councils work and what was the difference in atmosphere and form between a Council of Ministers, a 'Schloss Gymnich'-type meeting, and the European Council. She seemed interested in all this, no doubt hoping that, in the last at any rate, she would be a fairly early participant. At the end we got on to economic and monetary union for about ten minutes, in which John Davies, nice and well-informed man though he is, showed a certain capacity to get the wrong end of a point. She, if anything, seemed more pro monetary union than he did.

Then seven or eight other Commissioners joined us for lunch. The conversation was partly bilateral with me, which was quite easy, and then general. She was in no way tiresome, but left me with not the faintest sense of having been in the presence of anyone approaching a high quality of statesmanship, or even of someone who was likely to grow into this; she just seemed slightly below the level of events.

She then had meetings with other Commissioners before her press conference. Douglas Hurd was apparently rather worried about this press conference, and he proved to be right, as it seems she handled this fairly badly, both from her point of view and from ours; she sounded confused as to whether she had been visiting NATO or the Commission, and kept on making what were essentially strategic and defence points. But insofar as she let anything emerge it was that while she intended to be more pro-European than Callaghan, she couldn't think of any particular ways in which she was going to be so, and indeed chose – or allowed herself to be driven into – subjects of discussion on which she is just as uncooperative as the present British Government.

MONDAY, 5 DECEMBER. *Brussels.*

The European Council began with the King's lunch at the Palais de Bruxelles. The King as usual was immensely friendly and expressed almost as much pleasure at having received a leather-bound copy of *Nine Men of Power* as if I had given him a new kingdom. It was a beautiful day with a sparkling sun over the Parc de Bruxelles. The food and drink were obviously specially chosen as a prelude to a hard-working afternoon, the main course a cold *marbre de boeuf,* which Guiringaud with typical French respect for 'nos amis Belges' disparagingly described as bad pâté.

It was also over surprisingly quickly, but, in spite of this, we managed to start the meeting nearly half an hour late. Tindemans, after a brief statement of his own, asked me to introduce the papers on the current economic situation and economic and monetary union. I spoke for just over half an hour, which was longer than I had intended but it seemed to hold people's attention: not only the small ones, but Callaghan and Giscard, who was notably friendly and attentive throughout this Council. Only Schmidt looked as though he was asleep, which he mostly does when anyone other than himself or Giscard is speaking. Then we had a *tour de table*. Tindemans, Jørgensen (notably and rather surprisingly), Andreotti, den Uyl and Lynch all spoke enthusiastically.

Giscard was a shade cooler in substance, though not bad in manner and saying very precisely that he accepted the Commission's paper. Schmidt then spoke rather reluctantly and not very well and not on any subjects of any great relevance. However, he made no frontal attack or attempt to dismiss our proposals, though it could not possibly be said that he directly endorsed them, despite the fact that he had come up to me at lunch and said that he thought his ministers had been being too negative and that he would try and correct this. Callaghan was more enthusiastic, although a shade less so in the semi-public of the meeting than he had been to me in private after my introduction when, graciously and surprisingly, he had come round the table and said that he thought it was the best opening he had ever heard at a European Council.

However, we got enough of what we wanted for the moment on EMU, and also, by the skin of our teeth, we got our Community loans facility through. This was well supported by nearly all those I have mentioned previously, except for den Uyl. Giscard, however, was the disappointment. We knew that Barre was in favour and hoped that Giscard would speak in the same sense. However, what he did was to say that he himself was unconvinced but that some of his own Government seemed to take a different view and therefore he wasn't going to oppose it. But this didn't in any way amount to applying effective leverage to Schmidt who had expressed himself still more sceptically. However, at the end Schmidt said he was not going to stand out and, rather ungraciously it would seem from most people (though he thought he was being gracious), said, all right, if we wanted it we could have it, provided that other things, like the Regional Fund, were settled on a reasonably satisfactory basis; he was not going to be raped twice.

Dinner at the Palais d'Egmont. The Belgians foolishly applied exactly the same seating arrangements as at lunch, which meant that everybody had the same neighbours, except that the King having been removed, Schmidt and Giscard were next to each other. I had Andreotti and Michael O'Kennedy,* the Irish Foreign Minister, and we had all had enough of each other. So certainly had Giscard of Andreotti and, it appeared as the meal went on, even of Schmidt, so that towards the end he began some general conversation round the table, surprisingly immediately getting on to my books, announcing to everybody that he had read them all and talking for about ten minutes rather funnily, or at least wittily, about the Dilke book, showing a surprising knowledge, indeed almost an obsession with every detail of that strange story. His command of the subject was only impaired by the fact that throughout he referred to 'Dilkie', talking the whole time in French. Indeed he talked French and hardly any English throughout almost the whole of this European Council, and Schmidt also talked more German than I had known him do before.

TUESDAY, 6 DECEMBER. *Brussels.*

European Council at 10 o'clock. In the early part of this we got a rather farcical, but nonetheless quite satisfactory and surprisingly easy solution to the Article 131 dispute. Then we went on to the Regional Fund. This was less satisfactory and was indeed the worst aspect of this European Council.

We looked at one stage as though we might get a settlement at 620 million units of account. Probably I then made a considerable tactical error. I thought this was a bit on the low side, and by arguing for more got involved in a considerable dispute with Schmidt about the basis on which we calculated inflation. He thought we were doing it in regard to the high-inflation countries, which we were not: we were doing a weighted average. But in the course of this

*Michael O'Kennedy, b. 1936, Irish Foreign Minister 1977–9, and Finance Minister 1979–80. Member of the European Commission 1981–2.

argument it emerged that I was calculating it, as I thought was eminently reasonable, from the beginning of 1974, which was when the last programme came into operation, but he totally refused to do this and would only accept a recalculation from the beginning of 1977.

So this issue having suddenly exploded, not in a particularly ill-tempered way, but having taken a surprising turn, he went back to a much harder position in which it looked as though we might get only a very small amount indeed out of him. As his agreement to the Community loans facility was dependent on a satisfactory (for him) solution to the Regional Fund, we were in considerable difficulty and really had no alternative but to accept, and indeed accept somewhat gratefully, Giscard's proposal of 1850 million European units of account over a three-year period, split on a basis which started with 580 million for 1978. The Italians and the Irish were surprisingly unrigorous in fighting for a higher figure, as indeed were the British, but this was partly – to an extent I had not fully realized, but ought to have done – because the recipient countries were gaining enormously from the transfer to the European unit of account, which followed from the settlement of the Article 131 dispute, and very substantially put up their receipts in their own currencies.

We then bounded through a number of other items more or less satisfactorily, and the whole thing ended about 1.15, after which I did a large press conference with Tindemans, who had been a successful chairman. The Council had not been inspiring, but there had been quite a good atmosphere, some considerable success in settling practical disputes, and a fair if not tremendously enthusiastic wind behind our monetary union proposals. I think that my tactic of not having a great row with Ortoli and not presenting the European Council with too hard a choice at this stage has been correct, although much criticized.

WEDNESDAY, 7 DECEMBER. *Brussels.*

Commission, followed by a Socialist lunch at the Parc-Savoy, which is almost my least favourite of the grand Brussels restaurants and an extraordinarily lavish place to be chosen by the Federation of European Socialist Parties. They had disinterred old Sicco

Mansholt* to preside and had about five or six others, Fellermaier, Prescott, etc. The object was to launch a considerable attack on the Socialist Commissioners, but particularly upon me, for not being more political in the worst sense of the word, i.e. that we didn't run the Commission on a more party-political basis, that we didn't have more purely party votes, that we didn't devote ourselves enough to doing down the dirty Christian Democrats, Liberals, etc.

It was really all pretty good nonsense, particularly coming from Mansholt whom I like personally but who is a tremendous old attitudinizer. I forbore from asking him what particular Socialist policies he had introduced during his many years in the Commission, except for building up the worst excesses of the CAP during his period as Agricultural Commissioner. But, this apart, I replied with some vigour – provoked the more by the fact that Cheysson had made a ridiculous intervention slavishly agreeing with them. (When have you ever split from Ortoli on an issue touching French national interests, I asked him.) Vredeling, Vouël and Giolitti, however, were a great deal more helpful and reasonable. Having denounced the nonsense of what our assembled hosts had been proposing, I left in something of a hurry but with some satisfaction, feeling that the lunch hadn't done any harm, apart from being digestively too elaborate.

THURSDAY, 8 DECEMBER. *Brussels, Bonn and Brussels.*

A special Commission meeting from 9.45 to 1.30 to deal both with Mediterranean agriculture and the general CAP price proposals for 1978. It was a remarkably productive morning in which we got through the whole of the substantial Mediterranean agriculture proposals and settled the main price issues. There was a curiously evenly balanced division on this and had I organized against Gundelach I could undoubtedly have got a 1 per cent as opposed to a 2 per cent increase through. However, this might have been counterproductive. There would be no point in sending him into the Agricultural Council with a figure which he regarded as unrealistic.

To Bonn by car for my dinner with and speech to the German

* Sicco Mansholt, b. 1908, Dutch-nominated Commissioner 1958–73, President of the Commission for the unexpired portion of the resigned Malfatti's term 1972–3.

Institute for Foreign Affairs. As with nearly everything in Bonn it was in the familiar Königshof Hotel. Agreeable company, with Birrenbach* on one side and Weizsächer,† whom I always greatly like talking to, on the other. An audience of 350, which filled the ballroom, and a talk by me for very nearly an hour on EMU as seen after the European Council, with an attempted reply, particularly in the crucial German context, to the post-Florence criticism; and then a half-hour of quite tough but useful questioning. One or two, Ehmke notably, were sceptical, but the general atmosphere not at all so. Back to Brussels by midnight.

FRIDAY, 9 DECEMBER. *Antwerp and Brussels.*

Antwerp at noon for my official visit to the docks and the city. A short ceremony at the Stadthuis and the presentation of two rather nice Rubens reproduction etchings, a short speech before getting on to a motor launch where we had an elaborate lunch during a long tour of the docks until 3.45. Bonham Carters arrived to stay for the weekend.

SATURDAY, 10 DECEMBER. *Brussels.*

Left at 12 o'clock for Bruges. We missed the turning off the motorway for some reason and found ourselves half-way between Bruges and Ostend and therefore went on and drove round Ostend which I had not been to since I was aged six. A rather striking Gare Maritime and, even in the pouring rain, quite an attractive *petit port* and seaside town. Back to Bruges for lunch and the normal walking tour of Bruges, the canal banks, the Memling house, etc. A dinner party that evening with Tinés and others. It went on much too late mainly owing to Jacques Tiné seeming so pleased at getting away from his NATO diplomatic colleagues that he stayed until 1.30.

MONDAY, 12 DECEMBER. *Brussels.*

Lunch for Constâncio and the other members of the Portuguese negotiating team, mainly a return for their welcome to us in Lisbon

---

*Kurt Birrenbach, a CDU M.d.B with strong business and international connections, who had been a participant in most major international conferences since the 1950s.
†Richard von Weizsächer, b. 1920, President of the Federal Republic since 1984.

and also an expression of our appreciation of the quality of Constâncio, his frankness, competence, and the work his team had done. He gave us a realistic appraisal of the Portuguese position following Soares's defeat. He also made it pretty clear that they were going to settle with the IMF.

Denis Howell* for a drink for an hour and was glad to have Birmingham and political gossip with him. He was splendidly critical of nearly everybody in the British Cabinet and I found him friendly and enjoyable, not at that stage knowing how truculent he had been in the Environment Council that day.

Dinner at the Château de Val Duchesse for the first time this autumn, which may be why the autumn has been relatively agreeable. This was with the Agriculture Ministers – never having been to an Agricultural Council I thought that this was rather a good way of seeing them. I sat between Méhaignerie, the French minister, and Dalsager, the Dane, with Humblet, the Belgian President, opposite, with Gundelach on one side of him and Gibbons, a caricature of an Irish face, but very nice, on his other side. Lighthearted speeches (by agricultural standards at any rate) afterwards.

TUESDAY, 13 DECEMBER. *Brussels and Strasbourg.*

7.19 TEE to Strasbourg. Agreeable journey apart from a yodelling and dancing waiter who leapt about and shouted in what he thought was a highly dramatic way as we breakfasted without a hint of dawn through the Forêt de Soignes. Three hours' solid work before Strasbourg – much better than going by air if it is possible. Lunch for Colombo, President of the Parliament. Then by far the best question time I have had. The grouping of questions at last began to work, so that I had a whole hour to myself. I got through only three or four questions, with endless supplementaries, but at least I was able to develop a certain swing and pattern.

Then the last of my political dinners for the group which calls itself 'Communist and Allies', the 'Allies' being mainly a curious Trotskyite Dane, who was looked at rather askance by the others for he was dressed like an amateur revolutionary, and two Italians, the

* Denis Howell, b. 1923, MP for Birmingham, Small Heath, since 1961 and for All Saints before that, and always a great pillar of sporting (and pro-European) good sense within the Labour Party.

irrepressible Spinelli* and a woman journalist from Milan, who was on one side of me. Ansart,† the principal Frenchman there, was on the other. They were all very anxious to be pleasant. I had a good talk with Ansart about French Socialist/Communist history in the twenties and thirties, the Congress of Tours, etc.; he was surprised I knew anything about it.

WEDNESDAY, 14 DECEMBER. *Strasbourg.*

Early Commission before the Parliament sitting, at which Simonet began with a report on the European Council. I followed for fifteen minutes, and then listened to the debate before leaving for a lunch at the Hôtel de Ville which Pflimlin, the last Fourth Republic Prime Minister and Mayor of Strasbourg for twenty years, had surprisingly and agreeably decided at short notice to give in my honour. Attractive eighteenth-century Mairie; short informal speeches afterwards.

THURSDAY, 15 DECEMBER. *Brussels.*

Addressed the Economic and Social Committee as a beating-up-of-support exercise for EMU. Back to the Berlaymont for a particularly useless COREPER lunch; the ambassadors were at their worst. I think Nanteuil is the best, awkward although he can be.

Australian Ambassador (Plimsoll) at 3.30, who was obviously anxious to remove the acerbities which Fraser had created in our relations. American Ambassador (Hinton) at 4.15 who, in his usual ponderous but well-informed way, wanted a preliminary run over the subjects for the Carter visit on 6 January.

FRIDAY, 16 DECEMBER. *Brussels.*

A large (and for once mixed) luncheon party in the Berlaymont for the Japanese. This had started as an occasion for Nishibori, the

*Altiero Spinelli, 1907–86, was imprisoned by Mussolini 1927–43, a European Commissioner 1970–6, a 'Communist and Allied' Member of the European Parliament 1976–86, and as the author of the Spinelli Report, one of the few people to have driven Europe forward in the early 1980s.
†Gustave Ansart, b. 1917, was a French Deputy 1956–8 and again from 1972. A Member of the European Parliament 1977–81.

Ambassador, to thank him for the help he had given on the Tokyo visit; but it coincided with the visit of Ushiba* (new trade nego-tiator) which we had pressed for very strongly following im-mediately on his Washington visit so we somewhat changed its nature. Ushiba I thought nice and able, a little exhausted after his Washington trip.

Unfortunately the lunch was almost completely inedible: the worst meal which I have ever known served in the Commission dining room. There was an indifferent fish course and then a veal chop, which seemed to be an attempt by Davignon to dispose of some of his surplus steel products. Nobody could get their teeth into it. How much the Japanese noticed I don't know; perhaps they merely thought that if we intended to be nasty we could be very nasty indeed.

SATURDAY, 17 DECEMBER. *Brussels*.

Drove with Charles† and Jennifer in brilliant sunshine down the familiar autoroute over the Meuse at Namur to lunch at the Val Joli at Celles. Afterwards a walk to see the old marooned, swastikaed tank marking the furthest point of the German advance westwards in the Battle of the Bulge on Christmas Eve thirty-three years ago. Whether Rundstedt went to the Val Joli for *réveillon* I do not know; but his *élan* had fortunately died away by Christmas Day.

MONDAY, 19 DECEMBER. *Brussels*.

The beginning of the last week of this long, fifteen-week autumn term. Jennifer left to try to go to London at about 9.30, but after spending the whole day at the airport, with a mixture of fog in Brussels and fog in London, came back and then went by the night ferry. Yet another special Commission meeting to tie up still further the ends of the Davignon steel and textile proposals.‡

Foreign Affairs Council at 3.00. We dealt quite well with a few

*Nobuhika Ushiba, 1909–86, was a Japanese diplomat (former Ambassador to Washington) who was seconded to this role.
†Charles Jenkins, b. 1949, is our elder son.
‡In 1977 steel and textiles were both in a state of depression as a result of declining markets leading to overproduction and cheap supplies washing about the world trying to find a home at almost any price. Commission policy was directed to anti-dumping rules, fixed 'reference prices' (for steel), restructuring and use of the Social Fund for conversion and retraining schemes.

internal items, and then the question of the Greeks, who had turned up in Brussels again. Papaligouras* made a fairly discontented statement, though in my view with some justification, about the state of the negotiations. Then, after a fairly wearing five hours in the Council, we had to go to a dinner which the Greeks were giving in the Carlton Restaurant. I sat next to Papaligouras and listened to various complaints from him, which I am on the whole disposed to take quite seriously in spite of his state of advanced neurasthenia. During the course of the meal, at which he ate practically nothing and drank nothing either, he must have lit and put out between twenty and thirty cigarettes, and his whole manner was totally in line with this. Back to the Charlemagne at 11 o'clock for another two hours in the Council on steel, which Stevy (Davignon) handled very well.

TUESDAY, 20 DECEMBER. *Brussels.*

A continuous meeting of the Foreign Affairs Council from 10.00 to 5.30. A mixed day: first we disposed of the textile issue quite satisfactorily, the British withdrawing their opposition to the Commission proposals. Then we got the Germans to say that they would accept the 32 million units of account (for steel) *ad referendum* to their Cabinet, but with a strong implication that this would be all right.

Then into a discussion on the Regional Fund; this was far from all right. The Germans and the French were determined to get the Commission committed to the figure of 1850 million units of account, which had been proposed by Giscard and agreed at the European Council. There wasn't any real issue of substance, for we had no intention of challenging this by putting forward different figures in our preliminary draft budgets. But equally we strongly took the view that as an independent institution we could not just say, 'Yes, yes,' to any last-minute decision of the European Council and give our acquiescence in the minutes of the Council without even a Commission meeting considering this seriously. Such an acceptance might indeed place us in considerable embarrassment *vis-à-vis* the Parliament, and also considerably limit our ability to

*Panayotis Papaligouras, b. 1917, was Greek Foreign Minister 1977–8, having previously been Governor of the Bank of Greece and Minister of Planning.

play a mediatory role, which we had on the whole done very well during the early part of December, between the Council and the Parliament, in the event of a future dispute.

The Germans and the French, although united in wanting some commitment from us, had, as is typically the case, rather different motives. The Germans were concerned with the money; they didn't want to be under further pressure to provide more, and they wanted to have guarantees that we would not put them into a corner over this again. The French position was much more theoretical and constitutional; they wanted us, being present at the European Council, to accept ourselves as being bound by its decision, on the ground that any challenge of it – most of all from the Commission – would be almost *lèse-majesté* towards Giscard.

We had about two hours' rather difficult argument before eventually – after an adjournment – we arrived at a formula which was slightly softer and more acceptable from our point of view than the one I had offered half an hour before. The Council accepted 1850 million units of account as its programme for three years; the Commission 'took note' and said that it would 'act in consequence', which was precise enough in my view to be committing in practice, but imprecise enough to raise no great questions of principle.

It emerged during the adjournment that the Germans would accept anything that the French would accept; it emerged also that the French very typically had spent the adjournment going round muttering that if we persisted in being difficult not only would a very bad view be taken in Paris, but the whole question of our future participation in European Councils would be raised. The French are always great ones for using dark threats of this sort, and it was also typical that when the issue was over, Dohnanyi, who had been leading for the Germans, was extremely agreeable and said it was all very satisfactory and he totally understood my position, whereas Deniau, ex-member of the Commission though he is, went on looking dark and said that he thought the issue might have done great damage in Paris. Deniau is an able, vain, difficult man; Nanteuil had also been flapping round a great deal during the interval, but he, unlike Deniau, was worried and anxious to be helpful.

To the far end of the Avenue Franklin Roosevelt for my dinner of well-deserved thanks to Simonet for his presidency of the Council. Home under a great moon and a hard frost.

WEDNESDAY, 21 DECEMBER. *Brussels and London.*

Commission from 10.10 to 1.25 without any great difficulty. Then a festive Commission lunch to which all but two came. There were complaints from Cheysson and Davignon that there was no Christmas pudding, which was a pity as I had thought of having it but decided that it would be regarded as too heavy and too English.

Commission again until 4.30, when we satisfactorily rounded up the business with a normal exchange of compliments between myself and Ortoli on behalf of the others. Very well and warmly done by Ortoli, as indeed had been the case at the end of the summer. Ten minutes' drinks for my immediate staff, and the 6.25 plane to London. More or less on time for once. Then to the Savoy Hotel where I gave dinner for Edwin Plowden's now slightly ageing but still very powerful group of businessmen, who had entertained me so often since 1968. Apart from Plowden himself, there were Orr of Unilever, Pocock of Shell, Geddes of Dunlop, Wright of ICI, Partridge, former Chairman of the CBI and former head of Imperial Tobacco. A good discussion on EMU at the end. They were all in favour of it but totally sceptical as to whether it would be possible for the politicians ever to do anything so imaginative.

There was also an interesting discussion about the political situation: broadly they were satisfied with the Government's performance over the past year and equally apprehensive for the future under either a Thatcher Government or a Callaghan Government or any other Labour Government with a large majority; a typical view I think of a large and influential sector of British opinion. I was also struck by the extent to which the prospect of continuing and rising unemployment over the next decade was oppressing all their minds and striking them very sensibly as being the central economic problem.

The new flat at Kensington Park Gardens being only semi-habitable with builders in, I spent the night in the Savoy, the first time I had stayed in a London hotel since I had stayed in the same hotel nearly thirty-three years before, after our wedding in the Savoy chapel. Then we had the diversion of several V2s falling quite near.

FRIDAY, 23 DECEMBER. *East Hendred.*

Soggy, incredibly warm morning; temperature 59°, one of the warmest December days on record. Horrible weather, in my view. No remote possibility of frost or snow; there unfortunately seems now to be a regular pattern, a cold Advent, followed by ten days of nondescript weather with no winter quality over Christmas.

SATURDAY, 24 DECEMBER. *East Hendred.*

Oxford for an hour's not very effective shopping, then lunch with Arnold Goodman at Univ. Michael Astors,* Stuart Hampshire,† Jennie Lee and Hilde Himmelweit‡ (whom I had put on the Annan Committee on Broadcasting but never met before); the two last ladies staying with Arnold for Christmas.

WEDNESDAY, 28 DECEMBER. *East Hendred.*

Luncheon party of Bradleys,§ Rodgers' and Gilmours. Bradleys on particularly good form, Tom being extremely funny; also the Gilmours, Ian very easy and agreeable. I am not sure how happy Bill is, although full of hope, almost of complacency, for the future.

FRIDAY, 30 DECEMBER. *East Hendred.*

To lunch at the Wyatts'¶ at Connock, forty miles away. Clarissa Avon,‖ Weinstocks** and John Harris at lunch, the Weinstocks and Clarissa all being surprisingly agreeable. I used not to like Arnold Weinstock but I have greatly come round to him and now find

* Michael Astor, 1916–80, was the third son of Waldorf (2nd Viscount) and Nancy Astor. MP 1945–51, but much more interested in the London Library, the Arts Council and his own writing and painting.
† (Sir) Stuart Hampshire, b. 1914, philosopher, was Warden of Wadham College, Oxford, 1970–84.
‡ Hilde Himmelweit was Professor of Social Psychology at the London School of Economics 1964–83.
§ Tom Bradley, b. 1926, MP for Leicester, Labour 1962–81 and SDP 1981–3, had been my Parliamentary Private Secretary at the Ministry of Aviation, Home Office and Treasury 1964–70.
¶ Woodrow Wyatt, b. 1918, became Lord Wyatt of Weeford in 1987. A Labour MP 1945–55 and 1959–70, a friend since the 1940s.
‖ Countess of Avon and widow of Anthony Eden.
** Sir Arnold Weinstock, b. 1924, cr. Lord Weinstock 1980, has been Managing Director of the General Electric Company since 1963.

him thoroughly interesting, partly I think because he listens better. Netta Weinstock has always been a nice woman. Clarissa Eden out to be pleasant to a really quite remarkable extent. Woodrow I thought a little subdued.

SATURDAY, 31 DECEMBER. *East Hendred and Hatley.*

Drove with Jennifer to stay with Jakie (Astor).* Arrived at Hatley for lunch, croquet from 3.00 to 4.00, then the Rothschilds to dinner just before 8 o'clock. Quiet New Year's Eve, although Victor in some ways on obstreperous form, but very typically insisting on leaving at about seven minutes to twelve, thereby avoiding any midnight celebrations. Although he complains about it a good deal, he seems rather fascinated with the minutiae of the gambling Royal Commission, and I therefore feel less guilty about having pressed him into chairing it.

It has been an extraordinary year and in some ways a great strain, both on Jennifer and me. Looking back, it is now almost impossible to imagine the atmosphere of oppressive strangeness in the first days of January. Certainly my mood for the greater part of the year was such that I would not have made the decision to go to Brussels had I been able to see things in advance. The job is more difficult to get hold of and less rewarding than I thought. Also in many ways I am not particularly well suited to doing it, lacking patience, perhaps at times resilience, certainly linguistic facility which, while not essential, would be a considerable asset (this notwithstanding the fact that my French has improved a lot during the year). The number of opportunities to make a persuasive impact is also smaller than in domestic politics. The Parliament, although I have got increasingly to feel at home there as the year has gone by, does not compare as a sounding board with the House of Commons, and the

* (Sir) John Jacob Astor, b. 1918, is the fourth son of Waldorf (2nd Viscount) and Nancy Astor. MP 1951–9. Chairman of the Agricultural Research Council 1968–78. My House of Commons 'pair' in the 1950s, he became, and remains, an exceptional friend.

opportunity to do effective television appearances on a multinational scale is much less than on a national scale in the United Kingdom.

On the other hand I think I am able to run the Commission itself, as opposed to the Berlaymont, reasonably well. The contacts with Parliament, with other bodies like the Economic and Social Committee, and the outside speeches and lectures go reasonably well, as do on balance the contacts with the heads of government. I find the most difficult gathering to be the large, inflated, sprawling Council of Foreign Affairs. I considerably prefer, despite the fact that there is always a lot of strain associated with them, the much more restricted meetings of the European Council, and greatly prefer the informal Foreign Affairs Ministers' meetings of the 'Schloss Gymnich' type, particularly under Simonet's chairmanship. What I think have gone really well have been the contacts outside the Community, relations with the Americans in particular, although the Japanese trip also seemed to come within this category; also with the Portuguese and the Spaniards.

The year has been sharply divided into two parts, with the first seven months being on the whole dismal. Since 5 September, the date of the return from the holidays, although there have been setbacks, my sense of direction (provided by EMU) and morale have improved greatly.

1978

1978 was the year of the creation of the European Monetary System, and as a result the best of my four in Brussels. The trigger was the fall of the dollar. In October 1977, the month of my Florence speech, a dollar bought 2.30 D-marks. By February 1978 its value was down to DM 2.02 (it went further down to DM 1.76 by that autumn). By the standards of 1987 this was not a precipitate decline. But in the late seventies, when the era of dollar omni-potence was only a decade behind, it seemed like a collapse of the verities. It produced considerable inconvenience as well as com-petitive disadvantage for Europe. It also confirmed Helmut Schmidt's view that President Carter was abdicating from the leadership of the West. And the German Chancellor was less inhibited about filling the monetary than the political gap, and even better qualified to do so.

On 28 February, at what I expected to be a fairly routine meeting with him in Bonn, he electrified me by announcing his conversion to a major scheme of European monetary integration. What he proposed was well short of full monetary union. But it went about 30 per cent of the way down the ambitious road which I had charted at Florence. It was a wonderful 'turn-up for the book', a sharp contrast with the attitude of mildly benevolent scepticism which he had taken at the Brussels European Council only three months earlier, and a transformation of the Community landscape. Germany was the one country which could make a reality of monetary advance.

Schmidt normally coordinated his European moves with Giscard. But in the late winter of 1978 the French President was preoccupied with his legislative elections, the first round of which was due on 12 March. He was widely expected to lose his majority and find the second half of his presidency as hobbled as President

Mitterrand's was between 1985 and 1988. This did not happen, but its prospect affected events both by making Schmidt's initiative dependent on the left not winning in France (hardly a signal example of Socialist solidarity) and by making Giscard remote from the very early formative stages of the EMS.

Schmidt therefore used me as his main non-German confidant (and on 28 February he said that he had only two or three German ones) to a greater extent than he might have done if 'my friend Valéry' had been more secure and available. The question of confidentiality was a teasing factor throughout the incubation of the EMS. Schmidt was a naturally indiscreet head of government. But this did not mean that he liked other people betraying his confidences before − and sometimes even after − he had done so himself.

I am not sure that I was instinctively any more discreet than he was, but I knew what a big fish I had on my monetary union line, and I was certainly not disposed to shake it off with talkative clumsiness. I had the advantage of a reliable *cabinet* (mostly trained in the British Civil Service) and the disadvantage of having to keep in some sort of informal array both the traditionally leaky Commission and six or seven other governments who saw no reason why they should respect secrets of which their big brothers had mostly not bothered to inform them directly. Difficult choices about whether to inform X of what Y had said about Z consequently constituted a slightly comical sub-plot throughout 1978.

Once the EMS was into the phase of discussion between governments it became very much the creation of European Councils. It remains the most constructive achievement, and one which in itself justifies, this early institutional innovation of President Giscard's. One of the main reasons, in my view, why the EMS was able to be so quickly implemented (only sixteen months from Florence, twelve months from my Bonn conversation with Schmidt) was that it did not require a multiplicity of formal, unanimous decisions by the slow-moving Council of Ministers. Heads of government provided the direction and the will, while the central bankers handled much of the detail. Although no one could accuse the latter group (particularly the nodal figure of Otmar Emminger, the President of the Bundesbank) of unseemly enthusiasm, they were at least used to operating informally and quickly. The need for unanimity was obviated by Britain, the only country of the Nine not to participate in the exchange-rate mechanism, the central feature of the system, simply standing out and not attempting to veto what others did.

The staging points in the fairly rapid journey were Copenhagen on 7/8 April, where under the Council's Danish presidency the purpose and scope of a monetary integration scheme were first expounded to most of the governments; Bremen on 6/7 July, where in the first days of the German presidency the scheme was given a fairly precise shape and it was agreed, with some British reluctance, that governments would study this particular scheme as opposed to ranging all round the intellectual horizon and give their answers at the next meeting; and Brussels on 4/5 December (that next meeting) where, still under the German presidency, the great advances of the year appeared to dissolve into futility at what should have been the exact point of fulfilment. Giscard there became mysteriously sullen, Schmidt became defeatist, and (temporarily) negative answers were received not only from Britain, which was expected, but also from Italy and Ireland, which most certainly was not.

Fortunately, however, the solidity of the previous advances was too great for it all to disintegrate into chagrin and disappointment. The Italian and Irish Governments had fairly rapid second thoughts and announced their renewed adhesion before Christmas. Giscard remained sulky, and held up, nominally on a complicated point of agricultural finance, the inauguration of the scheme which was due for 1 January. Eventually this problem was not so much unravelled as left to dissolve, which process did nothing to explain why it had briefly been given such importance, and the EMS came into operation on 1 March. But this development belongs to 1979. 1978 closed with the system kicking lustily as it moved into its tenth month of pregnancy, but with one of its parents (which Giscard had an adequate claim to be) suddenly cool about its birth. As tends to be the case, such belated coolness was ineffective – except to prevent the child being born *en beauté*.

For the rest, 1978 was a year in which enlargement problems were increasingly prominent on the Community agenda. Greece, which I visited in late September, was by far the furthest down the road to entry of any of the candidate countries. It was also in my view the least qualified for membership, but it was too late for that view greatly to signify, particularly as it was balanced by the high regard which I developed for Konstantinos Karamanlis, then the Greek Prime Minister.

Spain was the most interesting (partly because both the biggest and the one with the strongest tradition of political influence) of the three candidates. I went to Madrid in April, having been to Lisbon the previous November. There was considerable latent opposition within the Community to Iberian enlargement. France was the most hostile, while the Benelux countries were reticent, and Italy uncomfortably torn between Latin solidarity and the rivalries of Mediterranean agriculture. I was firmly of the view that Spain and Portugal met all the three qualifications for membership (they were indisputedly European, democratic – even if only recently – and had a settled desire to join), and that rejection or undue delay would be damaging to them and discreditable to the Community.

Outside Europe my visits of the year were to the Sudan and Egypt in January, to Canada in March and to the United States in mid-December. It was a measure of the dominance of the EMS issue that I went away so little.

In July the Bonn Western Economic Summit took place. There was no trouble on this occasion about my attendance at all the sessions. This Summit was centrally concerned with trying to get an agreement for concerted economic growth. As ten years later, the Americans and most of the others wanted the Germans to expand. Eventually a sensible if not very precise plan was agreed. But it was aborted as a result of the oil price increase which set in a few months later.

The political situation in France has already been described. In Germany politics were reasonably stable. No Federal election was due until 1980 and the SPD/FDP coalition was showing no particular signs of strain. Schmidt/Genscher relations appeared tolerable if not warm. In Britain the Callaghan Government briefly enjoyed its period of greatest stability between late 1977 and the summer holidays of 1978, but subsequently began to look near its end. The avoidance of an election in October 1978 created bewilderment rather than confidence, and even before the 'winter of discontent' a change of government in 1979 became the general expectation.

The Italian Christian Democrat Government survived the tidal wave of Aldo Moro's murder after kidnapping in April and paddled along reasonably steadily under the subtle presidency of Giulio Andreotti. Forlani was Foreign Minister throughout the year. Pandolfi, when he became Treasury Minister in March, made more external impact. In the Netherlands there was a fairly sharp political move to the right, with van Agt (Christian Democrat) having replaced the Socialist den Uyl as Prime Minister in December 1977. The new Government was just as easy to work with on European issues as the old one had been.

In Belgium some fresh twist to the communal problem led to the European fame and oratory of Leo Tindemans being replaced in October by the less distinguished but more direct Vanden Boeynants, a multiple butcher from Ghent. Gaston Thorn (Liberal) continued as both Prime Minister and Foreign Minister of Luxembourg. Anker Jørgensen (Socialist) and Jack Lynch (Fianna Fáil) were equally undisturbed at the head of the governments of Denmark and Ireland.

The weather (always a preoccupation of mine) was rather better than in 1977. The winter was briefly severe in February, the summer was tolerable without being noteworthy and the autumn was superb, warm and settled until mid-November, and then cold and settled until into Advent.

TUESDAY, 3 JANUARY. *London.*

Andrew Knight, editor of the *Economist*, to lunch at the Athenaeum, the first time that I had been there since being elected a member under their special semi-honorary arrangements. Knight agreeable to talk to and indeed we went on upstairs until after 4 o'clock; he was well-informed about Brussels, though not exactly exhilarating in his appraisal of prospects.

WEDNESDAY, 4 JANUARY. *London.*

Kingman Brewster, American Ambassador in London, for a drink at Brooks's at 12.30. I had not seen him for over five years and not at all since he had been in London, and was agreeably surprised by an approach from him the day before saying that he much wanted to see me (mainly about European monetary union) during the few days I was in London. Very quick and well worth talking to. Then William Rees-Mogg to lunch. I found William much as always, perhaps ageing a little though he has always looked at least ten years older than he is, and having moved, as he expressed it, somewhat to the right on economic affairs, but politically quite pro-Government: thought Callaghan was doing very well; was detached from but not anti-Mrs Thatcher, and thought the whole prospect for the next election was very open. I did not feel as close to him in outlook as I have done at times in the past.

In the evening Jakie Astor and I gave our dinner for Solly Zuckerman* at the Capitol Hotel. This was Jakie's idea with which I happily fell in, not because there was any special event to celebrate – many people thought it was some great birthday of Solly's, but in fact he is seventy-three and a half, which is not a particularly notable time for celebration, nor has he for once received any recent honour – he has them all – but we were both in his debt from an entertainment point of view, like him very much, and thought it would give him pleasure, which I hope it did. The others present were Victor Rothschild, Robert Armstrong, Jacques de Beaumarchais, Christopher Soames, Sebastian de Ferranti, Eddie Playfair, Gordon Richardson[†] and George Jellicoe.

Soames, booming away, managed to get the thing going very well with general conversation towards the end of dinner, mainly by insulting everybody in sight. 'Tell me, Solly,' he said, 'why was your advice on nuclear matters, and indeed on all defence questions, invariably wrong? Was it primarily stupidity or cowardice? I have often wanted to know.' Solly made a very good response to this and thereafter the evening hardly looked back.

FRIDAY, 6 JANUARY. *Brussels and East Hendred.*

At 10 o'clock a rather difficult meeting with Ortoli, who came in in a fair state saying that he wished to complain about the arrangements

---

*Lord Zuckerman, OM, b. 1904, was Scientific Adviser, first to the Ministry of Defence and then to the Government, 1960–71. Secretary and then President of the Zoological Society of London, 1955–84. His greatest fame rests upon his nuclear knowledge and scepticism.

†Gordon Richardson, b. 1915, cr. Lord Richardson of Duntisbourne 1983, KG, was Governor of the Bank of England 1973–83.

for the debate on EMU in the Parliament in twelve days' time. What he mainly wanted was that he should open it with me, both speaking one after the other, which I think is a foolish idea. The basis of his complaint was that he feels outmanoeuvred since the acceptance of the compromise paper in November by my continuing to proclaim the high road of monetary union while he went on with the details. He was not willing, he said, to play Martha to my Mary (his phrase), and this was accompanied with faint threats that he might not wish to stay in the Commission. He was not disagreeable, as has never been the case with Francis, but his complaint was obviously the result of a lot of brooding over the Christmas holidays.

Francis is a very nice and instinctively loyal man, but he pushed too hard to keep near to his version of the paper in November, and a bit of reaction of this sort is almost inevitable. The trouble is that he likes detail himself and yet doesn't like to feel that he is being left only with the detail, while the broader lines are sketched in by me. Also he is instinctively a very cautious man who likes working in the Finance Ministers' club, and doesn't like sticking his head above parapets in relation to governments and taking risks of this sort.

Then to Zaventem to meet Carter. Waited about twenty-five minutes before his slightly late arrival, talking partly to Simonet, partly to Tindemans, partly to Luns, partly to the King, who arrived very quietly, almost sidled up, and began talking in his soft, agreeable voice with his nice shy smile about his holidays, about Spain politically and various other things. Speeches from the dais, the King doing rather well in English, Carter, also in English, doing I thought less well, getting much too much boom from the microphones, and also making an extraordinary solecism by referring first to 'Your Majesty' and then to 'Your Royal Highness' and 'Her Royal Highness' – who on earth writes his texts I can't think. He then came round and greeted us all with considerable warmth.

Carter drove up to the Berlaymont after a couple of hours with NATO at 2.25. He is a tremendous one for paying attention to crowd impact. As soon as he got out he climbed up – perhaps in order to give himself extra height – on the step of his car and waved enthusiastically, looking away from the welcoming party to the crowd, and all the way round he was very ready for instant response to anyone who was willing to cheer him, which a substantial number of people were. Also, on coming out of my office before moving to the Commission room, he spotted Alexander Phillips, Hayden's eight-year-old son, and immediately went over to him, saying, 'Do you work here?', which was, needless to say, a great success with him and, indeed, with his mother.

First we had the so-called 'restricted session' with five people on either side. I had Haferkamp and Ortoli, Hayden and Fernand Spaak, and he, Brzezinski, Cooper, Deane Hinton (his Ambassador) and Bob Strauss. He asked me what I thought were the main issues for the Community in the next few months; and we talked about the Multilateral Trade Negotiations, relations with the Third World, and then went on to enlargement and monetary union. Also the date of my next visit to Washington, which he hoped would be within six months.

At the Commission meeting itself he and I each read out our formal statements with a little improvisation around them. We then had some fairly brief discussions on MTNs, on energy, and then I asked him to say a word about the future of the dollar on which he was fairly reticent and did little more than whistle into the wind about the underlying strength of the American economy and therefore of the currency (there is a good deal of long-term truth in this). Ortoli got in a good point at the end, saying what we very much looked for was a consistency of support for the dollar now that such support had started so that we knew where we were and could plan and proceed on this basis. Carter left punctually at 4 o'clock. I then did a forty-minute press conference.

I left the office at 7.10 and made a remarkably quick journey: 7.35 from Zaventem, London Airport at 7.25 (English time), and an hour after that, at 8.25, I walked into the house at East Hendred.

SATURDAY, 7 JANUARY. *East Hendred.*

To Sevenhampton for lunch with Ann Fleming, who had the Donaldsons, Diana Phipps and John Sparrow.* We returned via Buscot, as I wanted to drive round the park for the first time since

---

* John Sparrow, b. 1906, was Warden of All Souls College, Oxford, 1952–77.

Gavin's* death and see what it looked like under the new Lord Faringdon. On the way round one of the back roads we got into the most appalling skid, which I suppose was due to my going slightly too fast on mud, so that the heavy car started slewing and I had great difficulty in preventing it plunging into one of the tree trunks which lined the road. I think we did five or six slews before I was able to get it back under control. Back at home we had my old protection officer (Ron Rathbone) for a drink – a pity he wasn't protecting us at Buscot. Beautiful day, wonderful winter light, which was partly the reason we nearly killed ourselves.

TUESDAY, 10 JANUARY. *Brussels.*

At 12 o'clock I spoke to about a hundred people organized by a European Federalist propagandist body, of which George Thomson had just handed over the presidency to Gaston Thorn. Quite an excitable little gathering. My reception at a gathering like this has been much improved by the Florence initiative.

An interview with Perlot,† the spokesman for the Italian Permanent Representation and their very strongly supported candidate as a replacement to Ruggiero as head of our Spokesman's Group. As a result of the Italians making it so clear that they much wanted him to have the job, I started a little biased against him, but in fact found him an extremely engaging and intelligent man and therefore swung in his favour.

WEDNESDAY, 11 JANUARY. *Brussels.*

A short and relatively easy Commission meeting from 10.10 to 1.20. Lunch with Hayden, going on a long time while he argued with compelling logic that he thought he ought definitely not to stay much beyond the end of the second year, that if he was ever going to leave me it would be time to go, that five years was about long enough to work for anyone, otherwise one became too much

---

*The 2nd Lord Faringdon (Gavin Henderson), 1902–77, a Labour peer of aesthetic tastes, had inherited Buscot Park in 1934.
†Enzo Perlot, b. 1933, was Italian Ambassador to Portugal 1984–7, and is now Political Director at the Italian Foreign Office.

their creature. It was all done in the nicest possible way. I regretfully think it a sensible decision. God knows what it will be like without him, however.

THURSDAY, 12 JANUARY. *Brussels*.

An important and potentially difficult lunch with Ortoli rue de Praetère, not made easier by the fact that he was drinking nothing, which is unusual. However, after a slightly sticky start, the occasion definitely went rather well and was worthwhile. Rather typically with him, we did not get final agreement at the end as to exactly when we should speak in the EMU debate in the Parliament. He said he would reflect upon it, but we were obviously *en bonne voie*. He made it quite clear that he was anxious to build bridges and relations perked up a good deal as a result of the lunch. Lesson: it is particularly worth seeing people at times when a looming dispute makes one loath to do so. As he reasonably hinted, if I had had a talk alone with him at an earlier stage this difficulty would probably have been avoided.

Dinner party composed of Davignons, Tugendhats, Ebermanns of my *cabinet*, and Laura. The best evening I have had with the Davignons; Francie out of her summer purdah and animated, and Stevy very funny; a lot of anecdotal conversation about world political figures, particularly Americans, over the past fifteen years or so; it was mostly Stevy and I who were talking after dinner. We all sat over the table until midnight.

FRIDAY, 13 JANUARY. *Brussels*.

Lunch for the five or six British journalists, which was all right from a conversation point of view, not I thought as interesting as the one they had given me a few months ago, but worth having and no great knots or difficulties, but no great theme either. However, they expressed a desire to go on with the series. Jennifer to Brussels in the early evening.

SATURDAY, 14 JANUARY. *Brussels*.

Drove to Henri Simonet's house in the country at Gooik, on a dismal day, for what turned out to be a rather grand Belgian luncheon party with the Boëls* and various other notabilities, about twelve people altogether. The house itself was rather elegantly done but it is a curious place to have a country house as it is only about ten miles from their Brussels house and rather on the same side of the city. It is a little like having one house in the Hampstead Garden Suburb and another in Barnet. However, the lunch was excellent, and the conversation rather good too.

TUESDAY, 17 JANUARY. *Brussels and Luxembourg.*

Foreign Affairs Council at 10.00. Three hours there before leaving by train for Luxembourg. I spoke to the Parliament almost immediately after arrival on economic and monetary union; a speech of about half an hour, followed by what I thought was going to be a substantial debate but in fact, owing to the mysterious working of the Parliament, turned out only to last one and a half hours and to involve no very serious contributions from the floor. Therefore the response was a bit disappointing. Ortoli, however, intervening at the time we had eventually agreed, spoke well and warmly. A drink with the Socialist Group, which was intended to be for Hayward and Underhill from Transport House, but they were hopelessly fog-bound, proceeding from Brussels in a coach, apparently, and did not turn up.

WEDNESDAY, 18 JANUARY. *Luxembourg and Khartoum.*

Commission from 9.00 until 10.00, with no great difficulties, sat in the Parliament until 11.30; met a deputation of Spanish MPs and then off to the airport to leave by an avion taxi which had come down from Brussels containing Jennifer for a flight to Munich to pick up the Lufthansa plane to Khartoum. Munich was sunny but covered in snow and we took off late. An easy flight via Cairo, arriving at Khartoum at 11.30, with filthy food. The temperature both in Cairo and Khartoum was almost perfect, absolutely clear sky. Drove to Government Guest House No. 1, which was slightly reminiscent of, although less luxurious than, Lee Kuan Yew's guest house in Singapore.

* Comte René Boël, b. 1902, was former President of the European League for Economic Cooperation and a patriarch of Belgian internationalism.

THURSDAY, 19 JANUARY. *Khartoum.*

Flew for about thirty-five minutes soon after 9 o'clock to visit the Gezira irrigation and general development scheme in the triangle between the Blue and the White Niles. Walked around this for too long and then flew back for a luncheon with the Vice-President and Foreign Minister on a Nile boat. Nice temperature, perhaps nearly 80° but no humidity and quite pleasant provided one was not actually in the sun. Altogether rather a good river trip, surrounded partly by diplomats and partly by a variety of other Sudanese ministers, as well as the host.

At 5 o'clock to the opening of the International Fair. This was a fairly chaotic occasion. No speech from President Nimeiri,* as a result of which indeed neither I nor Jennifer was at this stage quite clear which he was, but various manifestations of bands, processions on camels, etc. Then suddenly a wild rush and movement from the dais in the square where this was all taking place, through to the European Pavilion where the next phase was about to occur. We managed with some difficulty to get our way through the crowd and to arrive more or less intact for me to make my speech there. I spoke for about twenty minutes to again a rather chaotic gathering of a few hundred people, with Nimeiri and all the Government listening quite carefully, and the speech appeared to go all right.

FRIDAY, 20 JANUARY. *Khartoum.*

A long morning meeting with various ministers: a mixture of discussion about fairly hard bilateral subjects with a broader perspective on the renegotiation of Lomé† and the progress of North/South dialogue. Then visited the Commission delegation and planted a tree; then a brief tourist visit to the Presidential Palace which is an attractive Blue Nile-side building, built originally, I

---

*Gaafar Mohammed al Nimeiri, b. 1930, was President of the Sudan from 1971 until he was overthrown by a coup in 1985.

†The Lomé Convention (named after its place of signature in Togo and replacing the Yaoundé Convention negotiated by the original Six) was a non-reciprocal aid and trade agreement between the Community and forty-six African, Caribbean and Pacific states (now grown to sixty-five) which had been signed in 1975 and was due for renegotiation eighteen months before its expiry in 1980. This renegotiation began in the summer of 1978 and led to Lomé II which has now in turn been replaced by Lomé III. The renegotiation was already looming by the beginning of 1978.

suppose, in about the late 1870s, a good deal changed, but still with a certain atmosphere of Gordon, and retaining the horseshoe staircase on one side of which he was killed.

Then to Khartoum North on the other side of the Blue Nile for a lunch given by the German Ambassador as the acting President of the Community ambassadors (no Danish Ambassador in Khartoum). He proved an extremely intelligent man. Back to the Fair, where I had to give a long reception in our pavilion. Then to a late supper party at the residence of Watterson, Commission representative, British, forestry expert, ex-Sudan Civil Service.

SATURDAY, 21 JANUARY. *Khartoum and Luxor.*

Meeting with Nimeiri in the Presidential Palace from 9.00 to 10.15. I rather liked him. Slightly ponderous, conversation a little slow to get going, but quite sensible; seemed reasonably sure of himself, but at the same time not full of pomposity, ideas of grandeur or deity; very anti-Communist, indeed rather seeing 'reds under the bed' and feeling himself surrounded on every side except the Egyptian one. Perhaps the most surprising indication of feeling surrounded was his view that Kenya was becoming very penetrated and might easily go over when Kenyatta went. Nevertheless he thought it desirable that Kenyatta should go as soon as possible, because this was the only possibility of pulling the country together again at all as it was now deteriorating very rapidly under his corrupt régime. Nimeiri was quite sensible about Sudanese development possibilities, neither too utopian nor too grandiose.

Then drove to Omdurman, crossing the White Nile for the first time for an hour-long press conference. Then to the airport for a great ceremonial goodbye from the Vice-President, various ministers, all the ambassadors, etc. Eventually set off, after too long a wait, in a tiny new Cessna plane (which we had privately hired) for the four-hour flight to Luxor, a long time to be in a small plane unable to move; and a horrible long time it would have been had the weather been disagreeable. However, it was perfect all the way. The plane flew at 7/8000 feet and as a result we had a magnificent impression of the Nile Valley; occasionally going about a hundred miles away from the river, cutting across bends, but basically it was a flight down the Nile, first over the scrubland on the East bank, then across the river near Atbara and into real desert for the first time, then over Abu Simbel, Lake Nasser, and down to Luxor in the evening light between 4.30 and 4.45. We drove into Luxor and installed ourselves in the Winter Palace Hotel, which is extremely agreeable, quite good rooms, beautiful view over the Nile and out beyond towards the Valley of the Kings and the Valley of the Queens on one side and on the other a view over the old garden, rather reminiscent of that at the Marmounia Hotel in Marrakesh.

At 6.15 a *son et lumière* performance at Karnak, which was good to begin with but got both cold and boring towards the end with over-colourful text and over-sonorous voices. Dinner at the hotel with a few local dignitaries, the deputy Governor, Mayor, Chief of Police etc., plus our two pilots who were both Sudanese, extremely black and dervish-like, but who seemed excellent pilots and turned out to be absolutely charming men who spoke more than anybody else at dinner and gave us a much more vivid impression of what life in Khartoum was like than anything we had gained on the spot.

SUNDAY, 22 JANUARY. *Luxor.*

Morning expedition to the Valley of the Kings and the Valley of the Queens. Omelette lunch in the hotel garden, followed by a swim in the cool pool. Then a visit to the Luxor Museum. Dinner in the hotel, as on the previous evening, was, alas, very bad: typical English 1930s seaside hotel food which lingers on in ex-colonial places from Singapore to Cyprus. The Egyptian wine – Château Ptolemy it was called – was also pretty nasty with a particularly disagreeable bouquet which suggested there was a good deal of the mud of the delta in it. (Nanteuil told me that he had found Château Lafite in the Winter Palace on one of his honeymoons. He must have drunk it all.) However, the hotel produced very good dry martinis. These small difficulties apart, Luxor is a most wonderful place. At this time of the year there is perfect, apparently totally reliable weather, no humidity, temperature down to about 40° at night, up to about 75° in the day, not much wind, wonderful views and absolutely top-class sight-seeing. Agreeableness does not necessarily go with such sight-seeing, and the combination here was quite exceptional. It is a place and a hotel to which I would much like to go back.

MONDAY, 23 JANUARY. *Luxor and Cairo.*

Karnak again early for nearly two hours. Then a quick and cold swim, lunch in the hotel garden, followed by ping pong, my beating Laura by two games to one which was a great shock to her and a great pleasure to me. 5 o'clock plane to Cairo. A protocol reception, plus ambassadors, etc., at the airport, even though the Egyptian part of the visit was semi-private, and then to the Sheraton Hotel and a fine high view. An immediate request to go to the Ministry of Foreign Affairs and see the State Minister. I was a bit reluctant to be so summoned but eventually thought that I had better go and hear what he had to say. Boutros-Ghali, who is a highly intelligent man, had been present at the talks in Jerusalem and Ismailia* and gave me a good run-down, clearly from the Egyptian point of view – but there is a great deal to be said for the Egyptian point of view – of the position as he saw it. Then to a Foreign Ministry dinner at the Tahir (old Mohammed Ali) Club, where Farouk used to spend a lot of his time.

Then a midnight drive to the pyramids and the sphinx, which were surprisingly near, under magnificent moonlight. Cairo is an enormous city and a great metropolis, falling apart with the immensity of its problems, but there is no doubt about its dominant metropolitan position in the Middle East. If the rich Arab states were sensible they would put a great deal of money into it, housing, sewerage, underground railway, telephone systems, etc., which would be a very good thing for the area and for the world as a whole.

TUESDAY, 24 JANUARY. *Cairo and Brussels.*

8.30 Sabena plane to Athens and Brussels. Half-way across the Mediterranean we ran into rain and storm, which persisted all across Europe. Brussels just after 2 o'clock. An afternoon visit from George Thomson.

---

*In November President Sadat had visited Jerusalem for peace talks with the Israeli Government. In late December the Prime Minister had paid a follow-up visit to Sadat in Ismailia.

THURSDAY, 26 JANUARY. *Brussels*.

Sigrist, the German Permanent Representative, to see me at 11.30 with a letter from Helmut Schmidt announcing that it was his intention to invite everybody to a Western Economic Summit in Bonn in about mid-July, no precise dates. We were slightly discriminated against in the sense that the letter he gave me was a copy of the letter sent to the heads of government, rather than a direct letter to me, but still this is a vast improvement on the May position; there is obviously no doubt about our presence for a large part of this Summit.

A COREPER lunch in the Charlemagne building at 1.15. COREPER in my view no better than it usually is; bitty, lacking any leadership, and I feel it a slight waste of time to see them so often.

FRIDAY, 27 JANUARY. *Brussels*.

I received Karamanlis,* the Greek Prime Minister, at 11.30 downstairs, and brought him up, first for a talk *à deux*, then for an hour's meeting with the Commission and then for a lunch going on until about 3 o'clock. I liked him, found he had none of Papaligouras's neuroses and was much better to deal with. We moved just far enough in giving a political impetus to the negotiations, with a commitment to break the back of them by the end of 1978, to leave him moderately satisfied. Quite an impressive man.

SATURDAY, 28 JANUARY. *Brussels*.

A bad day. The cough and cold which had started near the Pyramids on Monday night had become acute. A meeting with Ushiba and his Japanese team between 11 and 12 o'clock, after which we adjourned for him to have more detailed talks with Haferkamp. The meeting seemed to go quite tolerably at the time, but subsequently led to a lot of rather mystifying ill-feeling. I don't know whether he was offended that I did not give him lunch and left Haferkamp to do this. There was in fact not the slightest reason why I should have

---

*Konstantinos Karamanlis, b. 1907, had been Prime Minister three times between 1955 and 1963, when he started an eleven-year exile in France. With the fall of 'the Colonels' he became Prime Minister again 1974–80, and was President of Greece 1980–5.

done so. I had when he came in December and it was quite appropriate that Haferkamp should on the second occasion, which indeed was exactly the routine we had followed with Bob Strauss. I thought after the meeting that maybe if anything I had pressed him rather too hard, though some of his subsequent complaints, which came out partly in the press, partly in reports back from the Japanese, and partly what he said in Paris, indicated that we hadn't pressed him hard enough, except on points of detail. (The whole incident was very odd. Ushiba, I think, finds it difficult to understand what is the split between Community and member state competence, prefers dealing with the Americans to dealing with us, reacts somewhat, not altogether surprisingly, to being kicked around from capital to capital in Europe and complained to about the success of the Japanese economy; and also has a mind which while intelligent seems to operate in an odd and indiscreet way.)

I left the Berlaymont feeling dissatisfied and drove with Edward and Jennifer to Ghent, where we lunched late with the Phillips' before going to see the great Van Eyck triptych in the cathedral.

MONDAY, 30 JANUARY. *Brussels.*

Henry Plumb,* President of the National Farmers' Union, to lunch with Jennifer and me rue de Praetère. A nice, sensible, solid Warwickshire farmer, now with a great deal of NFU experience behind him and, as I had thought when he was one of my vice-presidents in the Britain in Europe Campaign for the 1975 Referendum, a very good person indeed. He obviously feels he is near the end of his time as President of the NFU, which he has done for eleven years, and is looking, rather interestingly, at the possibility of running for the European Parliament, where he would undoubtedly be a great asset.

TUESDAY, 31 JANUARY. *Brussels.*

11.15 meeting with the House of Lords Select Committee (on European Community matters); about eight of them, Tony

---

*Sir Henry Plumb, b. 1925, cr. Lord Plumb in 1986 after being elected President of the European Parliament, of which he had been a Member since 1979.

Greenwood* in the chair, but Humphrey Trevelyan† the leading figure. A good discussion on enlargement. Then I saw Cobbold, ex-Governor of the Bank of England and a member of the Committee, on his own for quarter of an hour about EMU.

At 1.15 I gave a lunch for the new Court of Auditors (*Cour des Comptes*)‡ based in Luxembourg, with their nine members, one from each national state; a necessary but not exciting occasion. As it turned out also a tragic one, because Mart, the very nice Luxembourg ex-Minister of Finance who had been appointed to the Court, left before the end as he had just received a message that his wife had been seriously injured in a motor crash on an icy road and he didn't know what he would find when he got back. Alas, he found that she was dead.

Tried rather desperately to think of something to say for my third speech at the COREPER twice-yearly 'change of presidency' dinner that evening, and arrived only half-prepared. There was much better food than is usual at Val Duchesse, and this seemed to put everybody in a good temper so that the speech went slightly better than I thought it deserved. Van der Meulen didn't speak for too long afterwards and Riberholdt,§ who had just got up from a 'flu bed to which he quickly returned, delivered a whimsical Nordic speech, but nonetheless all reasonably satisfactory.

WEDNESDAY, 1 FEBRUARY. *Brussels.*

Commission meeting which proceeded in the normal way until just before 12 o'clock. I then went downstairs to greet the President of Mauritania, Oudh Daddah. We had an hour with him in the Commission and then went off to Val Duchesse again to give him lunch. He was much the nicest of the francophone Africans I had met: small, distinguished-looking man, talked rather well but, more than that, talked interestingly because he was happy to talk

*Lord Greenwood of Rossendale, 1911–82, had been a Labour MP 1946–70, and was a Minister in the first Wilson Government.
†Lord Trevelyan, 1905–85, had been Ambassador to Cairo at the time of Suez and subsequently to Moscow.
‡The *Cour des Comptes* had been established in October 1977 with an Irish Treasury official, M. N. Murphy, as President and Sir Norman Price, former Chairman of the Board of Inland Revenue, as the British member.
§Gunnar Riberholdt, b. 1933, was Danish Permanent Representative to the European Community 1977–84, when he became Danish Ambassador in Paris.

about his early life, quite unlike Mobutu. Daddah was keen to tell me how he had been born in a tent and had effectively been a nomad until the age of twelve or thirteen.

To the Cinquantenaire for the Commission's New Year diplomatic reception; stood up and received from 6.30 to 8.00, as did Jennifer. The last two days have been the height of the Commission winter season!

THURSDAY, 2 FEBRUARY. *Brussels and London.*

Coffee with Reg Underhill and Joyce Gould of Transport House at 11 o'clock (direct elections). The Egyptian Ambassador at 11.45 – a foolish man, alas.

I then saw the Israeli Ambassador from 4.00 to 5.00, partly complaints about citrus fruit, but also no doubt a deliberate visit, arranged with great *empressement* on his part to counteract any harmful effects of my visit to Egypt and indeed the Egyptian Ambassador's call that morning. He gave me the Israeli position, which needless to say was fairly hard, but not absolutely rigid; an intelligent and reasonable presentation.

6.25 plane to London. Encountered Willie Whitelaw* at dinner. He came in rather late and then started to tell me how absolutely ghastly life was with that awful woman, how he was thinking of resigning (from the Shadow Cabinet), what was my advice, etc. So I said, 'On the whole, don't resign, Willie.' 'Oh, good,' he said. 'No, don't resign,' I said, 'but distance yourself.' 'Quite right, quite right,' he said, 'quite right. It's better not to resign, but distance myself. That's right.' A long and typical conversation with him, not to be taken too seriously.

SUNDAY, 5 FEBRUARY. *East Hendred.*

Owens to lunch, for the first time for just over a year. They were both extremely agreeable – Debbie as always but David more so than he can be. He was a little bruised by some of his recent experiences and perhaps slightly nicer as a result. There were

---

* William Whitelaw, b. 1918, cr. Viscount Whitelaw 1983, was then deputy leader of the Opposition and was to be Home Secretary 1979–83, and Lord President of the Council and leader of the House of Lords 1983–8.

obviously a few subjects on which we did not agree, but no tension or any difficulty and perfectly agreeable conversation. Then a good game of tennis with them.

MONDAY, 6 FEBRUARY. *London*.

Called on Shirley Williams* at 12.15 at the Department of Education and Science near Waterloo Station, where I had not been since once going to have a drink with Reg Prentice three or four years ago. Shirley was very friendly and it was a great pleasure to see her, and we then drove together to the Charing Cross Hotel where I gave a lunch for twelve or fourteen members of the Labour Committee for Europe and had some informal exposition and discussion afterwards.

In the evening the annual Guildhall dinner of the Overseas Bankers' Club, at which I last spoke almost exactly ten years ago in my first year as Chancellor. In the meantime they have desirably cut down both the number of courses and the number of speakers, but not the size of the audience, which is still quite remarkable, at about seven hundred. John Baring† was in the chair, the Lord Mayor spoke briefly, I spoke for twenty-five minutes, and Gordon Richardson spoke for about fifteen. A very grand occasion, with a sung grace, loving cups, etc., particularly impressing Michel Vanden Abeele, the new Belgian member of my *cabinet*, who came with me.

TUESDAY, 7 FEBRUARY. *London and Brussels*.

8 o'clock British Airways plane from London Airport for the Foreign Affairs Council in Brussels. We had a mad pilot who would not take off for about twenty-five minutes because the plane was not clean. I had a conversation with him in which I felt rather torn, for he kept saying, 'We've got to keep up standards; this airline is going to pieces,' a proposition with which in general I rather agree, but not to the extent of making everyone twenty-five minutes late in order to have bits of the carpet re-Hoovered. However, I eventu-

---

* Shirley Williams, now Mrs Richard Neustadt, b. 1930, was then Secretary of State for Education and Science, and became President of the Social Democratic Party 1982–8.
† Sir John Baring, b. 1928, is now Chairman of Baring Brothers and of the Rhodes Trust.

ally got into the Council soon after it had begun. There until 1.15; not particularly exciting or demanding. I made several interventions during the morning, lunched with them, and then went back to the Council for another two hours. I then saw the Jamaican Foreign Minister, a rather dynamic figure called Patterson, and went to a male dinner party with the Canadian Ambassador, preparatory to my visit to Canada.

THURSDAY, 9 FEBRUARY. *Brussels.*

10.00 meeting with the Socialist Group of the Parliament on economic and monetary union. Only British and Germans spoke and they in their differing ways were both pretty sceptical. Then on to a meeting with the executive committee of the ETUC. About twenty-five people present, Vetter in the chair, Len Murray* arriving rather late: a rather better meeting with them.

SATURDAY, 11 FEBRUARY. *Brussels and Northern France.*

A new pattern of weather now; quite different from anything we have had since the early winter before Christmas. Cold and freezing hard and on the whole sunny, with occasional cloud and slight snow. Left at 12 o'clock to drive via the Namur citadel to lunch at Les Ramiers in the valley at Crupet. Then on and over the French frontier near Sivet to dine and stay at Auvillers-les-Forges.

SUNDAY, 12 FEBRUARY. *Northern France and Brussels.*

Drove to Laôn, very cold on the hill, though with a little cloud coming up; spent an hour there looking round the cathedral and the town, which was better than I had remembered. Then on to Reims where (in spite of heavy restoration) the cathedral is magnificent, particularly the glass. It came on to snow during lunch and we drove back in rather mixed weather to Brussels, arriving about 6 o'clock.

*Lionel Murray, b. 1922, cr. Lord Murray 1985, was General Secretary of the Trades Union Congress 1973–84.

MONDAY, 13 FEBRUARY. *Brussels and Strasbourg.*

Entertained the Labour Party Regional Organizers – all of them –
for a quick drink at 12.30. (I am certainly working hard on direct
elections.) 4.17 TEE to Strasbourg. Deep snow over the Ardennes,
slight snow in Strasbourg. To the dismal old Sofitel.

TUESDAY, 14 FEBRUARY. *Strasbourg.*

I made my Programme speech in the Parliament from 10.15 to
11.00. Dullish speech, which I delivered in a fairly low key but
thought it was quite well listened to. Back to the *hémicycle*, where
the debate continued mostly in a fairly desultory way, although
there were one or two good speeches, notably from Mark Hughes,
the Labour MP for Durham. The most critical speech came from a
German Christian Democrat, chairman of the Budget Committee. I
wound up from 5.40 to 6.05 and then went to the Château de
Rohan for the Museum of the Year Award, jointly sponsored by the
Council of Europe, UNESCO and IBM, and made the presentation
to the Ironbridge Gorge Museum at Telford.

WEDNESDAY, 15 FEBRUARY. *Strasbourg.*

Easy and routine Commission meeting from 9.00 to 11.00, and
then, feeling in need of some exercise, for a long walk round the
Orangerie and out beyond it, getting rather lost, through a vast
housing estate, and the new university area of Strasbourg, which
brought me out on to the canal, or one of the rivers, the Ill perhaps,
down below the cathedral. Five miles altogether.

   I gave a dinner for the British Labour Group. It was memorable
mainly for a tremendous row between Mark Hughes, who becomes
an increasingly admirable man, and Gwyneth Dunwoody,* which
led to her flouncing out before the end.

THURSDAY, 16 FEBRUARY. *Strasbourg and Brussels.*

Brussels by avion taxi for a pre-lunch meeting with Vouël, Ortoli,
Vredeling and one or two officials about how we should handle the

* Gwyneth Dunwoody, b. 1930, Labour MP for Exeter 1966–70, and for Crewe since
1974.

deputation of van Agt* and most of the Dutch Government which was coming that afternoon to try and reach an agreement with us about their Bill on investment aids. Then the normal, rather pointless COREPER lunch, and then the huge Dutch delegation from 3.30 to 5.30. Van Agt I thought rather impressive. From 5.30 to 6.30 an hour-long interview with *Die Zeit*'s foreign editor (Dieter Bühl). An agreeable small dinner party for Fredy Fisher, editor of the *Financial Times*, with the Jonquières† and Tickells.

FRIDAY, 17 FEBRUARY. *Brussels, Copenhagen and Brussels.*

Plane to Copenhagen, arriving at 8.45 in cold, sparkling weather. Greeted on the tarmac by Jørgensen (Prime Minister) and drove to the Christiansborg where we talked mainly about plans for the European Council, but also about wider economic problems for two and a half hours. Then a lunch for about thirty people in the Parliament building before going into a question session with the Danish EEC Committee. This went on from just after 2.00 until 4.15 and was exhausting but otherwise quite satisfactory. Rather good general questions and all my careful preparation of specific Danish issues proved unnecessary. Then a press conference followed by a drive round Copenhagen for about half an hour. It looked a handsome city as always; it was snowing hard, which suited it. Then to the airport where I thought we were rather lucky to get off at all, but we did so only a few minutes late. Rue de Praetère by 8.00.

SUNDAY, 19 FEBRUARY. *Brussels and Paris.*

Left home just before 11 o'clock to drive to Paris. Near the frontier we ran into quite a considerable snowfall, saw about twenty cars in the ditch, and had slowly to follow a snow-plough for nearly thirty miles north of Senlis. To the Train Bleu restaurant at the Gare de Lyon for lunch with Edward; good décor, expensive, moderate-quality food, quite fun however. To the Embassy in the afternoon.

*Andries van Agt, b. 1931, was Dutch Minister of Justice 1971–7, and Prime Minister 1977–82. Subsequently Community Representative in Tokyo.
†Guy de Jonquières, b. 1945, was *Financial Times* correspondent in Brussels 1976–9, and is now its international business editor. Diana de Jonquières became my research assistant 1984–8.

Nicko had a drinks party with Pierre-Brossolettes,* Courcels,†
Beaumarchais', two or three Embassy couples, one or two Paris
grandes dames, Odette Pol Roger and another; quite agreeable. Then
to the Brasserie Lipp for a dinner alone with Nicko, and afterwards
sat talking with him in the Embassy for another hour and a half
until nearly 1.00.

MONDAY, 20 FEBRUARY. *Paris.*

Jogged around the Embassy garden on a beautiful morning from
8.45. Hard freezing snow without any real *pistes* established and, as
it proved, disastrous going for my ankle. In the afternoon I drove
over difficult roads to see Jean Monnet at Houjarray, near Montfort
L'Amoury. Monnet looked immensely frail. He came into the room
very slowly on a stick, helped by his wife, and sat down surrounded
by rugs like a passenger on a pre-war Atlantic liner, although these
were very necessary as the heating had collapsed, and I sat in some
considerable chill. But in conversation, certainly in the length of it,
he was less weak than I had expected and, having been told that
half an hour was about all that he could do, found that he kept me
for two and a quarter hours.

There was a lot of talk about his book, by the English edition of
which he was absorbed. Also, towards the end, some general
European conversation. I am not sure that he said anything of
particular penetration, which is not surprising at the age of eighty-
nine, although he was remarkably sharp in his comments about
other people in the early days. Uri‡ and Hirsch§ were first-class, but
apart from them there was hardly anybody of any use. Schuman¶
didn't really understand the treaty which bore his name, and the
German members of the Commission – and indeed those from
other nations – were pretty useless. However, it was very nice to see
him and, curiously, I left on this occasion with less of a feeling that it

* Claude Pierre-Brossolette, b. 1928, was a *Finances* adjutant of Giscard's who became his
Secretary-General at the Elysée 1974–6, and then head of Crédit Lyonnais 1976–82.
† Baron Geoffroy de Courcel, b. 1912, was French Ambassador in London 1962–72, and
Secretary-General at the Quai d'Orsay 1973–7.
‡ Pierre Uri, b. 1911, was Economic Adviser to the Common Market 1958–9.
§ Etienne Hirsch, b. 1901, was President of the Euratom Commission 1959–62.
¶ Robert Schuman, 1886–1963, was Prime Minister of France 1947–8, and Foreign
Minister 1948–52.

was the last time I would see him than I had on some previous occasions.

TUESDAY, 21 FEBRUARY. *Paris and Brussels.*

A substantial thaw during the night. Worked all morning in the Embassy. To the Elysée for my meeting with Giscard at 5 o'clock. Found him with a cold, dressed rather peculiarly for a Tuesday afternoon in a tweed suit, and perhaps not looking as svelte as usual but otherwise quite relaxed, in spite of election pressure. Talked to him for about an hour. Crispin was present but Giscard had no one. He had however an agenda which he wished to work through, and did so quite effectively, leaving time for me to raise any points. Nothing tremendously significant, except for his suddenly saying that the French were entirely on the side of the British about agricultural prices and believed that a 2 per cent increase was too high, that 1 per cent would be better, and that he would be prepared to fight for this. We shall see. The French are, of course, now in the British position so that they can give their farmers an increase by dismantling their Monetary Compensatory Amounts* without a general rise in the price level. A friendly conversation on the whole. No discussion – not raised by him and obviously not at this juncture by me – about the French internal position and electoral prospects. On economic and monetary union at the end he was favourable in theory, non-committal in practice, but not discouraging.

6.45 train from the Gare du Nord. Rue de Praetère by 9.30.

THURSDAY, 23 FEBRUARY. *Brussels, London, Dublin and London.*

After a meeting with Ortoli to tell him about the Giscard talk and generally review EMU progress, I took the 10.45 plane with Crispin to London for David Bruce's memorial service in Westminster Abbey. The service was brought alive by one or two good hymns

---

*Monetary Compensatory Amounts are, when positive, the adjustments which make a green pound or a green franc worth more than an ordinary pound or franc, and, when negative, make a green D-mark worth less than an ordinary one. A country with positive MCAs can improve its farmers' incomes without any increase in Community agricultural prices (although at a cost to its own food price index) by reducing them.

and by Harold Macmillan's reading of the second lesson, which was a spectacular piece of ham acting and show-stealing, but very well done.

4.25 plane to Dublin. Met at the airport by Michael O'Kennedy, Minister of Foreign Affairs, and drove in for three-quarters of an hour with the Taoiseach, Jack Lynch, and found him pleasant to talk to though a bit too concerned with fairly detailed Irish points. Then an hour's meeting with four or five ministers presided over by Colley, the Minister of Finance and deputy Prime Minister, with a lot of Irish complaints on four or five specific points, but all done perfectly agreeably. Then a dinner with Lynch and these other ministers all in Iveagh House before leaving in a hurry for the airport and the 10.15 plane. Escorted out (fortunately he was not at the wheel) and on to the plane by an extremely drunk deputy Chief of Protocol who kept on trying to tear up my airline tickets and came down the aisle of the aircraft to say goodbye to me on, I think, four separate occasions, the last two messages of farewell being mysteriously delivered in French. Kensington Park Gardens by 11.30.

FRIDAY, 24 FEBRUARY. *London, Cardiff and East Hendred.*

A party at the Commission office for the Monnet *Memoirs*, at which I wish I could have stayed longer, as there were a lot of people there I was very glad to see: Hugh Thomas,* David Watt,† George Brown, and indeed old Michael Stewart,‡ as well as two or three other journalistic or literary figures of note. Richard Mayne§ has a good intellectual drawing power. Left for East Hendred just after 12.30. Afternoon train from Didcot to Cardiff to preside over the annual meeting of the UWIST court for just over an hour. Hurried departure for return train and East Hendred by 8.00.

---

*Hugh Thomas, b. 1931, cr. Lord Thomas of Swynnerton 1981, was Professor of History at Reading University 1966–76.
†David Watt, 1932–87, was a *Financial Times* and *Times* columnist, and Director of the Royal Institute of International Affairs at Chatham House 1978–83.
‡Michael Stewart, b. 1906, cr. Lord Stewart of Fulham 1976, was Foreign Secretary 1965–6 and 1968–70, as well as holding other senior posts in the first Wilson Government.
§Richard Mayne, b. 1926, had worked on Monnet's staff and translated his memoirs into English. He was head of the Commission office in London 1973–9.

SUNDAY, 26 FEBRUARY. *East Hendred*.

To Sevenhampton for lunch with Ann Fleming, Bonham Carters, Arnold Goodman and Susan Crosland, the first time I had seen her since Tony's death. I was delighted to do so and found her forthcoming and friendly. She and I must have talked for an hour and a half. She didn't ask me about Tony's earlier life,* as apparently she had been asking one or two others like Raymond Carr,† but was nonetheless fascinated by any conversation about him, and particularly by the story which I eventually decided to tell her about my two dreams, the one in Rome on 19 February 1977 and the other on the same day this year. On both occasions he appeared vividly and we talked for some time, the first being almost at the exact moment of his death and the second its exact anniversary.

MONDAY, 27 FEBRUARY. *East Hendred and Brussels*.

9.55 plane to Brussels. A late lunch with Gundelach, rue de Praetère, for a general review of agricultural problems. I found him as usual persuasive, easy, agreeable and worthwhile to deal with, but it all being a little *insaissisable*, partly because everything is so much in his mind, so little on paper, so little confided to his officials or even his *cabinet*. Sarah Hogg of the *Economist* for a 'major' interview on EMU from 5.45 to 7.25, which was at least giving her good value in time.

TUESDAY, 28 FEBRUARY. *Brussels, Bonn and Brussels*.

A farewell lunch to the Chinese Ambassador, Huan Hsiang. A party of six: he and his Counsellor, Crispin, Roy Denman and Franz Froschmaier, Haferkamp's *Chef de Cabinet*. The Ambassador spoke very good English, having been in London for some time, and was quick and indeed funny; therefore an agreeable and probably worthwhile occasion. Back to the office for a short time before motoring to Bonn with Etienne Reuter for my 5.30 meeting with Schmidt, which started five minutes late and went on until 7.20.

This was a dramatic meeting. After a normal session with

---

* She was writing a biography of him.
† (Sir) Raymond Carr, b. 1919, was Warden of St Antony's College, Oxford, 1968–87.

photographers and almost as soon as we were alone, Schmidt plunged in, almost blurting things out. What he broadly said was: 'You may be shocked, you may be surprised at what I intend to do, but as soon as the French elections are over, probably at Copenhagen* – assuming that the French elections go all right and that there aren't any Communists in the Government – then I shall propose, in response to the dollar problem, a major step towards monetary union; to mobilize and put all our currency reserves into a common pool, if other people will agree to do the same, and to form a European monetary bloc. There will be great risks', he added, 'if it all goes wrong, then maybe the Community will fall apart. Do you think it is worthwhile?'

I of course said, 'Yes, certainly,' and we then discussed in considerable detail how it should be managed, what the currency should be called, whether the European unit of account should be used, etc., the detail he supplied showing that he was serious about what he was saying. I asked him what degree of secrecy he wanted preserved, and he said, 'A great deal, I have discussed it with nobody except Emminger of the Bundesbank and the new Minister of Finance [Matthöfer]. There may be a lot of opposition here; there probably will be. I am not sure whether I can get away with it, but I am prepared to try. Do you think there is a chance of the British moving?' I said, 'Maybe; doubtful; I am not sure.'

I also assured him that I would not inform the Commission at this stage. He particularly asked me not to tell Ortoli or Haferkamp, at least until he had had a chance to consult Giscard. I asked him what he thought would be the position if, as seemed to me quite likely, there was a confused result after the French election. He said he would be guided by the advice of Giscard. He still had great faith in Giscard, as indeed he said he had in Barre. He would not necessarily mind having Communists in the Italian Government, but he could not go ahead with this with Communists in the French Government. He spoke reasonably warmly about Callaghan, much more critically than I had ever heard him about Healey, whom he thought showed an excessive, almost nauseating, eagerness for eating his own words without the slightest sense of shame, and, more importantly, with deep hostility towards Carter, whose be-

*The next meeting of the European Council, due on 7 April.

haviour over the dollar was intolerable, whose behaviour over the neutron bomb was vacillating, whose behaviour in the Middle East was ineffective, whose behaviour in the Horn of Africa was weak, etc. etc.

The anti-Americanism – or anti-Carterism, because Schmidt is basically pro-American – was in a way worrying, although if the dollar crisis is such an *amorce* for economic and monetary union, I am prepared, up to a point, to go along with it. At the same time he was anxious to stress that if we made such a move there might be suspicion that Europe was becoming inward-looking and therefore it should be an additional reason for our taking a liberal attitude on trade questions at Geneva and, he added, for not pressing the Japanese too hard.

He was gloomy, as usual, about German politics. 'Oh, things have gone pretty badly, with the near defeat over the anti-terrorist bill,' and this was having a bad effect on the standing of the Government, with a real danger that it might be left as a lame-duck administration. He asked how much progress I thought we could make at Copenhagen. I said a certain amount; that Jørgensen would certainly be anxious to be helpful, but that we should probably not envisage getting a major commitment tied up there, but should rather see Copenhagen as a very important stage towards the following European Council under the German presidency at the beginning of July, which he had decided to hold in Bremen.

On the Western Economic Summit later in July, he expressed scepticism as to whether Carter would come. I told him that I disagreed with this. I thought Carter would come and I thought that the Summit could be extremely important but could take place in appallingly difficult circumstances with, if we made the worst of a series of assumptions, confrontation between Europe and Japan, virtual breakdown of the multinational trade negotiations, great weakness and uncertainty in France and a further and more intensive dollar crisis.

Rather typically he brightened up at this catalogue of gloom and agreed that this was an additional reason for having a strong Community front. We parted on very friendly terms; indeed he gave me a medal on the way out, but not by premeditation and just one of his own collection, i.e. a spontaneous present and not a decoration! After the meeting, with Etienne to the Königshof Hotel where I needed a quick drink to help me digest all this, and then back to Brussels by 10 o'clock, where Laura and Crispin came to a late supper and I rather excitedly informed them of this great turn-up for the book.

WEDNESDAY, 1 MARCH. *Brussels.*

I was sufficiently exhilarated by my Schmidt meeting to attempt a run in the Bois at 8.15. A great mistake for my ankle. A long Commission morning from 10.10 to 1.25, and then off to the depths of Uccle for an Australian Embassy lunch for Garland,* their new Trade Minister, to whom I was determined to be agreeable in order to try and put relations on to a better personal footing. I did not find this too difficult as he is an agreeable man.

Resumed Commission meeting from 3.45 until 7 o'clock. A fairly wearing Commission day, particularly as my ankle was being extremely tiresome. In the morning we had quite a difficult one and a half hours on enlargement. In the afternoon we had Ortoli being fairly blatantly nationalist on the French demand that we should freeze their MCAs despite the pre-election fluctuations of the franc. He insisted that we waited until 7 o'clock for a report from Gundelach, who was seeing the French Minister of Agriculture (who had descended on him in the Berlaymont).

Back to rue de Praetère just before 8.00 to let (Dr) Ann Phillips have another go at my ankle. Marietta Tree,† who was staying, brought three of her 'collaborators' for a drink, and then at 8.30, everybody overlapping with everybody else, we had a dinner party for her with Hintons (the US Ambassador to the Community), Dillons (Irish Permanent Representative) and Perlots. It became like an opera scene with too many people doing different things on the stage at the same time.

THURSDAY, 2 MARCH. *Brussels and Edinburgh.*

10.40 plane to London. In the VIP lounge at London Airport I met, by accident, Douglas Wass, the Permanent Secretary of the

---

* (Sir) Victor Garland, b. 1934, became Australian High Commissioner in London 1981–3.
† Marietta Tree was married to Ronald Tree (pre-1945 MP and Churchill's host at Ditchley Park during the wartime weekends of the full moon) until his death in 1976. She had been a United States representative to the United Nations 1961–6.

Treasury, and Bill Ryrie, now Economic Minister in Washington and my old private secretary at the end of my time at the Treasury, and had quite an interesting exchange of views with them. They were very concerned to know what Schmidt was thinking about monetary questions and I was forced to give them a somewhat guarded reply. 11.40 shuttle to Edinburgh. Lunch with the Scottish Development Council in the North British Hotel. Then a fairly hectic hour of TV and radio interviews. To the university to deliver my Montague Burton Professorial Lecture at 5.15. It wasn't a great lecture, but the audience was extremely good. The lecture theatre was packed with six or seven hundred people. Then a large reception and finally a university dinner. An agreeable conversation with old Lord Cameron, the Scottish Judge, on one side, about Scottish and English legal systems, etc., and with the acting Principal, on the other (the Principal had died six weeks before), about American twentieth-century history. John Mackintosh* was also present. The dinner was notable for the fact that it was in a room surrounded by about eight very well-lit Raeburn portraits; he paints heads much better than hands.

FRIDAY, 3 MARCH. *Edinburgh, Newcastle and East Hendred.*

A good train journey along the East Lothian coast and down through Berwick-on-Tweed to Newcastle at 11.45. Then to the Northumbrian Water Authority offices for a presentation of the Kielder Water Scheme, a huge enterprise, costing in total over £100m, with a very big Community contribution, both from the European Investment Bank and the Regional Fund. After lunch with them, which Geoffrey Rippon attended, helicopted for an hour up into the North Tyne valley over the area to be flooded and down to a point on the long pipeline which they are driving between the Tyne and Tees valleys. Back to Newcastle at 4 o'clock to open the Newcastle Polytechnic Library. Ted Short, now Lord Glenamara,† was there – the first time that I had seen him since we

---

*Professor John Mackintosh, 1929–78, was Labour MP for Berwick and East Lothian from 1966.

†Edward Short, b. 1912, cr. Lord Glenamara 1977, having been Lord President and leader of the House of Commons 1974–6. He had succeeded me as deputy leader of the Labour Party in 1972.

ceased to be together in the Cabinet. An odd but nice man. 6.30 plane to London, and to East Hendred.

SUNDAY, 5 MARCH. *East Hendred.*

To London for a *Weekend World* programme with Brian Walden: a preliminary film and then half an hour's interview with him on economic and monetary union. Lunched late with the Gilmours at Isleworth, and returned to East Hendred through a spectacular evening light at 5.30.

MONDAY, 6 MARCH. *East Hendred and Vancouver.*

Met Crispin, Noël and other officials at London Airport for the noon plane to Calgary and Vancouver. Nearly two hours late taking off. However, we flew almost the whole eight hours and twenty minutes from London to Calgary (over Iceland and Greenland) in clear light, sunshine and snow, and Air Canada gave us the best food I have had in a plane for a year or more.

Then a disagreeable hour's flight from Calgary to Vancouver. A complete change of weather when we got to the continental divide: great thick swirling clouds going up to 40,000 feet, above our height at any rate, and down on to the Rockies and right down to the coast at Vancouver. So we arrived on a dark, oppressive, rainy afternoon, and experienced no change in the weather while we were in Vancouver. At the airport I was rather surprisingly asked for a TV interview in French.

To the Four Seasons Hotel, where we were magnificently installed on the top floor and from where the view would have been splendid had the cloud not been so obfuscating. Then a brief and perfectly agreeable dinner given by the British Columbian Government. Afterwards, however, I became gloomily aware that the trip was going to be dominated, and maybe rather ruined, by the question of a non-visit to francophone Canada. The Canadian Government were resolved that we should not go anywhere inside the Province of Quebec because they thought that Lévesque*

---

*René Lévesque, 1922–87, was a television reporter who became the militantly francophone and semi-separatist Premier of Québec Province 1976–85.

would turn up and make some sort of inflammatory separatist speech, perhaps even asking for admission to the Community!

The Canadians had also been difficult about passing on my messages to him in reply to his several messages to me. However, what had been agreed was that they would ask him to come and see me in Ottawa, but it seemed fairly unlikely that he would do this and there had already been some rather adverse criticism in the francophone press, which was a little over-zealously relayed to me that night by Heidenreich, ex-Messerschmidt pilot and high-quality Community representative in Ottawa.

The Quebec problem was the reason we were in Vancouver and why we were to go subsequently to Halifax. The natural pattern for a short official visit to Canada is Ottawa, Montreal and Toronto. If Montreal was out, Toronto was out too, and we had to have the two balancing and much longer arms of Vancouver and Halifax.

TUESDAY, 7 MARCH. *Vancouver and Ottawa.*

At 9.30 I had a meeting with most of the British Columbian ministers. Then a harbour tour in a very smart launch. In good weather it would have been excellent. If it had only stopped raining, which apparently it rarely does, Vancouver would have appeared a very striking place.

At 12.30 to a lunch organized by the Vancouver Board of Trade in the Vancouver Hotel, one of those green-tiled semi-skyscraper railway hotels which cover Canada. A good audience of 200/250. Left at 4.15 to fly to Ottawa by a Canadian Government plane, which enabled them to give a free ride not only to our party, which was large enough, but to most of the West Coast politicians who wanted to go to Ottawa. As a result there was animated conversation over dinner about Canadian politics, which are by no means without interest. Ottawa, with a three-hour time change, just after midnight. It was a cold, moonlit night, temperature about 15°F, and we drove five or seven miles along a hard frozen canal, through great piles of snow to the Canadian Government guest house at 7 Rideau Gate, a colonial-style house, well and agreeably furnished.

WEDNESDAY, 8 MARCH. *Ottawa.*

On a sparkling, freezing morning I went to the Parliament building — I am rather impressed by the official buildings in Ottawa — and saw Trudeau alone at 9.45 for about an hour. I had last seen him at the Summit, having before that not seen him for eight or nine years since he came to East Hendred soon after taking office. We talked mainly about his internal politics: he certainly intends to have an election in the summer and, I would judge, is quite reasonably confident of winning it;* about Quebec separatist problems; and about prospects for the Summit.

His relations with the Carter administration are obviously good, much better than Ottawa/Washington relations have been for some time past, and this is a consideration which has to be taken into account in all Community dealings with him. He was rather shocked that I had been sent to Vancouver. He half-apologized for this and also expressed some scepticism as to whether it was necessary to keep me out of Quebec. However on balance, he said, it might be wise and there was something to be said for seeing both ends of the country and not just doing the places that everybody went to.

He was tolerably relaxed about Lévesque himself, partly because he thought that his support was declining, though he surprised me by the extent to which, he said, a lot of people, particularly in the prairie states, and indeed in British Columbia, believed that he, Trudeau, was more or less hand-in-glove with Lévesque and was trying to force francophone/Papist influences on to the whole country. Speaking without great passion but with considerable resentment, Trudeau expressed himself shocked at the way Giscard and the French Government had received Lévesque, mainly, he said, because it was so different from the dismissive way (about Lévesque) in which Giscard had always spoken to him.

Then to the Department of External Affairs for an hour's meeting with Don Jamieson,† the Newfoundlander who is the Minister and whom I had met on several occasions before and liked. At noon he and I presided jointly over the formal session of the Committee of

---

*In fact he postponed it to the autumn and lost it.
†Donald Jamieson, 1921—86, was Minister for External Affairs 1976—9, and Canadian High Commissioner in London 1983—5.

Cooperation between Canada and the Community. By this stage I was beginning to be struck by how strenuously anglophone Canada now attempts bilingualism. Jamieson began his speech in the most appallingly bad French, so I had quickly to change the opening of mine.

Then an official luncheon of about two hundred in a room with a good view – wide horizon, snowbound landscape, brilliant sunshine – at the top of the building. An unexpected speech by Jamieson at the end, and therefore an impromptu one from me. Next a visit to question time in the Parliament building, and was called on by the Speaker to stand up in the gallery.

Then a substantial discussion with the Defence and External Affairs Committee. Following this I went to see Jean Chrétien, the relatively new Québécois Minister of Finance. Quite a tough, impressive man, who apparently could speak no English until a few years ago, and is still not fluent. Then a visit to the Commission office and staff.

Dinner party of about twelve with Trudeau at his official residence. An agreeable, informal atmosphere. His three children were all there when we arrived and seemed friendly enough, though very resistant to Trudeau's efforts to speak French to them. 'Aw, shucks, Pop, I wish you'd talk English,' was the reply of one of them to 'Dis à Monsieur Jenkins quel age tu as.' Slightly high-falutin conversation, led by Trudeau, but he getting me to do most of the talking and confining himself largely to asking questions about world trends, world unemployment problems, whither the world economy, etc., all geared in a general sense to the prospects for the Summit.

THURSDAY, 9 MARCH. *Ottawa and Halifax.*

Another brilliant morning, though with perhaps only about 10° of frost, and the Canadians consequently beginning to talk about spring arriving. To the Parliament building yet again for a so-called round-table breakfast, presided over once more by Jamieson, with about five or six ministers and officials present. I found myself involved (i) in making a speech for about twenty minutes which I hadn't altogether expected; and (ii) in answering a lot of moderately but not excessively difficult questions for nearly one and a half hours. Then a brief meeting with the ambassadors of the Nine. Then an hour's meeting with the Premier of Ontario, Joe Davis. Quite an effective little man who had come up specially from Toronto, I think mainly because the Government wanted to show that Premiers were invited and that one at least would come, even if Lévesque would not.

Then rather hurriedly to call on the Governor-General, Léger, a brother of the former Cardinal Archbishop of Montreal, himself an ex-diplomat, primarily francophone clearly, who has been in office three or four years: an interesting man despite the fact that I had been warned that he was very difficult to talk to since his stroke. I did not find this, except that his stroke had the most curious effect of making it easier for him to speak English than French.

Next a rather grand lunch, about fifty, all at one table in the early nineteenth-century Residence. Léger opposite me, I flanked by Mitchell Sharp, the former Minister both of External Affairs and of Finance, who had been my chairman at the previous day's meeting in the Parliament, and whom I much liked talking to; and, on the other side, by Joe Clark, the leader of the Opposition, whom I had met in London just over a year before and whom I thought had not gained much authority meantime.

3.15 press conference. No questions at all, so quickly do issues die, about the non-visit to francophone Canada, or about Lévesque, until somebody asked me one on the way out, which I replied to without great difficulty.

Took off for Halifax at 4.30 in a Canadian Government Viscount, which seemed a little unprepossessingly antique. However, it was very comfortably fitted up, having a middle section with a few vast armchairs, in one of which I sat, opposite the Minister of Veteran Affairs, Daniel MacDonald, who came from Prince Edward Island and who had been deputed to accompany me on the Nova Scotian part of the tour. He had lost both an arm and a leg in the war, which seemed almost excessive type-casting for a Minister of Veteran Affairs, and at first I thought that he was a rather typical small-town Canadian politician. I was utterly wrong. He turned out to be an absolutely charming man with great breadth of view and interest, whom I liked enormously on the flight, at dinner that night, and subsequently.

In Halifax we were driven to Government House, built in about 1810, in good dark stone curiously reminiscent of Halifax, Yorkshire. Dinner at the Château Halifax, a relatively new hotel, which was made more agreeable by the fact that at least two of the six or eight local notabilities present had been enthusiastic readers of *Asquith*.

FRIDAY, 10 MARCH. *Halifax and New York.*

At 9.15 a meeting with Regan, the Premier, which was intended briefly to precede a long serious discussion meeting about Nova Scotia's economic problems with him and his ministers. I was not quite clear what we were going to talk about. However, this again did not prove difficult. He began by saying that he wanted to ask me a very serious question, and I thought, 'Oh, God, what horror are we going to have about steel imports or something of the sort.' Instead of which he said, 'Could you tell me exactly what you really think were Asquith's relations with Venetia Stanley?' There must be nothing to do in Halifax except read *Asquith*. So we gossiped around literary questions for a little time, and then proceeded to the meeting with the other ministers which again was relaxed and easy.

Then a tour of the harbour before a luncheon of 150 with speeches back at the Lieutenant Governor's residence. A press conference at 3 o'clock, again not too difficult, and then back to the old Viscount for New York. After a nice evening over Boston we flew into thick cloud as we approached New York and hovered around in this for about twenty-five minutes – before coming out of it just above the runway of what I assumed was La Guardia, where we were supposed to arrive and where we were to be met. I thought as we landed that Manhattan, which one could see in a curious orange light, looked rather far away, but took no great notice of this until Sue Besford came down the plane announcing, for some curious reason as though this was a great achievement, that we were at Kennedy and not La Guardia.

I subsequently discovered that when we were on the glide path with La Guardia about ten miles away, the control tower there had rejected us on the ground that they had no immigration facilities. This apparently is a fairly well-known New York trick with Canadian planes; they had messed up an Andreotti visit a few months before. As it was, we were more or less stuck on the tarmac at Kennedy with no terminal anxious to take responsibility for us, quite apart from the considerable hazards which must have been involved in changing from one glide path to another in thick cloud at the busiest time of the busiest day of the week in the busiest bit of air space in North America, or indeed any other continent. However, we were eventually rather ungraciously let through Immigration and into a taxi, in which we drove off to Marietta Tree's in Sutton Place South, where both Crispin and I were staying.

SATURDAY, 11 MARCH. *New York.*

After lunch to the Frick for an hour. A beautiful day, quite warm, about 45°. New York this weekend is looking better than I have known it for several years past. Later there was a large and enjoyable Schlesinger dinner party. I sat between Alexandra Schlesinger and Shirley Maclaine. There was generally a slight showbiz atmosphere, as is normal with Arthur's parties, but no Sam Spiegel for some mysterious reason. Arthur made a pretty bad speech – he is addicted to speeches – and I made an equally bad one in reply.

SUNDAY, 12 MARCH. *New York.*

Marietta and I walked over to pick up the Schlesingers at 1 o'clock and then went with them to lunch at the Urquharts',* whom after quite a long interval I was delighted to see. A large party of twelve or fourteen. To the Metropolitan Museum for an hour in the afternoon, and looked mainly at the new French furniture rooms at the back, mostly recently given by the Wrightsmans. A rather grand Marietta dinner party of about thirty people, the Kissingers, Jackie (Kennedy), Evangeline (Bruce), the Spaaks, whom I had asked up from Washington, the Schlesingers, etc. etc. The party was somewhat interrupted by the French election results, which began to come through, although very badly presented on American television, just after dinner. It looked as though, against the odds, 'the majority' had won (a curiously tautological phrase), Giscard had escaped intact, and Schmidt's main condition for our monetary scheme had been met.

* (Sir) Brian Urquhart, b. 1919, was a member of the secretariat of the United Nations from 1946 to 1986, an Under-Secretary-General for the last twelve of these years.

MONDAY, 13 MARCH. *New York and Paris.*

10.30 Air France Concorde from Kennedy. Paris in 3 hours 24 minutes. Fast obviously, on the whole smooth, but not very agreeable: shuddered rather nastily for ten minutes when going supersonic, landed rather fast, and definitely cramped inside despite the fact that there were only 26 passengers in space for 110, which meant we each had two seats to ourselves. Food not very good. The only advantage apart from speed, and that by chance a rather striking one, was that the first edition of that day's *France Soir*, the Paris evening paper, was available at 10.00 in the morning at Kennedy, having come over by the westward Concorde. It was almost the only day in four years when I wanted to read that unimpressive newspaper for more than two minutes, for it contained all the detailed results, constituency by constituency, and I spent most of the journey studying exactly what had happened in the various French Departments.

Dined at the Coupole with Edward, Laura, Hayden and Crispin, at 10 o'clock, unfortunately only about two and a half hours after Crispin and I had finished lunch. Back to the hotel about 12.30 a.m. (7.30 p.m. New York time) not wanting to go to bed, but was restrained from calling on either Nicko or the Beaumarchais' to give them my election views.

TUESDAY, 14 MARCH. *Paris and Strasbourg.*

Horrible morning, windy, wet, cloudy. Also Concorde a complete flop for the avoidance of jet-lag. I felt worse than after a normal transatlantic flight. It required a great effort to catch the 11 o'clock train from the Gare de l'Est to Strasbourg. I could not even get any pleasure out of the French countryside. Answered questions in the Parliament from 5.00 to 6.00. Later gave a dinner for parliamentarians particularly interested in economic and monetary union, during which I woke up briefly and even spoke with some animation.

WEDNESDAY, 15 MARCH. *Strasbourg and Brussels.*

9 o'clock Commission meeting which, despite Concorde-lag, I got through without too much difficulty by about 10.20, and then had

a brief meeting with Ortoli and Davignon about the papers we were putting in for the European Council. Avion taxi to Brussels accompanied by Ortoli just after 12.00. Mildly disagreeable flight in bad weather, but nothing out of the way. Briefly to rue de Praetère, where I had not been for almost two weeks, and then to lunch with the group of British journalists with whom I now have this regular fixture. Although relations with them are now much better than they were, I still don't find them an immensely rewarding group, partly because I think – slightly under Palmer's* leadership – they always behave so depressingly professionally. They immediately started asking detailed questions as though they were at a press conference. They seem to have no sense at all that they would get more out of me if they allowed a little general conversation to develop.

Back to the office to receive Calvo Sotelo,† the new coordinating minister in the Spanish Government for relations with us, and was quite impressed by him. In particular, I think that he appreciates the link between the Spanish desire for accession and their need to work fairly closely with us both on industrial and agricultural policy and the renegotiation of the 1970 Convention, whereas previously these interlocking subjects were dealt with by the Spaniards as though they were in watertight and mutually contradictory compartments.

THURSDAY, 16 MARCH. *Brussels, Luxembourg, Liège and Brussels.*

To Luxembourg by car at 10.00. By the time I arrived to lunch with Thorn I was feeling more or less human for the first time since leaving New York. He was rather late for lunch, having been to Brussels for a meeting that morning and flown down in a delayed and bumpy aircraft. It was not quite clear why we could not have lunched in Brussels. Crispin said the answer was that the Luxembourgeois attach importance to being visited in their own country, which I suppose is understandable.

Thorn quick and quite funny as usual, but deeply depressed about everything and therefore becoming too cynical and hopeless,

*John Palmer, b. 1938, was *Guardian* correspondent in Brussels throughout my years there and has now returned to this post.
†Leopoldo Calvo Sotelo y Bustelo, b. 1926, was Spanish Minister for EEC Relations 1978–80, deputy Prime Minister 1980–1 and Prime Minister 1981–2. Now an MEP.

as at one stage I gently pointed out to him. He was even slightly sceptical about direct elections, though this is a good deal linked with his worry about Luxembourg losing the Parliament as a result of the bigger membership. He was depressed about the post-French election prospect, not about what he thought would be the outcome of the next round, but because he thought even the Giscard victory would leave a divided, weakened and hesitant France. He was fairly sceptical about any move forward from Schmidt. I hope I managed to cheer him up a bit towards the end.

Drove to Liège for a dinner speech, and back to Brussels at 11.30.

FRIDAY, 17 MARCH. *Brussels*.

An additional meeting of the Commission from 10.10 until 12.25. It produced a rather good discussion on the draft of the 'fresco'* enlargement paper. Then to the Hôtel de Ville for my official visit to Brussels, which began by my being shown the treasures of the city, which indeed are quite magnificent in the form of tapestries in particular, but furniture, panelling, paintings, as well. Then to the Maison Patricienne, a little eighteenth-century house belonging to the Ville de Bruxelles, where we had an agreeable lunch. A speech at the Hôtel de Ville but not, fortunately, at the lunch.

SUNDAY, 19 MARCH. *Brussels*.

Spent nearly the whole day preparing a 1500-word letter to heads of government, which was intended to ring some alarm bells and create an apprehensive but adventurous mood for Copenhagen.

MONDAY, 20 MARCH. *Brussels*.

A meeting with Cheysson for which he had asked the previous week and which I had deliberately postponed until after the result of the second round of the French election. He was in a buoyant, agreeable, sensible mood, and said that the result was for him a political disappointment, but a personal relief as well. In a Socialist Government he would certainly have been Foreign Minister

---

*A word which, with no great respect for the literal Italian meaning, had become Commission jargon for looking at the overall problems of the admission of Greece, Portugal and Spain as opposed to the bilateral ones with each of them.

(Mitterrand had confirmed it to him only three or four weeks before), but this would have been extremely inconvenient for his family, and therefore he did not personally mind the outcome too much, particularly as, so he claimed, he was greatly enjoying his Commission work. He was also in a buoyant mood about the Commission, thought we were doing much better now and generally making a good impact in the press and elsewhere. It was Cheysson at his best. He was also sensible about French politics, thought it was a considerable personal victory for Giscard, which he hoped he would exploit by consolidating the centre.

Went to the Ecofin Council at 12.30 to listen to Ortoli presenting his paper, which he did well, and then lunched with them, an occasion at which no serious business was done, though I had a quite interesting talk with Lambsdorff* on my one side and, on the other, Boulin,† the French minister who had narrowly scraped home at Libourne. At the resumed meeting of the Council, Denis Healey talked too much, as even Ortoli remarked to me. He embroiled with Lambsdorff in a highly counterproductive way, which merely had the effect of driving the Germans into a more stubborn corner, resulting in the press the next day giving the impression that they had firmly repulsed British, or indeed any other, pressure to make them move further in an expansionary direction.

TUESDAY, 21 MARCH. *Brussels, The Hague and Brussels.*
8.37 from the Gare du Nord to The Hague. A slightly depressing journey in horrible weather, the Low Countries looking very low. No breakfast car, contrary to the indications. At Rotterdam the train broke down. However, a good meeting with van Agt and van der Klaauw,‡ the Foreign Minister, followed by lunch with a lot of ministers and general discussion. I like the new Dutch Government even more than the old one. 2.10 train back to Brussels for a deputation of five Arab ambassadors – the Moroccan, the

* Otto Graf Lambsdorff, b. 1926, was German Minister of Economics 1977–84, when he resigned following allegations about business contributions to his party funds.
† Robert Boulin, 1920–79, was French Minister-Delegate for Finance (so called because Barre, the Prime Minister, was really in charge of the department) 1977–8, then Minister of Labour until October 1979 when he committed suicide.
‡ Christoph van der Klaauw, b. 1924, a professional diplomat, was Dutch Foreign Minister 1977–81, Ambassador to Belgium 1981–6, and to Portugal since 1986.

Anthony Crosland in the Foreign
Office during the last weeks of
his life.

Jennifer with Secretary of State Vance
in Washington, April 1977.
Fernand Spaak is behind.

President Carter visits Brussels, January 1978. Hayden Phillips and Alan Watson
(later President of the Liberal Party) behind.

The Boyhood of Helmut,
or How Chancellor Schmidt
Discovered Economic and Monetary
Union. Bonn, February 1978.

An unrelaxed press conference
with President Valéry Giscard d'Estaing,
Strasbourg, June 1979.

François Mitterrand, on his Commission
visit in May 1977, looks wary.
Haferkamp is the third person.

The King of the Belgians at the Berlaymont, 1977.

Exchanging gifts with Japanese Prime Minister Fukuda, July 1978.

I get a waterfall.   He gets a celestial globe.

The drawing room at 10 rue de Praetère.

East Hendred.

Jordanian, the Syrian, the Egyptian and the Somalian – who came to see me to protest about the Israeli invasion of the Lebanon. I just listened.

WEDNESDAY, 22 MARCH. *Brussels and London.*

Commission meeting 9.30 to 1.30, and got through a long agenda without the need for an afternoon session. Then a late lunch with COREPER, which was better than most of these luncheons. More *grandes lignes*, less trivia. I told them of my letter to heads of government, which they took perfectly well. Then back to the office to see Ortoli and show him my draft, with which, with a few minor amendments, he expressed himself content, and then saw Davignon for the same purpose. 6.25 plane to London. Dined at the Gilmours with Carringtons, Gordon Richardsons and Peter Jenkins (but not Polly).*

FRIDAY, 24 MARCH. *East Hendred.*

My new library being complete and my ankle still precluding any other exercise, I started on two days of obsessive book-arranging. Quite hard work physically, but even harder mentally, as it is always difficult to decide how to categorize books and where to place them. However, as a result of about eight hours on both this day and the next I managed to get it more or less complete.

MONDAY, 27 MARCH. *East Hendred.*

Gordon Richardsons to lunch, both of them very friendly and forthcoming. I gave Gordon my letter to heads of government to read after lunch, and, although I am not quite sure how precisely he took it in, he seemed generally favourably disposed.

FRIDAY, 31 MARCH. *East Hendred.*

Another depressing day of pouring rain, as throughout this Easter holiday. Lunch at home. A thirty-five-minute telephone call from

*Peter Jenkins, b. 1934, has been a political columnist on many newspapers and is married to Polly Toynbee.

Callaghan just before 6 o'clock. We had a reasonably satisfactory, fairly friendly, pre-European Council conversation. He was mainly concerned to tell me how well he had got on with Carter in Washington and how he had put his five points to him and had them well received, etc.* I was concerned to see what effect Schmidt had had on him a few weeks before. I decided that they had passed like ships in the night, Callaghan being concerned only to get Schmidt's blessing, or at least friendly acquiescence, for his visit to Washington, and not concerned to listen to what Schmidt had to say about European monetary stability. Equally, Schmidt had been more concerned to tell him about this and had probably not appreciated the extent to which Callaghan's mind was more on transatlantic approaches. I tried to open up his mind on the Schmidt point, but I suspect with only marginal success.

SUNDAY, 2 APRIL. *East Hendred and Brussels.*

The David Watts to lunch, he having recently moved from the *Financial Times* to his new job as Director of Chatham House. Both of them very good luncheon guests. I left just after 4.30 for Brussels. Just time to go to rue de Praetère and get to the Palais des Beaux Arts to receive the King and Queen for the European Youth Concert at 8.20.

The Youth Orchestra played remarkably well. Heath conducted the first short part, mainly the overture to *The Meistersingers*, and then after a rather long interval Claudio Abbado came on and conducted Mahler's Sixth Symphony. It was the first time I had heard Ted conduct and he appeared to me to be perfectly competent, although there was an element of Dr Johnson's dog about it. When Abbado took over afterwards there was not unnaturally a certain marked difference of style, quality of definition, etc.

A reception afterwards for the King and Queen, Heath, various ambassadors, etc., and then most of the others adjourned to a party at the British Embassy, but I went home for a late supper, rue de Praetère, with Laura, the Tickells and the Phillips', during which we

---

*Callaghan had put a paper to Carter suggesting that the summer Summit in Bonn should concentrate on the five issues of: commitment to growth, maintenance of world trade, currency stability in the long term, use of capital surpluses and the conservation of energy. There was an element of being against sin about it.

settled the final draft of the perhaps over-prepared letter to heads of government.

MONDAY, 3 APRIL. *Brussels and Luxembourg.*

10 o'clock meeting with the Chinese Foreign Trade Minister before the joint signature by him and Haferkamp of our 'framework'* trade agreement with the Chinese. He delivered a pressing invitation to me to visit China, which I intend to do before the end of the year or at the beginning of next year. Avion taxi to Luxembourg, giving a lift to K. B. Andersen and the main Danish officials. Had them to lunch at the Golf Club until 2.30, when Andersen left to preside over the Foreign Affairs Council, in which I spent the afternoon. Tugendhat did well on the budget. It was a useful and friendly discussion with Andersen, as usual.

At 6.15 we had an hour or so's negotiations with the Greeks, which was a curious procedure, less formal than on some previous occasions as there was some substantive negotiation, yet all done rather jerkily, as indeed was bound to be the case with the neurotic Papaligouras negotiating from one end of the table next to me in this huge room. I then dodged the formal dinner with the Greeks and dined instead, enjoyably and successfully, with Simonet – it was his party – Dohnanyi and Lahnstein, a junior but highly able German State Secretary.

TUESDAY, 4 APRIL. *Luxembourg and Brussels.*

Foreign Affairs Council all day. Simonet and Dohnanyi are becoming the dominant and most effective figures in this body.

The Council rather ground on during the afternoon. Davignon did a fluent and informative but over-long exposition of the steel position. I decided to leave at 5.15 as everything seemed in reasonably good shape, even the difficult Japanese issue, on which Haferkamp, contrary to what I had believed at first, had done right and shown cool nerve by signing the communiqué with the Japanese ten days before. Train to Brussels.

*I.e. an outline without at this stage much substance.

WEDNESDAY, 5 APRIL. *Brussels*.

Commission from 10.15 until 12.40. Then a Commission lunch for Emile Noël's twenty years as Secretary-General. I spoke very briefly, got Haferkamp to make the main speech, as he had been there the longest and I had already done a tribute in the Commission in the morning. Emile replied with tears in his eyes.

Commission again from 3.30 until 6 o'clock, with a preliminary run-through of the enlargement 'fresco'. Then received an ETUC deputation, a somewhat formal occasion, as they were having a day of symbolic European strike against unemployment. Afterwards half an hour's pre-Copenhagen Summit talk with Ortoli, during which I had to steer a fairly difficult course as I was still not free to tell him all that had passed between Schmidt and me, yet wanted to give him some steer so that we could approach Copenhagen together on good terms. I was equally not able to tell him that I was sending a document to Schmidt, prepared largely by Michael Emerson, which contained our proposals for a possible immediate advance, grouping the other currencies round the Snake, but keeping the Snake, using the European unit of account as a reference point and envisaging interventions in this way between Community currencies and, indeed, in dealings between Community currencies and the dollar. That document went off to Bonn by special messenger that afternoon.

Rue de Praetère dinner party composed of Simonets, Tugendhats, Haferkamps, etc.

THURSDAY, 6 APRIL. *Brussels*.

A day of preparation for the European Council interspersed by a series of visits *de tous azimouts*. At 10.30 I had Sir Mark Turner of Rio Tinto Zinc to see me. He at least was very quick. At 11.15 I had the Prime Minister of Cape Verde, who was perfectly agreeable, but no more. At 12 o'clock I went to see Tindemans, whom I had not seen for a little time, to talk over with him the prospects for the European Council. As usual a good, friendly talk with his saying that he was going to present some proposals for currency advance, which I knew had been prepared in the Belgian Finance Ministry and which were agreeable to us (though in the outcome he did not do so).

Then back to the Berlaymont, where Harold Wilson had arrived. He wanted to come to Brussels in connection with his City of London inquiry,* and I was naturally happy to receive him. I had him met at the airport by a *cabinet* member (Etienne Reuter), and Hayden talked to him until I got back from Tindemans. I had Haferkamp, Noël, Vouël, Crispin, Hayden and Donald Maitland to lunch with him, and most of his conversation must I think have been totally incomprehensible to the three non-British present, as it was full of muttered asides about recondite details of English politics, which hardly anybody except him and me, and not always both of us, could be expected to understand. He was anxious to be very friendly, including producing some wonderful flights of fancy, such as that he had specially timed his resignation in order to be as helpful to me as possible, so that I could have the run which he knew I had to have, but which he feared would not be successful, and still take the European job.

However, he was at pains to urge me not to cut myself off from British politics now. I might well be needed in the future, he said. Callaghan was too old, Owen was too young. The whole outlook was very bad. He was filled with dismay. He did not think there was much future for the Government, or indeed the Labour Party. A coalition government would almost certainly be necessary; he would bless it from outside, but not serve. I, however, would undoubtedly be needed. Taking all this with several pinches of salt, I kept the conversation going in a way which I trust was reasonably agreeable to him, and indeed I believe was so, except when we got on to the question of voting or non-voting in the Commission and I compared it with voting practices in the British Cabinet. He looked most pained and said, 'There was never voting in the Cabinet in my day.' I allowed fantasy to triumph over fact and did not pursue the matter.

After lunch Wilson went to see Ortoli, I saw David Marquand and did a little work, and then took Wilson down to the front door.

---

*A committee under the chairmanship of Sir Harold Wilson had been appointed in January 1977 by his successor to inquire into the functioning at home and abroad of the financial institutions of the United Kingdom. It finally reported, without great excitement or import, in May 1980.

FRIDAY, 7 APRIL. *Brussels and Copenhagen.*

Avion taxi to Copenhagen, accompanied by Ortoli, Crispin, etc. To the Royal Hotel. I worked hard in the plane and a little in the hotel on an opening statement, although I was not quite clear when it would be made or what the exact order of business would be. Soon after 12.30 Ortoli and I drove to the Amalienborg Castle for the Queen's lunch. I was rather reluctant to go so early as the invitations only said 1 o'clock, but protocol, police, etc., were insistent that that was the right time to arrive for the photograph. Callaghan arrived as I did, and immediately got into a very bad temper, not particularly with me but in general on discovering that the other two 'big ones' had not turned up, and that Schmidt indeed was not due to touch down at the airport until about five minutes later. All the little ones, plus the Italians, had, however, assembled.

Schmidt eventually arrived at 1.20, followed by Giscard at least seven minutes after this. Gaston Thorn had typically and correctly pointed out that there was no question of Giscard arriving before Schmidt and that probably his car was tucked into a side road on the way in from the airport waiting to see Schmidt go past. If so he might at least have come along a minute or two behind him. However, they all seemed tolerably tempered during lunch at which I sat between van Agt and Genscher and had a better conversation with Genscher than ever previously.

We then went to the Christiansborg for the opening session of the Council, which occupied itself with rather minor items of business for an hour. Then the heads of government and I drove out to Marienborg, a nice castle about twenty miles from the centre of Copenhagen (plenty of castles in Denmark). We were supposed to start there at 6 o'clock and I arrived about five minutes early on a most beautiful evening. However, we did not start until 6.30 not, as Thorn again suggested, because Callaghan would this time be at least half an hour late in order to get his own back (in fact he was there on time, as on this occasion were Giscard and Schmidt), but because van Agt was extremely late. We eventually had to start without him, and when he was then asked at dinner if he had got lost or if he had mistaken the time, he blandly said no, he had been having a press conference and the Dutch press were the most *exigeant* in the world. Rather a good cool performance, I thought.

When we started there was no one in the room except for the ten of us and a *chuchotage* interpreter for Andreotti. Later a Danish official came in, I think because Jørgensen was not fully understanding all the rather complicated exchanges in English and was getting understandably worried about losing the drift of the matter for the record which he would subsequently have to provide.

Jørgensen opened very briefly and then I spoke for about fifteen minutes. Callaghan and then Giscard spoke for about the same. And then Schmidt went off into one of his long soliloquies, which with a certain amount of interruption took forty minutes. It was mainly about the problems of the German economy in an improvident world, but it contained one or two splendid side-swipes, such as complaining at one stage that he could not understand English English. Mine was the worst, Callaghan's almost equally bad, Lynch's an improvement, but only Giscard's impeccably pellucid. After this, Jack Lynch alone was able to get in about a seven-minute speech before we adjourned for dinner just after 8.00.

It had been a good-tempered, analytical, slightly gloomy discussion. Giscard was the most constructive in opening up some lines for the future. He did a rather good analysis of the six groups in the world, the three parts of the developing world and the three main groups in the industrialized world, ending up by saying that of the three industrialized groups we in the Community had recently done by far the worst for growth and general economic performance, and that he could not dissociate this deterioration in our performance from the new era of world currency instability, with us the only one of the three developed groups which had such instability not merely between us and the other groups, but internal to our Community itself. It was a helpful analysis.

However, in this part of the discussion we did not get very near (except for some trailing remarks on my part) to discussing any hard scheme for advance towards a possible exchange-rate bloc. Schmidt at this stage intended to hold his hand until the tripartite breakfast he was having with Giscard and Callaghan the following morning. As recently as ten minutes before the start of the session he had told me that these were his tactics and that while he did not mind how much I opened the subject up, I should not expect him to say much in even such a restricted session as the one which we were having.

Dinner was rather pointless. Callaghan and Lynch were not there until the end as they were having a bilateral discussion about Northern Ireland outside. Nobody seemed to have much to say to their neighbours or anybody else until Giscard tried to start some general conversation, which began on this occasion not with a reference to Sir Charles Dilkie (sic), but by his suddenly asking me if I had ever read 'un livre par une Américaine, Mademoiselle Tugwell, ou un quelconque nom, qui s'appelle, je crois, *Les Canons d'Août?*' So I said, 'Yes, I have indeed read *The Guns of August** by Barbara Tuchman,' and this led on to a long semi-general discussion about World War I and II commanders, the different effects of the wars upon differing countries and a variety of related subjects, ending up with a discussion of why, in England, there were now no generals or commanders whose names were known to the public, which Giscard slightly implausibly claimed was not the case in France.

We reassembled upstairs at 9.45 and went on until 11.30. Schmidt, whether through boredom or for some other reason, had completely changed his mind, his plan, or his tactics. He opened the discussion, and after only a very few preliminary words proceeded to spill the whole beans. He deployed his plans for dissolving the Snake in the new arrangement, using the European unit of account far more extensively, both for transactions between the member governments, for joint interventions against the dollar and third currencies, and possibly indeed for providing a full parallel currency, which could deal in stocks of raw materials and in which OPEC money might be encouraged to invest.

It took me a little time to realize that he was in fact giving a full *exposé* and therefore my own notes were not as coherent as they might have been. Broadly speaking, what he said was a firm repetition of what he had said to me in Bonn five weeks previously, except that at Copenhagen he did not offer to commit *all* reserves, only suggesting a significant proportion of the dollar reserves of all the participating countries, although, he implied, an almost limitless quantity of their indigenous currencies. What had however moved on very significantly since the end of February was the state of the play with Giscard. It was obvious that Schmidt's visit to Rambouillet the week before had completely lined up Giscard.

---

* Or *August 1914*, as it is called in the English edition.

Giscard in some ways went further than Schmidt, and provided a more coherent, intellectual framework to the argument than Helmut himself did on this occasion.

In the two-hour session there were no participants except for Schmidt, Giscard, Callaghan and me. The others all remained absolutely silent, including Tindemans, who probably rightly did not produce his plan, for what Schmidt had proposed went rather further than what he had in mind. Lynch, Thorn, van Agt did not speak either. Andreotti intervened only at the end to make an irrelevant point about Mediterranean agriculture. Jørgensen summed up in a not very convincing manner. Callaghan was taken aback, I think, because although he had been given a fair rehearsal of what Schmidt had in mind on his own visit to Bonn about two and a half weeks previously, I do not believe that he had then taken things in at all completely (for the reasons which I gave earlier).

Nevertheless Callaghan handled himself well, expressed interest, was polite, non-committal, but didn't turn things down out of hand, or make any foolish statements. He concentrated on his fear that what was proposed might appear as anti-dollar and might therefore be divisive from an Atlantic point of view. Although I believe that at the fundamental level this is the reverse of the truth, the fact that he should take this point could at least be understood, because Schmidt had spoken in strongly anti-Carter terms, saying that the whole management of the dollar by the American administration was absolutely intolerable. At one point indeed he said that no American President could lead the Alliance while presiding over such degradation of the dollar as he had witnessed during his period as Federal Chancellor.

When we were breaking up Callaghan said that he was not sure that he had taken in everything completely and could I therefore go round to his hotel that night and go through it with him, to which I naturally acceded, though admitting that I was not sure that I had got every Schmidt detail myself. Accordingly, late though it was, Crispin and I saw him in a room in which John Hunt with a very bad cold, two Private Secretaries (Stowe and Cartledge) and Ken Couzens,* the Finance Second Permanent Secretary, as his

*(Sir) Kenneth Couzens, b. 1925, was a Second Permanent Secretary (Overseas Finance) at the Treasury 1977–82, and Permanent Under-Secretary, Department of Energy, 1982–5.

Treasury title now is, were present. I summarized what Schmidt had said for about ten minutes. Callaghan then went through his own notes which tallied almost exactly.

He next asked other people what they thought. I said I had probably better leave for that discussion. He said, 'No, no, do stay.' But nobody had much to say, certainly not Hunt. Couzens looked rather pole-axed and kept on repeating, 'But it is very bold, Prime Minister. Did the Chancellor really go as far as that? It is very bold. It leaves the dollar on one side. I don't know what the Americans will say about it. It's very bold, Prime Minister.' After about twenty-five minutes of this, we went back to the Royal Hotel where I talked to Crispin before going to bed, in a state of some excitement, for it had been a remarkable day, at 2 o'clock.

SATURDAY, 8 APRIL. *Copenhagen and Brussels.*

Ortoli came to see me at 8.45, and I gave him an account of what had taken place. It had been agreed in the meeting that very little, if anything, would be said outside, and it was suggested indeed that in the follow-up arrangements each of the heads of government should consult only one collaborator, though this was a prescript which had hardly been followed by Callaghan, who had immediately debriefed five, and I do not suppose was followed by any others either.

The full European Council reassembled in the Christiansborg at 10.10 and went on until 12.40. Not a great deal of useful business was transacted. Jørgensen was an uncertain chairman. An interesting *vignette* was that towards the end of the morning, when Giscard was holding forth about French dissatisfaction with the degree of progress which we had been able to make with the Japanese, and was addressing some courteous but slightly critical remarks about the Commission (rather for the record, I thought) specifically to me, Schmidt came round the table and said, 'Could you quickly come and have a word with me?' I paused, being hesitant as to what to do, but then decided that a talk with Schmidt about monetary advance was more important than listening to Giscard on Japan, and therefore got up and talked with Schmidt in a window with both our backs to the Council and indeed to the continuing Giscard. Giscard allowed this to go by without comment or sign of umbrage.

If one is so foolish as to believe in the equality of the European Council, one has only to think how differently he would have reacted if it had been, say, Lynch or Thorn who had come round the table and taken me away.

What Schmidt had to say to me, however, was of considerable importance. He wanted to tell me about that morning's breakfast, which had not advanced things a great deal, except that Giscard had made it absolutely clear that if Callaghan did not come in, he (Giscard) would go along with Schmidt, and that France would be prepared to re-enter the Snake and stay there as from July. He, Schmidt, wanted me to know this, and to realize that Giscard was absolutely serious about it and he hoped that the British would realize the same. I was able to use the opportunity to tell him what I was proposing to say at the press conference afterwards, to which he said that he had no objection provided that it did not upset Callaghan, whom he wished to propitiate until he had had a private go at bringing him along. So I took the opportunity subsequently of telling Callaghan too what I intended to say, which he in turn took perfectly friendlily. Schmidt told me that his next step would be to talk to Callaghan, indicating that he would prepare a paper before this (though in fact he did not do so), and would keep in touch with me after that, as of course he would with Giscard.

After the session we had a hurried lunch with the three or four small-country Prime Ministers who had stayed (it was again typical that the big ones had gone), and I then gave an hour-long press conference (for about six hundred journalists) with Jørgensen, who did much better here than he had done as chairman. I apparently gave the impression of being extremely pleased with the outcome without saying too much. Left just after 4 o'clock by avion taxi for Brussels. An agreeable flight embellished by an hour's cultural conversation with Ortoli in French, which he, being in as ebullient a mood as I (but more surprisingly), seemed determined to have.

SUNDAY, 9 APRIL. *Brussels.*

A perfect day, one of the very few this spring. Jennifer and I picked up Helena Tiné and drove down the Namur autoroute to picnic in the same field near Maillen, with a good open view across the lower

Ardennes, in which we had picnicked on the last warm Sunday of the autumn in mid-October after my return from Japan.

MONDAY, 10 APRIL. *Brussels*.

Dinner in the *Economist* flat on a top floor in the rue Ducale, with their correspondents Stephen Milligan and Christopher Huhne, plus the Simonets. Milligan was obviously anxious to find out about Copenhagen. I decided to be too clever. I gave him a lot of circumstantial detail about who sat where, who talked a lot, who didn't, etc., but nothing of substance. However, as he subsequently published all the circumstantial detail, as well as a good deal of substance which he had picked up from elsewhere, it looked, not unnaturally, to Schmidt and others, as though I had told him the main story. Home at about 11.30, Solly Zuckerman having arrived to stay for three days.

TUESDAY, 11 APRIL. *Brussels and Luxembourg*.

9.20 train to Luxembourg with Hayden, I suffering a post-Copenhagen exhaustion. To the Court of Justice where we thought we were lunching with Kutscher, the President. We discovered the building almost completely empty, certainly exuding an appropriate atmosphere of judicial calm. Everybody, secretaries, justices certainly, clerks, most of the *huissiers*, everybody in fact except one doorman and the Italian Advocate-General had gone to lunch. No sign of any lunch there or anywhere else. Hayden telephoned increasingly frantically and eventually discovered that the lunch was at Kutscher's flat about three miles away. No car by that time. We stood outside on a bright but extremely cold day waiting for the car for a long time, and eventually got to Kutscher's flat fifty minutes late. My temper uncertain by then. However, Kutscher and his wife were as always extremely nice and perfectly understanding, though rather a brief lunch with them and others from the Court because I had to answer questions in the Parliament at 3.00. Later, after a series of interviews, I gave a pointless dinner at the Golf Club for some parliamentarians allegedly interested in External Affairs.

WEDNESDAY, 12 APRIL. *Luxembourg and Brussels.*
Commission from 8.30 to 9.30. Then into the Parliament, first to listen to K. B. Andersen's report on the European Council and then to give my own report. Lunched with Colombo in the Parliament building and received the President of the Spanish Cortes in the afternoon. Listened to and replied briefly to the debate from 4.00 until 6.00. A particularly bumpy avion taxi ride to Brussels, where I arrived too late to listen to Michael Palliser's lecture at the Institut Royal but went to the reception for it briefly and then took Solly Zuckerman out to dinner.

THURSDAY, 13 APRIL. *Brussels and Berlin.*
Flew to Berlin, with a change of plane at Frankfurt, over lunch time. To the Kempinski Hotel, where the City government had installed me in a magnificent suite at the top. Then to the Schöneberg Rathaus for a call on the Governing Mayor, Dietrich Stobbe, from 3.30 to 4.45. Mainly political talk with him about the Russians. I liked him very much.

Next to the Senate Guest House for a meeting with Mrs Juanita Kreps, the American Secretary of Commerce, whom I had not met before. She had asked for the meeting, and proceeded to behave in the most extraordinary way. Her object was to discover exactly what had happened at Copenhagen. Her method was to come into the meeting accompanied by seven or eight officials, of whom four were engaged in taking a verbatim note, and immediately, without establishing any sort of relations, to ask me what had there taken place. When I pushed the question away, she seemed rather miffed. But it was a most bizarre idea that I would suddenly spill the Copenhagen beans to somebody I had never met before who (i) showed no understanding of the subject, and (ii) sat around with a whole series of hard-faced note-takers.

On from there to the Chamber of Commerce, where I gave quite a good lecture for about forty-five minutes, attended a reception, and returned to the Senate Guest House for a fairly hard-working dinner with thirty guests for two hours or so.

Then back to the Kempinski for a talk with Lambsdorff, the German Economics Minister, from 10.30 to midnight. I had not known him well before and found him easy and agreeable, much more so than one might at first think. Physically, and even mentally, he is like a curious mixture of Iain Macleod and Donald Tyerman, the ex-editor of the *Economist* whom I nearly succeeded.

FRIDAY, 14 APRIL. *Berlin and East Hendred.*

A splendid morning panoramic view from the top of the Kempinski, with the Berlin weather as splendid as usual. Further talks at the Schöneberg Rathaus, made memorable by the deputy Mayor, who spoke the most excellent English, suddenly announcing that one of the major social problems in Berlin was the presence of two or three hundred thousand immigrant 'turkeys', who apart from anything else made a great deal of noise in the streets. I said 'What, after Christmas, as well as before,' and then, such is the English juvenile sense of humour, and our capacity for expecting linguistic perfection from others while not even attempting it ourselves, we all found it very difficult not to giggle for the rest of the meeting. Then a press conference and afterwards the signing of the Golden Book in the Schloss Charlottenburg with a nice gracious speech from Stobbe and a reply from me which was one third in German. An official lunch there, and then the 3 o'clock plane from Tegel. East Hendred via Frankfurt by 7.45.

MONDAY, 17 APRIL. *East Hendred and London.*

Motored to lunch with about forty American correspondents at the Waldorf Hotel. Made them an unprepared speech for about fifteen minutes and answered questions. I stressed that we were not pursuing an anti-American course by wanting somewhat to reduce the role of the dollar in world monetary affairs and to do something of our own in Europe, rather than merely complaining about what the Americans did or did not do. At 6.45 I went to Eaton Square for a forty-minute worthwhile monetary talk with Harold Lever,* whom I had not seen for some time. He wanted a little reassurance on the American point, but was sensible, sympathetic and generally helpful.

*Harold Lever, b. 1914, cr. Lord Lever of Manchester 1979, had been my Financial Secretary at the Treasury 1967–9, before entering the Cabinet as Paymaster-General. He also served in this office (and the Cabinet) 1974–9.

Then to address a grand European League for Economic Co-operation dinner of about two hundred people, a very powerfully representative gathering, marred typically by the twelve or fourteen MPs present having to go off in the middle of the speeches to cancel each other out in a vote in the House of Commons: the speech was both well received and well reported.

THURSDAY, 20 APRIL. *Brussels.*

A meeting with Doko, the very old President of the Japanese employers' organization, and the delegation he had brought. I am not sure how much progress we made, but I suppose it was worthwhile. Then a luncheon for the chairmen or the managing directors of about twenty-five European television chains. They all seemed keen on monetary union, but not as much so as my 3.30 deputation from the European Cooperative Savings Institute who came specifically to express their strong support.

FRIDAY, 21 APRIL. *Brussels and East Hendred.*

12.35 plane to London (late), and to East Hendred. Worked quite hard on my speech for that evening at the Vale of the White Horse Council's annual dinner in Abingdon. They had assembled a great European turn-up from Lucca, Montreuil, and the other twinned towns. I had assembled what I hoped was a number of apposite quotations, two from Chesterton and one from Matthew Arnold, but I suspect I would have done better if I had devoted the time to putting on a tail coat with decorations, which all the top table except me were wearing, rather than the dinner jacket which I thought was enough.

SATURDAY, 22 APRIL. *East Hendred and Birmingham.*

Motored to Birmingham in the early evening for a Stechford farewell party to Ruby and Oliver Rhydderch (two former council-lors). It was quite unlike last summer, no great sense of regret at going back to Birmingham, no sense of how awful it was that I was no longer MP there. They were extremely pleased to see me, though equally all extremely pro-Terry Davis (my successor), who was there, and who obviously turned up at everything; not that they criticized me for not doing that.

MONDAY, 24 APRIL. *East Hendred and Brussels.*

Stayed at East Hendred for the morning, not rushing back to Brussels, as I am increasingly of the view that I don't get much real work done in the Berlaymont. 3.30 plane, and to an International Medical Services dinner in the Amigo Hotel, to which David Ginsburg* persuaded me to go. I made them rather a dull speech after the first course. Belgian service excelled itself and was so incredibly slow that when I left at 11 o'clock the last course was still unserved.

TUESDAY, 25 APRIL. *Brussels.*

A noon meeting with the Portuguese Foreign Minister (Victor Sá Machado), who came into the Government following its widening to a coalition, and is not a socialist. He speaks very good English, unlike most Portuguese, mainly I suppose because he was Secretary-General of the Gulbenkian Foundation – or perhaps the other way round. The good news was that the long-drawn-out negotiations with the IMF were at last settled and that the Portuguese expect to sign in the near future.

Bob Maclennan,† Professor Maurice Peston,‡ David Marquand and Michel Vanden Abeele to lunch rue de Praetère. Peston I found an impressive man: I liked him very much indeed. He used to work for Reg Prentice and was rather fed up with what Reg had done, though still speaking of him with sad affection. We had a useful discussion about various points around the monetary union issue.

At 3 o'clock I went to the External Affairs Committee of the Parliament, opened for half an hour, listened to their comments, and wound up for twenty minutes at the end. I like this format of opening fairly informally, listening to what they say and then weaving what points one chooses into a reply.

*David Ginsburg, b. 1921, Labour and later SDP MP for Dewsbury 1959–83; a friend since Oxford days.
†Robert Maclennan, b. 1936, Labour and then SDP MP for Caithness and Sutherland since 1966, in 1978 a junior minister, leader of the SDP 1987–8.
‡Maurice Peston, b. 1931, cr. Lord Peston 1987, has been Professor of Economics at Queen Mary College, London, since 1965.

I saw Christopher Tugendhat for an hour on a number of his points, but also because I wished to tell him I had now decided, fully in accordance with his wishes, to relieve him of the Personnel portfolio with the intention of giving it to Vredeling. He made no difficulty about this.

WEDNESDAY, 26 APRIL. *Brussels.*

Six rather tiresome hours in the Commission, particularly at the end of the morning on a Vouël paper on State Aids (to industry), which had been badly prepared by the *Chefs de Cabinet*. I was much worse briefed than I usually am on what is likely to come up. However, no disasters, although mildly irritating.

An Economic and Social Committee dinner at Basil de Ferranti's* flat, mainly for Leslie Murphy, Ryder's successor as Chairman of the National Enterprise Board. There were various other people like le Portz of the European Investment Bank, Provost, President of UNICE, and Debunne, the chief Belgian trade unionist. A general discussion after dinner, which I had to lead and which was not too bad. Murphy a bit sceptical on monetary questions. But Provost and one or two others obviously excited at what they thought had been the real progress at Copenhagen and how it had followed on from my Florence speech, which was encouraging.

THURSDAY, 27 APRIL. *Brussels and Madrid.*

1.40 plane to Madrid. First a meeting of one and a half hours with Calvo Sotelo, the minister in charge of the negotiation, and various members of his *équipe*. To the Ritz Hotel to change and see Jennifer who had arrived from London, and then to an hour's meeting at the Palacio Moncloa with Suárez, the Prime Minister. Found him as impressive as at our previous meeting. He afterwards gave a dinner of about forty people, remarkable for the fact that he had the leader of the Socialist Party, Felipe Gonzales, the Secretary-General of the Communist Party, Carrillo, and the deputy leader of the Catalan Nationalist Party, as well as most of the major ministers, round the table. As I said in my brief speech after dinner, there were not many countries in the Community, or indeed in the world, where such a

* Basil de Ferranti, 1930–88, was Chairman of the Economic and Social Committee (of the Community) 1976–8, and a (Conservative) MEP 1979–88.

cross-section could have been assembled, although I suppose Britain is one of them, and Italy another, but it would certainly not have happened in France, and probably not in Germany. Home very late, dinner not starting until nearly 11 o'clock.

FRIDAY, 28 APRIL. *Madrid.*

Left at 9.15 for the drive out to Zarazuela, the King's semi-country palace. It is in fact more a large modern villa than a palace, though set in a big park about fifteen miles from the centre of Madrid. An hour's talk alone with him, in which he struck me, much as in Brussels six months before, as being agreeable, quick, with a non-regal manner, shrewd rather than intellectual. He expressed some concern about the coolness of Spanish public opinion in the street towards Europe, which was more than any of his ministers said to me.

Back to the centre of Madrid, indeed into the old town for the first time, for a meeting at the Foreign Ministry with Oreja, young, bright, quick, if not heavyweight, on a wide range of foreign policy questions. Then back to the Ritz, where Calvo Sotelo came to see me to follow up how we were to deal with one particularly difficult point relating to the renegotiation of the 1970 agreement which had arisen the evening before.

Then, at 1.15, to the Danish Ambassador's residence to brief the ambassadors of the Nine, including Antony Acland, Bobbie de Margerie* and others not known to me. I liked them rather better than the Community ambassadors in Portugal. Then, at 2.15, to a lunch of industrialists (or *empresarios* as they are rather surprisingly called in Spanish), which took place in the Financial Club, a newish institution at the top of a fourteen-storey building with a very good view over Madrid and out into the barren countryside beyond the edge of the city, which remains fairly concentrated, even though the population has now gone up to four million.

A dullish but not testing press conference at 4.45, and then to the Cortes for a meeting with the President and his various Deputies. A rather stilted discussion with them with inadequate interpretation and therefore a good deal of bad French.

*Emmanuel (Bobbie) de Margerie, b. 1924, French Ambassador to Spain 1977–81, became Ambassador in London 1981–4, before being transferred to Washington.

Back to the Ritz and then, at 9 o'clock, a Calvo Sotelo dinner for about thirty people in the Palacio Fernan Nunez, an old Madrid *hôtel particulier*, built about 1750 and then done up rather sumptuously in the height of the style of the 1840s and taken over some time in the last thirty or forty years by Spanish railways, of which Calvo Sotelo had in the 1960s been President.

SATURDAY, 29 APRIL. *Madrid and Toledo.*

To the Prado for an hour. The Velasquez and Goya rooms immensely impressive, but I found El Grecos *en masse* rather disappointing. He curiously fails to gain from being displayed in great quantity. Then a short walk through the Plaza Mayor. Left for Toledo just after noon. After a tedious drive on a bad road, through dismal suburbs with heavy traffic, low cloud and a nasty light, we installed ourselves in the extremely comfortable Parador Nacional de Conde de Orgaz. That evening there was still a disagreeable hard light, though the view across the Tagus Valley to Toledo from the parador, with the cathedral, the Alcazar, and the other buildings rising on a hill above a bend of the river, is quite remarkable.

We had the Aclands to dinner, and much enjoyed seeing them again, although I thought them only moderately happy in Madrid, partly because a fourteen-storey bank is being built with great noise and dust alongside their embassy.

SUNDAY, 30 APRIL. *Toledo.*

Sight-seeing expeditions across the valley in the morning (the cathedral and the Alcazar), and again in the early evening (the Hospital de Tovero outside the walls of the town, and Santo Tome with the magnificent El Greco, the burial of the Conde de Orgaz). From 7.30 to 9.00 I sat working and reading, partly on the balcony and partly in my room with the window open, in one of the most magnificent lights I have ever seen, a complete contrast with the evening before, still cold, still windy, but the clouds had broken up, giving a brilliant late-April sharpness, with snow-covered mountains to the north of Segovia (nearly a hundred miles away) clearly visible in the last hour of sunlight.

MONDAY, 1 MAY. *Madrid and Brussels.*

Made to leave Toledo for Madrid airport much too early, which I hate doing. We were there over an hour before the plane was even due to take off. We hung about in the VIP lounge, with various members of the send-off party trickling in, and it was therefore not possible even to get down to any useful work or reading. Calvo Sotelo wisely left his arrival (to say goodbye) until the last possible moment, saying he had been held up by the traffic – a very sensible man in my view. Brussels at 1.15. To lunch a little late with the Danes: Foreign Minister, Permanent Secretary, Permanent Representative.

TUESDAY, 2 MAY. *Brussels.*

Foreign Affairs Council at 9.30 and all day including lunch until 5.30, when I left. There was a slightly obscure debate about protectionism, mainly between Lambsdorff and Owen, in which Owen uttered some of the most protectionist sentiments – unprepared, I think – that I have ever heard.

Then, towards the latter part of the morning, I introduced the 'fresco' on enlargement, which was surprisingly politely received by all the ministers. I rather feared that they would think we had been a mountain in labour and had produced a mouse, but although there were some points of disagreement about the transitional periods and some desire for more detail on economic matters, they all accepted the document as a good beginning and welcomed the fact that we kept it to twenty pages. Genscher was particularly forthcoming.

Dined with the Nanteuils in their new large suburban villa at Tervuren, with which they seemed very pleased compared with their previous less convenient but more distinguished town house in Ixelles. After dinner I was given an interesting little lecture by Huré, the French Ambassador to the Kingdom of Belgium, about the difference between the state and the nation in French political thought. Giscard, he thought, was too concerned with the nation, whereas the French desperately needed the state to hold them together as they were inherently febrile and undisciplined. Hence the need for Napoleon, de Gaulle, etc. Debré,* from the death of whose father the conversation started, exaggerated appallingly but nonetheless such exaggeration was necessary for the balance of French politics. It ended up by Huré saying that Pompidou – partly because he had more humble origins – understood the state as opposed to the nation much more than did Giscard, i.e. was much more of a Napoleon, whereas poor Giscard was left to be a Louis Philippe!

WEDNESDAY, 3 MAY. *Brussels.*

Five and a half hours of Commission. The long item in the morning was on the agricultural price position, with a report from Gundelach as to the result he saw being arrived at the following week. Everything seemed reasonably satisfactory except for wine, on which he had gone substantially further than authorized in the Commission a few weeks before. A slightly acrimonious exchange with him, but the Italians and the French being of course solid with him, and not much fight in anybody else, there was no chance of doing more than pulling him back very marginally. In the afternoon a moderately good discussion on the draft of the first part of the 'opinion' on Portugal's application for membership.

A monetary affairs lunch with four *cabinet* members, rue de Praetère. A drive and walk in the Forêt de Soignes for an hour before dinner; a beautiful evening, the weather having changed at lunchtime, and for the first time this year we saw the sun slanting through the light green beech leaves which are the best feature of Brussels in May.

THURSDAY, 4 MAY. *Brussels and London.*

Having decided not to go to Aachen for the Karlspreis Ceremony, and it being a Commission holiday, I went to London in mid-morning with Jennifer, and there worked on my speech for the Reform Club banquet that evening, which was to mark their having made me one of their few honorary members. It was a gathering of about a hundred and fifty, including I think six of the Nine

---

* Michel Debré, b. 1912, had been the first Prime Minister of the Fifth Republic 1959–62, and was subsequently Minister of Finance and then of Foreign Affairs 1966–9. His father, Professor Robert Debré, was a leader of French medicine.

ambassadors, Michael Palliser, etc. I had prepared a speech for the occasion with a lot of Reform Club references, with only a little serious stuff at the end. However they indicated during the day and on arrival that they hoped I would give them a full-scale serious European talk. I therefore had to do a combination of the two and, as a result, took forty-five minutes.

FRIDAY, 5 MAY. *London and Oxford.*

Another filthy day, pouring with rain from morning till night. In the afternoon I motored to Oxford to deliver the Cyril Foster Memorial Lecture. Tea in Michael Howard's* room in All Souls and then across to the South School of the Examination Schools, where to my amazement there were about five hundred people, including one or two surprising figures like Ann Fleming and the Michael Astors, and also the Hayters† and a lot of undergraduates. The lecture seemed to be curiously and jointly presided over by Raymond Carr, Warden of St Antony's, and Robert Blake, Provost of Queen's, he in his capacity as one of the pro-Vice-Chancellors. It was a solid lecture, lasting fifty-seven minutes, about relations with the Third World. There was some quite interesting material in it and it was well listened to by the audience, but it was certainly not sparkling. An early dinner at St Antony's for about forty.

MONDAY, 8 MAY. *London and Manchester.*

Peter Preston, editor of the *Guardian*, to lunch at Brooks's. I found him remarkably agreeable: not difficult to talk to as I half-expected, very European, well-informed, and sensible on practically everything.

5.20 train to Manchester. Installed in the same suite in the Midland Hotel in which John Harris, Irwin Ross‡ and I had sat gloomily sipping whisky and sweating prodigiously on the hottest English evening I can remember after a bad meeting (Manchester meetings mostly are) in the Albert Hall in June 1970, and where I

* (Sir) Michael Howard, b. 1922, was then Chichele Professor of the History of War and has been Regius Professor of Modern History 1981–9.
† Sir William Hayter, b. 1906, was British Ambassador in Moscow 1953–7, and Warden of New College, Oxford, 1958–76.
‡ Irwin Ross, b. 1919, is a New York journalist/author, whom I have known since 1953.

had begun to wonder whether that election really was in the bag after all.

On this occasion there was a dinner for about thirty people, given by the *Sun*,* with brief speeches. I sat between Larry Lamb† and a Tate and Lyle director called, surprisingly, Tate. Lamb and all the *Sun* people were in very buoyant mood, as they had just got news that they had decisively passed the *Mirror* and become the largest circulation newspaper – a considerable feat in such a short time – meaning, as I indicated in my speech, that the decision of the old *Mirror* Group to put the *Sun* on to the market was one of the most ill-judged acts in the history of British journalism. To have kept it there like Hemingway's fish, fastened to their boat, gnawed at but protective, would have been much wiser.

TUESDAY, 9 MAY. *Manchester and Strasbourg.*

A brilliant morning with spectacular Manchester sunshine, but I saw little of it as we were incarcerated in the Midland Hotel for the *Sun*-organized seminar on the Common Agricultural Policy. A rather good and worthwhile gathering. I spoke for thirty-five or forty minutes at the beginning, then we had 'the assessors', Neil Marten MP,‡ plus a rather good farmer from Cheshire, plus Professor John Marsh from Aberdeen plus a Co-operative Wholesale Society manager. I replied to them for twenty minutes and then left by avion taxi for Strasbourg. I arrived in the Parliament just after 4 o'clock, where I received the news of the death of Aldo Moro§ at the hands of his Italian kidnappers. Recorded a brief television statement on this shattering event for the Italian state and government, and therefore, indirectly, for the Community.

WEDNESDAY, 10 MAY. *Strasbourg.*

An easy Commission meeting from 9.00 to 10.00. Then into the Chamber, luckily, as little Fellermaier without any notice got up on

*Then quite radical, and with more political content than today.
† (Sir) Larry Lamb, b. 1929, was editor of the *Sun* 1975–81, and of the *Daily Express* 1983–6.
‡ (Sir) Neil Marten, 1916–86, was the anti-Common Market Conservative MP for Banbury 1959–83.
§ Aldo Moro, 1916–78, had been Prime Minister of Italy 1963–8 and 1974–6, and was at that time President of the Christian Democratic Party.

a complicated point of order which turned out to be a justified complaint about the very poor attendance and performance of the Commission at question period the previous day. Only Burke and Vredeling had been there. We had discussed this at the Commission meeting that morning, deciding that we must strengthen the team for Thursday and in future. I therefore had an answer, but felt I had to change my plans, stay in Strasbourg and do Thursday questions myself. I also settled down to a Wednesday in the *hémicycle*, making a series of brief speeches up to 7.30 p.m.

In one interval I took David Wood of *The Times* to lunch, mainly gossiping about British politics of the past. And in another interval I had a useful drink with Dohnanyi and discovered that he was keen to present some paper to the German Government about a very substantial increase in European Investment Bank funds to be used as a sort of mini-Marshall Plan for the applicant countries. Good as far as it goes, which may be quite a long way.

My change of plan had defeated the Sofitel (though this was not entirely a bad thing in view of our opinion of it) who could not have us for another night. We therefore went to Illhaeusern.

THURSDAY, 11 MAY. *Strasbourg and Brussels.*

Left Illhaeusern at 7.45, though not quite early enough, to drive hectically to Strasbourg Cathedral for a memorial Mass for Moro. Just squeezed into the front row between Colombo and Natali. It was a longer service than I had expected, nearly a full hour, good music, splendid setting, high Mass and communion service for everybody; a fairly good attendance. And then a quick breakfast in the Place de la Cathédrale before spending the morning in the Parliament. In my afternoon question hour I answered five out of six questions, all going reasonably smoothly, and, as in December, quite enjoying the occasion.

FRIDAY, 12 MAY. *Brussels.*

Hilda and George Canning (my Stechford chairman) arrived to stay. John Harris and Jennifer were also due to arrive, but they were diverted by a strike and indeed had a ghastly journey as the driver missed them at Lille.

SATURDAY, 13 MAY. *Brussels, Rome and Brussels.*

Jennifer took the Cannings to Walcheren, Middelburg and Vlissengen in order to see some of the scenes of George's exploits in the Navy during the war. I left for Rome by avion taxi just after 1.00 for the grand Moro memorial Mass. Two in a week was perhaps rather much, but the Italian Government had made it fairly clear that they would greatly appreciate my presence. John Harris and Hayden came with me for the ride. Met by Forlani, the Foreign Minister, and Natali, as well as by the rather typical news that the ceremony had been put back by half an hour on security grounds. (It was not clear why keeping the congregation waiting for a longer time in St John Lateran was going to help security.)

We arrived at the basilica, which is of course magnificent, at 3.45. The Mass started late even for the postponed time of 4.30. The Pope (Paul VI) made an exceptional appearance outside the Vatican* and was borne in on his ceremonial chair carried by ten men who, although presumably practised, were a little unsteady. This did not impair the dignity of his blessing as he swayed around six feet above the ground; no doubt he is used to that. His presence and demeanour were impressive. The service was beautiful, with haunting music, though, to me, cold, but perhaps that was because I did not know Moro. It took a long time and it was 5.45 before we left the church. Not many heads of government – Thorn and Tindemans I think were the only ones – but there was a fairly substantial representation nonetheless. Elwyn-Jones (Lord Chancellor) for the British, Peyrefitte (Minister of Justice) for the French. There was also a remarkable turn-out of Italian politicians. All the Christian Democrats, apart from poor Cossiga† who had resigned as Minister of the Interior and was not there, but also Berlinguer as well as most of the Socialists.

Rather a jam of the planes of various governments at Ciampino so that we did not get into the air until just after 7 o'clock Italian time (8 o'clock Brussels time). Nonetheless we got to rue de Praetère in time for dinner with the Cannings and Phillips' at 10.15.

---

*I think his last; he died twelve weeks later.
†Francesco Cossiga, b. 1928, was Italian Minister of the Interior 1976–8, Prime Minister 1979–80, President of the Senate 1983–5, and has been President of the Italian Republic since 1985.

TUESDAY, 16 MAY. *Brussels.*

Henri Simonet to lunch. As usual it was a pleasure to talk to him. He seemed at that stage on perfectly good form and not unduly apprehensive of what was happening in Zaïre, although taking the mistaken view that while the Belgians might have to do something, the French were unlikely to move.*

WEDNESDAY, 17 MAY. *Brussels.*

Seven hours of Commission, with a COREPER lunch, which is by no means a relaxation, in the middle. I gave the Commission a great lecture in the morning about inadequate attendance at the European Parliament.

Arrived late with Jennifer to dine with the Australian Ambassador for the Whitlams, who were visiting. A curiously mixed party, with the Papal Nuncio apparently substituting for the Ambassador's non-existent wife. The Whitlams in buoyant form as usual. I enjoyed talking to Mrs Whitlam, who really is a rather splendid figure. He is going to give up politics and become a professor at the National University at Canberra. Also present were Roy Denmans and Marquands. David Marquand is now finally going, having got his chair at Salford. He has written two or three extremely good speeches for me, but I do not think that he has found quite enough worthwhile to do.

THURSDAY, 18 MAY. *Brussels.*

I gave a lunch for the *Daily Telegraph* – William Deedes (the editor) plus the foreign editor, plus a leader writer. I enjoyed the occasion. Deedes is not a scintillating man (although he has other virtues), nor were the other two, but they seemed favourable and friendly and therefore it was worthwhile. Then a two-hour session with the Political Affairs Committee of the Parliament about enlargement.

At 6 o'clock I saw John Palmer of the *Guardian*, who asked

---

*On 11 May 4000 Zaïre rebels with alleged support from Russia, Cuba, Libya and Algeria had invaded Zaïre from Angola and captured the town and airport of Kolwezi. On 17 May the French decided to send in paratroops to restore the situation, and presented the Belgians, who believed they had special responsibility for the old Belgian Congo, with a *fait accompli*. Eventually, on 19 May, Belgian troops arrived too.

curiously desultory questions, but we got on in a reasonably friendly way, which is at least an improvement on a year ago. I had in fact been extremely nice about him (although I have no idea whether he knew that) to Peter Preston ten days before, saying, which is indeed the truth, that he was much the best informed of the British correspondents in Brussels.

Wayland Kennet* and Jacques Tiné and three or four others to dine. Jacques Tiné on very good and funny form, apparently delighted to get away from his NATO society, which I think bores him considerably. Wayland is keen to stand for the European Parliament, but he is not at all clear where he is going to find a seat he can win. Nor am I.

SATURDAY, 20 MAY. *Brussels and Nyborg.*

Avion taxi to Odense and then helicopted to Hesselet, near Nyborg, for the Danish 'Schloss Gymnich' meeting, which was held in a very smart, curiously Japanese-style hotel on the edge of the sea. When I got into the helicopter at Odense, David Owen and van der Klaauw, the nice Dutch Foreign Minister, were already sitting in it. Van der Klaauw was as agreeable as ever, but David was apparently in a very bad temper and scowled most ferociously at everybody in sight. Ostensibly that was because Simonet was not coming. However, David's temper, performance and general agreeableness improved substantially as the weekend went on. Simonet's absence persisted.

There was a considerable general to-do over lunch about this. Guiringaud had not arrived, but was definitely coming during the evening, and it was thought very desirable to have them both together to hear what each had to say about Zaïre and to try and patch up the difficulty which had arisen between them. I spoke to Simonet on the telephone during lunch and got a promise out of him that he would come at 7 o'clock, but he then went back on that, claiming that there was a special Belgian Cabinet meeting (there was one floating around, but it never took place). What is more likely is that Henri, finding himself in a rather impossible situation, decided to go to ground.

*The 2nd Lord Kennet, b. 1923, has been a Labour and then an SDP peer.

In the afternoon we had a discussion on enlargement, which was an agreeable seminar but not much more. Then I had a walk and long talk with Genscher. We had two further sessions, one from 5.15 to 7.00, and another from dinner until midnight. In the latter we listened to a long and extremely impressive *exposé* by Guiringaud of the French position in Zaïre. It was much the best thing that I have heard Guiringaud do. He spoke for about forty minutes, quietly, slowly, very clearly, with great knowledge and therefore great conviction; great knowledge of exactly what had happened from hour to hour, and of the position on the ground, although I think he had never been to Kolwezi.

SUNDAY, 21 MAY. *Nyborg, Hamburg and Copenhagen.*

I flew to Hamburg in the early afternoon for the DGB (German trade unions) Conference. An audience of about two thousand, speeches by Vetter and then by Scheel, the Federal President. Scheel's was very long, almost exactly an hour, and certainly not a conventional speech from a head of state. I would guess he had written it all himself. He tried to deal with the balance between growth and ecological and environmental considerations, and did so interestingly if in some ways naïvely. I spoke for twelve minutes, the first two paragraphs in German. When at the end of them I announced, 'I am now going to turn to English, which will perhaps be as big a relief to you as it is to me,' there was tumultuous applause, but it was a little ambiguous whether this was a tribute to my German, or an expression of deep relief.

The Conference had a remarkable turn-up of German politicians (and of some others, including Jack Jones). Apart from Scheel, there was also Carstens, the Christian Democrat President of the Bundestag, Kohl, leader of the CDU, as well as most of the SPD ministers, Apel, Matthöfer, etc. Then back to Denmark by avion taxi, arriving at the Hôtel d'Angleterre in Copenhagen just after 7 o'clock.

MONDAY, 22 MAY. *Copenhagen and Greenland.*

Airport at 10.30 to be informed that the plane was at least an hour and a half late. I therefore insisted on doing some sight-seeing and went first to Koger, a former Dutch settlement on the sea looking across to Sweden, next to the Francis Church, with the winding exterior staircase going up to the copper spire, to the bottom of which Laura and I climbed, and then back briefly to the Angleterre for a drink, until we were summoned to the airport and arrived exactly seven minutes before take-off at 1 o'clock: a satisfactory defeat of airport time-wasting.

Then a flight of just over four hours to Søndre Strømfjord, across Iceland, then over the very high mountains of western Greenland, then across the endless waste of the Ice Cap and into Søndre Strømfjord, in quite good weather, at 1.10 Greenland time. A quick turn-round and off in a helicopter for nearly two hundred miles to Sukkertoppen (Sugarloaf). Remarkable scenery, all off the Ice Cap, but flying over a sunny, snowbound landscape (ground temperature probably about 38°F) down fjords of quite remarkable length, steepness and complication, mainly frozen up but a little less so as we got to the sea.

At Sukkertoppen we were greeted by a demonstration, though it didn't seem a very serious one, being mainly composed of school-children out for the afternoon, organized indeed by the bearded deputy headmaster, but with lots of slogans like 'No Rome rule', 'Go home Father Christmas Jenkins', 'Greenland out of the EEC'. The deputy headmaster made a speech, I made a speech in response, it was all quite good-tempered, although by walking slowly in front of us they blocked our way down from the landing pad to the public hall, where we had a meeting with the town council, who were all rather friendly and constructive. I think the Green-landers could be persuaded to stay in the Community, but whether that is good for them or for us is another matter.

We then helicopted on to Atangmik, a settlement of about 180 people on the sea, a bleak place, where we wandered around in slushy snow and saw a rather pathetic fishing hut where they produced cod's roe and also dried cod carcases which hang up and are then exported to – of all places – Nigeria. Then we had a sort of village meeting, rather reminiscent of some election meetings, in which about sixty people shuffled in rather reluctantly and stood at the back. The mayor, if that is the right word, made quite a good, sensible speech, which he had typed out, and I responded. What they made of my speech I cannot think, particularly as it had to be translated via Danish into Greenlandic.

Then on into Godthåb and to the Hotel Grønland for a brief pause before going to dine with the Governor in a party of about twenty, with good food round a crowded dining table in a clapboard house built about 1800. I was getting a bit tired by the end of dinner (11 p.m. local time, 3 a.m. Copenhagen time) although it was still broad daylight.

TUESDAY, 23 MAY. *Greenland.*

A morning tour of the projects mainly paid for by the Community: a new airstrip, a fish packing factory and a technical college. Then an early lunch in the hotel given by the municipality of Godthåb (or Nuuk as it is called in Greenlandic). This was rather like a Chinese meal, with a splendid series of optional dishes. The first course was composed of herrings, eels, plaice, shrimps, ham and a variety of other things. Then there was a whole range of hot courses: a duck, liver and bacon, slices of pork, lamb chops, with nearly everything in sight imported from 2000 miles away. With the subsidy they get (partly from us, but mainly from Denmark) no doubt they can afford it.

There was a nice speech from the deputy mayor (the mayor was in Canada) and a substantial response from me. Then a 2.15 meeting with various politicians, officials, etc., during which the Governor told us that bad weather was moving in fast from the south, and that we might be stuck for days if we did not get away quick. Accordingly, after a press conference, we took off for Søndre Strømfjord at 4.30. We dined at the fairly basic hotel there with the large contingent from the Danish Ministry of Greenland which was accompanying us, the only slightly smaller one from the Danish Foreign Ministry, the Governor, who had flown out and was indeed coming back to Copenhagen with us for no very good reason, and a few politicians, including Motzfeldt, who was the leader of the left-wing opposition to the EEC and the most intelligent politician I met in Greenland.

WEDNESDAY, 24 MAY. *Greenland and Brussels.*

An expedition down to the port which was about 14 kms away, and which was still frozen up but which will become ice-free within

three or four weeks and remain so until mid-November. Then up to
a high point above the airfield with a magnificent view looking up
to the remarkable phenomenon of the Ice Cap, which begins about
twenty miles away. It extends over 90 per cent of the country, is
about 1700 miles long and 900 miles wide, has a depth in places of
10, 11 or even 12,000 feet, and nobody is certain what exactly is
underneath it. It contains such a volume of frozen water that, were
it to melt, the level of the sea all over the world would go up about
17 metres, which would obliterate a good number of major cities.

One o'clock plane to Copenhagen, where we arrived just after
9 p.m., and Brussels by avion taxi an hour and a half later. Fernand
Spaak, our Washington representative, called for a late-night talk.

THURSDAY, 25 MAY. *Brussels.*

An hour's meeting with Ecevit,* Turkish Prime Minister. He presented a series of detailed demands, which I think I turned reasonably, while stressing that we wanted very much to put things on a
better basis and that we had no intention of allowing the Greeks to
import the Aegean quarrel into the Community. A lunch of twenty
people for him, with speeches afterwards, in the Berlaymont.

FRIDAY, 26 MAY. *Brussels and Lucca.*

Plane to Milan for my Whitsun holiday. It took off late but then,
almost unbelievably, I got from Brussels to Pisa, including a change,
in two hours. Jennifer and the Gilmours were still at the airport,
having been much more delayed, so we drove out together and
arrived at La Pianella at 2.30. As we mounted the drive it typically
began to rain and poured for the rest of the day.

FRIDAY, 2 JUNE. *Lucca and Paris.*

Uncertainly better weather. 5.15 plane from Pisa to Paris via Milan.
Over an hour late at Orly. Drove to the Embassy where, with the
Hendersons out to dinner, I worked until midnight on boxes of
papers which had arrived from Brussels. A perfect evening in Paris,

*Bülent Ecevit, b. 1925, was intermittently Prime Minister 1974–9, and intermittently
imprisoned, following the military coup, 1980–2.

the continuation of the spectacular period of weather which had been going on all over Northern Europe while we had been rained upon in Italy.

SATURDAY, 3 JUNE. *Paris.*

Worked in my room all the morning and then lunched with Nicko, Mary and Jennifer on the terrace. Dined at the Brasserie Lipp with the Hendersons, Alex Grall, the head of the publishers Fayard, and Françoise Giroud.* I liked him very much indeed. (I had met her before.) We drove back round the Île St Louis and the Île de la Cité on a very warm summer evening with Paris looking splendid, the streets full of people and a greater sense of animation than I had felt there since the thirties.

MONDAY, 5 JUNE. *Brussels.*

A quite interesting 10.30 meeting with the Yugoslav Ambassador. The Yugoslavs present a problem no less than the Turks at the moment, and there is therefore a need to treat them with considerable sensitivity in view of their hinge position and the possible complications of Tito's death, whenever that comes.

Downstairs to receive Morarji Desai,† Prime Minister of India, first for a private talk and then for a lunch with about half the Commissioners. I had not seen him since the Commonwealth Finance Ministers' Conference in 1968. I remembered particularly his very graceful reply to my toast in the Painted Hall at Greenwich. In spite of a lot of fuss beforehand about what he could or could not eat, with his own chef being sent in and some worry on our part as to whether *we* ought to have alcohol, it was a particularly agreeable lunch, Desai making a striking impression. Whether he is a great man or not, I don't know. What he is, more surprisingly, is an extremely agreeable man, who talks very freely about Indian and world politics, perhaps slightly self-righteous, but with enough sense of humour to make it tolerable. We had a normal meal, with

*Françoise Giroud, b. 1916, was a State Secretary in the Giscard Government from 1974–6, first for Women's Affairs and then for Culture.
†Morarji Desai, b. 1896, had been deputy Prime Minister and Minister of Finance 1967–9, was imprisoned by Mrs Gandhi from 1975 until 1977, and then became Prime Minister 1977–9.

wine, about which he seemed totally unconcerned. The Indians with him mostly had normal meals but without alcohol. He had his own meal, composed of bits of garlic, bits of milk, bits of curd, bits of God knows what else, but with no sign of his special recycled drink. Towards the end of the meal one of our more sodden and less bright elderly waiters swayed towards him trying to pour out a large glass of Rémy Martin. 'No, no,' I said hurriedly, 'I don't think that would be quite right for the Indian Prime Minister.' Desai thought it rather funny. He made an agreeable speech afterwards, and it was generally a good occasion.

An afternoon's work, a 6 o'clock meeting with Ortoli, and then to a dinner with the Confederation of European Socialist Parties, to which most other Socialist Commissioners came. Robert Pontillon, the International Secretary of the French Socialist Party since Guy Mollet's day, was in the chair. It was *just* a worthwhile occasion, with a tolerable but not very exciting discussion afterwards.

TUESDAY, 6 JUNE. *Brussels, Luxembourg and Brussels.*

Avion taxi to Luxembourg at 8.15. A quick meeting on the agenda with K. B. Andersen and into the Foreign Affairs Council. No hiccups in the morning, and then a Council lunch largely taken up by my giving them an account of my meeting with Ecevit, in which they were unusually interested. Council again from 2.45. Desultory at times, blockage on the Regional Fund between the Italians and the Germans, which I almost, but not quite, alas, managed to solve. I was tired of the Council by 7.45 and went back to Brussels (even though it went on until 9.30) by avion taxi.

WEDNESDAY, 7 JUNE. *Brussels.*

Commission for seven and a half hours. Lunch with Henri Simonet who was just a little battered I thought about Zaïre, but not more than that.

I had Francis Ortoli to dine alone, rue de Praetère. Rather good conversation, probably more French than English, but a lot of it about linguistics. He claimed, surprisingly and I think hyperbolically, though no doubt flattering in intention, that he could always understand my English very well, much more so, he claimed, than either Tugendhat's or Burke's,* mainly, he said, because our minds operated so similarly that he could always tell the direction of my thought even though my language was complicated!

THURSDAY, 8 JUNE. *Brussels and London.*

An 11 o'clock meeting with the Austrian Foreign Minister (Pahr), who was a very sensible and worthwhile man with whom I had an hour's conversation. Then I saw Ronald Butt of *The Times/Sunday Times*. I have never been a fan of his, but he was friendly and sensible on this occasion. Then, suddenly, a request from Sigrist, the German Permanent Representative, to pay an urgent call. He arrived to explain that Genscher had made a diary cock-up for the following week and could not fulfil his luncheon engagement with me for the following Tuesday in Strasbourg. Would I accept Dohnanyi in his place and have Genscher to lunch a few weeks later? It hardly seemed to warrant a special ambassadorial visit, but this was I suppose courteous.

A COREPER lunch which was much as usual. At 3.15 I saw Garland, the Australian Minister for Special Trade Negotiations, an agreeable, youngish man whom I had met before. We had decided beforehand to give him slightly rough treatment in view of the way Fraser behaves and to tell him that there was no future in this. We wanted to improve relations with Australia but we would be damned if we would be bullied into doing so, and if they went on making disobliging statements after every meeting it would make it very difficult to achieve anything. I was not sure how taken aback he was. I think his Ambassador may have warned him, but at any rate he was uneasy and never recovered the initiative. I was able to end the interview more graciously by taking him to the lift and talking about one or two mutual acquaintances.

6.25 plane (semi-punctual) to London, and to the Harlechs† by 8.15 for the dinner preceding their ball. The dinner was for thirty-two or thirty-six, with a curious mixture of strands: Mrs Onassis, Sam Spiegel, Droghedas, David Cecils, Lee Remick, Peter Hall, for

* Cf. Helmut Schmidt, entry for 7 April 1978.
† David Ormsby Gore, 1918–85, succeeded as the 5th Lord Harlech in 1964. He was British Ambassador in Washington 1961–5. He married Pamela Colin as his second wife in 1969. (Sissie, killed in a car accident in 1967, was his first wife.)

example. I sat between Pamela Harlech and Jackie, about which I could not complain. Jackie was at her best, I have never had a better conversation with her, not only very friendly but also interesting, with a lot of talk about White House life, mostly when Jack was President, but also her return visits there and her relations with LBJ, towards whom she was surprisingly friendly and favourable, and with Nixon, to whom she was much less so.

Jack, she said, except occasionally, did not much like formally arranged dinner parties, because he could not decide in advance whom he wanted to see. But he would often ring up at 5 or 6 o'clock and say, 'Get somebody for dinner.' He did not greatly like having Ethel and Bobby, not because he didn't like Ethel, he did rather, and certainly not because he didn't like Bobby, but because Bobby was too much his conscience and kept demanding to know what he had done, what he had decided about this or that, telling him what he ought to do in the future. Bradlees (*Washington Post*), who turned out to be snakes-in-the-grass, were there a lot. But David and Sissie Gore came more than anybody else, she said, so much so that it became difficult because David would always chuck everything else, which in my view was probably his duty (the main duty of ambassadors is to have close contact with the heads of the government to which they are accredited) but which led to his breaking long-arranged dinner engagements at which he was to be the guest of honour and created some Washington ill-feeling.

Then the dancing guests began to arrive and the whole thing became rather overcrowded and hot for a time, but I sat this out, and subsequently had an extremely agreeable evening – as indeed did Jennifer. We stayed, amazingly, until 3.45, and walked home in the dawn, a thing we haven't done for many years. I even danced three times, led on to the floor the first time by Mrs William Rees-Mogg.

FRIDAY, 9 JUNE. *London and East Hendred.*

I had a morning of London errands, including buying some books in Hatchards, where I had a conversation as on a stage with Pam Hartwell, i.e. addressed by her to the whole shop. I then met Robert Armstrong at Brooks's before driving to East Hendred in the afternoon. The Beaumarchais' arrived to stay at 7 o'clock.

SATURDAY, 10 JUNE. *East Hendred.*

At 11.30 the Beaumarchais' and I went to Oxford and did a quick tour, including climbing to the lantern at the top of the Sheldonian, which I discovered only six months ago and which gives a splendid view. It is curious how many people one meets in the street in Oxford; between us we saw Isaiah Berlin, Oliver Franks,* Roger Makins (Sherfield),† and one or two others. Eric Rolls and the Douglass Caters‡ to lunch at East Hendred. Drove the Beaumarchais' over the Downs to the Blue Boar on a most beautiful evening.

SUNDAY, 11 JUNE. *East Hendred.*

Took the Beaumarchais' to Sevenhampton, where Ann also had Bonham Carters, Levers and Mark Amory§ for lunch. Then a tremendous afternoon of games. I played croquet with Mark Amory, who is a very good games-player, but who didn't know croquet very well, and beat him rather easily; then three sets of tennis (again a satisfactory result), and then croquet again. Stayed until 7.30. A perfect day, not very hot, but strong sunshine, and altogether very satisfactory.

WEDNESDAY, 14 JUNE. *Strasbourg and Paris.*

Commission meeting at 9.00, then into the Parliament for a short time before reluctantly leaving for Paris by avion taxi. To a luncheon at the Quai d'Orsay given by Guiringaud for the OECD ministers. A confused, disorganized lunch. I admittedly had not said that I was going until that morning, but at first there was no place for me, nor was there a place for Blumenthal (US Secretary of the Treasury) or for the Austrian Vice-Chancellor (Androsch), but eventually things were vaguely sorted out.

*Lord Franks, OM, b. 1905, Ambassador to Washington 1948–57, Provost of Worcester College 1962–76.
†Sir Roger Makins, b. 1904, cr. Lord Sherfield 1964, was Ambassador to Washington 1953–6, and then Permanent Secretary to the Treasury 1956–9; Chancellor of Reading University since 1970.
‡Douglass Cater, b. 1923, American academic and writer, was vice-chairman of the (London) *Observer* 1976–81.
§Mark Heathcoat Amory, b. 1941, subsequently edited the letters of Evelyn Waugh as well as those of Ann Fleming herself. He is now literary editor of the *Spectator*.

In the afternoon to the Château de la Muette for a series of bilateral meetings which were the purpose of my Paris visit. First, three-quarters of an hour with Blumenthal, in which I ran through my thoughts about European monetary stability, explained what we had in mind, and got a very satisfactory acceptance by him that the Americans were in effect perfectly happy about this.

Then a meeting with Malcolm Fraser of Australia. Perhaps as a result of my meeting with Garland and pressure from his officials, he was for once out to be pleasant. He wished to have a wide-ranging conversation about the Summit, the Third World, etc. That went more or less all right, and at the end we had a quick exchange of views about bilateral relations in which I stated our position, and we broke up without too much difficulty.

After this I had a meeting with Vance, who is very good, compared with Fraser or Blumenthal, at making these courtesy bilaterals easy and interesting. There was a curious element of American grandeur, not in his manner at all – very much the reverse – but in the room: the standard of the United States, the standard of the Secretary of State, the seal of the United States were all erected behind the desk in this rather small, temporary room in the Château de la Muette which he was occupying for thirty-six hours, and there was even half a platoon of marines outside. With three or four other people present we talked mainly about MTNs and the forthcoming Summit.

Then I went into the Plenary Session for twenty-five minutes and made a perfectly sensible, pointless seven-minute speech, which the officials were very keen that I should make, about the trade pledge.* I then left at about 6.30 escorted by two *motards* and had the most terrifying, ludicrous, ridiculous drive to Le Bourget. It was the peak of the rush hour around the Périphérique and the traffic was absolutely jammed up. But these two motorcyclists carved their way through so that we got there in twenty-three minutes, mostly going between 50 and 70 miles an hour, with the chance of a major accident at least one in five I would have thought. How ordinary French motorists put up with this behaviour I cannot understand. The *motards*, given the fact that they were trying to perform this lunacy, did absolutely spectacularly; they thumped

*Not to impose restrictions on imports from Third World countries.

and occasionally kicked small cars out of the way, with their feet off the pedals of their motorbikes.

I couldn't look most of the time. I fastened my seat belt in the back, a thing I have never done before, and tried to read the newspapers. We hit one car a glancing blow and bounced off a sort of balustrade on another occasion. However, we eventually got there without any grave damage to anybody, but I do not think it is a sensible way for the French police to behave, and it is certainly a disagreeable way to go through Paris on a particularly beautiful early June evening. I suppose it cut an hour off the drive, but this was hardly worth it, particularly as I had nothing serious to do at the other end.

I never thought I would find a little avion taxi such a haven of peace, like a hammock in a summer garden. We flew off into a cloudless sky, over the valley of the Marne and the plains of Champagne, through Lorraine, over the Vosges and down into Colmar. Drove to La Clairière (hotel) at Illhaeusern, where Jennifer, Hayden and Laura already were.

THURSDAY, 15 JUNE. *Strasbourg and Brussels.*

Drove into Strasbourg and to the Parliament at 11.15. Then with Jennifer took Tam Dalyell* to lunch. We much enjoyed talking to Tam, who, although slightly dotty, is in a curious way a first-rate man, with great self-confidence and interest. To the Parliament to answer questions for forty-five minutes mainly about languages in the enlarged Community, and then back to Brussels by avion taxi.

FRIDAY, 16 JUNE. *Brussels.*

A day of Berlaymont meetings, including two with Gundelach. These were intended to be a general run round agriculture and fisheries policy and also something of an attempt to repair one or two slightly damaged bridges between him and me. I find it very difficult to make up my mind completely about Gundelach. His

*Tam Dalyell, b. 1932. Labour MP since 1962. Member of the European Parliament 1975–9.

qualities are great; is his trickiness equally so?* Home at 7 o'clock, where the Jakie Astors had arrived to stay.

Saturday, 17 June. *Brussels.*

A remarkable three-hour expedition to the battlefields in the Ypres salient. We had a key prepared in Donald Maitland's office, which was extremely valuable, for otherwise I think we would have been completely lost. We went to Menin and then along the Menin Road between there and Ypres and turned off and saw a system of trenches and a museum. Then on to Hill 60, Hellfire Corner, and into Ypres itself to see the Menin Gate with its vast panels of names (56,000, I think) of those who did not have individual graves. Then on to Passchendaele, to the huge cemetery there. The whole expedition was interesting, even fascinating, but harrowing and oppressive, and we were glad at the end to get out of the area. Why does Waterloo have no similar effect? Is it a difference of numbers or a difference of a hundred years? We drove to Bruges where we lunched without much appetite, went to see the Memling and returned to Brussels.

Sunday, 18 June. *Brussels.*

We took the Astors (and Phillips' with children) on a surprisingly beautiful day and picnicked in the field near Maillen in the near Ardennes where we had been before. The site wasn't as successful as previously because we had forgotten that in June, as opposed to April or October, the 'corn is as high as an elephant's eye', and as a result the view was almost blocked out. After lunch we played cricket on the road, organized by Hayden, interrupting – or interrupted by – a local bicycle race, so that there was a certain clash of English and Belgian cultures. However, no trouble.

Monday, 19 June. *Brussels.*

A 12.30 meeting with the President of Mali. An agreeable man, accompanied by two or three others in magnificent robes. There was not a great deal to talk about.

* Gundelach, I had been told by some kind friend, had been making disobliging remarks about me in London. But see also the entry for 10 December 1979.

Then with Hayden and Roger Beetham to give Larry Lamb and the *Sun*'s political editor (Anthony Shrimsley) lunch. It ought to have been more successful than it was. Lamb, who had impressed me greatly in Manchester six weeks before, seemed on rather bad form. Shrimsley quite intelligent, but the whole thing not as pointful as it should have been.

TUESDAY, 20 JUNE. *Brussels.*

10.30 meeting with Raymond Vouël, who complained, with some justification, about Davignon running around and organizing all sorts of cartels which were offending the competition rules of the Commission. Then Andreas Whittam Smith, the City editor of the *Daily Telegraph*,* who was an extremely good interviewer, agreeable, and taking points very quickly. And then, at noon, an extraordinary ceremony organized by the Anciens Combattants de l'Europe, who gave me a medal. It was mainly got up by the French, but there were about eight high British Legion officials, and the actual presentation was made by Rommel's Chief of Staff, who not surprisingly was extremely old, an *echt* Iron Cross German General, who did it all with considerable style.

WEDNESDAY, 21 JUNE. *Brussels.*

Day-long Commission over by 6.00. Dinner for the change of presidency from the Danes to the Germans, which, at Astrid von Hardenberg's† good suggestion, we had arranged at the Maison d'Erasme in Anderlecht. I don't think Erasmus had actually lived there for more than six or seven months – did he ever live anywhere for much longer? – but it is an attractive sixteenth-century house, well run as a museum, and a good place for a dinner. The dinner went very well. I had Madame de Nanteuil and Frau Sigrist on either side of me. I made a rather erudite speech, partly about Erasmus, partly about the Vikings, partly about Greenland, which Hayden had prepared very well for me, and we then listened to a good, sensible, rather long speech from Riberholdt, followed by a somewhat misty one about the Nibelungen from Sigrist.

* Andreas Whittam Smith, b. 1937, became the founder editor of the *Independent* in 1986.
† Gräfin von Hardenberg was the Commission's deputy Chief of Protocol.

THURSDAY, 22 JUNE. *Brussels, Paris and Brussels.*

11.43 TEE to Paris with Crispin. Worked extremely hard all the way and then lunched very late in Paris. At 4.45 to the Elysée. Giscard rather impressively received us two minutes ahead of time, and we talked for about an hour and a half. It was one of the best conversations I have had with him. We talked a little about economic growth, in which we agreed that we had the tactical and cosmetic problem of making the Bremen European Council seem worthwhile while knowing that Schmidt was not willing to say very much until he got to the Bonn Western Summit. Then we went on to monetary arrangements in Europe, in which Giscard was extremely hard and firm and clearly determined to go ahead. The curious effect of this was that, perhaps because he was more interested, because we were discussing something more closely, interrupting each other a good deal, he became, if anything, rather smaller, less like a would-be Louis XIV, or even General de Gaulle, and more as I remember him as a Finance Minister; less making pronouncements as a head of state, more discussing a real subject.

Towards the end he suddenly raised the question of the reform of Community institutions, saying that this was a personal view of his, a lot of the French Government didn't share it, etc., but he was particularly worried about the presidency of the Council of Ministers and of the European Council and thought these ought to be done on a semi-permanent basis by someone who had been a major figure in the national government of a big country. I wasn't clear whether he intended this to be something – which indeed it might be – which would greatly devalue the Commission, or something which could be amalgamated with the presidency of the Commission, though I doubt this.

From the Elysée I went to see first the Hendersons and then the Beaumarchais' before travelling back to Brussels alone on the 8.30 TEE, dining – or rather ordering dinner, because it was almost completely uneatable – along the Oise. But I still like rolling across the plains of northern France on a long summer evening, even with a lot of clouds, which at least produce constantly changing light.

FRIDAY, 23 JUNE. *Brussels*.

Into the office late to see Ambassador Harriman, not, however, Averell, but an agreeable Nigerian who is the United Nations Commissioner for Anti-Apartheid. I then gave a drink, with a speech and questions, to fourteen Dutch editors, lunched at home with Jennifer alone, and returned to the office to give an interview to an allegedly 7-million-circulation Japanese newspaper: a rather formal visit from the editor and three supporting journalists, but fortunately it seemed at the time to go rather well and lasted no less than one and a half hours.

Woodrow and Verushka Wyatt arrived to stay the weekend, but I had to go to the Palais d'Egmont for a dinner for the Federation of Socialist Parties which was meeting to draw up a direct elections manifesto. I had bilateral conversations with Brandt and den Uyl before dinner, at dinner with Mitterrand and Craxi,* and after dinner with Soares of Portugal (for a long time), and Gonzales of Spain (for a short time). It was a good round-up of the great and the good of the European Left. There were brief speeches at dinner from Simonet, who was giving the dinner, Pontillon, who was the nominal President, and Brandt, who was much the most senior man there.

SATURDAY, 24 JUNE. *Brussels*.

Took the Wyatts for my regular *giro* of Brussels, from the Forêt de Soignes to the Grand'Place. K. B. Andersen, the Danish Foreign Minister, accompanied by Ersbøll and Riberholdt, arrived for an hour's meeting at home before dinner. Then, at 8.30, we turned this into a social dinner as a mark of appreciation of K. B. Andersen's presidency of the Council of Ministers. This went very well. The Wyatts got on excellently with the Danes, and the Danes were nice and sensible, as they nearly always are. Half seriously they attributed Danish prosperity to the fact that they had never had any basic industries worth speaking of to run down: no coal, no steel, no shipbuilding, no textiles, no heavy engineering. All done on pigs, beer and porcelain.

*Bettino Craxi, b. 1934, had become General Secretary of the Italian Socialist Party in 1976. Prime Minister of Italy 1983–7.

MONDAY, 26 JUNE. *Brussels and Luxembourg.*

Jennifer left for London after a fourteen-day visit to Brussels. Following the new Chinese Ambassador, I saw Talboys,* the deputy Prime Minister of New Zealand, whom I like very much indeed and whom I got without great difficulty to say quite clearly that the sheep meat regime, as at present proposed, caused them little difficulty. It was possible future changes which worried them.

Avion taxi to Luxembourg for the Foreign Affairs Council, which sat for five hours until nearly 10 p.m. There was a good deal of wrangling about the treatment of human rights in the Lomé Convention, of which most notably David Owen, but several other people too, were making very heavy weather.

TUESDAY, 27 JUNE. *Luxembourg and Brussels.*

I took time off from the Council to see John Davies, the British Conservative foreign affairs spokesman, and give him some briefing about our attitude towards Australia and New Zealand. He was easily reassured on these points and anxious to be helpful, being more concerned about African questions and Soviet penetration there.

Lunch for Genscher and two of his collaborators at the Golf Club, the postponed meal from before he took over the presidency. Not a great deal of business was discussed but he was interesting in an anecdotal way.

Back to the Council from 3.15 to 6.30. I then decided I had had enough and returned to Brussels by avion taxi. I had Charlie Douglas-Home† to dinner and enjoyed talking to him, partly about Iberian enlargement and partly about the royal prerogative in Britain, on which he is writing a book.

THURSDAY, 29 JUNE. *Brussels and Bath.*

12.35 plane to London, and then in the early evening of a day of pouring rain had a horrible slow drive to Bath, for the university

---

*Brian Talboys, b. 1921, was Foreign Minister and Minister for Overseas Trade as well as deputy Prime Minister of New Zealand 1975–81.
†Charles Douglas-Home, 1937–85, was then foreign editor of *The Times*. He became editor in 1982. He was married to Jessica Gwynne.

dinner before my honorary degree the following morning. I enjoyed the dinner, liked the Vice-Chancellor and his wife and the Mayor and Mayoress of Bath, as well as the Chancellor, Lord Hinton, and delivered quite a reasonably successful twenty-minute speech of the occasion to an audience of about 150/200.

SATURDAY, 1 JULY. *East Hendred.*

To Buscot Parsonage at 9.15 p.m. for Diana Phipps's great opera ball. It really was a most extraordinary occasion, dinner for five hundred people, at tables of ten or twelve, all placed. My only concession was my Abruzzan cloak over a dinner jacket, and there was a fair number of other people who were dressed as no more than the conductor or the audience. There were some spectacular costumes, some successful, some not. George Weidenfeld,* as some vague eighteenth-century figure, looked surprisingly convincing, Claus Moser† arguably a little less so because he had a more elaborate costume. Noël Annan as Prince Gremin also looked surprisingly authentic, as though he was in a perfectly natural uniform for him to wear as Vice-Chancellor or Provost.

The most spectacular-looking woman was Jessica Douglas-Home as the governess in *The Turn of the Screw*, who arrived in a governess cart with her two children, quickly disposed of for the evening, though the horse remained and was rather a nuisance. The Harlechs were paired as the Pharaoh and Phareen from *Aïda*, and poor David, who was sitting next but one to me at dinner, was so encrusted in golden armour that he had to spend most of his time trying to get bits of breast-plate off in order to be able to talk, eat, or do almost anything (he had already removed his helmet). Dinner went on for the greater part of the time we were there. We left about 12.45, as we were both tired. The weather was sad. Nonetheless it didn't ruin the occasion, which was a fantastic feat of organization (and extravagance) on Diana's part.

* George Weidenfeld, b. 1919, cr. Lord Weidenfeld 1976, London and (now) New York publisher.
† Sir Claus Moser, b. 1922, Professor of Social Statistics at LSE 1961–70, and head of the Government Statistical Service 1967–78, was Chairman of the Royal Opera House 1974–87. Warden of Wadham College, Oxford, since 1984.

MONDAY, 3 JULY. *East Hendred, Warwickshire and London.*
Accompanied by Nicko Henderson, I drove to Stoneleigh to open
the Royal Show at 11.15. A curious, rather enjoyable, gathering. I
addressed an audience of somewhere between two and four
thousand, who were some distance away from me on a cold, windy
morning. They listened surprisingly well to some tough warning
words about milk, and some more acceptable ones about European
monetary arrangements. Then a tour of part of the Show, which
was impressive. Then a press conference, which I had been reluctant to do, at which rather sensible questions were asked, and then
lunch in the Royal Pavilion, where the admirable Henry Plumb sat
surrounded by two duchesses, the old Duchess of Gloucester and
the less old Duchess of Devonshire.

Then with Nicko by train from Coventry to Euston for my
meeting with Callaghan from 6.00 to 7.20. On European monetary
advance he was obviously rather 'miffed' (indeed I think this was,
rather surprisingly, the word he actually used) that he hadn't been
more closely consulted, although in fact (unless he took the view
that Schmidt and Giscard should never meet on their own without
him) he had nothing to be 'miffed' about, because he had already
been sent (whether he had read it I was not sure) a version of the
so-called Schulmann/Clappier paper,* which was more than I had
seen at that stage, or indeed the Italians or the Little Five. However,
the significant thing was that he *felt* 'miffed' and announced that he
was declining the invitation to come before lunch to Bremen on the
following Thursday in order to have a tripartite meeting. He
claimed that it was very difficult because of a Cabinet meeting, but
not with much conviction. As usual, on these recent occasions, he
was agreeable, sensible, affable.

At the end of our discussion Callaghan kept me back alone for a
short time, and then asked what I wanted done about my renomination as President.† He didn't want there to be any suggestion, as there had been last time with the French, that they were

* Horst Schulmann was a senior official in Schmidt's Chancellery; Bernard Clappier was
the Governor of the Bank of France. They were both Summit 'sherpas'. Their paper was a
semi-secret Franco-German statement of methods and objectives for the Bremen
European Council.
† For 1979 and 1980. A Commissioner is nominated for four years, but a President only
for two, although he is normally then reappointed.

hanging back so far as Ortoli's renomination was concerned. Would I like him to propose it at Bremen? I said I hardly thought this was necessary, and it was not exactly the same position as with the French in 1974, because he was not occupying the presidency (of the Council). However, it ended by his saying that he would do anything I wished, and adding: 'Would you be all right if Mrs Thatcher were to be there after October?' In all electoral conversations I have had with him, most of them conducted tangentially in this way, he has never given the impression of overconfidence, which is very sensible on his part.

TUESDAY, 4 JULY. *London and Luxembourg.*

Took off from Northolt for Luxembourg just after 8 o'clock, entirely alone apart from the two pilots in the little plane, and a pretty disagreeable journey it was with the whole of Western Europe covered in endless layers of dirty cloud of almost limitless cubic capacity.

To the Parliament at 10.15, only a little late for the beginning of the Genscher speech, and sat in until 1.00, when I made a brief intervention. In the afternoon I worked in the Cravat Hotel, trying to clear my thoughts by writing a sort of letter to myself in advance of the Bremen Summit. Then I saw Deane Hinton, the American Ambassador, he having come to deliver some sort of *démarche* which I, or indeed he, didn't take too seriously, about the dangers of the MTNs going wrong in Geneva. This was a predictable artillery barrage before the engagement.

In the evening I drove in pouring rain down to Ehnen on the Mosel and the German frontier, where I had last dined on a baking evening almost exactly two years ago, and where on this occasion I gave Gaston Thorn, Prime Minister of Luxembourg, a three-hour dinner. I discovered that he had been fairly well briefed, but not shown the paper, about the Clappier/Schulmann work, having received a visit the previous day from Clappier. Clappier had done Luxembourg and Rome, and Schulmann it appeared had been to Belgium, Holland and Denmark. Nobody, alas, had thought to go to Ireland.

WEDNESDAY, 5 JULY. *Luxembourg, Bonn and Brussels.*

A difficult Commission meeting from 9.00 to 10.15. Ortoli tried to make a great row with Vredeling because of the insulting remarks which Vredeling had made about the French Government at a press conference in Rome following the breakdown of the Social Council, at which the French had been isolated and intransigent. Vredeling had some justification, although he had obviously blown off rather foolishly. What was striking on this occasion was that this hot-tempered, irascible man didn't rise much to Ortoli's complaint, which, as Francis told me subsequently, was a great disappointment to him. Vredeling confined himself to saying that he had been mistranslated, that he had used the Dutch word 'dum', which he implausibly claimed meant 'without reasons given', rather than, as one might assume, 'stupid', 'imbecile'. (I was subsequently assured by the Dutch Foreign Minister that what it meant was precisely 'stupid', if not something stronger.)

Crispin and I then left to motor to Bonn. Rather good country between Trier and Coblenz, though the weather was dismal as on every recent day. Bonn at 1 o'clock (German time) for lunch with Schmidt, for once not alone, but he with Schulmann and I with Crispin. This lasted until 3.40 and was immensely worthwhile. Schmidt began by saying, not altogether untypically, that he was feeling very unwell. He had got some bug in Zambia, as a result of which he could not eat much. He drank a rather eccentric mixture of port and coca-cola, and ate at least as much as I did, but this was because the meal was, by any standards, strictly inedible, and he was presumably used to it. At one stage he told us how he ran the whole of Germany from the Chancellery with a staff of, I think, thirty-eight, and it was at least clear that none of the thirty-eight was a qualified chef.

However, the conversation more than made up for this. He described his various plans for Bremen, and who had been consulted and who had not. I told him about Callaghan's slight sense of being left out and warned him he ought to try and deal with this. He gave us the paper, and also gave us some British paper which had been sent to them but of which I had never heard previously, and indeed never heard of again. We also talked about MTNs, about which he expressed some apprehension, having obviously been pressurized by the Americans a little, as we had, and being quite willing to give way to them, but I said the moment for that had certainly not arisen. But it was altogether a highly satisfactory and friendly conversation, in which at one stage he went out of his way, which was peculiarly gracious for him, to say that I underestimated how much an influence I had had at our various meetings on the whole development of his thought on European monetary affairs and, indeed, European affairs in general.

Crispin and I then drove back in filthy weather to Brussels and went into the office for about an hour and a half. Ortoli insisted on coming to see me at 7.15 and I gave him a brief rundown on Bonn, including, with slight hesitation, showing but not giving him the Clappier/Schulmann paper. Schmidt had given it to me with great stress on secrecy, saying, which was true, that the Little Five, and indeed I believe the Italians, had not actually seen the paper, which made me a little hesitant about showing it to anyone else, particularly knowing the state of Schmidt/Ortoli relations.

THURSDAY, 6 JULY. *Brussels and Bremen.*

12.15 avion taxi for Bremen and the European Council. The proceedings began with a lunch in the Rathaus, a magnificent building, three hundred years older than the Hamburg late nineteenth-century edifice. There was a notable absence, which was generally interpreted as being deliberate, of Callaghan and Owen. Then a very good speech from the Burgomeister, a slightly less good one from Schmidt.

We started the Council in another room in the same building at 3.30, the British having arrived just before, marching in in single file, like a jungle expedition,* first Callaghan, then Owen, Palliser, Hunt, Couzens, McCaffrey,† McNally,‡ etc., and then about fifteen bearers carrying thirty red despatch boxes. God knows what they were all supposed to have in them. The afternoon meeting lasted

* Appropriate in view of the almost continuous tropical downpours with which the Bremen climate welcomed this European Council.
† (Sir) Thomas McCaffrey, b. 1922, became chief information officer of the Home Office under me in 1966, was inherited by James Callaghan and subsequently served him as his principal press officer throughout his public career.
‡ Tom McNally, b. 1943, was political adviser to the Prime Minister 1976–9, and subsequently first Labour and then SDP MP for Stockport 1979–83.

until 6.30, which was longer than I expected, and dealt, *inter alia*, with the Ortoli paper on concerted growth which I introduced and about which there was not too bad a discussion.

Then we reassembled − it was not clear whether for an early dinner or for a meeting of heads of government and me before dinner. The 'Big Three' were missing and so the rest of us chatted away in our usual desultory fashion. The first of the 'Big Three' to arrive, as indeed was appropriate as he was the host, was Schmidt, looking very gloomy, who came up to me and said, 'Things have gone very badly with Callaghan.' Ten minutes later Giscard arrived and gave Thorn, Tindemans and me an equally dismal report, though rather differently expressed, saying that he had had another go at Callaghan after the tripartite talk and it seemed as though he wished to stand out; nothing more could be done with him.

Then Callaghan arrived, obviously not in a very good mood either, and, indeed, his demeanour at dinner, when he sat at the end of the table in a way at once aloof and dejected, can best be described as surly. However, nobody's mood was very good so that we had a thoroughly pointless dinner, neither gossiping nor transacting any business. Nobody, not even as on some previous occasions Giscard and I, managed to get any general conversation going at all, partly because I was feeling too gloomy about the news to want to try. Whether he was equally gloomy I don't know.

At about 9.30 we settled down for the restricted meeting proper. This continued until midnight and went much better than I would have expected from the pre-dinner reports and the atmosphere at dinner. Schmidt began by asking Giscard to introduce their joint paper. This was put round and there was an adjournment while people read it. During this I told Giscard across the table that he had left out one rather important point: that was the deposit of equivalent amounts of national currencies to the amounts deposited in gold and dollars with the European Currency Fund. This he accepted perfectly well, and then asked me, rather surprisingly, whether I had shown the paper to Ortoli, to which I simply said, 'Yes.'

We then settled down to a general discussion. In contrast with Copenhagen three months before, a substantial part was played by Italy and the Little Five. There was no question of it being just a foursome between the Big Three and me. Andreotti, Thorn, Tindemans, Jørgensen, van Agt and indeed Lynch all spoke quite a bit. Callaghan attracted the most attention. They wanted to see which way he would jump, and on the whole he did not jump too unfriendlily. At one point he raised the question: 'What was the relationship of the problems of convergence and the transfer of resources with the currency point which was being put first? Ought they not all to advance together?' He put this question to Giscard, who said I had better answer, so I did, incomprehensibly to everybody else – at first at any rate – but successfully from Callaghan's point of view, by quoting the old bit of Walcheren doggerel:

> Great Chatham with his sabre drawn
> Stood waiting for Sir Richard Strachan.
> Sir Richard, longing to be at 'em
> Stood waiting for the Earl of Chatham.

In other words, waiting for everything to advance together was a recipe for never advancing at all.

This went rather well with Jim because he knew the jingle, though got it wrong when he tried to requote bits of it back to me, but it put him in a good humour, and generally from that moment onwards things went rather better. Towards the end of the evening it seemed possible to draft a highly constructive introduction to the paper itself which would enable it to be published, without any definite commitment on anybody's part, except a definite commitment to work on *this* scheme, to refine it by 31 October and to take a decision in December. Eventually I got a form of words accepted by everyone including Callaghan as a working hypothesis.

Then, a curious sub-committee, consisting of Schulmann as one of the authors of the paper (Clappier was not there), Lynch because he had been particularly concerned about transfer of resources, and me, sat down at the end to try and put into detailed words what had been agreed. Schmidt stayed behind, hovering around us, and, eventually, after about twenty minutes, I got something written out which was accepted as being satisfactory and was taken away to be typed. Bed only at 2.15 (3.15 Belgian time) but in a state of considerable exhilaration at the dramatic upturn after the low point of dinner.

FRIDAY, 7 JULY. *Bremen and East Hendred.*

To the Rathaus for the so-called 'family photographs' at 9.45. We assembled for these in the Sea Captains' Hall, comparable in scale to the main hall of the London Guildhall, and so named because it is where a traditional banquet to say goodbye to the sea captains was held. But the main thing that we appeared to be saying goodbye to that morning was the degree of agreement which we had reached the previous evening. Schmidt came up to me saying that Callaghan was running out on what he had agreed and was getting some support from Andreotti and maybe van Agt. This was confirmed by a brief interchange which I had with Callaghan himself and a word which I overheard him having with Andreotti. Their reasons for caution were quite different. Callaghan was not much in favour of the scheme politically, Andreotti was very much in favour of the scheme politically, but was doubtful whether Italy could sustain a place in it without substantial support.

The session began at 10.00 in an intimate and satisfactory little room, and we quickly got down to the European currency part of the communiqué and argued over this for, I suppose, two and a half hours. At times things got rather bad-tempered between Callaghan and Schmidt, less so between Callaghan and Giscard, mainly I think because Giscard cared less than did Schmidt whether Callaghan came along. From a fairly early stage it was possible to see verbal compromises which could be satisfactorily incorporated and this was what we eventually did. But Schmidt and particularly Giscard were leaving Callaghan to wriggle on his hook at this stage, and saying that they wanted no papering over of cracks where real differences existed.

The essential point which I stressed several times was that the British should agree to study *the* scheme put forward, if necessary to try to amend it, but not just to tour all round the intellectual horizon, and this was what was eventually accepted. Callaghan was slightly tiresome in saying he thought the draft produced the evening before went far beyond what had been agreed, which was not remotely true, and indeed was strongly contested, particularly by Giscard who said the draft was wholly accurate, as did at least five other people who spoke.

The tiresomeness lay in challenging the accuracy of the draft;

there was nothing wrong in Callaghan retreating a little, as it is reasonable and indeed fairly normal to have overnight thoughts on matters of this sort, even when less important, at sessions of the European Council. However, in spite of having said that my draft went beyond what had been agreed, Callaghan, as well he might have been, was extremely agreeable to me throughout and thanked me very warmly at the end for having been helpful to him, as indeed did Schmidt and Giscard and the others. It was a very wearing but on the whole satisfactory meeting, with the Commission in a far more nodal position than at previous European Councils.

The session lasted until 2.30 p.m. After a snack I did the press conference with Schmidt, which was huge and lasted no less than eighty minutes. This was mainly because Schmidt read out an extremely long and boring statement and was also pretty diffuse in answering his own questions. (I had a few, but he had more.) I think for some reason or other he was anxious to be as boring as he could be. He was certainly not sparkling, although – what was more important – he had done extremely well in the Council. He and I then parted on excellent terms. He had offered to take me to Hamburg in his helicopter to get a plane from there, but the long press conference scuppered this plan. So I went to Bremen airport and spent a long but contented time there waiting for a later plane. East Hendred just before 9.00.

SUNDAY, 9 JULY. *East Hendred.*

Gilmours, Willie Whitelaws and Hugh Thomas's to lunch. A perfectly agreeable lunch, though Willie talked rather too much about Conservative Party politics without saying anything very interesting. He and Hugh Thomas apparently didn't get on very well together; no doubt he thought Hugh Thomas had become too right-wing! The Gilmours, who brought the Whitelaws because they were staying with them, seemed curiously oppressed by their presence.

MONDAY, 10 JULY. *London.*

Lunch with the Labour Committee for Europe. Quite a successful gathering, though some of them were surprisingly unaware of the significance of Bremen. At 6.00 I went to see Ted Heath in Wilton Street in order, which was not difficult, to line up his support for the Bremen initiative. I found him enthusiastic and anxious to make a speech later in the week. I may say that Willie Whitelaw and Ian Gilmour had been perfectly sound the day before, in considerable contrast with the non-committal statement which had been issued by Geoffrey Howe* on Sunday and which foreshadowed Mrs Thatcher's indifferent line in the House of Commons.

A dinner at the Savoy Hotel for my former Permanent Secretaries, Sir Richard Way, Sir Charles Cunningham (I hesitated over whether to ask him† but decided there should be no exceptions; he accepted, I put him on my right and was very glad I had had him), Sir Philip Allen (now Lord Allen of Abbeydale), Sir William Armstrong (then Lord Armstrong of Sanderstead), Sir Douglas Allen (now Lord Croham), Sir Sam Goldman, who was never a full Permanent Secretary but of equivalent rank in the Treasury, and Sir Arthur Peterson, of my second period at the Home Office, with Sir Robert Armstrong, never a Permanent Secretary of mine but now one (he was a Private Secretary and a Deputy Secretary of mine) to make up what I thought would be an appropriate balance of present as well as past. The only one who couldn't come was Sir Frank Figgures. I enjoyed the occasion and was very glad I had organized it.

TUESDAY, 11 JULY. *London and Brussels.*

9.25 plane from London Airport. I gave lunch to the British journalists, whom I found about as boring as usual. After some routine work in the office I went home at 6.45, where Jennifer had just arrived from London.

It was the evening of our dinner for the King and Queen of the Belgians. The other guests we had assembled were the Tinés and the Tugendhats. We had intended to have the Dohnanyis, but they chucked in stages, she at two weeks' notice, Klaus the day before. We asked Laura as soon as Frau von Dohnanyi had cancelled, and we then luckily managed to replace Dohnanyi with Giolitti, whom

* Sir Geoffrey Howe, b. 1926, was then shadow Chancellor of the Exchequer, became the real Chancellor 1979–83, and has been Foreign Secretary since 1983.
† Our Home Office relations had not been altogether smooth in 1965–6.

by rather convoluted logic we thought singularly appropriate as he had just failed to become President of the Italian Republic after a brief period as favourite. The main problem was seating, for it became clear that if Giolitti was to sit on Jennifer's left, which she was insistent should be the case, the only thing which really worked was for Laura to sit next to the King, which she claimed to be apprehensive about but appeared to enjoy. The King and Queen were agreeable and easy. Marie-Jeanne cooked unusually well. I feared her nerve might have cracked, as she was very excited by the occasion, but not at all. They stayed until nearly 12 o'clock, talking animatedly, and the whole occasion was satisfactory.

WEDNESDAY, 12 JULY. *Brussels.*

Commission completed in the morning, owing to a light agenda. I then had an agreeable lunch with Brunner and Ralf Dahrendorf.* Dahrendorf talks very well and Brunner, despite his faults, is also a good conversationalist. It was a great contrast with the gloomy lunch I had had at the same restaurant with the British a few months previously.

SATURDAY, 15 JULY. *Brussels and Bonn.*

In the early evening Crispin and I drove to Schloss Gymnich, this side of Bonn, for the Western Economic Summit. We dined there with the Canadians: Trudeau, Jamieson, the Foreign Minister whom I know quite well and like, and Chrétien, the fairly new Finance Minister whom I met in Ottawa and who can hardly speak English. An agreeable but not enormously pointful dinner.

SUNDAY, 16 JULY. *Bonn.*

A beautiful morning: cool (maximum temperature that day was 63°F), settled sun and low humidity, a remarkable and lucky combination for the Rhine Valley in mid-July. Helicopter to the Chancellery grounds. The first session was from 10.00 to 12.30. In

---

*Ralf Dahrendorf, b. 1929, had been a German-appointed member of the European Commission 1970–4, before becoming Director of the London School of Economics 1974–84, and Warden of St Antony's College, Oxford, in 1987.

sharp contrast with the London position fourteen months before, there was no question of my being excluded from any of the meetings. The only mild indignities were in relation to meals, where I was not allowed to lunch or dine with the heads of government, except at the large general lunch given by Scheel, and invited to do so with the Finance Ministers. But in the meetings, which was far more important, I was given full treatment as a head of delegation, and invited to speak frequently by Schmidt. Callaghan, a little brazenly I thought, passed me a note early on saying, 'Isn't it extraordinary that all that trouble that Giscard made about your attendance last year should now have disappeared so completely?'

At the first session we devoted most of the time to a general *tour de table*. Quite good, quite short contributions were made. I hadn't prepared anything, but thought it essential to speak, and therefore made a ten-minute intervention after the heads of delegation.

We reassembled from 3.15 until 4.20, had a break for Schmidt to go and brief the press, and then met again from 4.50 to 6.35. This third meeting was the crucial one at which we discussed inter-national monetary matters. It did not go very well. This was partly but not entirely bad luck. Giscard opened at Schmidt's invitation, and while he was doing so Schmidt passed me a note saying that I must 'back up Valéry' on this as it was very desirable to get something helpful in the communiqué.

I pondered exactly what to say, but did not for the moment have to do anything because after Giscard's opening Fukuda spoke and made some highly critical remarks about the dollar, delivered quietly and politely but nonetheless biting home quite hard, and saying, which is probably exaggerated, that the main reason why everything had not gone well since the London Summit – in the Japanese case at any rate – was due to the neglect of the dollar by the Americans. This nettled Carter, who replied rather defensively, and I think put him in a bad temper altogether. I then spoke after this, and tried to still American and to some extent – though this was less necessary – Japanese fears about the EMS, and I hope did so reasonably persuasively, but I am not sure.

After this Schmidt himself spoke at considerable length, and I thought too provocatively against the Americans, and for once not persuasively at all. He and Carter got involved in a sharp argument, which certainly made Carter sound much more reserved towards the EMS scheme than we were told afterwards he was briefed to be or had intended to be. The American officials went round the corridors that evening saying that the US position was more favourable than the impression which had come out. But, of course, the fact that the Americans sounded so reserved in the session itself eased the position of the British, and certainly gave Callaghan, Healey and Owen the feeling that they were less in a corner than they might otherwise have been.

After this unsatisfactory session I set off to go back to Schloss Gymnich by helicopter. No sooner had we taken off than one of the pilots came plunging back into the cabin of the large helicopter looking panic-stricken, losing his helmet on the way, and scrabbled about at the back, failed to do what he was trying to do, and then came forward signalling desperately to the other pilot to put the machine on the ground, which he proceeded to do in a cornfield just the other side of the Rhine.

Apparently a door was open. I wasn't greatly frightened, though thought it disagreeable, and was glad when we were on the ground and knew what was happening. However, after that we got back safely to Schloss Gymnich, had a quick change and returned to Bad Godesberg where I dined, not particularly rewardingly, with the Finance Ministers in Le Redoute, a familiar place from old Königswinter days and, indeed, other meetings since. I think there was no conversation of any particular significance, except for one or two of Denis Healey's pronouncements. Denis said that he was certain there would be an election in October. He was confident of the result, but he would not remain Chancellor of the Exchequer after a Labour victory. Dinner was over early but it was too dark for helicopters. I gave Jean Chrétien a lift back to Schloss Gymnich having to talk French the whole way, because it actually seemed easier than his strangulated English.

MONDAY, 17 JULY. *Bonn and Brussels.*

Up early on a fine morning and ran from 7.30 under the somewhat bewildered gaze of the many security guards standing around in the agreeable grounds of Schloss Gymnich. A meeting on MTNs with Denman and Crispin at 9 o'clock, and then helicopted in for the third Summit session, which took place from 10.30 to 1 o'clock. After a preliminary period on hijacking and anti-terrorism measures we got down to the MTN discussion, which I opened. The Trade Ministers – Strauss of America, Deniau of France, Lambsdorff of Germany, Dell of Britain – were wheeled in instead of their Finance Ministers for this item. There were obvious differences within the Community, which meant that after the opening I felt I had to lie back. The French were quite skilful – particularly Giscard, though Deniau to some extent as well – and undoubtedly moved the Americans a little without getting into any sort of *impasse*. They presented their case better than did the Germans and had some reason to be pleased with themselves afterwards, as they noticeably were.

We then walked across to the Villa Hammerschmidt for Scheel's ceremonial lunch, which went on too long so that the afternoon session did not begin until 3.30. It then continued on until 6.15. This was mainly communiqué stuff with problems about energy and the Third World, though the more specific remaining point to be settled was the figure for the various growth targets, and the German one in particular; eventually it was agreed that this should be raised by 1 per cent of GNP, whatever exactly that means.

So the much-heralded Summit came to an end. It was not vastly exciting, but probably better than the London one because more precise. It was certainly better from our Commission point of view, and just good enough to present to the press and the world as an achievement rather than a setback. Then we went off to the press conference which was held in some vast auditorium, but I think was deeply unrewarding for the press because it merely took the form of nine statements with no questions. (It was agreed that I should sit in the front row but not make a statement, although I at least had a microphone, unlike in London!) This was over by 7.20, and we all 'ran for the bus', in my case a Mercedes to Brussels.

TUESDAY, 18 JULY. *Brussels.*

I saw Ortoli at 11.15, and had a brief meeting about Italian steel problems with Donat-Cattin, the only disagreeable man in the Italian Government.

I then had Willy Brandt at noon for an hour's talk followed by an enjoyable lunch. Then, at 3.55, Fukuda arrived early so that when I got downstairs he was already out of his car but that, as the Japanese were very free to admit, was their fault and not ours. I had a reasonably satisfactory private meeting with him for nearly an hour, and then received the presentation of a large picture of a waterfall by the 'second best-known artist in Japan', as they quaintly put it. We gave Fukuda in return a rather beautiful late eighteenth-century Italian celestial globe, with the signs of the zodiac, which Crispin had cleverly bought. Then an hour's Commission meeting with Fukuda, followed by a forty-five-minute press conference, and after that a respite.

To Val Duchesse in good time (this time) to receive the Japanese and, after dinner, partly at the prompting of Crispin, who thought they had been slightly offended by Haferkamp, I made a prepared, warm, friendly speech, which was generally thought to have smoothed any ruffled feathers, and meant that they left in a good humour and reported themselves subsequently as very pleased with the visit.

WEDNESDAY, 19 JULY. *Brussels and London.*

Commission for three hours. Then to Simonet's house in Anderlecht, where he gave a useful and enjoyable lunch for Van Ypersele, the Belgian Chairman of the Monetary Committee, Professor Robert Triffin,* Lahnstein of the German Finance Ministry and maybe one other. An optimistic discussion about the state of play after Bremen and Bonn.

Commission for another three hours, which was long without being killing, and I then saw Vredeling who told me, not entirely to my dismay, that he had decided not to take on Personnel from Tugendhat. 8.35 plane to London. A substantial amount of late-night work in Kensington Park Gardens on my Essex degree speech, which was intended to be one of substance about the post-Bremen position.

---

* Robert Triffin, b. 1911, is a Belgian-born economist who had been Master of Berkeley College, Yale, and achieved world fame as an international monetary specialist. Having returned to live in Brussels, he was of great assistance to us in the run-up to the EMS.

THURSDAY, 20 JULY. *London and Colchester.*

11.30 train from Liverpool Street to Colchester and up to the university for an enjoyable lunch with old Rab Butler,* the Chancellor, on one side of me, and Mollie Butler on the other. Rab looked in an appalling condition, with bits of him coming off, but interesting to talk to as always. A short congregation in the afternoon, during which I spoke for about twenty minutes, as far as I could tell quite successfully, then a quick tea and a train to London.

FRIDAY, 21 JULY. *London and East Hendred.*

To the Bank of England to lunch and address their EEC Committee, a gathering of about seventy to whom I spoke without a text and, as a result, better than usual. After that, feeling that I had broken the back of the summer's work, I drove with Jennifer to East Hendred.

SATURDAY, 22 JULY. *East Hendred.*

It should have been a very good day for morale, having got so much work over, but, alas, I woke up with a sore throat and a cold which I didn't at first take at all seriously, but mistakenly so.† Robin Day‡ came at 12.30, and I put to him the proposition that he might become head of the Commission's London office. He seemed attracted, while rightly reserving his position.

MONDAY, 24 JULY. *Brussels.*

Formal opening session of Lomé II, from 10.30, a vast gathering – which went on until about noon, and at which I had to make rather a routine speech. Lunch with the Council of Economic and Finance Ministers, which was mildly interesting because it gave me a good idea of how their follow-up meeting at Bremen had gone.

A Coordination Meeting,§ fairly brief, before the Foreign Affairs

*R. A. Butler, 1902–82, cr. Lord Butler 1965, KG, holder between 1941 and 1965 of almost every Cabinet office except that of Prime Minister. Master of Trinity College, Cambridge, 1965–78. Chancellor of the Universities of Sheffield and Essex.
†It persisted for three and a half weeks.
‡ (Sir) Robin Day, b. 1923, was already a political television interviewer and presenter of note, although not quite so pre-eminent as today.
§ The purpose of such meetings was to decide which Commissioner handled which item and to determine some consistency of line.

Council. A farewell call from David Marquand, three ambassadors with credentials, an hour's meeting with Dohnanyi and the Germans and then a dinner with him alone. This was enjoyable in spite of my cold.

WEDNESDAY, 26 JULY. *Brussels and London*.

Final Brussels morning of the summer. Commission from 10.10 to 1.05, going along rather well and easily apart from a slight difficulty about 'Crisis Cartels'* at the end, which we had to adjourn until the afternoon. Lunch with Crispin and Hayden, to discuss the autumn term, and Commission again until 5.45. We got through Crisis Cartels, having twisted Davignon's arm, but it was time that that was done on this issue. However, it was a more difficult Commission to bring to an end in time than had been the previous pre-holiday ones, and I eventually left in some disorder, without being able to say goodbye to anyone much, let alone have the customary glass of champagne with the *cabinet*. Just caught the 6.25 plane to London, got home in time to go to Solly's very agreeable Zoo dinner of about twenty for us. I sat between Joan (Zuckerman) and Caroline (Gilmour) and afterwards had a long talk with Evangeline (Bruce) for the first time since David died. A very good evening, but late.

THURSDAY, 27 JULY. *London*.

To the opera with the Mosers (also Jennifer and the Donaldsons) – Bellini's *Norma*. A fairly but not spectacularly enjoyable performance, much though I like the opera, a very weak tenor, but Bumbry acted magnificently throughout and sang well in the second part. And anyway my cold was fairly awful.

FRIDAY, 28 JULY. *London and East Hendred*.

I gave a long background interview to Stephen Milligan for his Granada television programme on the various Summits, which is to

*Under Article 85 of the Treaty of Rome a derogation to the ban on market-sharing agreements could be temporarily permitted to ease problems of overproduction. A request for such a derogation was first made by the synthetic fibres industry. Consideration of the validity of the request occupied much of the time of the various Community institutions in the second half of 1978.

be presented in December. Lunched with the Bar Council at Grays Inn because their President, David McNeill, was an old Oxford acquaintance and he had there assembled about twelve legal luminaries, including Leslie Scarman, whom I was particularly glad to see, Elwyn-Jones and Peter Rawlinson. I drove to East Hendred on a rather attractive day, not settled weather, but good light and good, clear sky, thinking that I had a long and not undeserved summer holiday ahead.

MONDAY, 31 JULY. *East Hendred.*

The day of my *cabinet* meeting at East Hendred, which last year had been held in the garden in such spectacular sunshine that poor Renato Ruggiero nearly melted. This year there was pouring rain, which never ceased throughout the day. They struggled in, some from Brussels and some from London, in time for us to start at 11.40. We were thirteen altogether, including Jennifer, and John Harris from outside. In the morning we mainly discussed plans for reorientating the work of the Commission so that it concentrated on major issues where there was a chance of progress rather than flogging horses which were minor as well as dead; this meant certain consequential changes in personnel policy and greater flexibility in moving people around. In the afternoon we dealt with the Common Agricultural Policy and questions of the transfer of resources to poorer countries. I did not think the discussion was as good as last year, but the others seemed reasonably satisfied by it. We ended at 6 o'clock and most people left pretty rapidly to catch their planes.

FRIDAY, 4 AUGUST. *East Hendred and Norfolk.*

Drove via Kettering (lunch Bradleys) to stay with the Zuckermans at Burnham Thorpe for four days.

MONDAY, 7 AUGUST. *Norfolk.*

Solly, Jennifer and I drove over to the rather oppressive shrines of Walsingham about 6.00. Then back for a young man whose work was much admired by Joan Zuckerman (though less so by Solly) to attempt a drawing of me. He was very dissatisfied with the result and refused to let me have it and went off in a state of gloom. We rang him up during dinner and said that he could come back the next morning and have another go, which he duly did. Dined in and then stayed up late that night writing the greater part of the foreword to Joan Zuckerman's book on Birmingham (which I finished the following morning), having just previously written a *Times* piece about John Mackintosh, who, alas, had died the week before.

TUESDAY, 8 AUGUST. *Norfolk and Suffolk.*

Weather still as awful as ever. We left at 12.15 and drove to Norwich, which was immensely crowded, I suppose because so many people had been driven in from Cromer, Yarmouth, etc. by the appalling weather. I have never seen a church so full of sodden people as was the cathedral. We lunched in the Maid's Head Hotel, a splendid old fossilized 1930s (if not earlier) restaurant. Very bad food, rather nice service, with two tables looking as though they were occupied by people out of the film of *The Go-Between*. Then drove, still in pouring rain, to the Rothschilds at Rushbrook, near Bury St Edmunds, for dinner and the night.

FRIDAY, 11 AUGUST. *East Hendred.*

Lunch with the Rolls, who had Kingman Brewsters (the American Ambassador in London), Robert Marjolin and Michael Stewarts (ex-Ditchley)* to lunch at Ipsden. The good view I had formed of Brewster on the brief occasion when I had had a drink with him in London a few months before, was sustained. Not primarily serious conversation, though about half an hour on the political aspects of monetary union.

MONDAY, 14 AUGUST. *East Hendred.*

Diana Phipps, George Weidenfeld and Nicko Henderson to lunch with Jennifer at the Blue Boar. An enjoyable lunch, Nicko ebullient, George agreeable and unpushing in every way, I suppose

*Sir Michael Stewart, b. 1911, Minister in Washington 1964–7, was Ambassador to Greece 1967–71, before becoming Director of the Ditchley Foundation 1971–6.

because his ambitions are now fulfilled. I have never known him so well informed on a wide range of issues. The Annans came to East Hendred for several sets of tennis between 5.30 and 7.30.

TUESDAY, 15 AUGUST. *East Hendred and Sare.*

Plane to Bilbao. Drove across the French frontier to reach the Beaumarchais' at Sare by 6.00. Jacques had his foot in a plaster case as a result of a broken bone and was therefore rather immobile and subdued.

THURSDAY, 17 AUGUST. *Sare.*

The first fine day for a long time. I collected the Tavernes* from Bayonne Marina and brought them back to the Beaumarchais' for lunch. They were on very good form, both elegant with completely grey hair, Dick Viking-like in a sort of naval casquette, but balanced and sensible in his judgements: a highly attractive and intelligent man.

MONDAY, 21 AUGUST. *Sare.*

The weather had cleared again. I drove into Biarritz with Jennifer and Marie-Alice and swam, then lunched in, read, and worked on a review of Arthur Schlesinger's *Robert Kennedy*. Dined at the Fagoagos' (a local doctor) to meet the Spanish-Basque nationalist leader, Monzón, who has lived in St Jean-de-Luz since the civil war, and was a typical exile, interesting culturally, but totally unrealistic politically. He wanted an independent Basque state, which would form some sort of loose Iberian federation with Spain on the same basis as, he suggested, Portugal should do. He slightly reminded me of old Gwynfor Evans.†

WEDNESDAY, 23 AUGUST. *Sare.*

Drove into Biarritz earlier than usual, with Jennifer and Robert and Serena Armstrong (who had arrived to stay), swam in the usual

*Dick Taverne, QC, b. 1928, was Labour and then Democratic Labour MP for Lincoln 1962–74. He served with me at the Home Office and the Treasury 1966–70, and was the forerunner of the SDP.
†Gwynfor Evans, b. 1912, was Welsh Nationalist MP for Carmarthen 1966–70 and 1974–9.

bouncing breakers, went into the Hôtel du Palais to show the Armstrongs the plaque commemorating Asquith's kissing hands there with King Edward VII on his appointment as Prime Minister in 1908, and noted again that although only about fifty words long it contains two mistakes.

Chaban Delmas'* to lunch. Chaban, although looking somewhat older than when I had seen him last two years ago, seemed more vigorous and, although talking desultorily during lunch, was striking afterwards. His perspective of French politics was at once traditional and personal. He was indifferent to Giscard, but in favour of maintaining the prerogatives of a President of the Fifth Republic, and bitterly critical of Chirac, whom he thought the embodiment of all evil, for opposing him, a curious reversal of positions since Chirac supported Giscard in 1974 and scuppered Chaban's own candidature as a result. Chaban believed that Mitterrand remained in a powerful position, still full of ambition for the 1981 election, but that when he had gone, which he thought would not be until after that, the French Socialist Party might well split up as there would then be nobody to hold it together.

THURSDAY, 24 AUGUST. *Sare and East Hendred.*

We left just at 11.00, getting into Spain in an hour. We got slightly lost on the way to Bilbao airport, but this at least gave us a view of Bilbao, which reminded me of Pittsburgh, Pennsylvania, before they got rid of the smog. East Hendred at 5.00 on a fine but cool afternoon. The visit to Sare had been a great success. It was, as always, a great pleasure to be with the Beaumarchais', and the Armstrongs made a *bonne-bouche* at the end. I think Jacques needed guests and I suspect if he remains immobile for much longer and Giscard blocks his having anything to do, he may go into a slight decline, which would be very sad indeed.

FRIDAY, 25 AUGUST. *East Hendred and North Wales.*

Left mid-morning to drive to Talsarnau and stay with the Harlechs. We went via Cirencester, Gloucester, Ledbury and Leominster, just

* Jacques Chaban Delmas, b. 1915, Mayor of Bordeaux since 1947. President of National Assembly 1958–69, 1978–81, 1986–8. Prime Minister of France 1969–72. Candidate for the presidency 1974.

beyond which we picnicked in a field with a good Herefordshire red soil view and the sun coming out on a beautiful but cool day. Then on to Ludlow, and to Craven Arms and Bishop's Castle, through my old 1940 forestry camp area over the road up which David Ginsburg and I (Anthony Elliott joined us next day) had bicycled on a warm mid-July evening in 1940, stopping at a pub for supper and hearing one of Churchill's most famous 9 o'clock Sunday evening broadcasts – I think the 'fight on the beaches' one.* Then on through the rolling open countryside of Montgomeryshire into the tiny town of Montgomery where I had never been before, and to Bala, which looked a little less bleak in the sunlight than I had ever seen it, but which was true to form in refusing us a drink because we were too early (normally it is because it is a Sunday). Glyn at 6.30.

SATURDAY, 26 AUGUST. *North Wales.*

A perfect day, strong sunlight, quite cool. Tennis morning and evening. Lunch in the garden. At the end of the afternoon I went for a short drive down to the sea to see the view of the mountains. After tennis it was such a perfect evening that I then drove alone once again to the sea at 8.15 and saw a memorable sunset over the Lleyn Peninsula.

MONDAY, 28 AUGUST. *North Wales.*

A difficult drive via Beddgelert and Caernarvon to lunch with the Cledwyn Hughes'† on the edge of Anglesey at Trearddur Bay. Of all my close friends in the House of Commons I think he was the only one whom I hadn't seen since leaving and I was anxious to fill the gap. He is not standing again and therefore has probably been in the House of Commons for the last time as a member. He said he was bored with the House, most of his friends had left and he thought he preferred to get out at sixty-one rather than sixty-five and get other things to do, of which I think he will find a considerable number.

---

*Not exactly. That had been earlier in the House of Commons. This one (14 July 1940) said: 'Should the invader come ... we will defend every village, every town, every city ...'
†Cledwyn Hughes, b. 1916, cr. Lord Cledwyn of Penrhos 1979, having been MP for Anglesey from 1951, and a member of the Cabinet from 1966 to 1970. Now leader of the Opposition in the House of Lords.

Indeed he had already been asked, most surprisingly, to be Ombudsman but, wisely I think, had turned it down. He had had Callaghan on the telephone on Saturday night who was obviously wavering considerably about an October election, although it was Cledwyn's view that it was still more likely than not that Callaghan would come down for October and that this would be wise.

We then drove back across the island to call on the Angleseys* in their new flat at the top of Plas Newydd, they having evacuated and turned over the rest of the house to the National Trust.

WEDNESDAY, 30 AUGUST. *East Hendred.*

Shirley Williams for lunch from 1.30 to 4.45, all in the garden. I found her buoyant. The rumours that she was disenchanted with politics and was going to give up, although not specifically denied by her, did not seem to me to fit in with her mood, which was one of considerable commitment. She is very pro Bill Rodgers, but fairly critical of most other people, particularly David Owen, but Hattersley† too. She thought Denis (Healey) would not become leader unless the whole thing was absolutely made for him by Callaghan. He would only succeed as heir in very propitious circumstances. He would not have enough people fighting on his side to get him through a difficult contest, and if Callaghan – as he might well if he won – stayed on two or three years, that would probably see Denis out.

She, I think, was rather in favour of a spring than an autumn election, but not very certain about this. She was thoroughly sound on all European questions and anxious to be briefed on monetary issues, having had some quite long talks with Blumenthal (whom she had found wobbly and wavering) at Aspen where she had spent the summer, and she thought the American attitude was crucial for a UK Government decision.

---

*The 7th Marquess of Anglesey, b. 1922, author and Chairman of the Historic Buildings Council for Wales, had married Shirley Morgan, daughter of the novelist Charles Morgan; she was then Chairman of the Welsh Arts Council.

†Roy Hattersley, b. 1932, has been Labour MP for Birmingham, Sparkbrook since 1964, was Secretary of State for Prices and Consumer Protection 1976–9, and has been deputy leader of the Labour Party since 1983.

Thursday, 31 August. *East Hendred*.

An incredibly dismal, dark, cold morning. We turned the heating on in the house and I lit a fire before lunchtime. Jennifer went to London for the day. In the evening we drove to West Wick near Pewsey to dine with the Devlins,* who produced a (mainly) Oxford and legal dinner party with, as always, very good food and wine. Enjoyable evening.

Friday, 1 September. *East Hendred*.

I had a long telephone talk with Bill Rodgers, with whom I had not been in touch for some time, and also a call from Debbie Owen saying that David was very anxious to see us, which slightly surprised me.

Saturday, 2 September. *East Hendred*.

Edmund Dells and Michael Jenkins's to lunch. It was the first time that Edmund Dell had ever been to any house of ours, and I had asked him – strange, shy, rather silent, good man that he is – mainly because I had been told by so many people that he was unsound on monetary union. I had therefore spoken to him at the Council of Ministers in July and said that I had heard that this was so, and why was it? To which he rather sweetly replied, 'Well, perhaps it is because you haven't talked to me enough.' So I thought that maybe a talking session would be a good idea. Hence the lunch.

He proved more talkative and agreeable than I had expected on general subjects – China, music – and they were both good guests. I had a go at him on the central subject afterwards but I am not sure that I made much impression, not at the time at any rate. He produced a remarkably complicated and oversophisticated, also highly pessimistic – perhaps the two are the same – reason for his opposition. It was that he thought we would get too much German subsidy, too much German money, which would act, rather like North Sea oil, as a false cushion for us and go on making it unnecessary for British industry to make the fundamental changes, without which it was assuredly doomed.

*Patrick Devlin, b. 1905, cr. Lord Devlin 1961, was a Lord of Appeal in Ordinary 1961–4 before unexpectedly retiring to authorship and occasional inquiries.

SUNDAY, 3 SEPTEMBER. *East Hendred and Dublin.*

The end of the long holiday and, alas, almost the brightest and best morning we had had. Crispin arrived to take me to the 12.50 plane to Dublin. He appeared vigorous after his Himalayan and Tibetan holiday in spite of having been bitten by a dog in some remote Asian country and consequently having to have a series of rabies injections.

On arrival in Dublin we drove to the hurling ground where, at the pressing invitation of the Taoiseach, we were to watch the all-Ireland championship finals. When asked to this event I had imagined that it was a sort of rustic occasion, with some traditional game being played on a village green. (I am not sure that I was absolutely clear of the distinction between hurling and curling.) Instead of this there was a ground the size of Twickenham or Cardiff Arms Park and a crowd of seventy thousand. It was obviously a great Irish state occasion, with not only the Taoiseach (Jack Lynch) but his predecessor Liam Cosgrave, Burke (my Commission colleague) and all sorts of Irish dignitaries present in the boxes. I found the game highly enjoyable, a curious mixture of hockey, lacrosse and rugger. I got a sufficiently clear view of the form by half-time to bet Colley, the Minister of Finance, that Cork would be the victors over Kilkenny, and this was not just a wild guess. I would gladly have invested more than £5, which was what I won. However, it was a well worthwhile bet for it became much publicized, as did my part in the whole occasion, which was, I suppose, good for the Commission profile in Ireland.

MONDAY, 4 SEPTEMBER. *Dublin and London.*

Left the hotel about 10.00 to go and see the Taoiseach in his normal rather dismal offices. He did not seem on his brightest form. I think that, an old Cork hurling player himself, he was exhausted from his celebrations both at the match and in the evening with the team. He is definitely in favour of coming into the European Monetary System, but not very precise about what he wants out of it, although attaching more importance, as did his ministers subsequently, to Irish growth not being cut back than to any immediate transfer of resources or increase in the Regional Fund.

Then a meeting with three or four of the other main ministers: mainly Monetary System but some slightly more detailed issues as well. The Irish were much less inclined to grumble than the last time I saw them, and indeed went out of their way to say that their relations with the Commission and the Community were now excellent. After a lunch given by the Taoiseach in Iveagh House, we went for a drive and a walk round Phoenix Park on a most beautiful afternoon. Then a plane to London, and Kensington Park Gardens just before 6 o'clock.

David and Debbie Owen came for a drink. They were both thoroughly agreeable. David, although he had been rather in favour of a spring election, obviously thought that one for early October was now definitely fixed. Equally obviously he thought that he would not be Foreign Secretary after the election whatever happened, because if Labour won Healey would take over. He was rather disappointed at the thought of the election cancelling the Labour Party Conference, at which he believed he might have got a very good vote for the National Executive Committee.

Jennifer and I then went to the Capitol Hotel for dinner with the Soames's, at which were present, amongst others, Carringtons, Gordon Richardsons and John Harris's. Soames very tough and firm on Europe and on the Monetary System, Gordon reticent, a bit wobbly, but not in my view too bad, Carrington rather hopeless about his ability to deal with Mrs Thatcher and indeed very depressed about the prospects, saying quite firmly that he thought she would be against and that there would not be enough pro-European strength in a Tory Cabinet to carry her along.

TUESDAY, 5 SEPTEMBER. *London and Brussels.*

To the National Westminster Bank in the City where I addressed their main board and their various regional boards (a total of about fifty people) on the EMS. 3.30 plane to Brussels and the new term.

THURSDAY, 7 SEPTEMBER. *Brussels, Rome and Bussento.*

8.40 plane to Rome. Drove to the Eden Hotel where the Italian Government had reserved a suite for us, and worked there from 11.00 until 12.30. Then to the Palazzo Chigi for a meeting with Andreotti and Forlani and three or four other people. Andreotti was on typical form, looking tired, pasty, unhealthy, but agreeable and on the ball; he hadn't had much holiday, but I don't think he likes holidays; and he was talking in a more clearly focused way than at our last meeting. He is eager on economic grounds, and determined on political grounds, to come into the European Monetary System, but he not unnaturally wants to get as much out of it as possible. The Italians are more specifically demanding than the Irish. The thrust of his demand, to an extent which surprised me, was on changes in the Common Agricultural Policy rather than on the transfer of resources as conventionally defined. The discussion continued over lunch with about four ministers, including Pandolfi,* the Minister of the Treasury, whom I had met once or twice before and of whom I think very highly, until about 3 o'clock. There was an informal 'on the hoof' press and TV conference as we left the Palazzo Chigi.

Hayden, Laura and I left by self-drive hired car, but with police escort, and made good progress south in deteriorating weather. As usual there were heavy downpours around the Bay of Naples. We then drove on down a very crowded and wet motorway until we turned off and began a difficult twenty-six-mile drive over the hills to arrive at Bussento (and the Bonham Carters) at 9.15.

SUNDAY, 10 SEPTEMBER. *Bussento and Rome.*

The third very good day of weather. Left after lunch for Naples (a two-and-a-half-hour drive), deposited our car at the Excelsior Hotel and were then rushed through the streets with a quite unnecessary screaming police escort to the Mergellina Station where we caught the *rapido* to Rome. To the Hassler Hotel and to dinner in the roof restaurant, where we were joined, at his urgent request, by Emilio Colombo. Laura feared that he was coming to complain about something – apparently we hadn't replied to some point which he had raised in a letter. But this (as I suspected) could hardly have been less accurate. What he wanted us to do was to provide him with some facts and preferably even a draft speech for the Jean Monnet Lecture at Florence, the successor to mine of the previous year, which he was going to give and which he wanted to be as helpful as possible.

*Filippo Pandolfi, b. 1927, Italian Minister of the Treasury 1978–80, and later of Industry and of Agriculture.

MONDAY, 11 SEPTEMBER. *Rome and Brussels.*

Breakfasted on my balcony at 7.45, looking over a slightly misty and autumnal but very warm and sunny Rome: a spectacular view. 9.45 plane. Flew in beautiful weather to about Coblenz and then bumped for twenty minutes into Brussels on as nasty a day as one could easily imagine.

Peter Carrington to lunch. Rather a good talk with him, perhaps because he is a particularly good listener. However, he obviously thinks that if they win in the spring there is a 60–70 per cent chance of his becoming Foreign Secretary. He doesn't totally exclude the Heath possibility but thinks it unlikely; doesn't wholly by any means exclude the John Davies possibility either, but hopes that won't happen. Does clearly exclude the Soames possibility, and is also unenthusiastic about the view which I canvassed to him, which I had previously canvassed to Soames the week before (where it was greeted with more enthusiasm), that Soames might become Minister of Agriculture for eighteen months or so. Carrington says this is because he thinks there couldn't be two ministers – particularly two ministers concerned with Europe – in the Lords. (He may feel a bit that he couldn't control Soames.) However, he was very anxious to discuss what he could most usefully do, as Foreign Secretary in a future government, in the Council of Ministers, etc., and anxious to know how he could make a favourable European impact. At the same time he was not at all confident how effectively he could direct a Conservative Cabinet in such a direction. As always he was gloomy and critical about Mrs Thatcher, and surprisingly pro David Owen.

WEDNESDAY, 13 SEPTEMBER. *Luxembourg and Brussels.*

An easy Commission meeting between 9.00 and 10.00, then into the Parliament for Genscher's long-delayed statement on Bremen and Bonn (no previous opportunity); quite well done, not too long. I followed with twelve minutes on the same subject. I then listened to the debate both morning and afternoon, which was almost entirely devoted to the EMS. Sixteen speakers out of nineteen were in favour, and to some considerable extent seized the real issues. It was a great contrast with our December attempt to get the Parliament to debate it, when they weren't taking it seriously.

I took Christopher Tugendhat to lunch and found him half attracted by the idea of an outside inquiry into the Commission* but half worried for his own portfolio responsibilities.

I wound up the Bremen/Bonn debate with an impromptu speech of ten minutes, and then returned to Brussels by avion taxi at 7 o'clock. It was a most beautiful day in Luxembourg, not very warm but absolutely clear sky, extremely low humidity, the first perfect day of autumn. At rue de Praetère I found Robert Marjolin whom I had asked to dine and stay the night. I had a three-hour dinner with him alone. He is an extremely nice man, looks fifty-five and is now nearly sixty-eight, on the board of a number of very high-class companies, Royal Dutch, Chase Manhattan, General Motors, American Express. He is a bit cynical, both about Europe and about French politics, but well worth talking to; I got him on to the subject of what one should do with the Commission and found him favourable to what I had in mind about an outside inquiry. He was willing to make some suggestions about names, but would not undertake it himself. 'Like you,' he said, 'I am interested in policy, not in organization.' He first suggested Pierre Dreyfus, ex-head of Renault, as a possible chairman, but then withdrew his name in favour of Witteveen, ex-Managing Director of the IMF.

THURSDAY, 14 SEPTEMBER. *Brussels.*

Lunch with Crispin for Calvo Sotelo, the Spanish Minister for European Affairs, and Bassols,† their Ambassador; two and a

---

* Over the summer of 1978 I decided that the internal working of the Commission and its *services* needed improvement, particularly through a loosening of the rigidities which prevented the most effective deployment of personnel. This was the first point discussed that year at the *cabinet* strategy meeting at East Hendred in late July. A small outside committee of inquiry seemed to me the best chance of overcoming national defensiveness and innate conservatism. This committee took shape under the chairmanship of Dirk Spierenburg, a Dutch diplomat and former Coal and Steel Commissioner, with British (Dick Taverne), French, German and Italian members.

At about the same time President Giscard d'Estaing conceived the idea of having 'Three Wise Men' to look at the relationship to each other of all the European institutions. This obviously embraced the external powers of the Commission, but not its internal working. The two inquiries were slightly confusingly parallel to each other, but not strictly overlapping. Neither transformed Europe, but I think mine produced more practical result than did his.

† Raimundo Bassols y Jacas, b. 1925, was Spanish Ambassador to the Community throughout my presidency and later Ambassador to Morocco.

quarter hours' detailed conversation in French. However, Calvo Sotelo, as I thought in Madrid in April, is a solid, considerable, sensible man with whom to deal. We talked about a wide range of things, including not least the Giscard letter to heads of government and to me, which had arrived the previous day, proposing that 'Three Wise Men' look at the future of European institutions. I had known this was around for some time, and of course it was all part of the subject he had broached with me in our June talk. However, I regret the exact timing because it coincides with my idea of an outside inquiry into the Commission. However, I don't intend to be put off because of that; his inquiry and mine have different terms of reference, and indeed a different subject.

As I told Calvo Sotelo, I am not too agitated about the letter, although I know some members of the Commission, notably Natali and Davignon — both of whom wanted to issue denunciatory statements — are excited against it. Vredeling, whom I would have expected to be most agitated, is not so. No doubt there is a desire in Giscard's mind to cut down the power of the Commission, to reduce or eliminate our political role, our connection with Parliament, and half to amalgamate us with the Council secretariat and with COREPER, and thus to make us all into servants of the European Council. This must clearly be resisted and some others will no doubt resist the other thought at the back of his mind, which is to revert to the old *Directoire* idea and to reform the Council of Ministers so as, after enlargement, to give greater power to the major countries, particularly France and Germany, maybe Britain. However, I don't believe in taking the rigid defensive view that everything is perfect (it is certainly far from that) and that therefore we should resist any change. I am sure it would be foolish for the Commission to take up this position. Altogether the Giscard initiative requires delicate playing.

I talked also with Calvo Sotelo about his worries that the Greeks might try to veto Spanish entry, or might be put up by the French to do this, and tried to reassure him.

After a long meeting with Davignon, partly about the Giscard letter but mainly to disclose my ideas to him before our Commission strategy weekend, I had an hour with Siad Barre, the President of Somalia, before the small dinner we were giving him in the Berlaymont. He is one of the few Africans who is neither francophone nor anglophone, though he speaks both, but Italian better than either. Although a good linguist, he is not a vastly intelligent man, an old Marxist, who has quarrelled bitterly with the Russians in the course of the past year. I had a desultory conversation with him at first, but he got better over dinner. I made a brief three-minute speech of welcome, to which he said that owing to his English not being perfect he was not sure that he could manage an adequate reply, and then produced a spate of more or less coherent words for thirty-two minutes.

FRIDAY, 15 SEPTEMBER. *Brussels and Comblain La Tour.*

A meeting with Gundelach, mainly about agriculture but also about the agenda for the weekend, and found him, too, pretty good and firm. Then I saw his new Director-General, Vilain, a Frenchman of course as is regrettably 'obligatory' in DG6, but was surprised, expecting to see an elegant *Inspecteur de Finance,* to discover a rather young, stolid-looking man who might be a policeman. Gundelach had told me that he seemed rather 'square' but I wasn't quite sure of his use of the word in English; however it seemed a good description. Vilain seemed agreeable enough to get on with: unable to speak English.

At 12.15 I received Warren Burger, the Chief Justice of the United States. He being the Third Citizen, it was held that I should go down and meet him, which I did, and then had three-quarters of an hour's conversation before taking him in to lunch. Conversation is perhaps not exactly the right word. I thought vaguely of what I might talk to him about, perhaps telling him a little about how Community institutions work, but found this happily totally un-necessary, as he talked the whole time – but well – about Supreme Court affairs. He looked rather like Asquith approaching his dotage but was quite a personality.

At 3.30 I saw Ortoli for the last of my conversations with Commissioners and found him more or less all right, perhaps a little less enthusiastic about reform (of the Commission) than the others, but certainly not proposing to have a row about it. Drove with Jennifer to the Hostellerie Saint Roch at Comblain La Tour in the valley of the Ourthe.

SATURDAY, 16 SEPTEMBER. *Comblain La Tour.*

The morning session opened with Tugendhat's paper on budget balance and future resources, a paper of Giolitti's, some contributions from Ortoli, moderately good this first half. Then Gundelach gave a very long but really rather brilliant *exposé* of the agricultural position. We got almost complete agreement on no fundamental upheaval but a very tough anti-surplus price policy, particularly on milk products. Afternoon and early evening sessions on direct elections, the part the Commission should play in them, whether Commissioners should stand, etc., and the organization of the work of the Commission.

SUNDAY, 17 SEPTEMBER. *Comblain La Tour and Brussels.*

A final session for three and a half hours, almost exclusively on personnel policy and the outside inquiry. We drove back to Brussels via Villers-le-Temple. A dinner party, rue de Praetère, for Christopher Soames who was staying with us, and Simonets amongst others. Christopher on boisterous form and the evening was easy and agreeable. His arrival caused great excitement in Marie-Jeanne, our excellent but not young Belgian cook, who had worked for him. She not only produced even better food than usual, but had her hair done specially.

MONDAY, 18 SEPTEMBER. *Brussels.*

To the Ecofin Council hoping to discover, as we all were, exactly what had happened at the Franco-German meeting at Aachen. The ministers of both countries were reticent. Healey made a fairly effective row about this, but eventually it emerged that nothing too hard had been settled and the slight *morosité* evaporated. The eight (i.e. less Healey) were then prepared to agree upon the Belgian compromise with the parity grid system for intervention, but with the 'basket', as it were in reserve behind it, providing the basis on which it could be decided who was responsible for an imbalance and who should act to correct it.

WEDNESDAY, 20 SEPTEMBER. *Brussels.*

Haferkamp at 7 p.m. to tell him that Tugendhat had referred to me the question of Madame van Hoof's* visit to China as one of his party, and that I thought he would be unwise to press ahead with it. However, I said that I would not veto it in the last resort.† At first he seemed rather inclined to give way but said he would talk about it with her and with Denman (his Director-General). I don't believe he wants her to go but I have little doubt he will be frightened by her into agreeing.

THURSDAY, 21 SEPTEMBER. *Brussels.*

Lunch at home for Georges Berthoin, the previous representative of the Community in London and the new Chairman of the European Movement. Berthoin was surprisingly interesting, though slightly disturbing. He is very worried about the Giscard initiative. If they got rid of the political role of the Commission, the overall European interest would go by default, he said. It is essential this should be the starting point, even if national governments subsequently whittle it away somewhat. If it is all left to national governments, nothing will emerge except for a series of horse-trading deals. He is also worried that no government (certainly no major one) is inclined to fight hard for the Commission. He is of course a great defender of the previous system, but still there is a good deal of sense in what he says and he put it very well.

It also emerged from this conversation that the great Commissions of the past were not all that powerful. Hallstein, he thought, started the rot by having an extremely ill-judged joust with de Gaulle which led to his defeat and decline; and that indeed way back in the traditionally great days of the Coal and Steel Community, Monnet had resigned because he felt he had lost control of the Commission.

Then for yet another session with a committee of the Parliament,

---

*Renée van Hoof was (and is) the head of the excellent Commission interpretation service. She became Madame Haferkamp in 1986.

†I did not think that I could dictate to a senior vice-president who should and who should not be in his party for a particular visit. He said that he needed her for interpretation purposes, not with the Chinese but within his multinational team.

this time the Legal Affairs Committee, presided over rather fruitily by Sir Derek Walker-Smith;* quite an enjoyable encounter. Home at 6.30 where Jennifer had Ken Galbraith for a drink. I had not seen him for eighteen months and he looked very well in spite of his approaching seventieth birthday and seemed as buoyant as ever.

FRIDAY, 22 SEPTEMBER. *Brussels and East Hendred.*

An early meeting with Haferkamp, who said he had had many long discussions with Denman and Renée van Hoof, particularly with Renée, and had decided she ought to go. So I reluctantly approved this. Jennifer and I then proceeded to miss the 12.35 plane to London. They had forgotten to put my suitcase in the car and I made the disastrous decision to go back to rue de Praetère and get it, believing that we always caught a plane in Brussels. It was a ludicrous attempt: leaving the Berlaymont at 12.10, even with an extremely lucky journey, we only got to the airport at 12.32 and they refused to take us. It was the first time† I missed a plane in Brussels. We eventually got away in rather bad order at 4.30, no first-class seats, no protocol – I think they were rather fed up with us for being so late – and then had a very good journey, beautiful weather at London Airport, and we arrived at East Hendred less than two hours later. I played croquet with Edward in a magnificent sunset.

MONDAY, 25 SEPTEMBER. *London and Brussels.*

To the Dorchester Hotel at 9.00 to address the opening session of the World Planning Conference. It was quite a good, slightly futuristic speech, written partly by Stanley Johnson,‡ about oil dependence and the possibilities of escaping from it, relations with the Developing World, etc. Some rather anti-motor car remarks which had been put into it attracted a good deal of attention, particularly on the BBC, and led to an exaggerated report that I had

*Sir Derek Walker-Smith, b. 1910, cr. Lord Broxbourne 1983, Conservative MP for Hertfordshire and a middle-rank minister 1955–60, was a Member of the European Parliament 1973–9.
†And as it turned out the only time.
‡Stanley Johnson, b. 1940, was an official in the Commission's Environment and Consumer Protection Service 1973–9, a Conservative MEP 1979–84, and is now back in the service of the Commission.

urged the abolition of the motor car, which however didn't do any great harm, though it reverberated on for a bit.

3.35 plane to Brussels and one and a half hour's interview there with Nick Stuart, Department of Education and Science and ex-Number 10 Private Secretary, as a possible replacement for Hayden. I found him, as I expected, bright and quick, although knowing practically no French, but eager to come, and I think on balance that he is the better candidate.*

Rue de Praetère dinner party for the Lee Kuan Yews, with Tickells, Brunners and the Singapore Ambassador and wife. As often with Lee, a slightly sticky beginning but then a highly enjoyable evening; we had mostly general conversation with a lot of anecdotes about world politics.

TUESDAY, 26 SEPTEMBER. *Brussels.*

One and a half hours' more serious conversation than the previous evening with Lee Kuan Yew before giving lunch to the President of Cyprus and then having a meeting with him from 3.00 to 4.00. I am afraid that Mr Kyprianou and I rather bored each other. Crispin thought that in the afternoon meeting we were both liable to fall asleep with our heads meeting and cracking in the middle. However, we just kept apart and the conversation going.

THURSDAY, 28 SEPTEMBER. *Brussels and Athens.*

Plane to Zurich and on to Athens. It was pretty cold in Brussels, and incredibly cold in Zurich. Athens at about 4.45 Greek time, where it was an absolutely perfect day, temperature 75°, no wind, which I regard as the bane of Greece, and a general atmosphere of balm. I was met at the airport by Karamanlis himself, as well as a great horde of other people, and there did a very brief press conference with him before driving to the Hôtel Grande Bretagne. I was then able to pay a quick visit to the Acropolis in wonderful light and with not many people about. Athens appeared more agreeable than I remembered it.

A serious meeting with Karamanlis from 7.45 to 9.15. There was

---

*I had seen a Home Office man the previous week.

a friendly atmosphere and I think a reasonably good relationship was established. I find him an impressive and agreeable man, although we had a fair amount of argument, particularly in relation to the length of the transitional period for bringing Greek agriculture into the Community system. They had been unofficially talking about requesting no transitional period at all, which would be disastrous, as it would drive the French and the Italians into demanding an excessively long one, which would bog down the whole negotiations.

I explained this to him very carefully and I think moved him on it. His main approach to all questions of Greek membership is essentially political, one of prestige, though not in a petty sense. He has devoted nearly twenty years of his career to Greek Europeanism and does not want this to be dissipated by Greece being treated in a second-rate category, i.e. given less favourable treatment than he thinks was extended to the previous three enlargement candidates. He is also very anxious to differentiate the Greek position from that of Spain and Portugal, and included in this conversation some slightly uncalled-for barbed remarks about the stability of Portuguese and Spanish democracy, with Italy thrown in for good measure, and even a few side-swipes about the difficulties of getting governments together in the Netherlands and Belgium!

However, we were broadly able to agree on the further timetable – break the back by Christmas, leave a few things over, get the *accords* ready for signature by the summer holidays – but all this depending on the negotiations going well over the next phase, which he recognized could be difficult, and during which he agreed to strengthen his official contacts with Brussels and keep in closer personal touch with us.

Then after this on to a largish (fifty or so) mixed dinner party at the Prime Minister's official residence. Fairly formal speeches, with television (there was heavy television and newspaper coverage of the whole visit). The conversation with Karamanlis at dinner was all right, but not terribly easy linguistically. (At the serious meeting he had talked Greek and I had talked English and we had been interpreted by his *Chef de Cabinet* – very well done for a non-professional.)

Karamanlis is indeed linguistically very odd. He has lived for ten years in France. He left Greece in 1963 before the Colonels came and did not return until 1974, when he immediately became Prime Minister again. He had close and influential French friends, Debré particularly, Couve de Murville to some substantial extent too, and even a quite close and useful acquaintanceship with the General himself. Yet he can hardly speak French at all. At one stage during dinner I thought I would try him in French to give him some slight relief from his halting English. So far from being a relief to him, it was absolute agony, and a look of total puzzlement came over his face as I addressed to him the most simple questions. This caused me some collapse of linguistic morale as I think my French, while not elegant, ought to be comprehensible. I was therefore greatly relieved when on the drive home that night Roland de Kergorlay, the chief official dealing with enlargement who, whatever else he can or cannot do, can certainly speak French, suddenly said to me, 'Karamanlis can hardly understand a word of French, you know. I found I had to talk English with him because he was just not understanding anything I said in French.' I have never felt more pro-Kergorlay!

FRIDAY, 29 SEPTEMBER. *Athens.*

9.45 call on the President of the Republic,* a little intellectual who was very agreeable to talk to. He gave me the amazing news that the Pope had died:† so amazing that at first I misunderstood him. 'The Pope has died,' he said rather inconsequentially. 'Oh, yes,' I said, 'yes, indeed I would like to have gone to his funeral, but unfortunately it was not possible.' 'No, no,' he said, 'the new Pope is dead.' 'Good God, you can't mean it?' I said. But of course he did.

Then a meeting of ministers, about six of them, presided over by the large Cretan, Konstantinos Mitsotakis,‡ the other most notable ones there being the Minister of Agriculture, Boutos, of whom I thought rather well, and Kontogeorgis, the minister in charge now of relations with Europe, who is nice but not impressive. This lasted two hours and was quite a serious meeting, with a lot of points –

*Konstantinos Tsatsos, b. 1899, philosopher and lawyer, was President of Greece 1975–80.
†Pope Paul VI had died on 6 August. His successor Pope John Paul died on 28 September.
‡Konstantinos Mitsotakis, b. 1918, was Greek Minister of Coordination and Planning 1977–80, of Foreign Affairs 1980–1, and has been leader of the new Democratic Party since 1984.

particularly the agriculture transition points – being gone into in considerable detail, and quite complicated arguments having to be deployed. I hope I shifted their minds a bit.

Then a luncheon at the hotel of sixty to seventy people – ministers who had been at the morning meeting, plus a collection of industrialists, bankers, trade unionists, heads of agricultural federations, etc. I made a short speech to them afterwards which led into a discussion.

Press conference at 4.00. This was expected to be formidable, as there are a lot of Greek newspapers (with very tiny circulations) and a high reputation for 'yellowness'. However, I found it reasonable, although long and crowded. It produced some fine misquotations the next day, which I hope did not do too much harm.

After a routine debriefing of the ambassadors of the Nine in the scruffy little German Chancellery, there was a reception in the rather grand Parliament building given by the President of the Chamber. Mavros* and indeed Karamanlis came, but not, slightly to my disappointment, Papandreou.† I had declined the offer of an official dinner and had intended to go off quietly with my Brussels team, but it became obvious that Karamanlis was free, so I asked him if he would come and dine with us, which he accepted with alacrity, but then not unreasonably turned the dinner party into one of his own. We all went off to some taverna below the Acropolis, where we dined in a party of about fourteen from 9.30 to midnight.

I had an agreeable conversation with him, his English seemed to have improved, and the evening went along buoyantly; the fact that he had wanted to do it was obviously a sign that the visit had gone rather well. He expressed great disappointment that I was going back the next morning, which indeed in view of the perfection of the weather I was beginning to feel myself, accentuated by the fact that he made it clear that the cruise on which he had wished to take Jennifer and me was to be on the old Onassis yacht, *Christina*, which now apparently is the official property of the Greek Prime Minister.

*George Mavros, b. 1909, had been a Minister or Governor of the Bank of Greece for much of the time between 1946 and 1966 and again briefly in 1974. Imprisoned under the Colonels. In Opposition in 1978.
†Andreas Papandreou, b. 1919, was leader of the Opposition 1977–81, and has been Prime Minister of Greece since 1981.

SATURDAY, 30 SEPTEMBER. *Athens and Brussels.*

Another perfect morning. I returned alone by the 8.50 plane (forty-five minutes late), leaving the others to the pleasures of the cruise. We had the most beautiful flight, with the sea absolutely still and a very faint haze, but otherwise a spectacular day, over the Peloponnese and Corfu to Brindisi, up the east coast of Italy where we ran into wisps of cloud about Ancona and over Venice. There was dappled sunlight over Germany before the usual wall of thick cloud settled in somewhere between Bonn and Liège. Brussels at 11.30, and home in cold rain. Afternoon expedition to Louvain with the Beaumarchais', who were in Brussels for a conference. Jacques somewhat better, although having got much worse after we left Sare. They and Hayden and Laura to dinner, rue de Praetère, and we had an enjoyable time compensating for Athens sunshine with very good wine.

MONDAY, 2 OCTOBER. *Brussels.*

Received Stobbe, the Governing Mayor of Berlin, for a meeting and lunch. I like him and think he is a very impressive young man. He is only about forty and has rather a stolid appearance, but is bright and quick. At 3.30 a meeting with about fifty representatives of the Berlaymont unions to explain to their somewhat suspicious minds what we were planning to do about the review body as a result of Comblain La Tour. Not sure to what extent I persuaded them; certainly they were not enthusiastic for change, but they could hardly be expected to be, as they know how inefficiently some of them are sitting on golden eggs, if that is not a mixed metaphor.

An hour's talk with Sam Brittan* which was quite satisfactory though he is more pro full monetary union than he is pro the EMS. Then, as an act of courtesy, I went to listen to Stobbe's lecture to the Institut Royal, where he had a good audience. He gave a dullish short lecture in English, which left time for lots of questions, which he answered brilliantly, with a great delicacy of touch and some emotional force, on quite difficult subjects.

*Samuel Brittan, b. 1933, has been principal economics correspondent of the *Financial Times* since 1966.

Tuesday, 3 October. *Brussels, The Hague and Brussels.*

Train to The Hague. A meeting from 12.30 to 1.30 with a lot of ministers, presided over by van der Klaauw, the Foreign Minister. That went very well. The Dutch are nice and sensible, and also I had an agreeable feeling, which I certainly would not have had a year ago, that I have a greater command of the various issues of Community business than any of them – although that obviously should be the case. Van der Stee, the Minister of Agriculture, I liked very much as on previous occasions. Van Agt, the Prime Minister, joined us just before the end of this meeting, and between it and lunch I had a quarter of an hour alone with him and van der Klaauw, during which we talked a bit about the Giscard letter, with a fairly good common approach, and I also tried out the idea of Witteveen on them, about which they were enthusiastic. Back to Brussels by the afternoon train.

Thursday, 5 October. *Brussels and Manchester.*

Five ambassadors with credentials. Then a meeting with fifteen British agricultural journalists, and then over to the Charlemagne, very reluctantly, for a COREPER lunch. The lunch was one of the most dreary of the series. We spent the time discussing pointless detailed issues about the agenda for the Council of Ministers.

Home, cutting it rather fine, to change into a dinner jacket, before catching the 6.10 plane to Manchester. It was the only sensible way of arranging things, although it seemed an odd dress for an air journey (almost unknown since the days of Imperial Airways, although I believe passengers then mostly dined on the ground). To the Midland Hotel and the Manchester Chamber of Commerce dinner. It was a large gathering of about three hundred packed into the room, and was generally a good occasion. My speech, although a bit long, was about the Community's industrial policy and the best I had delivered for some time.

I started by replying to the comments on my wishing to abolish the motor car, accompanied as it had been in some papers by suggestions that, in that case, I might start by giving up either the Mercedes or the Rover. The point was use not possession. I was a devoted train traveller. When I had been on an official visit to The

Hague two days before, and they had very kindly brought a motor car on to the station platform in order to drive me the short distance to the Catshuis, I said, 'Do you always do this for official visitors?' And they replied, 'We don't know. No official visitor, except you, has arrived by train for twenty years.'

I was joined after dinner by Jennifer, who had been addressing the Victorian Society in Manchester.

THURSDAY, 6 OCTOBER. *Manchester and Paris.*

A rather beautiful morning. The weather in my experience is always good in Manchester. Plane to Paris, to the Embassy at noon, and then to the Paris Hilton for a luncheon speech to the Cercle de l'Opinion. Oddly it was the first public speech I had made in France (apart from to the Parliament in Strasbourg), and was therefore of some importance. There was a large audience of over five hundred, including a lot of notables – Poher, President of the Senate, Maurice Faure, Couve de Murville, Lecanuet, Pontillon, Olivier Giscard d'Estaing (Giscard's brother, who is Chairman of ELEC which is associated with the Cercle).

It was an exhausting occasion. They kept on having speeches all through lunch; fortunately they suspended service for mine, although it was before the main course, and there was good attention for thirty minutes. The question period afterwards was chaotic and unsatisfactory. On balance the occasion was worthwhile.

Back to the Embassy and worked in the garden before a short walk around the Concorde and the Rond Point. We dined with the Hendersons and Marie-Alice de Beaumarchais (Jacques being ill again, although only with 'flu).

SUNDAY, 8 OCTOBER. *Paris and Brussels.*

The weather as perfect as ever. This October is the most exquisite month imaginable at any season of the year. Jennifer and I did a pre-lunch drive through south-east Paris, Boulevard de Montparnasse, Boulevard de Port Royal (where I stayed in the two summers before the war), Avenue de Gobelins, Place d'Italie, Bois de Vincennes, and then up to the heights of Bellevue and

Ménilmontant near Père-Lachaise and back through the Place de la République. It is a segment of Paris redolent of 1870–1939, yet largely hidden from foreigners today. Another lunch in the Embassy garden with the Hendersons alone. 5.44 TEE from the Gare du Nord. A splendid sunset on the way out of Paris but dark for most of the journey. A very satisfactory weekend in Paris. The Hendersons were extremely welcoming, and I thought more reconciled to retirement than when we last saw them there in June, and therefore talking much more (and with enthusiasm) about returning to England.

THURSDAY, 12 OCTOBER. *Brussels and Milan.*

Plane to Milan for an official visit. Three hours late because of fog there, which is only too usual in that distinguished city I fear; it was a beautiful day in Brussels. Got to the Savini Restaurant very late for my lunch with eight or ten Italian editors and the Lombardy industrialists who were organizing the visit. Most of the editors had waited, and we had a rather good discussion with sensible questions. Then to the Hotel Principe e Savoia before a call on the Prefect, a bouncy Sicilian of conversational verve (an interesting appointment to Milan). And then on from there to the Municipio for a meeting with the Syndico, a little right-wing socialist. Last there was a dinner with a not frightfully good speech from me on monetary union and a few questions.

FRIDAY, 13 OCTOBER. *Milan and East Hendred.*

A quite testing round of meetings (regional council, Lombardian industrialists), little speeches, press conference, TV interviews, etc. from 10.00 until 4.00, including a Confindustria lunch.

Then on the most beautiful afternoon I squeezed in a visit to Santa Maria delle Grazie to see the *Last Supper*, which I had not done for about fifteen years. It is noticeably deteriorating, the balance of the composition is still absolutely spectacular, but the colour and the line and the detail and the clarity have almost totally gone.

My plane for London took off at 6.30, only an hour late. Then we were stacked over Kent for nearly one and a half hours, because London Airport was only half open. East Hendred after a misty drive at 10.30.

SUNDAY, 15 OCTOBER. *East Hendred and Brussels.*

Donaldsons, Harlechs, Douglass Cater, Caroline and Jane Gilmour to lunch. I left with the Harlechs, who dropped me at London Airport for a Brussels plane which yet again was over an hour late. Rue de Praetère just after 9 o'clock for a postponed three-hour dinner alone with Pandolfi – the fairly new Italian Minister of the Treasury. He is very much a Lombardian, from Bergamo, I think. He speaks good English and we had a satisfactory talk about Community affairs in general, but obviously and particularly the EMS. His will to come in is very strong, and, whatever Italian hesitations there may be, I believe he will try and overcome them. The Italian main interest in the 'concurrent studies'* field seems to have switched from a shift in the balance of European agriculture (although they still attach some importance to that) to a large programme of loans with subsidized interest rates for major infrastructure projects. He talked about a nationwide environmental improvement scheme, which sounds a little airy-fairy, but I don't think, as conceived in his mind, it is so. Indeed he took exactly this view himself about a Messina Straits bridge, which he thought was far too ill-defined a project at the moment for vast sums of public money to be committed to it.

MONDAY, 16 OCTOBER. *Brussels and Luxembourg.*

Motored to Luxembourg to attend the Ecofin Council all morning and again for an hour after lunch. It was a depressing and disturbing meeting. I listened but didn't speak at all in the morning and only briefly in the afternoon to warn them that they were all drifting away from the objectives of the Bremen communiqué. In contrast with the September Ecofin meeting, when there was a solid front of eight countries, with the British isolated but not too intransigent, at this meeting there were about three floating groups with different positions on a whole range of issues and, if anything, it was the Germans who were becoming isolated on an excessively hard line, put forward in particular by Emminger, the President of the Bundesbank.

* Rather a euphemism for the transfer of resources to the poorer countries to encourage them to come into the EMS.

At the September meeting, mainly as a result of the Aachen arrangement between Giscard and Schmidt, there were eight countries for moving from the 'basket' to the 'grid' so far as the system of intervention was concerned. This had been subsequently modified by the so-called 'Belgian compromise', which was more favourable to German 'hardline-ism'. Having won this victory, the Germans ought to have been content. Instead, they tried to use it as a jumping-off ground for a further retreat (from Bremen), and also produced an extremely unconvincing scheme for, in effect, getting away from the 25 billion *écus* (European Currency Units) of credit, although pretending that they were not in fact doing so.

As a result of all this Healey was able to recover a good deal of the initiative, which he exploited skilfully to get support from Pandolfi and from Colley (Irish Finance Minister) and also on some issues from Monory* (French Finance Minister), and even, occasionally, from the Belgians and the Luxembourgeois. Only the Dutch and the Danes were solid with the Germans. Matters improved a little, but not much, in the afternoon, when Lahnstein rather than Emminger was leading for the Germans. Emminger is, I fear, anxious if he can to block the EMS and, if he cannot, to be dragged into it only by his hair, screaming, and with as puny a scheme as possible.

I then moved into the Foreign Affairs Council, which met for five hours and did a certain amount of routine business. As a result the three-a-side dinner that Dohnanyi was giving me at the Hostellerie Gastronome did not start until 10.30. However, he was as agreeable as ever and so indeed were those with him, even Sigrist being almost sparkling. Unfortunately they had ordered an elaborate dinner of five courses, which we were forced to sit through until about 12.30.

TUESDAY, 17 OCTOBER. *Luxembourg and Brussels.*

I attended a Concertation Meeting† on the Regional Fund between representatives of the Parliament and of the Council. The Council were giving remarkably little to the Parliament, although the

*René Monory, b. 1923, was French Minister of Industry and Trade 1977–8, of Finance and Economics 1978–81, and of Education 1986–8.
†Technical term for an attempt to reconcile differences between the two arms of the budgetary authority.

previous evening, to my surprise, the Danes had proposed a significant move forward which the Germans had been willing to accept, which we had supported strongly, but which had been blocked by the French and the British. At this Tuesday morning meeting Dohnanyi presented the Council position softly and rather well, and was then replied to by a combination of the Irish Senator Yeats and Donald Bruce,* who did his piece well without being too bad-tempered, but pointed a finger firmly at the British and the French. I think he was more concerned to have the British in his sights, but the French took it as a tremendous attack on them and *lèse majesté* against Giscard.

Luc de Nanteuil in response put on a peevish performance, first ostentatiously putting *Le Figaro* up in front of his face and then, getting bored with that journal, throwing it on the table, crossing and recrossing his legs, and generally miming a man in a bad temper. However, when I saw him in the afternoon he seemed to have completely recovered his good humour. He is a strange man; in most ways I like him very much, but he is not good at translating the sometimes extreme instructions of his government into firmness without petulance.

I later spoke to Johannes Witteveen on the telephone in Houston, Texas, and tried, I fear unsuccessfully, to persuade him to accept the chairmanship of my outside review body for the Commission.

At 6 o'clock we had the formal opening of the Portuguese negotiations for about an hour, at which Dohnanyi and I made speeches, followed by the new Portuguese Foreign Minister (Correia Gago) who seemed a bright and agreeable man. The questions at the press conference were, as nearly always, asked by the British more than anybody else, the inevitable Château Palmer starting off, and rather to my surprise they were mostly directed at me. Avion taxi to Brussels.

WEDNESDAY, 18 OCTOBER. *Brussels*.

Saw Gundelach on the difficult issue of whether we were going to take the British to court on several fish conservation measures. I

---

* Donald Bruce, b. 1912, cr. Lord Bruce of Donnington 1975. Labour MP 1945–50, MEP in the last years of the indirectly elected Parliament.

was sceptical on the major one, not because I was against taking the British to court but because I feared that on the legal opinion we would not win. Gundelach was clearly under considerable pressure from the Danish Government and also believed it might strengthen his negotiating hand with the British. Eventually we agreed to set in train the legal process in all four cases, but not to get ourselves into a position from which we could not draw back from any one of them.*

A short-notice dinner party, rue de Praetère, for Maitlands, Denmans, Tinés and Laura. Donald Maitland was far more relaxed than I had seen him before. It was obviously rather a good idea to have him to a 'scratch' party. He has become a new man in the last few months: (i) he is much more courageous *vis-à-vis* London, (ii) he is more *communautaire*, and (iii) he is much funnier. Jacques Tiné as agreeable and funny as ever. As a result they stayed much later than I had intended.

THURSDAY, 19 OCTOBER. *Brussels and London.*

11.15 plane to London. I arrived to discover Jennifer in (for her) a considerable state about the ludicrous build-up of the story which had begun as a trickle in *Tribune* and then, the British press feeding off itself as usual, became a flood, announcing that we had not paid our Labour Party subscriptions for several years. It was wholly untrue, the subscriptions had been paid by banker's order, and the whole thing had obviously been motivated by a malicious Trot. in the North Kensington Labour Party. By this time we had had about five separate, quite prominent newspaper stories and two (rather funny) cartoons, and our attempts at denials had been quite unable to stem the flood. We eventually sent off a rather good, non-portentous letter to *The Times*, which gradually achieved the staunching operation.†

A dinner speech at Grosvenor House to the Council of British Shipping. This turned out to be almost the biggest dinner I have

---

* Curiously, it subsequently emerged that the British thought they were on stronger legal ground on one or two of the minor ones than on the major one – the size of the so-called Norway pout box (an area closed to fishing for this type of fish) – on which our own legal services were so doubtful.

† I suppose, in retrospect, that we were sensitive to the story because, while strictly *non vero*, it had its *ben trovato* element.

ever addressed, with about 1100 people. Agreeable neighbours in the shape of Ronald Swayne, the chairman, and John Ropner, whom I hadn't seen since we crossed the Atlantic together on the *Queen Mary* on my first visit to the United States in 1953.

SUNDAY, 22 OCTOBER. *Rome.*

Dressed in the extraordinary costume of white tie, evening tailcoat, black waistcoat, decorations, which was required for the Papal installation,* I set off for St Peter's just after 9 o'clock. The Mass (in the open air) began at 10 o'clock and went on until 1.15 in steadily improving weather, so that the umbrella I had cautiously taken manifestly became unnecessary by about 11 o'clock. Most of the first hour was taken up by the homage of all the cardinals, and I wished that I had a key to them. Emilio Colombo (next to me) wasn't bad and pointed out about fourteen, but even his knowledge seemed far from perfect. The Duke of Norfolk, in the next row, offered pungent comments about one or two of them. The second hour was taken up by introductory parts of the service and by a half-hour sermon, delivered seated but with great force by the new Pope, who has a remarkable linguistic ability. There were passages in French, Spanish, German, English, Serbo-Croat, Polish obviously, Russian, Czech I think, and Portuguese, all thrown in on the Italian base and all rather convincingly done.

In the third part of the service, the Mass itself, communion was distributed by an immense fleet of priests to everyone in the reserved area, and so far as I could make out also to vast numbers of people in the crowd below the bottom of the steps, which was said to number 250,000. The music was on the whole good, though not quite so memorable as it had been in San Giovanni in Laterano at the Aldo Moro service. It is more difficult to get the peculiarly haunting lilt of the Roman Mass music in the open air.

The ceremony over, we got away with quite remarkable speed. I walked out with Andreotti and Forlani and was in my car and moving off within ten minutes. Lunch (changed) soon after 2 o'clock with Laura and Crispin and Delli Paoli (our protocol man) in the most beautiful weather. Delli Paoli succeeded in getting the

* Following the death of Pope John Paul I on 28 September, his successor Pope John Paul II, formerly Cardinal Wojtyla of Cracow, had been elected on 16 October.

restaurant to move one table outside for the sun-worshipping English. Then a very good expedition for one and a half hours to two basilicas, San Giovanni and Santa Maria Maggiore, plus the Janiculum Hill (for the view) and the Campidoglio.

The British Ambassador (Alan Campbell), Leslie Benson* and Milton Gendel,† amongst others, to dinner at the Bolognese in the Piazza del Popolo. Raymond Barre was also dining at the restaurant.

MONDAY, 23 OCTOBER. *Rome and Brussels.*

A half-hour interview on general subjects for Italian television on the balcony of the Hassler. I then dressed again in the elaborate costume of the day before, improved slightly on this occasion by my wearing one of Laura's black silk scarves as a cummerbund to cover the gap between my hired black waistcoat and my semi-stiff shirt. The audience ceremony (at 11.30) turned out to be much too long and rather a bore. The Pope was late arriving, having given private audiences to the King of Spain and one or two other heads of state. He made a quite good but, in the circumstances, rather too long speech in French, and then started on his list of individuals who were each taken up to the throne and had perhaps two minutes with him. The European Community counted as an international organization, so came towards the end with NATO, the United Nations, etc. at about 2 o'clock. By then I was anxious to have it over, and so I suspect was the Pope though he showed no signs of boredom. When I mounted the steps of his dais he paused to see what language I would talk in, and as he had sounded equally good in English and French I started in English, but found him more halting than I expected, although still a forceful personality at close quarters as at more distant ones.

I then bolted, before the end of the ceremony, and was escorted by *motards* to Ciampino. Brussels by 5.00.

*Lady Benson, 1907–81, was married first to Condé Nast and then to the English banker, Sir Rex Benson. She was the mother of Leslie Bonham Carter and the owner of Bussento, the house in the south of Italy which we frequently visited.
†Milton Gendel, b. 1924, is an American art historian who is the widower of Judy Montagu, the daughter of the recipient of so many Asquith letters.

WEDNESDAY, 25 OCTOBER. *Brussels*.

Commission for seven hours. A substantial discussion on EMS which Ortoli opened with a speech lasting sixty-five minutes which reduced everything to the level of a very flat plain and greatly underestimated the importance of concurrent studies. I decided to adjourn and go back to it in the afternoon, when I made a short intervention putting a slightly different emphasis on where we were, the dangers of the position and the importance of concurrent studies.

THURSDAY, 26 OCTOBER. *Brussels*.

The first morning of rain for weeks. I saw in succession the President of IBM, then Signora Badua Glorioso, the new Italian Trade Union Chairman of the Social and Economic Committee (very good indeed) and then Robert Stephens, the now elderly diplomatic correspondent of the *Observer*. I took Christopher Tugendhat to lunch, Chez Christopher appropriately enough, and had an agreeable talk with him. Back for the presentation of six hundred Community medals to those who had served twenty years. An enormous ceremony, it being twenty years after the Treaty of Rome.

It was also the twentieth anniversary dinner of the European Investment Bank, which sounded rather a ghastly occasion and to which I had reluctantly agreed to go, but which turned out to be agreeable and worthwhile except for, as usual in Belgium, there being too many courses and the service too slow.

FRIDAY, 27 OCTOBER. *Brussels, Bonn and Brussels*.

Avion taxi to Bonn. I did not want to drive three times along the autobahn in twenty-four hours. I regretted the decision as soon as we got to the airport and were told that Bonn was in thick fog. However, we persuaded them to take off. When we got near we could see a thin layer of dense mist just over the Rhine Valley. Until Cologne we were in full sunshine and could see the tops of the hills and even of the spires. However, the pilots went in (the advantages of a small plane) and we suddenly saw the runway about ten feet below us. They flew above it for a bit (presumably to make sure it wasn't an autobahn) and then came down quite safely. On the ground there was practically no visibility at all, less than 100 metres I would guess, and aeroplanes parked alongside us on the apron were just dim shadows.

We drove to the Bundeskanzlerei and I saw Schmidt from 10.00 to 11.20. Peripheral matters for fifteen minutes: MTNs, fisheries, free movement of labour in relation to the Greek negotiations, and then had an hour on the EMS. He said the meeting with Callaghan had produced remarkably little; it had been a non-discussion. His assumption now was that the British were not coming in. However, he thought we would certainly get Ireland in and probably Italy too, the latter with wider margins. He was quite forthcoming about what he could do for them on concurrent studies, provided he didn't have to do it for the non-participant British as well.

Giscard, he said, was quite firm, the determination on his part very strong. There were difficulties with the Bundesbank and this put a sharp limit on the extent to which he (Schmidt) could move on the basket as opposed to the parity grid; he couldn't move either on automaticity of intra-marginal intervention. He could win over the Bundesbank he thought, on the question of the back-up resources available (he agreed it must be 25 billion to start with) and on what he might do in the way of concurrent studies, where he was primarily thinking in terms of loans at subsidized rates of interest, mainly through the EIB.

It was a precise, worthwhile discussion. We also touched on the CAP, on which he thought he could accept a price freeze for German farmers but not an actual reduction in income such as might be involved with a combination of price freeze and reductions of MCAs. Back by avion taxi and into the Berlaymont at 12.45.

SATURDAY, 28 OCTOBER. *Brussels and Bonn.*

By car with Crispin to Schloss Gymnich. A full turn-up of Foreign Ministers, except for Simonet who didn't arrive until 4.30. A good lunch, but horrible little rooms. Schloss Gymnich is basically a nice place, but it is furnished in such a way as to create maximum inconvenience – absolutely nowhere to put anything, no writing table, only one tiny table covered with flowers and bowls of fruit, which I firmly put outside the door. Equally, the only shelf in the bathroom was covered with costly toilet preparations. Despite the fact that the place is done up in the utmost luxury, with gold taps, etc., it is neither convenient nor elegant.

A fairly desultory discussion (though some useful business was done) during the afternoon on the Giscard letter, in which there was no tendency to turn it down out of hand, but a substantial desire to get it under control. Several countries were anxious that the Three Wise Men should be Four, and should be the four presidents, i.e., me, Colombo (Parliament), Kutscher (Court) and the President in office of the Council of Ministers. This was supported by Italy, Luxembourg and, more surprisingly, Germany. I was unenthusiastic.* An inconclusive outcome on this. The Dutch, and indeed the Danes for almost opposite reasons, were insistent that the Wise Men should be precluded from recommending an upset in the balance of Community institutions, which was helpful from the point of view of safeguarding the Commission position.

Then we succeeded in getting a fairly satisfactory compromise solution for a weighted voting formula when the Greeks come in. We got away from the principle of eighteen votes continuing to be a blocking minority, on which the British, the French and the Danes had been trying to insist.†

Boring conversation at dinner: a sort of review of the world done without any sinews of logic or originality of thought. It would have been regarded as a disgrace in intellectual or journalistic circles in most major capitals. Each Foreign Minister just chipped in with some titbit of information he had picked up about some country, and the whole thing became almost like a shop-girls' exchange of gossip. 'And then there's Iraq. They are carrying on with the Russians. And, Afghanistan, shocking behaviour there too.' Perhaps such a banal exchange of views has something to be said for it, but not much.

---

*It was advanced as a ploy to teach the French not to play anti-*communautaire* games, and while I thought it a good joke, I did not have time to spare to serve on a leisurely committee of inquiry.
†The four big countries had ten votes, the Netherlands and Belgium five, Denmark and Ireland three and Luxembourg two. The importance of getting away from eighteen was that it set a precedent for flexibility when Spain and Portugal came in.

SUNDAY, 29 OCTOBER. *Bonn and East Hendred.*

Session from 9.30 until 11.20, mainly on Africa, but also a long report from Guiringaud on his recent discussions with Gromyko in Paris. Also a return to the Giscard letter. As soon as the meeting was over we helicopted to Wahn, from where I got a lift with David Owen to Northolt. I had a tolerably interesting conversation with him during the journey. He was much better on EMS than the night before, and was generally being extremely friendly. Almost for the first time he asked my advice on something, but, alas, on Africa, on which I am singularly ill-equipped to give him any. East Hendred for lunch, where I started a week's *Toussaints* holiday.

WEDNESDAY, 1 NOVEMBER. *East Hendred.*

I spent the whole morning and afternoon writing an *Observer* article on the EMS, the first article (as opposed to a book review) I had written myself for a long time. Perhaps as a result of unfamiliarity I thought it was better than it was.

To Oxford to dine in Worcester hall with the Briggs'. A talk with Richard Cobb, remarkable writer on French eighteenth- and nineteenth-century history, before dinner. I was much struck by the change in the undergraduates (perhaps Worcester is traditionally exceptional in this respect) who had an extremely conventional appearance, now looking much more like undergraduates of the thirties than those of the sixties. But they are much less political, or if political more right-wing, than then. The proportion from independent schools is rising quite substantially, owing I fear to the end of the grammar schools and the comprehensive schools not mostly trying for Oxford.

THURSDAY, 2 NOVEMBER. *East Hendred, London and East Hendred.*

To London for a one-and-a-half-hour meeting with Callaghan in Downing Street. On EMS I got the impression that he was not coming in, though I was by no means certain of this. He was genuinely engaged with the subject, genuinely torn in his mind. When I said I appreciated his political difficulties, he rejected this firmly, saying: 'No, no, if I was convinced it was right I would do it. It *isn't* a question of politics.' But I thought he protested a little too much on this. Perhaps the most interesting thing he said was to ask at the end why I thought that Giscard, without a tremendously strong economy, was very willing to do it. I said, 'Because France is much more self-confident than Britain. They believe they can make a success of things, whereas we don't.' He rather sadly said that perhaps that was right and perhaps he agreed. We covered a few peripheral subjects, with him not unnaturally showing great interest in the CAP and also in budgetary contributions.

SATURDAY, 4 NOVEMBER. *East Hendred.*

Drove to Oxford where I voted (unsuccessfully) for John Sparrow in the Professorship of Poetry election. An unexpectedly large turn-out. I was surprised to meet Anne and Mickey Barnes queuing to vote, also, on the way out, Douglas Jay and Patrick Reilly arriving from All Souls. Douglas was remarkably cool and unfriendly. It is astonishing how his mind is dominated by the one question of Europe which prevents his being friendly even in a casual encounter, the first for nearly two years, despite old friendship.*

MONDAY, 6 NOVEMBER. *East Hendred and Brussels.*

Morning plane (late) to Brussels. EMS lunch speech to a Brussels establishment gathering at the Cercle Gaulois. In the afternoon I recorded a ninetieth birthday television tribute to Monnet.

That evening I had Finn Gundelach to dine alone, rue de Prae-tère. He seems less tense than a few months ago. We agreed satisfactorily on the sort of paper we should put in to the European Council. He wants it to be short and firm, and he is quite hard on a price freeze. He had two other points of interest. The first was personalities within the Council of Agricultural Ministers. The one he dislikes most is Ertl,† with Silkin a strong second. The one he has

*A few years later this disappeared, and after my return to the House of Commons in 1982 my relations with this angular and insular but exceptional and distinguished English eccentric (b. 1907, Labour MP for Battersea 1946–83, President of the Board of Trade 1964–7, cr. Lord Jay 1987) were happily repaired.
†Josef Ertl, b. 1925, a Bavarian member of the FDP, was German Minister of Agriculture 1969–83.

the highest regard for is van der Stee, the Dutch Minister, and after him the Luxembourgeois and the Italian, Marcora.

His second interesting point was what the pattern of European agriculture would be if we had no CAP and allowed production to find its own level. Our imports, in his view, from most countries would not be much greater. The North Americans would do all right, the Canadians very well indeed because of hard wheat. Nobody else would achieve much, certainly not the New Zealanders and the Australians. Our level of production would be lower, but this wouldn't very adversely affect agriculture down to, say, Rome. Southern Italy would do very badly. So would the Celtic fringes. I rather encouraged him to work this out in more detail and put it down on paper.

THURSDAY, 9 NOVEMBER. *Brussels*.

It being the most exquisite, sun-drenched autumn day, I drove myself to the Bois de la Cambre and sat reading and looking at the leaves and the lake for most of the morning. I then went into the office only at 12.30 to see Paul Loby of Agence France Presse. I then joined at short notice a lunch party of Hayden's at the Cercle Gaulois (my second visit that week) in a rather nice garden room with the sun streaming in. Hayden apparently thought that he was a member of the Cercle Gaulois by virtue of his being a member of Brooks's, but discovered after inviting his guests that this was not so. However, he managed to get the table by talking about the President's *cabinet*. That goes better at a Brussels club than it would in St James's Street.

At 7.00, we had Bob Strauss, accompanied by four other Americans, including Ambassadors Alonzo McDonald and Hinton, in for a talk about the waiver dispute.* A rather successful hour's talk. We didn't quarrel but were very firm and kept them on the defensive throughout. Jennifer arrived in Brussels for the first time for a month.

---

*The power of the American Government to waive so-called 'countervailing duties' was due to expire on 3 January 1979. Unless they took urgent legislative steps to extend this power the effect on European imports into the USA was likely to be considerable and the climate in which MTNs were carried on substantially worsened.

FRIDAY, 10 NOVEMBER. *Brussels*.

The weather still being spectacular, I went for a walk with Jennifer at Groenendaal, and then lunched with her and Crispin at the Chalet de la Forêt.

Shortly before leaving the office at 7.00, I got ensnarled with Tugendhat who rang up making, as I thought, the most ridiculous fuss about his not being treated properly for the Prince of Wales's visit. The point was that the subjects which the Prince had asked to be discussed in his meeting with the Commission did not include one which Christopher could naturally introduce. I got rather impatient with him, I think rightly so. It is extraordinary the unbalancing effect which royalty has even on the most normally sensible people. Unfortunately during my testiness I rather forgot that we were dining with the Tugendhats that evening. However, Christopher rose splendidly above the issue at dinner and both he and Julia were totally agreeable and had other interesting people there as they mostly do.

SATURDAY, 11 NOVEMBER. *Brussels*.

My fifty-eighth birthday. Drove to Auvillers-les-Forges just over the French frontier to meet the Beaumarchais' at the good restaurant there. Unfortunately the weather had changed into cold, freezing mist and the Beaumarchais' had a dreadful fog-bound drive from Paris. They came back to Brussels with us and the four of us dined alone, rue de Praetère.

SUNDAY, 12 NOVEMBER. *Brussels*.

Took the Beaumarchais' to Groenendaal for a pre-lunch walk, again in spectacular weather, very cold now, but with perfect sunshine again and the leaves at their very best. This first fortnight in November the leaves have been better than I ever remember them on this side of the Atlantic.

MONDAY, 13 NOVEMBER. *Brussels, Basle and Berne*.

Early train to Basle for lunch with the Central Bank governors and then my Swiss official visit. The train collapsed between Luxembourg and Metz, and we had to get into another extremely cold one before chugging into Basle at 2.35 instead of 1.00. The governors were just finishing lunch but they waited while I ate hurriedly and I had a good discussion with them until about 4.20. Zijlstra,* the Dutchman in the chair, was very good I thought. Gordon Richardson helpful, as one would expect him to be. Clappier said not a word, a rather useless and ineffective performance for Giscard's vicar at a rather crucial EMS discussion. The sceptics (predictably) were Baffi[†] and Emminger. The Americans, Volcker[‡] and one other, were quite helpful. It was worthwhile and not as technically formidable as I feared it might be.

In the afternoon, a beautiful day again in Basle, I went to the Drei Könige Hotel before my lecture at the university at 6.15. This went surprisingly well, although it was not a brilliant lecture, but the large audience received it friendlily. Then a long reception, and then dinner at the Schützenhaus which was where we had lunched. There were brief speeches after dinner, mine willingly given as it was in response to the presentation to me of a spectacular little book – a 1520 edition of the Latin epigrams of Sir Thomas More with a Victorian binding.

We then drove to Berne, where we were installed in the excellent Bellevue Palais Hotel. Grand Swiss hotels of the first third of this century have a remarkable quality. They are built with the solidity of the Drake in Chicago and furnished with the elegance of the Paris Ritz.

TUESDAY, 14 NOVEMBER. *Berne and Strasbourg.*

An early meeting with Fritz Honegger (effectively Economic Minister) and various members of his staff, including Central Bank people. A quite intense discussion, they showing considerable interest in the EMS and a desire to enter in the future,[§] though not to rush it, partly because they suspected, probably rightly, that the

---

*Jelle Zijlstra, b. 1918, was Prime Minister of the Netherlands 1966–7, and head of the Dutch Central Bank 1967–81.
†Paolo Baffi, b. 1911, was Governor of the Bank of Italy 1975–80.
‡Paul Volcker, b. 1927, was President of the New York Federal Reserve Bank 1975–9, and Chairman of the Board of Governors of the Federal Reserve System 1979–87.
§Ten years later that particular bit of the future has still not arrived.

French might veto them as they had once vetoed their entry into the Snake.

Then a joint meeting with the President, Ritschard, and the Foreign Minister. The presidency rotates on I think a two-year basis amongst the Federal Councillors, and Ritschard continues to discharge his normal responsibilities, which in his case are fairly mundane ones, public works, etc. However, he is a rather impressive man. I had quite an interesting discussion with them both. It is extraordinary how they manage linguistically: the President talked in German and was interpreted, the Foreign Minister talked in French and was not. I talked in a mixture of English and French, which the President understood, and indeed he understood some English too, but not completely. Most of the other meetings, however, were satisfactorily conducted in English.

Two other less pointful meetings and then a lunch given by the President in a seventeenth-century house with a good view. We had drinks on the terrace – it would indeed have been warm enough to have lunched outside in full sunshine; quite extraordinary for 14 November. I much liked all those I spoke to and indeed found Switzerland surprisingly agreeable, and Berne a particularly attractive town. I had never been there before. Then a press conference, a drive to Basle and a train to Strasbourg.

THURSDAY, 16 NOVEMBER. *Strasbourg and Brussels.*

The weather seems to have broken at last (after six weeks) and I sat and worked in the hotel on a rainy morning until 12.30. Then I took Donald Bruce to lunch. He has a staccato mind, works hard, but there is some curious deficiency. However, he is an effective member of the European Parliament, and having been anti-European says he is now anxious to cooperate. I did an hour's quite enjoyable question session in the Parliament, and then took an avion taxi back to Brussels, where I arrived in time (i) to go home, (ii) to see the Lancashire Mayors who had come over about textile problems and who were extremely protectionist (but who would not be in their position?), and (iii) to have a 7 o'clock meeting with the new President of Kenya, arap Moi, and then give him dinner. He was more agreeable than interesting. The more memorable man in his team was the very flashily dressed Attorney-General, Njonja, whom I remembered from my visit to Nairobi five years before, who tries to be a sort of black Elwyn-Jones – indeed he had been a pupil of his – though a good deal more flashy.

FRIDAY, 17 NOVEMBER. *Brussels and East Hendred.*

An hour with Dirk Spierenburg, former Dutch diplomat, ex-member of the Coal and Steel Commission, an experienced, urbane, firm figure, whom I have got to be chairman of the external review body for the Commission. 12.30 plane to London. East Hendred at 5.30, where we had the Simonets coming for the weekend. Despite the great efforts of Peter Halsey (my driver) to show them how VIP treatment should really be done at airports, with the hope this might encourage Henri to make Zaventem better, they did not arrive until 9 o'clock.

SATURDAY, 18 NOVEMBER. *East Hendred.*

Took the Simonets into Oxford for a brief tour, including a visit to the lantern at the top of the Sheldonian. Henri bought a lot of books at Blackwell's, which made us late for lunch at Sevenhampton with Ann (Fleming) who had the Bonham Carters, Derek Hill, whom Ann wants to paint my portrait but who is very expensive, and Stuart Hampshire who arrived even later than we did. We returned on a dismal afternoon by way of Buscot. I had to work before dinner and could not get Henri to settle. As he is Foreign Minister, why does he not have a lot of despatch boxes from the Belgian Foreign Office? Perhaps they don't have them. Enjoyable dinner with them alone.

SUNDAY, 19 NOVEMBER. *East Hendred and Brussels.*

Saw the Simonets off at 11.15. The weather had been awful but the brief weekend was otherwise very successful. Gilmours, Wyatts, plus John Harris to a rather hilarious lunch. Woodrow, John Harris and I played croquet in the twilight until Jennifer and I left for the 7 o'clock plane to Brussels.

MONDAY, 20 NOVEMBER. *Brussels*.

To the Ecofin Council, mainly listening to Ortoli doing well in a general EMS discussion, which however failed in its main purpose of eliciting what the British were going to do. In the afternoon to the Palais d'Egmont for the great conference with the ASEAN (Association of South East Asian Nations) Foreign Ministers which Genscher has been so keen to organize. I made an opening speech, as did he, and then went back to the Ecofin Council. Val Duchesse dinner for the ASEAN ministers. I sat next to General Carlos Pena Romulo, the Philippine Foreign Minister, aged nearly eighty, one of the San Francisco signatories of the UN Charter, President of the General Assembly in the early 1950s, and the longest serving Foreign Minister in the world after Gromyko. He made a rather good speech after dinner. His oratorical style might be described as early Stevenson, though with a much harder line and without the jokes.

After dinner Genscher insisted on organizing a discussion which I thought was going to be a disaster, but wasn't, mainly because two or three of the ASEAN ministers spoke extremely well. All of them were notably more anti-Russian (though rather pro-Chinese) than were the European Foreign Ministers. So the discussion turned into Genscher and others excusing themselves to these Third World gentlemen for being relatively soft with the Russians because of the problems over Berlin, etc. A curious evening.

TUESDAY, 21 NOVEMBER. *Brussels*.

A meeting with Abela, Secretary-General of the Maltese Ministry of Foreign Affairs, who is said to be the most sensible of the Maltese. However, he was by normal standards quite remarkably foolish (and tiresome), complaining about everything, at once aggressive and boring, so that eventually I said to him, 'Do you think that Malta gets a worse deal from the Community than do other countries?' He predictably answered, 'Yes.' So I then said, 'Well, why don't you change your tactics, which are well known to be the most objectionable in Europe, since you think they do you so little good?' No coherent reply emerged.

FRIDAY, 24 NOVEMBER. *Brussels.*

Spierenburg for another talk about the various members for his review body. I sold him Victor Rothschild and accepted one or two of his. Then, I had a meeting with the Gambian President followed by a Berlaymont lunch for him. It was not a particularly interesting or purposeful occasion, but no doubt necessary.

SUNDAY, 26 NOVEMBER. *Brussels and Paris.*

Drove on a cold misty day, it having quickly reverted to the high pressure freezing weather, to a village about twenty miles beyond Huy in the near Ardennes where the Jonquières have Fernand Spaak's country house temporarily at their disposal. They had a large luncheon party for Roderic Braithwaite, a departing British diplomat.

5.17 TEE with Crispin to Paris, and installed ourselves in the Embassy. It was a beautiful clear cold night.

MONDAY, 27 NOVEMBER. *Paris and Brussels.*

A talk with van Lennep* at OECD, and then to the Elysée for a meeting with Giscard. This followed the normal pattern: a guard of honour in the courtyard, a fairly punctual ushering in, though not as absolutely so as usual, and an hour's discussion. François-Poncet, whom everybody knew was about to be appointed Foreign Minister, was still present and still 'avec la tête dans ses blocnotes', but was supplemented on this occasion by Wahl, the new Secretary-General of the Elysée, so that we were five altogether, with Crispin on my side.

The conversation was perfectly friendly, though, as is always the case with Giscard, without warmth. Not a great deal about the EMS. He said it was all satisfactorily fixed: he didn't think the British would come in, but maybe from their point of view they were wise. This was done rather dismissively (indeed he was rather lofty throughout) and was in contrast with the Embassy impression that the Callaghan visit had been a great success. So in a sense it had

*Emile van Lennep, b. 1915, Treasurer-General of the Dutch Ministry of Finance 1951–69, then became Secretary-General of the Organization for European Economic Cooperation and remained there until 1984.

been, but mainly because Giscard didn't want to argue with Callaghan and was perfectly willing for him to stay out. Giscard's clear assumption that the System would come into operation on 1 January. He assumed too that the Italians would come in, although the wider margins for them were a mistake, but if they wanted it, so be it. And so far as assistance to them and the Irish was concerned, he thought that subsidized loans through the European Investment Bank should be the main mechanism. I ought probably to have contested this elliptical dismissal of the Regional Fund, but I wasn't too anxious to get into a detailed argument with him about this and other budgetary questions, and, perhaps mistakenly, I rather let that go.

We had a certain amount of conversation, but obviously not very deep, about agriculture, about fisheries, and about MTNs, on which he appeared to be taking a rather milder line than Deniau and not objecting to any particular timetable, but merely saying the quality of the package was what mattered. Then we talked about his 'Three Wise Men', in which he was forthcoming about names, saying that for a Frenchman he had in mind Marjolin, about which I knew, of course, or, as a second choice, Soutou, retiring General Secretary of the Quai d'Orsay, which I did not know. He also mentioned Brinkhorst* (he wasn't quite sure of his name but we got to him by a roundabout route) as a possible Dutchman, leaving the third slot probably for an Englishman, as to whose identity he expressed no particular preferences.

We also discussed my 'Five Wise Men' for the external inquiry, in which he showed some interest, but was firmly against Spierenburg's first choice (and therefore at that stage mine also), of Fontanet, French ex-minister, on the ground that he had received so many recent setbacks, electoral and otherwise, that he was a used-up man. On the other hand he was firmly for Delouvrier,† the second man on Spierenburg's and my list, currently head of Electricité de France. So, having put the issue to him, whether wisely or not, I clearly have to go for Delouvrier.

I returned hurriedly from my Elysée meeting to the Château de la

---

*Laurens Brinkhorst, b. 1937, was Netherlands State Secretary for Foreign Affairs 1973–7, deputy leader of D66 (a new political party) 1977–82, and European Community Ambassador in Tokyo 1982–6.
†Paul Delouvrier, b. 1914, was Prefect of the Paris region 1966–9, and Président Conseil d'Administration, Electricité de France, 1969–79.

Muette for a large OECD lunch with all their many ambassadors. I had a good talk with van Lennep at lunch, who, throughout the day, I liked rather more than I had previously. After lunch but at the table there was a fairly intensive discussion, with an opening statement by me and a lot of questions from ambassadors which I wound up with a general answer at the end.

5.44 TEE to Brussels. Dined with Michael Jenkins, whom I am very glad to have back in Brussels.

TUESDAY, 28 NOVEMBER. *Brussels, Rome and Brussels.*

Avion taxi to Rome accompanied by Crispin and Plaja, the Italian Permanent Representative, for lunch with Andreotti. We arrived in dismal weather and drove straight to the Palazzo Chigi where we started with Andreotti and two or three officials, Ruggiero, who seems to be coming up in the hierarchy, La Rocca* as usual, and Plaja of course; Pandolfi (Minister of Finance) was with us for part of the time.

The Italians, both Andreotti and Pandolfi, sounded extremely positive about EMS and gave the impression that while they had previously been somewhat influenced by British hesitations they were now moving away from them and were on the brink of a favourable decision. I got them on to some detailed discussion about concurrent studies. They were less interested in agriculture than they had been when I had last seen Andreotti in September. They were not even overwhelmingly interested in the Regional Fund. Their clear first interest was in subsidized loans. They wanted the subsidy to be 4 per cent off the normal interest rate and they wanted a good deal of money (although they weren't anxious to say exactly how much), which was to be specifically directed to infrastructure projects in the Mezzogiorno. They implied they had had helpful conversations not only with Schmidt but also with Giscard about all this.

Immediately after lunch we left for Ciampino, from where we took off on a nasty rainy day just after 3.30. After several hours in the office, I went to Tervuren to a fashionable dinner party of the Ullens de Schootens, she Swedish and Prince Bernadotte's daughter. After dinner I had about half an hour's talk with the Chinese

* Umberto La Rocca, b. 1920, was Political Director of the Italian Foreign Ministry at this stage and closely associated with Andreotti. Later Ambassador to the United Nations.

Ambassador, who was a rather incongruous guest, and I suppose that was quite useful, though not exactly relaxing after my long Roman day.

THURSDAY, 30 NOVEMBER. *Brussels, Bonn and Brussels.*
Received Al Ullman, Chairman of the Ways and Means Committee of the House of Representatives, a curious figure, in his sixties, though looking younger with a somewhat trendy hairstyle, though rugged face. I found him friendly and intelligent and thought it well worthwhile having seen him.

Then at 11 o'clock, I went downstairs on a bitter, freezing day, to receive the Prince of Wales. I brought him up to my room and had half an hour's easy private talk with him. He was anxious to be informed about what life in the Berlaymont and the Community was like and showed interest in the details of operation, which I found sensible and agreeable. He gave me a photograph of himself in a rather nice self-deprecating way, saying, 'I am told I ought to give you this. I don't suppose you want it, but I hope you won't do the same as Trudeau, who immediately stuffed it into a drawer which was crammed full already of ones of most other members of my family.' So I said I would not do exactly that and gave him a leather-bound copy of *Asquith* in return, with which he seemed pleased.

Then I took him into the Commission room for a meeting lasting about fifty minutes. I made a little speech of welcome, to which he responded nicely, and then several of the Commissioners performed, with him being given an opportunity to ask questions at the end of each. First, Ortoli, who kept saying, 'Donc, Monseigneur, deuxième [or troisième or quatrième] hypothèse,' but on the whole did well and wasn't too long. Then Gundelach, then Tugendhat, who got in not because I changed my mind but because the question of the budgetary contribution had become of immediate relevance and was an appropriate subject to have; then Stevy Davignon, who performed brilliantly, the best of the four, whereas Gundelach rather surprisingly was the worst. Davignon gave a four-minute thumbnail sketch of industrial policy and what we were trying to do. The Prince asked a few questions. And then at the end he asked one or two more general questions not directly relating to what had been said, including one to Cheysson, to whom I thought it was misdirected but it shrewdly wasn't, about the Atlantic Colleges of which he has become chairman following his Uncle Dickie.

Then I conducted him into the *'cathédrale'*,* where we had a reception for a selection of the British staff – they had all been chosen by lot so it ought to have been fair – which he did well for forty or forty-five minutes. Then we went on into lunch with the Commission where he was placed *en face* to me and had Ortoli on one side and Gundelach on the other. The lunch went perfectly easily, though without any tremendously penetrating discussion. Afterwards I saw him off, just before 3 o'clock, walking most of the way to the Charlemagne with him, where he was about to see COREPER. There were a lot of people about, mainly photographers I think.

I immediately went to Zaventem to take an avion taxi to Bonn, and got into the Chancellery for a meeting with Schmidt at 4.30. This went on until 6.00 and was a good, useful, optimistic meeting.† He thought and hoped that everything would be all right with the Irish and Italians, though not with the British. He said he had had a lot of very difficult negotiations with the Bundesbank, and that indeed a lot of opinion in Germany was against him on the issue, which considerably restricted what he could do in making concessions on the operation of the exchange rate mechanism in the new system. He indicated clearly what were his limits, which were certainly not intolerable. He had just come back from a long and exceptional session with the Board of the Bundesbank at Frankfurt, the first time for years a Chancellor had attended. He was however prepared to be pretty forthcoming on concurrent studies, although he was much more reserved on our tough agriculture paper, which I left with him. He said firmly, what I think he had said to me before, that his position *vis-à-vis* Ertl was such that while he could agree to a freeze he couldn't agree to a combination of a freeze and the dismantling of positive MCAs, which he interpreted as meaning an actual reduction in German farmers' incomes (it would not necessarily).

*Commission name for the large reception hall on the thirteenth floor of the Berlaymont.
†Too optimistic as it subsequently emerged. See pages 349–53.

On concurrent studies, however, he was willing to contemplate two windows: one on the Regional Fund, in which he mentioned an increase of 200 or 250 million units of account, to be shared among the less prosperous participating countries, although *if necessary* letting this be distributed according to the established key if that got over a particular difficulty with the British; and, second, he was willing to do a significant sum in subsidized loans, with interest rate subsidies of the annual order of 400 million for a few years. He didn't like a 4 per cent subsidy, would have preferred 2 per cent, but thought one might settle at 3 per cent. So everything seemed in reasonably good shape from this point of view. He was rather more forthcoming than were Schulmann and Lahnstein, who were there, but I assumed that he could get his way with Federal Government officials.

The question was would he get his way with Giscard? I said, 'What about the Regional Fund? Are you going to be able to move Giscard on that?' 'I don't know, I think so,' he said. 'I am going to telephone him now.' And, indeed, at the end of the interview I left the room with the call to Giscard starting and my assuming that, on the basis of their relationship, Schmidt, apparently firm on this, would prevail.

Back, reasonably satisfied, to Wahn and a quick return to Brussels, where I got into the office at 7.10 and did an hour's work before dining at home with Jennifer who had arrived from London. On balance I was pleased with the day.

SATURDAY, 2 DECEMBER. *Brussels.*

After breakfast I went to see Vanden Boeynants, the new Belgian Prime Minister. I found him quite impressive and incisive, much more so than Tindemans, his only disadvantage being that he cannot speak English.* Nonetheless I had a good hour's talk with him in French, which he speaks very clearly in a Flemish sort of way. He gives the impression of being more on the ball about the European Council than Tindemans did, even when he, Tindemans, was in the chair. Vanden Boeynants was anxious to be helpful, but was reserved on agriculture (not unnaturally with Belgian elec-

* Not a very good judgement as he has since been in considerable legal trouble.

tions coming up) and also a little more reserved than the Germans on the Regional Fund. But in general he was quite forthcoming, though expecting difficulty with the French, particularly in view of the adverse vote on the sixth VAT directive which had taken place in the French Chamber the night before, which was a dangerous defeat brought about by an unusual alliance of Communists and Gaullists.

A lunch party, rue de Praetère, for Averell and Pamela Harriman, plus André de Staercke, the old Belgian diplomat. The Luns' were also supposed to come, but didn't turn up. A telephone call at 1.30 elicited great confusion and abject apology from him – he thought it was Monday. 'Never have I done such a thing in my life before,' he said. But I subsequently discovered from Jacques Tiné at dinner that evening that he had done almost exactly the same thing in Paris ten days before, so perhaps elderly absent-mindedness is beginning to affect the mind of even that Great Dane of a Dutchman.

Averell, who was off to Russia the next day, was on remarkable form for eighty-seven. He had had an endless programme of dinners in Brussels but seemed thoroughly fit on them. He was wearing a large pair of very new expensive shoes which is surprising if you have been a multi-millionaire all your life and therefore presumably accumulated quite a lot of good old shoes. Such a purchase at the age of eighty-seven seemed to point to an unusual combination of confidence in the future and meanness in the past.

SUNDAY, 3 DECEMBER. *Brussels.*

I had a long pre-dinner meeting with Ortoli and his Director-General, and Crispin and Michel Vanden Abeele from my *cabinet*. It was not particularly useful or well structured. Francis, as he does sometimes but not often, talked too much and not very purposefully. His only good remark was: 'Everything is too well set up for this Summit. It is too well prepared. I think it will go wrong. They generally do in these circumstances.' I went to bed with a distinct sense of apprehension about the following day.

MONDAY, 4 DECEMBER. *Brussels.*

To the Charlemagne at 1.30 for lunch there and the beginning of the European Council. The heads of government turned up more or less on time and we got down to a working lunch by 2 o'clock. This was partly concerned with the agenda, although the shape of this was not discussed sufficiently rigorously, and partly with general economic problems, during which Giscard threw out the sensible idea that the Commission should produce a study of the shape of the European economy in relation to the world division of labour in 1990, to which I gladly acceded.

The Council session began at 3.45. Quite unexpectedly, instead of being a short session leading on to a meeting of heads of government and me, as had been the successful pattern at Copenhagen and Bremen, this developed into a long, grinding niggle which ran until 8.15, dealing almost entirely with the internal mechanics of the EMS. There was a lot of slow argument about detailed points – the balance between short- and medium-term credits, a semantic argument about the 'presumption of intervention', or stronger or weaker words, when a currency was on the margin of divergence, and an Italian point, which caused a lot of difficulty, about a request for a specially loose obligation of repayment in the case of 'involuntary debtors'.

It was all detailed and in my view manifestly soluble stuff, which should never have been allowed to take so long and block us from what were clearly the more difficult points about transfer of resources. It was also all done without anybody being asked to make a firm declaration of position as to whether they would come in and, if so, in what circumstances. Callaghan was never throughout this four and a half hours asked to say whether or not he was joining the central mechanism; and he volunteered no information. Schmidt chaired this long session, as he chaired the Council throughout, with good humour, detailed patience and a certain shrewdness, but without in my view having satisfactorily thought out his game-plan for the two days.

Dinner in the Palais d'Egmont, with only the heads of government and me, from 8.45 until 11.30. This at least settled the 'Three Wise Men'. Giscard firmly proposed Marjolin. There was a certain amount of havering about who the Dutchman should be. The

Italians suggested that a Greek might be appointed (Andreotti had tried this out unsuccessfully on me on the previous Tuesday, but didn't press it hard when it was not well received by the others). Callaghan turned down Heath, I think understandably in his position, and Soames and Thomson for less adequate reasons, and then suddenly produced the name of Edmund Dell. This was not very well received because everybody except Schmidt said that they had never heard of him; but he was eventually supported by me on the ground that he was an admirable man even if somewhat anonymous, and it then went through.

The Brinkhorst suggestion seemed to have died for we heard no more of it, but there were two possible Dutch names, van der Stoel, on whom I have never been very keen because of his rigidity, and Biesheuvel,* the man who was eventually appointed. It swung away from van der Stoel because as Dell and Marjolin were nominally members of Socialist parties (though I told Giscard that in fact I knew Marjolin had voted for him and not the Socialists at the last election – about which he, Giscard, was doubtfully pleased in the context) it was decided that the Dutchman had to be right of centre.

The question of Euro-MPs' salaries was also settled, after a good deal of misinformed comment, on the basis of the lowest common denominator, i.e. national salaries but European expenses, which will no doubt be a good recipe for organized hypocrisy.

Then we went back to the Charlemagne for a continuation of the Council from 11.45 p.m. until 2 a.m., everybody getting tired though not particularly bad-tempered. We ploughed on through the remainder of the mechanism of the working of the System, actually reaching decisions on most although not quite all points.

I went to bed at 3 o'clock, feeling neither particularly satisfied nor overwhelmingly dismayed. I thought it was all very slow and in danger of losing both momentum and direction.

TUESDAY, 5 DECEMBER. *Brussels.*

The European Council began at 10.20 a.m. and proceeded to sit with no proper adjournment but occasional breaks of twenty

*Barend William Biesheuvel, b. 1920, was Prime Minister of the Netherlands 1971–3.

minutes or so until 9.20 in the evening. Again, strategic chairmanship was lacking. There were altogether four brief breaks, but no lunch was served at any normal time; eventually cold meat and glasses of wine were brought in at 4.15.

We got on to the concurrent studies issue at a fairly early stage in the morning. We had a quick *tour de table*, but it was not done in any very sensible order. The Danes and the Belgians who came first had nothing much to say. Callaghan had at last to make it clear that he was not coming in to the central mechanism and therefore was in no position to ask for much. The Irish and the Italians asked for a good deal, the Italians probably for rather too much, though I am not certain that this was a major tactical error. They asked for 800 million units of account a year (in interest rate subsidies), but as they could well have expected at least half of that there was something to be said for a high opening bid.

Giscard then made it clear that he was unwilling to contemplate any such sum. He climbed on Callaghan's back to block effectively and decisively the Regional Fund window, because Callaghan made it clear that the British would not give up their 27 per cent share. Giscard then said, 'Well, that being so, perhaps even without that being so, the French, who were asking for nothing special and who were taking on the full obligations of the System, could not contemplate giving up their share.' But even beyond that, if the Regional Fund were to be increased he would have to ask for a larger French quota, which had always been in his view desirable for France and indeed had been recommended by the Commission in the early days. Therefore there would have to be a renegotiation and that being so it was quite impossible, in view of what the British had said (and in view of what he had said), for there to be any advance at this meeting on that front, and so we might as well stop talking about it.

This, though depressing, had manifest force with two major countries in a blocking position. We were therefore forced to concentrate on the other point, the subsidized loans, with the subsidy bunched in the early years so as to amount to a sizeable initial grant. Schmidt suggested a total, to be divided between Italy and Ireland, of 400 million units of account a year — I think it was over a three-year period that it was then contemplated. Giscard then said he couldn't go over 200 million, so the whole elaborate construction looked as though it was grinding to a halt. Andreotti and Lynch looked extremely depressed, Andreotti's head sank even further into his body, and poor Jack Lynch was almost on the verge of tears.

Schmidt made a gloomy little speech saying that it all seemed absolutely hopeless and he wasn't sure that it was worthwhile going ahead with EMS at all, Germany would be better off without it in any case. I then intervened for about five minutes saying that so far from anybody being better off without it, the whole Community would be in a disastrous position, far worse off than if we had never launched the scheme. The sense of dismay, disaffection and falling apart would be overwhelming; we would find everything else, from enlargement to handling the directly elected Parliament, much more difficult to deal with. It would be a worse moment than for many years past. Giscard did not like this much because it didn't suit his book, and he said coldly that he did not share the rather dramatic interpretation of the President of the Commission, but I think that most other people thought I was right.

At this stage we had an adjournment. Both the Irish and Italians told me that the expectation of their public opinion was such that they did not think they could possibly go ahead on this basis. Schmidt came up to me in rather a gloomy way, rather agreeing with my cataclysmic speech, and we had a long friendly talk, my saying, 'Why don't you put greater pressure on Giscard? You and Giscard are the parents of the scheme, you have this special relationship, surely you can do something about it.' 'No, I can't move him on this,' he said. 'His internal position is too difficult.' It remains my view, however, that throughout this Council Schmidt did not press Giscard nearly as hard as he ought to have done.

Somewhat at my suggestion, Andreotti asked for a bilateral meeting with Giscard during this adjournment, and told him that his Government might well fall whether they went in on these terms or whether they stayed out, and that therefore one could have a position exactly in line with what I had said about things being at this stage much worse than if we had never started the enterprise; we would have Italy unable to come in but with its delicate political balance gravely upset as a result of the difficult choice presented to it. However, my suggestion of this bilateral was not a good idea. It did not go well, Giscard merely saying that in view of the Italian position maybe they would be better to take a British point of view and remain outside the mechanism for the time being, which was neither helpful nor, in my view, sensible.

We then resumed and went round the table rather gloomily once again. Schmidt proposed a compromise (he would certainly have gone, as he made clear to me, much further himself) by which we should do 200 million of subsidies *for five years* and that this should be concentrated on the two countries and divided between them according to whatever formula seemed appropriate. He asked me for one and I eventually said that two to Italy and one to Ireland might seem appropriate. This was accepted but we ground on for hour after hour on the total sum. Eventually 200 million for five years stood as the final offer, even though the Italians and Irish were still looking extremely miserable.

The whole issue had in fact become ridiculous, whether looked at from either one side or the other. What was perfectly valid in the French (and ?German) point of view was that the sum we were discussing – the difference between 200 and 400 million units of account shared between Italy and Ireland – was certainly not going to make the difference to the ability of those countries successfully to come into the System and stay there. On the other hand, the contributions required to ease the way in of Italy and Ireland by giving them the cosmetic presentation they said they needed for their public opinion, partly because of the expectations which had been built up (not unreasonably so in view of the bilateral conversations which Andreotti – and Lynch also – had had with Schmidt and Giscard) were quite small from the point of view of the richer countries. It was therefore a narrow schism, unimportant in itself, but with great capacity for damage.

In this rather bad atmosphere we went on to one or two other items. Schmidt judged that we couldn't at this stage have a proper discussion about our agriculture paper, but then got into it backwards by mistake so we half discussed it but without it being properly presented. Giscard then got very difficult about another item, fastening on to a Danish objection to our scheme for introducing the *écu* into agriculture in such a way that it should be neutral from the point of view of the operation of MCAs. He tried to insist on getting in the communiqué a point that no new permanent MCAs should be created; they should be dismantled very quickly and automatically. We in turn insisted on getting in a balancing sentence about having regard to the agricultural price effects (i.e. this should not be a back-door method of giving a big increase to French farmers) and eventually this was agreed. Giscard, to an extent which was not immediately apparent, was playing for something which could be used later in the Agricultural Council.

Eventually the whole sorry proceedings terminated just before 9.30 p.m. There were little final speeches round the table, the Italians and the Irish were sad, the British almost gloating that things had fallen apart, and Giscard singularly maladroit, saying what a splendid symbol the *écu* was in French history and announcing that he was going to have some specially minted for presentation to those present, which fell like a damp suet pudding on the already heavy atmosphere. However, without any actual insults being exchanged (it might in some ways have been better if they had been), we wound up.

Schmidt and I then did the press conference. Helmut was manifestly tired but not as depressed as he ought to have been. He tried to get me to answer most of the questions, which I did, and by some miracle did them rather well, so that he said, 'I can't think how you remember the detail so well,' whereas I had always thought that the detail of the EMS was exactly what I was weak on. Putting the best face I could on things, I described the result as being 'a limited success, successful in that we had got something which could be in place on 1 January, but limited because we were not sure that we had more than six members'. I carefully refrained from being more pessimistic than that because I had a slight feeling even then, which was confirmed in one or two talks on the way out, that the Irish and the Italians, though dismayed, might well come round on more mature reflection.

WEDNESDAY, 6 DECEMBER. *Brussels.*

Into the Berlaymont for the normal Commission meeting which, luckily, had a short agenda which I was able to complete in the morning. Everybody was a bit gloomy, but there was no disposition to quarrel with the general appraisal of 'limited success', with slightly more stress on 'limited' than on 'success'.

At 6 o'clock there was a ceremony in the Berlaymont for the

presentation of the Prix Bentinck to me (mainly, ironically, for my efforts on the EMS). I made a largely impromptu speech, which was a bit sombre. The prize was nice to have as it is quite valuable and has a certain amount of prestige. We dined – for the prize – with the Camu's at Aalst in a party of about forty, with various notabilities, and speeches after dinner, including a good funny one by Gaston Thorn.

THURSDAY, 7 DECEMBER. *Brussels.*

Deep gloom had set in by this morning. I had Ortoli for half an hour before lunch. He was also vastly gloomy, thought we had a great Community crisis ahead of us, and said that he hadn't slept at all during the night. He was agreeable, as he nearly always is, and he made one constructive though minor suggestion that we should have a dinner of the four (in his view) most intelligent Commissioners before we separated for Christmas to try and look at the bleak prospect ahead – the four being him, me, Gundelach and Davignon.

To lunch with COREPER at 1.30, where I gave them a general rundown on what had happened, expressed in fairly mordant terms. Fortunately, this could not last very long because at 3.00 I had to go to the UNICE, i.e. European Employers, Twentieth Anniversary, preside over a panel discussion, and later listen to Schmidt's surprisingly good semi-impromptu forty-five-minute English speech. I then drove with him to the airport for half an hour's private talk. I found him more gloomy than on Tuesday night, and inclined to question whether he had done things right – this is an attractive side of him. 'I am not sure I arranged it very well, but I don't see quite how I could have done it otherwise. Ought I to have put stronger pressure on Valéry?' 'Well, I think a bit,' I said. 'But it's very difficult, you know. I don't think I could have budged him in view of the internal position.' 'Well, you might have tried harder.'

He had a faint gleam of hope that something more might be done for the Italians and the Irish, and was still regretting that the Regional Fund window had been blocked, and suggesting, remarkably unrealistically I thought, that while there was nothing he could do with Giscard, nothing probably anybody could do with

Giscard, I might be able to move Barre, who might be able to move Giscard. He urged me to telephone Barre, a suggestion which on reflection I discarded, I think rightly, because (i) no indirect approach to Giscard would have worked; and (ii) my information was that Barre was harder on the Regional Fund than Giscard.

FRIDAY, 8 DECEMBER. *Brussels, London and East Hendred.*

The Turkish Foreign Minister, Ökcün, came to rue de Praetère at 9.30. Half an hour's talk with him. I had met him before and he seems a nice, agreeable man who likes looking at books but is not tremendously on the ball at any rate so far as his country's economic problems are concerned. He brought a letter from the Prime Minister and required various reassuring remarks from me. London for lunch and doctor. Then to Paddington at 5.00, believing that the new high-speed train which had so impressed me in September would be a good way to escape the rush hour. So it might have been if the wretched thing hadn't broken down between Slough and Taplow, so that it eventually limped into Didcot at 7.17.

As a result of lunching in a London restaurant, being on this long-delayed train and, presumably, appearing on British television a good deal during the previous week, I had a lot of encounters with semi-strangers who were all very sympathetic, but, it emerged after a moment or two's conversation, for the wrong reason. They nearly all began, 'You must be very disappointed, aren't you?', to which I would say, 'Yes,' and they would then say, 'A great pity Britain not coming in,' so that I realized that they thought this was why I was disappointed, whereas it wasn't the reason at all, as I had long since reconciled myself to this foolish and typical British decision, a repetition of the same mistake for the third time in twenty-five years. Why do nations never learn? My disappointment was due to the fact that we appeared to have lost the Irish and Italians and that therefore there was a deep split down the middle of Europe which, with enlargement on the horizon, would undoubtedly mean that we were on a straight road to a two-speed Europe.

SATURDAY, 9 DECEMBER. *East Hendred.*

Left at 11.30 to drive to Warwick University for the honorary degree they were giving me. We arrived for an agreeable lunch with Leslie Scarman, the Chancellor, whom I much like, and a perfectly easy occasion. I made a short impromptu speech after lunch and there was no speech at the ceremony.

MONDAY, 11 DECEMBER. *London and Brussels.*

A Labour Committee for Europe lunch at the Charing Cross Hotel. 3.35 plane to Brussels. There I saw Calvo Sotelo, the Spanish Minister for Europe. Two points primarily were dealt with. First, I had to tell him how badly the Commission had reacted to the attempt on the part of the Spanish Government to say that they didn't like our suggestion of an Italian called Papa, who had been our delegate in Ankara, as the head of our Madrid office. Their objection was apparently based on the fact that he had been an active member of the Italian Socialist Party, and they therefore thought he would interfere in Spanish politics. I said that this had not created a good impression at all in view of the extent to which we were firmly saying what a pluralist democracy Spain had become. He took this quite well and said he would consult the Foreign Minister and reflect upon it. The second point was that he stressed to me that it would be a great advantage for Spain if they could have the formal opening of the negotiations by March, and that if this could be achieved they would then be content for nothing much to happen for several months after that.

TUESDAY, 12 DECEMBER. *Brussels and Luxembourg.*

Excellent news during the morning that the Italian Government had firmly decided to enter the EMS; a considerable retrieval of the previous position.

Avion taxi to Luxembourg, which produced the worst flight which I have had on any occasion in the past two years. We bounced around in the new turbo-prop Conquest, fortunately for only thirty-eight minutes, but it was extremely disagreeable. I was not feeling sick, as Hayden and Laura were, but was mildly frightened, as they were also, and definitely felt rather unsteady when I got out. The pilots obviously thought that it had been fairly rough and apologized profusely, though in fact they had managed a feather landing despite being unable to get the plane straight on a line with the runway as the wind was blowing so hard that they had to go in crab-wise.

A meeting with Emile Noël who told me that Tugendhat's speech on the budget controversy had gone rather badly, but I didn't take that too seriously. Then I presented 112 medals to those who had served twenty years or more. I then staggered off to talk to the Political Committee (of the Parliament) about the results of the European Council and to answer a number of questions, some good, some rather foolish.

I then went briefly to a drink at the British Embassy as I had not been there since the new Ambassador, Patrick Wright, ex-Number 10 Foreign Office Private Secretary,* had taken over. I liked both the Wrights very much. I had a brief word with Thorn but not to any particular point, and rather more sensible words with various other people about the state of opinion in the Parliament on the budget issue.

WEDNESDAY, 13 DECEMBER. *Luxembourg and Washington.*
Another day of pouring rain and howling gale. An easy Commission meeting, a short speech to the Parliament, a late quick lunch, an attempted afternoon sleep in the hotel, from which I awoke feeling gloomy and mildly intimidated by the prospect of the evening's solitary journey,† and then an avion taxi to Charles de Gaulle at 6.00. Changed to the Concorde and took off at 8.10 for Washington. I worked furiously the whole way, being very behind-hand with the American briefs, and was no more impressed with the comfort or food of the nearly full Concorde than I had been coming east eight months before. Worst of all, it was slow, nearly four hours for the *trajet.* As a result we never quite caught up with

---

*(Sir) Patrick Wright, b. 1931, Ambassador to Luxembourg 1977–9, Saudi Arabia 1984–6, Permanent Under-Secretary at the Foreign Office since 1986.
†This was exceptional in my European life, except from Brussels to London and vice versa. The explanation on this occasion was that my staff for the Parliament (Hayden Phillips and Laura Grenfell) had gone back to Brussels, and Crispin Tickell had gone ahead to Washington.

the day; we could see it vaguely hovering over the tropics in mid-Atlantic and we could see it disappearing in the west as we came over land between Boston and New York, but it was quite dark when we got on the ground at Washington.

We were met by various protocol people, plus Fernand Spaak, Deane Hinton, Crispin, etc., and drove to the Hay Adams Hotel, where we arrived at 7.15 American time. We talked for an hour or so, and then, with a great act of will, I declined to go out for dinner, let Crispin and Fernand go alone, and went to bed instead. As a result I slept remarkably well until 6 a.m.

THURSDAY, 14 DECEMBER. *Washington.*

The Hay Adams is a comfortable hotel, subject on this occasion to two remarkable deficiencies, (i) the kitchen had been burned down so that they could produce no breakfast, and (ii) there was one pane missing from the window in my room, which for me was a slight relief as I like fresh air, but would have driven most Americans into a state of insanity as it was fairly cold outside. It was a most beautiful morning. The dawn was golden and the sun came up out of a cloudless sky. I worked until 7.45 and then Crispin and I walked up the road and had a very good breakfast at the Carlton Hotel. Then at 9.15 we went to see Bob Strauss and the inevitable Ambassador Henry Owen in Strauss's Special Trade Commissioner's office.

First, Strauss and Owen got me alone and asked me to endorse their handling of a request by Jean-François Deniau, the French Minister of Trade, to come to Washington and, as it were, do a bilateral MTN deal on the side, seeing Strauss and the President as well. They had refused this but said that Henry Owen would go to Paris and see Deniau on the following Monday morning.

Were they not right in refusing to let Deniau see the President? (A remarkably undiplomatic question, I must say.) I replied that it was no part of my duty to decide which ministers of member states the President of the United States saw, but that I had no complaint to make about what they had done. I obviously thought the negotiations should be with Haferkamp and his team, though equally I thought it would be foolish to refuse information which might be helpful to the French, and that I therefore welcomed the discussions which they had offered in Paris. The whole issue, on which the Americans are quite capable of reporting my remarks back to the French, was a frightening minefield for causing trouble between us and Paris.

Perhaps with this in mind I used the semi-formal meeting which followed to make the point strongly that the French were not in as isolated a position as the Americans thought; it was quite wrong to think in terms of eight to one, it was much more the shading of a spectrum and that if we didn't get a better package than was now available, it would not just be the French, it would be several other countries, perhaps the majority, who would be against it. But if we got a good package I thought we could carry everybody along, and this was more important than the date, though the time was ripe for us to try to conclude the negotiations by the end of the year.

On this relatively happy (and, as it turned out, rather too optimistic) note we separated. I had hoped to have forty-five minutes to myself for a little further reflection before seeing the President, but Henry Owen, who can be egregious as well as ubiquitous and inevitable, said that he wanted to come with us, so we took him to the Hay Adams, whose incinerated kitchen was incapable of producing even coffee, before driving across to the White House just before 11.00. We had the usual hold-up at the gate, when the guards looked amazed at any suggestion we were expected, and became very suspicious of Henry Owen when he said he worked there, but eventually let us through, after which with unexpected speed I was in the Oval Office with the President.

He greeted me as warmly as ever, seeming I thought more at ease than on previous occasions. We had about ten minutes together, he, Crispin, Owen and me, before we proceeded to the larger meeting. He was mainly concerned to talk about the Deniau point, and a bit about Guadaloupe,* and to ask me how Callaghan stood after his defeat in the House of Commons the night before – a few issues of that sort – and to express general friendship and desire to keep very close relations. Then we proceeded to the Cabinet Room and had our across-the-table meeting with a total of about twenty people. He made a speech of welcome, I responded, and then we went into a discussion of issues, MTNs, the European Monetary System (for which he expressed at this stage – differently from

*The venue of a Giscard-organized four-power meeting which was pending in January, and attendance at which did James Callaghan so much accidental harm.

Bonn – warm and unqualified approval), followed by our sub-agenda of scientific items.

Towards the end, rather unexpectedly, he enquired about our relations with China, camouflaging it a little by also asking about our relations with Comecon and Yugoslavia. But it was the China answers he was interested in, enquiring exactly what was the 'framework agreement', when I was going there, etc., which should have alerted me to the events of the following evening* more than in fact it did.

Then to the State Department, where we had an early lunch, presided over by Warren Christopher, acting Secretary of State (Vance being in the Middle East). Christopher, whom I had met only once before, is an extremely sensible and nice Californian, who organized the lunch very well. It was a working occasion, with discussion pretty well the whole time, but he did not make me talk too much, so that I was able to eat something, and he orchestrated it well so far as participants and subjects were concerned, between people on their side like Press, the President's Scientific Adviser, Cooper of the State Department, and Bergsten of the Treasury.

Disturbing news from Luxembourg that Vredeling (acting President in my absence – it rotates between the vice-presidents) had called an emergency Commission for 11 p.m. to pronounce on the budget crisis which had developed between the Parliament and the Council. I doubt if a night meeting under his emotional chairmanship is likely to promote cool reflection.

Our next appointment was with Schultze, Chairman of the Council of Economic Advisers, and we found him depressed though fluent in his always overheated office. He thought that growth in the US economy might well be down to zero and even possibly technically a recession (two quarters of negative growth during the year).

Then Blumenthal, who had Tony Solomon† with him, and was slightly more optimistic. He was firmly pro-EMS, quite different from his Bonn position. The US Government had at least coordinated itself on this, although there was a slight suspicion in my

---

*An announcement of full diplomatic relations between the United States and the People's Republic of China came on Friday, 15 December.
†Anthony Solomon, b. 1919, was Treasury Under-Secretary 1977–80, and head of the New York Federal Reserve Bank 1980–4.

mind that their firm benevolence was a matter of tactical teeth-gritting rather than spontaneous enthusiasm. This I think was certainly so with Solomon, who fastened on one vulnerable point, about the level at which gold deposits were to be valued, and the general effect of this. Blumenthal, whom I always like, was very willing to admit past errors about the dollar but also anxious to express total confidence for the future, saying the whole position since 1 November was qualitatively different.

On from there, flagging slightly by this time, to the Federal Reserve Board, to meet Miller,* the Chairman, for the first time. Crispin, who is normally at least as critical as I am, was rather impressed by him. I was not. I thought he produced a fine series of clichés in a not very well-structured conversation, but no doubt this was at least as much my fault as his. The following meeting, at 5 o'clock, was with Larosière† and the five or six top officials of the IMF, which he, Larosière, had asked for and at which they wished to sniff around with reasonably benevolent suspicion at the possible impacts of the EMS on them.

Fernand Spaak's dinner for me, which was a large and fairly well-chosen affair of thirty-six: the Chief Justice, who looks more and more like Asquith, and who, in spite of his not very liberal reputation, I much like, partly because he talks well about historico/legal matters on both sides of the Atlantic; also a couple of fairly important Congressional figures, as well as a good George-town sprinkling – Kay Graham,‡ Evangeline Bruce, Alsops, Bradens,§ Brandons,¶ etc. It was a good dinner, my only irritation with Spaak – and it is rare for him to cause one – being his *placement*, in which he decided, saying it was necessary on protocol grounds, despite my expressed scepticism, to give me both the Congressional ladies. I think it was a mistake on any grounds; it would have been

*William Miller, b. 1925, was Chairman of the Federal Reserve Bank 1978–9, and Secretary of the Treasury 1979–81.
†Jacques de Larosière de Champfeu, b. 1929. Under-Secretary of the Treasury 1974–8, Chairman of the Deputies' Group of Ten 1976–8. Managing Director and Chairman of the Board of IMF 1978–86; Governor of the Banque de France since January 1987.
‡Mrs Katherine Graham, b. 1917, has been the proprietor and publisher of the *Washington Post, Newsweek* etc. since the death of her husband Philip Graham in the 1960s.
§Tom and Joan Braden have straddled Washington since the beginning of the Kennedy presidency.
¶Henry Brandon, b. 1916, was *Sunday Times* correspondent in Washington 1950–83. His wife since 1970 has been Mrs Reagan's social secretary.

much more sensible to give me Kay Graham on one side, who certainly considers herself, as do I, a more important lady. However, the two Congressional ladies were not in fact too bad, although one of them was a religious maniac and the other appeared to be slightly drunk.

FRIDAY, 15 DECEMBER. *Washington and New York.*

German Embassy at 9 o'clock, where I was due to brief the ambassadors of the Nine. Despite the diplomatic pre-eminence of Washington, they were not on this occasion a very impressive group, though it was perhaps unfair to judge them as both the Frenchman, Laboulaye, and the German, Von Staden, were away. Peter Jay, who now looks very much the part, certainly has the best appearance. He asked no questions round the table, but was forthcoming afterwards. Of those who spoke, the Dane was the best, and the French substitute, the commercial *attaché*, the worst. Then to Capitol Hill, where I had a meeting on MTNs with Ullman's committee. Fortunately we didn't get into too much technical or controversial detail, but discussed mainly the timetable with general expressions of goodwill.

Then there was an interval before my luncheon at the National Press Club. Fernand Spaak's other untypical mistake of the week had been to announce at our conversation on the Wednesday evening that the essential rule for a National Press Club speech was to open with an extremely funny story. At that stage I took it calmly, but as the time approached I found it totally impossible to think of any remotely appropriate joke.

In this interval I therefore paced up and down desperately to try and think of something funny to open with. Absolutely nothing came. I arrived in despair. However, the whole occasion gave me the impression from the beginning as being friendly and likely to be helpful. It seemed a much better atmosphere than when I had last been there twelve years before as a young Home Secretary. It was much fuller for one thing, and when I actually got up to speak several entirely impromptu mild jokes of the occasion came to me, so that the first five minutes were a great success and thereafter the speech followed through rather easily. Then a good question period, fast, easy questions, and so off with high morale for the 3 o'clock shuttle to New York. We drove on a beautiful New York afternoon to Marietta Tree's apartment in Sutton Place.

From 5.15 I went to the Links Club and talked to a dozen bankers assembled by George Ball. They were all personally agreeable and basically friendly to the EMS. They were certainly a high-powered lot, including the main people from Chase, City Bank, Hanover, Chemical, etc., plus the head of IBM. At 8.00 Marietta had a large dinner party (thirty-four) with a fairly predictable grand New York mixture: Kissingers, Schlesingers, Betty Bacall, Kitty Carlisle,* Bill Paley,† Brooke Astor,‡ Mrs Agnelli.§ I much enjoyed it.

SATURDAY, 16 DECEMBER. *New York.*

A day off in New York. Took the Brian Urquharts to lunch at the Caravelle, went to the Metropolitan and the Frick in the afternoon, and dined on the West Side with the Irwin Ross's.

SUNDAY, 17 DECEMBER. *New York, Ann Arbor and Brussels.*

8.30 plane to Detroit. Drove to Ann Arbor for lunch with the President of the University of Michigan and about forty other people at about 12 o'clock. It was a ghastly luncheon, not a drop to drink at the long reception beforehand – I hadn't expected anything at lunch – totally inedible food, and speeches, which again I hadn't expected, after lunch. Then over to the theatre for the commencement and honorary degree ceremony and my address to an audience of about four thousand. To be honest, I don't think the address went very well: it was a good speech, but too long, thirty-four minutes, and slightly too elaborately prepared, as well as trying to say too much. In any event I always find commencement addresses difficult, and the total absence of alcohol didn't help either. However, it passed off, the ceremony was over and we got away just after 4 o'clock and drove back to Detroit Airport on a sparkling, cold, clear winter afternoon.

*Kitty Carlisle (Hart), actress and singer, is the widow of the impresario Moss Hart.
†William Paley, b. 1901, was President of CBS 1928–46 and Chairman 1946–83.
‡Mrs Vincent Astor, née Brooke Russell, the last station on the mainline of the Mrs Astors of New York.
§Princess Marella Caraciolla de Castagneto, married to Giovanni Agnelli since 1953.

La Guardia at 7.30, and the 8.45 Sabena plane from Kennedy to Brussels. Dinner and two hours' sleep before I awoke over Ireland.

MONDAY, 18 DECEMBER. *Brussels.*

Another special Commission meeting at noon to try and extricate ourselves from any damage which might have been done by Vredeling's late-night one on Thursday. However, good work had been done over the weekend and it was fairly clear what view we should take on the budget. There had been irregularities in the Parliament's handling of the matter, but illegality should not be compounded with further illegality, and we should accept as a fact that the budget existed, and was certified as valid by Colombo as President of the Parliament, which was within his constitutional rights. This was our firm view, without any clear dissenters.

I gave lunch to Klaus von Dohnanyi, Sigrist and a third German. Klaus was more or less on time for once and we had an agreeable lunch with rather good talk. I lectured them a little on being pushed around by the French, which I hope they took reasonably well.

TUESDAY, 19 DECEMBER. *Brussels.*

Foreign Affairs Council with lunch from 10.30 a.m. to 8.15 p.m., which was more than long enough. It was never tremendously productive and pretty boring for much of the time. What was not boring, but not agreeable either, was a 5 o'clock meeting, which I had at my request, with François-Poncet. I found him in a highly excitable state about the budget and everything else. He was at least trying to be agreeable most of the time and arguing with himself in some ways more than with me, saying, 'No, I am a man of conciliation, I want to seek a solution, a political solution if possible. But if this goes wrong, the possibilities of damage are enormous, the Commission will be in the same position as the Hallstein Commission. We could call off direct elections, it could affect the whole future of the Community.'

The French do get into an enormously overexcited state and find it difficult to believe that there can be different interpretations of things and that people who don't agree with them are not necessarily knaves or fools. They treat people as craven, threaten them too much, and believe that they will succumb to a 'thunderbolts of Zeus' treatment. I think that it stems from the fact that the French Government is too hierarchical and authoritarian, and that they are all terrified if they can't bring home to Giscard exactly what he wants. This corrupts people like François-Poncet, who is in general a decent, sensible, intelligent man. The whole interview left a disagreeable taste in my mouth.

WEDNESDAY, 20 DECEMBER. *Brussels.*

A morning Commission to 1.35, by which time we had succeeded with a little difficulty in completing all the business. Then a Commission Christmas lunch. Last year they complained that they hadn't been given enough traditional English food, so this year we organized Christmas puddings with brandy butter, mince pies and, of course, turkey. It was all quite successful, I thought, except the turkey, which was pretty badly cooked, appallingly carved and filled with what was supposed to be chestnut stuffing, but which tasted to me rather like stale liver pâté. However, that apart, the occasion wasn't too bad.

In the afternoon I went to the Greek negotiations from 4.45 to 6.30, which Natali was conducting very well. Then I saw Bassols, the Spanish Ambassador, who came in to announce (i) that the Spaniards were extremely pleased that we had got them the formal opening of the negotiations on 19 February, and (ii) that on reflection they would be extremely glad to work with Signor Papa as our representative in Madrid – a very typical example of the way in which one can get sensible results from Calvo Sotelo, though he would have done better not to have got into an untenable position to begin with.

Then home to the quadripartite dinner, with Ortoli, Gundelach and Davignon, which flowed from Ortoli's conversation with me when he was so apprehensive after the European Council. I think the occasion was worthwhile. They all talked well. It was certainly a social success and they stayed a good deal too late, until 12.45. We argued round the problems of relations with the French in particular, including the row, mainly between the French and the Germans, which had broken out over MCAs in the Agriculture Ministers Council. I am not sure that we arrived at any firm view about how to proceed, except that we all thought that the Community faced a fairly critical six months in which the Commission had to steer a difficult and narrow course, but one could no doubt have predicted that without the dinner.

SATURDAY, 23 DECEMBER. *East Hendred.*

I had a fairly excited evening telephone call from Cheysson, he having seen François-Poncet for two hours that morning, who was obviously going on trying to fulminate against the Commission, though not to my mind in any way more disturbingly so than he had done the previous week.

SUNDAY, 24 DECEMBER. *East Hendred.*

To Oxford for an early evening drink in Univ. with Arnold Goodman. He had Ann Fleming and at least two other ladies staying, and we could feel mounting tension on Ann's part, although Arnold, always apparently blandly indifferent to atmosphere, was dispensing generalized benevolence and rising splendidly above this.

MONDAY, 25 DECEMBER. *East Hendred.*

Mild and soggy, as usual on Christmas Day. For the first time ever, I think, I played tennis on Christmas afternoon.

THURSDAY, 28 DECEMBER. *East Hendred.*

Lunch with the Wyatts at Connock. Arnold Weinstocks were also there. I continue to like him much more than I used to. We played croquet on a damp afternoon for too long, well into the twilight. I played with Weinstock, who was absolutely hopeless but, rather interestingly, instead of getting impatient with the game became anxious to go on and on, with a determined but misplaced faith that if he did he would quickly master it.

SATURDAY, 30 DECEMBER. *East Hendred and Hatley.*

Hatley, with snow beginning to fall, at 4.30. Jakie had the Rothschilds to dine, bringing with them Alan Hodgkin, the new Master of Trinity and an exceptionally agreeable man, plus his American wife. I had a long talk with Tess (Rothschild) at dinner, who delivered elaborate apologies and nervous reactions from Victor about whether I was very offended with him for not finally agreeing to join the external review body. The answer is that I was somewhat fed up with his havering but certainly not to an extent of it causing continuing offence.

1978 has undoubtedly been immensely better, despite the setback in December, than 1977, though that perhaps is not saying all that much. For 1979 the prospect looks less good, more like 1977 I suspect, though I hope not as bad.

1979

Of my four Brussels years, 1979 was the least dominated by one or two clear themes. In the first months of the year the EMS, which had been the *leitmotif* of 1978, was still waiting to be brought into operation. The French Government forced a delay because it proclaimed itself dissatisfied with the agro-money arrangements by which Monetary Compensatory Amounts could make the rates of exchange at which agricultural products were traded different from those generally prevailing. By early March, however, it allowed this problem, still unsolved, to be moved aside, thereby confirming my feeling that it was more a symptom of a burst of general Elysée *morosité* towards the Community than a root cause.

This *morosité* came at an unfortunate time, for it coincided with the French turn to assume the six-month presidency of the Council of Ministers (and consequently all the other inter-governmental institutions in the Community) at the beginning of January. The authority of Council presidencies varies substantially. A new member country can be overawed, a small country overstrained (in its diplomatic resources), and even a big old member country like Germany can suffer from a lack of coordination within its government. France was neither new nor small, and its government, whatever else could be said about it, did not suffer from a lack of coordination. The tradition and the expectation therefore were that France provided the most authoritative presidency of the Nine, good for Europe if the mood in Paris was constructive, extremely bumpy to work with for everybody, but above all for the Commission, if it was not.

The auguries at the beginning of 1979 were not good. At the Brussels European Council in December 1978 Giscard had shown unusually little concern for the susceptibilities of Italy or Ireland, or even of Germany. The French had been further excited by the old nominated Parliament passing its last budget in a form which they (and several other governments) regarded as illegal, by Emilio Colombo as President of the Parliament nonetheless certifying it as valid, and by the Commission accepting this as a fact. The imminence of direct elections for the Parliament (due in June) did nothing to assuage these feelings. The French had never been keen on this advance, although loath to block it, and they rightly opined that the new Assembly (they insisted on denying it the name of Parliament) would be more presumptuous in general and more critical of the French agricultural interest in particular.

In addition there was Giscard's almost *ex-officio* determination that the Commission should not play too independent a role. De Gaulle had put down Hallstein. He, by contrast, had failed to keep me out of the Summits which were his own creation. But he was certainly not going to encourage the authority of the Commission. This had been a large part of his motivation for launching his idea of a *comité des sages* or 'Three Wise Men'. He had got the proposition through the other governments but only in a form which meant that he quickly lost faith in the ability of those nominated to do the job he wanted done, which was to turn the Commission into a strengthened secretariat of a European Council to be presided over by a permanent President. He also, I think, wanted to use the French presidency to curb the independent prestige of the Commission.

He was not wholly alone in this desire. The British were basically with him but, perhaps surprisingly, concentrated more on form, leaving the substance to Paris. The French had no difficulty about according me a guard of honour whenever I went to the Elysée, but objected if I did not speak as the servant of the European Council. The British did not seem to mind what I said, but their Foreign Secretary sent a minute around the Foreign Office (in 1978) instructing his officials to desist from the growing practice of referring to me as 'President Jenkins'.

The French approach was more serious. It was obvious at the turn of the year that the six months of the French presidency were going to be a test of nerve such as no other presidency had provided. And so it proved to be. It was like living under the constant threat of an artillery bombardment. It was not in fact very damaging when it came, but one never knew when it was going to recommence, and this did not make for a calm life.

Then, at the end of January, there appeared in the sky a totally different cloud, at first no bigger than the proverbial man's hand and never of much real importance, although it managed to consume a vast amount of time and morale over the next nine months. In late January the *Economist* published a couple of paragraphs complaining about the extravagance of Haferkamp's travelling expenses and also pointing a finger at the inappropriateness of Madame van Hoof having accompanied him to China (see pages 314–15 *supra*). There was in addition a side-swipe at Vredeling.

The issue was widely re-reported in the British and continental press, there were questions in the European Parliament and the newly initiated and rather overgunned and underoccupied Court of Auditors (or *Cour des Comptes* as it was habitually referred to in all languages) was wheeled in to conduct a detailed inquiry into the expenses of all Commissioners. This kept the issue simmering beneath the surface until it erupted again in August and provided another two months of convulsions before finally subsiding because of a combination of boredom and an inadequate supply of scandalous lava.

The 'scandal' was debilitating because it touched what was thought to be a vulnerable flank of the Commission. Particularly in Britain, but in some other countries too, it was widely regarded as a symbol of 'fleshpot' living. No doubt my own predilections assisted the caricature. But in fact it was largely unjustified. The Secretary-General of NATO lives immensely more grandly in Brussels than does the President of the Commission for the very good reason that he is provided free with a house and a household establishment, whereas the President pays for them out of his own income. Equally, the main difference between ourselves and governments in the use of private aircraft (which became another point at issue) was that we hesitated because we had to hire them specially, whereas they used them more habitually because they were permanently at their disposal.

Haferkamp had undoubtedly behaved foolishly and sometimes extravagantly, although never dishonestly, but even his hotel bills needed to be seen in the context that he was the nominee of almost the richest country in the world, and that his choice of *caravanserai* in, say, New York was no more opulent than that of the then deeply indebted British Government.

The only amusement which I derived from this sad saga was the light which the *Cour des Comptes* reports shone upon the differing peccadilloes and prejudices of the several nationalities. The German temptation was undoubtedly the grand Babylonian palace hotels of the world. The Italians, *per contra*, wanted only to go home, as frequently as possible, and preferably at public expense. The French were addicted to a lavish supply of flowers for their offices, a minor vice one would have thought, even if accompanied, as it was, by an iron determination not to give the names of those whom they entertained in their reasonably modest use of their expense accounts. The Belgians were equally reticent here. The British, I have to recall, were boringly impeccable. Christopher Tugendhat was spotless.

The late spring was dominated for me by two elections, the British one on 3 May, and the Community-wide first direct election for the European Parliament on 7/8 June. I took no part in the first, but made speeches in all the nine countries except France (where I judged that an intervention would not be welcome) for the second. These speeches were directed to the importance of the constitutional development and not to support for particular candidates or parties.

The British election resulted in the beginning of Mrs Thatcher's long government. I had mixed feelings about the result, believing on the whole that a change of government would help Britain's relations with the rest of the Community. With the new Government my relations were on the whole good. I often disagreed with Mrs Thatcher, but I found her friendly to deal with, undismayed by such disagreements, and in no way resenting my not being an agent of Whitehall. With the new Foreign Secretary my relations were, paradoxically, closer than they had been with the outgoing one.

My hopes for Britain becoming much more *communautaire* were however substantially unfulfilled. Mrs Thatcher did not take to Europe like a duck to water. She was a duck who remained on a bit of offshore land. Furthermore she was almost immediately involved in a dispute with the Community which was to dominate the remainder of my presidency and to absorb much of the energy of the Community for at least four years after that. Britain, one of the poorer countries of the Community, made a net budgetary contribution almost as large as that of Germany. This was essentially for two reasons: we imported more from outside the Community than did the others and therefore paid more in import levies; and our small (but efficient) agriculture made few demands on Community outgoings. The so-called 'renegotiation' of 1974–5, which produced the minimum results with the maximum ill-will, had made only a small impact on this problem, which had however conveniently disappeared underground in 1976–7. It resurfaced during 1978, and Callaghan expressed concern to me at our meeting of 2 November (see page 333 *supra*).

It was a nettle which Mrs Thatcher had to grasp, and her hand did not flinch. The question is whether she grasped it skilfully. I thought not, from several points of view. The micro reasons emerge from the diary, although perhaps more strongly in 1980 than in 1979. The macro one was that she caused a justified but limited dispute (the total Community budget within which her marginal argument took place has never been more than 2 per cent of the member countries' public expenditure and substantially less than 1 per cent of their national income) totally to dominate the Community for five years and to run into the sand any hopes of, or ambitions for, a British leadership role within the Community.

The European elections produced from Britain an appallingly low poll and a vast Conservative preponderance. From the rest of the Community a greater sense of European commitment and a fairer electoral system produced a much higher participation and less distorted party balances. For the Commission, however, it produced a potentially formidable new Parliament, twice the size of the old, which we approached with a mixture of respect and apprehension. In retrospect I think our hopes were better founded than our fears. The directly elected Parliament had at least a good first six months.

In late June I went to Tokyo for my third Western Economic Summit. It was dominated by the second oil shortage and price increase, which had already destroyed the Bonn Summit plans for coordinated growth, and which the world statesmen there assembled, with all the prescience of flat-earthers who saw no reason why spring should follow winter, assumed would be permanent. Tokyo also provided the background for the last bumps of the rather queasy six months of the French presidency.

During the autumn the two inquiries which had been set up at the end of 1978 completed their reports. Giscard's *trois sages* had, however, so disappointed their instigator that the French Government lost interest in the publication of that report. They had at least done no damage and provided some sensible reflections. The findings of my Spierenburg inquiry were available to us by early October, were accepted by the Commission, and substantially implemented. The rigidity which kept some people in useless sinecures while others of equal rank were overworked was modified. So was the national grip on particular posts. But the firm and sensible recommendation that as the Community was enlarged big countries must give up their right to nominate two Commissioners withered on the bough. So the position of too many Commissioners chasing too few jobs, with which I was confronted in 1977, was exacerbated by Greek entry in 1981 and Spanish and Portuguese entry in 1986.

Enlargement negotiations probably absorbed less of my time and attention than in 1977 or 1978. The Greek treaty of accession was signed in Athens in June, and that was that for the time being. The Spanish and Portuguese negotiations were in a midstream calm, although by inviting the Spanish Prime Minister (then Adolfo Suárez) for a Brussels weekend in December I made a reasonably successful attempt to give them a new momentum.

I travelled outside Europe more than in 1978: a three-country West African trip in January; a major visit to China in February; Japan for the Summit in June; and Egypt in October. It was, however, the only year of the four in which I did not go to the United States. In Europe, outside the Community, I went only to Greece in June and Austria in October.

Over the summer and during the autumn a substantial part of my interest began to move back to British politics. My working assumption during 1977 and 1978 was that I had finished with them, even though I would stay only the normal four years in Brussels. After that I had little idea of what I would do, although I was sufficiently confident in March to reject without hesitation both James Callaghan's kind suggestions of a peerage and of the governorship of Hong Kong.

Then (this, and the reverse, can sometimes be the case) horizons began simultaneously to widen in several directions. An invitation to give the Dimbleby television lecture (on any subject that I liked, although I think the expectation was that it would be a European one) came in May, and my thoughts gradually settled on the idea of using it to propound a new, anti-party approach to British politics. Much of my working leisure, to coin an oxymoron, of the late summer and autumn was devoted to composing what I wished to say.

At the same time there was an agreeable boomlet fostered by some governments and by some Commissioners in the view that I should stay on as President, breaking the post-Hallstein pattern, for a further two or four years. I was flattered but not particularly attracted by this prospect, except insofar as flirting with it might enable me to avoid a lame-duck year. I had come to think of the Commission presidency as a sort of Grand National course, with the fences and the ditches occurring at predictable intervals, and four times around it seemed to me enough. But it was agreeable to have a prospect of the option and this, together with the blood-coursing effect of Dimbleby, meant that I approached and survived the Dublin European Council (Mrs Thatcher's charge of the Light Brigade, except that she had more resilience than Lord Cardigan) and the turn of the year 1979/80 in a higher state of morale than at any of the times under survey except for that period of 1976 when I had the illusion that Europe was open before me, and the spring/summer of 1978 when, with less illusion, I believed we were quickly fashioning the European Monetary System.

MONDAY, 1 JANUARY. *Hatley.*

Francis Pym,* the new Conservative foreign affairs spokesman, came over for a drink and a talk. Although I had been in the House with him for years and indeed had an old Monmouthshire connection, our fathers having been members for adjacent constituencies

---

*Francis Pym, b. 1922 (cr. Lord Pym 1987), had been Conservative Chief Whip 1970–3, and Secretary of State for Northern Ireland 1973–4. Despite this entry he was Defence Secretary 1979–82 and only Foreign Secretary 1982–3. His father was Leslie Pym, MP for Monmouth 1939–46.

and, across parties, quite close, so that Pym's father gave me a wedding present, I had hardly ever had any direct talk with Pym himself. I found him rather impressive, firmly pro-Europe although not starry-eyed. He thought the European cause was quite a difficult struggle but one which had been allowed to go much too much by default in the Conservative Party. He is brisk, quite self-confident, no great intellectual range, no great phrase-maker in conversation but everything said sensibly, succinctly, even powerfully, and there was clearly complete confidence on his part that, unlike the previous shadow, John Davies, who was probably destined (illness apart) to be only a shadow, he, Carrington or no Carrington, Soames or no Soames, would be Foreign Secretary in a Conservative Government.

FRIDAY, 5 JANUARY. *London and Brussels.*

I became extremely depressed on reading the newspapers, and decided that the French monkeying around on MCAs and holding up the start of the EMS meant that Europe was in danger of falling apart and that I had better try and do something about it. Therefore I did some vigorous telephoning to Brussels and set up a meeting for the Sunday morning in Paris with Barre with the intention at least of trying fully to understand the French point of view. The commercial planes being totally unreliable, I set up an avion taxi from Northolt to Brussels at 3.45.

In the meantime I had an early lunch with Harold Lever at Brooks's and found him buoyant and very sensible on nearly everything. My agreement with him, as with Shirley, is now very close indeed. He is of course much more interested than Shirley in economic and monetary matters and remains a firm partisan of EMS. He is depressed about the Government, but not excessively so, and thinks it might easily win the election. He intends to stand himself again and is obviously quite keen to go on in the Cabinet if he can. But when I suggested to him at the end that if they were still in office after Nicko* and wanted to make a political appointment to Paris he and Diane would do it well, he responded rather enthusiastically.

* Sir Nicholas Henderson was due to retire as Ambassador to Paris in April 1979.

SATURDAY, 6 JANUARY. *Brussels and Paris.*

To Paris by plane in the early evening. To the Embassy and then out to dinner at Lipp with Nicko. I had a long talk with him about the mysteries of the French switch of line, why they had become so adamant about MCAs. I am not sure that he understood things a great deal better than I did, but referred to some important conversation which Barre had had with the German Ambassador in which he had laid down the position, and said that I would no doubt discover more about it in the morning. He was, however, in some ways as exasperated by the French as I was. He also said that he thought François-Poncet had been made Foreign Minister partly because Giscard wanted to get rid of him from the Elysée, but that may be unreliable hearsay.

Then, Nicko having gone off to catch a night sleeper to Grenoble, I called on Ortoli in the rue de Bourgogne and went over the whole business with him. He had been seeing a lot of people and was clearly nervous about forthcoming rows with the French Government. However, we managed to hammer out a common position on which he was perhaps just a little wobbly but to which I think he will hold at any rate for the time being. He said that there was a view in Paris that the Commission was too frightened of a vote of censure in the Parliament. It was not absolutely clear to me why we shouldn't be a bit concerned about that, though no doubt 'frightened' is not the right impression to give. I stayed the night in a completely empty Embassy surrounded by a frozen Paris, one or two servants, but no Hendersons, no other guests, a rare experience.

SUNDAY, 7 JANUARY. *Paris and Dakar (Senegal).*

To Matignon to see Barre at 10.30. Barre received me as friendlily as ever and we had quite a useful talk for fifty minutes mainly in French. Crispin and Barre's man, Jean-Claud Paye, were there taking notes. I explained that our interest was overwhelmingly to get the EMS in position as quickly as possible, that we were very disappointed at the delay, which we found extremely surprising, and I feared that whatever had happened the French hold-up had prevented it being born *en beauté*. However, that was so. What I now wished was to see it in place, but my other, and equal, priority was not to let any agreement undermine the essential need for freezing farm prices otherwise we would be in a hopeless position with surpluses.

Barre attempted to explain why MCAs were of such importance to them, but this was a general statement based upon a long-term objection to the unbalancing of the market between France and Germany and certainly did not amount to any explanation of what had happened between 7 December and 31 December to make them become of such dominating short-term importance. On a price freeze he was reasonably sympathetic, without absolutely committing himself. On the budget, he said that they would be as hard as a rock in principle, particularly in relation to the future, but would seek compromise on the present budget. He was not I think too well-informed about this and didn't contradict any of the arguments which I put forward, including my view that while we wanted to avoid a resort to the Court, because we thought a political solution was much better, if a political solution was not forthcoming I did not see how we could avoid ending up in the Court. On the EMS, in response to a request from me, he specifically denied that the French were using MCAs as an excuse. He denied that there was any French cooling off on the basic desirability of the scheme.

At 1.00 I took an Air France Concorde to Dakar* where it was a rather nasty cloudy day with the sort of clouds which would produce rain in Europe, but apparently don't in Dakar at this time of the year. The city, more or less surrounded by sea, looked reasonably agreeable. There was a ceremonial welcome by the Prime Minister at the airport and we then drove to the Residence Medina, a government guest house; not a very attractive building, I fear, and sited, for some mysterious reason, on almost the only spot in Dakar from which you cannot see the sea.

One and a half hours' meeting with the Prime Minister (the second man, the President being the head of the Government) who seemed to me agreeable and sensible.† He is enormously tall, very black, and known as 'the Giraffe'. Dinner with the Commission delegate.

*For the start of a six-day 'Lomé' tour of two francophone and one anglophone African countries.
†Abdou Diout, b. 1935, was Prime Minister from 1970 until 1980 and has been President of Senegal since then.

MONDAY, 8 JANUARY. *Dakar.*

A call on Senghor, the President, from 11.00 until 12.15. He is a little, bright man, looking much younger than his seventy-two years, completely French having been a Socialist Deputy for fifteen years before independence, having lived in France during the pre-war period, having had, as he is very fond of telling one, a lot of literary *salon* life, and still being a great *littérateur*, composer and translator of poetry. However, on this occasion the conversation was mainly political, and largely carried on by him. He expounded a hard anti-Communist line, complaining that the West did not take the Russian threat nearly seriously enough and didn't do enough in Africa to combat it. He didn't necessarily want European troops, but when he put Senegalese troops into Zaïre it would be a great advantage if we gave them some financial support. He expressed interest in a West African defence community though without the 'Marxist/Leninist states' in it. He made an attack on Algeria for racist policies, and put forward a whole series of views, some of them sensible, some of them less so, but worth listening to.

Lunch at the rather magnificent residence of the French Ambassador which we were told had been built by Louis de Guiringaud, but was hardly a constructional success as nearly all the pigeons of Dakar congregated under the roof.

In the late afternoon we went by motor launch across a narrow strait to the island of Gorée which has been occupied by almost everybody, Dutch, Turks, Danes, British and French, from about 1500, and which has achieved great recent fame as a result of *Roots* drawing attention to its position as a departure point for slaves. We made a rather gruesome but notable visit to the Maison d'Esclaves, seeing all sorts of horrors. It is now run as a sort of black museum with a lot of American visitors. The whole island, apart from being too windy, had a considerable quality of its own and was well worth visiting.

Dinner with Senghor in his Presidential Palace. A party of about ten, including four of Senghor's ministers. It was quite a remarkable occasion, epitomized by the authoritarian choice of drink: before dinner there was only Jack Daniels Sourmash, and at dinner only an excellent pink champagne. Senghor led the conversation, for two and a quarter hours, before, over, and after dinner, without raising any political subject. It was entirely cultural, general intellectual conversation, a little pretentious I thought occasionally on his side, as no doubt he did on mine. He claimed not to be able to speak English, but to read it fluently, as he had translated the poems of Gerard Manley Hopkins, Dylan Thomas and T. S. Eliot into French, which would by any standards require a very remarkable command of written English.

I asked him who he thought were the two outstanding French poets of this century and he mentioned two people of neither of whom I had ever heard. He then asked me who I thought were the two outstanding French novelists, and I swallowed and said Proust and Simenon (treating 'French' as embracing Walloon). He said, 'Proust naturellement, mais pourquoi Simenon?' It would have been more original to have put it the other way round. We had a good deal of Proustian conversation later in the evening linked to his wife's property between Caen and the sea, which, as I pointed out, meant that it was very near Cabourg, and we then both of us tried to remember what Cabourg was called in *À la Recherche*. I had it on the tip of my tongue, but I had the impression that it was a little further back in the recesses of his mind. However, on the way out I suddenly remembered Balbec, and announced it to him, by which he seemed remarkably struck.

It was a somewhat stilted dinner and I went away with some doubt as to whether anyone so self-consciously intellectual and literary has not an element of the bogus in him.

TUESDAY, 9 JANUARY. *Dakar and Bamako.*

Ambassadors of the Nine for a briefing, and then a press conference. The Prime Minister came at 11.30 to take me to the airport, bearing various farewell presents with him, including the Grand Croix of the Légion d'Honneur of Senegal – an enormous green sash with a star and God knows what, and a letter from Senghor conferring this upon me and making it fairly clear that it was done mainly on the basis of my literary knowledge and in particular my ability to produce the name of Balbec!

We then flew to Bamako in Mali in a very luxurious private Senegalese plane. We were greeted by a whole stream of ministers and, so far as one could tell, a large part of the Malian army, with flashing helmets, some of whom formed various guards of honour for inspection. Also there were all the Western ambassadors, in other words two: the German, who was broadly in charge from the Community point of view, and a little American career lady (a French Ambassador exists, but was away).

To the Hôtel de l'Amitié, an enormous fourteen-storey building set back half a mile from the River Niger, which at that point is nearly a mile wide, thousands of miles from the sea though it is, and were installed on the top floor in a very comfortable suite with a good view. We were informed by the Commission delegate (a fairly elderly Italian with great knowledge of African culture and African art and several books to his credit – but not, I thought, a great grasp of actuality) that a *coup*, a peaceful *coup* he opined, was imminent and might easily affect the head of state. However, we became increasingly sceptical of this because the ministers with whom we had dealings, including President Traoré himself, didn't seem particularly nervous.

First, I had a short meeting alone with the said Youssouf Traoré, then a drive up the hill to a sort of ministerial compound, where we had what seemed a very long meeting, mainly because the Minister of Planning made a complaining speech lasting nearly an hour and going into immense detail, which was obviously thought in-appropriate by his colleagues. Then to a large garden party in the dark at the house of the Commission delegate. Afterwards to dinner with the German Ambassador (Schraepler), a nice man of unusual charm with an agreeable French wife.

WEDNESDAY, 10 JANUARY. *Bamako, Timbuctoo and Bamako.*

Took off at 8.20 in a curious twin-engined, high-wing, old Russian plane which I viewed with apprehension and dismay, but which in fact proved to be extremely stable for the three-hour slow journey, diverting in order to see things like the Silingué Dam and to follow the course of the River Niger to Timbuctoo (Tomboctu in French and therefore in Mali).

I was greeted at the airport by the military governor, mayor, etc. and then at the entrance to the main square, five miles away, by two Nubian maidens, one of whom presented me with some dates, which I ate, and the other with a bowl of camel's milk, which I put to my lips but refrained from drinking as it had the most nauseous smell. Then into the square where the whole population seemed to be lined up. Fortunately the population of Timbuctoo is now only about 8000, as compared with 100,000 in 1500, so it was not quite as formidable a gathering as it might earlier have been. A lot of music and cheering, though quite whom or what they thought they were cheering I am not sure. Then I walked round the square and decided that the only thing to do was a Richard Nixon, plunge in, shake hands and then move on fifty yards and plunge in again.

Then a tour of the town with an excellent guide, seeing the mosque, which was very old, various houses where European explorers of the early nineteenth century had lived (and mostly died), and the starting point of the old caravan routes across the desert. I rode on a camel for a mile to lunch. It was my first camel ride since c. 1928 at the London Zoo, and a distinctly hazardous enterprise.

We had a rather nasty lunch in a rather nasty hotel. After having consumed bits of three or four courses I assumed that the lunch was over, but there was then a sudden stirring at the windows which were thrown open, with the curtains widened, and in came the most enormous roast camel, trussed like a sort of monstrous turkey, though about seventeen times as big, borne in upon a stretcher and laid down with great cheering. Then they performed the old desert trick of taking a whole roast sheep out of the inside of the camel, a whole roast chicken out of the inside of the sheep, a little pigeon-neau out of the inside of the chicken, and an egg out of that, and one had to eat a little of everything. The camel seemed to me to have rather a bland taste, not nearly as objectionable as its milk. Then back to Bamako for a Government dinner with speeches and the presentation to me of another Grand Croix du Légion d'Honneur. (Crispin got a Chevalier.)

THURSDAY, 11 JANUARY. *Bamako and Accra.*

A meeting with President Traoré at 8.30. He showed no signs of having been deposed during our absence in Timbuctoo and indeed, though saying nothing memorable, seemed to me a good deal more self-confident and also rather more interesting than when he had come to see me in Brussels.

We took off for Accra at about 12.30 and got there at 2.15, arriving in steaming heat quite different from the relative coolness of Dakar, the moderate heat, 75° perhaps, of Bamako, and the considerable but very dry heat of Timbuctoo, where it may have been 85° in the afternoon. But in Accra (mysteriously January is the warmest month of the year, despite it being 8° north of the equator) it was 93°, sticky and horrible.

We were met by the Chief of the Defence Staff, in effect the Prime Minister in a presidential system, called General Hamadu, whom I saw a lot of and got rather to like, and the new lady Foreign Minister, of whom I didn't think much.

No sooner had we got out of the airport than the most dreadful thing happened. I had thought it would happen sooner or later on one of my visits because of the ludicrous way in which motorcycle escorts behave. One of them shot out from the airport into the main road to hold up the traffic, utterly failed to do so and was completely crushed by a huge lorry which came down upon him. Fortunately, I suppose, I didn't actually see the accident, though I saw the corpse afterwards, but most of the others did, including the General who was with me and who was a good deal upset by it, as he ought to have been.

We first had a meeting with the General, the tiresome lady Foreign Minister, and an excellent man called Dr Abby who is the Commissioner for Economic Planning and a highly sophisticated economist with a lot of English and American training.

Then we went to see the head of state, Colonel Akuffo. This was an unsatisfactory meeting, mainly because it was foolishly organized, with about thirty people sitting in the room, apart from a press of journalists who were allowed to stand inside the door. The Colonel was talking so quietly that they could hardly hear what he was saying, but I was louder. A slightly stilted three-quarters of an hour, partly about the Lomé Convention, partly about the state of Ghana. He announced himself firmly resolved that they would hand over power to the civilians in the summer, though obviously not overconfident about the result. He was very critical of his immediate predecessors but less so of Nkrumah.

Indeed the general note about Nkrumah at my various meetings was surprisingly favourable. He has gone through a process of considerable rehabilitation, mainly by reference to how badly things have been run since, though in fact there is only too much evidence of his extravagant, grandiose and unattractive building mania. The whole town looks full of stadiums built in cracked, discoloured concrete. The whole country looks appallingly run down: great laagers of cars unable to move through lack of spare parts, for example. There is a strong sense of near-disintegration, and needless disintegration, as Ghana is inherently quite rich, but with an inflation rate of 150 per cent; the complete neglect of basic products, notably cocoa, has brought its obvious result.

Then a dinner given by General Hamadu at army headquarters. Hamadu raised a surprising point for a General, the undesirable pressure of Western arms salesmanship in Africa, which, in his view, was doing great harm.

I then spent two late-night hours finishing *The Sea, the Sea*, feeling that the combined effect of staying in this rather gimcrack State House in this steaming, rundown country, and Iris Murdoch's phantasmagoria, was having a distinctly unsettling effect on me.

FRIDAY, 12 JANUARY. *Accra and Paris.*

Quite a good morning expedition to the Kpong Dam about fifty miles away. It is a major enterprise, with a lot of Commission money in it, and was worth seeing. Also it was an opportunity to get some impression of the countryside of Ghana, which is much more scrubby, less vegetated than that of Nigeria. I travelled in the car with Abby both ways and had quite a useful talk with him. He is fairly pessimistic and thinks maybe there is about one chance in three of pulling the country round. He was critical of many things, like the foolishness of trying to run a chain of state hotels, which merely means that ministers run up bills they don't pay.

Lunch with the French Ambassador to meet the other six Community ones, who were quite an impressive lot. The German (Herbert Weil), as is often the case in African countries, was probably the best, an old wartime refugee and BBC employee in London during the war.

UTA plane to Paris via Lagos at 9 o'clock.

SATURDAY, 13 JANUARY. *Paris and Brussels.*

Roissy at 7.25 a.m. France was covered in snow and freezing as when we left. Rue de Praetère at 11.30. Lunched with Jennifer alone. There was a lot to talk about, what with Africa and what had been happening in England about which I was signally ill-informed. She was surprised that I hadn't realized how the country seemed to have plunged into chaos during the previous week and how there was a mood of deep *morosité* and how ill-judged Callaghan's remark about 'What crisis?' had been as he returned from Guadaloupe the previous Wednesday or Thursday.*

FRIDAY, 19 JANUARY. *Brussels.*

Dinner party, rue de Praetère, for General Haig plus wife. We expected the Harlechs, who were due for the weekend, but had been frustrated by British Airways. Therefore we had a slightly truncated party with only the Tickells and the Davignons to help entertain the Haigs. It went just tolerably well, I think, no more. It was a little difficult to get it to jell, but things improved later on. Haig is a strange man, with a simple manner and very right-wing views, very critical of Carter, full of political ambition and I think rather overrating his chances. She is more agreeable than I had thought on the previous occasion.

MONDAY, 22 JANUARY. *Brussels and London.*

To London, taking four or five hours, for a meeting followed by dinner with the Labour Committee for Europe. I had an interesting bilateral conversation with Shirley at dinner, who was in a great state of political gloom and was disposed to agree with me that the big mistake we had made was not to go and support Dick Taverne in 1973; everything had got worse since then. By an irony we hadn't supported Dick when we ought to have, and we had supported Reg Prentice, and although neither of us regretted this, there was a good deal less compelling a case, in retrospect at any rate, for having done it. She thought the election lost whenever it came and that the party would be in a very bad state after it, and she was thinking very clearly in terms of splits and anxious for me to come back.

*This was the peak (or trough) of the 'winter of discontent'.

TUESDAY, 23 JANUARY. *London and Brussels.*

I was due to make a speech in Dublin to the Irish Confederation of Industry, lunch with them, and see the Taoiseach in the afternoon. We awoke to quite thick snow and I was told that the avion taxi which we had ordered could not possibly get into Northolt and that no commercial flights were running. Therefore I firmly cancelled the Irish expedition (Crispin was fortunately in Dublin already and able to perform on my behalf) and set about the difficult but necessary task of getting back to Brussels. London Airport was announced as closed until 1 o'clock. When I got there at about 12.30 I was told that it was now closed until 4 o'clock and so went away to lunch until then.

There then seemed a good prospect of a Sabena plane leaving, but an endless sub-farce set in. We got on the plane, but were told that the plane was iced up and they couldn't find any de-icing equipment, and we would have to get off. Then we were told that they had borrowed some de-icing equipment from KLM (Benelux solidarity), then we were told that the de-icing equipment wouldn't work, so that we *would* have to get off the plane. So we got off the plane and were off it for about three-quarters of an hour, during which I had some quite useful telephone conversations with both Callaghan (who seemed surprisingly pleased to hear from me) and with Gundelach in Brussels.

Then we got back on the plane again. Then came a frenzied request that passengers should please sit down in any seat as the plane was moving away and if we missed the slot we might easily be there all night. Then it was eventually discovered that there were five passengers for whom there were no seats. An attempt was made to get the five people who had got on without boarding cards to own up, this being put in high moral terms, the steward saying, 'There are five of you here not entitled to be on the plane. Unless you identify yourselves you may prevent 110 people who are entitled to be here from getting to Brussels at all tonight.'

Eventually one man, looking rather like a young version of Christopher Mayhew, did own up; the other four did not. Thereupon an announcement was made that the only alternative was to clear the plane and re-check everybody – although fortunately not first-class passengers. This enterprise needless to say took a good forty minutes. Passengers came back on, having been cleared, looking as though they had had a successful interview with the Parole Board and were being allowed their freedom again, half sheepish, half pleased. Eventually we got into Brussels at about 10.30, having spent literally the whole day trying to do this simple journey.

THURSDAY, 25 JANUARY. *Brussels*.

In the late afternoon Noyon, head of the Commission Security Service, accompanied by a British security officer, came in to see me in great agitation and secrecy. Apparently the Belgians had been informed through British sources that there was a serious IRA plot to assassinate in the fairly near future a senior British representative (as it was put) in Brussels, and they had narrowed the list of possible targets down to me, Tugendhat, Crispin rather surprisingly, the three ambassadors and, I think, two generals.

There were a few hazy clues, such as that they had set up some sort of watching/firing post quite some time previously outside the house of the person who was the target and that they had reported that his habits were somewhat irregular – which is not true of mine. My morning walking or running habits are only too regular, particularly as this report came from before Christmas, before the snow introduced a certain irregularity. And they also reported that near the house in question there was a school, which posed certain dangers of shooting the children by accident. That seemed to rule out rue de Praetère, although, on the other hand, of all the targets mentioned, I (to the IRA) was much the most obvious one, as well as, presumably, being the best known generally. Crispin, on the other hand, did have a school near him, although on other grounds he seemed the least likely target.

Noyon took it all very seriously and said that we must take much heavier precautions. Obviously I couldn't ignore the matter completely, particularly as they stressed it was a real threat and that the attack was likely to be made in the course of the next few weeks.

I went home for a short time, rather rushing across the pavement in an embarrassed way, and, looking round the house, realized how incredibly exposed it was for shooting through a window for it is overlooked on all sides.

FRIDAY, 26 JANUARY. *Brussels and East Hendred.*

I saw the *comité des sages*, Robert Marjolin, quite well known to me, Edmund Dell, also quite well known to me in a different way, and Biesheuvel, Dutch ex-Prime Minister, who was unknown to me but who, in some ways, made the best, most agreeable and constructive impression of the three. I talked to them in a fairly animated way, leading them on to subjects rather than waiting for them to ask questions, for two hours. I formed the impression that Biesheuvel had the concept closest to us, that Marjolin though very sensible on many things had a typical French antipathy to the Parliament, which he refused to regard as a significant institution, and that Dell, although broadly a European, was pretty firmly against any form of more effective decision-making and rather complacently satisfied with the Council from his experience of it. What effect I had on them I didn't know. However, it was a more agreeable two hours than I had expected.

Then to London by a plane which was only one and a half hours late, and to East Hendred.

SATURDAY, 27 JANUARY. *East Hendred.*

On a very cold beautiful sunny day I walked in deep snow over the Lower Downs for three miles. Then with Jennifer to Sevenhampton to lunch with Ann Fleming, who had the Lees-Milnes,* John Sparrow and a keeper of manuscripts at the British Museum called John Gere, whom I liked very much. I also liked the Lees-Milnes more than on previous occasions and much enjoyed the whole occasion. We returned in a perfect winter sunset at 4.30.

THURSDAY, 1 FEBRUARY. *Brussels, Paris and Brussels.*

I left at 9.30 in lowering skies and heavy rain to drive to Paris for the lunch of the four Presidents which Giscard had summoned, and, arriving at the Etoile by about 12.15 I decided to call unexpectedly on the Beaumarchais'. Even so, I arrived slightly too early at the Elysée, the first of the Presidents. Kutscher arrived soon afterwards and then Colombo. Giscard, accompanied by François-Poncet, only

---

*James Lees-Milne, b. 1908, was on the staff of the National Trust 1936–66 and has been a prolific author during and after these years.

descended when we had all assembled – rather typical behaviour. However he was out to be gracious and to smooth some of the many feathers already ruffled by the French presidency. It was a bit overdone because he began by saying to me, 'Ah, Monsieur Jenkins, vous parlez admirablement le français maintenant, il y'a quelqu'un qui me l'a dit au cours des dernières semaines, j'ai oublié qui. Non, non, je me souviens, c'était le Roi d'Espagne.' I said, 'C'est un peu étrange, Monsieur le Président de la République, parce que le Roi d'Espagne et moi avons toujours parlé en anglais.'

We then proceeded into lunch, which was in its way agreeable, in a small dining room on the ground floor with a burning fire which slightly illuminated the gloom of the day. The conversation was moderately serious, mainly conducted by Giscard and me. It was in French, which was indeed the only remotely common language of everybody, but was a disadvantage for Kutscher and me, as Kutscher is much better in English than in French, and to some extent a disadvantage even for Colombo, though he is no good at all in English.

It was partly about agricultural prices, Giscard advocating some small increase, and my saying firmly that we were against this. Giscard asked at one stage whether I was not worried by having the Commission isolated with the British alone on the price freeze, which was a slightly malevolent way of putting it, and to which I replied that I did not think this would be the case. The Italians and maybe some others would be with us, but, in any event, I had opposed the British sufficiently firmly when I thought they were *wrong* and I was certainly not going to move from a position I was convinced was *right* merely because the British happened to share it.

After lunch we had a further forty-five minutes, in another room, mainly about the budget. This gave me the opportunity to say, as I had wanted to do for some time, that the fundamental error which had been made was both for the council to try and control the maximum rate of expenditure (which in my view was not unreasonable since even national parliaments on the whole did not have the ability to spend money except in agreement with the executive – and in any event they had the responsibility of raising the money in a way that the European Parliament did not) and, something else, which in my view *was* totally unreasonable, which was to try to combine this with control over Parliament's priorities. It had been clear for some time past that Parliament was giving priority to the Regional Fund, and to resist this on the basis of the sacred texts of the European Council's decision of fourteen months before was to make a nonsense of Parliament as part of the budgetary authority. If it was intended to try and restrict them in both ways then it was hardly worth pretending that the Parliament had any budgetary powers at all, and certainly a mistake to move to a directly elected Parliament.

Giscard accepted this to a surprising extent and said, 'Yes, within a ceiling I see that Parliament must have freedom to manoeuvre.' I also trailed the possibility that the Commission would put forward in due course a supplementary budget. It would be necessary because of the EMS arrangements, and we might do it in such a way that we went above the total of 11,000 million units of account which Parliament had voted. Giscard and Poncet did not look very pleased but took no violent exception.

We also had some pronouncements from Kutscher about the competence of the Court if the budget issue was put before it, to which on the whole he gave an affirmative answer, with Giscard warning that France would not necessarily recognize the validity of this and a very grave position might consequently arise, etc.

Despite all this, we left on reasonably good terms, with Giscard courteously coming out with us, although we soon discovered that this was because there were a lot of television cameras outside to which he duly spoke and then turned, first to me and then to Colombo and then to Kutscher, for us to add a few words.

I also gave a brief interview to Reuters and then drove off taking Colombo with me in my car as I wished to ask his advice on some parliamentary point. A slight farce then set in. I was proposing, in response to a note Nicko Henderson had sent to me at the Elysée, to go and see him at the Embassy. For some extraordinary reason, however, we also had in my car, accompanying Colombo (whose car had not turned up), François-Poncet's *Directeur de Cabinet*, and I was not anxious for it to look as though I ran straight from the Elysée to the British Embassy. I therefore rather unconvincingly dropped them in the rue du Faubourg St Honoré, made another time-wasting circuit by the rue Boissy d'Anglas and left myself only ten minutes for Nicko.

We then drove back to Brussels through pouring rain and a sodden landscape. Berlaymont at 6.45, where there was rather a lot of work, as well as a speech to get into shape for a Val Duchesse change of presidency dinner at 8.30. The dinner followed the regular pattern of these occasions. I had Hedwige de Nanteuil on one side and Signora Giolitti on the other. I made a rather serious speech, more so than the last time, which probably wasn't a bad idea. Sigrist as the outgoing President of COREPER had no difficulty in being equally serious, curiously apologizing for the incompetences of the German presidency, and then Luc de Nanteuil made, if not exactly a frivolous speech, one which was not remotely about policy or substance, but which was exceptionally nice about me, much more so than anyone else had been previously at these dinners.

FRIDAY, 2 FEBRUARY. *Brussels.*

Drove to Leuven where I was being given an honorary degree. It is an intensely Catholic university. At the Mass in the cathedral everybody except me took communion, including all the professors. Then a two-hour ceremony in a rather nice hall.

The other degree recipients were the ex-President of Venezuela (Caldera), the Cardinal Archbishop of Kinshasa (Malula), and the Polish composer Penderecki. I had to make the principal speech near the beginning, which was neither very good nor very bad. Tindemans then did an allocution about me, and towards the end the ex-President of Venezuela made a rather good speech in French which is not however the best language for Leuven. Then lunch with the Tindemans and back to the Berlaymont at 3.30, where two days away had produced a pile-up of work.

SATURDAY, 3 FEBRUARY. *Brussels.*

On a beautiful clear, cold morning I drove Neil Bruce* (staying) and Jennifer to Crupet beyond Namur where after a half-hour's walk up to and round the village on an extremely slippery surface we lunched at Les Ramiers and then drove back to Namur via the river

---

*Neil Bruce, b. 1919, was a Balliol contemporary who was subsequently a BBC foreign correspondent and a lecturer in international politics at Keele University.

and walked for another half-hour on the Citadel. A small dinner party for Neil and the Plajas (Italian Ambassador). A lot of talk with Plaja after dinner about the Italian position and some of my complaints about the way the French presidency was conducting itself so far, although my views had been a little assuaged by Thursday's Elysée luncheon, which had undoubtedly done some good.

MONDAY, 5 FEBRUARY. *Brussels.*

At noon I addressed a group of about eighty so-called US leaders, who were people from business working in government for a year, or vice versa. They looked quite bright, I spoke to them without a text and spoke quite well, but they then asked very boring questions, mainly about the technical details of tariffs affecting the industries from which they came.

Then to a lunch of about ten for the Spanish Foreign Minister Oreja which Simonet gave in the Palais d'Egmont. The anecdotal conversation was all in French, which meant that I couldn't tell as many anecdotes as I might have liked! My command of punch lines in French is inadequate.

At 6 o'clock we had the formal opening of the Spanish negotiations, a long speech from François-Poncet, a shorter but in some ways better one from me, and a good and serious reply from Calvo Sotelo. Then a dinner for the Spaniards at the Val Duchesse, at which François-Poncet and Oreja spoke, but not me, and at which I had a good talk with the latter, whom I was next to, and decided that he was an exceptionally nice and intelligent man with a wide range of interests. After dinner I had a prearranged forty-five minutes with François-Poncet alone, during which we went through the agenda for tomorrow's Council and made it clear on which we were going to have difficulty. I told him what we would have to say on the budget and also warned him that we were bound to have a major clash on Euratom questions, where there could be no question of our not upholding the Court ruling, which the French must understand absolutely clearly.* He took all this fairly

*The Court of Justice ruling of November 1978 had in effect upheld the Commission's right to insist on a Community Agreement for the supply of nuclear materials from Australia, assuring the same terms to all users, and denied France's asserted right to conclude a parallel bilateral agreement.

well and there was certainly a vast improvement in atmosphere from my very unsatisfactory meeting with him before Christmas.

TUESDAY, 6 FEBRUARY. *Brussels.*

Still beautiful weather, very cold and clear. Jennifer went to London and I spent the morning in the Foreign Affairs Council. Then lunched with the Council and had another four hours in the afternoon. It was quite a good Council from my point of view and rather morale-boosting. I made an intervention summing up the budget debate in the middle of the morning, then carried on the Euratom argument in the afternoon, getting support from nearly everybody except the French, and eventually putting them into an oddly pleading position of saying would we accept this, would we accept that. We had a long-drawn-out negotiation on this and eventually reached a slightly inconclusive but much more satisfactory outcome than might have been expected. Dohnanyi played his hand well and helpfully on both occasions.

I saw Richard Mayne and was greatly relieved to discover that he was happy to accept retirement from the London office with goodwill and that there was no unpleasantness there. I dined with Davignon, Ortoli and Gundelach (who joined us rather late from the Agricultural Council). Morale was slightly higher than when the four of us had met before Christmas, but not vastly so. I gave them an outline of the Haferkamp affair, and they cluck-clucked in a suitable way, though Ortoli made the perceptive but depressing comment that things would probably swing round on to Willy's side and that he would be regarded as a persecuted semi-hero and that the rest of us would get nearly as much mud as he did himself without deserving it.

WEDNESDAY, 7 FEBRUARY. *Brussels.*

Pouring with rain. I had noticed a ring around the moon in an otherwise clear sky when walking back from the Charlemagne to the Berlaymont at 7.15 the previous evening. It is the most reliable of all weather signs.

Commission for three hours in the morning and four hours in the afternoon. The afternoon session was rather exhausting, with one or two difficult items. I persuaded them with only a little difficulty that we should not present a new budget at this stage. Then there was an unexpected raising of the Haferkamp affair by Cheysson, who did it nominally in helpful terms but who only has to see any bubbling pot to want to stir it. And then an unexpected and tiresome defeat on GSP* for China. Haferkamp presented it fairly badly. I thought it was all arranged, but to my dismay, Ortoli, Gundelach, Davignon and Cheysson (Cheysson was expected, the others not) all came out in a rather hostile way, so there was nothing to do except half accept a negative decision for the moment but say that I would have to come back to it before I went to China: a boring end to the meeting.

THURSDAY, 8 FEBRUARY. *Brussels.*

A difficult meeting with Aigner,† who is Chairman of the Budget Control Committee, about the Haferkamp affair and its repercussions. Then had Francis Pym, accompanied by Crispin, to lunch, rue de Praetère. He was extremely anxious to learn not only about Brussels, but how to be Foreign Secretary which, as I recorded at the beginning of January, he is quite confident that he will be, although he is not necessarily expecting an election before the autumn. I felt a bit like Lord Melbourne with Queen Victoria, although apart from a certain dumpiness they do not look exactly alike. However, I think Pym is nice and straightforward, even if not intellectually sparkling. Crispin liked him too. Then to Bruges, where I spoke and answered questions at the College of Europe for an hour and a half. I enjoyed the meeting which was attended by all their 180 students.

---

*The Generalized System of Preferences (GSP) is a means of giving tariff preferences on behalf of developed countries to developing countries. The GSP was agreed in 1968 at the Second Session of the UNCTAD in New Delhi. The preferences are non-discriminatory, autonomous (i.e. not contractually agreed) and non-reciprocal. The European Community began such arrangements in 1971, the USA in 1976. The Community scheme applies to 128 independent countries and more than twenty dependent countries. China has benefited from the Community scheme since 1980.
†Heinrich Aigner, b. 1924, had been a CSU (Franz Josef Strauss's Bavarian party) member of the Bundestag since 1957 and of the European Parliament since 1961.

FRIDAY, 9 FEBRUARY. *Brussels.*

Cheysson at 9.45 to try and move him, not very successfully, on GSP for China. I then saw Napolitano,* and a delegation of about five from the Italian Communist Party, who had made a great issue about coming to see me. Napolitano was talkative, svelte and moderate, and indeed agreeable and sensible, as I had thought when I had seen him in London about three years before; most of the others were silent.

At 12.30 I had Klose, the Governing Mayor of Hamburg, for half an hour's talk and a lunch. Unfortunately before seeing him I made the mistake of reading the summary of the German press comment on the Haferkamp affair, which Tugendhat had sent me, and was horrified and depressed to find how anti-British, anti-Tugendhat, and indeed how anti-me the German press comment had turned into after its initial, but brief, anti-Haferkamp phase. How right Ortoli was. Therefore I started in a gloomy and not very pro-German mood. However, Klose is a nice agreeable man, though he doesn't get on with Schmidt I am afraid, nor with Apel.

After lunch I saw George Thomson and wept a little on his shoulder about the Haferkamp affair as he had done on mine over the Rhodesian sanctions affair the year before. Then I got the figures for which I had asked for various forms of expenditure, and discovered the horrific bit of news that our 1978 expenditure on avion taxis was more than twice the previous year's, and that as a result we were over our budget for this part of Commissioners' travel and accommodation expenses, though not over the budget for either representation expenses or travelling expenses in the Commission as a whole (that is including officials). After seeing Tugendhat about this bad beginning to the weekend I went home, where Caroline had arrived to stay and where we unusually had a purely English dinner party.

MONDAY, 12 FEBRUARY. *Brussels and Luxembourg.*

I saw the acting Egyptian Foreign Minister, Boutros-Ghali, for just over half an hour at 10.30: an agreeable, intelligent man. Then I

* Giorgio Napolitano, b. 1925, a member of the Camera dei Deputati, was President of the Italian Communist Group (in the European Parliament) 1979–86.

attended a reception which Brunner was giving for Heath and the European Youth Orchestra, spoke briefly to Ted and listened to one or two rather good little performances.

At 12 o'clock I saw Greenborough* and two or three other people from the British CBI and then, at 12.30, Vredeling, to lobby him successfully about reversing the previous Wednesday's GSP decision for China. Crispin had done a good and much more difficult job with both Davignon and Gundelach the previous week.

After this I gave lunch to a highly distinguished body of Norwegian parliamentarians containing at least two ex-Prime Ministers and, so I was told, either one or two future Prime Ministers – that is always more difficult to tell. At 3 o'clock I saw Ortoli on several matters, including telling him that I was going to try and change the GSP decision, which he accepted with neither enthusiasm nor complaint. He was not going to be at the meeting on Wednesday so he was not of crucial importance, but I thought it necessary to tell him.

4.27 train to Luxembourg and worked all the way, mainly on my draft statement relating to expenses, while Nick Stuart and Laura did a breakdown on the dreaded avion taxi figures. We arrived in filthy, gloomy weather and I went to see Colombo to discuss various bits of business for the week with him – a friendly conversation as always.

TUESDAY, 13 FEBRUARY. *Luxembourg.*

Delivered my not very exciting Programme speech to the Parliament at about 10.15. A tolerable debate during the morning, except for a notably ungracious speech from Fellermaier, the leader of the Socialist Group, who I am afraid likes me as little as I like him. Then I found myself rather unexpectedly called upon to reply to half the debate at about 12.10, and then went out to lunch at Hostert with the Tickells and Nick. I took a minor debate (about Eurobaromètre – a public opinion poll commissioned by us in which a foolish and embarrassing question had been asked) at 6.00, and then did a ten-minute TV interview with Robert Mackenzie.†

---

* (Sir) John Greenborough, b. 1922, a senior Shell man, was President of the CBI 1978–80.
† Robert Mackenzie, 1917–81, was an LSE professor of Canadian origin who achieved considerable fame as a BBC political commentator and inventor of the 'swingometer'.

WEDNESDAY, 14 FEBRUARY. *Luxembourg.*

The weather still filthy. A two-hour Commission meeting at 9.00, longer than usual during a Parliament week, but not altogether unsatisfactory. I told them about the avion taxi figures, which reduced them to a state of stunned dismay – most of them at any rate. I got the GSP decision satisfactorily reversed, had a rather gloomy interview with Tugendhat, who is even more depressed than I about the Haferkamp affair, and spoke to Robin Day on the telephone for a *World at One* recorded tribute to poor Reggie Maudling, whose death had been announced that morning. Then, at 12.30, I recorded a Southern Television interview with Stephen Milligan, the author of all the Haferkamp trouble, whom I treated fairly frostily.

In the afternoon I appeared before the Budget Control Sub-Committee, which I had had to promise Aigner I would do. I had arranged with Aigner that I would merely make a brief statement, telling them what I was going to say in the Parliament the following afternoon, and then withdraw, and it would all be done without publicity. He interpreted this sufficiently freely that the room was crammed with television cameras and the Committee seemed to have swollen to about four times its normal size, and I had, with the support of a number of other members, to get the television cameras removed before I would start. However, I eventually made a brief statement and they did at least observe the no-questions agreement, mainly due to British Tory and Labour members (Bessborough and Bruce) being particularly helpful.

At 5 o'clock I saw the Australian Ambassador who had come partly to complain about us and partly to complain about his Government, as is usually the case with that admirable man. Then I saw Donald Bruce and thanked him for his help in the afternoon. He thinks that he has got no chance of being directly elected and would like a job in my *cabinet*, which is perhaps why he was so helpful, but one should not be too cynical.

I dined with Laura at the St Michel and had the most cheerful meal of this long Luxembourg visit. I decided that I really must bounce up and not allow this dreadful cloud of Haferkamp affair gloom to suffuse me; whether I will stick to this excellent resolution remains to be seen.

THURSDAY, 15 FEBRUARY. *Luxembourg and Brussels.*

Listened to and wound up with a twenty-five-minute speech the second half of the debate on my Programme speech. Lunched with Laura and Nick, going back to the Parliament rather early to be ready for questions at 3.00. The only one I took was that relating to the Haferkamp affair, on which I made a statement of about seven minutes. This was quite well received with only Fellermaier producing a slightly snide question (which probably turned out to be rather helpful) asking what were the national motives of the *Economist.* I replied that I had no idea, but one thing I greatly deplored was the introduction of this nationalist note into the dispute, and spoke rather emotionally about my attachment to Anglo-German friendship, and that we must really grow up as a Community. It was unimaginable that if an attack on a New York politician appeared in a Chicago paper it would be regarded as an Illinois plot against the East Coast. It was not very carefully considered, but probably worth saying and went rather well.

Back to Brussels by car, still in horrible weather.

FRIDAY, 16 FEBRUARY. *Brussels.*

A morning Commission meeting on the budget. The issue was whether we did a budget which was purely supplementary, to which I half inclined the night before, or one which was lightly rectifying as well as supplementary. The two French, Ortoli and Cheysson, both wanted a heavily rectifying budget, and the two Italians a purely supplementary one. Eventually there was no alternative but to compromise on a lightly rectifying one, which indeed Tugendhat had put forward and expounded rather well, and was eventually agreed with dissent from Cheysson from one side and Natali and Giolitti from the other, but not with formal dissent from Ortoli. Therefore a reasonably satisfactory outcome.

Jennifer and I had Ortoli to lunch, rue de Praetère. The purpose of the lunch was to discuss with him things which might happen while I was away* and, in particular, the paper − not wholly satisfactory − which he had prepared on convergence for the

*I was due to go to China for ten days on 20 February.

European Council. In view of my impending absence, it was not possible to do more than suggest that he made about four moderately significant changes of presentation, to which he agreed.

About 4 o'clock I went across to the Commission TV studios, thinking I was due to do a ten-minute interview with Michael Charlton. It turned out to be a major programme, lasting forty minutes, with not only Charlton, but Malcolm Rutherford and MacIntyre, the BBC man in Brussels, as well. I began in dismay, totally unprepared for a long interview. However, most mysteriously, although I was somewhat worried when it was over, subsequent responses suggested it was one of the better things I had done on television for a long time.

I saw Davignon at his request for three-quarters of an hour to talk about MTNs, on which he was fairly depressing. Dined at home with the Beaumarchais', who had arrived to stay.

SATURDAY, 17 FEBRUARY. *Brussels*.

Jennifer having put her back out the previous day, there was extreme uncertainty as to whether or not she would be able to come to China. She stayed in bed. I took the Beaumarchais' to Crupet (once again; it is the only near Ardennes restaurant open in February). We had a short walk (still on ice) before lunch. It was not a bad day. Returned via Namur. Snow started to fall quite heavily in the evening and I drove the Beaumarchais' with difficulty to the Nanteuils' christening party. I learnt there that war had broken out between China and Vietnam, which was a highly inconvenient time and raised a question of whether we should still go to Peking on Tuesday.

MONDAY, 19 FEBRUARY. *Brussels*.

At noon I had a meeting with the Chinese *Chargé d'affaires*, the Ambassador being in Peking waiting for us (we had made a definite decision during the morning that we should go to China rather than postpone the visit; Jennifer fortunately somewhat better, having seen doctors) and did some visit planning with him, including the abandonment of the boat trip through the Yangtse gorges on the ground that three days was too long.

Bill Rodgers came for a drink at 7.30. He was on very ebullient form, although he said he was depressed after the action, but he clearly thought that he had had, as Peter Jenkins put it, 'a good war' during the strike period* and was exhilarated by having made a public breakthrough and the feeling that he had performed effectively, which he certainly had. He is a great fighting colonel.

TUESDAY, 20 FEBRUARY. *Brussels, Paris and Karachi.*

A snow run in the Bois, then some fairly frenzied packing before leaving rue de Praetère at 9.50 to address the joint twentieth anniversary of COPA, the European farmers' union, and two other agricultural organizations down near the Gare du Nord. The President of COPA spoke too long, so that I was only just able to get in my short speech (a rather good, tough speech written by Graham Avery) before driving to the Gare du Midi for the 11.43 to Paris, accompanied by Jennifer, Crispin, Celia Beale, Enzo Perlot and Etienne Reuter (Emile Noël, Roy Denman and Endymion Wilkinson, Tokyo-based Sino-expert and good Chinese speaker, joined at subsequent points), lunching on the way. Then to Charles de Gaulle and the 4.10 plane. I did some hard work on briefs during the early evening. We arrived in Karachi after seven and a quarter hours flying and spent an hour and a half on the ground there, standing out for a large part of the time on the platform at the top of the steps. It was a cool, agreeable night, starlight, waning moon and the temperature about 60°F.

WEDNESDAY, 21 FEBRUARY. *Karachi and Peking.*

I slept for quite a long time – well on into the light – before putting on fresh clothes and breakfasting only a short time before a 2.30 p.m. arrival in Peking on a greyish day, no snow, temperature about 32°. We had done the whole flight quickly, in thirteen and a half hours flying time from Paris.

We were met on the tarmac by the Minister of Foreign Trade and various other Chinese dignitaries, including the Ambassador in

---

* 'The winter of discontent'.

Brussels; Sung, the old Ambassador in London, now more or less permanent head of the Foreign Office; and the ambassadors of the Nine or rather the seven there represented (no Luxembourgeois, no Irish), less the Italian who was away and represented by his Counsellor. Drove, accompanied by the Minister of Foreign Trade, to the guest house in the western part of the city (the grandest one, they claimed), where we arrived at 3.15. Then we had some programme discussion, unpacked, and went over a speech for the banquet that evening.

Arnaud, the French Ambassador, came by a slight confusion just as we were leaving. We had asked him, were told he could not come, and then had a summons to be at the Great Hall of the People earlier in order to have a talk to Gu Mu, the Vice-Premier who was host, before the banquet at 7 o'clock. So there was a slight embarrassment, but not greatly so, for Arnaud is an agreeable man. I drove with him in the car for the quarter of an hour to the Great Hall, and consulted him as to what I should say on Vietnam in my speech. I talked rather formally with Gu Mu for fifteen minutes or so and we then proceeded into the banquet soon after 7 o'clock. It lasted, including the speeches, for the statutory two and a quarter hours. The food was not as good as I remembered Chinese food on our last visit (1973), partly because apparently it never is very good in the Great Hall of the People and partly because it belonged to no particular *cuisine* but was an all-China *mélange*.

Gu Mu made a perfectly tolerable speech, rather short. My speech was longer; maybe given the fact it had to be translated after each paragraph it was a bit too long (ten minutes plus ten minutes' translation). On Vietnam I stuck firmly to the declaration of the Foreign Ministers of the Nine, issued on the Monday morning.

Bed at 10.30 and then, after about four and a half hours I woke up sleepless. I noticed that there had been a considerable fall of snow, the first apparently in Peking since well before Christmas, and then heard and saw two tremendous explosions accompanied by great orange flashes in the sky, the first a loud bang like a V2 going off about two miles away, the second a still louder bang which made the furniture shake in the room, like a V2 going off half a mile away. I was not frightened for some reason or other, thought it unlikely that a Soviet air attack had begun, but wondered in a rather detached way what on earth was happening. After that I worked until 5.00, writing out some notes for an opening statement at my meeting with Gu Mu the following morning and generally clarifying my thoughts on a number of points. Then back to bed and slept heavily until 8.00.

THURSDAY, 22 FEBRUARY. *Peking.*

I had great difficulty in gearing myself up from a state of extreme somnolence for the meeting with Gu Mu at 9.00. Fortunately we were told that this had been put back because of the snow, and, rather surprisingly, his difficulty getting to the Great Hall (where does he live?), but then we were summoned only about twenty minutes late. There were hundreds of people hurriedly clearing up the streets of the snowbound city.

The meeting lasted three hours and was held in a conference room round a table. After a welcome, Gu Mu invited me to open as he had indicated the previous evening that he would do. I then made a statement about the world situation, sounding a fairly sombre note, and ranging over matters from Iran, Africa, the Middle East, American leadership or lack of leadership, progress within the Community, normalization of Chinese relations with America, Chinese/Japanese friendship treaty, to Vietnam. Vietnam I coupled with the decline in American self-confidence, and said that that unhappy country had already contributed enough to world instability in the last ten years and therefore the Chinese embroilment causes us considerable concern and I hope very much that when you say it is limited in space and time that that will indeed be the case and the time will be very short. That will make things much easier for the 'friends of China', of whom I count myself one.

I then went on to a description of developments within the Community, EMS, direct elections, enlargement, etc., and then, in the third part of my statement, I came to Chinese/Community trade relations, saying that their modernization programme could certainly be amongst, and perhaps *the* major development for the remaining years of this century* and was something in which we wished to participate fully and which might indeed play a significant part as an impulse to growth for which the industrialized world

*I think this is proving to have been an exaggeration.

had been looking. This all took, with translation, a good hour.

Gu Mu replied at least at equal length, covering even a wider range of subjects, most of them fairly predictable, all predicated on a strongly anti-Soviet position of course, but this not put in particularly violent terms. The Vietnamese, he said, had become 'little hegemonists' (a phrase which I felt somewhat contradictory but did not bother to take up subsequently). After his long statement, I came back with various comments, assuring him in the first place that he need have no doubt of our awareness of possible Soviet threats. We had indeed been aware of them longer than most, having lived through the Czechoslovakian *coup* in 1947 and the attempt to strangle Berlin in 1948, and had set up NATO as a result, which still remained in good order, etc.

The interesting part of the trade discussion was on the relative shares of the market which the main powers might hope to occupy. I indicated that we expected a larger share than the United States in view of the present pattern of trade and our longer history of diplomatic and commercial relations with the People's Republic, and a significant share in relation to Japan, although Japan would no doubt be their main trading partner. Gu Mu then rather surprisingly said that our share should be as large as that of Japan or the United States – in other words, equal thirds. I said this was fine *vis-à-vis* Japan, but *vis-à-vis* the United States we expected more, for the reasons given. This interchange ended inconclusively but perfectly amicably. The meeting was generally thought to have been good and useful.

Back to the guest house soon after 12.30. There were as many bicycles as ever but a good deal more motorized traffic in Peking than I remember from the last occasion; I would think about twice as much. More trucks, but also a new element, a sort of small jeep, Chinese made, which now occupy about as big a proportion of the traffic as taxis do in central London, and are apparently owned by government departments, agencies, rural communes, etc.

Lunch alone with our team of nine at the guest house. Very good food, much better than the night before. Then back to the Great Hall of the People for a slightly over-long meeting with the Foreign Minister, Huang Hua. Having talked so much in the morning I was rather anxious to get him to talk, and opened by asking him about Chinese/American and Chinese/Japanese relations, which produced only too long an *exposé* on his part. However the conversation got more interesting in the second half of the two-and-a-quarter-hour session.

In justifying the Vietnamese operation – 'against the Cubans of the East' – he complained that we had not done enough to combat the activities of the Cubans in the West in Africa. 'France', he suddenly said, drawing Emile Noël into the conversation, rather as though Emile were a parachute colonel attired in képi and battle-dress, 'France had acted decisively in Zaïre, but nobody else had done much.' I said the Belgians had done something and, in any case, we were necessarily somewhat inhibited against African intervention by our imperialist past. He said that China for her part would maintain her tit-for-tat attitude towards the Soviet Union and her accomplices. Now China was teaching a lesson to Vietnam. The boundaries were comparatively unimportant. What was important was the overall strategic concept, in which context it was necessary to see China's punitive action against Vietnam. She was battling not for selfish motives but for the general interest in containing Soviet expansion.

There was some talk about the PLO at the end, which I raised, saying that they were undoubtedly a destabilizing influence in the Gulf and possibly in Saudi Arabia and what were the Chinese doing about this. Huang Hua said it was a rather disparate organization, but they exercised what restraining influence they could. Huang Hua, as I discovered subsequently at dinner, spoke and understood extremely good English, having been at the UN for five years, but we nonetheless did the whole conversation with translation which at least made it more leisurely.

To the Peking opera from 7.30 to 10.00. There were three separate little operas; all of them classical, i.e. set in the eighteenth century or earlier. The first was a sort of duelling match in the dark and more ballet with an element of acrobatics than opera; the second, apart from the music, was reminiscent of an overstylized Mozart production; the third, *The Monkey King*, was again ballet and still more acrobatically orientated. All three, the music apart, were rather good. The costumes were elaborate, quite different from anything we had seen five years before when this form of classical opera had been heavily frowned upon. There was an auditorium for about 1500 people, fullish but not packed, with a fairly high proportion of foreigners, including a number of tourists, but a fair number of Chinese as well. The applause, as indeed tends to be the case with Chinese applause, was moderate rather than enthusiastic.

Dinner at the guest house and bed at 11.30. During the day we had been given the official explanation of the explosions and illuminated sky of the night before, which was that a boiler had blown up in an apartment house. I suppose true, for I cannot think of any other plausible thesis. But it must have been a very big boiler and very damaging to the apartment house.

FRIDAY, 23 FEBRUARY. *Peking*.

Up again at 8 o'clock, again with difficulty. A meeting with Deng* at 10.00. We first had a photograph and then settled down for one and a half hours of extremely fast, taut, intensive conversation. Compared with when I had last seen him five and a half years ago, when Jennifer and I talked to him for the same length of time, the first foreigners that he had been allowed to see after his first period of disgrace, Deng looked younger, despite the fact that he is now seventy-four, and he has gained enormously in authority. He is now an extremely tough, impressive personality by the highest world standards, with a great grasp of the details of international affairs, accompanied of course by an extremely hard line. Unlike the meetings with Gu Mu and Huang Hua there was no question of long *exposés*. Neither of us spoke for more than two and a half minutes at a time and the interchanges were fairly evenly balanced. He began by asking about the progress of the Community and showed his knowledge by asking one or two extremely shrewd questions, such as: 'Would the new directly elected Parliament, frustrated in its ability to have greater nominal powers, not take it out a little on the Commission?' I said, 'Maybe yes, but their real target would be the Council of Ministers.'

*Deng Xiaoping, b. 1904, was Secretary of the Central Committee of the Chinese Communist Party 1956–67, when he was removed from office in the Cultural Revolution. He was restored to favour as a member of the Politburo 1973–6, at the beginning of which period we had been offered our unexpected interview, and then again disgraced as an 'unrepentant capitalist roader' by the Gang of Four in April 1976. He returned to the Politburo in 1977 and became Chairman of the National Committee of the Chinese Communist Party in 1978.

We then moved over the whole world scene with considerable speed. The only point on which I thought he was unrealistic was a Middle Eastern settlement, and unrealistic there because of his unwillingness to allow the Soviet Union any place in the world scheme. He therefore thought that while there must clearly be a Palestinian state on the West Bank, while there must clearly be recognition of the integrity of the rest of Israel and its right to exist; a guarantee for this need not be provided by great powers but should be provided by some non-aligned powers. I would put the likelihood of the Israelis accepting, say, a Yugoslav/Indian/Malaysian guarantee at about zero.

On Vietnam, he gave me the impression that things were going fairly badly. I asked him about the equipment of the Vietnamese army and he gave a neutral answer, saying that one machine gun, one rifle, was very much like another, and air power was not involved. What was, however, the case was that the Vietnamese troops were much more battle-experienced than the Chinese troops. Nobody in the Chinese army had fought for twenty years, and those who had fought then had all become 'old fat generals'. He stated that the Chinese were not going far in, they could extricate themselves whenever they wished, whenever they had taught the Vietnamese a lesson, had shrunken 'their swollen heads'.

He said that the risks of a Soviet intervention had been very carefully calculated. There were various possibilities: that of a minor deployment of force against the north or the north-west of China; and that of a more major activity there. They had calculated on both possibilities. Neither had happened. There were, however, some people in China who thought that the fact that nothing had happened so far might indicate a stronger rather than a weaker reaction at some stage in the future. I said that what I would fear more from a Chinese point of view was that the Soviet Union would continue to do nothing and that if the Chinese got bogged down for any length of time in Vietnam, world opinion – perhaps nervous and fickle in their view but no less real for that – certainly in the Third World and to some extent in the West, would be alienated from the Chinese position and this would militate against the building up of the broad front against 'Soviet hegemony' which they so much desired.

I don't think he liked this point very much, and said: 'Well, no doubt the Chinese would have a bad name for some time, but this was better than to behave in the inactive way against which they had been preaching in other theatres.' And so we left the Vietnamese topic.

We talked briefly about trade relations, but he made it clear that he mainly delegated these to the Minister for External Trade, whom I was seeing that afternoon. We then had an hour's pause for reflection before proceeding right across the city to the extreme eastern part where is the new diplomatic enclave. There the French Ambassador had a lunch for his six European colleagues and us. This was the one Western meal we had in China; the French wine was more welcome than the food.

I gave them a slightly expurgated briefing, for the European ambassadors in Peking are notoriously leaky as they have nobody much to talk to except Western journalists and I did not want my impression of the Deng talk relating to the Chinese doing badly in Vietnam to appear immediately in the press.

Then once again to the Great Hall of the People for our detailed meeting with the Minister for External Trade, Li. This was reasonably satisfactory. Roy Denman did some of the talking, though not much. Li gave the impression of not being particularly well-informed, and has a maniacal laugh, but is probably quite shrewd. On most of the points on which we wanted detailed agreement, the Business Seminar in Brussels in the summer of 1980, the Trade Centre in Peking, we were able to get agreement quickly. On textiles* we neither expected nor achieved much progress. We held out to them the prospect of generalized special preferences, which they did not ask for and did not snatch at, so we were able to put it in a fairly tentative form. With great difficulty we extracted their estimates of Chinese annual imports by 1985, which by a process of elimination and short bracketing we were eventually able to establish as $25/$30 billion as opposed to the present total of just over $10 billion.† Altogether it was a useful, pedestrian meeting.

That evening we gave a cocktail party in the Peking Hotel for the European press, the diplomats, and some 'Chinese friends' who

* More of which they wanted to export to us but which we did not want to receive.
† In fact their 1985 imports turned out to be $33.4 billion, with the difference between 1979 and 1985 prices more than bridging the discrepancy.

were not quite senior enough to be asked to our banquet the following evening. I talked a bit to all three circles, and it was over by about 7 o'clock. We dined in the guest house alone with our party.

SATURDAY, 24 FEBRUARY. *Peking.*

A beautiful morning following two rather cloudy days after the snow on Thursday and Friday; temperature still about freezing point. I addressed the Institute of Foreign Affairs at 9.00, the same body which I spoke to five years ago. There was a larger audience than last time, about 150, although I was rather curiously expected to speak to them sitting down. I delivered not a bad prepared speech which, with translation, took almost exactly an hour, and then answered questions (last time there were no questions) for forty-five minutes. Most of them were planted and prepared, as they so carefully and methodically covered the main areas one would have liked to have been asked about in relation to the Community: enlargement, EMS, direct elections, etc. But there was one unprepared one from a Chinese lady, who asked it in English and attracted slightly Batemanesque glances, but more I think because of the nature of the question and because she was not on the list than because of her asking it in English and not Chinese. This was about events in Iran and how damaging they were to us. Then a cold, sunny, very rapid walk through the Imperial Palace and to the top of Coal Hill. Lunch in the guest house and a necessary hour's sleep in the afternoon.

Then our final important meeting – with Chairman Hua – from 5.00 to 6.20. Hua is very different from Deng, much less fast-talking and quick-comprehending, but in his way quite impressive. In a sense it was a rather intelligent head of state performance, not a head of state in the Carter or Giscard sense, nor in the Queen's sense, but rather like talking to Scheel, compared with talking to Schmidt. We talked a certain amount about China geographically, where everybody on their side came from; talked a bit about our delegation, with Hua trying to identify the different nationalities in our team.

He then gave a long *exposé*, but also listened with apparent interest to my *exposé*, in which I developed more strongly than I had done previously the need for a stimulus to the Western economies, which gave us not only a friendly interest, but also a self-interest, in helping with Chinese modernization. He seemed quite interested in this analysis, which followed naturally from what he had just been saying about his study of Western economies.

On Vietnam, which he raised without prompting from me, he gave the impression that they had had some further bad news in the past twenty-four hours. Contrasting with what we had been told on the Thursday – and even what Deng had said the previous morning – he was hesitant about a date for coming out, saying that this depended on two sides, and that they wanted to be assured that the Vietnamese would not pursue them over the border if they extricated themselves, or words very much to that effect.

Hua had read (or been briefed on) my speech that morning and commented friendlily on my remark that China was neither wholly a part of the first world, the second world, or the third world, but potentially part of all three.

The Hua meeting over, we had our press conference at 6.30, which was easy to the point of being dull.

Then, upstairs a little early for the banquet we were giving in the Great Hall, where we had most of the same guests as on the Wednesday evening, except that the Foreign Minister came as well as Gu Mu and the Minister for External Trade; and we also had the stars from the Peking opera, the main lady from the Mozart-like piece in the middle and the Monkey King himself. The food was rather better than they had provided and all done at a cost of not much more than £300 for about fifty people (which makes it still more mysterious what Haferkamp did with his £1800 in China last autumn). The banquet conversation was interesting but only mildly so. Huang, on my left, talked English very well, and delivered one message, saying that he greatly hoped that if Eric Varley* (who had just arrived in China) told him that Britain couldn't sell Harriers for the moment, he wouldn't bring a lot of false excuses, but would just say that public and parliamentary opinion made it too difficult while the Vietnam war was going on. If it was put frankly in this way the Chinese would accept it, but if it was cocooned in a lot of unconvincing excuses they would be offended.

*Eric Varley, b. 1932, was Secretary of State for Industry 1975–9. He withdrew from politics and became Chairman of the Coalite Group in 1984.

Gu Mu, on the other side, complained a good deal about interest rates, which led to certain reflections on my part as to how interest rates operate when you are lending from inflationary economies to an allegedly non-inflationary one. The exchange rate ought to deal with this, but if the exchange rate is totally managed, and is that of a currency without any world market, does it? This, however, was a little too complicated for the interpreter, who was one of the weaknesses of the trip, and was not as good as we had on our private visit in 1973.

However, it was worth noting that the Chinese were very hooked on the interest rate point and will do their best to break any Western consortium to hold the line on rates of interest on long-term credits. They have a slightly naïve approach to interest rates, rather like the arguments I used to have with my Birmingham constituency party in the 1950s, with the claim that housing could be much cheaper if the money were free of capitalist usury. It is one of few remaining bits of anti-capitalist dogma in China.

After the banquet we went to the French Embassy and completed the briefing of the ambassadors. On the whole they are not a very impressive lot, although Arnaud is agreeable and the German (Wickert)* intelligent. Cradock wasn't there on this occasion (because of Varley) so he is not involved in this judgement, although I do not find him exciting. The Dane looks like a caricature of the Chinese view of nineteenth-century 'foreign devils' – large, red-faced, carrot-coloured hair.

I then had my first good night's sleep of the trip. The talks had been completed and on the whole we thought they had gone well; certainly they had been held at the highest level and had been of very considerable interest, and I think we had improved relations without disguising our concern and apprehension about the Vietnamese position, not so much on moral grounds as on the possible weakening effect on China's position in the world.

SUNDAY, 25 FEBRUARY. *Peking and Cheng-Tu.*

We took off just after 11.00 in a private Chinese Government Trident – a vast improvement on the old Ilyushin we flew in last

*In 1981 (English edition 1983) he published an excellent book on China entitled *The Middle Kingdom*.

time – for Cheng-Tu in Sichuan Province. A surprisingly long flight of two and a half hours, first over a snowbound landscape, then the snow dying away, then some mountains with more snow, then the Yellow River, then another range with little snow, and then down into the extremely green mountain-rimmed plain of Cheng-Tu. We drove in about ten miles from the airport, through this rich agricultural area, looking slightly like the plain of Lombardy before industrialization and pollution, to a guest house or hotel – it was never quite clear which it was – just inside the town and across a bridge over the river. We lunched there on hot spicy Sichuan food.

At 3.15, it being the most beautiful, balmy, early spring day, with a particular quality in the atmosphere and light, and the temperature about 65°, we went off on two semi-cultural expeditions, the first to the 'cottage' of Du Fu, who was a well-known Chinese poet of about the year 800 and whose poems go on being printed throughout the world, so much so that they have there made an interesting collection of about 150 of the 500 known editions of his works, approximately two-thirds of them in Chinese and going back to the eleventh century, and the others from a whole variety of foreign languages. It is not a 'cottage', but a series of pavilions and rather well laid out and interesting and attractive.

Then we went across the city to the Temple of Zhu Ge Liang, a still earlier figure, a statesman and sage of the time of the Three Kingdoms, i.e. after the end of the Han dynasty in about the third century AD.

At 7 o'clock there was a banquet, still in the guest house or hotel, which lasted only until 8.30. The host, the Chairman of the Revolutionary Committee, was an old bald man, looking rather like a mixture of Lords Denning and Morris of Borth-y-Gest, with a slight partisan Chinese touch as well, if one can imagine the combination. Like all such chairmen, who are moved around like French prefects, he had been there only a relatively short time, having last been in Chungking.

I made rather a good speech about Sichuan culture, based on what we had seen in the afternoon, and Sichuan's special place in China, and only hope that the interpreter was up to getting it mildly right. Those who could understand English laughed quite a lot – and in the right places. Jennifer and I went early to bed, but most of the others went for a night walk, in the course of which they succeeded in assembling around them, under an isolated street lamp, a high proportion of the language students of Cheng-Tu. How they did it, I cannot think. But it was clearly a great success and ended with Enzo Perlot rendering Puccini arias to an enthusiastic audience who joined in the choruses.

MONDAY, 26 FEBRUARY. *Cheng-Tu and Chungking.*

We left at 9.30 on another beautiful day and drove for about one and a quarter hours through the attractive countryside of the Cheng-Tu plain; attractive both because of the extreme greenness and intensity of the cultivation, and because of the appearance of the small towns, and even more of the groups of farm buildings, which had a certain French style about them – good grey stone, good tiles, but a lot of thatch as well. In the last part of the journey we began to get into some hills, and arrived at the Juan Xian Irrigation Works. These are quite a remarkable scheme, because although modernized and developed recently they have existed as irrigation works for nearly two thousand years, at first watering only a limited area, but now covering several thousand square miles. The area of the scheme itself was a mixture of temples, dams and bamboo bridges. We wandered agreeably for two hours.

Lunch with the local Revolutionary Committee in their offices. We got back to Cheng-Tu about 3.00, and visited a large park, which, like all parks in China, suffered from having far too many people in it. This I suppose is a good thing and shows the parks are used, and if you have a population of 900 million they are bound to be somewhere. This park was remarkable for its varieties of bamboos.

At 4.00 we took off on the 200-mile flight to Chungking. Although equally in Sichuan, Chungking is utterly different from Cheng-Tu. The region is mountainous, rather like the more precipitous South Wales valleys, with great gorges, hardly any level soil, the airport a long way from the city even with the help of a substantial recently constructed tunnel.

At 7.30 we were entertained to the statutory banquet in our guest house. The Chairman of the Revolutionary Committee, after the usual speeches, took us off to visit the city from 9.30 to 10.30. This meant an eight-mile drive to the junction between the Chialing River and the Yangtse. Chungking has this remarkable site – I can think of no wholly comparable site in the world (Pittsburgh is perhaps the nearest) – where two great rivers join, but not in a plain. The Chialing is about a thousand miles long, the Yangtse three and a half thousand, and Chungking is about half-way along its course and therefore nearly two thousand miles from the sea, although it is already a big river, nearly a mile wide. The Chialing is much clearer than the rather muddy Yangtse.

Chungking was of course Chiang Kai-shek's capital during the war and it still has a faintly 1940-ish atmosphere about it, and indeed seems now rather rundown. A great deal of heavy industry was moved here when the Japanese occupied Wuhan in 1938, but the industry has not been doing very well, which is largely attributed to the Gang of Four, but I suspect there are other causes as well. I had thought of Chungking during the war as having a hard continental winter, but in fact it has rather a soft climate. The day we were there, although exceptional for the time of the year in being clear and sunny, was not exceptional in temperature, which was 65° or 68°, with the nights much cooler.

TUESDAY, 27 FEBRUARY. *Chungking and Wuhan.*

First we went to visit the house, now a museum or shrine, in which Chou En-lai lived for six years over the wartime period, partly as an organizer of the Communists in the south-west of China, and partly as a liaison officer with the Chiang Kai-shek Government. This house, downtown near the Chialing, was interesting, with some good photographs, and well worth seeing. Then after that to the rather larger house, where Mao and indeed Chou also stayed during the period from the end of August 1945 to the middle of October that year, when Mao came to Chungking immediately after the end of the war with Japan, negotiated with the Chiang people and arrived at an agreement known as the Double Tenth Agreement, because it was signed on 10 October 1945. This was slightly less interesting than Chou En-lai's house, but this may be partly due to the fact that I always find Chou a much more attractive and interesting figure than Mao. Although one doesn't *hear* much of Mao now, one still *sees* only too much of that moon-like face staring down from placards.

We then drove for more than an hour to visit a glass factory at Bei-Bei on the west bank of the Chialing River. The drive out was through a lot of industrial suburbs, passing some coalmines, a large steel works, interspersed with areas of intensive cultivation, all in the tightly enfolded countryside. It was easy to see that Greater Chungking had a total, though scattered, industrial population of about six million. The visit to the glass factory was mercifully fairly short. It seemed to be moderately successful, some successful designs, mostly taken over from the Czechs or the Canadians apparently; some hideous modern Chinese designs. There were skilled workers, but the standard of management, I would guess, was not very good; and the general factory conditions were rather like early Victorian England, with practically no industrial safety and a great deal of molten glass being twirled round by workers without masks or proper protective gloves, and twirled round pretty close to the visitors too. After that another twenty minutes' drive to the North Hot Springs, again alongside the Chialing, and a very spectacular sight. There we were entertained to lunch, saw some temples which were interspersed with the springs, in which some of our party bathed in a hot and overcrowded swimming pool.

Then to the airport and an hour's flight, which brought us over the totally different landscape, much covered in lakes, of the three cities which together form the conurbation of Wuhan. It was a beautiful, slightly misty spring evening. We drove, crossing two rivers, the second being the Yangtse, to Wuchang, the third of the towns, where we stayed in a much more lavish guest house, somewhat garishly furnished, than either of the two in Sichuan, or indeed the one in Peking.

Our Revolutionary Committee host at the statutory banquet was a pretty well-known man called Ling, who had previously been Mayor of Shanghai and had got into deep conflict with the Gang of Four and had been confined to his house for eight years, and his wife, also quite a powerful figure, for six years. He had been an extreme 'capitalist roader' in the eyes of the Gang of Four, and was bitterly hostile to them and the whole previous Shanghai position, as he made clear when we told him we had been there in 1973. This aroused no agreeable nostalgia in his mind.

After dinner there was an acrobatic performance for an hour and a half. It was interesting to compare it with the one which we had seen in Shanghai five years before. It was incomparably more elegantly and artistically presented. Apart from there being no nudity, it was rather like a Paris music hall performance of thirty to fifty years ago, the Folies Bergères or Alcazar. However, it was not as spectacular as in Shanghai, partly because the stage was smaller and gave less of an impression of danger; it was more a performance based on incredibly delicate and extremely impressive feats of balance and contortion. Women played a far more dominant part than in Shanghai.

WEDNESDAY, 28 FEBRUARY. *Wuhan and Peking.*

The day began with a mercifully brief visit to a machine tool factory. Those who knew slightly more about machine tools than I thought that it was pretty antiquated, though very large, with a work force of nearly eight thousand.

The manager said what a terrible time he had had under the Gang of Four, particularly towards the end. When I asked what this amounted to he gave quite an interesting and substantial reply, saying that those then in power had tried to undermine his authority in every possible way, they were only interested in talking and not in production and regarded him as a 'capitalist roader' because he was interested in the factory actually producing something. Now that they had got rid of the Revolutionary Committee in the factory the whole thing worked a great deal better, though it still had a long way to go.

Then a cold visit to the East Lake. It was a remarkably clear day – the weather had changed overnight – a north wind having blown out all the mist of the previous evening. It was rather like a spring day in Chicago. From the lake we went to the Archaeological Museum, where we were taken round by an extremely intelligent curator and shown things which had come out of a recently discovered 2600-year-old tomb, including a whole variety of domestic utensils, but also a great set of bells on which they played a rather haunting version of 'The East is Red', which hardly achieved an authentically contemporary note, but nonetheless brought out the quality of those ancient and variegated bells.

An early lunch at the guest house, and then a visit to a remarkable Buddhist temple, which was more reminiscent of India than

China. Then a drive round the centre of Hankou, which of the three towns is the one with the most metropolitan animation and which, c. 1900, had a series of international concessions like Shanghai, and which still has the air of a city of that sort. Unfortunately we never got to the Bund, alongside the Yangtse, mainly because the Chinese local officials are moved about so quickly that they don't know their way about the towns they are administering.

Then to the airport to return by our Trident to Peking. Peking was still under snow, but it was a beautiful evening with a splendid red sunset. We reached the guest house at 6.30 and dined there.

THURSDAY, 1 MARCH. *Peking and Karachi.*

Leisurely morning visit to the Temple of Heaven in the south of the city, the best of the Peking monuments. We lunched with Kang, the Ambassador in Brussels, and various other people who had accompanied us on the tour round, at the Imperial Restaurant.

Then back to the guest house, where Li, the Minister for External Trade, came to say goodbye. This turned out to be a rather serious conversation, in which he obviously thought he ought to say one or two things which he had omitted at the meeting the previous Friday afternoon, such as what great importance they attach to GSP and how good their silk was. So the conversation was a curious mixture of courtesy and rather excessive detail. Before leaving we made presentations to various people from Kang downwards, the interpreters, the Chief of Protocol, the head of the Security Service, my bodyguard, the cook at the guest house, etc. We had brought a lot of clocks with us, and there were also signed photographs and books.

Sung, the old Ambassador to London, came to drive with me to the airport and I had a rather good talk with him on the journey. Then at the airport we had the ambassadors, or at any rate five or six of them, and also the deputy Minister of Foreign Affairs. The French did much better than the British, who in spite of requests produced no newspapers, whereas the French produced a complete set of *Le Monde* for the days we had been away.

We took off at 5.45, with one and a half hours of sunset and then dinner over South-West China. It was a slow flight as there was a great head wind of 160 knots, so that we took eight and a half hours to reach Karachi.

FRIDAY, 2 MARCH. *Karachi and East Hendred.*

Athens at 5 a.m. The light came up over Yugoslavia and we got into Charles de Gaulle just before 8.00 French time, an hour and a half late. A quick change round and on to the plane to London, with newspapers, boxes, etc. We were typically stacked over Heathrow. Filthy weather in Paris, slightly better in London. East Hendred by 10.00, feeling surprisingly well.

SUNDAY, 4 MARCH. *East Hendred.*

Bonham Carters came about noon to drive over with me to lunch with the Briggs' at Worcester (College).

It was a typical large Briggs Sunday luncheon party – twenty-two in all, I think: Berlins, John Sparrow, the American Ambassador and Mrs Kingman Brewster, Janet Suzman, Catherine Freeman, all an agreeable lot of people, although rather too many of them. However, I like the Briggs' very much. We walked in the Worcester garden for a bit, and then did a drive around Oxford, going in particular into the new St Catherine's, which I don't think Mark had ever seen.

MONDAY, 5 MARCH. *East Hendred, Brussels, Bonn and Brussels.*

8.25 plane to Brussels, caught with difficulty as the motorway was jammed from near Maidenhead. An hour's Coordination Meeting for the Foreign Affairs Council, and then back to the airport and an avion taxi to Bonn for a talk with Schmidt.

Lunched with Oliver Wright* at the British Embassy, the first time I had been there since the Hendersons left. It was a good lunch, sitting at a little table in the window of the dining room looking across the river to the sun-bathed (for once) Siebengebirge opposite. Wright is a curious man, a good presence, well informed and shrewd about German politics, but lacks subtlety or breadth of vision. He is perfectly friendly and yet without warmth (towards me, at any rate).

*Sir Oliver Wright, b. 1921, was Ambassador to Bonn 1975–81, and to Washington 1982–6.

Then to the Chancellery, where we had Schmidt for a full two hours. It was not a particularly illuminating talk. He was in one of his gloomy, complaining moods, not fortunately much about us, but about the world and almost everybody in it, although Carter had a special place in his demonology list. He was not particularly friendly towards Callaghan, indeed asking whether I thought a new British Tory Government would be more 'predictable', which is now his favourite favourable word. There was not much reference to 'my friend Valéry' either, though surprisingly little criticism, considering the way the French had messed up the start of the EMS.

We had a good deal of discussion about the CAP, on which he is a mixture of fundamental good sense and rather supine acceptance of being locked in to no reduction in German farm prices, which he interprets as being the same as no reduction in farmers' incomes, which it is not. However, a certain amount of progress was made on these subjects, although there was a complete unwillingness on his part to take the lead at Paris the following week and try to force through a solution to the still held up MCA/EMS problem. 'I tried in Brussels,' he said. 'It wasn't a success. I can't try again; now it's up to Giscard. He is the chairman. I mustn't interfere with him.' I tried on leaving to put a bit more enthusiastic backbone into him, but I am not sure it was successful. However, as a ground-clearing enterprise the talk was worthwhile.

Brussels by 6.30, and into the Council for one and a half hours. François-Poncet with Nanteuil and a young private secretary to dine, rue de Praetère. I was accompanied as usual on such occasions by Crispin and Christopher Audland. It was a surprisingly successful three-hour dinner, with really very good talk with François-Poncet, partly general conversation mainly about France socially, geographically, historically, and partly some business talk relating to the Council. It was a vast advance on relations in December and I thought we had got on pretty good terms for the first time. On this occasion at least, he was an agreeable, sensible, highly intelligent, well-informed, talkative man.

TUESDAY, 6 MARCH. *Brussels*.

A rather belated press conference on China. Then the Council for two hours. The discussion was mainly on the state of progress in the

MTNs and was not as bad as I expected. The opposition, from Deniau for the French, and to some lesser extent from the Irish and Italians, seemed broadly containable. Haferkamp and Davignon, particularly the latter, did well, and I intervened at the end to make it clear that while we would try to deal with one or two of the peripheral points which had been raised, there was no real chance of getting any substantial change in the package before we came back to them in April, when they would have to take a firm decision.

In the afternoon there was a long-drawn-out Concertation Meeting, with five or six representatives of the Parliament, on the budget question. François-Poncet dealt with this with great tact giving nothing in substance but being extremely polite, so that they left in a tolerable temper.

WEDNESDAY, 7 MARCH. *Brussels.*

Commission meeting for three hours in the morning. Then to Comme Chez Soi with Simonet, where all the family and staff were on particularly good form because they had just had advance notice of their third Michelin star. Their cup of joy would have been overflowing if they had also heard that the Villa Lorraine had lost its third star, but that was not the case. Henri (Simonet) was firmly convinced that there would be a Belgian Government under Martens the following week, hopeful that he (Henri) might stay on as Foreign Minister, and more than hopeful that Martens being too busy in Brussels he might be allowed to go to the Paris European Council alone and thus have the heady pleasure of dining with heads of government. He was as friendly and agreeable as usual.

Three and a half hours of Commission in the afternoon. Dinner at home for John Sainsbury,* with Nanteuils (Luc being on particularly talkative form and agreeable in a way that would have amazed most of his COREPER colleagues), Brunners, etc.

THURSDAY, 8 MARCH. *Brussels and London.*

12.30 plane to London. Lunch with Hayden at Brooks's. One and three quarter hours with Callaghan at 4 o'clock. He was, as in

* (Sir) John Sainsbury, b. 1927, has been Chairman of J. Sainsbury Ltd since 1969, and of the Royal Opera House, Covent Garden, since 1987.

several recent interviews, immensely friendly, quite different from two years ago, and keen to talk on a whole range of issues, British internal ones to begin with. He was not very well informed or focused on the issues for the Paris Summit, but quite anxious to be told about them and not making any fuss about the bilateral issues which he raised with me, except for a hard continuing note of complaint about the British share of the budget being unfair. He tried to shrug off the devolution *débâcle** but was not particularly optimistic about the political situation generally.

I then went to the City to give a lecture to the Overseas Development Institute in the headquarters of Barclays Bank. A rather good audience of about two hundred: Michael Palliser, Ronald McIntosh, George Jellicoe, Leo Pliatzky. The lecture almost got off to an appalling start because I suddenly realized during the chairman's introduction that I had got the wrong text in front of me, the original one and not the one which I had laboriously amended on the way over. I signalled wildly. Crispin, whom I had warned that I may have eaten a bad oyster at lunch, assumed I was becoming desperately ill, but Roger Beetham, not being aware of this, made a more sensible judgement and came up with the proper text. So all was saved but not without the incident being fairly obvious and causing some amusement.

Home at Kensington Park Gardens where I discovered most surprisingly a letter of tentative invitation to be Master of St Catherine's College, Oxford – they must have seen me casing the joint the previous Sunday. I am not, however, tempted by being head of a college.

SUNDAY, 11 MARCH. *East Hendred and Paris.*

10.30 plane to Paris with Jennifer. To the Embassy where we are staying a night for the last time in the Henderson régime (they only have three weeks to go) and possibly ever,† as it is unlikely we will have close friends there in the future. Lunched with them alone, worked in the afternoon and walked in the twilight. Crispin came at

---

*The Government's proposals for devolution of powers to Scottish and Welsh assemblies had been submitted to referenda on 1 March and had resulted in the narrowest possible victory, on a low poll, in Scotland and overwhelming defeat in Wales.
†True, so far.

7.00 and we went through various points for the European Council, and then dined with him, the Hendersons and Jennifer.

MONDAY, 12 MARCH. *Paris.*

A rather desultory morning's work until I left the Embassy at noon
and moved into the Ritz.* Lunched with Jennifer, Crispin and
Michel Vanden Abeele, before moving up, under motorcycle
escort, to the Kléber, where the European Council began fairly
punctually at 3.10 and sat for four hours. We ran through a range of
subjects: the economic situation of the Community, world trade
relations, Japan, energy, and then a general clutch of social papers,
all introduced by the Commission, i.e. Ortoli or me.

In the first discussion Callaghan made a prepared and subsequently heavily leaked statement of position, mainly on the CAP
and the budget. It all sounded too electoral, although he did not do
it badly. The note of the Council was distinctly low key, and Giscard
to my surprise did not appear to be trying to get very much out of his
summing up on the social *volet*,† or indeed energy, where I would
have expected him to go for a more positive outcome.

The room was not satisfactory. It was bigger than the ones in
which we normally meet, so that Giscard and François-Poncet were
isolated at one end of the table, Ortoli and I at the other, with four
delegations down either side, Schmidt and Giscard for once not
sitting next to each other.

A heads of government dinner at the Elysée at 8.15. The *place à
table* was rather more satisfactory from my point of view than
usual; *au bout de la table* inevitably when alone with heads of government, but on this occasion between Schmidt and Callaghan,
which was a change from between Thorn and Andreotti, to which I
had become rather too used. However, that mattered little as the
conversation was almost entirely general and not very good at that.

Giscard opened rather typically by asking about the Queen's visit
to the Middle East, and there then developed a discussion conducted mainly between him and Callaghan, Giscard taking a
fairly hard, pro-Arab line, i.e. more extreme than the Egyptians,

---

*I would not have thought it wise to stay in a British Embassy for a European Council. It
would have given the impression of too close a national affiliation, most of all in Paris.
†Using the Social Fund to ease the consequence of the rundown in the steel industry.

Callaghan being certainly pro-Egyptian, even pro-Israeli. There was some discussion at the end about Turkey, on which Schmidt reported depressingly.

Then after dinner, 'round the fireside' as it is quaintly called, there was first a discussion about China, on which I was asked to report. Then a discussion about the French desire to have a new look at the Euratom treaty, not to amend it they were careful to say, but to see if any adaptations of interpretation were necessary. This was pretty coolly received by the others (in many ways more favourably by me than by most, except for my saying extremely firmly that we had competences in the non-proliferation field, which the French were inclined to deny), with the outcome that it should be discussed at the French Schloss Gymnich, but without, I think, anybody expecting much to happen.

Giscard's launching of his great Euro/Arab/African dialogue plan was also coolly received, with a suggestion from Schmidt that it was perhaps best to start with the Africans before one brought in the Arabs, and that the whole thing should not be done on too grandiose and clumsy a scale. However, there was no great ill feeling on any side, and we broke up at about 11.30 in reasonably good order.

TUESDAY, 13 MARCH. *Paris and Strasbourg.*

To the Kléber by 9.30. Everybody arrived more or less on time, except for Callaghan and Schmidt who had breakfasted together (on defence matters) and, somewhat inconsiderately, didn't turn up until 10 o'clock, so that even Giscard was kept waiting for half an hour. I had a good deal of conversation with him during this time. Throughout the whole of this European Council he was quite friendly, and he was obviously going to make no difficulty about my presence at the press conference, as he asked me for how long I thought, on previous experience, it should last.

When the session eventually started, we opened with agriculture, on which I made a fifteen-minute statement, distancing myself from Callaghan, for obvious reasons, by putting in a certain general defence of the CAP, but then being extremely hard on the need to deal with surpluses by a price freeze. We discussed this for an hour, with I thought a rather good reception round the table.

Callaghan kept fairly quiet, though he was obviously on our side on practical matters even if not on matters of theory. Thorn was silent. Lynch, Jørgensen, Andreotti and even van Agt expressed general approval for our position. Schmidt didn't say yes and didn't say no (he picked a rather pointless semi-argument with Callaghan on the assumption that Callaghan was advocating deficiency payments, which he was not), but the general thrust of what he was saying was favourable to our point of view and anti the farm lobby.

Giscard's summing up was clearly hostile but contained a good deal of *legerdemain*, which he developed later in the press conference, differentiating between products, differentiating between countries in which surpluses were produced, and generally trying to lose our hard proposal in sophistical refinements. The remainder of the morning was occupied with the communiqué.

Just before the end of the Council, Callaghan and I both went out and coincided in the loo, whereupon he made to me the most fanciful offer, saying, 'Would you like to be Governor of Hong Kong? I could possibly persuade Murray MacLehose to stay on until nearly the end of your time in Europe.' I said, 'Certainly not, Jim. I have never heard a more preposterous suggestion.' However, in a curious, rather heavy-footed way, he went on, saying, 'Oh, it's a very important job, you know. You would be good at it. What do you want to do when you come back to England? You'll go to the House of Lords, I presume.' I said, 'I am not at all sure, as I told you when you last suggested that to me. Not for the moment, certainly. I want to come back and look around and keep options open.' 'Well,' he said, 'You might find it quite difficult to get back into the House of Commons.' 'Certainly,' I said. 'And you might not like it when you got there,' he said. 'It has changed, it has deteriorated a lot.' I said, 'Yes, yes. All I intend to do is come back and look around at the political landscape, Jim, and certainly not become Governor of Hong Kong.'

The Council over, I asked Giscard what time the press conference was to take place. He said, 'In five minutes,' so I waited outside, perhaps not spending as much time as I should have on a draft which Roger primarily, but Crispin also, had produced, expecting Giscard at any moment. In fact he did not return for twenty-five minutes, no doubt working on his text, and then disappeared again for another ten minutes. However, we eventually got into the *salle de presse.* The conference was fairly large and Giscard made a statement of about twenty minutes, rather dull I thought, though I was probably only half listening to it, but in which he certainly gave an over-hard impression of the anti-price-freeze view of the Council. What was true of course was that the Council had not specifically endorsed it, but he came very near to giving the impression that it had rejected it. Then, at the end, he said, 'I will now answer questions, either on behalf of the Council or on behalf of France.' I indicated then that I wished to speak. He, without great resistance, but equally without any enthusiasm, said, 'Monsieur le Président de la Commission veut ajouter quelques mots.' So I then spoke for five or seven minutes, slightly galloping through the text I had before me, making a few cuts, and as a result possibly coming out slightly more sharply against Giscard on agricultural prices (not in substance, but in form) than I would have done had I felt less rushed.

Then there were questions, all of them to Giscard, except for one from an Italian journalist to me, saying, 'Are you maintaining your position on the price freeze after the Council?' To which I said, 'Yes, certainly. On the whole I was rather encouraged by the discussion.' Then as we walked out, Giscard said, 'You didn't say exactly the same thing as me,' not particularly disagreeably. I said, 'There is often a difference of emphasis. I speak for the Commission; you speak for the Council.' And then, as we walked further out and I said goodbye to him, he took up an argument of substance, saying, 'Yes, yes, I see your point on products in surplus, but why do we have to have a freeze for products not in surplus?' To which I said, 'We don't necessarily, but they aren't products of any great significance. We can of course look at what you can find in that category but certainly not milk, certainly not sugar, certainly not cereals, and, indeed, not beef at the moment. Maybe one or two other meat products.' Then we parted, reasonably amicably, though I suspect he was not at all pleased, one, with the fact of my intervention, and, two, with the form of it. However, we shall see.

5.15 train from the Gare de l'Est to Strasbourg. Still very dismal weather, so that the long journey up the Marne valley was not as agreeable as it might have been.

WEDNESDAY, 14 MARCH. *Strasbourg.*

A very bad night's sleep. The retained heat of the beastly Sofitel is appalling. In addition, Monsieur Pflimlin, who no doubt thought he should keep the square outside the hotel particularly clean, sent the most appalling dragon of a cleaning machine round, which was with us hissing away from 5.00 to 6.15.

A Commission from 9.00 to 10.30 without great incident. Then, at noon, I had Johansen, the Danish member of the *Cour des Comptes*, who is in charge of the investigation into the Haferkamp affair, to see me. He seemed a sensible man, but what will come out of it I can't tell. Did a not tremendously exciting question time. Read the French press. 'Passage d'armes courtoises', *Le Monde* said, 'entre Président Giscard et M. Jenkins.' I dined very briefly at the little restaurant opposite the hotel, got back to the Parliament at 9.00 and took an hour's China debate in a very empty house.

THURSDAY, 15 MARCH. *Strasbourg and Brussels.*

Statements on the European Council from François-Poncet for an hour and from me for ten minutes. Then a debate until 1 o'clock; quite good but not vastly significant. Afterwards an official lunch given by François-Poncet for Colombo and the enlarged Bureau of the Parliament. I sat between François-Poncet and Geoffrey de Freitas,* and found Poncet a little cool. Atmosphere disseminates itself quickly down the French Government hierarchy.

Avion taxi to Brussels at 6.00. It was a very long flight, mainly because the landing conditions in Brussels were absolutely appalling, and suddenly just at the end (the pilots had warned us of this beforehand) they said, 'We don't think we can go in. Where would you rather go, Charleroi or Ostend?' I said, 'Preferably Antwerp.' Almost as soon as I had said it, we were twenty feet over the ground and on the runway – in Brussels. So I asked, 'Why did you suddenly ask that?' and they replied, 'Because a British Caledonian plane ahead of us just overshot, so we assumed we might have to do so as well. But we got in. Wasn't that good?' I said, 'Yes, very good,' but

---

*Sir Geoffrey de Freitas, 1913–82, Labour MP 1945–61 and 1964–79. High Commissioner to Ghana and Kenya in the interval. A Strasbourg figure since 1951 and President of the Assembly of the Council of Europe 1966–9.

thought it would have been even better had I not believed that Jennifer was on the British Caledonian plane. However, it turned out that she wasn't, and had got in with difficulty just earlier, and was at home by the time I arrived there after an hour in the office.

FRIDAY, 16 MARCH. *Brussels.*

I saw Hinton the American Ambassador, who came in with a great statement from Carter, which was obviously being put out by all American embassies, urging us in the strongest terms to use our influence in favour of the Israeli/Egyptian peace settlement, and indicating that the United States would attach great importance to what their friends did on this occasion. Not primarily a matter for us, although obviously there are going to be difficulties within the Nine, with the French, as so often, taking a much harder position than anyone else.

At noon I went down to receive the President of Guinée-Bissau who was an agreeable if not impressive head of state. I had a brief private talk with him and then took him into the Commission for a formal three-quarters of an hour meeting, and then to lunch at Val Duchesse, which lasted until about 3.15. Back in the office I saw first Haferkamp and then the new Japanese Trade Minister, Yasukawa, who seemed to me to be an improvement on Ushiba. Home early, where the Zuckermans had arrived to stay.

MONDAY, 19 MARCH. *Brussels.*

A meeting with Murphy,* the Irish President of the *Cour des Comptes*, mainly about some fairly abstract questions of Court and Commission competence, but also about the Haferkamp affair with the news, mildly but not totally unwelcome, that Colombo had written with the Aigner request that they should widen their inquiries into travel expenses as well as representation expenses. I said that was acceptable to us, but that it was extremely desirable to complete the whole report by the date they had said, which was the end of April, and to have it dealt with in this Parliament.

I saw the Chairmen of the EEC Select Committees of the House of Lords and the House of Commons, Tony Greenwood and John

* Michael Murphy, b. 1919, was the first President of the *Cour des Comptes* 1977–81.

Eden,* with two officials; both of them were perfectly agreeable and neither of them was penetrating.

In the afternoon I saw Peter Parker† of British Rail and found him as bright as I have always thought him; then the Israeli Ambassador, who mainly wanted to invite me to Jerusalem as he had heard I was going to Egypt; Tad Szulc of the *New York Times*, whom I had last seen in Washington in 1963 when I was doing a first anniversary piece for the *Observer* on Cuba II, who turned out to be very good value; and finally Tugendhat.

That evening, without great enthusiasm, I had a dinner for the Confederation of Socialist Parties. They were mostly as tiresome as ever. Mansholt started off with his old song that the Commission should be much more political in a party sense; there was a Socialist majority (which is doubtful, but maybe) and we should decide all issues by votes on party lines. I replied as robustly as on a previous occasion and was agitated afterwards, thinking I had been too *cassant*, but Nick Stuart who was there said, 'Not at all, I think you behaved like a saint under great provocation.' However it produced, as rows always do upon me, the effect of making me wake full of *angst* at 5 a.m. and not sleeping again.

TUESDAY, 20 MARCH. *Brussels, Paris and Brussels.*

11.44 TEE from the Gare du Midi to attend the Monnet funeral at Montfort L'Amaury, Michael Jenkins accompanying. One could tell from the beginning that the train was no good. It left nine minutes late, and limped to the French frontier. There were continual works along the line. We stopped on three occasions at least for a full five minutes and it was amazing in the circumstances that we were not more than forty-one minutes late at Paris. That left us exactly forty-four minutes to get from the Gare du Nord to the church in the country to the west of Paris, which would be rather like trying to get from Liverpool Street to near Maidenhead in an equivalent time.

However, Peter Halsey had taken a more than spectacular initiative. Realizing from the arrival board that we were going to be late,

*Sir John Eden, b. 1925, cr. Lord Eden of Winton 1983, was Conservative MP for Bournemouth 1954–83 and a middle-rank minister 1970–4.
†Sir Peter Parker, b. 1924, was Chairman of British Rail 1976–83. Now Chairman of the Rockware Group and a member of many other boards.

he tried to get *motards* from the police station at the Gare du Nord, but failed. So he had rung up the British Embassy and they had succeeded. The two *motards* had arrived literally three or four minutes before we got in; if we hadn't had the last maddening stoppage outside Paris we would probably have set off, disastrously, without them. As it was, after not too hair-raising a drive, we arrived at the church at 3.26. Schmidt arrived at 3.27, Giscard arrived at 3.28. The honour of the Commission was saved.

It was a striking service; an attractive, medium-sized French country church, full, of course. The opening was the Battle Hymn of the Republic, a recording, sung in English, and Schmidt (for whom it didn't matter) arrived and then Giscard (for whom perhaps it did) came and sat on his little throne between the body of the church and the altar to this transatlantic cadence. Most of the rest of the service was to me not tremendously moving (the Mass I find slightly impersonal on these occasions), but there was a good haunting hymn towards the end, called 'Dieu, je crois en toi'.

Then back to the Gare du Nord for the 5.44, and rue de Praetère at 8.30.

FRIDAY, 23 MARCH. *Brussels and Kent.*

No run on security grounds because of news the previous day of the assassination of Richard Sykes,* the British Ambassador in The Hague, and the still more threatening news (for us) the evening before that a Belgian had been shot dead, probably from the circumstances in mistake for John Killick (Ambassador to NATO), and thus tying up with the intelligence we had received about possible threats six weeks before, but had typically forgotten about in the meantime. On the good old principle of shutting the stable door, the Belgian police were thronging rue de Praetère, and I proceeded to the office at 9.30 with screaming police cars, motor-cycle escorts, and a guard of about fourteen policemen. Fortunately I was due to go to London that morning for a weekend in Kent with the McIntoshes.

---

* Sir Richard Sykes, 1920–79, had been a Deputy Under-Secretary in the Foreign Office before going to The Hague in 1977.

MONDAY, 26 MARCH. *London*.

In the afternoon I spent nearly two hours in Brooks's preparing in some detail a speech for the ELEC gathering which I was to address at the Reform Club in the early evening. It was rather a lot of effort for a twelve-minute speech to about 120 people, but I judged it to be worthwhile because of the likely quality of the audience. I was right. After the speech I talked to John Barnes, ex-Ambassador to The Hague (who always looks sprightly and rather Fred Astairish, but even more so than usual on this occasion, perhaps because he was congratulating himself on having no longer been in The Hague the previous week), Robert Armstrong, David Watt, Peter Jenkins, Dora Gaitskell (who for the first time was looking somewhat older),* Douglas Hurd (sensible, nice, a little gloomy as usual), Ian Wrigglesworth, Bob Maclennan, and Con O'Neill (argumentative, but very high quality and whom I had hardly seen since the European Referendum campaign).†

TUESDAY, 27 MARCH. *London and Brussels*.

9.25 plane to Brussels. In the afternoon I did a rather tricky interview for the *Figaro*. It was tricky because it was to some extent a reply to the same paper's previous week's great attack on me for my incredible effrontery and impertinence in contradicting the President of the Republic in public, etc., signed by an old Gaullist minister, Georges Gorse. Then, after an hour's *tour d'horizon* with Davignon at his request I went to dine with the Chinese Ambassador, a sort of reunion dinner for our February visit.

WEDNESDAY, 28 MARCH. *Brussels*.

Between the normal two Commission sessions I gave a lunch at rue de Praetère for the largely unoccupied *Times* journalists‡ whom Charlie Douglas-Home had brought over, the various European

---

*Baroness Gaitskell, cr. 1963, is the widow of Hugh Gaitskell.
†Sir Con O'Neill, 1912–87, twice resigned from the foreign service before becoming Ambassador to the EEC 1963–5. Director of the Britain in Europe campaign for the 1975 referendum.
‡The paper was closed down from November 1978 to November 1979.

correspondents – Peter Nichols from Rome, who is rather a good man, Charles Hargrove from Paris, about whom I have mixed views, our local correspondents, Patricia Clough from Bonn – and one or two other people from London. It was all perfectly agreeable, as indeed I always find anything with Charlie Home.

In the evening a dinner primarily for Hugh Thomas, with Laura, the Tickells and Helena Tiné. We came out after dinner and listened with bated breath, as they say, to the BBC sound commentary, given by Nick Stuart's father,* on the result of the division in the House of Commons. At first it sounded as though the Government, as usual, had won, which would have been an anti-climax, but then there was the news of the Opposition victory by a single vote, and therefore Callaghan's announcement that he would recommend dissolution the next day. I had no feeling of exhilaration in the sense of wanting to take part in the campaign, but a satisfaction that the anti-climax of another narrow Government victory had been avoided, and that the Government's life, long past its useful term, wasn't just going to drag on indefinitely.

Hugh Thomas – despite his occasions canvassing for me in Stechford – is now a dedicated Thatcherite Tory, but didn't seem too certain about the result. Laura and the Tickells – and me probably – were all in a way rather torn, Laura slightly Tory but firmly anti-Mrs Thatcher, Crispin keeping his counsel, Helena naturally not having many views. However, an election in five or six weeks and a new Government whether Labour or Tory after that, rather than one just hanging on, will certainly be a good thing.

FRIDAY, 30 MARCH. *Brussels.*

Leslie Bonham Carter arrived for the weekend just before lunch (Mark coming from Germany tomorrow). A 3.30 coordination meeting for the Foreign Affairs Council next week. In the course of it Crispin gave me the news that Airey Neave† had been blown up in his car coming out of the House of Commons, which was fairly shattering. He was our East Hendred Member of Parliament. I neither liked nor disliked him, but thought he had a slightly bad

---

*Douglas Stuart was a well-known BBC commentator.
†Airey Neave, 1916–79, was Conservative MP for Abingdon 1953–79, and Opposition spokesman on Northern Ireland from 1975.

influence politically. I had always found him agreeable, but not constructive. However, an assassination at the House of Commons was a most terrible thing, and a dreadful beginning to an election campaign.

SATURDAY, 31 MARCH. *Brussels.*

The last day of the wettest March (so *Le Soir* informed me) in Brussels there had ever been since records started at the beginning of the Kingdom. March 1914, which had previously held the twentieth-century record, had been overtaken fairly comfortably about 25 March, and it was touch and go up to the night of the 30th whether the previous all-time record of 1836 would or would not be surpassed. However, it narrowly was and an absolutely filthy month it has been, raw, but not the exhilarating cold of January and February, and almost continuous cloud and pouring rain. This last day showed no improvement.

We left for Aachen at about 10.30, and met Mark at the railway station there. Then on a very raw day we walked round the cathedral and the Rathaus, the Rathaus looking curiously different, particularly the great hall upstairs, than on the occasion of the Karlspreis ceremony.

We recrossed the frontier and lunched at St Hubert near Eupen where we were the only customers, apart from our accompanying policemen. The restaurant was in one of those slightly ugly, bogus châteaux in a little park looking on to suburban villas which are a particularly nasty feature of some parts of Belgium.

TUESDAY, 3 APRIL. *Luxembourg and Brussels.*

Foreign Affairs Council at 10.15 on MTNs. A moderate round-table discussion. I then asked for a restricted session (because we were engaged in negotiations) before the replies, which Stevy Davignon and Gundelach gave very well indeed. The Council resumed at 3.30 and went on until 8.30. I thought we were then very near to completing the MTN package. But François-Poncet suddenly announced that we must adjourn and deal with the Greeks. I said, 'No, no, it is impossible to stop at this stage,' and, being supported by the Germans, we got an agreement that we should split the Council (no dinner except for those who were dealing with the Greeks) and that Poncet would take the negotiating council with the Greeks, and Deniau would preside over the MTN council.

I had intended to go back to Brussels, first on the 5.30 train, then on the 9.15, and therefore just went down to see the beginning of the MTN council. But I was persuaded by Davignon to stay – rightly, I think, not because there was much of great value for me to do, except that I was able to take the lead on any procedural point and hold the ring for Davignon and Gundelach to deal with the detail. At 2 a.m. we eventually got the package through. The Italians were the most difficult, but not impossibly so. We got them away from outright opposition after they had spoken to Andreotti in Rome on the telephone, and into no more than a holding reserve, partly by my threatening to speak to Andreotti myself (he, poor man, probably thought that the prospect of having to talk to me in French over the telephone would be even worse than his Italian political difficulties, and softened his line considerably).

At 2.15 a.m. we set off to drive back to Brussels. There was light snow falling as there had been during the day, but I did not take April snow seriously. Twenty-five miles out, just beyond Arlon, it became difficult to maintain this view. Going up the first slope to the Ardennes, there were stranded lorries all over the place, almost blocking the road, and we were very near the point of turning back (which was a discouraging prospect). It did not look as though we would get to Brussels before 8 o'clock; whenever we tried to go faster than 25 mph we took a nasty lurch across the road, and the only two cars which passed us ended up in the ditch. However as we came down the slope, somewhere near Marche, the snow died away. It is curious how subject to snow are those relatively low Ardennes hills.

WEDNESDAY, 4 APRIL. *Brussels.*

A postponed Commission at 11.00. I had the Westminster Bank chairman – Leigh-Pemberton,* an agreeable man – and two other directors to lunch, rue de Praetère, and then did a press conference on the MTNs with Haferkamp, Gundelach and Davignon before

*Robin Leigh-Pemberton, b. 1927, has been Governor of the Bank of England since 1983.

another two hours of Commission. Then I went to a Monnet Mass which we had, rightly, decided to arrange in Brussels at the instigation of Ortoli and Davignon – neither of whom however turned up, despite the fact that they were at the Commission until the end and, indeed, dined with me that evening. In fact, practically nobody turned up. It was in a very bleak modern church, which was, I would guess, about 11 per cent full, approximately the same proportion as voted 'Yes' in the Welsh Referendum. However, the Papal Nuncio did it well, but no one could say it was an inspiring occasion in view of the attendance. There were very few diplomats, a curious mixture – Eugenio Plaja, the wife of Riberholdt, a few black men and the Swiss Ambassador. From the Commission, Vouël, Tugendhat, Brunner and me.

Then to rue de Praetère for the third of my 'Four Horsemen'* dinners. Gossip, but agreeable gossip, over dinner, with Ortoli as usual being very animated. He had every reason to be more animated than the rest of us as he had not spent the night trying to get back from Luxembourg. Some interesting conversation at the end, when Ortoli, strongly supported by Davignon, and up to a point by Gundelach (though he was getting sleepy by that time) said that immediately after the British election, whatever the result, it was crucial to solve the problem of Britain's relations with the Community, getting Britain to accept an enthusiastic commitment in return for dealing with her legitimate grievances, budget and otherwise. In that way the sore could be prevented from festering, but if it was just allowed to go on festering for even six months or so, they thought there would be a real danger to the future of our membership – perhaps to Britain's desire to remain a member, but even more to the desire of others that we should.

THURSDAY, 5 APRIL. *Brussels, Birmingham and Glasgow.*
11.25 plane to Birmingham for a Chamber of Commerce lunch speech which most curiously took place at the St John's Hotel, Solihull. An audience of about 250, I think, and the speech went rather well. Then on to Glasgow to deliver the Hoover Lecture

*My mildly mocking name for the Ortoli, Gundelach, Davignon, Jenkins quartet.

(financed by vacuum cleaners rather than by the ex-President, I think) at the University of Strathclyde.

A text for my lecture had been sent down to Luxembourg, where Crispin and I both thought it fairly awful on first reading. It had then been redone by Nick Stuart, who was with me, but I still didn't think much of it. However, with a little improvisation it turned out to be a quite good lecture, so I must have been rather jaundiced about it. I got apprehensive when reading the correspondence in Birmingham and discovering, which I had not previously noticed, that so far from being a little faculty talk, it attracted a fee of £2000, enormous by British standards, which, although I felt I had to give it away, partly back to Strathclyde, inevitably – although perhaps wrongly – made me take it a little more seriously.

After the lecture I dined agreeably with the academic weight of Strathclyde, and then returned to the Central Hotel. It really is a rather magnificent hotel, old railway style at its best, expressing all the self-confidence and splendour of 1890s Glasgow: tremendously good polished woodwork, downstairs and upstairs, and a comfortable sitting room, bathroom and bedroom, not at all rundown.*

SATURDAY, 7 APRIL. *London, The Hague and Brussels.*
9 o'clock plane to Amsterdam, cursing myself for having agreed to do a direct elections speaking engagement in The Hague, without which I could have gone quietly to East Hendred. However my morale improved when we arrived at Amsterdam in the first good weather I had seen for five weeks, and drove fairly dangerously, under motorcycle escort, to The Hague. And it improved further when I spoke to a rather good audience of about two hundred, including a lot of notabilities (den Uyl, van der Klaauw, Brinkhorst, Berkhouwer, etc.). But it declined again with an absolutely filthy lunch, a sort of sitting-down snack, all of it quite inedible, and nothing to drink until I asked for a glass of beer, which they brought. Whereupon, van der Klaauw, the Foreign Minister, sitting next to me said, 'Where did you get that from? I wish I could have one.' I assured him that he could, if he asked. The Dutch, although stubborn, are often undemanding.

*It survived eighty years of railway ownership much better than it has since survived eight years of privatization.

Laura and I then drove to Scheveningen, had a walk on the sea front, and went on past Delft, round Rotterdam to the sea at Veere, and back across the ferry – it was still a beautiful day – from Vlissingen to Breskens. Brussels at about 8 o'clock.

MONDAY, 9 APRIL. *Brussels.*

At last the last half-week of this seemingly endless (partly owing to calendar, partly owing to weather) Christmas/Easter term. Plaja at 10.45, with Italian complaints about MTNs. I was reasonably sympathetic but think they may be pushing their luck a bit. I then saw rather a good delegation from the Italian Republican Party at 12.30, and afterwards took Spierenburg to lunch and was rather encouraged by the way he seems to be getting on. I found him agreeable and think his ideas are *probably* sensible, although he is a little too interested in the wider questions of how the Commission should be appointed, and what its relations with the Parliament should be, and not quite interested enough in the duller ones of internal bureaucratic organization.

Dined with Deane Hinton at a farewell party for General Haig, and had some serious conversation with both of them afterwards. Haig appeared as usual as a nice man, plenty to say, right-wing views, but not offensively so. He has been a good SHAPE commander, and believes, though I have my doubts, that he may have a great political future, but he is not to my mind remotely a great man.

TUESDAY, 10 APRIL. *Brussels.*

On a most beautiful day – it had suddenly become 70° – Crispin and I lunched at a little restaurant on the corner of the Petit Sablon. Then an afternoon and early evening of clearing up in the office before going off to the Wakefield* dinner (new British Ambassador to the Kingdom). That was rather enjoyable; it is a splendid house, almost as good as the Paris Embassy, which I hadn't been in since coming to Brussels. I liked both the Wakefields very much; they are a great improvement. It was a slightly predictable group, mainly of

*Sir Peter Wakefield, b. 1922, came to Belgium after three years as Ambassador to the Lebanon. Since 1982, Director of the National Art Collection Fund.

Belgians apart from the Killicks: the Burgomeister, the Grand Marshal of the Court, etc. After dinner I talked for a long time to old Sir James Plimsoll, the Australian Ambassador (he is not in fact as old as he looks), whom I always like.

FRIDAY, 13 APRIL. *East Hendred.*

To the Berlins for lunch with Annans, Quintons, Michael Astor, John Sparrow and Arnold Goodman. After lunch, walked round Addison's Walk with Jennifer and also through Christ Church.

MONDAY, 16 APRIL. *East Hendred.*

Lunch with the Gordon Richardsons just west of Cirencester, who had Kit McMahon, former Magdalen economics don, former economic adviser to the Bank, now executive director, plus wife, staying. McMahon nicer and less thrusting than I had thought him to be, and the Richardsons on excellent form. A grand but rather unused house. Drove back through appalling traffic, with Bibury a scene of congested chaos, to see the Tickells at Ablington. The third day of perfect Easter weather.

FRIDAY, 20 APRIL. *East Hendred.*

Davenports, Michael Astors and Hendersons to lunch. Nicholas (Davenport)* beginning to age at last. Michael Astor seemed in surprisingly rude health in spite of his winter of illness. Nicko violently right-wing, much more than anybody else, on the election. In the evening I watched without enlightenment or inspiration various political broadcasts.

TUESDAY, 24 APRIL. *Brussels, Frankfurt and Strasbourg.*

I flew to Frankfurt to speak at a European Election demonstration in the Rathaus there. There were about five speeches, including a good one from the Minister President of Hessen. We then motored

---

*Nicholas Davenport, 1893–1979, was a radical stockbroker and financial commentator, whose heterodox views did not prevent him making enough money to acquire a regicide's fine mansion near Faringdon in which he much entertained, *inter alia*, Hugh Dalton and Richard Crossman.

Prime Minister (now President)
Mário Soares of Portugal comes
to Brussels, March 1977.

With Pierre Elliott Trudeau
in Ottawa, March 1978.

With the King of Spain in Madrid, April 1977.

Willy Brandt in the Berlaymont, July 1978.

The European Council meets in Brussels, December 1978.
Seated left to right: Andreotti, Michael O'Kennedy, Jack Lynch, Jean François-Poncet, Giscard, Schmidt, Hans-Dietrich Genscher (reading newspaper), Jørgensen, Christophersen, Vanden Boeynants, Simonet and, next to me, the back of van der Klaauw.

With Jennifer at the Temple
of Heaven, Peking, March 1979.

Talks with Deng Xiaoping in the Great Hall of the People.
(On my right, Emile Noël and Crispin Tickell.)

With Prime Minister (later President) Karamanlis at the signing of the Treaty for the
Accession of Greece, Athens, May 1979. (In the background, Natali, Sir Donald Maitland,
Andreotti and O'Kennedy.)

From Greenland's icy mountains,
Sukkertoppen, May 1979.

To Afric's golden sand,
Timbuctoo, January 1979

The Tokyo Summit, July 1979. Real or willow pattern?
Left to right: Jenkins, Clark (Canada), Carter, Okira, Schmidt, Giscard,
Mrs Thatcher, Andreotti.

down past Heidelberg and Karlsruhe and got into Strasbourg at 5.30. I had Fellermaier, the leader of the Socialist Group, and Manfred Michel, the secretary, to dinner. Fellermaier, absolutely typically, turned up an hour late, with some less than adequate excuse. However, I had a useful period of preliminary conversation with Michel about Socialist Group affairs and likely figures in the new Parliament.

WEDNESDAY, 25 APRIL. *Strasbourg.*

Saw Cheysson at 11.30, partly to rebuke him for the ridiculous telegram which he had sent to Nkomo the week before, which was singularly ill-judged.

John Ardwick* to lunch. He is a nice and intelligent man who has been very helpful in the European Parliament and it was intended as a thanks on departure. Quite what he will do in the future I don't know. Interesting gossip about King, Cudlipp, Wilson, Gaitskell, etc. He remains a very firm old Gaitskellite in spite of the curiously close personal relationship which he had with Wilson over a large number of years.

Then I saw Christopher Tugendhat to talk about some of his budgetary problems, mainly next year's. This year's budgetary dispute between Parliament and Council has resolved itself well, the only disadvantage being that our additional applications for staff have got lost down an *oubliette*, though I don't think there is much we can do about that at this stage.

THURSDAY, 26 APRIL. *Strasbourg, Luxembourg and Brussels.*

I saw Rowling, the ex-Prime Minister of New Zealand and currently leader of the Opposition, for a slightly inconsequential chat, and then motored to Nancy with Nick Stuart. Nancy was absolutely magnificent. Curiously I had never been there before, though often through it by train. The Place Stanislas is one of the supreme urban sights of Europe.

---

*John Beaven, b. 1910, cr. Lord Ardwick 1970, was London editor of the *Manchester Guardian* 1946–55, editor of the *Daily Herald* 1960–2, and political adviser to the *Mirror* Group 1962–76 (hence his interest in Cecil King and Hugh Cudlipp).

After lunch we drove on to Luxembourg, where I delivered a direct elections speech, with questions, in the television head-quarters building before a smallish, but quite notable, audience. Accompanied by the excellent Mart, the Luxembourg member of the *Cour des Comptes*, who would make a good Commissioner, I dined *à trois* with the Grand Duke in his Palace. Very good dinner and engaging *tour d'horizon* conversation. The Grand Duke I found agreeable, relaxed and intelligent. Avion taxi back to Brussels at midnight.

FRIDAY, 27 APRIL. *Brussels and East Hendred.*

A long meeting with the President of Bangladesh. He was a reason-ably amiable military gentleman who said that he was very inexperienced in politics, and who was also slightly slow and inarticulate, but sensible and seems resolved (we will have to see what exactly happens) on returning the country to democracy. They seem also to be beginning to make a little economic sense.

Rue de Praetère luncheon for Calvo Sotelo, with his Ambassador and one other Spaniard, for a discussion of the Spanish position, the form of negotiations, etc. Calvo Sotelo, as always, impressive, sensible, and francophone.

Evening plane to London for an unexpected weekend at East Hendred. This was because we had decided, four or five days before, to postpone an Egyptian visit as there wasn't much to discuss with them, the meeting was rather badly set up (thanks largely to their incompetent ambassador in Brussels whose only possible qualifi-cation is that he is the brother of the Prime Minister), and the Egyptians, no doubt because they had a lot of other things on their minds, hadn't given the long-previously requested *agrément* to our delegate in Cairo, so we had nobody to organize things there.

MONDAY, 30 APRIL. *East Hendred and London.*

Lunch with the Gilmours at Isleworth. Ian thought the Conserva-tives were probably winning the election, though wasn't over-whelmingly confident, and told me more strongly than when I had seen him before Easter that he was pretty committed to accept the number two job at the Foreign Office, under Carrington. The night they had won the no-confidence vote in the House of Commons, he had rashly agreed over a late-night drink with Carrington that he would do this, which greatly strengthened Carrington's claims to the Foreign Office, which now seem fairly clearly established. The difficulty is that whoever is number two there ought not to do Europe. The Foreign Secretary ought essentially to do that himself, and this makes the job, apart from the disadvantage of not being head of a department, in my view a less good one than Ian ought to have.

Sir Michael Palliser for a serious talk at Brooks's from 6.45 to 8.00. Acting on the assumption of a change of government, which both of us thought likely but neither of us thought certain, we then discussed how things should be played. He thought that Carrington was likely to be Foreign Secretary and would be marginally better, because more experienced, than Pym. Quite a good and sensible talk with him, including a satisfactory interchange about Crispin's future. I said very firmly that Crispin should be given a substantial embassy as soon as he came back from me (and a KCMG too) in order that he might have the opportunity to move up fairly quickly to one of the three top jobs by the end of his career, which he was certainly good enough to deserve. Palliser has Mexico City in mind for him.

TUESDAY, 1 MAY. *London and Brussels.*

To the Maudling memorial service at St Margaret's. It was absolutely packed, and a good, rather moving service. Ted (Heath) gave an impressive and generous address, done remarkably without notes, and there was also a good reading by Sandy Glen.* I walked out with David Steel and told him how well I thought his campaign had gone and that he really had done the best of the three, though I had no idea how many votes it would bring him. I had a brief word with Harold Macmillan and with Ted afterwards.

Plane to Brussels with Jennifer where we had a rue de Praetère dinner for Senator Ed Muskie,† whom I had not talked to since the memorable occasion in Douglass Cater's house in Washington

---

*Sir Alexander Glen, b. 1912, was Chairman of the British Tourist Authority 1969–77.
†Edmund Muskie, b. 1914, was Governor of Maine 1955–9, Senator for that state 1959–80, and US Secretary of State 1980–1.

seven and a half years ago when he had been so completely carved up by Dean Acheson, the last occasion on which I saw Acheson. We also had Hinton, the American Ambassador, one person whom Muskie had brought with him, and Edmund Dell, who is one of the *trois sages*, plus his assistant, a very bright Foreign Office lady called Alison Bailes, who had been sitting in the car with Sykes when he had been assassinated in The Hague. It was altogether an interesting dinner. Muskie was very agreeable and more impressive than when I had seen him with Acheson; rather protectionist, however, despite being very close to the President. Dell seemed friendly and reasonably sensible on his affairs.

WEDNESDAY, 2 MAY. *Brussels.*

Pressing messages from Philippe de Rothschild saying he must see me urgently on some highly important personal matter. I thought it was to do with Jean-Pierre de Beaumarchais and therefore thought I should see him, and persuaded Jennifer a little reluctantly to have him to lunch. And then during the morning he kept ringing me up about the arrangements and also asking if he could bring Joan Littlewood* with him. I agreed to this reasonably enthusiastically as I thought she might be quite interesting; she turned out to be moderately so. The only thing he wanted was to try and get me to sponsor some wine (i.e. Mouton) art exhibition in London.

In quick succession at about 7.30 I had frantic telephone calls from Bill Rodgers and Shirley Williams, both of whom had had Number 10 on to them saying there was a tremendous rumour circulating in the City that I was about to come out with a pro-Tory statement. I assured them that I was coming out with no statement at all during the election. They seemed relieved. (Nor did I vote. Jennifer voted Liberal.)

Dinner, rue de Praetère, with John Harris who was staying, Jennifer and Laura. John pretty convinced, but by no means absolutely so, that the Tories would win. He and I stayed up talking about the future and what I might or might not conceivably do in politics.

* Joan Littlewood founded the Theatre Workshop in 1945 and subsequently did many productions at the Theatre Royal, Stratford. Went to work in France 1975 and was largely responsible in the early 1980s for an unfortunate autobiography published by Philippe de Rothschild.

THURSDAY, 3 MAY. *Brussels*.

A rue de Praetère luncheon party for the Chinese Ambassador and his wife. We also had Thea Elliott who was staying with us and was an old China hand, having had one child born in Peking in the late 1950s, plus Denmans, Tickells, and Plaja, the Italian Permanent Representative. I was surprised and pleased that the Chinese had come to lunch on their own, without any 'interpreter'. The Ambassador showed no signs of resentment that the follow-up to my Peking talks are not as yet going terribly well, mainly because of the French taking up a very restrictive view on the textile agreement and one or two other governments being difficult on GSP.

A visit from Lathière, the French head of the Airbus consortium. He is the most surprising man, *Enarque, Inspecteur de Finance*, had been *Chef de Cabinet* to Jacquet when I was dealing with him on Concorde in 1964–5, looked like a butcher, talked a most undistinguished English fluently, and was obviously an extremely effective head of Airbus. Then just after 7 o'clock I went to the Brussels Hôtel de Ville and made a brief direct elections speech and then wandered around the stalls which had been laid out in the Grand'Place, one for each of the numerous Belgian parties competing in the election. But my insular mind was slightly more on other elections that day.

Sat up listening to the results with Jennifer, Laura, Thea and Celia, which began to come in seriously about 12.40 Brussels time. I eventually went to bed at 5.45, having waited to hear the Stechford result, but, Birmingham being as incompetently late as ever, had failed to do so. It was clear that the Tories were set for a substantial majority which would last a full Parliament. I had mixed feelings at the end, though on the whole I think a change of government is better for Britain's relations with Europe, but I cannot find pleasure in it. Thea I think was the most solid Labour supporter amongst us, though we were all somewhat torn.

FRIDAY, 4 MAY. *Brussels*.

In the afternoon I heard the totally unexpected and dreadful news of Shirley Williams's defeat, and then went home for a sleep before the Beaumarchais' arrived to stay at about 8 o'clock. Late-night telephone conversations with Shirley and Bill Rodgers.

SUNDAY, 6 MAY. *Brussels.*

Did some English telephoning, to Ian Gilmour, Peter Carrington, one or two other people, including David Owen, who had got a good result personally, rather surprisingly so. To bed very early. The post-election weekend definitely exhausting, draining and not very satisfactory.

TUESDAY, 8 MAY. *Brussels and Luxembourg.*

In the margins of the Foreign Affairs Council I had a substantial talk with François-Poncet, mainly about the agenda for Mercuès, the French 'Schloss Gymnich', and also on some difficult nuclear matters, the French having decided to take the nuclear question off the Mercuès agenda thinking it was too sensitive in advance of direct elections. I agreed to this but said we couldn't leave it for too long. François-Poncet was reasonable and quick and I was definitely pro him on this occasion.

At the end we disposed of Cheysson's telegram to Nkomo, which over the weekend had shown signs of escalating into a major row with the French, although they knew perfectly well that I had not approved of it. However, Poncet agreed that we could now leave it where it was. But in the typical French way of getting in a parting shot, he said as we were walking out that there was great sensitivity about Commission political activity. Some people – not, he implausibly alleged, the French as much as the Germans – had raised eyebrows at the high degree of political content in my China talks.

At lunch Christophersen (Danish Foreign Minister) made the most ridiculous fuss about the leaked Denman working paper on relations with Japan, which had contained the famous phrases about 'workaholics', 'rabbit hutches', etc. I replied robustly, saying it was a pity it had leaked, but I was far from sure that it had done any harm, I had since received several friendly communications from the Japanese Prime Minister, and in any case it was much better that people should write in vivid phrases than in the usual awful Europe bureaucratese. I was strongly supported in this line by Dohnanyi and Simonet, both of whom were excellent, but nonetheless it took a very long time to persuade the stubborn Christophersen not to raise the matter in open Council during the afternoon.

The Council spent all day grinding its boring way through the negotiating brief for the final stages of the Community/ACP* negotiations. This very detailed work, which ought to have been done by COREPER, was a clear example, as I told François-Poncet, of the way in which the Council downgraded itself and became no more than a glorified COREPER, with a consequent bad effect upon the attendance of Foreign Ministers who just sent their under-secretaries who could not take decisions: a classic vicious circle.

I then drove to Luxembourg on the most perfect evening, a long overdue improvement in the weather, to make a valedictory statement to the departing nominated Parliament on the following afternoon.

THURSDAY, 10 MAY. *Brussels, London and Edinburgh.*

London for my Open University degree at Guildhall. Kingman Brewster, the American Ambassador in London, and I were jointly honoured, and Asa Briggs was installed as the new Chancellor. I saw the Wilsons going into the lunch, and Mary, amazingly, more or less confirmed the story in Harold's notorious interview that she had intended to vote for Mrs Thatcher.

Then to Edinburgh in filthy weather for a dinner with the Consultative Committee of the Coal and Steel Community, presided over by Derek Ezra† and attended by a fair collection of Scottish notabilities, including the new Secretary of State, George Younger.‡ I spoke without a text for about twenty minutes. I sat between Ezra and Gormley, Gormley making a great number of centre party noises.

SATURDAY, 12 MAY. *East Hendred and Cahors.*

To Northolt to get a lift in Peter Carrington's plane to the French 'Schloss Gymnich' at Mercuès, near Cahors. I gave Peter a rundown on the various other Foreign Ministers and encouraged him at some fairly early stage to make a general statement of European

*African, Caribbean and Pacific (i.e. Lomé) countries.
†Sir Derek Ezra, b. 1919, cr. Lord Ezra 1983, was Chairman of the National Coal Board 1971–82.
‡George Younger, b. 1931, was Secretary of State for Scotland 1979–86, and is now Secretary of State for Defence.

commitment. The weather improved spectacularly just south of
Paris and we landed at Toulouse on the most perfect warm spring
morning. There was a reception there by prefect, mayors, the new
British Ambassador (surprisingly) etc., and then into a helicopter
accompanied by one or two other Foreign Ministers for a rather
long journey to the Château de Mercuès. When we got there we
found a most spectacular place, an old castle turned into a very high
grade hotel on a cliff overlooking the Lot about seven miles out of
Cahors.

Three-and-a-half-hour session, mostly outside. Peter made his
statement of intent or commitment, and made it very well. He then
went on and more or less told us that they were very loath to keep
on Rhodesian sanctions beyond the autumn. This was received in a
rather reserved way by Genscher, Simonet, van der Klaauw, and to
some extent by Forlani. But François-Poncet, Christophersen and
Hamilius, the Luxembourgeois who was substituting for Thorn,
were more forthcoming. However, Carrington got away with it
better than he would otherwise have done because everyone was
so pleased with his preliminary statement.

At dinner there was the usual tour of the world, no more
inspiriting or profound than previously. I got to my room fairly
early. It was a perfect night, full moon, and I sat by my window
reading for two hours.

SUNDAY, 13 MAY. *Cahors and Brussels.*
A spectacular early morning, with the dark smooth-moving river
looking incredibly beautiful. The south-western French countryside can have a peculiarly benign and smiling quality.

Another *alfresco* session for two hours. François-Poncet raised his
complaints about the European Court but got virtually no support,
and in the course of it, rather surprisingly, paid an enormous tribute
to the Commission, and to me in particular, for the help we had
given in solving the (Community 1979) budget problem.

Maurice Faure, Mayor of Cahors and former patron of François-
Poncet whom he had introduced into the area, plus the prefect,
came to lunch. I had quite an amusing conversation with Faure,
François-Poncet and the Simonets about the Kennedys, on which

subject they were all curiously ill-informed, and I held forth for some time.

Faure then insisted on taking me on a tour of the local sights, driving himself very fast with his chauffeur in the back. He drove rather as I do, I suppose, except that he went over all the red traffic lights, vaguely waving to the local population. Very long flight back in Simonet's turbo-prop plane. He had been told the Belgian jet couldn't get in to Cahors, as the British had also been told, but found that his Dutch colleague had a perfectly good jet on the tarmac, as indeed did François-Poncet. This produced a spark of Benelux jealousy.

MONDAY, 14 MAY. *Brussels and Copenhagen.*

On my way back from my Bois jogging I read the *Guardian* lead story which stated that there were now new Commission estimates that the budgetary cost to Britain in 1980 would be up from £1000m to £1500m, but that I, after consultation with the Commission, had suppressed this estimate in the meeting that I had had with Mrs Thatcher the previous week. The story was a total fabrication because apart from anything else I hadn't seen Mrs Thatcher, it was probably malevolent coming from Palmer, and in my view was highly defamatory. I therefore decided to act extremely heavily, partly to try and stop any repetition from Château Palmer. So I rang up Preston, the editor, and began by saying firmly, 'You grossly libelled me this morning.' He sounded absolutely terrified, as though he had been shellshocked, and we then dictated to him a statement which had to appear on the front page the following morning.

I then left for Copenhagen, first for an hour's meeting with Anker Jørgensen, the Prime Minister and a nice man, and then my direct elections meeting and address to the Danish Foreign Policy Society. They produced a remarkably good audience, absolutely packed, I should think about 250 people in the Hôtel d'Angleterre. The audience seemed to have a complete comprehension of English, and there were some good questions afterwards. Dinner in the Parliament with K. B. Andersen (now the Speaker).

TUESDAY, 15 MAY. *Copenhagen, Munich and Brussels.*

10.45 plane to Munich to address the ETUC conference. The audience was a great contrast with Copenhagen. It was a much bigger room, probably rather more people (about five hundred) but they were all sitting at desks shuffling papers around, the acoustics were rather bad, and I got the impression that I was talking through a wind to a non-listening audience. However, rather to my surprise, they applauded quite well at the end, and they listened to me at least as well as they listened to any of their own leaders.

I then had a very good sight-seeing tour of Munich: the Frauen-kirche, the old Rathaus, the new Rathaus, the Opera House, the Hofgarten, Nymphenburg, which was closed, but which we were able to walk round: an attractive, surprisingly early building, about 1680 (I thought it was later) with great wings spread out, rather as at Versailles or Blenheim, to make it look as big as possible. The disappointing building was the Amalienburg, which I had always heard was rather good. Then back to Schwabing, which is now the smart, 'left bank' quarter. Brussels by just after 11.00, having had three of the last four meals on aeroplanes, which is too much by any standard.

MONDAY, 16 MAY. *Brussels and London.*

6.35 plane to London and to Grosvenor House for my CBI dinner speech. It was one of the most formidable gatherings I had ever addressed, about twelve hundred people, including almost exactly half the Cabinet – Howe, Joseph, Maude, Nott, Howell, Prior* and various others I can't remember – plus most of the Permanent Secretaries, plus Shirley Williams, plus Bill Rodgers, plus Denis Healey, plus Roy Mason. My speech, which was mainly European, but also had a good plug for centrist politics, telling the Government not to make major legislative changes unless there was good reason to believe the changes would survive the next tilt of the political balance, went rather well. It was moderately reported in the press and very well reported on the BBC the next morning, but slightly to my regret more the European part rather than the warning to the Government to spare us too many queasy rides on the ideological big dipper.

* Not many of them now left.

I drove Shirley home and discovered that her views on her own future are very sensible. She was not rushing back into the House. She wasn't sure she was going back at all, but certainly wanted to stay out for the rest of this year. She has lots of things to do, including an autumn's teaching at Harvard. She wants to look around, and I suppose let people seek her rather than vice versa.

THURSDAY, 17 MAY. *London and East Hendred.*

To the Monnet memorial service at St Margaret's. It was not very well attended in numbers, although it was quite a distinguished gathering, with Callaghan rather surprisingly there, plus Alec Home, plus Ted, who gave another of his noteless, even if not wholly impromptu, addresses. I thought it rather a good service, in spite of unfamiliar hymns.

SUNDAY, 20 MAY. *East Hendred and London.*

Jennifer and I went to Lew Grade's great Euro Gala at Drury Lane. We had Dickie Mountbatten and Ted Heath in the box with us, Mountbatten boisterously friendly as usual, Ted reasonably friendly to me though basically in a very grumpy mood, partly because he had had his snarl-up with Mrs Thatcher over her incredibly foolishly sending him a written offer of the Washington Embassy. A delicate sounding might have been one thing, a formal written offer was ludicrous. I sympathized with him but got into slight difficulty, knowing that Nicko Henderson had been decided on a week or so before, and *nearly* telling him that I knew, but withdrew into saying only that I thought they had now got a candidate. He showed every sign of wanting to pursue this with understandable vigour.

MONDAY, 21 MAY. *London.*

A noon meeting with Mrs Thatcher, the first time I had seen her since the election, and indeed, apart from perhaps three meetings with her as leader of the Opposition, almost the only time that I had talked to her seriously.

She was anxious to be pleasant, came downstairs to meet me,

arriving very faintly flustered two seconds too late to be at the door, and we then had beaming photographs taken and moved to the upstairs study, where I had spent so much time with Wilson and even a certain amount of time with Callaghan. Rather to my surprise she began by offering me a drink, which Callaghan certainly wouldn't have done at noon, and I'm rather doubtful about Wilson too. I rather primly refused, saying it was a little early. She looked rather disappointed, so I made what I thought was a tactful recovery, saying, 'Let us have one at 12.30. It will give us something to look forward to if the conversation goes badly.'

However, it didn't go too badly at all. We started off with some general conversation about Chequers, her pattern of life, etc. Then she went into her rather *simpliste* European lecture, which I let run on for ten minutes or so when it slightly died away, and then after that she listened as well as talked and I should think I had 60 per cent of the remaining hour. She was fairly rigid on a number of things, notably fish, but was however very anxious to strike a constructive note on others: very determined to get something on the budget; willing I think to give something – I'm not quite sure what beyond general cooperative goodwill – in exchange for this; anxious to grasp points of detail and quite quick at doing so; thinking always a little too much in terms of the EEC and NATO as two bodies which ought to be amalgamated; and making one or two frankly foolish remarks about starving the Arabs to death by cutting off North American wheat supplies, or something equally silly. However, the general impression was quite good and certainly friendly.

TUESDAY, 22 MAY. *London, Birmingham and Brussels.*

To Birmingham for George Canning's inauguration ceremony as Lord Mayor. Arrived early and therefore paid a visit to the Art Gallery. Warmly greeted by the curator, a number of people on the way round, and indeed by quite a lot of people in the street, both before and after the ceremony – a rather pleasant, warm, Birmingham-returning atmosphere.

George looked very smart, every inch a Lord Mayor. The speeches were good. Minnis (a Liberal) proposed and Clive Wilkinson seconded; then a very good speech from George himself.

All were full of warm references to me. There was time for a drive around Stechford before the 4.30 plane to Brussels.

WEDNESDAY, 23 MAY. *Brussels.*

Michael O'Kennedy, the Irish Foreign Minister, arrived at noon for his acclimatization meeting and lunch. We had quite a good meeting for one and a quarter hours, nothing very dramatic, his grasp being reasonable without being exciting. Then a Commission lunch for him at which, again, he acquitted himself quite well.

THURSDAY, 24 MAY. *Brussels, Aachen, Brussels and Milan.*

Motored with Laura to Aachen for the Karlspreis ceremony. Colombo received the prize and Tindemans made the allocution. Genscher spoke on behalf of the Government, and the Mayor of Aachen, Malangré, who is in the course of being elected to the European Parliament, also spoke. As three of the speeches, including Tindemans's, were in German and Colombo's was in Italian, I did not, alas, understand a great deal, and there were no translations. However, it is a nice hall and the ceremony strikes evocative chords with me.

Then back to Brussels and to Milan with Laura by 7.30. We were met by Giro, the head of our office in Rome who was in Milan for some other occasion, and were driven in by him in an immensely expensive, huge Mercedes, which he had hired on our behalf, but privately, as it wasn't an official visit, and which we then made the dreadful error of keeping to take us on half a mile to dinner, and which altogether cost £45 – an appalling waste of money.

FRIDAY, 25 MAY. *Milan and Lucca.*

Left early and drove in a hired car via Parma to the Gilmour house near Lucca in time for lunch. Jennifer, the Gilmours, Charlie and Sara Morrison,* and Hayden had already arrived from London.

* (Sir) Charles Morrison, b. 1932, has been Conservative MP for Devizes since 1964. Sara Morrison, b. 1934, is a director of GEC.

SUNDAY, 27 MAY. *Lucca.*

Ian (Gilmour) slept most of the weekend but was on good form when awake. He seemed to enjoy being a Foreign Office Minister and was full of splendid anecdotes about the early days of the Government. Sara Morrison very sharp, but quite amusingly so, about everybody, including old friends like Peter Carrington. She is still a dedicated Heath woman and therefore a dedicated anti-Thatcher one. Charlie Morrison slightly deaf (a good thing to be if married to Sara, who does talk almost without stopping) but nice and sensible and more intelligent than I had realized; an absolutely rock solid centrist-liberal on every issue one could think of – Europe, hanging, Rhodesia, race relations, indeed everything imaginable, which is surprising and impressive.

MONDAY, 28 MAY. *Lucca, Athens and Rome.*

Left with Laura for the 7.53 train from Pisa. Rome, after rather an uncomfortable journey without breakfast, at 11.00. First to the Hassler, then to Ciampino to join Andreotti on his plane. Athens, with a change of time, about 3.40. There was an enormous ceremonial greeting, with vast guards of honour. Mitsotakis, the Cretan deputy Prime Minister, took charge of me and drove me in to the Grande Bretagne. The ceremony* was well organized in a modern rotunda between the Parliament and the Acropolis. We had three speeches (François-Poncet, Karamanlis and me) and then the ceremonial signing. Giscard turned up, but did not speak. He sat beaming in the seat nearest the rostrum, looking like the mother of the bride.

Then to dinner at the Presidential Palace, where I was received with immense warmth by Tsatsos, the little President, mainly on the ground that he had read and enjoyed the *Asquith* which I had given him last autumn; and then, apparently, at dinner he got Giscard going on Dilke ('Dilkie' is Giscard's favourite subject), and was regaled with the whole story.

Dinner was for about three hundred people. I sat between François-Poncet (with whom I had quite an amusing conversation) and van der Klaauw. After dinner Karamanlis spoke again as well as

* For the signing of the treaty admitting Greece into the Community.

Tsatsos. Then Giscard spoke in Greek, which perhaps showed more gallantry than sense.

Then briefly to a spectacular reception, with tremendous lighting and illuminated alleyways in the garden of the old Royal Palace, until we left at 11.30, drove to the airport and took off at midnight for a rather sleepy return to Rome and the Hassler. It was satisfactory to have got it all done in one day. Very good hot weather, temperature about the same − 85° − in Rome and Athens, but slightly clearer in Rome.

TUESDAY, 29 MAY. *Rome and Lucca.*

9 o'clock plane to Pisa and back to La Pianella at noon, swam before lunch, and lunched in the garden on a perfect day.

FRIDAY, 1 JUNE. *Lucca and East Hendred.*

To England after a very successful holiday, spectacular from the weather point of view, in spite of the Athens interruption. We were immensely well treated at Pisa Airport and for once by British Airways.

SATURDAY, 2 JUNE. *East Hendred.*

The Rodgers' to lunch with Ann Fleming. They went rather better together than I expected. Bill was very funny and indiscreet about all Labour Party affairs, Callaghan, etc. After Ann went, the Rodgers', in improving weather, sat with us in the garden for another two hours. Bill was not too depressed by the election, very committed to politics, rather complacent I thought about shadow Cabinet elections: the Manifesto Group were only putting up nine candidates, they didn't wish to score too crushing a victory, etc. He was quite realistic about his own position, thought he would get on, but in eighth, ninth, tenth position − something like that.

MONDAY, 4 JUNE. *London and Brussels.*

Lunch with Victor Rothschild. I found him on only tolerably good form. Only the subject of the Dimbleby Lecture, which he did last year and about which he had a great row, and I have agreed to do this year, really animated him.

Back in Brussels in the early evening I did a long British sound radio phone-in programme in the Brussels studio, which lasted no less than one and a half hours. There were surprisingly good questions, intelligent, friendly and rational. Apart from those who were listed to appear, Judith Hart,* about to be a Dame, insisted on coming in and asked a long-winded question, to which it was not difficult to reply.

TUESDAY, 5 JUNE. *Brussels.*

I saw Gundelach, followed by Hinton the US Ambassador, followed by the Pakistani Ambassador, who wanted me to go and visit his country, which I have no intention of doing in view of their general behaviour and treatment of Bhutto in particular; and then lunched with Crispin, with whom I hadn't had a talk for some time.

Dined with Léon Lambert, with his splendid pictures, statuary and wine, for Ken Galbraith. I was very pleased to see Ken, after a long interval, and who now, though aged seventy-one or -two, was looking much better than I had seen him for quite some time past, and talking rather well without trying to hog the conversation. I am very fond of the old thing.

THURSDAY, 7 JUNE. *Brussels.*

Lunch with the new Belgian Prime Minister, Martens,† in his *hôtel particulier.* He is a nice, agreeable young man — about forty-two — not well-informed about European questions, though generally favourable like all Belgians. He is essentially an expert on the communal (i.e. Walloon/Flemish) question, which is I suppose what counts in Belgium at the present time. He is a Flemish Christian Democrat from Ghent. He listened while I talked most of the time, and alas I found myself addressing more and more remarks to Van Ypersele (the great Belgian monetary expert who is

* (Dame) Judith Hart, cr. Baroness Hart of Lanark 1987, was Labour MP for Lanark 1959–87, and holder of various middle-rank offices at periods between 1964 and 1979.
† Wilfried Martens, b. 1936, has since been Prime Minister of Belgium 1979–81, 1981–5 and from October 1985.

his *Chef de Cabinet*) because he understood so much more what I was saying.

At 3.15 I saw Ortoli for a rather difficult meeting. All difficulties with Ortoli arise about drafts, and we were arguing about whether a paper on the 1990s for the European Council should be on the basis of his draft (which he claimed was his *cabinet* draft, but which in fact he had done himself) or the draft which Michael Jenkins had done for me. I thought ours was better (it was really a clash between English and French stylistic and schematic approaches) but he was stubborn about his. I was inclined to be stubborn too.

However, by the time I got back from a one-and-a-half-hour visit of inspection to DG10 I had decided that it wasn't worth having a great row with Ortoli about the drafts. Both were tolerably good, neither was brilliant, and these papers are not read with sufficient attention that it is worth treating them as works of art. I therefore gave in to him, subject to our being able to make amendments to his version. I did a half-hour pre-Summit Japanese television interview, which is supposed to balance with one from Carter and is therefore quite important, and then had an hour with an Australian parliamentary delegation, led by Billy Snedden,* who was pushed out by Fraser as leader of the Liberal Party and is now Speaker. Snedden was appropriately anti-Fraser. We then dined with the Tugendhats, a large party of about thirty, obviously their great summer fête.

FRIDAY, 8 JUNE. *Brussels, Paris and Brussels.*

7.30 train to Paris. The TEE was, as usual, about twenty minutes late. A meeting with Giscard from 11.00 until 12.15.

He had not only Wahl, François-Poncet's replacement as Secretary-General of the Elysée, present as a note-taker, but also François-Poncet himself, which seemed to me slightly over-egging the custard. I had Crispin. It was a perfectly tolerable meeting in form, though not a particularly good one in substance. And, indeed, even on the form, as Crispin remarked afterwards, while Giscard is mostly polite, he is never warm. He made it clear early on that he wished to discuss the European Council at Strasbourg, rather than that and Tokyo together, this no doubt being an

---

* Sir Billy Snedden, 1926–87, had led the Liberal Party in opposition 1972–5.

expression of his reluctance to admit my *locus* in relation to Tokyo. However, he managed to link it to the reasonably persuasive argument, which indeed I had used the previous year, that Bremen (the European Council) should in no way be subordinated to Bonn (the Western Summit).

In practice this did not make much difference to what we discussed. We had a reasonably constructive discussion on energy, though it emerged curiously that Giscard's position on a number of issues was closer for once to the American than it was to the German. Then we had a discussion about the British budgetary problem arising out of his meeting with Mrs Thatcher two or three days before. He expressed himself, but again without warmth, as reasonably impressed by her, and indicated his willingness to give a remit to the Commission at the Strasbourg European Council to study this matter and bring forward proposals. But he then indicated, almost as an afterthought, though it certainly was not that, that this would be conditional on the British agreeing in Strasbourg (had it not been done previously) to an agricultural price settlement, involving a light increase – 1½ to 2 per cent, he implied – for agricultural products, possibly exempting milk, but certainly nothing else. I said bluntly that this was not acceptable to us as a Commission, but if he could get the rest of the Nine to agree I suppose he didn't need us.* He let this pass without challenging our Commission determination to stick to the overall freeze. He also added that a British willingness to settle on fish would be a condition for the Dublin European Council (in December) agreeing to any recommendations which we might bring forward.

Then, in a slightly embarrassed way to be fair to him, he said: 'There is just one issue to which I must refer, and that is the question of the Strasbourg press conference. I was very surprised when in Paris in March you made a statement slightly different from mine, and then in your answers to questions took a quite different view. I am sure you will understand, as an *homme de politique*, that it is not possible for the President of the Republic to share a press conference with anyone else.'

I looked surprised at this, and said, 'It is absolutely habitual that, under all other presidencies, we share the press conference, and at

* A unanimous decision of governments is required to override the Commission on such a matter.

the two European Councils under Schmidt I did exactly as I had done in Paris in March. Indeed, at the press conference at the end of the Brussels Summit, when he was rather exhausted, I answered nearly all the questions at his request.'

Giscard then said, 'I see two possibilities: either that you can, if you wish, give a totally separate press conference on your own, or that you may come to mine and I will make my statement and answer questions, then I will leave, and you can make your statement and answer any questions there may be to you.'

I said I would reflect upon which I considered was the better of these two not very attractive proposals. I thought either of them would give rise to adverse comment. However, I knew already that I would not be anxious to have a great row with him about this immediately before Tokyo, where we were supposed to be jointly representing the Community. We then parted on reasonably polite terms.

Lunch with François-Poncet at the Quai d'Orsay. A third of the way through, we got down to the difficult Euratom issue. Not a bad discussion on this, a statement of position on both sides, no complete agreement, but no ill-temper either. He, to my surprise, showed himself ill-briefed on one particular question, but otherwise was as competent as usual. I said that an early French approval of the Australia/Euratom agreement would lead to a great improvement of atmosphere. He clearly didn't totally exclude this. I said that I had divined since our last meeting that the approach of Niger to the Commission for a general agreement had been somewhat difficult for France and we had no intention of interfering with the France/Niger agreement.

Train, even later than the morning TEE, back to Brussels, where the Harlechs had arrived to stay.

SUNDAY, 10 JUNE. *Brussels.*

Took the Harlechs to Waterloo, where, for the first time since my childhood, I climbed up the mound to the lion and wondered why on earth I hadn't done it during my previous two and a half years in Brussels. It may have obliterated the sunken road, but it gives a very good impression of the battlefield. Then to the farm at Hougoumont, which is always rather moving to see. Then on to a picnic place at Villers-la-Ville where we had arranged to meet the Tickells and the Andrew Knights (editor of the *Economist* and considerable friends of the Harlechs). We climbed up above the abbey and picnicked in sunny but slightly heavy weather, on a very good site.

The Harlechs left to catch their plane at 5.20. They had been very good guests, easy and enthusiastic – David always easy, Pamela always enthusiastic, and both of them a bit of the other. David, however, has the advantage of extremely wide interests and is determinedly pleasure-seeking, but in the best sense, and never gives the impression of being bored. He was remarkably calm in view of the fact that his much-publicized mission to the African states to try and soften up their position on Zimbabwe/Rhodesia was due to begin the following evening.

I had to go into the Berlaymont shortly before midnight to receive the results of the European elections and make some comments on radio and television. The results were extraordinarily badly presented by the elaborate organization we had set up there, and clearly the British poll, 31 per cent, was a deep disappointment, much worse than I had expected. However, the polls from other countries, most notably Italy, were much better. In Britain the Labour Party did slightly better than expected, winning seventeen seats, whereas I thought they might win only eight.

MONDAY, 11 JUNE. *Brussels.*

A meeting with Gundelach so that he should know of the salient points Giscard had made to me before his (Gundelach's) meeting with the French Minister of Agriculture that afternoon. (Gundelach then lunched with Andrew Knight and leaked it all to him, which however did not come out in a too damaging form, but which I had carefully refrained from doing with Knight the day before.)

Then to lunch with the Australian Ambassador – a long way out – for Peacock, their External Affairs Minister: an agreeable man, as I have always thought him, and very keen to get on with us. Gundelach had improved the atmosphere a good deal in his talks with the Australian Government, but Peacock was at no pains to conceal his differences with Fraser, or indeed his pleasure that he had come out better than Fraser in a recent public opinion poll.

TUESDAY, 12 JUNE. *Brussels, Luxembourg and Brussels.*

Foreign Affairs Council in Luxembourg. It began very late – the French presidency is particularly bad at beginning late. The new British Government was represented for the first time. Carrington was not there, but Ian Gilmour, Nott, the Minister of Trade, and Douglas Hurd were. Nott, I thought, did rather well. Ian only had to make one brief intervention. I had a drink with him afterwards, during which he pressed on me the importance the UK Government attached to the UK/Australian uranium agreement. Douglas Hurd, vastly pro-European, found himself with a very restrictive brief on Lomé questions, and locked into an even more isolated position than the Labour Government had mostly occupied.

Back to Brussels by train and dinner rue de Praetère with Laura, for the last time as she is off in thirty-six hours. Rather sad.

WEDNESDAY, 13 JUNE. *Brussels.*

A farewell party of about fifty for Laura, rue de Praetère. A moderately good speech from me and a better one from Laura. Then a dinner for Lee Kuan Yew, the Prime Minister of Singapore, and his wife (plus Laura). Harry Lee may have political faults but he is almost unique amongst world leaders in being an extremely good talker and a very good listener as well, so I enjoy seeing him very much. His wife is also highly intelligent.

THURSDAY, 14 JUNE. *Brussels, Paris and Brussels.*

7.30 train to Paris for the second time in a week, for a visit to OECD which I am each year pressed to do and which each year seems equally or more pointless to me. It is a day of diplomatic contacts without specific purpose, rather like publishers milling around at an international book fair. I began with an hour's bilateral meeting with Warren Christopher, Cy Vance's deputy at the State Department. I thought him, as always, a highly sensible, agreeable man, though we didn't in fact have much of great importance to talk about. Then I went into the session for a short time and listened to some rather boring speeches and afterwards had a forty-minute meeting with Blumenthal, the American Secretary to the Treasury, and found him, curiously in view of the current low popularity and authority of the Carter administration, more confident and more relaxed than on previous occasions. Perhaps the general decline of the administration improves his relative position.

Then back again for a very short time into the session. Before lunch I had moderately useful talks with Geoffrey Howe, with Pandolfi the Italian Minister of Finance, and with two or three others. After lunch I walked up and down the terrace with the Turkish Foreign Minister, feeling and looking like a bad caricature of a diplomatic stage set. What he (the Foreign Minister) wanted was that I should be firmly in favour of a visit to Turkey of Haferkamp, accompanied by the Foreign Minister of the country holding the presidency. It was a modest ambition. I said I would endeavour to set that up. This he seemed extremely pleased with.

Then I had a meeting with the Portuguese Foreign Minister, de Freitas-Cruz.* He gave me a pessimistic but intelligent analysis of the Portuguese position, and I in return told him to make sure he had a talk with Larosière, the Managing Director of the IMF, who was there, as there appeared to be some misunderstanding on his part as to whether or not the Portuguese were prepared to settle.

Back to Brussels by the 5.44 TEE, and rue de Praetère just before 8.30 where I had David Steel to dinner. A rather gossipy talk with him, more about the election than the current and future political situation. He was pleased with his election campaign, although disappointed with the votes obtained, and went rather out of his way to tell me that, as a result of it, he had become a major public figure, possibly the best known after Callaghan, Heath and Mrs Thatcher. In other words, he was, I think, underlining in the nicest possible way that in any future political arrangement he wasn't to be treated as an office boy. Very strongly anti-Thorpe. Anti-Mrs Thatcher, still rather pro-Callaghan.

FRIDAY, 15 JUNE. *Brussels.*

A special all-day Commission meeting at La Prieuré† to discuss our relations with the directly elected Parliament. Some sensible decisions were arrived at, not the least of which was Burke's sudden

---

* João de Freitas-Cruz, b. 1925, a professional diplomat, was Portuguese Foreign Minister 1978–80, and Ambassador in London 1980–3.
† La Prieuré was a sort of pavilion in the grounds of the Château de Val Duchesse.

announcement that he was going to hand in the Parliament port-folio. He might have told me beforehand, but that was as nothing compared with the relief that he had vacated this now important job which we had reluctantly given him in 1977, and which was not at all his *métier*. A few other sensible decisions were made, such as that Commissioners should have their individual names on replies to written questions. What had hitherto been the practice was that they were just answered in the name of the Commission and that what was everybody's responsibility became nobody's responsibility, except that of the rather insensitive *services*.

The evening was taken up with the visit of President Senghor of Senegal: a substantial meeting and then a Val Duchesse dinner for him and his wife, with no speeches at his special request. I found him agreeable, sensible, very moderate on Rhodesian questions, but perhaps not quite so interesting as in Senegal four months before.

SATURDAY, 16 JUNE. *Brussels and the Somme.*

An expedition to the battlefields of the Somme with Jakie Astors. We met them for lunch at Roye just off the Paris motorway. In the afternoon we drove around the huge Lutyens memorial and then a Canadian memorial, with a lot of remains of trenches, but half grown over so that they looked (the shell holes in particular) almost like bunkers in a well-kept golf course. Then we went through Albert and had a remarkable view across country to Amiens Cathedral about twenty miles away – at least as good a view as that of Chartres across the Beauce. Stayed in an hotel near Compiègne.

MONDAY, 18 JUNE. *Brussels.*

I began to deal with the question of Burke's replacement as Commissioner responsible for relations with the Parliament. In view of the composition of the new Parliament it clearly had to be, in the currently developing jargon, a centre-right Commissioner, i.e. it would not be sensible to appoint a Socialist, and this meant that there were only three possibilities: Natali, who was probably the most obvious one, apart from linguistic difficulties; Davignon, who was very heavily charged already, but manifestly capable of doing this or any other job; and Tugendhat, who had the disadvantage of being the same nationality as me, but the advantage of being already linked with the Parliament owing to his budget responsibilities.

I had a sneaking fear that Natali would be too nervous of the Parliament, as he had somewhat illustrated by his behaviour in the budget crisis in the spring; and that with his pessimistic and worried, though extremely agreeable, general demeanour he might keep us all in a constant state of apprehensive gloom. I decided therefore to have Davignon in and sound him out. He immediately announced that he was against Natali for much the same reasons that had caused me to hesitate, that his candidate was Tugendhat, but, when asked by me, agreed that he might do it himself.

TUESDAY, 19 JUNE. *Brussels.*

Interviews for *Die Welt* and the Kyoto (Japanese) News Service. Vredeling to a fence-mending lunch at home alone, as I had been told that he was feeling rather miserable and neglected. He wasn't disagreeable and talked quite interestingly on one or two points. Then I saw Ortoli to talk to him about the Commissioner for the Parliament. He was in favour of Natali, but when I told him Davignon might do it, thought that Davignon would be even better, but said he would be perfectly happy with either of them. He was against Tugendhat.

I next saw the oddly named Eddie Mirzoeff from the BBC, who turned out to be extremely nice, to discuss, a long time in advance, arrangements for my November Dimbleby Lecture. Dined at Léon Lambert's, a big dinner of farewell for General Haig. I had quite a long post-dinner talk with Haig. He is clearly still harbouring high political ambitions. He is rather in favour of a German as Secretary-General of NATO when Luns goes, though he thinks this will not be soon. He was not against an Englishman, but certainly not in favour of any Englishman. I don't think Ian Gilmour's kind idea of Mulley* would run with him.

---

*Fred Mulley, b. 1918, cr. Lord Mulley 1984, was Secretary of State for Education 1975–6, and for Defence 1976–9.

WEDNESDAY, 20 JUNE. *Brussels.*

I saw Natali before the Commission. I had a perfectly agreeable conversation with him. He clearly wants the Parliament job. I told him that I wasn't sure he wasn't too busy what with enlargement and his need to travel to Italy a great deal, and that Davignon was a possibility and I was hovering between the two and hadn't made up my mind. He took this quite well, though obviously a bit disappointed.

The morning Commission meeting was extremely difficult at the end because of the question of the United Kingdom/Australia uranium agreement. Last July the British Labour Government had submitted to us the terms of such an agreement which were unacceptable in a number of ways. Brunner had written to them pointing out these objections, which they had dealt with by modification. They had therefore come back to us expecting (Maitland particularly) a clear run through. However, in view of a Court judgement having intervened, we did not think we could endorse even their modified agreement without risking the Commission position falling apart, unless they were willing to put a time limitation on it. Crispin was extremely keen on forcing this, and very courageously keen, as the British – and in particular UKREP*– were very hot on the issue and blaming him for the hold-up.

In the Commission itself Davignon argued strongly in favour of the time-break clause; Tugendhat argued in favour of the British position and was supported by Brunner, who gives way to everybody but who is the responsible Commissioner; and Ortoli, no doubt on French grounds, was in that direction too. Therefore it was extremely difficult to hold the position, but I just succeeded in doing so, saying that I would have a hard go at negotiating the break clause with the British Government, which I thought there was a chance of doing provided there was no leak of the split position in the Commission. (Needless to say this was a slightly overoptimistic hope, though in fact no leak appeared in the press, but it certainly got back to UKREP.)

Home late for lunch with Nicko Henderson on a pre-Washington briefing visit to Brussels, with, rather ironically, two of my pro-

*Neologism for British Permanent Representation to the Community.

British Government adversaries of the morning, Brunner and Tugendhat. Nicko was informed and a little probing, but frustrated by me.

Back to the office to receive a portentous telephone call from President Murphy of the *Cour des Comptes*, telling me that the dreaded report was ready and that he was willing to come to Brussels, either on the Thursday, Friday or the following Monday, secretly but ceremoniously to hand a copy over, and indicating that it was going to be pretty tiresome. 'The press will have a field day,' he said lugubriously. I arranged for him to come on Monday.

I then saw Nicoll of the UK Representation, Maitland already having gone to Strasbourg for the European Council, and made a little statement to him following the Commission meeting, which he received disappointedly.

THURSDAY, 21 JUNE. *Brussels and Strasbourg.*

Avion taxi to Strasbourg accompanied by Ortoli, etc. Then to the Terminus-Grüber Hotel opposite the station, where the French Government had put us up. It was said to be a resort of ill repute but in fact turned out to be an improvement on the Sofitel.*

Giscard gave us lunch at the Préfecture. I was placed, surprisingly, between Peter Carrington and Mrs Thatcher, Giscard no doubt thinking it was good to have all the English cuckoos in the same nest, but it was amazing that at her first European Council he didn't have her next to him. Peter Carrington started by saying, 'I am very angry with you.' I said, 'Oh, yes, I suppose it is about UK/Australia, but you certainly should not be angry as there is no reason at all why you shouldn't agree to what we want.' He then made no pretence of being seriously angry and listened to what I had to say without I think knowing much about it.

Mrs Thatcher didn't mention it. She, however, was quite chatty at lunch and concerned as to how she should open up the budget contribution question and eager to have it first in the afternoon, which apparently she had just more or less arranged with Giscard. I told her that this was a mistake. She must have it the first day, certainly, but to start on it cold was not in my view right. However, she had arranged it on the agenda, so I supposed it had to be done.

* So much so that we changed from the Sofitel to the Terminus-Grüber for the subsequent eighteen months of our visits to Strasbourg.

After lunch Giscard suddenly announced that the Foreign Ministers would go off somewhere or other, but the heads of government
and me (at least I presumed I was included) were to do a walk round
the old part of Strasbourg. This we proceeded to do in extremely
chaotic fashion for an excessive time. It lasted twenty-five minutes
in a temperature of well over 80°F and a great deal of pushing and
shoving. Giscard, Mrs Thatcher and Schmidt were in the front row,
the rest of us in the second or third rows; it was not agreeable but
mildly amusing. I was told subsequently that Giscard decided on it
at short notice because he thought Mrs Thatcher might do a walk-
about on her own – perhaps he was confusing her with the Queen.

Then four hours of session in a good room at the Mairie – not
quite as good as the Bremen Rathaus room but, that apart, the best
we have had. Giscard did not give Mrs Thatcher a chance to open, as
she thought he had said he would. I think she was lucky, but she
subsequently thought he had cheated her.

The first item of substance was a report from the Governor of the
Bank of France, Clappier, on the working of the EMS, a neutral,
reasonably optimistic report. A brief discussion on that in which
Mrs Thatcher announced that they would be making deposits
(which she expected to have a better effect than it did) and I
suggested that we ought to have a serious discussion at Dublin with
a view to moving on to the European Monetary Fund, but Giscard
indicated that he thought this too early.

Eventually we got on to the convergence/budgetary issue, which
he asked me to open. I did so, moving fairly rapidly on to the
budgetary aspect of convergence and putting the matter in a
reasonably but I hope not excessively pro-British way. Mrs
Thatcher, who I thought had been quite good in her previous
interventions, immediately became shrill, and even more so in her
quickly following second intervention. The prospect began to look
distinctly uncertain, as Giscard was wavering, and van Agt,
Jørgensen, and indeed Lynch were back-pedalling and asking only
for a study to be made, i.e. no proposals requested from the
Commission.

Mrs Thatcher meanwhile had got into an argument with
Schmidt, which was silly as he was absolutely crucial to her getting
the result that she wanted. She also had circulated bits of paper
which looked as though they had come from the Commission;

indeed she said they were Commission figures, but I had firmly to deny responsibility for having put them around, as although I thought they were broadly correct I was not going to be cross-examined on them, which Schmidt showed a certain tendency to do. When Mrs Thatcher tried to intervene for a third time, I had to stop her by intervening myself instead (which she accepted fairly graciously) and proposing the solution which was eventually accepted, that we should go to the Ecofin Council with a neutral statement of the facts, and then, not waiting for their authority, prepare a programme of remedies to present to the next European Council. She accepted this gratefully and graciously as indeed she should have done. It was not a bad afternoon and, on balance, not a bad performance on her part, except for this one fairly major tactical mistake on what was, after all, much the most important subject for her.

Dinner on an immensely hot evening at the Château de Rohan. Before dinner there was a typical little Giscard ploy. In the afternoon he had announced that he was giving *écus* to everybody, adding, with the unintentional bad manners which are curiously natural to him, that there were gold ones for the heads of government and silver ones for the Foreign Ministers, but believing that he had balanced it by saying this was merely an indication of French attachment to bimetallism. Therefore, there was a certain amount of doubt as to which I would get. However, he advanced upon Schmidt and me before dinner, with two golden *écus* in boxes in his hand, presented one to Schmidt and then presented the other to me, saying, 'Ah, but Monsieur Jenkins, there is just one difficulty: yours is not inscribed. If therefore you will let me have it back, I will have it appropriately inscribed and sent to you as soon as possible.' I suppose he could not decide until the last minute whether I was to get a gold or a silver one!

The dinner was rather grandly done. A beautiful room with everything manifestly brought down from the Elysée – plates, wine, not food I presume, but chefs certainly – and typical Giscard elaboration. There was fairly desultory foreign affairs conversation at dinner. Mrs Thatcher, still more surprisingly again not placed next to Giscard, did rather well on Rhodesia. Talk after dinner about China, Euro/Arab dialogue and one or two other subjects, but nothing very conclusive.

FRIDAY, 22 JUNE. *Strasbourg and Brussels.*

Three-hour European Council session in the morning on a variety of subjects – the communiqué obviously, relations with Japan, our paper for the 1990s, on which I opened with a statement about demographic changes and the speed of advance of high technology in Japan and the United States and the danger of our being left behind and uncomfortably squeezed in the middle.

There remained the question of the press conference, following Giscard's embarrassed *dictat* at our meeting in Paris two weeks before. However, when I asked what time he was going to start it, he asked if I intended to make a statement, and I said, 'Yes, indeed, but it is not finally prepared. However, I will be quite happy to show it to you before we go in.' He then said, 'What I think we will do is this (it is a slight modification): I will make my statement and answer any questions to me. Then I will stay for your statement and if there are any questions for you afterwards I will leave at that stage.' A ludicrous finessing, but I suppose a mild improvement.

In fact, everything passed off perfectly smoothly. So a ridiculous but potentially nasty corner was turned not too unsatisfactorily. He and I parted on surprisingly good terms for once, saying that we looked forward to seeing each other in Tokyo.

Back to the Berlaymont at 5 o'clock, where the report of the *Cour des Comptes* had arrived. I had changed my plan and got Murphy to deliver it by special messenger, as I thought it was a mistake to be waiting for it all over the weekend. I had read it by about 6 o'clock. It was not a very good report. The first part, written in English on *frais de représentation*, was better and fairer than the second part, written in French, on *frais de mission*. The general impression was neither very good nor very bad.

MONDAY, 25 JUNE. *Brussels and Anchorage.*

At 11.00 I saw Murphy of the *Cour des Comptes*, he anxious to be friendly, I rather chilly and pointing out what I thought were the weaknesses of his report. A little feeder plane at 2.10 from Zaventem up to Amsterdam for the 4.15 JAL plane for Anchorage and Tokyo. The dismal weather of the Low Countries persisted the whole way, giving the impression of a world almost totally enshrouded in cloud. However, a relatively comfortable journey because of the good and comfortable sleeping berths which JAL had made out of the hump of the jumbo.

TUESDAY, 26 JUNE. *Tokyo.*

Tokyo at 4.30 in the afternoon (9.30 a.m. Brussels time). Helicopted in to within half a mile of the New Otani Hotel. The security precautions were prodigious. The Japanese had virtually closed down a sector of the city about the size and nature of that from Hyde Park Corner to Kensington High Street. We had to enter the hotel through the older part and walk through an immensely long arcade of about 250 yards, with shops on either side and a hundred or so guards, a lot of them female, standing silently with their backs to us the whole way along. This was quite apart from the posse of ten or twelve armed policemen who accompanied us.

I was installed in a large suite on the thirty-eighth floor, with a considerable view over a large part of the city, and surrounded by the rooms of the rest of our party which filled that antenna of the hotel. The *Cour des Comptes* would not have liked it, had the Japanese not been paying, but what else we could have done, even if they were not, I do not know. Despite cloud and rain the temperature was around 90° (a weather combination about as unpleasant as possible) but the air conditioning was quite good.

WEDNESDAY, 27 JUNE. *Tokyo.*

At 11.00 I went to see Ohira, the Japanese Prime Minister, almost the only time we went out of the hotel during that long dismal day of waiting. A moderately useful conversation with rather stately consecutive translation. The Japanese briefing after this meeting, I think unintentionally, was rather tiresome, as it indicated that I had said (which indeed was a phrase I did use) that the European oil import target was not a *fait accompli* – i.e. it depended upon what others would do – whereas they interpreted it as meaning that it was something which was not firm. However, this caused only a mild ripple in (typically) the French press, but not more than that.

Back in the hotel I went down one floor to see Joe Clark, the new Canadian Prime Minister, before lunch. I had met him twice before. He had been to call on me in London in 1976 and had sat next to me at the Governor-General's lunch in Ottawa in 1978. I had found him quite good in London, rather unimpressive in Ottawa, but now on this third occasion better than I expected: fluent, seemed in reasonable command of himself and fairly firm in what he wanted. He was anxious to be friendly to the Community, but did not dissimulate when I raised with him the question of ordering the Airbus and said (1) that they had a firm policy of not interfering with state corporations, and (2) they were pretty sure that Air Canada was going to buy Boeing.

At 6.30 James Schlesinger (US Energy Secretary), Cooper, and Henry Owen came to see me. By this time I was in a fairly bad temper, partly through having spent the whole day incarcerated in the hotel and partly because it had become by then abundantly clear that Giscard was not going to relent and ask me to the European dinner which he had organized for Mrs Thatcher, Andreotti and Schmidt that evening. It was a silly discourtesy as it made it extremely difficult for me to know what was going on in the European camp, and indeed caused mild irritation amongst all the others.

I therefore worked off a certain amount of my bad temper on these three Americans, Schlesinger in particular deserving it as he talked a great deal of nonsense, appealing for sympathy because American indigenous oil was becoming exhausted as they had used it up so fast in order to help Britain during the war. 'Oh, God,' I said, 'surely we don't have to have that "blood on the oil" history at this stage? I can't attach a different moral value to one barrel of oil than another.' He looked mildly shocked by this, but came off his line very quickly, and, indeed, we were told subsequently that this meeting had led to their going back to Carter saying that the Americans must be more forthcoming than they had hitherto intended to be. So bad temper for once brought some benefit.

Crispin went to dinner with some of his Summit 'sherpas' and I rather gloomily and uselessly went to a restaurant with Audland and Fielding.* Returning, I met Schmidt at the beginning of the long corridor and had about ten minutes' talk with him. He seemed rather fed up with the European dinner, and implied it had been useless, which was a slight comfort.

* (Sir) Leslie Fielding, b. 1932, was then head of the Commission Delegation in Japan and is now Vice-Chancellor of Sussex University.

THURSDAY, 28 JUNE. *Tokyo.*

Up at 6.15, last-minute work on Summit papers, but diverted by Mount Fuji, which for the first and only time during our visit suddenly came up clear on the horizon for about an hour and then disappeared again. Then to the first session of the Summit, which started at 9.45. The session took a rather extraordinary form. Ohira opened with a brief statement, outlined a sort of agenda, and then asked if we would like to go round the table on the agenda, with five-minute statements. Carter spoke for about five minutes, Giscard spoke for about five minutes, Andreotti spoke for about four, Mrs Thatcher spoke for about ten. Schmidt then spoke much along the lines he did in Strasbourg, quite well, but for twenty-five minutes. Then Clark, then me, also for about ten minutes, doing a review of how things had gone in a variety of fields since Bonn, and coming on to specific energy points at the end.

Ohira made a few remarks himself and then said he thought we ought to adjourn for coffee, which amazed everybody as it is not the practice and we had only been going for at most one and a quarter hours. The coffee break took a good forty minutes and when we reassembled he said, 'At this point on the agenda we are supposed to discuss the macroeconomic situation, but it seems to me that that was covered to a substantial extent earlier this morning. Collaborators are not yet quite ready with the communiqué on energy, so it is rather difficult to know what we should do.'

Mrs Thatcher then said she would like to make a few remarks on inflation, and made them quite well, saying that she was against it and announcing that Keynes was out of date. Schmidt then agreed with Mrs Thatcher in substance but sprang to the defence of Keynes, saying it was not Keynes who was out of date but Keyn*en*sianism as he rather curiously called it. There then followed a slightly academic exchange of views between Giscard, Schmidt and me about the extent to which Keynes would be a Keynesian today, followed by a point of mine, which Mrs Thatcher took up, about it being desirable to have a price index which excluded energy price increases, otherwise trying to restrain inflation and trying to restrain energy consumption ran head-on into each other.

When we came to the end of this somewhat desultory conversation, at 12.10 exactly, Ohira said, 'Lunch is at 1 o'clock and I think perhaps we all need some rest before that, so I suggest we now adjourn and assemble for the photograph at 12.45.' This we proceeded to do, totally at variance with previous Summit practice which is to go on talking and talking and always adjourning late, and obviously rather to the displeasure of those who particularly like talking. Nobody tried to prevent my being photographed with the heads of government, although Giscard looked slightly baleful. Perhaps that particular aspect of the comedy is behind us – but not others.

I lunched with the Finance Ministers. The heads of government were in the same room, but stayed on at their table, so that the session did not resume until 4.15. This led to a considerable cock-up as it was not at all clear what they had been agreeing to or not agreeing to over the luncheon period. Giscard, to the annoyance of Mrs Thatcher, the embarrassment of Andreotti, and indeed I think even the mild irritation of Schmidt, had propounded – which the Americans and the Japanese wanted – individual European country targets within the total of 470 million tonnes for the Community as a whole,* provided the Americans would make some unspecified concession. But nobody seemed quite clear exactly where we were and Giscard indeed at one stage, as became apparent during the afternoon session, had been prepared to agree with the Americans that a 1979, instead of a 1978, base should be taken. This would have been disastrous for the Community, for whereas we were just on the 470 million tonnes in 1978, we might be as low as 425 million in 1979, and would therefore either have a figure which we could not hold until 1985, or we would be in the ludicrous position of having to import oil we did not need during the second six months of 1979 in order to preserve a statistical base.

On these sorts of points we negotiated, not very successfully – the meeting at times breaking down rather like the merry-go-round in *La Ronde* – for several hours. It wasn't really a discussion session but a sort of negotiating conference on figures in the communiqué, with it not being clear from time to time whether we were in session or not. There was a general impression of mild chaos amongst the Europeans because, despite our firm overall Community position,

*I.e. they wanted to have a German, French, Italian etc. figure for oil imports in the communiqué and thus be able to complain to an individual government if it was over its level, whereas we wanted to keep room for *virement* within the Community.

it was not remotely clear what hand Giscard (as the President-in-office of the European Council) was playing, though it was certainly not a Community hand or, indeed, a very effective hand at all.

Giscard, in my perhaps prejudiced view, was on notably unimpressive form throughout this Summit. I think it was because he was not treated as the belle of the ball. The Japanese made a considerable fuss of everybody, including me, of whom in all their papers (which had vast supplements about the Summit) they had a full biography, just as with the heads of government. But amongst the heads of government Carter was the most important one to the Japanese, because when they think of a President of another country, they think of the President of the United States as being, as it were, their President. Also, he had been paying a three-day state visit and got a lot of publicity from this. Next, insofar as there was an individual who aroused particular curiosity, it was Mrs Thatcher, because she was new and a woman. And third, insofar as the Japanese think of a European country with which for a mixture of good and bad reasons they feel affinity, it is Germany, and therefore Schmidt was at least as big as, probably a bigger figure in their eyes than Giscard. Giscard therefore ended up only about number four, not really much more prominent than Andreotti, Joe Clark or me, which isn't at all what he likes.

Schmidt got increasingly impatient and bored throughout the proceedings, partly because when Giscard behaves badly Schmidt switches off, rather like a husband who pretends not to notice if his wife gets drunk, and partly because he was frustrated by not being able to make his long quasi-philosophical *tours d'horizon*.

Carter was subdued, spoke very quietly, not a great deal, but when he had to speak did so quite effectively and did not seem jumpy or on edge: diminished but not neurotic was how I would describe the general impression he made. Ohira, partly but only partly for language reasons, was an appalling chairman. The Japanese just don't think in terms of the normal discussion meetings of which we are so fond, they don't like rambling around the intellectual horizons themselves and probably don't therefore see why anyone else should do it; and they may be right. However, his chairmanship was sufficiently bad that I think even he noticed it, and indeed at the end he apologized, as the translator put it, 'for my inadvertent chairmanship'.

One advantage of his 'inadvertent chairmanship' was that the sessions were mercifully short. We were back in the hotel by 6.30, despite the fact that I had been held up for a few minutes by having to walk out to her car with my new friend Mrs Thatcher, who asked if I was leaving and hoped we could leave together in order to protect her I think from being surrounded by the press to whom, quite sensibly, she didn't want to give 'on the hoof' conferences. She had done quite well during the afternoon, though she was expressing considerable impatience with the form of the meeting and, in particular, with Giscard's performance.

Then we had the Emperor's dinner at the Imperial Palace. Here again, so far as I was concerned, there was Giscard-ordained segregation. In other words the heads of government were received by the Emperor and the other members of the Royal Family in one room and then came and joined the Foreign Ministers, the Finance Ministers and me after about twenty minutes. However, whether accidentally or not, the Emperor frustrated this by sending the Court Chamberlain to bring me up to him and I had a good ten minutes of imperial conversation before we went into dinner. As in 1977, I quite enjoyed talking to him. It is done through an interpreter but it is about quite serious subjects, about Japan in a sort of socio-geographical sense, and he is serious, well-informed and reasonably easy.

I also had a rather good *place à table* at dinner, between the wife of the Emperor's younger brother, who looked rather younger than she could have been as she had stayed at Buckingham Palace under King George V on her honeymoon in 1931, and a former Prime Minister, who was curiously interested in what one might call English Gaitskellian politics, had known Hugh well and indeed Tony Crosland also.

FRIDAY, 29 JUNE. *Tokyo.*

A morning session from 9.50 until 12.10 once again mainly negotiations on the communiqué and particularly on the energy parts of it. Then an hour's pause before lunch, during which I asked François-Poncet to come and see me, because I had been worried by a development at the end of the morning in which Carter led Schmidt off into the idea of putting in some denunciatory stuff about OPEC in the communiqué. While not against denouncing OPEC, I wasn't keen for us all to get hooked on a Carter line hoist largely for internal American political reasons (as subsequently emerged very clearly) and to have it done rather hot-headedly – and Schmidt was certainly in a hot-headed mood by this time – in a heads of government drafting session, which is never a good recipe for good sense.

A final afternoon session for an hour and a half. The difficulty at this stage was that Andreotti was insisting very firmly and pertinaciously that the Italians would only accept a country target (rather like the Japanese who were in the same position) if it was made so loose as to be almost meaningless. In other words, he wanted a footnote saying that it was all to be seen within the context of the Community target. In the circumstances Mrs Thatcher came in and said wasn't it much better if we just all jointly stuck to the Community target, and I supported her on this. It would in fact have suited Schmidt much better too, but he was leaning back. Then Giscard intervened, very bad-temperedly; whether against Mrs Thatcher or me, or both of us, was not absolutely clear saying, 'No, this is an intolerable going back on what we had decided hitherto,' etc. He then moved round the table to talk to Andreotti. I had a draft to offer and, irritated by Giscard, firmly refused to go on talking until he had gone back to his place and was prepared to listen. Mrs Thatcher was much shocked by his display of bad manners and bad temper, I less so.

Ohira announced that at the press conference there would be no questions but statements from everybody, including me. So I had progressed from sitting at the press conference with no microphone in London, to sitting silent at the press conference with a microphone in Bonn, to sitting at the press conference with a microphone and being allowed to make a statement at Tokyo!

Most of the statements were very bad. Probably Mrs Thatcher's was the best, although she rather tailed off. I at least was short. Giscard and Schmidt were both notably bad, Schmidt just seeming bored. Then I did my own press conference (as did the others) from 6.30 to 7.00, with I suppose about 150 pressmen present, as opposed to the thousand or so we had had for the general occasion, and answered a few questions.

We could not helicopt to the airport as it was after dark, so we were driven out to the old airport about ten miles away, put on a special plane and flown round for forty minutes until we landed at the new airport, a most remarkable performance between what were alleged to be airports for the same city. The JAL plane was in the air at 9.45, and I managed to arrange that on this journey I should not be brought downstairs at Anchorage. Needless to say, however, I awoke at Anchorage where, mysteriously, it was 10.30 in the morning on Friday the 29th, the day on the evening of which we had left Tokyo, and for once the sun was shining.

SATURDAY, 30 JUNE. *Anchorage and East Hendred.*

London at 6.00 in the morning (3 p.m. Japanese time) and East Hendred at 7.15. Began early telephoning of the Little Five: first, Thorn, then van der Klaauw (van Agt being characteristically away on a bicycle tour), then the Taoiseach, Jack Lynch. Later that morning I got Martens, the Belgian Prime Minister, but failed to get the Danes until Monday. I think this is a worthwhile exercise.

Jennifer and I went to lunch with Ann (Fleming) at Sevenhampton where there was a large party composed of, amongst others, Mark Boxer,* Katie Asquith,† the Levers, Patrick Trevor-Roper,‡ etc.

TUESDAY, 3 JULY. *Brussels.*

Saw Tugendhat at 10.30, he anxious to lobby hard for Natali as the parliamentary Commissioner. He was not anxious to do it himself, but would much prefer Natali to Davignon, and argued persuasively, indeed I think decisively, in favour of this course.

After the annual *cabinet* luncheon at rue de Praetère. I returned to the office to see Davignon, having made up my mind over lunch, and to tell him that it was to be Natali and not him, which he took thoroughly well. At 7.45 I was warned that Mrs Thatcher wished to talk to me on the telephone and Crispin came around in order to help deal with that. It was about the UK/Euratom arrangement and, without too much difficulty, I was able to negotiate a satis-

---

* Mark Boxer, 1931–88, cartoonist (Marc), and editor of the *Tatler* from 1983.
† Lady Katherine Asquith, b. 1949, is the great granddaughter of the Liberal Prime Minister.
‡ Patrick Trevor-Roper, b. 1916, is an ophthalmic surgeon and author.

factory settlement with her. She is fairly crisp at negotiating, but perfectly sensible. She also, I think slightly prompted by Woodrow (Wyatt), who had been trying to organize a meal at his house, asked me if I would come to Chequers for a quiet dinner to talk about European Councils, Summits, etc.

WEDNESDAY, 4 JULY. *Brussels.*

I told Natali he was to get the Parliament job, which he accepted with pleasure but not ecstasy. The Commission received it at least as enthusiastically as he did, but even more so the news of our settlement with the British, which was received with almost incredulous pleasure. I telephoned Colombo (President of the Parliament) about the wretched *Cour des Comptes* report, finding him as agreeable as usual but extremely vague as to what ought or ought not to be done about it.

To the Château de la Hulpe, which I had decided upon for the change of presidency dinner (essential to change the scene if you can't change the cast). My speech about the French presidency was based upon a rather elaborate comparison with a bottle of Château Lafite 1897, given me by my Bristol wine merchant, which I had approached with a mixture of respect, apprehension and anticipation. When my son Charles, with whom I had shared it, asked me the next day what I had thought of it, I had said, 'Very remarkable, but one wouldn't want to drink it every day, would one.' This was received just tolerably by the French, well by the others.

THURSDAY, 5 JULY. *Brussels.*

A visit from the President of Colombia, the impressively named Julio Cesar Turbay. I had a not very satisfactory quarter of an hour with him in my office, mainly because he was interested in trying to draft a communiqué, to which they attached particular importance; we don't normally have them for such meetings. Then a rather more successful Commission meeting with him for one and a quarter hours, and afterwards a very successful lunch, when he proved to be a solid, interesting, agreeable man, who sat back in a most curious way from the table to eat – about two feet away from it – but this was a minor idiosyncrasy.

SATURDAY, 7 JULY. *East Hendred.*

At 10.15 we left for Reading, for an honorary degree ceremony. No speech was required, therefore a restful occasion. The large audience received me with apparent enthusiasm. (Perhaps they hoped I would provide the university with some Community money, but that is an ungrateful thought.) Roger Sherfield was the Chancellor and I enjoyed talking to him at lunch, I had previously and mistakenly thought him unforthcoming.

MONDAY, 9 JULY. *Brussels.*

A call from Lamb of the US Mission (Deane Hinton being in Washington). He, we had been warned, was coming in under instructions to ask exactly what we thought the country targets accepted at Tokyo meant, in particular in the case of Germany, and, indeed, whether it included North Sea oil, or whether it was only imports from third countries. Our view was that it was only imports from third countries, but there seemed some confusion between the French and the German positions on this, another indication of the way that Giscard had slightly cocked things up at Tokyo and Schmidt had allowed him to get away with it. However, our line with the United States was perfectly clear. We could only speak on the Community target as a whole. This applied to imports from third countries only, in other words it did not include North Sea oil (any more than their imports included Alaskan oil), but that so far as the individual country targets were concerned, queries on these points should be addressed to the individual governments. This was a perfectly tenable line and one which Lamb both expected and accepted.

TUESDAY, 10 JULY. *Brussels.*

A meeting lasting about an hour with Plaja, Nanteuil and Murphy, the second man in the Irish Permanent Representation (Dillon being away). I decided to have them in as representatives of the present, past and future presidency of COREPER, because there had been several signs of growing morosity on the part of COREPER, several reports of mutterings at meetings about things the

Commission had or hadn't done. Certainly while I had been away in Japan the Commission had made a cock-up of the *agrément* to a new Greek Ambassador and future Permanent Representative, and some people in the Commission – Haferkamp, Natali, Cheysson (a curious mixture) – had been in favour of refusing *agrément*, which we had never done before. The man concerned (Roussos)* had apparently been in Brussels under the Colonels, but he had been serving successfully and satisfactorily as Ambassador in London for the past three or four years, and it seemed to me that if Karamanlis was satisfied with his record under the Colonels, there was no reason why we should not be.

THURSDAY, 12 JULY. *Brussels, Cardiff and East Hendred.*

To Cardiff for the UWIST degree day ceremony. A most beautiful morning, quite nice in Brussels and spectacular in England. The drive across the Downs and then on through Gloucestershire and Monmouthshire was as beautiful as anything I had seen for a long time. It was even high tide in the Severn, which seems rare.

Two one-and-a-half-hour degree-giving sessions, interspersed with Principal Trotman-Dickenson's lunch party. Then to the Angel Hotel, where, after a certain amount of sweaty preparation, I did a thirty-minute interview for BBC Wales with Vincent Kane, with whom I had done things in Luxembourg and Strasbourg and think rather good.

To the City Hall for the Welsh Development Corporation dinner, a huge gathering of nearly five hundred. Thirty-five minutes from me (broadcast live by Radio Wales) and then the new Secretary of State for Wales (Nicholas Edwards) made a surprisingly partisan speech, although in quite a good voice.

SATURDAY, 14 JULY. *East Hendred.*

Lunch at Buscot Parsonage with Diana Phipps, who had George Weidenfeld and the Charlie Douglas-Homes.

Drove myself to Chequers (where I hadn't been for several years) for the Thatcher dinner engagement mentioned by her on the

---

* Stavros Roussos, b. 1918, was Ambassador to London 1974–9, and became Secretary-General of the Greek Foreign Ministry 1980–2.

telephone and surprisingly vigorously followed up. I was greeted by Denis Thatcher and led into the medium-sized sitting room on the ground floor, where the Prime Minister and Woodrow (Wyatt) were already deep in conversation. I had no idea who was going to be there, but apparently she had settled for this odd quartet.

Perfectly agreeable general conversation before an early dinner at a small table in the window of the big dining room. Quite a good meal, and interesting enough political conversation. Towards the end of dinner we began to get into the middle of things. Hitherto we had been talking principally about what she thought of Strasbourg and Tokyo, to which the answer was not much: she had thought a lot of Schmidt on both occasions and very little of Giscard, whom she thought petulant, vain and rather ill-mannered. I told her that she had seen him at his worst, certainly at Tokyo, and when all was said and done, although she was right in a lot of her complaints, the good side was substantially greater than she allowed for, for he was highly intelligent, on the whole his policies went in the right direction and on the whole they did so effectively; and that, therefore, one ought (although my instincts were often very much like hers for he could be absolutely maddening) to try to suppress these feelings, and realize there was a good deal to put in the credit balance. It was a pity, though, that he spoilt such a large credit balance by these rather silly – but nonetheless deep – fissures of character. She seemed willing to agree with this.

At any rate, somebody – Woodrow or her – said, towards the end of dinner, arising out of something I had said, 'How do you think the British hand should be played *vis-à-vis* Giscard, Schmidt and the others?' I replied, 'Well, that is rather a big question which I would prefer to open up on, not just as we are leaving the table, but when we settle down afterwards.' Whether or not she took this as a suggestion that I wanted to talk to her alone, I don't know, but she then said, 'Ah, well, let Roy and me go off and have twenty minutes alone, while you, Woodrow, have coffee with Denis.' And so we separated.

The twenty minutes almost inevitably multiplied itself by four, during which I expounded to her my view that, without in any way wishing to encourage bad Franco/German relations (good Franco/German relations being essential for Europe) we should nonetheless endeavour to break up the endless exhibition waltz between

Schmidt and Giscard which had been going on for too long, and which left the Little Five, and indeed Italy as well, as rather bored wallflowers sitting at the edge of the room. The conversation obviously wasn't only this, but this was a central part of it.

She then collected the other two from the terrace and we all four talked for another hour. This last part of the conversation was largely politico-industrial gossip, whom she might get to run various things, etc., all fairly indiscreetly done. Some of her ideas were pretty silly (some of the silly ones encouraged by Woodrow) though not all of them. She wanted to get rid of Villiers from the British Steel Corporation, which may well be right; but she also wanted to get rid of Ezra from the Coal Board, which would be a great mistake. She was also rather keen to get a job for George Brown (she thought he was much younger than he is, for some reason) but, of all things, suggested making him chairman of the BBC, where she wanted somebody who would take a tougher line. Anything less suited to George, at this or indeed any stage of his career, I can hardly imagine. I felt in a slightly embarrassed position, because I did not want to do George down but I knew this would be hopeless for him, as the qualities it requires are steadiness and calm day-to-day judgement, which are exactly the qualities he does not possess. This is not incompatible with the fact that he has very good longer-term judgement. I tried to steer away by saying that he might be better at a more executive job.

I was struck throughout this conversation by three things: first, Woodrow is on very close terms with her, talks freely, easily, without self-consciousness, says anything he wants to; secondly, Denis Thatcher, while a caricature of himself in some ways, is not in the least afraid of her and talks a good deal. But he doesn't always talk foolishly, quite shrewd comments on the lines of 'Old JD of BP told me . . .' The self-caricature aspect came out even more strongly when he said goodbye to me on the steps and I noticed his somewhat notorious Rolls standing at the side of the courtyard and said, 'Ah, I see you've got your Rolls-Royce here.' 'Yes,' he said, 'I've got to give the old bus a spin from time to time. I know *she* doesn't like it very much, but the old cylinders you know get choked up if you don't give her a spin. Lovely bus, lovely bus. Mind you, that's a beautiful little Boche job you've got over there. I'd really rather have that; that's a real modern car.' Funny man.

Whether he is exactly out of his depth I don't know. He is his own man, I think. He remains a moderately prosperous suburban businessman, who is perfectly self-assured with her. Not an unfavourable impression at all.

The third thing that I retained from the conversation was that she talked extraordinarily freely, although she was only critical by implication of my particular Cabinet friends, Gilmour, Carrington, Whitelaw, because she pointedly left them out of a list of the sound men – Howe, Biffen, Joseph, Nott, and could there have been one other? – who were fighting tooth and nail on her side for public expenditure cuts. I left just before 11.00.

MONDAY, 16 JULY. *East Hendred, Brussels and Strasbourg*.

To Brussels in the morning and to Strasbourg in the evening with the prospect of meeting the new Parliament looming heavily.

Gave Willy Brandt a long enjoyable dinner alone. He was looking thin, almost young, slightly febrilely bright-eyed. I would be sceptical about his future health, but he is for the moment tremendously agreeable and easy to talk to, a good deal more so than he used to be when Chancellor. Not critical of Schmidt, except occasionally by implication, but not tremendously optimistic about the future of German politics. He didn't quite see where the leadership in the SPD was going and thought there was a slight tug to the right. He thought Apel probably the most likely successor. Schmidt thought Matthöfer possible, but he (Brandt) didn't think this remotely possible. Apel was not great but better than I thought he was. Dohnanyi was emerging as a faint possibility for the leadership, about which I expressed enthusiasm. He was encouraging about the work of the Commission. He agreed, under a little pressure from me, that he would stay and make a speech on Thursday.

TUESDAY, 17 JULY. *Strasbourg*.

A most gloomy, hot, sticky, dark day for the opening of the new Parliament. The *doyenne d'âge*, Mme Louise Weiss, aged eighty-six, Gaullist but before that a politician of the Third and Fourth Republics, delivered an extraordinary Gallic address of bidding, lasting a full hour, which was redolent of the spirit of Geneva in the thirties. The only appropriate person to have replied would have been Philip Noel-Baker, with whom no doubt she used to dance tangos on the terrace of the Beau Rivage c. 1932.* In a slightly ludicrous way, it was not a bad performance. The Parliament then adjourned in order to begin its various manoeuvres for the election of its President.

Just before 10 p.m. we heard that Mme Veil[†] had been elected on the second ballot, with only three votes to spare, and went back to the Parliament to hear her brief acceptance speech.

WEDNESDAY, 18 JULY. *Strasbourg*.

I made my formal speech to the new Parliament at 11.00. It lasted only fifteen minutes, had some rather good phrases, and particularly as it followed an extremely long and boring speech by Lynch, the Irish President-in-office of the European Council, went all right. Lunch at Valentin Sorg which Donald Maitland was giving for Soames, who had turned up in a silent but representational role for the British Government.

At 4.15 I paid a long formal call of congratulation upon Mme Veil. She was pleased to be elected, ill-informed about parliamentary and European affairs, agreeable, totally francophone. Afterwards I saw Russell Johnston,[‡] who had come on a protest mission from the British Liberals about their non-representation in the Parliament owing to the absence of proportional representation. I received him sympathetically.

THURSDAY, 19 JULY. *Strasbourg*.

I spent the morning in the Parliament supposedly for my speech of substance, but in fact the three hours were taken up with a procedural wrangle raised by Pannella[§] and his sidekick Signora

* Philip Noel-Baker, 1889–1982, cr. Lord Noel-Baker 1977, intermittently a Labour MP 1929–74, spent much time in Geneva on League of Nations business in the twenties and thirties (and was a great dancer).
† Simone Veil, b. 1927, French Minister of Health 1974–9, President of the European Parliament 1979–82.
‡ (Sir) Russell Johnston, b. 1932, has been Liberal MP for Inverness since 1964.
§ Giacinto Pannella, b. 1930, had founded the Movement for Civil Rights and Freedom 1974, member of the Camera dei Deputati 1976–86, MEP since 1979.

Bonino about the non-recognition of the ragbag of Italian Radicals, Franco-Bruxellois, and God knows who else he had put together. This was thought to be Parliament at its worst, but I didn't wholly think so. It was minorities asserting themselves (presenting Mme Veil with an initial taste of the problems of the presidency, which she did not handle particularly well), but was also Parliament behaving like a Parliament and therefore I wasn't wholly impatient that my speech and the others were held up until after lunch.

I eventually spoke from 4.25 until 4.50. I had to make a decision as to where to speak from. There was no rostrum on the first day. It had been installed on the second day and O'Kennedy (Irish Foreign Minister) automatically used it. I used to do so in the old Parliament when I was making a speech of importance. But I suddenly decided that it was better to be more part of the Parliament than the President of the Council of Ministers, and slightly to differentiate myself from this long drone from the rostrum, and therefore spoke from my place at the end of the first bench, which I think I shall stick to unless something very exceptional happens.

Brandt spoke immediately after me, a considerable oratorical performance, and one immediately had a real feeling of the value of the new Parliament. A speech could get a response from somebody of real significance in his own country and indeed in Europe as a whole. It was not like the previous Parliament where I felt that I was throwing words into a Chamber without an echo and where the most likely response was for little Fellermaier to get up and complain that the translation of my speech in Danish had not been circulated seventy-two hours beforehand.

FRIDAY, 20 JULY. *Strasbourg and Cardiff.*

I listened to Tugendhat's good opening of the budget debate, gave a radio interview for IRN, had a brief word with Barbara Castle,* and a talk with Ann Clwyd, a new Labour member. (The few Labour members seem much more agreeable than I expected.) I took an avion taxi back to Brussels and on by commercial flight to London

---

* Mrs Barbara Castle, b. 1910, was MP for Blackburn 1945–79 and a fellow member with me of both Wilson Cabinets. She had been elected an MEP in June 1979, and became leader of the Labour Group in Strasbourg.

for Cardiff, where I was due to speak at a University of Wales dinner before my honorary degree the following morning.

We drove the same route as eight days before, but in less good weather. I struggled into my dinner jacket in the back of the car and tried frantically to put a speech together. I was intimidated by the thought of speaking, unprepared and noteless, with my mind on other things, immediately before the Prince of Wales, who I had been surprised to be told was a spectacularly good after-dinner speaker. He had apparently done very well at a Royal Opera House dinner at the Guildhall.

A dinner of about sixty, after which Goronwy Daniel, the Principal of Aberystwyth and the current Vice-Chancellor of the university, made the first speech, and spoke extremely well, with a sense of timing worthy of a considerable actor. I then rose and said I was aware that I would have to speak before the Prince of Wales, who was one of the most accomplished after-dinner speakers, I was told, in England, but I did not realize that I would be sandwiched between him and a Vice-Chancellor who was undoubtedly the most accomplished after-dinner speaker in Wales. Then, for some reason or other, my speech rather took off, I got on to a vein of impromptu semi-jokes which couldn't go wrong, and bumbled on for about fifteen minutes with curious success.

This left the poor Prince with two difficult speeches to follow as well as my excessive and embarrassing tribute to him. He had a pedestrian little speech prepared for him, on which he improvised rather well. He is a nice young man and almost certainly the most intelligent male member of his family since Prince Albert.

SATURDAY, 21 JULY. *Cardiff and East Hendred.*

Three-mile walk before breakfast to visit Llandaff Cathedral. Then to the National Museum of Wales, where we saw the Rubens cartoons which they have just bought, and also the spectacular collection of Impressionists which the two Misses Davies of Gregynog left to them at varying stages in the forties and fifties. I suppose it was the first museum I ever visited, and I doubt if I had been in it since the thirties, so it was a nostalgic expedition.

Then a good ceremony with twelve honorands, Graham Suther-land the other principal non-local one. I talked to him a lot, and developed an ambitious if rash hope that he might be prepared to paint a portrait of me.* This Welsh expedition, though it fell too quickly after the previous one, was exceptionally enjoyable both for Jennifer and for me. I don't know quite why, but it was.

Back to East Hendred, where the Rodgers' arrived unexpectedly for a drink and stayed for a scratch dinner. We had a more agreeable and relaxed talk with them than we had had for a long time, and were extremely glad that they had come.

SUNDAY, 22 JULY. *East Hendred and Brussels.*

To Brussels in the late afternoon, where Crispin and I had Giscard's *trois sages,* Dell, Marjolin and Biesheuvel, to dinner, rue de Praetère. There has been a curious shift in the balance of power within the group since I saw them in January. Biesheuvel, the Dutchman, seems to me now the dominant figure, whereas Marjolin was so earlier. Dell has always been somewhat in the middle, a little detached, but quite sensible.

MONDAY, 23 JULY. *Brussels.*

Lunch at home for Michael O'Kennedy, the Irish Foreign Minister, plus two other Irish. I was rather sleepy for some reason or other, and O'Kennedy seemed to me less good, less on the ball than I had expected him to be. No doubt he was rather nervous about his first chairmanship.

Then no fewer than six ambassadors' credentials – all done in sixty-five minutes. Then an hour with Soutou, ex-permanent head of the Quai d'Orsay, who, most surprisingly for such a senior diplomat, didn't speak English.

Home early for my British dinner for Carrington, Ian (Gilmour), Peter Walker† and Maitland. Just after 8.00 I was sitting at my desk thinking happily that I had got another twenty-five minutes, when Peter Walker arrived, having been told rather typically by some foolish man at the Embassy that it took half an hour to get to the

---

*This hope was never put to the test, for he died six months later.
†Peter Walker, b. 1932, MP for Worcester since 1961, has held a wide variety of Cabinet posts in both the Heath and Thatcher Governments. He was Minister of Agriculture 1979–83.

house, whereas it only took five minutes. After momentary irritation I was quite glad to see him, as I had originally thought of offering him dinner alone. He has not got the hang of how to deal with the Agricultural Council yet, and he certainly hasn't appreciated Gundelach or got alongside him.

The dinner was a great success. Everybody seemed to enjoy it a lot, much of it was very funny, but also useful at the same time. I gave Peter C. a lecture after dinner, slightly along the lines I had given to Mrs Thatcher, but done in a more post-prandial tone, telling him that he really had an opportunity if he played his cards right to be the greatest Foreign Secretary since Canning, I first said, but then quickly corrected it to Bevin. I then went to the loo. Whereupon Carrington, forgetting that Crispin was there, jumped up in a great state of exhilarated excitement at my comparisons.

TUESDAY, 24 JULY. *Brussels.*

Nothing of interest in the Foreign Affairs Council, apart from tributes in his absence to François-Poncet's presidency. So I thought I had better strike a slightly different note, particularly as O'Kennedy had been far too apologetic about it not having been done in June, which I said was largely my responsibility, but it was three weeks before the end of the French presidency and I always took the view that it was a mistake to tip the waiter too generously before one had finished the meal. The British thought this very funny, and so I think did most others. The French didn't seem offended; perhaps François-Poncet would have been. I said quite a lot of nice things about him, including that he had shown great skill at untying knots. Some of his skill was of course both necessary and understandable, because he had tied up most of them himself. But apart from these few glancing remarks, there were a lot of thoroughly friendly ones, because I like François-Poncet, but believe increasingly in teasing the French which is not done enough in Europe.

WEDNESDAY, 25 JULY. *Brussels and London.*

After a long morning's Commission, I gave COREPER an end-of-term lunch. They didn't have much to say, but weren't in any way disagreeable. Afterwards I saw Ortoli, partly to tell him that I wasn't circulating the *Cour des Comptes* report as it looked as though there was a good chance it might hold without leaking until September, though one couldn't be sure, and it seemed better not to give the press a free run in the empty newspapers of August.

Then to London for the long-awaited holidays. Sense of relief slightly diminished by having invited thirty people to dinner at Brooks's. It's very nice having a party the evening of return, but a great deal nicer if other people give it.

However, it turned out well. We had a great rollcall of the establishment: Carringtons, Soames', Gilmours and Norman Stevas from the Government. Shirley, Rodgers', Levers, Thomsons from the Labour Party. David Steel, Hartwells, Zuckermans, Bonham Carters, Peter Jenkins', Rees-Moggs. I think that was about it. It all went agreeably well until about 12.15, when Brooks's slammed the door on us with great relief (I do not think Fox would have approved of this puritanical attitude to late hours).

THURSDAY, 26 JULY. *London.*

Dinner at the Other Club. Callaghan was there rather surprisingly, looking at bit inspissated, but I didn't have a chance to talk to him. I sat between Robert Armstrong, who was very nice about Hayden, and Prof. Trevor-Roper,* who has become a peer for some not very clear reason and for some still more obscure reason wishes to call himself Lord Dacre of something or other, which is running him into trouble, not surprisingly, with Rachel Home.† There were one or two others whom I would like to have talked to, notably Jeremy Hutchinson‡ and Garrett Drogheda.

---

*Professor Hugh Trevor-Roper, b. 1914, cr. Lord Dacre of Glanton 1979, was Regius Professor of Modern History at Oxford 1957–80, before becoming Master of Peterhouse, Cambridge, 1980–7.

†Mrs William Douglas-Home, b. 1929, following (at some delay) the death of her father who had been known by a higher title, emerged as the Baroness Dacre (27th in line) in 1970. She was not enthusiastic about sharing it with Professor Trevor-Roper nine years later.

‡Jeremy Hutchinson QC, b. 1915, famous defence counsel, had been created Lord Hutchinson of Lullington in 1978.

MONDAY, 30 JULY. *East Hendred.*

Annual *cabinet* day at East Hendred. It began with Manuel Santarelli (Perlot's deputy) ringing from Brussels in a great state because of some story in *Le Monde*. I didn't take it terribly seriously, but nonetheless it was mildly disturbing as he was so agitated. There was apparently a headline saying 'Drôle de Jeu de M. Jenkins'. It was all totally without foundation, a bit of French fantasy about the Euratom affair. Crispin dealt with it rather well when he arrived.

The six hours' discussion including lunch was in three parts: first, a whole range of immediate questions facing us; second, institutional questions, relations with Parliament, Spierenburg, Three Wise Men, problems of this sort; third, slightly longer range policy issues. We covered the first two almost inevitably better than the third which we slightly galloped through at the end, but it was long enough, as this part of the discussion was unfocused by me.

WEDNESDAY, 1 AUGUST. *East Hendred and Palafragal.*

Left for Barcelona before lunch accompanied by Jennifer, Caroline Gilmour and her son Andrew. Did not get to the Griggs'* house near Palafragal until 7.30, rather hot and sweaty as the car (hired from Barcelona airport) was very small and very full of luggage and us. However, the house was splendid. A great 1928 villa, built by John's maternal grandfather, Lord Islington, with all the scale and lavishness of a villa of fifty years ago, perched high above the sea, commanding an unspoilt peninsula. We dined in with the Griggs,* and John Bayleys† who were also staying.

SATURDAY, 4 AUGUST. *Palafragal.*

Gerona at about 7 o'clock. A very spectacular cathedral, semi-fortified, at the top of an enormous flight of steps as approached from the west front. The broadest nave in Europe apparently.

---

*John Grigg, b. 1924, author and journalist, succeeded his father as the 2nd Lord Altrincham in 1959, then disclaimed the title when this became possible in 1963. Married to Patsy Grigg.
†John Bayley, b. 1925, has been Warton Professor of English Literature at Oxford since 1974. Married to (Dame) Iris Murdoch, philosopher and novelist.

TUESDAY, 7 AUGUST. *Palafragal.*

Left for Barcelona just after 11 o'clock, partly to look at it and partly to assist in the changeover of guests at the airport. Lunch was slow so that we only just got the two Gilmours on the plane to Milan and thence to Pisa. I then proceeded to try to re-find Patsy (our two cars had been left ill-parked together) but she was so agitated by the impending arrival of her mother-in-law and others that she seemed completely to have disappeared. After various brushes with the police, and having to put my car in the car park, I eventually found that her car was being hoisted on to a lorry and managed with some difficulty to get it de-hoisted for a relatively small payment of about £5. Eventually old Lady Altrincham, the daughter of the said Lord Islington, arrived in a pretty bad temper saying she had had the most filthy journey (she is a formidable old gorgon) plus Christian Smith, wife of John Smith, ex-MP for Westminster, with various children. Patsy, with great self-sacrifice, took her mother-in-law and left me to take the Smiths. We had a short look round Barcelona, visited the cathedral, which was quite good, and had a short drive round one or two good squares near it and a drink at the Colon Hotel.

FRIDAY, 10 AUGUST. *Palafragal and East Hendred.*

East Hendred for lunch. The weather coolish, but not bad, although it had clearly been very unsatisfactory while we were away. Our Spanish visit, however, had gone very well, with almost unbroken good weather, a little too hot if anything, the first time I had known it so in the Mediterranean for years: a splendid house and generally very satisfactory.

TUESDAY, 14 AUGUST. *East Hendred.*

Spent the morning trying unsuccessfully to start my Dimbleby Lecture.

WEDNESDAY, 15 AUGUST. *East Hendred.*

Lunched at home in the garden with Jennifer and apart from being stung, twice as it turned out, by a wasp, I was feeling rather relaxed and cheerful. Slept afterwards in the sun and awoke to discover that the *Cour des Comptes* report had leaked into *Der Stern*, a semi-scandalous German magazine: therefore the end of the period of relaxation. I had a fairly hectic evening on the telephone, trying to contact various members of my staff in their scattered holiday locations.

THURSDAY, 16 AUGUST. *East Hendred.*

A morning on the telephone, leading to the issuing of a statement both in Brussels and London. There had been some stories in the British papers that morning but on the whole they didn't show great signs of escalating. There was nothing on the *World at One*, for example. George Scott* in London was a great pillar of sense and stability.

Sat up late talking with Bill Rodgers (who was staying) about the future. He wanted me to come back into the House for a Labour seat, which curiously I possibly could get – several feelers have been put out from Northfield, although I don't think a different Birmingham seat would attract me, even if a Labour seat did at all.

FRIDAY, 17 AUGUST. *East Hendred and Anglesey.*

By Hereford, Newtown, Dolgellau and Caernarvon to Anglesey, where we arrived at 7.30. It was a good evening after an indifferent day, Plas Newydd looking splendid and the Angleseys' flat, which I had seen only briefly last year, turned out to be substantial with fine rooms and views. Amongst the three or four others staying was Laurence Whistler, younger brother of Rex, who is writing a biography of his brother and is particularly interested in Plas Newydd because of the great dining-room mural.

SATURDAY, 18 AUGUST. *Anglesey.*

The Cledwyns, as they should now be called, came to lunch. Cledwyn on tremendous anecdotal form.

---

* George Scott, 1925–88, editor of the *Listener* 1974–9 and frequent Liberal candidate, had become head of the London office of the Commission earlier in 1979.

SUNDAY, 19 AUGUST. *Anglesey and Harlech.*

Amabel Williams-Ellis, Clough's widow, John Strachey's sister, came to lunch, rather splendid at eighty-seven. The Harlechs came to dine at 8 o'clock and then we left with them at 11.30 for the hour's drive to Glyn and a two-day stay.

MONDAY, 27 AUGUST. *East Hendred.*

Bess (Church) gave me the shattering news of Mountbatten's assassination in Ireland. I had last seen him at the Euro Gala at Drury Lane in May, after fifteen years of quite close official association with him, not only over the prison inquiry in 1966, but also over various aviation matters before that; and indeed there had been a certain continuing relationship with him in Brussels. Dreadful though it is, I suppose that from his point of view it is not too bad as he had begun to give the impression of not knowing what to do with the rest of his life and might even have welcomed a dramatic death, although not one with these side-effects. He was a pretty remarkable man on the whole, not a great intellect but with exceptional drive and power to pull or push people along with him. He was also good at grandeur without pompousness. We watched this evening television tribute to him which was very well done by Ludo Kennedy.

TUESDAY, 28 AUGUST. *East Hendred.*

Christopher Tugendhat to lunch. Brilliant sunshine, basic temperature still low, but a remarkable swing – the thermometer having been 41° when I got up in the morning had become 91° in the sun by 4 p.m.

I had quite a useful talk with Christopher about the budget paper and other matters. He is agreeable, sensible, very well read and well-informed, occasionally slow-firing. On the whole he has been a very good Commissioner.

WEDNESDAY, 29 AUGUST. *East Hendred.*

The Owens to lunch. They had not been to East Hendred for eighteen months and we hadn't seen them since the election. David

was out to be pleasant and talked quite good sense about personalities and balance of power in the Shadow Cabinet, yet there is
undoubtedly a reserve over our relationship, even though this
occasion went quite well. I think I would find it very difficult ever to
be really close to him again, and indeed although pleasant and
reasonably sensible he does not appear to have in any way the
stature of an ex-Foreign Secretary. The only remark he made at all
critical about his own tenure of office was that perhaps he had got
there too young; on the other hand he referred to it complacently as
a period of very good relations when he and Britain were on such
good terms with everybody.

THURSDAY, 30 AUGUST. *East Hendred, London and
East Hendred.*

To London by train for lunch with Geoffrey Howe in 11 Downing
Street. We lunched downstairs, and I had an agreeable general talk
with him in the course of which we had perhaps thirty or forty
minutes about the handling of the budget paper, on which he
seemed to me sensible but not enormously well-informed on detail.
I tried to make some points on how I thought the Government
should play it and the need not to put all the eggs in the basket of the
Dublin Summit.

Afterwards I went upstairs at 11 Downing Street for the first time
since we had left that house on the early evening of Friday, 19 June
1970 – quite extraordinary that I had never previously been back.
The cartoons we put on the stairs are still there and the Howes,
unlike the intervening tenants, seem to like them and would be
glad to fill in the few gaps which remain.*

MONDAY, 3 SEPTEMBER. *East Hendred and Brussels.*

Left rather gloomily for the 9.45 plane to Brussels. The length of the
holiday does not increase the enthusiasm for return. I telephoned
Jack Lynch in Dublin to sympathize with him over his stinkingly
unfair English press following the Mountbatten murder, and to say

*Towards the end of our 1968–70 sojourn in 11 Downing Street we had assembled on
the staircase (with the help of [Sir] Roy Strong, then Director of the National Portrait
Gallery) a collection of cartoons of previous Chancellors. I think we had deliberately
avoided photographs in order to provide a variation from the No. 10 staircase decoration.

that I and a lot of people in England had considerable respect for him, etc. I thought that (i) he deserved some support because he is a nice man, and (ii) it was highly desirable not to get him into a bitter anti-British frame of mind. He sounded very friendly and I think was genuinely pleased to have been telephoned.

Went to a men's dinner at Luns's house for Henry Kissinger, with General Haig as well. I was between Luns and Haig, but was struck in the general conversation towards the end by the extent to which Haig cannot hold a candle to Kissinger when he (K) is in the room. He is still in a curious sense very much his old assistant of the White House days and has none of Henry's rather glottal sparkle. Henry on good form, I thought, though looking rather fat again. I had a good hour's talk with him alone after dinner. He is sniffing the political air, but it is not easy to see what he can do. He is playing with the idea of being Senator from New York, but he says he won't run against Jack Javits, although he thinks that Jack is quite old enough to give up. No doubt he thinks that he could be President at the drop of a hat had he been born a citizen. Haig is also sniffing his presidency prospects and clearly thinks they have improved a bit since last June, though in my view they were pretty non-existent then and are not much better now.

Kissinger, despite his supreme self-confidence, is enjoyable to talk to, although he has a lot of views with which I don't agree (not all of them very seriously worked out). He listens quite well – his vanity is not insensitive or indestructible – and we had a good conversation about writing memoirs.

TUESDAY, 4 SEPTEMBER. *East Hendred.*

During the morning I saw Gundelach and Ortoli to try and warm them up for the Commission's consideration of the reference paper on budgetary convergence* in the afternoon and thought that both of them seemed more or less all right.

A long and rather wearisome special Commission meeting for four and a half hours after lunch. Not only was it wearisome, but

* Current Brussels jargon for using the Community budget to help the poorer more than the richer countries. It therefore subsumed the problem of Britain's excessive budgetary contribution. 'Concurrent studies' and the 'reference paper' were other jargon phrases with the same meaning.

also extremely difficult, with grave doubts at the end of the day as to whether we were going to get a sensible paper at all. Natali made the tactical mistake, because he wasn't wholly satisfied with its strength, of coming out against the paper as a whole, and therefore played into the hands of Gundelach and Ortoli who wanted greatly to weaken it. Davignon talked in rather the same terms, and all round the table, apart perhaps from Giolitti, who for once was more sensible than Natali, and Tugendhat, there was remarkably little support for what we had worked on so carefully. However, I thought it could probably be put together again and that indeed proved to some extent to be the case. That evening I had a rue de Praetère dinner with Ortoli, Gundelach and Davignon, into which I staggered rather exhausted. After another three and a half hours it was fairly clear that they, having blown off, would the next time round be prepared to accept something at least tolerable, provided greater obeisances were made to Community mythology.

WEDNESDAY, 5 SEPTEMBER. *Brussels, London and Rome.*

To London early to attend the Mountbatten funeral. I was seated between Luns, who talked in a loud voice the whole time (two goes a week of Luns is more than enough), and Ducci,* who was representing the Italian Government and who talked in a soft voice some of the time.

The service, curiously, I did not find particularly moving, or even enormously impressive, though I suppose it was. The Prince of Wales read the lesson well and there were great, familiar, and moving hymns, but as nobody around me (being mostly foreigners) could sing them, the sound somehow did not swell up and rather got lost in the high roof of the Abbey. But it was an occasion. It was perhaps the last great funeral of its sort. Of those that I have attended, only Churchill's has been comparable, and I suppose Dickie would have been pleased with it. There was no great sense of loss about him, for his life had manifestly run its course, and therefore there was no special quality of poignancy, as, say, with Tony's service in the same place two and a half years before.

5 o'clock plane with Jennifer to Rome. It was a rather beautiful

---

*Roberto Ducci, b. 1914, was Italian Ambassador to London 1975–80.

evening. We stayed at the Grand Hotel – as opposed to the Hassler – for the Italian Government were putting us up.

THURSDAY, 6 SEPTEMBER. *Rome and Palermo.*

By Italian military aircraft to Palermo. Drove round the edge of the city to the Hotel Villa Igiea, which has a fairly splendid position on one side of the Bay of Palermo (though with slightly too good a view of the shipyards, which are very near on the right). Typically, in spite of all the talk about the unrelenting summer sun of Sicily which beats down from June to October, it was raining when we arrived.

Then I had an extremely hard day's work. A one-and-a-half-hour meeting with the President of the Regional Government and about twelve members of his junta, if that is the word. This I thought would be an informal exchange of views, but in fact he opened with a longish prepared statement, lasting nearly half an hour, quite tough though perceptive and well-informed. He was indeed in general quite a bright man, called Matarella, apparently the son of the old mafia leader in the western part of the island, including Palermo, where mafia rule prevails, but was thought not to be *mafioso* himself.* This meant that I had to make a substantial reply fairly impromptu, but this was not in fact too difficult to do, particularly as I had to be interpreted in chunks to the room, whereas the interpretation of his speech was merely whispered into my ear. His Regional Council was very well disciplined as none of the others spoke a word.

We then went to the Palazzo dei Normanni where there are some wonderful mosaics, both in the chapel and in the secular hall, which I do not recollect having previously seen. Next a lunch with short speeches, at which all the notabilities were present, the prefect, the president, the mayor, the cardinal (with whom I had quite an agreeable talk before lunch, he very non-Sicilian), local deputies, members of the European Parliament, a minister from Rome, etc.

Afterwards an interminable tour of the shipyards and harbour, enlivened only by the fact that the head of the Italian shipbuilding

---

*He was murdered four months later.

industry, Buccini, who had come down from Genoa, was extremely
intelligent and worth talking to. Sicilian labour is apparently
markedly unproductive compared with northern Italian labour,
partly because they take an average of forty-two days' sick leave a
year.

Then a still more exhausting meeting with the Chamber of
Commerce. There were 350 of them and all the speeches were of
reasonably good-mannered complaint about local issues. Unfortunately, the simultaneous interpretation, which was not provided by
our interpreter but by two girls they had got from Rome, was almost
completely incomprehensible. I really could not understand a word
they were saying. I was reduced to listening in Italian, which I could
understand more, and as what they all said was fairly predictable it
wasn't too bad. I then wound up for half an hour. Then a press
conference, which was a relative relaxation. Then a large reception
and buffet dinner at the Villa Malfattini.

FRIDAY, 7 SEPTEMBER. *Palermo, Catania and Taormina.*
Across to the eastern part of the island, along the coast for some
time and then through a very bleak inland area to Enna near where
we inspected a major soya bean experimental station, run by an
extraordinary self-made, very rich entrepreneur called Mario
Rendo, the whole thing allegedly run as a foundation. The soya
experiment was up to a point quite interesting, though Rendo
seemed to me totally unrealistic about the possible results of it. How
he has made so much money with such unrealism I do not
understand, for he was talking about it providing employment for
250,000 people.

Natali was standing rather gloomily, with his moustaches droop-
ing, on the edge of the field, God knows why exactly, but this no
doubt explains why he does so much travelling to and in Italy.
He didn't, despite being an ex-Minister of Agriculture, manage to
look very rural. An agreeable official luncheon at the Jolly Hotel,
Catania, from 2.45 to 4.30.

Then a brief rest before my lecture to the university at 6.15. Nice
building, good hall and they seemed reasonably appreciative. Afterwards we left for Taormina and the San Dominico Hotel – a

converted monastery. It was rather splendid, high above the sea, with a beautiful garden and good rooms.

SATURDAY, 8 SEPTEMBER. *Taormina.*

Rest day at Taormina. I spent most of it trying to write our response to the wretched *Cour des Comptes* report. Alas, the weather was not perfect. Etna was briefly visible in the morning, but then disappeared into a mixture of haze and cloud. We dined in the hotel, with our highly intelligent interpreter, Gesulfo, and the far less intelligent Italian protocol man, who had never previously been south of Rome in his life and obviously thought it rather degrading to have to do so. He came from Friuli where he has a wine-growing estate, and looked like a post-Risorgimento House of Savoy cavalry officer.

SUNDAY, 9 SEPTEMBER. *Taormina, Rome and Urbino.*

Back to Rome by military aircraft. Lunch with Malfatti at the Villa Madama. (Malfatti, my predecessor but two as President of the Commission, has become Foreign Minister in the new Cossiga Government.) I think somewhat inspired by my old friend Renato Ruggiero, Malfatti had worked himself up into a great state of excitement and was determined to have a great go at us about the totally unsatisfactory nature, from their point of view, of the paper on convergence. The Italians were very fed up that their budget imbalance had in fact disappeared, but were extremely bad at producing any precise ideas, at this stage at any rate, as to what further they wanted done. I don't like Malfatti enormously at the best of times, and I didn't think he did this particularly effectively, or even, in spite of a lot of protestations of friendship, particularly agreeably.

We set off for Urbino at 4.20 and had the most dreadful drive. The protocol department of the Italian Foreign Office had decided that the thing to do was to go across the peninsula on the autostrada to Pescara then drive up past Ancona and into Urbino that way. Had I looked at the map for a moment it would have been absolutely clear to me that this was crazy, but by the time I got hold of a map it was too late and we were already launched off towards L'Aquila. As a result we had a drive of 480 kms as opposed to the 260 kms which was all that was necessary, on a rather bad autostrada, screaming along dangerously, with sirens going the whole time, in a police-led and police-tailed convoy of about five cars, no fewer than two of which eventually broke down as well as another running out of petrol. We arrived shaken, exhausted and extremely bad-tempered just before 9.00.

I had been supposed to go to a great reception given by the *municipio* in the hall of the old ducal palace at 7.30, but we were desperately late for that. However, as they were all assembled I had to go there briefly and make a little speech. After a quick dinner we retreated to the not very good Montefeltro Hotel. Although the rooms were small and ill-furnished, there was at least a magnificent view over the moonlit Umbrian countryside.

Monday, 10 September. *Urbino and Rome.*

Degree-giving ceremony in the university at 11 o'clock. Substantial speech from me, but not a bad occasion. Both Colombo, who had driven up from Rome specially (by the right route, lucky man), and Forlani, who is a sort of local boss as well as an ex-Foreign Minister, came, which was kind of them.

Then back to the Grand Hotel in Rome by the correct route and with the greatest of ease in three hours despite entering Rome at the rush hour.

Tuesday, 11 September. *Rome and Brussels.*

To Castel Gandolfo for our audience with the Pope. Greeted there by the old French chamberlain, Archevêque Martin, whom I know somewhat from previous occasions. Castel Gandolfo has a fine position but is not an attractive building inside. It was not available to the Popes from 1870 until the Concordat in 1929, and it was then done up in a sort of Papal Mussolini style. On the way in Martin first made it clear that the Pope wished to have the main part of the audience with me alone, and that Jennifer and the others were to come in at the end to receive a blessing and have a photograph taken, which was possibly a slight disappointment to them, but was all right from my point of view. Martin also said, 'En quelle langue,

Monsieur Jenkins, aimeriez-vous parler avec Sa Sainteté? En Allemand?' he surprisingly added. 'Certainement pas,' I said. So Martin then said, 'Eh bien, le Saint Père est également à l'aise en Anglais ou Français.' So I said, 'If he is equally at ease, I am rather more at ease in English, so perhaps we might talk English.' 'I am sure the Holy Father would be delighted,' he replied.

I then had about thirty-five minutes with the Pope alone. He started in French, so I replied in French and we talked so for perhaps the first ten minutes. I did not have the impression that even his French, though he had a good accent, was perfect. He did a good deal of searching for words and, while he was certainly as good as or better than me, he did not give any impression of great fluency. This part of the conversation was agreeable but a little trite. Then when we got on to Northern Ireland, I asked him if he minded if we spoke English and he said certainly not, he would be delighted, and so we did most of the rest of the interview in that language, but this was possibly a slight mistake because his comprehension of English was very far from being perfect, and I suspect that he was not following a good deal of what I said.

However, I think he might have got the central point which I wanted to make, which was that his forthcoming visit to Northern Ireland was clearly an affair of the greatest possible importance particularly following so closely after the Mountbatten and other murders and that it could have very great impact. Perhaps not even he could influence the very small minority of those who were dedicated to violence for its own sake, and there was no doubt little need to influence the majority of the population who were against violence. But those whom it was extremely important to influence were the sizeable minority who gave passive support to violence. This phrase he certainly seemed to take in and repeated several times, 'Passive support, passive support, yes that's very bad.' So I hope that this at least, which was the central thing I wanted to say, got through.

He was perhaps a little less impressive than I expected to find him. He has a wonderful smile and, even without the smile, looks agreeable (forceful as well) and made of very good material. He didn't have anything of great significance to say and perhaps, particularly in the part of the conversation in English, but even to some extent in French, he let me lead the conversation so that I guess I was talking a good 60 per cent of the time. And while it was a much more agreeable, intimate talk than I had ever had with either of the two previous Popes whom I have met, the sheer human and intellectual impact upon me was less than I expected.

Then the others came in and he did his blessings very agreeably, gave a medal each to Crispin, Enzo Perlot and me, and a book to Jennifer, and we had some very good photographs taken – Vatican photographers seem excellent – and parted on suitably warm terms. He is not tremendously well informed about Community affairs and Western European matters, much less so than was his predecessor, but this is perhaps natural as he thinks much more in Pan-European or Eastern European terms. It appeared to me in one part of the Irish conversation that he was far from clear about the constitutional position by which both parts of Ireland were members of the Community, but Northern Ireland through the United Kingdom and the Republic of Ireland entirely separately.

Jennifer went to London and I went to see Cossiga, the new Italian Prime Minister, at 2 o'clock in the Palazzo Chigi. I hadn't seen him for three years, but had known him fairly well in 1975/6 when I was Home Secretary and he was Minister of the Interior. I thought him then a nice intelligent man and this impression was fully confirmed. Also, unlike most Italian politicians, he talks quite good English, but was not, however, quite naturally, anxious to do any very serious business except through an interpreter. We talked until 3.15, getting very hungry. He was much more reasonable than Malfatti had been and I think I was able to persuade him on a number of issues: first, that the Italians would make a great mistake to block any British solution, because their budget problem really had turned round, and though they had certain wider problems, they were on a somewhat longer time scale and the hope of solving these in a way satisfactory to Italy would certainly not be enhanced by taking a dog-in-the-manger attitude at this stage. Second, that it was essential that they should not just complain about the Commission's inability to propound solutions to problems which they did not formulate clearly, but that they must submit some more precise proposals, either by sending some high-level officials to Brussels, or by putting in clear papers.

We then adjourned to an excellent lunch (the *tartuffi* season is the peak of the Italian gastronomic year) before returning to Brussels.

WEDNESDAY, 12 SEPTEMBER. *Brussels*.

Lunch at home for Madame Veil. I found her a good deal different from my expectation following our July meeting. She is nicer and less sharp. Her conversation is engagingly babbling. There are never any silences, never any difficulty about finding something to say: things just come out as they come into her head, a mixture of gossip, how nice her penthouse suite in the Amigo Hotel was (I hope the *Cour des Comptes* don't get on to that too quickly), what she thought about Strasbourg, what difficulties she was having with various people, what she thought about Pflimlin, how she was going to deal with the problem of Parliament wanting to move. A mixture of quite important things and quite unimportant things, all spontaneously pouring out.

I think she feels somewhat lost with the Parliament, which is not surprising considering that she has never sat in a Parliament in her life, and is forming a fairly low view of most of the groups. The British Conservative Group she put at the top of the list, and probably rightly so, so far as coherence is concerned. She is very determined not to be intimidated by Debré, who had been firing heavy Gaullist guns on her flank about the inadmissibility, in his view, of the armaments debate which is scheduled for the September session. But she seemed fairly unshaken by that, and indeed generally gave the impression that the fears she would be Giscard's woman in the Parliament were misplaced. The real danger is that she will be a slightly incompetent President, not that she will be anybody's agent.

Then back to the Commission for a rather excessively long session, from 3.40 to 7.50. However, in the course of this, we satisfactorily disposed of the reference paper, which had looked in real trouble the week before, but as a result of some re-editing and a good deal of lobbying of the more important Commissioners we managed to get through in a tolerable form. Home pretty tired at 8.15, but no respite as the Spierenburg group arrived to dine almost immediately and stayed until nearly midnight. It was mainly a thank-you dinner to them towards the end of their work, but we had some interesting conversation and I found them all in quite good morale.

SATURDAY, 15 SEPTEMBER. *East Hendred, London and East Hendred.*

Edward's wedding day and a most beautiful morning. Motored from East Hendred to the Savoy Restaurant, the Grill being closed, and at 12.30 installed ourselves in the window and waited rather a long time – despite the fact that they had been anxious to be early – for the children, all of whom eventually arrived together, Edward with his very agreeable Canadian best man. Set-piece family luncheons are liable to be a slight strain, but this one was agreeable.

The wedding in the Temple Church went off very well. I suppose there were 150/200 people, an amazing proportion of them wearing morning coats. I was surprised at the number of our old friends, because I had encouraged nobody to do it, who turned up so attired (Mark Bonham Carter, Ronald McIntosh, Madron Seligman*), but what was far more striking was the very high proportion of the young who did so; they obviously rather like dressing up. The church was attractive and the presiding clergyman was good. So was the music, though a little unusual, and the scene was much improved by the fact that the west door, through which Sally came with her father (the guests had entered from a south door at the side), remained open throughout with crisp, clear, cool September sunlight streaming in the whole time.

Then we at first stood about in the piazza-like courtyard outside the church and I wished we had arranged the reception there – it would have been just about the right temperature. But eventually we moved into Middle Temple Hall where everything went on for a surprisingly long time, from 4.00 to 6.30 or so, but quite satisfactorily. The best man's speech was perceptive about Edward and funny in bits. The whole thing was tremendously traditionally done, to a far greater extent than I had expected, cutting the cake, champagne, confetti for the departure of the bride and groom and God knows what else.

MONDAY, 17 SEPTEMBER. *Brussels.*

Roy Mason, accompanied by Gavin Strang, his assistant agricultural spokesman, to dinner at home with Jennifer. Mason was in

* Madron Seligman, b. 1918, a friend from Balliol days, has been an MEP since 1979.

one sense very agreeable, very pro-European, even prepared to defend almost all aspects of the CAP, which seems to me to be pushing it a bit, and I think enjoyed himself (and wrote a nice letter afterwards). But he is incredibly obscurantist (straight Paisleyite, as Jennifer put it) on Northern Ireland, where his lack of imagination and inability to understand *any* of the Catholic case really were absolutely shattering. He just loves the Northern Ireland Protestants. Also he is a remarkably insensitive man in other ways. After dinner he held forth in a great set piece about the terrible rigours of his security protection and how he was under constant threat, which may well be so, but all done as though he were addressing three friendly members of his General Management Committee in Barnsley, with not the slightest hint of understanding that I knew anything about these security problems or had ever been Home Secretary.

TUESDAY, 18 SEPTEMBER. *Brussels.*

In the margins of the Foreign Affairs Council I had a good bilateral talk with Dohnanyi, which was interesting because he was very keen to get out of me what I thought was a sum on which it would be possible to settle with the British, and to tell him what I thought the scale of the problem was. I said I thought one could envisage a settlement at around 1000 million units of account. I couldn't be pinned to this, but if he wanted some idea of an order of magnitude, this is what I would insert into his mind.

THURSDAY, 20 SEPTEMBER. *Brussels.*

An interview with a lady called Miss Keays who has been recommended to us as a replacement for Patricia Smallbone when she gets married at Christmas. I thought she was rather good in spite of having a very Tory background, and pretty well decided to engage her. Celia is a bit worried about her because she thinks she is too strong a personality; she will find it very difficult to be as strong a personality as Celia!

SATURDAY, 22 SEPTEMBER. *Brussels and Fontainebleau.*

Drove to Fontainebleau, or more precisely the Hôtel Bas Bréau at Barbizon, and on a most beautiful, cool, sunlit day, lunched in the garden of this rather flash establishment. (A *'baiserdrome'*, the Beaumarchais' described it as when they arrived to lunch next day, though the appearance of most of the other guests didn't make this terribly plausible.)

At 4.30 on the outskirts of Fontainebleau we had the INSEAD ceremony for the opening of their academic year. There were several preliminary speeches, all quite good, one by Olivier Giscard d'Estaing, one by the President of INSEAD, one by Uwe Kitzinger,* who gave a striking and dramatic performance, starting in German and switching to English; and then mine.

SUNDAY, 23 SEPTEMBER. *Fontainebleau and Brussels.*

After running early in the forest, I was driven into Fontainebleau to buy the newspapers and had a cup of coffee in a café opposite the château. I had hardly been in Fontainebleau or at a zinc *comptoir* since 1938, and was suddenly transported back to Third Republican France. Then we drove to near the obelisk and got a most memorable 'September morn' view of the château (west facade). Lunch again in the garden of the hotel, during which Ortoli telephoned to say that they were locked in discussions with the Finance Ministers as there was the first EMS readjustment of currencies (certainly the Danish kroner, maybe the Belgian franc going down, the mark going up) being negotiated.† Back to Brussels by the early evening train from Paris.

TUESDAY, 25 SEPTEMBER. *Brussels and Strasbourg.*

8.16 train to Strasbourg (no avion taxis these days) feeling nervous of the new Parliament which we had hardly met in July and which, after two months away, would surely have sharpened its teeth. Even the two relatively easy questions which I had to answer filled me with apprehension. They passed easily, however.

After a late sitting of the Parliament I attended a dinner which

---

*Uwe Kitzinger, b. 1928, had been a fellow of Nuffield College, Oxford, since 1956, was then Dean of INSEAD (1976–80) and is now Director of the Oxford Centre for Management Studies and head of Templeton College.
†It was settled quickly and satisfactorily by that evening, in sharp contrast with pre-1971 'Bretton Woods' devaluations.

Mme Veil was rather ineffectively organizing. First I had invited her to lunch and she had riposted by saying it should be her lunch. Then she changed it to dinner. Then she asked all the other available members of the Commission without telling me. Then she changed the time on no fewer than three occasions during the day: first, it was to be 8.00, in an adjournment of the Parliament, then it was to be 10.30, then it was back to 8.00, then it was back to whenever the Parliament was adjourned. We eventually assembled in a slightly bad temper in the Sofitel at about 10.15. It was a highly franco-phone dinner, which is quite good for me from time to time, although the main conversation between Mme Veil and Ortoli and Cheysson I found a bit fast, but they are fully entitled occasionally to get their own back on us anglophones.

The main interest of the dinner emerged only in retrospect. Vredeling, the fourth member of the Commission present, was next to me and appeared throughout to be perfectly sober. However, at some stage after 12.15 a.m. he got involved in an affair with 'Chrystal'. I was not sure, when it was first reported to me, whether this was a form of glass or a German lady. It subsequently became clear that it was a question of glass, for in a fit of anger with some Dutch MEP at some unspecified time later in the night, he had picked up a heavy ashtray, thrown it, missed (I suppose fortu-nately) the MEP, lightly grazed the chandelier and shattered a plate glass window. The cost was £5000; the cost to Vredeling's morale was much higher.

THURSDAY, 27 SEPTEMBER. *Strasbourg.*

To the Parliament at 11.15 to attend the budget debate, begun by Christopher Tugendhat with a very good speech. Afterwards I gave lunch to the British Labour Group. They were all quite agreeable. They nearly all turned up, although, apparently and typically, they had had a great debate (I am not sure they hadn't even had a vote) as to whether or not they should come. It was almost like the legendary motion of sympathy on an MP's illness carried by nine votes to seven, with eight abstentions. However, there was no trace of this in their behaviour. Barbara Castle made a nice speech at the end of lunch, to which I responded.

MONDAY, 1 OCTOBER. *East Hendred and Vienna.*

To Vienna, to be met on the tarmac by Kreisky* together with a great array of lesser dignitaries. At the Imperial Hotel I was installed in enormous grandeur (thank God there was no question of our having to pay the bill). It was rather a pleasure to be back in Vienna, where I had not been for twenty-three years and which I found surprisingly unchanged.

At 3.00 a meeting with the President of the Republic, Kirch-schläger† a non-political former diplomat, who has been elected as an Independent (although a Socialist nominee) and who is a tall, distinguished man, who held an entirely appropriate head of state conversation with me. We discussed the evolution of Austria's foreign policy since 1945 in general but interesting terms and also the internal balance and the problems of one party holding power for a long time. It was a worthwhile talk in the splendid room where Francis II had worked and died at his desk, the ante-room being the bedroom where Maria Theresa had died. The Austrians have official buildings of extraordinary grandeur, greater I think than is so in almost any other country. The Italians are in a high class, the Germans in a low class for obvious reasons, even the French I think not quite as grand as the Austrians, nor the British.

Then across the courtyard for another hour's meeting in the Chancellor's office. This was the old Ballhausplatz of pre-1914 diplomatic fame. In the ante-room here is the spot where Dolfuss was shot. (There is no lack of notable death sites in Austria.) I talked with Kreisky about a variety of things, but not least the Labour Party, in which he is extremely interested from the Socialist International point of view, and the leadership of which he was rather naïvely asking me to go back and take over. I explained to him the impossibility of this and disclosed a little of my thought about the re-orientation of British politics, which was somewhat of a shock to him. Although he thinks the Labour Party is appalling, he nonetheless has a typical Germano/Austrian reluctance to comprehend any organizational break.

After that, a meeting with ministers, over which he presided,

*Bruno Kreisky, b. 1911, was Federal Chancellor of Austria 1970–83.
†Rudolf Kirchschläger, b. 1915, was Foreign Minister 1970–4, and President of Austria 1974–86.

which was detailed but not difficult. The problem of relations with Austria is that they are at once outside the Community and a crossroads of the Community. Perhaps we could give them some money to build a new autobahn on what is called the Gästenarbeiter route. It is appallingly overcrowded at the moment with traffic from the Community through to Yugoslavia and Greece, and it will become worse as a result of Greek accession.

To the Staatsoper for *Il Trovatore*, well sung by Ricciarelli and a Slav lady previously unknown to me, but with doubtful Karajan sets. The performance was enjoyable but not memorable.

TUESDAY, 2 OCTOBER. *Vienna and Brussels.*

At 11.30 I had a meeting with Kreisky and the ministers of the evening before, for which he had asked although it was not on the programme. I decided that it should be turned into a slightly wider ranging discussion than on the previous evening, and he had decided the same, so there was a rather happy coincidence of view.

He opened with quite a long statement saying how he wanted to get Austria much closer to the Community without actual membership, which was not possible, but in effect asking for the substance of membership without the form. I replied only moderately sympathetically, because this is difficult for us, but it was a good, general *tour d'horizon*. After that there was a press conference and a Ballhausplatz luncheon.

Then a meeting in the Parliament with the President and about a dozen others, including the chairmen of the main committees. Afterwards, with a little time to spare, we walked to the Karls-kirche, a remarkably secular church, certainly more dedicated to the Hapsburg dynasty than to God. When we returned to the hotel, Kreisky was waiting for me in a palm court and we had tea there for twenty minutes before setting off for the airport. Austria is a very odd mixture of grandeur and informality. It would be impossible to imagine Giscard or Mrs Thatcher eating cream cakes in the public lounge of the Crillon or the Savoy Hotel, or even Schmidt in the Königshof. However, it seemed perfectly normal in Vienna and nobody took much notice of Kreisky.

During this final conversation he was very keen to revert to our Labour Party discussion. He said he had thought about what I had told him, and maybe I was right, maybe I was not, but he hoped that I would reflect very carefully on all these things. At any rate, he and Brandt were anxious to promote my position, and whatever I was going to do they greatly hoped that I would come and address a major meeting of the Socialist International which they would organize in the last months of my period of office. At the airport he took me out to the plane.

THURSDAY, 4 OCTOBER. *Brussels*.

A most formidable session with the Control Committee from 3.00 until 6.00. Entering the room was like going into a Senatorial hearing of the worst sort. The large *hémicycle* of the Economic and Social Committee building was packed with about three hundred people and masses of television cameras. The disagreeable Aigner was in the chair, but opened not too intolerably. Then a flat report from Johansen, the Dane on the *Cour des Comptes*. Then a brief statement from me, followed by an endless list of questions from Brian Key (the *rapporteur*),* to which I replied perhaps at too great a length – I should think I was about forty minutes. But there was something to be said for saturation treatment. At any rate there followed a series of not altogether unhelpful interventions from the floor, and I had a strong feeling by this time that things were going better. Several more answers from me and a wind-up at the end. There was a general feeling that I had handled it robustly and a hope that the worst was over.

SATURDAY, 6 OCTOBER. *Villers-le-Temple*.

Commission weekend at Villers-le-Temple. We started just before 10.00, with Spierenburg there to present his report. It was intended that he should only stay for about an hour, but it quickly became inevitable that he should stay the whole morning.

Spierenburg opened hard and responded to any criticisms extremely forthrightly, I thought very sensibly, but perhaps not as persuasively as he might have done. As a result there was a good deal of criticism during the morning, partly from the fringes.

---

*Brian Key, b. 1947, was the strongly pro-European Labour MEP for South Yorkshire from 1979 to 1984, when he was not reselected.

Brunner, Cheysson, perhaps Natali, Tugendhat were all slightly hostile, even Ortoli on one or two points, and I began to feel doubtful as to whether the report would not be eaten up when we came to discuss it substantially on the following day.

In the afternoon (switching from Spierenburg) we had quite a good discussion, mainly on agriculture, balance of the budget points, etc. The British issue we got through without too much discussion, which I was anxious to do, merely turning the corner that we would put forward a paper with a whole variety of options, including issues on the payments as well as on the receipts side.

SUNDAY, 7 OCTOBER. *Villers-le-Temple and Brussels.*

We came back to Spierenburg. Things went much better than I feared they would. One or two people were still being tiresome, Brunner notably, but increasingly isolated, but Ortoli, Gundelach, Davignon and, notably, Giolitti, who made one of his best interventions, all came out firmly in favour, and therefore the feeling, quite satisfactorily, was that broadly Spierenburg was right. Jennifer and I lunched fairly quickly, and drove ourselves back to Brussels via Huy.

MONDAY, 15 OCTOBER. *Brussels.*

Peter Parker came with one or two other people from British Rail, plus some SNCF (French Railways) representatives, about the Channel Tunnel. Quite a good, sensible project put forward jointly by them and it was rather a good meeting. Then a lunch rue de Praetère for Parker and the SNCF Managing Director, Monsieur Gentil.

Mirzoeff, the BBC man in charge of my Dimbleby Lecture, came for a drink, supposed to be for half an hour, but in fact he stayed from 6.30 until 8.00. He obviously doesn't think a great deal of the incomplete draft, and is probably quite right too, though it mildly depresses me.

FRIDAY, 19 OCTOBER. *Dublin.*

To Dublin for a long early evening meeting with Jack Lynch, the Taoiseach. I am not sure that he is very sharply focused on how he is going to conduct the Dublin European Council, but he still has nearly six weeks to go and is very open to suggestions. I had an agreeable talk with him as usual.

Then to the Shelbourne Hotel where I had Garret Fitzgerald to dine. An immensely slow dinner, served by a very incompetent waiter, who was incapable of opening a wine bottle, an unusual Irish deficiency. Crispin was also there, and Garret as usual was on very good and worthwhile form. The conversation was wide-ranging and not particularly on political matters. He is obviously pretty confident of being able to win the next election, and his thoughts therefore (European orientated though he is) are natur-ally rather on Irish than on wider politics, but there was a lot of interesting talk about Irish life, modern Catholicism, the Pope, a whole range of issues.

SATURDAY, 20 OCTOBER. *Dublin and Ashford Castle.*

To the appropriately named Casement military airfield, from where we took off at about 10.30, accompanied by van der Klaauw, in an extremely small plane which chugged along on a rather beautiful clear morning over the midlands of Ireland, which I had never seen before. We landed near Ashford Castle, rather a magnificent hotel on the second biggest lough in Ireland, partly old, partly eighteenth-century, with a lot of nineteenth-century additions. It had belonged to various people at various stages, but most recently, like so many houses in Ireland to the branch of the Guinness family with the Browne and Oranmore title. Foreign Ministers trickled in by various routes, but there was I think a complete attendance, plus, for the first time at one of these gatherings, wives. This is so unusual in Europe that I had omitted to note that they were invited and therefore had not passed the suggestion on to Jennifer, who might have come.

A rather heavy lunch and then a session from 3.45 until 7.15, which was too long because we missed being able to go out on the most magical evening. Fortunately I was sitting facing the sunset, which was of outstanding quality, and was therefore able to take it in from the conference room. No real discussion about British budgetary questions and a fairly rambling discussion on a range of issues, Peter Carrington doing quite well, François-Poncet playing a curious hand about the report of the *trois sages*, which the French have been pressing for so urgently but the publication of which they now wished to postpone, and various other matters of this sort.

At dinner I had Mrs O'Kennedy and Mrs Genscher – a nice, jolly woman – on either side of me. Then a rather good, brief Irish folk performance, almost entirely by one family.

SUNDAY, 21 OCTOBER. *Ashford Castle and East Hendred.*

No morning session. Indeed, the whole Ashford Castle event, although thoroughly agreeable (perhaps the best place we have been to, with great lavish Irish presents and even wives) was more of a jaunt than any of the previous occasions, with remarkably little serious business transacted. We left by helicopter for Shannon, from where Peter Carrington gave me a lift to Northolt. It was a morning of wonderful clarity, and flying between Bristol and Chippenham one could see the whole of southern England, with the Isle of Wight standing out, outlined as on a map, as well as previously having had a magnificent view of the South Wales coastline and the valleys and mountains. East Hendred by just after 1 o'clock, where it was warm enough to have drinks in the garden.

MONDAY, 22 OCTOBER. *East Hendred and London.*

To 10 Downing Street at 11.30, for a rather wild and whirling interview with Mrs Thatcher, lasting no less than an hour and fifty minutes. She wasn't, to be honest, making a great deal of sense, jumping all over the place, so that I came to the conclusion that her reputation for a well-ordered mind is ill-founded. On the other hand, she remains quite a nice person, without pomposity. For example, when, after a series of particularly extreme denunciatory remarks about Giscard, but a great deal about other people too ('They are all a rotten lot,' she kept saying, 'Schmidt and the Americans and we are the only people who would do any standing up and fighting if necessary') she suddenly announced, after making some very extreme remark about Giscard, 'I don't think this had better be recorded. Indeed, I think the whole interview shouldn't be recorded.' I said, 'Oh, didn't you know, it is an absolute rule in the Community that when the President has meetings of this sort a *verbatim* account has to be on the desks of all other heads of government the next morning.' 'It's not really so, is it?' she said, at least half-believing. 'No,' I assured her, which she thought not exactly funny, but took perfectly well, whereas Callaghan would have got very huffy about a tease of that sort.

I came out, having maybe put a little sense into her head on one or two other points, but slightly reeling after this long tirade, not particularly against me but at various things she didn't like. I was left with no feeling that she had any clear strategy for Dublin, except for determination, which is a certain quality I suppose.

TUESDAY, 23 OCTOBER. *London and Strasbourg.*

Plane from London Airport to Strasbourg, where I arrived on a most beautiful day. Scott-Hopkins,* the Tory leader, to lunch. He is a curious man, quite an able leader, perfectly agreeable to talk to, although giving little sense of *rapport* or response. In the evening I gave Stevy Davignon dinner. He announced to my surprise how much he would like me to stay on as President of the Commission, saying that if I did he would stay on, but he thought if not, not. How much this means I don't know, and still less do I know whether I want to stay on, but it is nice that he should say so.

WEDNESDAY, 24 OCTOBER. *Strasbourg and Brussels.*

A longish Commission from 9.00 until 12.45, then an urgent telephone call from Nanteuil to deliver some not very urgent protests about something Cheysson had said. Afterwards a lunch for six or seven chairmen of parliamentary committees. Back in the afternoon to do a little lobbying. A great part of the Commission in the morning had been taken by the Commission discovering that the Control Committee was intending to freeze half the allowances (both *frais de représentation* and *frais de mission*) in the coming year until they had a report, about May, as to how the year was going. This obviously was extremely tiresome, not so much from a practi-

---

* (Sir) James Scott-Hopkins, b. 1921, was an MP 1959–79, and has been a Member of the European Parliament since 1973. He was leader of the European Democratic (Conservative) Group 1979–82.

cal as from a dignity point of view, and it galvanized and united the Commission, which was perhaps not very elevating, in a way that I had hardly seen anything do before.

We all agreed that we would try to get a substantial amendment put in, which would be moved by the Liberal Group, and that we would all corner various people. Several had been done in the morning but I in the afternoon did three or four, which was almost overkill because it was quite obvious that they were perfectly willing to be persuaded and that there was no difficulty in getting the offending passage removed. Indeed by the end I began to think that we might have added an addendum to our amendment saying that Herr Aigner should be expelled from the European Parliament.

THURSDAY, 25 OCTOBER. *Brussels and Cairo.*

Motored to Amsterdam and took a KLM plane to Cairo. Drove in on a beautiful evening to the Meridian Hotel on the island in the river. A briefing meeting with our delegate (recently arrived), a serious German called Billerbeck, who on the whole impressed me. He certainly took the briefing meeting very seriously, so much so that he wouldn't do it in the room, but insisted on going out on to the terrace (which was nice except for a slight mosquito threat) on a moonlit, reasonably cool, clear evening. Dinner with him and our party in the Palme d'Or restaurant in the hotel, done up in *Death on the Nile* style.

FRIDAY, 26 OCTOBER. *Cairo.*

A visit to the main museum, which I had not been to before, an extraordinary jumble, all laid out like Maples furniture basement, but with some remarkable things in it. We saw mainly the Tutankhamun tomb contents. Then to the Ministry of Foreign Affairs for one and a half hours with Boutros-Ghali, interspersed with the ceremonial signing of the accord setting up our delegation. Boutros-Ghali is nominally the deputy Foreign Minister, but he would be the Minister if he were not a Copt. He is a very bright man and I had a good talk with him, during which he more or less told us that the school of thought represented by him in the Egyptian Government would not greatly mind if we recognized the Tunis/Arab League, though they would prefer that we did not do it too quickly; and he also floated an idea for some Community help (mainly for symbolic rather than practical reasons I think) on the West Bank and in the other occupied territories.

Then a very good river boat trip over lunch with the whole of our party and a few accompanying Egyptians. We went up the Nile for about twelve miles to the older pyramids, the ones without the sphinx but with the steps. An official dinner given by Hamil el Said, the Minister of the Economy, who was our constant host and companion, and a party of about forty.

SATURDAY, 27 OCTOBER. *Cairo.*

At 11.00 we set off for the drive to the Barrage, where we had an hour's meeting with Sadat.* He is an optimist beyond the bounds of reason, and I suppose slightly dotty, but quite attractively so. He wore a sparkling blue suit, with knife-edge creases, and a sparkling white shirt. He announced that most successful meetings had been held between his Prime Minister and the Israelis in London, which had effectively overcome all outstanding problems. This proved to be quite untrue. He also suddenly announced, to the surprise and dismay of Hamil el Said, that he had agreed to supply a limited quantity of oil at guaranteed prices to the Israelis (which the British won't do to the other Europeans). Hamil said, 'Oh, dear,' or words to that effect, 'I hope you got something worthwhile in return.' 'My dear Hamil,' he said, 'I have got things beyond the confines of your narrow imagination.' He later launched into a great denunciation of the other Arab governments, saying that when he had finally sewn things up with the Israelis – which he expected to do well before May, probably in the early spring – he would return to this theme and launch denunciatory attacks on those who lived in vast luxury by exploiting their own people and everybody else.

The impression he made was more agreeable than this sounds. He is a considerable figure with remarkable qualities. Whether one would like to be his enemy in Egypt I doubt, or how much liberty of expression there is. At one stage earlier Boutros-Ghali had said to me, 'The trouble with dealing with Israel is that it is a *real* democracy,' and this I suppose says something about Egypt. However, Sadat

* Anwar Sadat, 1918–81, was President of Egypt from 1970 until his assassination.

is certainly one of the better people in the world at the present time and like all Egyptians has a degree of agreeable sophistication which helps to make Cairo for me an extraordinarily attractive city, in spite of the terrible messes which are associated with it – the squalor, and the fact that things don't work. (Nearly all the telephones are out of order: it is impossible to telephone the airport from the centre of the city, and purely a matter of chance whether one can telephone one part of the city from another.)

On this visit we are extremely lucky to have almost perfect weather. The humidity and the great heat have just gone and we had clear atmosphere with a maximum temperature of 80° and a minimum of 60°, which is about as nice as it can be.

Press conference at 6 o'clock, and then a debriefing of the ambassadors of the Nine at the Irish Embassy. This is in the so-called Garden City, the old, fashionable pre-1939 (perhaps even pre-1914) part of Cairo, but now very rundown. The Irish have a large flat in a turn-of-the-century block where all the other residents are French-speaking Egyptians (which means they speak French the whole time), the block slightly dilapidated and the Irish apparently unable to afford to mend a window pane, unless it is impossible to get somebody to do it, which I find difficult to believe.

From there to the British Embassy, where Crispin and I dined alone with Michael Weir,* plus newish second wife, she previously in the Foreign Office herself and a slightly assertive career girl, a bit like a woman in a Charles Addams cartoon, who greatly grew on me as the evening went on. Michael Weir, whom I had not met before, I thought effective and agreeable. I had never been to the Cairo Embassy before either, and was interested to see Cromer's house, which was built for £39,000 c. 1890. It was not cheap. £39,000 was a vast amount of money in those days – but what was remarkable was that it came out within £16 of the estimate.

TUESDAY, 30 OCTOBER. *Luxembourg and Brussels.*

Dohnanyi to lunch in Luxembourg. He was, for once, very shocked by the behaviour of the French – Bernard-Reymond† not François-

---

* Sir Michael Weir, b. 1925, was Ambassador to Cairo 1979–85.
† Pierre Bernard-Reymond, b. 1944, was a State Secretary at the Quai d'Orsay 1978–81. An MEP since 1981.

Poncet, whom I think he likes more, at some restricted session yesterday. Also he had I thought a rather foolish idea about trying to upgrade not the presidency of the Council as such, but the Secretary-General, and floated the idea of putting Thorn into that job when the useless Hommel retires in the summer. Certainly a change for the better would be desirable, but I doubt whether a political figure would be sensible. It certainly would not suit me from the point of view of the future of the Commission, but Thorn would not of course be there until nearly the end of my time.

Dohnanyi then left rather gloomily to take the charter plane to Lomé to which a number of them were setting off for the signature of the Convention there. I had firmly decided that enough was enough so far as travel was concerned and that it was unnecessary for me to go. Motored to Brussels and worked hard all evening with Michael Jenkins on the paper for tomorrow's Commission – the so-called reference paper – keeping open the various options for dealing with the British problem. I was nervous after our September experience as to whether it might come apart at the last moment. Ortoli, in particular, might well be dangerous, and you can never tell with Gundelach, but I was rather encouraged by the fact that Ortoli pressed me to have a lunch for the 'Four Horsemen' at rue de Praetère *after* the Commission, and I judged it extremely unlikely that he, who doesn't like rows, would want to lunch with me if he was going to be awkward in the morning; and this indeed proved correct.

WEDNESDAY, 31 OCTOBER. *Brussels and East Hendred.*

Saw Donald Maitland for a final farewell call. I am sorry to see him go; my opinion of him has gone steadily up during the past two years.

Commission from 10.10 to 1.30. Fairly early on in the discussion on the paper it became clear that things were not going to be too awkward. I introduced it myself, fairly firmly indicating where there were possible areas of compromise and where there were not. Ortoli, Gundelach and, indeed, Davignon responded by saying that the areas of compromise were desirable but that they weren't going to press for going beyond that. So without too much difficulty we turned this dangerous corner. As a result we had a fairly relaxed subsequent luncheon; but, apart from the fact that Ortoli always manages to get the conversation into French, he played no national hand.

6.45 plane from Zaventem for my truncated East Hendred *Toussaints* holiday.* Jennifer and I had decided that it was too difficult to get to Sare where we had intended to stay with the Beaumarchais', not having gone in the summer. We feared that they might be offended by this, but discovered that it did not suit them badly because Jacques had severe 'flu and they were not sure when they could get there themselves.

THURSDAY, 1 NOVEMBER. *East Hendred.*

Up early, with an awareness that this November – the latter part of it in particular – was going to be a very testing month, what with my Dimbleby Lecture on the 22nd and then the Dublin Summit, and could turn out to be a fairly disastrous or at the very least a deeply disappointing month.

I then got down to a great day's work on Dimbleby. I clearly had to get the back of it broken on this holiday and as early as possible. I had already written nearly enough to fill the whole fifty minutes, but I was still lacking hard proposals, let alone peroration and conclusion, had a lot of otiose stuff at the beginning, and knew that I could not get down to an effective job of getting it into proper shape until I had a draft of the whole. Therefore I worked hard from 9.15 until 1.00, went out to a pub lunch at Clifton Hampden with Jennifer, and then proceeded to work equally solidly from 3.15 until 8.15, in other words eight and three-quarter hours solid writing during the day. It is difficult to tell how good it is, but I was very pleased to discover that I could still concentrate as hard as this on writing something without a draft and produce nearly three thousand words in a single day.

I was exhausted but satisfied at the end of it, when the Rodgers' arrived to dine. After dinner I read Bill bits of the more controversial part at the end. I think he was sufficiently post-prandial not to be taking it in too meticulously, but at least he was fully warned of what was coming and certainly showed no sign of reacting with

*The Brussels habit was for All Saints Day on 1 November to form the core of a long holiday weekend.

deep shock or hostility. He had moved quite a bit since the talk we had had in the summer, when he was staying at East Hendred, and had tried to persuade me to come back into politics in the conventional way.

SATURDAY, 3 NOVEMBER. *East Hendred.*

Gilmours to lunch alone. I got Ian to read Dimbleby. He thought parts of the political stuff at the end were too right-wing, and in particular objected to my using the phrase 'the social market economy'! So I adjusted it for this and other helpful criticism. He was also against having the Yeats quotation in at the end (too hackneyed). On this opinion is divided.

SUNDAY, 4 NOVEMBER. *East Hendred.*

To Sevenhampton with Jennifer and lunched with Ann and the Donaldsons. The Donaldsons are very keen to come to the Dimbleby Lecture which I shall arrange.

MONDAY, 5 NOVEMBER. *East Hendred and Strasbourg.*

11.30 plane to Paris for Strasbourg. Held up all the afternoon at Charles de Gaulle by the French air traffic controllers' strike. Strasbourg only at 6.45. Yet another dinner for Ortoli, Gundelach and Davignon.

TUESDAY, 6 NOVEMBER. *Strasbourg and Brussels.*

Intensive telephoning between 10.45 and 11.45, partly to fix up with Robert Armstrong for Davignon to pay exploratory visits to him and to Wahl in the Elysée to see how much room there was for give on both sides,* which visits had been suggested at dinner the night before.

Late afternoon plane to Brussels (late in both senses, the French air traffic controllers' strike again), but much worse than that, it

---

*The subject, of course, as was becoming perennially the case, was the British budgetary contribution.

was really intolerably bumpy and disagreeable for the whole of the fifty minutes, so much so that they wouldn't serve any drinks. Just when one needed them most. I would have thought that some heroic girl might have crawled along the aisle handing out much-needed sustenance. Arrived in the Berlaymont feeling rather shaken but recovered and went to dinner with the Michael Jenkins'.

WEDNESDAY, 7 NOVEMBER. *Brussels.*

A highly unsatisfactory lunch with COREPER in the Berlaymont, at which they nearly all, with the exception of Noterdaeme, the new Belgian, and I think also Michael Butler,* the new British Permanent Representative, complained hard about the reference paper containing options rather than a single precise recommendation with a figure: Nanteuil, but also the little ones, Dillon (Ireland) in particular, Dondelinger (Luxembourg), Riberholdt (Denmark), Plaja (Italy) a bit but not excessively, Lubbers (Netherlands) I think keeping quiet. It was rather disagreeable to have them yapping away quite so much, though I replied very robustly partly because I am so convinced we are right. Riberholdt and Nanteuil would like to have had a single proposition which they could have shot down, and thus improve their tactical position: the others, particularly Dillon, but to some extent Dondelinger, etc., were fighting a battle for COREPER's dignity and for them to have a specific role, which is not a primary interest of ours. So I was not unduly shaken by them.

After a long afternoon Commission, I had a three-quarters-of-an-hour arranged telephone call with Schmidt. He very much likes these long conversations, which I don't. He is rather good at them and we had a thoroughly productive discussion about what might or might not be done *vis-à-vis* the British. His general line was that Mrs Thatcher had some pretty unrealistic ideas, but nonetheless he was anxious to help her to what extent was possible, but she really had to compromise and think about things much more sensibly and seriously or she would be in great trouble. Then at the end he made some odd remarks asking how much of a crisis I thought there was

* (Sir) Michael Butler, b. 1927, replaced Sir Donald Maitland as British Permanent Representative to the European Community in October 1979 and served there until 1985.

in France as a result of the Bokassa diamonds affair,* speaking in a rather more detached way about Giscard than he had done before: not exactly unfriendlily, but as though he was genuinely seeking information. It is very much his habit suddenly to ask questions at the end of a discussion about any range of issues which are in his mind.

A late dinner party, rue de Praetère, for the Michael Butlers. Ann Butler is a bonus, but whether Michael is an improvement on Donald Maitland is more doubtful. He does rather bang away at issues without great sensitivity or feeling, as he showed in the COREPER lunch today, but he is a highly intelligent man and perhaps in some ways has a wider range of interests than Maitland, including – not that that much excites me – a great collection of Chinese porcelain.

Saturday, 10 November. *East Hendred.*

At 7 o'clock David Marquand came for a general political discussion but also usefully to read Dimbleby. He is very anxious for us to make a move in politics. Dimbleby he was constructive about, though fairly critical, and in a way not very enthusiastic, but perhaps this was rather good for me, particularly as he made, not on that occasion but subsequently by telephone, what turned out to be an essential point, that I should talk about the radical centre and not just the centre as such.

Sunday, 11 November. *East Hendred.*

My fifty-ninth birthday. Hayden and Laura, Leslie Bonham Carter, Griggs, Thea Elliott and Charles and Ivana to lunch. Just as we were going in we were telephoned from Paris to be told that Jacques de Beaumarchais had died that morning in the Salpêtrière Hospital. It was an enormous shock, although we had had an underlying worry about his health for the last fifteen months, partly because everything had gone so wrong since he returned from his previously brilliant career and highly successful embassy in London.

*President Bokassa of the Central African Republic proclaimed himself Emperor and reigned for a fairly brief spell before being toppled from power with some French assistance. During his imperial period he was alleged to have given some unaccounted-for diamonds to President Giscard d'Estaing.

They were both of them immensely close friends of ours. There were hardly any of the barriers which there almost inevitably are between the British and the French. They had been here a great deal during their embassy, we had done four two- or three-day trips in England with them, we had stayed at Sare so often, and they had stayed in Brussels I think no fewer than four times during the previous year. We last saw him at Barbizon, where he seemed quite well when he came to lunch at the end of September. And we had intended to go to Sare the previous week.

TUESDAY, 13 NOVEMBER. *Brussels and Strasbourg.*

Early train to Strasbourg. Crispin and I gave lunch to Stevy Davignon. He was back from his mission to the French and the British, and I thought him rather overoptimistic.

Christopher Tugendhat kindly gave me dinner. I found him quite interesting on budgetary questions, both British and the wider Community ones, but gloomy and worried – as we all are a bit – about the Parliament prospect.

WEDNESDAY, 14 NOVEMBER. *Strasbourg.*

Up at 7.50 on a dark, wet morning with the rain driving across the Place de la Gare, so that it looked like an 'umbrella' picture by Boudin or Corot. A debate on the British budgetary problems and convergence generally, which I opened for twenty-five minutes and which was reasonably satisfactory, with certainly no significant criticism along the COREPER lines that we had not been more specific. I did another twenty minutes near to the end at about 9 p.m. Then yet another dinner for the 'Four Horsemen', Ortoli, Davignon, Gundelach, plus, on this occasion, Emile Noël and Crispin. Too late, moderately satisfactory, too expensive.

SATURDAY, 17 NOVEMBER. *Brussels.*

I had a meeting with Davignon, Ortoli and Crispin – Gundelach away in Italy, thank God (not thank God particularly that *he* was away: it would have been better if they had all been away) – which went on unbelievably from 6.30 p.m. until 9.00 achieving remarkably little, with Francis being at his worst. Therefore I was rather bad-tempered at dinner with our weekend guests.

MONDAY, 19 NOVEMBER. *Brussels, The Hague and Brussels.*

Train with Crispin from the Gare du Nord to The Hague, where we first had a meeting under van der Klaauw's chairmanship and then a luncheon in the Catshuis which van Agt joined. The meeting was with a number of ministers – perhaps six or eight of them – and the lunch was equally strongly attended. It was a singularly satisfactory encounter with the Dutch. Quite a good detailed meeting beforehand and then, at lunch, although almost completely sacrificing my food as a result, I was able to give them an exposition of the British problem and why it existed and why it had to be solved as far as one could, which I think was more persuasive and more reasonable than anything I had done before on the subject and undoubtedly shifted them considerably. It focused my mind more sharply than previously, and they seemed very pleased with all aspects of the meeting and expressed themselves very strongly in this sense.

I had a brief talk at the end alone with van Agt and van der Klaauw and we got very near to what it might be possible for them to do.* Also, when van Agt was briefly out of the room, van der Klaauw asked me whether I was a candidate to continue as President of the Commission, and I explained to him very firmly that I was not *a candidate* and probably not available, but not certainly so as I did not wish to be too much of a lame duck during the last year. He seemed to understand completely and van Agt, when he came back, I think took the same point.

Back to Brussels by train. Dinner at the Irish Embassy for Michael O'Kennedy, with the normal three on each side. There was serious talk over dinner and again an exposition of the British problem from me. Not as well done as in The Hague and they were more resistant, particularly Dillon who clearly has a very strong anti-English streak in him. I suppose the Irish all have to some extent and it is totally understandable.

* Which indeed led to van Agt being one of the most constructive people at Dublin.

TUESDAY, 20 NOVEMBER. *Brussels.*

Finally cleared and sent to London for release the text of the Dimbleby Lecture. God knows how it will go, but at this stage one can only hope for the best. A short, early lunch with Martens, the Belgian Prime Minister. It was an attempt at a repeat of the performance with the Dutch the previous day. Simonet who was present was, if anything, more difficult than Martens. It was another useful exercise, undoubtedly making some progress with them though they are a step or two behind the Dutch. Foreign Affairs Council all afternoon and then a longish and fairly difficult (British budgetary) meeting with Gundelach and Ortoli.

WEDNESDAY, 21 NOVEMBER. *Brussels.*

Three-and-a-half-hour Commission meeting. Lunched with COREPER at the Charlemagne. I don't know why these luncheons are coming so close together at the present time. This was a much easier and more constructive encounter than on the previous occasion two weeks before. Four-hour Commission in the afternoon, very long, late and wearing. The last three days have not been exactly the way to prepare and be fresh for Dimbleby.

THURSDAY, 22 NOVEMBER. *Brussels and London.*

The long-awaited Dimbleby day. I spoke to the European Youth Forum for about half an hour from 10.15. Afterwards to the Parliamentary Committee on Information, which I also addressed, again for about half an hour, and in this case had to listen and reply to a discussion of some length, for which I was not perfectly briefed. The 12.45 plane to London was fortunately late, so that I was able to stay with them until 12.35. Otherwise there could have been ill-feeling. Then, of all things, there was no drink and no lunch on the plane, on the splendidly inadequate ground that there were only three stewards instead of five. As there were only eight first-class passengers, they would not have had the slightest difficulty in serving drinks, and indeed lunch had they wished (tourist-class passengers don't get lunch in any case). Presumably there is some union rule about not being willing to do anything with fewer than five stewards. As a result all three of them did absolutely nothing for the whole flight, except make themselves coffee; extremely irritating.

To the Savoy Hotel, where I had taken a small suite and where I had a late, light lunch and a last read-through of the lecture, before going the few hundred yards to the Royal Society of Arts where John Harris met me at 4 o'clock. There we had a rehearsal of the walk-on and walk-off, and a run-through of a few pages to make sure that the timing was right. Our best calculations indicated that I should be about two minutes within the allocated forty-eight/ forty-nine minutes.

Back to the Savoy with John and Jennifer for a rest, change and a drink, and then back to the Royal Society at about 7 o'clock, and proceeded to deliver the over-matured lecture to a full and fairly distinguished audience. Amazingly, I suppose the response to having an audience, all our careful calculations went awry and it took fifty-two minutes, but as the whole of the top echelons of the BBC were sitting in the front row, they could hardly cut me off.

Afterwards, feeling reasonably pleased, I went downstairs for a party for perhaps half to three-quarters of an hour. Everybody was really pretty enthusiastic and interested, the only person manifestly hostile being a somewhat bleary Ian Waller (of the *Sunday Telegraph*) who apparently went round saying it was absolute nonsense. The journalists in general, however, were more sceptical than the others, this applying, for example, to Fred Emery of *The Times*.

Of the politicians present, none was hostile and some were enthusiastic. Bill Rodgers, who had had an extremely important lunch with John Horam* that day (who had had a great influence on him) said that suddenly in the course of the lecture he had had a vision of himself sitting in the headquarters of the new party with his sleeves rolled up, actually organizing things, which I took to mean – I hope rightly – that Bill had passed over some emotional watershed. Ian Wrigglesworth was there and was also enthusiastic, and Phillip Whitehead,† although much more detached, was certainly not hostile.

* John Horam, b. 1939, Labour and then SDP MP for Gateshead 1970–83. Bill Rodgers's, junior minister at the Department of Transport 1976–9.
† Phillip Whitehead, b. 1937, was Labour MP for Derby 1970–83. He did not join the SDP. A television producer, he is Chairman of the *New Statesman* and of *New Society* since 1986.

FRIDAY, 23 NOVEMBER. *London, Brussels, Paris and East Hendred.*

Inevitably woke up early full of *angst* and apprehension about what the newspapers would look like and what other reactions would be. In fact, the newspapers were by no means bad. A good deal of coverage and none of it or hardly any of it at this stage markedly other than what I would have wanted.

11.30 plane to Brussels – not that I wanted to go to Brussels, I wanted to go to Paris, but the wretched air traffic controllers' strike being still on and avion taxis being too extravagant (at any rate I had no excuse for one back from a private engagement), the only way to get to Paris was to go via Brussels, and motor.

Having achieved Paris, I went to the Elysée to see Giscard for fifty minutes. It was the usual sort of Giscard interview – polite, cool, even cold, though the coolness at least equal on my side by now to that on his. It was clear that he was willing to do a certain amount, made no complaint about our paper in the Commission's circumstances, clear equally that he wasn't going to do a great deal, clear that he was going to insist on a number of unrelated concessions in return for whatever he agreed to, clear too that he was leaning back and was going to be in a detached, passively awkward mood (perhaps the best way of putting it) at Dublin. This meeting was not in itself particularly worthwhile, but it was important that I had gone through the motions of seeing him beforehand.

Then to Avenue Franklin Roosevelt for a quick, early dinner with Marie-Alice. I found her in a fairly poor condition, I suppose. Shattered certainly, but also embittered by the two years of official neglect which had preceded Jacques's death. She was extremely hostile to the French powers that be, and showed me a sharp letter which she had sent to François-Poncet in response to the rather ludicrous typewritten letter which he had sent to her on behalf of the French Government. She fortunately completely understood why we hadn't been able to go to the funeral and was pleased with the piece which I had written about Jacques over the previous weekend and which had appeared in *The Times* on the morning of Monday 19th. She was unwilling – at first I thought only superficially – to have a memorial service in London because it would have to be organized by the French Embassy. But towards the end of dinner I became convinced that she was serious about this and therefore decided that there was nothing more to be done. Nonetheless I enjoyed seeing her, it was not as wearing as it sounds, and she is still very much the highly individual, indomitable, totally splendid Marie-Alice. 9.30 plane (late) and East Hendred at 11.45.

SATURDAY, 24 NOVEMBER. *East Hendred, London and East Hendred.*

To London to address the annual meeting of the European Movement, almost the last thing I wanted to do after the previous few days. There were three speeches, from George Thomson, Heath and me. I spoke pretty unprepared; I had a text but didn't like it. Lunch with the Gilmours at Isleworth. East Hendred at 4.30. I was very tired, but by this time, from letters and other responses, it was beginning to be clear that public reaction to Dimbleby had been better than the press reaction, though the press reaction had not been bad, and that the resonance was very considerable indeed.

SUNDAY, 25 NOVEMBER. *East Hendred.*

I did only a little desultory work in the morning. Although it was the weekend before a European Council – and a pretty crucial one – I felt I had done most of the preparation I could on this, knew the subject well, and in any event having two major events running so closely together meant that Dimbleby at least had the advantage that I could not worry too much about Dublin.

The Sunday press was not bad: an immensely long but slightly confused leader in the *Observer*; a very good leader in the *Sunday Times*; a hostile leader in the *Telegraph*, predictably and not woundingly so.

Bradleys to lunch. Tom managed to go on until 2.30 without mentioning Dimbleby. At first I thought it was not exactly because he strongly disapproved of it (if so he would have told me) but more because, in Tom's curious switch-off way, he had been so preoccupied with Kettering Town or some such thing, that he just hadn't noticed that it had taken place. But when, however, I at last raised it half-way through lunch, he was fully aware of everything and all the reactions to it, and pretty strongly approving. What he disapproved of desperately was that by some appalling accident he hadn't been invited to the lecture itself and, even worse, he had been approached by David Owen on Westminster tube station on the Wednesday evening, he (Owen) having got a copy of the lecture, from the press no doubt, and he (Tom) having very little idea what was in it.

However, Owen had almost totally retrieved the position by telling Tom how much he disapproved of it, and by saying that it was 'very unfair of Roy to do this to those of us who have risked our careers for him'. To which Tom reacted violently, and not unreasonably, saying, 'You've risked your career for him? You've risked nothing at all. What better career do you think you could have had? You are a walking career,' and stumped off. Owen had denounced the lecture in not exactly violent but in slightly disagreeable terms in a speech, I think on the Friday at lunchtime, which had appeared in the press on the Saturday.

MONDAY, 26 NOVEMBER. *East Hendred, London, Dublin and Brussels.*

To London by train and a little late (but we had warned her and she showed no sign of umbrage) to my hour's meeting with Mrs Thatcher: a shorter, more restrained, equally friendly, encounter than on the previous occasion. I could not quite make out whether she was prepared to compromise or not. I don't think she wants a break and she reiterated her point that there is no question of her leaving the Community, no question of an empty chair, no question of illegality. It is not clear either whether she will accept any sort of postponement.

Lunchtime plane to Dublin, and then an hour and a half's meeting with Lynch. This was almost entirely devoted to the agenda, although there was some discussion about where he had got in a previous meeting with Schmidt. I found him in very typical Lynch-like form, anxious to be guided on the agenda, though fairly pessimistic, and sensibly so, about the outcome of his European Council. There being a gap after this, we went to the Irish National Gallery, which was well worth doing, before our plane to Brussels. After dinner I went into the Berlaymont, where the lights would not work, and had a forty-minute telephone conversation with Schmidt. Sitting in total darkness, I rounded up things with him.

TUESDAY, 27 NOVEMBER. *Brussels*.

Studied the letters on Dimbleby which were pouring in from various addresses at this stage. They were remarkably favourable and of remarkably high quality. The numbers were not enormous (a few hundred) and never achieved vast proportions, but compared with previous big correspondences this one was notable for the complete conviction and commitment with which people wrote. And also for the fact that, whereas when, say, I resigned from the deputy leadership, they broke 70/30 favourably, these broke literally 99 to 1 favourably, with the 1 per cent being dotty rather than against.

I then gave lunch for Poensgen, the new German Permanent Representative. He had been Ambassador in Greece; he is an unimpressive-looking man and came with a reputation for being difficult. But I found him agreeable and sensible.

THURSDAY, 29 NOVEMBER. *Brussels and Dublin*.

To Abelag for an avion taxi to Dublin – we thought that even in present circumstances we could and should afford one on this occasion – with Ortoli, his *Chef de Cabinet* and my various staff in extremely cooped-up conditions. It was an extraordinarily long and roundabout flight, so that we had to go straight to the state luncheon in the President's house in Phoenix Park.

A rather good luncheon, but too large and too long. I sat between Martens and Simonet (very Belgian rather than very English this time). The Council started at 3.40 in Dublin Castle and went on until 8.10. There was a certain amount of routine stuff introduced by us first, which lasted longer than I expected (some, I think, were rather keen that it should do so). Then into the budget question about 6 o'clock, introduced briefly by me. Mrs Thatcher did quite well for once, a bit shrill as usual, but not excessively so. There was quite a good initial response. The Italians and the Irish, for instance, offered to pay their share and it was agreed without much question that we should fully apply the financial mechanism.

Schmidt started to cross-question me on how we could do things beyond that, which was difficult but not impossible. Then towards the end Mrs Thatcher got the discussion bogged down by being far too demanding. Her mistake, which fed on itself subsequently at dinner and indeed the next morning, arose out of her having only one of the three necessary qualities of a great advocate. She has nerve and determination to win, but she certainly does not have a good understanding of the case against her (which was based on the own-resources theory, or theology if you like), which means that her constantly reiterated cry of 'It's my money I want back', strikes an insistently jarring note. 'Voilà parle la vraie fille de l'épicier,' someone (I think Simonet) said. She lacks also the third quality, which is that of not boring the judge or the jury, and she bored everybody endlessly by only understanding about four out of the fourteen or so points on the British side and repeating each of them twenty-seven times. But that developed over the evening. Up to the 8.10 adjournment there was no real progress but no disaster either.

Dinner was at Iveagh House. Mrs Thatcher sailed in last, but behaving rather well, particularly as I gathered that she had had (i) an explosive row with her senior officials on the way over in the plane, so that it nearly blew up over St George's Channel, and (ii) another explosive row in the interval between the adjournment and dinner. But she came in looking in full command of herself.

She kept us all round the dinner table for four interminable hours. During the first part, the bilateral conversations over dinner, she mainly talked to me (I was next to her) in order to avoid talking to Giscard, who was on her other side. Then there was a general conversation about nuclear defence, in which she upbraided, in a rather uncomprehending way, the little countries for their pusil-lanimous attitude. She was somewhat supported by Giscard (who was not very comprehending or sensitive either), but not by Schmidt, who felt passionately, on her side, about the substance but felt forced to intervene with a statement saying that neither she nor Giscard could understand non-nuclear sensitivities, because they had been nuclear powers for a long time, but he understood them even though he did not agree with them. (During this conversation she vouchsafed her only awareness of Dimbleby. The Belgian Prime Minister was justifying his hesitancy about cruise missiles by citing his coalition difficulties. Mrs Thatcher turned to me with a mixture of belligerence, good humour and total self-satisfaction and announced to a slightly bewildered table – none of them elected by the British system – 'And *that* is all *your* great schemes would amount to.')

Back then to the budget question with her reiterated demand becoming more and more counterproductive. At times she was not bad and always maintained her temper though not her judgement, even under considerable provocation, particularly from Jørgensen who, partly because he can't speak English well, was at times behaving like a little street urchin calling out insults. Schmidt got frightfully bored and pretended (but only pretended) to go to sleep.

It was obvious to everyone except her that she wasn't making progress and was alienating people. Giscard was able to lean back, as he had in the afternoon, and shelter behind Schmidt, which is a bad position from the British point of view. There were no great rows, only the Jørgensen insults and Schmidt simulating sleep. Cossiga, attending his first European Council, was immensely active, perhaps talking a little too much, canvassing heavily the idea of a special February European Council (the Italian presidency begins on 1 January) as things couldn't be settled in Dublin, to which I was moderately favourable and one or two other people maybe were too. Back to the Shelbourne Hotel very late.

FRIDAY, 30 NOVEMBER. *Dublin and East Hendred.*

During the night or while dressing I came to the firm conclusion that the only thing to go for was a postponement. Postponement is sometimes a mistake, if it is done just for the sake of postponement, but it appeared to me (a) that if one were in a room and didn't like the furniture, and another room was offered, at least try it, and (b) that people were rather frightened of a great quarrel in the Community, and with all the pressures upon us from the Iranian situation and the American reaction to that situation, the general impending economic threat, etc., that postponement might produce a better atmosphere in February or March, and (c), which in a sense is part of (b), that all sorts of things might happen in the next two months – the Americans might conceivably think it necessary to make some sort of pre-emptive strike in the south of Iran, or something of this sort, and that therefore there could be circumstances in which we could reach a settlement later, which we could not do now.

I tried to telephone Schmidt to this end, but missed him. At 10.00 I went (at her request) to see Mrs Thatcher in Dublin Castle where she was installed (perhaps incarcerated is the better word), because the Irish felt that nowhere else would be satisfactory from the security point of view (all the rest of us were in embassies or hotels). It was an unforgettable scene. Those two important knights, Sir Michael Palliser and Sir Robert Armstrong, were sitting in inspissated gloom. The atmosphere was enlivened, if that is the right word, by a plaque upon the wall saying: 'In this room James Connolly, signatory to the proclamation of the Irish Republic, lay a wounded prisoner prior to his execution by the British military force at Kilmainham Jail and his interment at Arbour Hill, 12th May, 1916.' She wasted half the time on a harangue, which embarrassed her two knights and bored me (the worst aspect was the time it wasted) but her purpose was to say that she would accept a postponement.

Then the so-called 'family photograph', during which I was urgently and obviously talking to Schmidt, trying to urge the postponement upon him as he and Giscard were leaning back and saying there was no point in it. Then the Council met from 10.40 to 2.40. We had a Commission text which we eventually got adopted. The Belgians had a less good text, but they helpfully accepted ours. But Giscard and Schmidt were unwilling to accept a postponement until Mrs Thatcher had said that she would approach the next meeting in a spirit of compromise. This for some time she declined to do, just going on banging away at the old points. Eventually Peter Carrington (who was out of the room too much, with various other things on his mind) had a word with her, and in her next intervention she said – the words coming out of her with almost physical difficulty, but given her character having meaning nonetheless – 'Yes, I would approach such an early European Council in a spirit of genuine compromise.'

Giscard then said, 'I do not want there to be confusion between a compromise and a misunderstanding. You may think we have got a compromise, but what we may have is a misunderstanding which can lead to nothing but trouble for the future.' But he eventually agreed, though he was rather irritated by the draft which I put forward and indeed took Ortoli out to complain about it, having rather offensively asked: 'Is this the draft of the Commission, or the President of the Commission speaking personally?' I said I spoke with the authority of the Commission. It could manifestly hardly have been considered by the whole Commission, as they weren't there, but it was well within the terms of our paper. So it was eventually agreed that the Italians should make soundings as to whether the circumstances existed for having an earlier Council. We galloped through the remaining items not very satisfactorily, as some of them were important, notably Europe's weakening position in information technology. But the Council was wholly dominated by the British budgetary question.

Then a three-quarters-of-an-hour press conference with Lynch – a huge gathering of journalists as usual. He did it well, better than I would have expected. Questions came about equally to both of us. There was a certain amount of difference between us, enough to have excited Giscard had he been in the Taoiseach's position, but not to cause any drama with a modest, reasonable man like Lynch.

I flew to London in a howling gale, and, with a considerable feeling of relief, got to East Hendred by 7.00. It was nice to have both Dimbleby and the European Council over.

SATURDAY, 1 DECEMBER. *East Hendred.*

To Didcot to pick up Bill Rodgers, who was returning from South Wales where he had been making a striking and helpful speech at Abertillery, brought him back to East Hendred, where we arrived at exactly the same time as Shirley Williams from London. I talked with them for an hour or more before lunch and went over the position. There was a fairly good identity of view, though both of them – Shirley perhaps a little more than Bill – were anxious to say that it was always possible, although not likely, that things would go sufficiently well in the Labour Party that they would want to stay with it; but they were quite willing to contemplate all other possibilities. Bill in particular struck me as being emotionally committed (surprisingly for Bill) to a break. Shirley has always been in a sense more intellectually open to it than Bill, but has not yet passed over the sort of watershed that he did some time at the end of November – the day of my lecture, I think, though maybe a lunch with John Horam on that day was even more decisive than the lecture.

They both thought that if Healey were elected leader of the party, Callaghan going in perhaps a year's time, that would be a period of setback for us. There would be a tendency for people to rally to a new, tougher leader and give him a chance, but equally neither of them had any real faith in Denis doing anything new, giving any new direction, or had any loyalty to him. It was a very worthwhile talk. Bill even seemed keen to get down to almost small details of organization, which is a very good sign with him. But who can say what will happen?

SUNDAY, 2 DECEMBER. *East Hendred.*

Bonham Carters, Asa Briggs' and Wyatts to lunch. After lunch I talked seriously to Woodrow for perhaps twenty minutes or so, giving him a rundown on the Dublin Council. He had been on the telephone to Mrs Thatcher that morning and he spoke to her again after he had gone back and then telephoned me. I gave him a fairly accurate account of her performance, both the good and the bad parts.

THURSDAY, 6 DECEMBER. *Brussels and London.*

To London after yet another COREPER lunch. I travelled across with John Sainsbury, whom I was pleased to see. He seemed pro-Dimbleby. Other people I had seen in the morning, notably Chandler,* the Director-General of NEDO, had also been pro-Dimbleby. I had Colin Phipps,† ex-MP, who gave up his seat to seek a Euro seat but failed to get one and is now extremely anxious to be an organizing figure in some new party, to see me. I had always been a little suspicious of him, mainly because in the 1976 leadership contest he had done us a good deal of harm by first of all announcing that he was a keen supporter of mine because I would clean out all the dead wood from the Government, which meant that the many people who feared that they might be dead wood immediately became extremely suspicious of voting for me, and then, having done this damage, switched to Healey a week later. However, on this occasion he was impressive: agreeable, easy, had done a good deal of work, very optimistic about the possibilities, and seemed to have contacted a lot of people.

* Sir Geoffrey Chandler, b. 1922, came from Shell to be Director-General of the National Economic Development Organization 1976–82.
† Colin Phipps, b. 1934, an oil exploration executive, was Labour MP for Dudley 1974–9.

FRIDAY, 7 DECEMBER. *London and Dublin.*

12.10 plane to Dublin. Lunched at the Hibernian Hotel with Denis Corboy, the head of our Dublin office. Then to Trinity College to be robed and to take part, fortunately without a speech, in the degree ceremony. We were greeted in Dublin by the news that Haughey* had beaten Colley, by a fairly narrow but nonetheless decisive margin, for the leadership of Fianna Fáil and hence the Prime Ministership following Lynch's surprising (not in substance but in exact timing) two days' old announcement that he was resigning. Lynch very kindly came to the ceremony, as did Michael O'Kennedy, which like all TCD things was rather splendidly conducted, all in Latin, in a very good hall.

Then an hour with Jack Lynch in his familiar old office in which I have often seen him, and Cosgrave before then. He was sad to be going, obviously feeling slightly that he had been pushed out. He did not conceal his dismay at Haughey's election, but reminisced agreeably about the past few years. A nice man, but not I suppose an immensely dynamic or effective one. However, he has held the leadership for thirteen years, has been Prime Minister twice and has prevented a lot worse things happening in Irish politics. Not that I am convinced that Haughey, who is odd, colourful and possibly but not certainly dangerous, will be all that bad.

Afterwards I tried to cobble together a speech for the Trinity College dinner that evening. I had enjoyable conversations with on one side F. S. L. Lyons, the Provost and biographer of Parnell (which incidentally he, like me, pronounces *Par*n'll), and the Professor of Greek on the other. The whole occasion was very typically TCD, which is quite good at trying to make Oxford and Cambridge seem rather redbrick.

MONDAY, 10 DECEMBER. *Brussels and Strasbourg.*

I had Peter Walker for lunch, rue de Praetère. He was anxious to be friendly and made a most unfavourable impression. He opened fairly soon after we sat down at the table by saying, 'I know you

*Charles Haughey, b. 1925, having previously been successively Minister of Justice, Agriculture, Finance, and Health and Social Welfare between 1961 and 1979 then became Irish Prime Minister until 1981, from March to December 1982, and since February 1987.

think that I don't get on well enough with Gundelach, but what you ought to know, indeed you may have heard already because I asked Ian Gilmour to tell you [he wisely hadn't told me], is that although you are always very pro-Gundelach, Gundelach when he came over and saw me made the most disobliging, disloyal remarks about you.' I know this is not entirely out of character, alas, with Gundelach, as I had heard it once or twice before. I think it stems partly from the fact that he is constantly on the verge of exhaustion and from the fact that he can't bear not being the star of everything. He has a rather misty, Nordic vanity. I, however, was determined not to rise to this, showed no great interest and didn't ask Peter Walker to say what Gundelach had said, which he was obviously very keen to do.

However, Peter obviously thought that he was on to a very skilful ploy and followed it up with a number of other almost equally disobliging or unfortunate remarks. He disavowed Ted Heath, saying he had never been a close friend of his, though perhaps he ought to go and see him because he thought he was in a very poor condition and had taken to eating chocolate biscuits from morning until night, which was a very bad sign. He said my Dimbleby Lecture was no doubt interesting, but in the House of Commons people had said it was my taking the temperature and that at one time in the past – which is without foundation – I had launched the idea of forming a new party with Harold Lever, and then recoiled (quite untrue: much though I love him I would never start an organizational venture with Harold).

Conversationally, Walker was forthcoming, anxious to be friendly, and altogether left rather a nasty taste in my mouth: curious because he is quite an able man.

Then a very bouncy and full avion taxi ride to Strasbourg. It's very odd that the air between Brussels and London should always be so relatively calm – it is very unusual to bounce on that journey – and so frequently very rough between Brussels and Luxembourg or Brussels and Strasbourg. I think the meeting point between the Central European and the Atlantic weather systems must produce a concentration of unstable air.

The new Monday evening question time for an hour and a half, appallingly long. As I had rather thought, the new arrangement is likely to be the beginning of the end of question time: (i) a continuous hour and a half is not nearly as good as two three-quarters of an hour, and (ii) Monday evening means that not all that many people are there, and those that are there are mostly British because they are the only people who like question time.

Then I introduced the supplementary budget, in a rather dull speech of about fifteen minutes, but they seemed pleased that I had done it.

WEDNESDAY, 12 DECEMBER. *Strasbourg.*

Another filthy morning, and I worked rather gloomily on another speech, and then rushed up to the Parliament to be ready to open at 9 o'clock. Typically, this had been changed the night before without anybody telling us and in fact I didn't have to speak until just after 11 o'clock, when I delivered a fairly brisk, fifteen-minute report on the Dublin European Council and then listened to Lenihan,* the new Irish Foreign Minister. Gave lunch with Crispin to Henry Grunwald,† the managing editor of *Time*, and his interesting wife. We had quite a substantial meal, which was as well for we then returned for the Budget Council, which began at 3.20 and went on until just after 4.30 in the morning with nothing to eat at all and nothing to drink except for a few whiskies which I got from the British delegation at about 1 o'clock. It was a singular misapplication and waste of thirteen hours of continuous and exhausting session.

It was not a high-level Council. Lenihan was in the chair and in some ways was not bad, Lahnstein was representing the Germans, Bernard-Reymond the French, Nigel Lawson‡ the British, an Italian and a Belgian I did not know, van der Mei (as slow and stubborn as ever) for the Dutch, Ersbøll for the Danes. At first it seemed as though a compromise between Council and Parliament was likely, but gradually the hope of this faded away mainly because of the foolishness and chaos of the Council. The Parliament was less concerned with sums of money than with getting some effective control over agricultural expenditure for the future.

* Brian Lenihan, b. 1930, has been Irish Foreign Minister 1972–3, 1979–81 and since 1987.
† Henry Grunwald, b. 1922 in Vienna, to which he has now returned as US Ambassador.
‡ Nigel Lawson, b. 1932, has been Chancellor of the Exchequer since 1983, but was then only Financial Secretary to the Treasury.

Eventually we adjourned at 4.40, with the Parliament rep-resentatives saying that they would put the proposals to the Budget Committee at 8 o'clock in the morning, but with no great feeling that they were likely to be accepted. Mme Veil clearly wanted acceptance and a compromise, no doubt because of the delicacy of her position. The fact that the French had been somewhat more forthcoming than the Germans and the British undoubtedly in my view owed a great deal to an Elysée desire not to embarrass her. Bed only at 6 a.m. Up again just after 8 o'clock.

THURSDAY, 13 DECEMBER. *Strasbourg and Brussels.*

To the Parliament at 10.15. It was then clear that there was going to be a very heavy rejection of the budget. Hurried discussion with Davignon and one or two other Commissioners. Then in the early stages of the debate I hurriedly wrote out a very brief statement which I would make when the vote had been taken saying that the Commission naturally regretted that there was not a budget but carefully refraining from saying that we regretted what the Parlia-ment had done. The train was temporarily off the tracks and we would take full responsibility in the interests of the Community as a whole for trying to get it back on at the earliest favourable moment, and for this we would need the cooperation of both halves of the budgetary authority. This did not commit us specifically to produc-ing a preliminary draft budget, although in my own mind I already thought that it would be necessary, and it did not commit us either to a date, which was wise because the Parliament was not in a great hurry.

Impressive statements were made by several people on behalf of the groups, Dankert and Lange (Socialist), Bangemann (Liberal), Klepsch (Christian Democrat). Only Ansquer for the Gaullists and somebody for the French Communists, making the most extra-ordinary cliché-ridden speech (pretty close to the Gaullist line), spoke against. The worst speech was the opening one from Lenihan, in which he made an ill-judged appeal to the Parliament to behave responsibly and was greeted with some derision.

I had an extraordinary scene with Vredeling towards the end of the morning. Obviously in a great state (he hadn't gone to bed at all and had gone round looking for a group to harangue and found his way into early morning meetings of the Budget Committee and the Socialist Group and made badly received statements to both of them), he started to complain that we hadn't had a Commission meeting and that there was no collegiality. I said that there weren't enough Commissioners in Strasbourg to have a Commission, and all the few there had been consulted and all were in favour of what I proposed to do, except apparently for him. He said there would be a disaster and I would be howled down if I did not immediately promise a preliminary draft budget by a specific date, and if I did not do it he would get up afterwards and do it. I said, 'Very well, you do that and one of us resigns tomorrow and the Commission will decide which it is.' So he then declined into muttering and head-shaking, looking very hysterical, though in no way due to alcohol which he does seem to have kept off.

At the end, when the overwhelming vote had been announced, I got up and made my brief statement, which lasted only a minute and a half and which was very well received. After that I rather insufferably said to Vredeling, 'If only your judgement was as good as your heart, Henk, life would be much easier, wouldn't it?' He said, 'Oh dear, I was only being so anxious because I was afraid it would go wrong and I didn't want you to do it wrong.' So I patted his arm in a fairly friendly way and went off. A most extraordinary man, foolish but good-hearted.

Lunch with Fred Warner* and Jennifer at La Wantzenau. After-noon non-TEE back to Brussels: we could get seats neither on the aeroplane nor the evening TEE. Strasbourg transport is intolerable.

FRIDAY, 14 DECEMBER. *Brussels.*

Home at 6.30 feeling very exhausted and extremely loath to go to Château de la Hulpe and have our long evening with Suárez, Spanish Prime Minister, and Calvo Sotelo, whom we had invited, to have eighteen hours or so of talks. Laura and Hayden had arrived to stay at about lunchtime and it would have been a great deal pleasanter to dine with them and Jennifer.

At La Hulpe I had a longish talk with Suárez both before and during dinner, all through an interpreter which in some ways

---

* Sir Fred Warner, b. 1918, had been Ambassador to Japan 1972–5, before being elected a Conservative MEP 1979–84.

makes it more of an effort, but at least makes it more precise than if we were both talking bad French. Suárez made as favourable an impression upon me, in spite of the somewhat unfavourable circumstances, as he had done when I had last seen him in Madrid.

SATURDAY, 15 DECEMBER. *Brussels.*

To Château de la Hulpe for 9.30 and then a long talk with Suárez more or less alone. I put firmly our attitude to the negotiations, our desire to conclude them according to the timetable he had in mind, by the end of 1980 (the bulk of them at any rate) with a view to Spanish admission at the beginning of 1983.* This would require considerable effort and accommodating spirit on both sides. We wanted to strengthen not weaken the Spanish economy, but this must be done in a way which was compatible with membership of the Community. Equally there had to be certain changes in the agricultural policy or it would be impossible just to graft Spain on to it without having bankrupting sums of money involved in olive oil alone. Also they must take seriously our trans-Mediterranean preoccupations, just as we attach great importance and value to their special Latin American contacts and the strength which they could give the Community.

Then back to the general discussion which had been proceeding under the joint chairmanship of Natali and Calvo Sotelo and a round-up there until about 11.30. I then saw the Spaniards off in a howling gale although it was a rather beautiful morning with a clear sky and a good winter woodland view. As I drove back through the Bois a great tree came down on the other side, crushing a car and leading to the Bois being closed for forty-eight hours.

TUESDAY, 18 DECEMBER. *Brussels.*

Reluctantly received Dohnanyi for breakfast.† I had a moderately useful talk with him mainly about the British budgetary position, but also about the Parliament. He like all sensible men is rather enthused by the Parliament's rejection of the budget, but worried by difficulties to which it may give rise with the French. He quite

*This timetable subsequently slipped by three years.
†The reluctance sprang from breakfast as a working meal, not from Dohnanyi.

rightly says that the French are now extremely defensive and nervous as they fear a future in which a majority of the Parliament can unite with a blocking minority of the Council to take charge of agricultural expenditure (a very good thing, but I suppose it puts the Germans under some strain given their determination to remain close to the French).

WEDNESDAY, 19 DECEMBER. *Brussels and London.*

At last the last day of this almost endless autumn session, which has been going on for 107 days since 3 September. Quite a good Commission and very satisfying getting through it in the morning. A good discussion on the budget which, although certain issues of future difficulty were not opened up, revealed a more than reasonable coincidence of approach at this stage. After this, the Commission Christmas lunch, which passed off agreeably. I banned turkey, which was so badly done last year, and we had pheasant which was much better and the Christmas pudding was, as before, a success. Early evening plane to London.

THURSDAY, 20 DECEMBER. *London.*

Dick Taverne, Anthony Lester, Bob Maclennan, David Marquand and Michael Barnes, all of them expectedly, and John Horam, unexpectedly but extremely agreeably, came to Brooks's for a plotting meeting about radical centre, etc., and for dinner afterwards. They were all pretty good, with the exception of Anthony, whom I thought was rather downbeat (but that can be in his character). Taverne and Horam were particularly good, and Mickey Barnes very enthusiastic. They were all in a way enthusiastic, they all thought a split was inevitable and desirable. There was a slight difference in emphasis, but not more than that, as to the extent to which we were thinking in Labour Party or in broader terms.*

---

*I.e. whether the catchment area of any new party was to be Labour members and supporters or more widely drawn to embrace those of other parties or of no party. I favoured the latter approach.

MONDAY, 24 DECEMBER. *East Hendred.*

Charles and Ivana arrived at about 10.30, bringing clearing weather, and we then motored to Bath where we had an immensely enjoyable day, the city looking spectacularly good, better even than I remembered it, in bright, cold sunlight.

TUESDAY, 25 DECEMBER. *East Hendred.*

A memorable morning, hard white hoar frost with the mercury way down below the bottom of the thermometer (20°F). Drove to the Monument, and saw a splendid sunrise illuminating wide views, although there were little troughs of mist in the valleys. After church, I drove up again, with others. The light was different, but still very good, with a curious impression now that there was fog in the valley – though I don't think that it was fog – and with the tops of the cooling towers at Didcot Power Station and little elevations like the Faringdon Clump rising out of it like islands in the sea. I think it was a light refraction effect.

THURSDAY, 27 DECEMBER. *East Hendred.*

Lunch with the Eric Rolls at Ipsden. They had the Kingman Brewsters (US Ambassador), the Michael Stewarts, and Robert Marjolin, always their Christmas guest. An enjoyable long luncheon with a certain amount of good general conversation (but rather less productive than when I sold the EMS to Kingman Brewster there eighteen months ago) about America, Britain, France, the world, etc.

SUNDAY, 30 DECEMBER. *East Hendred and Cambridge.*

A particularly enjoyable lunch with the Bradleys at Kettering. Not much politics, though Tom indicated, for what it was worth, that on one occasion Hattersley had asked him if he could contemplate breaking with the Labour Party, and he had said, 'Certainly.' Then on to the Rothschilds' at Cambridge. Victor morally in better form than I had expected to find him, though with some kind of residual bronchitis and frequently taking his temperature, as a result of which he had to go to bed at about 9.30. Victor never goes out, sits in his shirtsleeves the whole time, and just shouts at Sweeney for dry martinis or Bucks fizz – a most incredibly unhealthy life. How he survives so well I don't know.

MONDAY, 31 DECEMBER. *Cambridge and Norfolk.*

Left after an early lunch and proceeded to the Zuckermans' at Burnham Thorpe. Upstairs before the New Year, after a dinner with Solly's spectacularly good wine. I sat reading alone over midnight. A change of decade, not merely of year. 1979 was not as good as 1978, but not intolerable either. The wretched, petty *Cour des Comptes* affair overhung some of it. The advent of the new Parliament began to look menacing in the early summer. But I was quite wrong. As the year turned out, the Parliament was a great advantage, showed its strength and muscle and improved the quality of Europe. The problem of the British budgetary contribution was in an important sense mishandled because it involved the creation at home by the Government of such a groundswell of anti-French but also general anti-European opinion. It was not skilfully played by Mrs Thatcher. However, I am able to take it reasonably calmly, partly because I think the Commission did its best at Dublin and came out quite creditably, but also because Dimbleby and thoughts of the future occupy my mind greatly. Goodness knows what 1980 itself, let alone the decade as a whole, may hold. Slightly intimidated by the thought of having let a genie out of its bottle.

1980

1980 was a year sharply divided into two halves. In the first half (accurately five months) there was little time for anything except the BBQ. (These initials were first used in the diary on 18 February; I think they were originally intended to stand for British Budgetary Question, but the alternative of Bloody British Question increasingly became the connotation in my mind.) Not only I but the whole Community was rarely allowed to think about anything else during this period. This was a pity for it was a time when Europe's economic performance was faltering badly, when East/West relations were tense following the Soviet invasion of Afghanistan, and when American leadership was unsteady.

It was also a time when the continued strengthening of Political Cooperation (printed with capital letters because it is the term of art for the attempt at foreign policy coordination which in 1970 was initiated within the Community but outside the Treaties) would have been particularly desirable. But there was little energy left for it. The *impasse* at the Dublin European Council had left the Community in a state of suspended crisis, and until it was resolved everything else seemed to the British at least, but to some extent to everybody, to be peripheral.

I believed that on the merits Mrs Thatcher had right broadly on her side, although she showed little sense of proportion, some of her favourite arguments were invalid, and her tactical sense was as weak as her courage was strong. All this, however, counted for little compared with the danger, of which I had become convinced in early 1979, that the issue, unless satisfactorily resolved, would alienate any British Government from the Community and do a good deal of harm to the whole European enterprise. I therefore gave as total a priority in the first half of 1980 to assisting a solution as I had done throughout 1978 to promoting the EMS — to which

Britain's continued non-adhesion was a considerable factor in reducing goodwill amongst the other eight.

'Assisting a solution' meant trying to get these other eight to contribute, beyond as it were the terms of the contract, to a special subvention of 1000 to 1100 million *écus* (approximately £700 million) a year to Britain, and trying to get Mrs Thatcher to accept the two-thirds of a loaf to which, from her point of view, this amounted. The trouble with her constantly reiterated 'it's my money I want back' argument was that this argument gave no recognition (surprisingly for the head of such a commercially minded government) to the fact that to forgive a bad contract involved some generosity on the part of those who were the beneficiaries.

The trouble with my position in 1980 as opposed to the other three years of my presidency was that for the first time I could be accused of playing a British hand and of putting my whole weight and attention behind it. I believed it was in the general European interest, but I doubt if this view of my motives was taken in Paris, and perhaps not in some other capitals too. In these circumstances attempts by the French Government to neutralize in advance such firepower as I possessed were only to be expected, and they were duly forthcoming, although more from the Quai d'Orsay, it appeared, than from Giscard or Barre. Perhaps more significant was the withdrawal of the Belgian Government from their advocacy of a renewal of my presidency (see the entry for 14 May).

What I am above all struck by, however, on a rereading of the diary, is the extent to which the dispute put under strain my relations with the other Commissioners, nearly all of them by that stage close and friendly associates. On one occasion I found myself in a minority of two in the Commission, with only Christopher Tugendhat supporting me. This was a position I had never previously been remotely near, indeed only rarely in even a strong minority.

It was the long-drawn-out nature of the dispute, I think, which built up the personal strains. At Dublin, Francesco Cossiga, as the head of government of the country about to assume the presidency (of the Council), had launched the idea of bringing the next European Council forward to February. However on the 18th of that month he and I decided that insufficient progress had been made and that we should revert to the normal date at the end of March. Then on 24 March he decided unilaterally on a further postponement. The European Council eventually met in Luxembourg on 27/28 April, when Mrs Thatcher to almost universal amazement rejected a very favourable offer.

There was then no alternative, unless the Community was to break up, but to begin a cosmetic operation to save Mrs Thatcher's face without overstraining the generosity of Chancellor Schmidt and the others who would have to pay. This meant dressing up approximately the same deal in a somewhat different form. It was this which was achieved in the Council of Ministers (not the European Council) on 29/30 May. Lord Carrington then showed himself a more skilful and sensible negotiator than his head of government. He knew when to settle. She did not.

It was the run-up to this final encounter which produced the real *morosité*. Everyone was tired, bored, and knew that the repeat performance was an unnecessary charade. However there were brighter aspects to the sorry saga. We were lucky that it took place during the Italian presidency, and we were doubly lucky with the composition of the Italian Government. Both Cossiga as Prime Minister and Emilio Colombo, who had taken over as Foreign Minister in early April, were consistently helpful. So was Klaus von Dohnanyi, the German Minister for European Affairs, who from this relatively junior position took great risks, negotiating well beyond his authority, in order to settle the damaging and divisive issue. The French were by no means bad at the end of the day, and other smaller governments were also surprisingly amenable, most notably the Irish, who forwent an opportunity to remember the wrongs of centuries.

When the settlement came (at the end of an eighteen-hour session) it did so with a sudden completeness. The issue went away like a summer storm. It was bound to resurface in the future, but not until well after my time as President. And there was little that my Commission could do about preparing for that resurfacing except to set in train studies on longer term Community financing (the so-called 'mandate') for our successors to pronounce upon. The governments would never have accepted unpalatable policy recommendations, on an issue not immediately pressing, from a dying Commission.

The beginning of June therefore saw a complete change of gear. The leaders of Europe had become both irritated and wearied by the issue. When it was over they went into a condition of stasis. The two June Venice meetings, first the European Council and then the Western Economic Summit, were flat. My own mood matched that of the Community. In early June I began to feel unwell, which happily I had hardly done during the previous three and a half Brussels years, and did not fully recover until well into September. The symptoms were vague, perhaps stemming more from general exhaustion than from anything else, but the net effect was a period when I approached issues with more dismay than zest. Luckily there was no major European issue with which to deal. After 30 May no dominating Brussels theme seized my attention.

Nor did I do much external travelling in the second half of 1980. In the first half I had been to New York and Washington for a week in January, to Yugoslavia in February, to Portugal in March, and to India for nine days at the beginning of May. I had intended to do a major South American trip in the early autumn, but cancelled it when my June/July exhaustion set in. I went only to Norway in July, Spain in October and Sweden in November. The Yugoslav, Norwegian and Swedish visits were because of the attention which the Commission devoted to relations with the small adjacent countries which had to live in water greatly affected by any movements of the vast hull of the Community. The Indian visit was to discharge a postponed commitment to the largest Third World country. The American visit was routine although I got much involved in discussions of their reaction to the Soviet invasion of Afghanistan. At the end of the year I felt that I owed the Americans a farewell visit, but was only able to fit this in during January, after I had ceased to be President.

With the BBQ out of the way, my thoughts inevitably turned increasingly to my impending return to England which had become far more associated with the political prospect than I would have believed possible twelve months before. On 8 June I delivered a follow-up to the Dimbleby Lecture in the form of a speech to a luncheon of the parliamentary press gallery. It raised more explicitly than did Dimbleby the forming of a new party. It received more press publicity than Dimbleby and by just over a year later had come back into my favour because of the inclusion of the phrases about the experimental aeroplane which might 'well finish up a few fields from the end of the runway' but which might equally well 'soar in the sky' and 'go further and more quickly than many now imagine'; and after the Warrington bye-election this seemed a happy juxtaposition with soaring much more likely than crashing.

Immediately after the event, however, this speech and reactions to it added to my gloom. I felt that I had somewhat misjudged the moment, which had not been the case with the November lecture, and had condemned myself to being stranded on a ledge halfway up a cliff, committed to some dramatic political action, but lacking the strength and resources single-handedly to launch a new political movement.

It would obviously be both a more attractive and a more feasible project if it could be done with some major collaborators. At that stage this meant primarily Shirley Williams and William Rodgers. David Owen I did not then regard as a likely ally. I knew that he had disapproved of the Dimbleby Lecture. I subsequently discovered that he was more favourably disposed towards the press gallery speech, having shifted his position when shouted at in the special Labour Party Conference on 31 May. The other two were in friendly touch with me and were already semi-detached from the Labour Party, although reserving their position until they saw the political developments of the autumn, both the decisions of the regular party conference in late September and the result of the leadership election (following James Callaghan's withdrawal) in early November. I was more than prepared to wait that length of time for them, although I would not have done so indefinitely.

The Labour Party political developments of the autumn, when they came, were as unfavourable for its own electibility and as favourable for the prospect of a new party as could easily be imagined.

Following this I had seen Bill Rodgers on 5 October and David Owen on 19 October. They had both moved substantially since the separate August meetings which I had had with each of them. However, I still inclined to the view that the odds were slightly against Bill making the break.

On 10 November the result of the second and final ballot for the Labour Party leadership was announced. The first ballot, a week before, had given Denis Healey a surprisingly insubstantial lead over Michael Foot. It was a position in which Foot could easily overtake him, and that was precisely what happened – by a margin of ten votes – in the second ballot. Apart from the strength of the left-wing challenge, Healey suffered from some right-wing defection.

From that date onwards I do not think that I doubted there would be a significant break-away from the Labour Party. On 29 November David Owen informed me that he was definitely prepared to be part of a new party, although he indicated very clearly that he did not think I should be its leader. This struck me as *menu détail* compared with the great news that he was willing to move. He said that he was fairly sure that Shirley Williams would do so too, although he had some doubt about Bill Rodgers. I, however, had a very satisfactory talk with Bill on 11 December.

So my last Brussels weeks passed to the accompaniment of sporadic pieces of news which made the British political prospect seem markedly more promising. It was a vast improvement on June and July. I no longer felt stuck on the cliff ledge.

From early November onwards everything began to be for the last time: my last visit outside the Community, my last Strasbourg session, my last European Council, my last Council of Ministers, my last COREPER lunch (rather a joy), and eventually my last night in the rue de Praetère house, which was dismantled from 15 December. In addition to these naturally occurring 'lasts' there was a whole series of more or less formal specially arranged farewells: to eight member governments (it seemed ludicrous to include the British on this occasion), to the Parliament, to the Council, to the Commission *huissiers* and drivers.

I went to England for Christmas on 19 December. I was still President until 6 January 1981, but effective power ceased with the beginning of the Christmas holidays. I returned to Brussels only for a brief two days on 4 January.

THURSDAY, 3 JANUARY. *London.*

Ian Gilmour to lunch at Brooks's. An enjoyable and, up to a point, useful talk. He is off on a great tour of all the Nine countries, presumably to try and arrange a compromise agreement, though his instructions are remarkably unclear, and the position is made more confused by the fact that Geoffrey Howe* is going to do four or five of them, not with Ian but more or less overlapping. Certainly the Foreign Office view is that they would settle for some reasonable compromise, but to what extent this represents a thought-out Cabinet view I don't know.

We talked a bit at the end about post-Dimbleby centre party issues. He seemed to have one main point that he wished to make to me, that it was a great mistake for me to give any impression – as apparently had appeared (though unobserved by me) in one or two newspapers – that I might come back from Brussels before the end of the year. It was crucial (to what?) to make clear that I would serve out the year. Equally he takes at once a slightly cautious view (as I would expect) about what we might achieve, believing, as he always has done, that one needs to have great interests behind one to succeed in politics. But at the same time also believing it just possible that we might achieve success more quickly than is within the bounds of my imagination. In other words, that we might find it very difficult to advance slowly but that it was just conceivable that the collapse of Conservative support would be so great that one might, in some sort of loose alliance with the Liberals, even win the first general election.

Another meeting later in the day with three 'conspirators' on new party matters, Jim Daly, GLC transport chairman, John Morgan, old *New Statesman* writer, Harlech Television figure etc., whom I didn't expect – it is curious how more people than you expect turn up on these occasions – and a man called Clive Lindley, who is one of those curious Welsh marches businessmen, rather

---

*Then Chancellor of the Exchequer, not Foreign Secretary. The subject requiring a compromise agreement was of course the British budgetary dispute which, post-Dublin, was all-dominating.

like Colin Phipps.* They were all quite sensible and I hope they are all right. It is going to be very difficult to manoeuvre everyone into position.

FRIDAY, 4 JANUARY. *London and East Hendred.*

George Scott's great press lunch (for editors to question me on European issues), at which nearly every editor in London turned up with the exception of William Rees-Mogg. We had Fredy Fisher of the *FT*, Peter Preston of the *Guardian*, Deedes of the *Telegraph*, Trelford of the *Observer*, Harry Evans of the *Sunday Times*, Charles Wintour of the *Evening Standard*, Molloy of the *Mirror*, Andrew Knight of the *Economist*, and the editors (whose names I cannot remember) of the *Express* and the *Evening News*, as well as one or two people from other papers. Only a moderately successful occasion. Nobody asked questions about British politics, except for the *Express* editor, who started off with a silly brash question, which rather killed the subject. After that a tolerable, not more, discussion on Europe.

Then, with clearing weather but not rising spirits, I motored with Jennifer to East Hendred. The first few days of January are usually one of the most depressing periods of the year.

SUNDAY, 6 JANUARY. *East Hendred.*

Tried to do my David Bruce tailpiece† before the Ginsburgs and Thea Elliott and the Wayland Kennets came to lunch: Wayland a great centre party man, and David Ginsburg sympathetic but cautious, and kept describing a lunch he had had with Denis Healey and insisting how important it was that Jim should be replaced by Denis: so far as I am concerned it is Tweedledum and Tweedledee.

---

* He turned out not to be at all like Colin Phipps.
† A small book had been compiled out of the letters of tribute which a remarkable variety of (mainly) American and British figures had written after his death. Evangeline Bruce asked me to write a summing-up, with which flattering but testing request I gladly complied.

MONDAY, 7 JANUARY. *East Hendred.*

Drove up to the Downs for the sunrise at 8.00. David Steel to lunch.
I had a good talk with him for three hours. He is very agreeable,
sensible and curiously mature. He also looks remarkably like
Hayden (Phillips), to an extent I hadn't realized before. He perfectly
understands that there is no question of me or anybody else joining
the Liberal Party. He equally is anxious to work very closely, and
possibly, if things went well, to consider an amalgamation after a
general election. He would like the closeness at the time of the
election itself to take the form not merely of a non-aggression pact,
but of working together on policy and indeed sharing broadcasts,
etc. He says that for this point of view he has overwhelming support
in the Liberal Party.

He agreed with my view that a lot of the calculations were based
too much on deciding how much water there was in the kettle, as it
were, and how it could be shared out, whereas there was a lot more
to be brought in from outside, people uncommitted to and unin-
volved in politics. He agreed that it would not be sensible to think
purely in terms of the Liberals having Tory seats and our having
Labour seats: this was too simple an approach. He fully accepted my
point that if, which I was not committing myself to in any way, I
wanted to fight a bye-election during 1981, it would probably be
much better to do this in a Tory-held seat than in a Labour-held
seat, and indicated that his people would make way for me in those
circumstances. Altogether a thoroughly satisfactory talk.

After he went I walked three miles to above West Hendred in
the twilight until I left for the Oxford Farming Conference at 7.00.
Brief drinks in Worcester and then on to the Randolph Hotel for a
rather excessive five-course dinner, sitting between the agreeable
chairman and Henry Plumb.

They accepted my speech, with its rather hard message, quite
well, but obviously not enthusiastically. However, it was at least as
well received as Peter Walker's speech, which was intended to be
more to their taste and was based on the fallacy that surpluses can
be dealt with in a way that is thoroughly acceptable to British
farmers, which I believe is nonsense. Somebody has got to be hurt,
including the British, if that problem is to be dealt with.

TUESDAY, 8 JANUARY. *East Hendred and Brussels.*

3.45 plane to Brussels. Dinner at home for Ortoli, Gundelach and Davignon, together on this occasion again, with Emile Noël and Crispin (Tickell). Gundelach more subdued than usual. I think the intractable problem of agricultural prices, plus probably his feeling that the next presidency (of the Commission) is slipping away from him, plus his normal state of semi-exhaustion, is having a slightly rattling effect upon him.

WEDNESDAY, 9 JANUARY. *Brussels and Paris.*

5.17 TEE from the Gare du Midi to Paris to see Marie-Alice de Beaumarchais, and dined with her near the old Saint-Eustache church of revolutionary fame.

THURSDAY, 10 JANUARY. *Paris and Brussels.*

At 7.00 I was driven swiftly through the dark, cold, fairly empty streets of Paris to the Gare du Nord, where I was able to equip myself, surprisingly early, with the English newspapers as well as some French ones. I read them over breakfast and watched a grey dawn across the plains of Picardy.

A curious man was opposite me in the restaurant car. He spent no less than one and a half hours reading every word of *L'Humanité*, a remarkable feat of slow concentration which pointed irresistibly to his being either a plodding functionary of the French Communist Party or, more probably, a member of the Deuxième Bureau, or whatever that organization is now called. He then read the *Canard Enchaîné* but got through that at a more normal pace, and then became very impatient to leave although there was no steward to pay. So he eventually got up and departed, I assumed to find the steward.

A few minutes later a young, non-French-speaking Dutchman arrived and sat in his place, whereupon the steward came and presented him with a bill. He said he hadn't had breakfast, the steward pointed unbelievingly to the dirty plates around him, I rashly intervened, 'Non, non, ce monsieur vient d'arriver. Ce n'était pas son petit déjeuner. Il y avait quelqu'un d'autre. Il avait la note à la main quand il est parti.' 'Dans quelle direction?' asked the steward. So I said I thought towards the rear of the train. The steward then accusingly said, 'He was a friend of yours?' I said, 'Certainly not.' He then said would I go with him and find the man. I said, 'Even more certainly not,' and the whole thing was on the verge of escalating out of control into a most ridiculous scene.

However, the train at least got to Brussels on time, and the incident provided me with a peg for my speech at the change of presidency dinner that evening at Val Duchesse. I was finding it desperately difficult to think of anything remotely fresh to say at my seventh dinner in this series.

FRIDAY, 11 JANUARY. *Brussels, Rome and Brussels.*

Took off for Rome just as dawn was breaking on a most beautiful, hard-freezing, clear-skied, Brussels morning. At 11.30 to the Quirinale to call on Pertini, the relatively new octogenarian Socialist President of the Republic, whom I had not met before. Slight worry as to what on earth I was going to talk to him about, for I assumed a statutory half-hour or so, but no problem emerged, for despite it all having to be done through interpretation and our sitting around in an awkward-sized group of about fourteen people, the conversation galloped along, with a great deal of history and a flood of personal judgements (he is tremendously impressed with Mrs Thatcher), accompanied by long expositions of his attitude to world politics stemming from his wartime experiences. A verbose, dynamic, interesting, unconventional little man; the interview, quite unexpectedly, lasted one and a quarter hours.

From the Quirinale to the Palazzo Chigi for a 1 o'clock meeting with Cossiga. Malfatti was also supposed to be there but had had another heart attack. As a result, Cossiga and I spent a long time alone, discussing what he should do about the Malfatti problem, I saying firmly that he must have a proper Foreign Minister to preside over the Council, that it couldn't be left to Zamberletti, the quite nice Under-Secretary. He agreed, said that he had to make a change and that he was sorry but Malfatti's health just wasn't up to it. Who, therefore, did I think he should appoint? There were two possibilities, Ruffini, the Defence Minister, and Pandolfi, the Finance Minister. Would it be a bad thing to move across the

Defence Minister? he curiously asked. Would it look too much as though it were a military appointment? I said, no, schematically there was absolutely no objection to this, though it was of course the case that Pandolfi was linguistically very good and well known and well respected in Community circles. I did not know Ruffini. So he said he would reflect on all this. I hope that he will go for Pandolfi.*

Partly as a result of this friendly conversation, we were able, when joined by a few others, to clear our thoughts for the next stage of the Commission paper with considerable ease and in a very good atmosphere and to move into lunch at 2.30. On the British budgetary question Cossiga was moderately but not excessively optimistic. He said that the conversations with Ian Gilmour had not gone particularly well the week before because the Lord Privy Seal had had nothing he was able to say to them. I pointed out firmly that this was not his fault, as he had been given a very narrow negotiating brief, but the Italians definitely left me with the impression that they thought it had been a great mistake to undertake this mission without giving it any authority to negotiate on a figure below the 1500 million units of account which the British were still demanding.

The best Cossiga and I could do was to agree that we would work hard on method, that it was very difficult to say that an early Summit would be worthwhile, though it was too early definitely to rule it out, and that we should be in close touch again at the end of the month after his visit to Mrs Thatcher in London and my visit to Schmidt in Bonn. A useful, agreeable meeting. Plane from Fiumicino and home to rue de Praetère exactly twelve hours after I had left.

SUNDAY, 13 JANUARY. *Brussels.*

Took George and Hilda Canning† to Tervuren and, for the first time, to the Musée d'Afrique Noire. On the Saturday we had taken them to Waterloo, where Jennifer and I had climbed up the Mound in bitter, sparkling weather. In the late afternoon we went to Malines

*In fact he went for Ruffini, who lasted only three months.
†See entry for 12 May 1978. On this occasion they were staying with us after an official Lord Mayoral visit to the Commission.

and found the cathedral more splendid than I had remembered. It was helped by a brilliant winter sunset. Dinner at home alone with the Cannings. George and I had quite a serious political conversation at the end, in which he assured me, without pressing which was good and nice of him, that he would support me in anything I did in the way of a radical centre party, etc. Quite a commitment for him to enter into, particularly as one knows how solid he is when he has said something.

MONDAY, 14 JANUARY. *Brussels.*

I saw Ian Gilmour for half an hour. I hinted to him that the Italian visit hadn't gone very well and discussed how one should handle things in the future. Afterwards I saw Tom Enders, the new United States Ambassador, an impressive, self-confident, over-tall Yale man, who I think is probably very good. In the afternoon I saw Dick Cooper, one of Carter's two envoys, Warren Christopher being the other, with the general US briefing about what they wanted us to do on Iran, Afghanistan, etc. I just listened.

A short late working dinner at home for the Italians, Ruffini, Zamberletti, Plaja, etc. It was rather a remarkable feat on Ruffini's part to have arrived at all, considering (i) that he had only been appointed, unexpectedly he told me, that morning, (ii) that he had to stay in Rome in order to meet Warren Christopher (who had only arrived at about 5.30) and see him at the airport. However, although I was impressed by his coming, he didn't quite seem to know whether he was on his head or his feet and while no doubt his knowledge of NATO matters, and, I daresay, Italian internal politics is good, his knowledge of Community affairs is distinctly sketchy. He also seems to me to show signs of being a rather stubborn man, but perhaps that is not a bad thing in an Italian. More serious is the fact that, alas, he speaks no word of English or French. He does not understand even the simplest French phrases.

TUESDAY, 15 JANUARY. *Brussels and Strasbourg.*

Foreign Affairs Council all day until 7.30. Ruffini not surprisingly a somewhat uncertain President. At the Council lunch I had more or less to preside. There was a long wrangle about a communiqué on Afghanistan. The French were very stubbornly for the *status quo* on agricultural exports to Russia, or even worse than the *status quo*, and the British tried much too hard to get a long-term change of commercial policy through, i.e. end of sales of subsidized butter to Russia (which they have always wanted) under the shadow of a particular political situation. However, eventually, after an adjournment and the solvent of boredom, a text emerged. Although at one stage there had been eight to one against the French and in favour of a harder line, they managed, by their usual combination of stubbornness and a certain degree of skill – plus the weakness of the others – to get the British into an equally isolated position by the end. Ruffini was a better chairman during the afternoon. Then to Strasbourg by an incompetent avion taxi which wasted two hours.

WEDNESDAY, 16 JANUARY. *Strasbourg.*

A meeting with Mme Veil at 12.15 and then lunch with her for Ruffini and Zamberletti. She had procured an interpreter for Ruffini but one who could only do French into Italian and, as he added rather pointlessly when we arrived, into German – but not English. However, it didn't matter because Mme Veil talked nearly all the time and at such a rate that there was no time for the interpreter, poor Ruffini hardly understood a word that was going on and the conversation passed between her (rattling along) and Zamberletti and me (both limping behind). Not a very pointful occasion.

Just before sunset I went for a forty-minute walk in the Orangerie with Nick Stuart. It was, I think, the coldest walk that I have ever had on this side of the Atlantic. We walked very fast and heavily clad round the frozen park, on a beautiful day (as all this period of weather has been), with the setting sun a great red ball glowing through the frost, but I was still agonizingly cold at the end, and had the impression that my clothes were disintegrating almost in the way that I experienced in Chicago ten years ago. The temperature was about 20°F, which is extremely low for the middle of the afternoon in Western Europe.

Dinner after a Commission meeting with the Fred Warners and the Frank Giles'.* Frank rather shocked by some of my remarks about Giscard.

*Frank Giles, b. 1919, was deputy editor of the *Sunday Times* 1967–81, and editor 1981–3. Married to Lady Katherine (Kitty) Giles, née Sackville.

With Crispin Tickell in the garden of rue de Praetère, July 1979. Over his shoulder: Michel Vanden Abeele, Belgian member, and Mrs Etienne Reuter, wife of Luxembourger member of my *cabinet*.

A medal from the Pope, Castel Gandolfo, September 1979.

I meet Giscard's *trois sages*, January 1979: Barend Biesheuvel, Edmund Dell, Robert Marjolin.

And receive the report of my Five Wise Men, September 1979: Dick Taverne, K. Buschman, Paul Delouvrier, Dirk Spierenburg, Giuseppe Petrilli.

The Dublin European Council, December 1979.
Left to right: front row, Werner, Giscard, Lynch, Thatcher, Cossiga;
second row, van Agt, Jørgensen, Schmidt, Jenkins, Thorn;
third row, van der Klaauw, Martens, O'Kennedy, Zamberletti (Malfatti was ill), Carrington;
back row, Simonet, François-Poncet, Olesen, Ortoli.

With Prime Minister Adolfo Suárez of Spain, Château de la Hulpe, near Brussels, December 1979.

Venice, June 1980, for the European Council and Western Economic Summit.

In session: left to right, Genscher, Ortoli, Jenkins, Jørgensen, Olesen.

Crispin Tickell and I look as though we are attending a Venetian funeral. Celia Beale and detectives in front.

Out of session: Carrington, Werner, Mrs Thatcher, Jenkins, Colombo and (over Colombo's shoulder) Renato Ruggiero.

The Queen at the Berlaymont, November 1980. Presentation of some *cabinet* members. Left to right: Nick Stuart, Etienne Reuter, Klaus Eberman.

The 'Gang of Four' launching the Social Democratic Party, 1981: Jenkins, David Owen, William Rodgers, Shirley Williams.

THURSDAY, 17 JANUARY. *Strasbourg and Brussels.*

Took Pieter Dankert,* the *rapporteur* of the Budget Committee, to lunch. I found him as I expected an able and impressive man, and certainly a remarkably good linguist. Yet, at the same time, I had the impression that there is some fault which may account for the fact that he has not achieved more in Dutch politics, and that – not that this is a bar to achievement in politics – he may not be as nice as he is able. We talked a little about the future Commission, and he told me the most extraordinary story: that Bernard-Reymond had been in Strasbourg canvassing the claims of Cheysson to be President. As the French spend most of their time putting in complaints to me about Cheysson's statements, this seems very odd indeed, even on the unlikely assumption that the French have any remote claim to the presidency. It must be some sort of ploy, I think. Then back to Brussels in the little *avion de ligne*.

FRIDAY, 18 JANUARY. *Brussels and New York.*

1 p.m. Sabena plane to New York.

At 8.30 I went with Marietta Tree to a most extraordinary dinner at a restaurant called Le Cirque given by a rich Texan wife, for about fifty people, most of whom she did not know, and in honour of the Kissingers, whom she had asked to choose the guest list. This turned out a remarkable, and in some ways uneasy, mixture of New York grand society and café society and one or two who belonged to neither. Her husband had unfortunately disappeared into hospital three or four days before, but she, an extremely bouncy lady of about forty, carried on with tremendous aplomb, even making a slightly contrived but by no means bad speech.

The *mise-en-scène* was that of a 1940s film, with three violinists playing throughout and a feeling that Adolphe Menjou should be the head waiter. Then suddenly the three turned into two who advanced up the room, doing a serenade to Kissinger, and I realized – though it took a moment or two to do so – that they weren't two of the three hired performers but were Isaac Stern and Zubin Mehta. Afterwards Stern made Mehta do an extraordinary

---

*Pieter Dankert, b. 1934, an MEP from the Netherlands since 1977, succeeded Simone Veil as President of the Parliament, 1982–4.

double-talk act with him, in which he said, 'Now I will make a little speech in which I shall start each sentence and my friend will have to finish it. Then he will start the next one and I'll finish that.' Mehta looked slightly apprehensive about this, but in fact did it extremely well: Stern did it brilliantly, and the whole thing was an extraordinary *tour de force* for about five to seven minutes.

I sat between Mrs Mehta and Happy (or Unhappy as she is now known, I fear) Rockefeller, with Kissinger on the other side of Mrs Mehta. A lot of people of some note present – Javits* inevitably, Jack McCloy† – I cannot really think who altogether. Baddish speeches, including a rather indifferent one from Henry, but not as bad as those a (to me) unknown Senator and an unknown Congressman had made earlier. The hostess's was well above the average, even including her extraordinary act of saying, 'Now we have got Henry's book, which is the greatest book for a very long time, but not perhaps as great as the Bible, therefore, I am opening the Bible on this higher stand and opening Henry's book on the other stand a few inches below it.'

SUNDAY, 20 JANUARY. *New York.*

At Marietta's large dinner party there was a bizarre interchange between Sam Spiegel‡ and Nicko Henderson, neither knowing who the other was, but neither being able to understand that they didn't know someone as notable as the other obviously was. It all arose over a discussion of the Christmas holidays, when Heath had somewhat surprisingly spent two weeks more or less alone with Sam Spiegel in the West Indies. Nicko couldn't think who this man was with whom Heath had spent such a long time; and Spiegel couldn't think who this man Henderson was who knew Heath so relatively well.

MONDAY, 21 JANUARY. *New York.*

To the vast, dismal Hilton for my dinner with the Economic Club of New York, which I had last addressed ten years previously. As is

---

*Jacob Javits, 1904–86, was Senator from New York 1957–86.
†John J. McCloy, b. 1895, former High Commissioner in Germany, Chairman of the Ford Foundation 1953–65, Hon. Chairman of the Council on Foreign Relations.
‡Sam Spiegel, formerly S. P. Eagle, 1904–85, was a film mogul who moved much in liberal political circles.

their habit, it was a double billing, with Reuben Askew, ex-Governor of Florida, Robert Strauss's replacement as Special Trade Commissioner. I greeted the occasion with foreboding, having been told by some rather foolish man the previous evening that it was a useless audience (which was contrary to my previous recollection) and the only thing to do with them was – as apparently old Lord Thomson (Roy not George) and done several years ago – to tell them an endless series of rather *risqué* stories, which was not my intention, desire, or capability.

In fact it turned out a very good occasion: an audience of nearly a thousand and I made quite a brisk speech, with even some oratorical flourishes. We then had a good question session, including one about what were my intentions in relation to a centre party in British politics. I recalled Al Smith's 1924 riposte, which was at least appropriate in New York, when he got off the Twentieth Century Limited from Chicago, was prematurely asked whether he was a candidate (for President) and said, 'I have not yet reached a decision upon that grave matter. But even had I done so I think it extremely unlikely I would wish to communicate it to the nation, through you, from this railroad platform.'

TUESDAY, 22 JANUARY. *New York and Washington.*

Nine o'clock shuttle to Washington. At 11.00 a curious meeting with Brzezinski and Vance jointly, in Brzezinski's White House office. It was never clear who was in charge.

Then, at 11.30, a three-quarters-of-an-hour meeting with Carter. I saw him first in the Oval Office alone and had the normal agreeable conversation and photographs, and then had a rather good exchange with perhaps a total of fourteen people round the table, fairly evenly balanced conversation and not difficult. He was looking on much better form than when I had last seen him in Tokyo at the end of June, but this is not surprising as that was a very low period for him, and this is an up period after his crushing defeat of Teddy Kennedy in the Iowa primary.

I then went to the State Department in Vance's car and had a half-hour's meeting with him, followed by a two-hour luncheon. The meeting was better than routine, partly because we completely floored him over sanctions against Iran. In a polite way I told him why I was sceptical about them and found to my surprise (it's a bad thing that the US State Department should think things out so incompletely) that he had no real answers, and not much conviction either. Over lunch we ran through a range of issues – Yugoslavia, Turkey, China. It was better than previous meetings at the State Department, because we had more to talk to them about and it was in no sense a contrived agenda.

At 3.15, I saw the Secretary of Commerce (Klutznick) who Carter told me would explain the exact US position about the restriction on the export of high technology to Russia, but discovered they were still in a totally confused state about this.

The Spaaks had a huge dinner for me, forty-eight I think, with his fairly normal but rather good selection of people, a few Senators, a few Congressmen, Harrimans, Chief Justice Burger, Vangie (Bruce), I think no ambassadors of the Nine (other than Nicko), a few White House people, Lloyd Cutler,* Henry Owen, Dick Cooper – all quite well done and well organized. The only difficulty was that Madame Spaak was distinctly gloomy, as she thought that when Fernand went back to Europe she would lose not only her embassy but her husband,† and therefore reproached me for agreeing to his return. (I had no alternative. He had done four very effective years and wanted a change.)

SUNDAY, 27 JANUARY. *East Hendred.*

The Rodgers' to lunch; found them on good and friendly form, Bill's political position not having changed much: i.e. much tempted by movement but had to wait until the autumn.

MONDAY, 28 JANUARY. *East Hendred, London and Brussels.*

A Savoy lunch at which I presented the Granada journalistic awards of the year. Then the 4.45 plane to Brussels, on which I easily beat all my records doing the door-to-door journey, central London to the Berlaymont in 1 hour and 41 minutes.

* Lloyd Cutler, b. 1917, Washington Democrat and lawyer, was Counsel to the President 1979–81.
† Alas, it turned out to be much worse. Sixteen months later she shot him and then killed herself.

TUESDAY, 29 JANUARY. *Brussels.*

At noon I received the Minister President of North Rhine Westphalia, Herr Rau,* for a talk alone, followed by a short luncheon. He seemed all right, not vastly exciting but quite interesting enough to go on with. A Social Democrat Landpresident in coalition with the FDP.

Made a brief speech at a farewell party for Alan Watson, Director of Television in the Commission – in which difficult job he has done very well.

THURSDAY, 31 JANUARY. *Brussels, Bonn and Brussels.*

Up at 7.40 with my speech on Afghanistan to the Political Committee of the Parliament (a great public affair with television, etc.) rather weighing on my mind. I worked rather frantically on it before going to the Palais d'Egmont for the much-publicized hearing at 10.00. The fifteen-minute speech seemed to go fairly well, and I had no great difficulty with the exchange of views afterwards, which went on for about two hours. Brandt made a rather wobbly speech, Scott-Hopkins a pompous one about butter, but up to a point I seemed to satisfy him. I was slightly concerned as to whether I had not, on butter and other agricultural export sales, gone a shade further in the direction of banning anything going to the Soviet Union than was compatible with the 16 January decision of the Council of Ministers.

Then a singularly ill-timed COREPER lunch. It was my lunch for them, but I arrived slightly late and more than slightly bad-tempered. I was immediately nobbled by Luc de Nanteuil with an attemptedly menacing complaint about my speech that morning. I don't think he had read it, but he kept on saying that it would be studied very carefully in Paris and if I had said we weren't going to sell butter there would be *remous* in Paris, and the French Government would deeply disapprove, etc., to which I was fairly off-hand, being fed up with Luc always treating Paris as the areopagitica of Europe, and just ill-temperedly and dismissively said, 'Quel dommage!'

However, the row persisted during lunch, when Dillon (the

*Johannes Rau, b. 1931, was subsequently the unsuccessful SPD candidate for the Federal Chancellorship in 1986.

Irishman) was at least as bad as Luc, and nobody was very helpful except for Butler who is somewhat counterproductive. I again got rather bad-tempered at one stage during lunch, saying that it would just firmly stick in my mind that the whole reaction of COREPER to Afghanistan was an argument about butter and they seemed unable to raise their gaze out of the milk churn.

I left feeling dissatisfied with them and with myself. They weren't all quite as bad as they might have been: Poensgen wasn't there, Eugenio Plaja was trying to pour oil on troubled waters and Riberholdt wasn't too bad. But Dillon and Nanteuil and one or two of the others were extremely tiresome.

Then I drove off with Crispin on a filthy day, all the external circumstances unpropitious at the moment, to Bonn for Schmidt at 6 o'clock. Schmidt was very late, not emerging from a meeting of the National Security Council until 6.45, having apparently been at it from 2.00. He complained a good deal about his health (he apparently has some nasty form of angina), but this didn't prevent his looking more or less all right and proceeding to have the most extraordinary wide-ranging, 'brain-storming' conversation, which lasted, first with Crispin and Horst Schulmann present, from 6.50 until 8.45, and then with Schmidt and me alone until 10 o'clock, so that the whole encounter was well over three hours with no dinner, one or two drinks I thought rather reluctantly brought in, a few *kleine essen*, and nothing else.

It was an amazing conversation, much of it fascinating, and it covered almost every subject under the sun: mainly the world strategic balance, his distrust of what the Americans had done in relation to Afghanistan, their lack of any overall concept, the closeness of his relationship with Honecker,* into which they had been forced by a mutual nervousness of their superpower leaders, the fact that there were very few people in the world to whom he could speak in great confidence – Gierek† (surprisingly) was one, Brezhnev was not, Mrs Thatcher was not, Giscard was, Carter was

*Erich Honecker, b. 1912, has been head of state of the German Democratic Republic since 1976.
†Edward Gierek, b. 1913, lived for almost twenty-five years in France and Belgium before returning to Poland in 1948 and becoming First Secretary of the Communist Party and leader of the régime in 1970. In 1980 he fell from power and was interned for a year from the end of 1981.

not, maybe Vance was, maybe Carrington was, he didn't know him well enough.

This led on to the one positive proposal to come out of the meeting, which was that I would try and arrange for him to have a private meeting with Carrington as otherwise I could see no way forward on the British budgetary question, on which he had become distinctly hard, moving back to a position less favourable than he had been prepared to take in Dublin. I therefore said, 'Let's see if we can't arrange a meeting, as you say you would like to talk to him about general things. It is difficult to do this in a normal way in London because you would then have to do it with Mrs Thatcher.' He said, 'It is difficult to do it in the normal way in Bonn, because I then ought to have Genscher with me and he is the touchiest man in the world.' So I said, 'Why don't you come to my house in Brussels? I will arrange a dinner there.' He replied, 'What about England?' and out of this began to germinate the possibility that he might come to spend the weekend, nominally seeing his daughter, who lives in London, and that we might arrange something at East Hendred. It did not seem to me likely that anything would come of this, but at least it seemed worth trying.

Although no practical progress was made on the wretched British budgetary problem, and although the conversation was basically depressing, I got closer to the nub of matters with him than I have perhaps done before, particularly the nub of the difficulty of the British position in Europe if the Franco-German position was as locked-in an alliance as, he quite frankly explained, it has inevitably become.

A part of the hour's private conversation I had with him alone was political, a reversion to the possible Carrington plan, some of it was what one might call gossip about our responsibilities, my talking to him about future German Commissioners, for instance, and some of it was just conversation, with his talking about his pattern of life, his reading (he had amazingly just been reading the complete plays of Oscar Wilde, and the night before had read a whole Agatha Christie novel during a long insomniac spell). He struck me as being in an attractive mood, in some ways a bit unhinged, but on balance, as always, an interesting and formidable man.

I left him feeling nearly as exhausted as he said he was. Crispin and I drove back on a still most filthy night, getting to rue de Praetère just after midnight. I went to sleep feeling distinctly uneasy about the Political Committee speech, the reactions to it, and the fact that I had probably been too *cassant* with Luc de Nanteuil and not much better with Dillon and the other members of COREPER. It had been an extraordinary day and no one could say that the interview with Schmidt was dull or that relations with him were inhibited. But these close personal relations don't seem to be leading to any solution of the budget problem.

FRIDAY, 1 FEBRUARY. *Brussels.*

Commission meeting at noon. Rather an awkward time on butter, as there was strong feeling, reasonably courteously put on the part of Gundelach, Ortoli and Cheysson, that I had gone too far on banning butter sales in the Political Committee the day before. No doubt some of them had been nobbled by their governments. However, I was able to hold the thing without too much difficulty, getting quite strong support from dear old Natali and fairly dear old Haferkamp. Still it was quite an awkward little storm, slightly bigger than in a teacup.

Then Henry and Shirley Anglesey arrived to stay the weekend. I went to the Berlaymont, first to telephone Cossiga in Rome, and then to have a short hour's meeting with Andov, the Yugoslav Trade Minister who was here to try and conclude our long-drawn-out negotiations for a contractual link agreement with the Yugoslavs. I was very keen on this happening, particularly as I proposed to go to Yugoslavia at the end of the month and had to get the agreement out of the way before this would be possible. Andov seemed at first a rather dour Soviet-looking little man, but I slightly warmed to him later when I took him to the lift.

SATURDAY, 2 FEBRUARY. *Brussels.*

Filthy weather, and Jennifer, seized with some awful stomach bug, was unable to get up. Angleseys and I left at 11.45 to try and do Waterloo before or after lunch, and to lunch at the now favourite Trois Canards at Ohain. Before lunch we did the Panorama and Hougoumont, but decided that the pouring rain was too much for the Mound. Then a successful and enjoyable lunch and back to the

Mound where, despite cold driving rain, we crept in through a hole in the hedge and clambered up the grass bank, a formidable feat.

After that into the town of Waterloo and the Wellington Museum, which in spite of a number of curious solecisms in the labelling is definitely interesting. Then we had the success of discovering on enquiry, but without too much difficulty, the burial place of the first Marquess of Anglesey's leg (Uxbridge when he lost it), which is more or less opposite the Wellington Museum, in a sort of water-closet in the garden of what now looks like a nursery school. A very successful day given the weather; Angleseys very good guests, full of enthusiasm and interest.

SUNDAY, 3 FEBRUARY. *Brussels*.

Still in filthy weather I took the Angleseys on an afternoon expedition to Malines, where, by remarkable luck, we coincided with the installation service of the new Archbishop, Cardinal Suenens's successor. A great Mass, a packed cathedral, with people climbing up on pulpit supports and any dais or ledge that they could find. There was a very wide age spread, Catholicism clearly thriving in Flanders. There was a great array of purple in front of the altar, including Cardinal Willebrands from Utrecht, Suenens and, obviously, his successor.

TUESDAY, 5 FEBRUARY. *Brussels*.

Peter Carrington and Crispin to breakfast, rue de Praetère, at 8.45. A satisfactory conversation on a variety of issues, but not least because he was enthusiastic about the idea of a meeting with Schmidt, though preferred it to be at East Hendred; and said that he then could handle Mrs Thatcher all right. He agreed with me, not exactly reluctantly, but extremely nervously, that if we could try and get a settlement around 1000 million units of account, maybe he could sell it to her, maybe it was reasonable, etc.

I sat next to Carrington again at lunch and had a further long talk about my future wishes in relation to the Commission,* and what I

---

* On which my position, a little harder than when I had talked to van der Klaauw and van Agt on 19 November 1979, just before the Dimbleby Lecture (see page 522 *supra*). was that I had no intention of staying beyond the four years but that I did not wish, in the interests of my own authority for the first part of the last year, to discourage too brutally the attempts to promote a further term which some governments, notably the Belgian, Dutch and Italian, were kindly making.

thought about a possible replacement as a British Commissioner.

In the Foreign Affairs Council Gundelach disposed of the butter issue, for the moment at any rate, rather satisfactorily. He is at his best on an occasion like that, looks confident, is persuasive.

WEDNESDAY, 6 FEBRUARY. *Brussels*.

We dined with Madame Feher, the widow of the Hungarian chemical manufacturer who made his business into the second chemical firm to Solvay in Belgium. Remarkably good pictures. The dinner was for General Rogers,* Haig's replacement, but I did not talk to him much. Talked most of dinner to Marie-Louise Simonet and after dinner to Hedwige de Nanteuil, with whom I had a sort of love-in with messages of how upset Luc had been because he thought he had had a row with me, which he hated, about butter, on which he was acting under instructions, and my sending a message back to him saying it was partly my fault, not on the substance, but I feared that I had shown a lack of courtesy to him before lunch: and there was a great deal of cooing all round, including for two minutes with Luc himself, at the end. It was as well, as we are dining with them tomorrow evening and I am in any event probably the person in Brussels official life who most likes Luc.

MONDAY, 11 FEBRUARY. *Brussels and Strasbourg*.

Schmidt on the telephone at 2 o'clock, with the rather surprising good news that he wanted to go ahead with the Carrington meeting and that he would like to dine at East Hendred on Saturday, 23 February.

Avion taxi to Strasbourg for the normal boring hour and a half of questions which didn't start until 6.20 and therefore didn't finish until 7.50. I thought that was supposed to be a fixed feast, but nothing, alas, is fixed in this Parliament. I did not have many questions and they gave no great difficulty. The only tricky point was when somebody tried to ask me a question not on the paper at the beginning and I had very firmly to say that if the Parliament

---

*General Bernard Rogers, b. 1921, was Chief of Staff of the US Army 1976–9, and Supreme Allied Commander, Europe, 1979–87.

conducted its business like that it would get into a great mess. There would be imprecise answers and it would be unfair to those who put questions down. They seemed to accept this.

TUESDAY, 12 FEBRUARY. *Strasbourg.*

I delivered my annual Programme speech at 10.00. Crispin, who can be quite a severe critic, said he thought it was the best of the four Programme speeches, but that perhaps wasn't saying much.

Then I had two people from the American *National Geographic* magazine (why?) for a remarkably dull lunch. After that a tedious and oddly wearing Commission meeting for three and a half hours. Then Peter Shore to dinner, because he had asked to see me and I thought I would quite like to hear his views. He was very late and not very apologetic, but I found plenty to talk to him about. I found him very anti-Benn, whom he thinks rather mad, skirting round the mountain of Healey, very pro-Foot. His view on world politics is that of an old-fashioned Atlanticist of the 1950s, very pro the Americans, on nearly all their attitudes, wise and unwise, which they have taken up over both Iran and Afghanistan. He is bitterly anti-Europe, particularly the French, where one has a bit of sympathy with him, but he goes much too far and regards them as not so much a nation as a conspiracy against the public weal. But the whole impression was one of somebody who is agreeable, intelligent, but miles off being a great man, and not very inspiriting either.

WEDNESDAY, 13 FEBRUARY. *Strasbourg.*

Michel Poniatowski* to lunch at the Maison des Tanneurs. Lots of gossip about French politics, he telling me exactly what he thought of everybody. The important people in the Government were those who had a certain influence outside their Department: Barre (obviously), Deniau, Giraud, and that I think was about it. François-Poncet was definitely not in this category. Poniatowski was very interested in movements in English politics, centre party, etc. He was surprisingly well known to the restaurant management, although he had never been there before; and a group of

* (Prince) Michel Poniatowski, b. 1922, MEP since 1979, was French Minister of the Interior 1974–7, and a roving ambassador for President Giscard 1977–81.

French publishers' salesmen at the next table was very interested to engage him in conversation about the termination of the French equivalent of the Net Book Agreement, which seems to be having the consequences which had always been predicted for such a change in England, i.e. the closing down of about half the serious bookshops of Strasbourg – and no doubt in the rest of France as well.

SATURDAY, 16 FEBRUARY. *East Hendred*.

Sevenhampton for lunch with Ann Fleming, Donaldsons, John Sparrow and Robert Blakes. I was pleased to see Robert Blake who is an interesting and serious man. Sparrow not in very good condition, though thoroughly agreeable. The Donaldsons looking remarkably fit'for their age, although rather Healeyite. They were strongly in favour of the centre party, but it depended a bit on Denis not being elected leader of the Labour Party.

MONDAY, 18 FEBRUARY. *East Hendred and Rome*.

To Rome for a meeting with Cossiga at the Palazzo Chigi at 5.00. I am not sure that he knows quite where to go on the British budgetary question (henceforward referred to as the BBQ). However, we were at least able to agree that there was no point in having an earlier European Council. Then to the Hassler Hotel before dinner at the British Embassy – the first time that I had been in the Villa Wolkonsky for nearly ten years – with the new Ambassador (Ronald Arculus) and Carrington, who was there with his very bright Assistant Private Secretary, Paul Lever.

TUESDAY, 19 FEBRUARY. *Rome and Brussels*.

Political Cooperation, which went on from 10.45 until 3.45, when I left to go back to Brussels. Though I say that it 'went on', this could hardly be described as a continuous process, because Ruffini, who is an absolutely hopeless chairman, occasionally left it quite unclear whether we were in session or not, in a way rather reminiscent of the Tokyo Summit last June. At one stage we just sat around for about half an hour, while he had a telephone brought in, attempted

to telephone somebody – God knows who; we were discussing the
Moscow Olympics, so perhaps it was Brezhnev, perhaps it was Lord
Killanin,* or perhaps it was Cossiga. And failing to get through –
most likely to Cossiga, I suppose – he at one stage threw the
telephone on the floor, with predictable results. Then another was
brought in and he eventually got through, and so in conditions of
some farce we proceeded.

The statement of Afghanistan 'neutrality' was disposed of quickly
and well, but then there were hours of unrewarding debate about
an Olympics statement. François-Poncet, who had been helpful on
the neutrality proposal, had obviously come with instructions on
the Olympics (i) not to agree to a statement, and (ii) not to get
isolated. The two objectives proved incompatible and he got fretful
and marionette-like, jerking his arms about.

THURSDAY, 21 FEBRUARY. *Brussels, London and East
Hendred.*

To the Cercle Gaulois for a lunch given by Heath in connection with
the European Youth Orchestra. Friendly, interesting talk with him.
He made quite a good little speech. Then saw Van Ypersele about
the state of play on the European Monetary Fund and other EMS
questions. 4.45 plane to London.

SATURDAY, 23 FEBRUARY. *East Hendred.*

The day of our Carrington/Schmidt dinner, Schmidt rather to my
surprise having stuck to his engagement and come to England
specially to do it. We had asked Edward and Sally, which somehow
made it easier to leave Schmidt and Carrington alone for some time.
Dinner went moderately well. Hannelore Schmidt nicer, easier and
more interesting than I had expected, speaks very good English,
ex-Hamburg schoolteacher, much interested in the preservation of
wild flowers and botanical conservation in Germany, but also in a
lot of other things too. Helmut, benign and looking rather better,
but as usual no small talk and both Edward and Jennifer found him
quite difficult to talk to.

*Lord Killanin, b. 1914, was President of the International Olympic Committee
1972–80.

Edward only seized his attention by asking him if he was going to blow up the world (hardly within the Germans' capacity now), to which he replied no, but that other people might easily do so. I left Carrington and him alone for an hour and a quarter after dinner, but then brought them into the drawing room and we went on for too long so that it was 12.45 before they all went. I think no business of great value was transacted. Schmidt was not well enough briefed on the BBQ to be able to discuss it in detail, Carrington said. But it was good from the point of view of personal relations and there was some interesting world politics discussion.

MONDAY, 25 FEBRUARY. *East Hendred, Dublin and London.*

10.40 plane to Dublin. Drove straight to a talk alone with Haughey, the new Taoiseach, whom by a series of accidents I had never met before. (The most notable 'accident' was in April 1970 when I went for an Irish holiday after my last budget on the day he was due to present his first budget. In the event he claimed he fell off his horse in the courtyard of his house, and the then Taoiseach, Jack Lynch, presented his budget instead of him. By the time we got back from Ballylicky a week later, when Haughey was supposed to give us lunch, he had not only fallen off his horse but been dismissed from the Government and faced criminal charges for gun-running, from which he was subsequently acquitted, it should be said. So Lynch gave us lunch instead.)

Found Haughey, as I had been forewarned, extremely engaging. Much quicker than previous Irish Taoiseachs, though perhaps (but I am not sure) less trustworthy. Very well informed about British politics, Dimbleby Lecture, etc. Mostly agreeable gossip before lunch. Lunch at Iveagh House, usual form, Foreign Minister, several officials and Crispin present, and quite good. Rather intensive but sensible arguments, mainly about agriculture but one or two other things as well.

Back to London by 5.00. To Michael Barnes's flat, where I had an hour's meeting with about ten 'new party' plotters. I thought the hour was rather good and brisk but apparently the discussion got all over the place later.

Then dinner at Bridgewater House, given by Edwin Plowden and attended by five or six of his senior businessmen. Of the old ones, there were John Partridge and David Orr, whom I think very good, and Peter Baxendell, the chief British man in Shell, and Maurice Hodgson, the Chairman of ICI. All of them I think sympathetic to proportional representation, some of them to the idea of a centre party if the Government failed, but still putting more faith in Mrs T. than I would have expected. Edwin rather to the left of the others. However, in response to a tentative query from me, they made it clear that there was little prospect of money. Big companies with many shareholders do not like political subscriptions, they said.

WEDNESDAY, 27 FEBRUARY. *Brussels and Belgrade.*

George Weidenfeld to lunch rue de Praetère. Mainly gossip about America, but George was also quite interesting and sensible on British politics, preoccupied by a mixture of who he might have to dinner with us in April, and how we might organize the centre party.

In the early evening an avion taxi to Belgrade, which was too fast so that we arrived well before the welcoming party was ready for us. Drove to the so-called Residence Villa, an old Prince Paul* *nid d'amour*, I would guess, on a low hill about two or three miles from the centre of Belgrade.

THURSDAY, 28 FEBRUARY. *Belgrade.*

A morning of hazy sunshine with the temperature just above freezing point. The physical atmosphere, which struck both Crispin and me during the next two days, was curiously like China, exactly a year previously. To New Belgrade and the large rather good building in which most Government offices seem to be situated for a meeting, followed by lunch, with Djuranovic, the Prime Minister, an effective but unmemorable Montenegran. In the past twenty-five years a whole new city with a population of about 300,000 has been built across the Sava from the old town.

The Yugoslavs were anxious to give an impression of calmness, business as usual, collective leadership already functioning and

*Prince Paul, 1893–1976, son of Prince Arsen Karageorgevich, was Regent of Yugoslavia 1934–41.

ready to take over full responsibilities in the face of the manifestly impending but slow death of Tito. They were pleased with their agreement with us and discussed quite sensibly the follow-up to it, and then gave us a long review of their approach to world affairs which suggests some justifiable apprehension but not panic about the exposure of their position. Their main concern is their quarrel with Bulgaria over Macedonia and the possible escalation which might arise from this. For the rest their relations with their Communist neighbours, Rumania above all, but also Hungary and indeed Albania, are quite good. They showed some disenchantment with the way in which the non-aligned movement has been taken over by Castro even while Tito, one of its two founder members, is just alive. This will push them towards a lower international profile in the future.

An interesting talk with the Foreign Minister Vrhovec, a bright little Croatian who had just returned from Delhi. He was very reserved towards the Carrington plan for the neutralization of Afghanistan (said the Indians were too), but took a definitely more favourable line when I explained to him that 'neutralization' was the wrong word and that 'neutrality', which was much more of a subjective state, was better. It was much nearer to non-alignment, provided that this was not 'non-alignment' in the bogus Cuban sense.

He also suffered from the illusion that the British Government was implacably hostile to Mugabe and would not contemplate a Zimbabwe Government with him in control, and the associated illusion that we were primarily concerned with our trading interests in Rhodesia. I told him that nothing would have pleased us better from an economic point of view than for it to have been obliterated from the face of the earth some time ago. British trading interests in Africa were those with Nigeria (growing) and those with South Africa (diminishing) but both of them very substantial and the whole difficulty of policy was to maintain some sort of balance between the two: a difficult enough problem without the complication of Rhodesia.

FRIDAY, 29 FEBRUARY. *Belgrade and East Hendred.*

Lunch given by Andov (the Trade Minister and our main host). Quite friendly, unbuttoned talk, rather typical of an end-of-a-visit lunch, during which I, for the first time for instance, talked about Ivana (my half-Yugoslav daughter-in-law), asking did they know this and discovered – I think genuinely – that only the Ambassador in Brussels knew it, and had not bothered to pass it on, which did not suggest a very neurotic régime. I was impressed by this. Plane to London at 5.30.

MONDAY, 3 MARCH. *East Hendred and London.*

Left on a most beautiful morning to visit, appropriately, the Meteorological Office at Bracknell: a Crispin enterprise. I found it fascinating, with a lot of interesting discussion about both weather and climate. Then to London and the Turf Club for lunch, once more with Peter Carrington,* and with Ian Gilmour. Useful but not memorable talk with them.

TUESDAY, 4 MARCH. *London, Paris and Brussels.*

Early plane to Paris. To the Brasserie Lipp where I met Crispin. Then disaster struck. I discovered that I had left my diary in the plane, or at any rate did not have it. At 11.30 I saw Barre at Matignon for an hour and a half. He was alone, relaxed and surprisingly confident, talking very much more as a head of government, very much less as Giscard's adjutant, than on previous occasions. This I suspect was not due primarily to the fact that Giscard was away for ten days, longer than ever previously, but much more to a feeling of confidence in his own position. I thought him a bit complacent about the French economy, but not quite as pedagogic as usual. He listened with interest to my exposition of what I regarded as a slightly subtle world macroeconomic case for an energy levy.

There was a good atmosphere throughout, as there generally is with Barre, and a hint of some progress on the BBQ. He told me that he did not see a solution at 1500 million units of account, that it was not only France that was blocking this. This was a great illusion. There were a lot of other countries, including Germany, who would not pay the amounts this involved. I said maybe, but that the Germans might well pay their share of, say, a thousand million

*We had both been at a large Briggs luncheon party in Worcester College, Oxford, the day before.

which might provide the basis of a solution if they thought they could carry the French with them. There was no contradiction or dissent from Barre. Merely a suggestion that we should put forward a solution (with a slight implication that it could be along these lines) about a week before the European Council. Then he took me round the lower rooms of Matignon, including that in which the 'Matignon Pact' was signed by Blum in 1936. Apparently Matignon only became the residence of Présidents du Conseil in 1935, Pierre Flandin being the first occupant. Then a very brief impromptu press conference *sur le perron*.

THURSDAY, 6 MARCH. *Brussels and Lisbon.*

Half an hour on the telephone with Dohnanyi, agreeably but not tremendously pointfully, about the BBQ at his instigation. 11.10 plane to Lisbon. Down into Lisbon at 1.15 in rather indifferent weather. Met at the airport by Sá Carneiro, the new Prime Minister and leader of the Social Democratic though rather right-wing party, plus the Christian Democrat Foreign Minister Freitas do Amaral, whom I had met in Luxembourg a few weeks before, plus their wives. Mrs Sá Carneiro, as we thought she was, was rather a good-looking lady who might have come straight off the Yale campus. In fact she turned out to be a Danish publisher. Mrs Freitas do Amaral was totally different, very Latin, also rather engaging. Jennifer's plane from London was rather later than mine and during the wait 'Mrs Sá Carneiro' enlivened proceedings by expressing distrust of TAP (Portuguese Airlines) and asking me if I knew that the initials were known (by whom?) to stand for 'take another plane'.*

An afternoon meeting with Sá Carneiro in the Prime Ministerial residence, the old Salazar house, though he (Sá Carneiro) does not live in it, where I had seen Mário Soares two and a half years before. Driving through the streets, Lisbon looked slightly tidied up, a little less like Calcutta than it had begun to do on the previous occasion. It seemed in better working order. This was certainly true of the hotel, which had abandoned *autogestion* since we were last there.

Sá Carneiro raised no subjects of great importance but talked

---

*This joke became macabre in my memory when she and Sá Carneiro were killed in an air crash outside Lisbon nine months later.

interestingly, well, and friendlily, and was amazingly well informed about my background, writings, etc. He is a very small man, about 5'3" I would think, but with great drive, and talks very good English, even better French and I think pretty good Spanish as well. I was definitely rather impressed by him, but maybe too much influenced by his going so out of the way to be particularly nice to me. Then I saw Freitas do Amaral for forty-five minutes. Quite a useful talk in which we discussed the timetable for the outstanding negotiations, but again did not get into substance.

Back at the hotel Soares came to see me for an hour. He had come back from Paris more or less specially that afternoon. Attractive, friendly, expressing himself well in imperfect French, but a little woebegone and complaining. He was in something of a 'we was cheated' mood, but his resentment was not against Eanes, the President of the Republic, who had dismissed him, but with whom he had clearly had a *rapprochement* and about whom he was anxious to speak friendlily, but against the Government, which he held to be exacerbating political differences in Portugal.

He added that his commitment to Portuguese adhesion to the Community was complete, but that with this polarization of politics he was beginning to have trouble on the issue with his own Socialist Party. He was clearly not happy in opposition, not personally bitter about Sá Carneiro, though complaining hard about some constitutional scheme of the Government, which sounds a pretty good bit of gerrymandering. They apparently plan to increase the number of seats – from four to perhaps thirty – for Portuguese emigrants, of whom there are about a million in the Community and two million outside. This could obviously be a fine recipe for producing a quiverful of pocket boroughs.

Then to Cintra where we had a dinner, as on the previous occasion, in the magnificent hall at the Palaccio da Vila with about 150 guests and speeches afterwards. I sat between 'Mrs Sá Carneiro' and Mrs Freitas do Amaral. 'Mrs Sá Carneiro', I had discovered in conversation with Soares, is not married to Sá Carneiro. They have been together for about two years. She is called 'Snou', has been in Portugal for about fifteen years as a publisher, is clearly quite a powerful and indeed agreeable lady, but Sá Carneiro is very bold in such a Catholic country to seek a divorce from the mother of his several children. ('When I marry Mrs Snou', only a slight variation from a line in an old American musical, kept occurring to me.)

This was the first occasion on which 'Snou' had appeared in public as his consort and this was no doubt provoked by Jennifer's coming and the banquet having to be made bisexual. I thought I detected a slight frostiness between Mrs Freitas do Amaral and her. The speeches went quite well, both Sá Carneiro's and mine.

FRIDAY, 7 MARCH. *Lisbon.*

Lunch was another grand official banquet – at the Foreign Ministry – sitting this time between the Freitas do Amarals. More speeches. Then to the Presidential Palace for a long interview with General Eanes. I had heard in the meantime that the Sá Carneiros were proposing to come out and lunch with us informally at Cintra the next day, as they wished to continue the talk. Perhaps inspired by this knowledge, Eanes kept the conversation going much more animatedly than last time. He was more unbuttoned and relaxed, seemed to me to have become a more rounded personality, but nonetheless made it absolutely clear that he was on pretty bad terms with his Prime Minister. No direct criticism but solid silence about him, accompanied by at least four or five tributes in the course of the hour to Soares.

Then towards the end he said he could go on as long as I liked. But when we came out about ten minutes late we found Sá Carneiro had been left cooling his heels. When I indicated to Eanes that it would be unwise for me to keep my press conference waiting indefinitely, he responded by saying that he was at my disposal any time during the weekend and would I come and see him again. Our weekend off was being rather seriously eaten into by competitive bidding from President and Prime Minister.

Then to the Italian Embassy, a very splendid late seventeenth-century building in a rundown quarter, and there did a rather exhaustive briefing of the Nine. I thought the ambassadors were rather an impressive lot for once. The 'Brit', as on the previous occasion, was Lord Moran, ex-John Wilson,* who wrote a good book about Campbell-Bannerman.

---

*John Wilson, b. 1924, succeeded his father, Churchill's doctor, as 2nd Lord Moran in 1977. Ambassador to Hungary 1973–6, and Portugal 1976–81, High Commissioner in Canada 1981–4. His life of Sir Henry Campbell-Bannerman had been published in 1973.

SUNDAY, 9 MARCH. *Cintra, Lisbon and Brussels.*

Drove in and saw Eanes in his private presidential apartments at noon. He was very friendly. I think he is an honest man but not nearly as quick as Sá Carneiro, and some of his explanations of the plots, etc. which are going on seem to me a little unconvincing. His basic view was that the divide between the parties should not be allowed to grow too wide: this is partly because he does not like parties and wants to strengthen his own position, but partly because he has a general and desirable commitment to holding Portugal together, and a particular one to keeping the European enterprise as a national and not a party enterprise. Then back to Brussels.

MONDAY, 10 MARCH. *Brussels and Strasbourg.*

Decided I must go on to a strict régime. Avion taxi in rather depressed mood to Strasbourg at 3.45. Listened to Gundelach's statement on butter sales to Russia which he did pretty well and which was accepted by the more sensible Tories and by the House generally. There were one or two shrill comments but a solid one from Henry Plumb, though balanced by a menacing willingness to vote for anything against anybody by the disagreeable Aigner. Question time from 6.00 to 7.30 which ambled on in its usual boring way. Then back to the hotel and as a substitute for dinner watched Mrs Thatcher on French television — there was a girl interpreter, possibly specially auditioned, with a peculiarly disagreeable voice.

WEDNESDAY, 12 MARCH. *Strasbourg, London and East Hendred.*

I had a lunch at La Wantzenau organized by Henry Plumb and Madron Seligman for six youngish Tory MPs, including some of the most difficult ones on the butter issue. Once or twice they were tiresome but it was well worth doing, I think. Evening plane to London.

MONDAY, 17 MARCH. *East Hendred, London and Brussels.*

One-and-a-quarter-hour meeting with Mrs Thatcher at Downing Street. This was a good deal calmer than on some previous occasions. Nothing very memorable was said, although she was clearly willing to contemplate a package deal at the European Council, provided the actual phrase was avoided, and willing also to talk at any rate in terms of two-thirds of the shortfall, or even a little less. It was perfectly friendly throughout and she showed more willingness to listen than previously. Jim Cattermole and Tom Ellis* and George Foulkes,† as the officers (the last two new) of the Labour Committee for Europe, to lunch at the Athenaeum.

Then to Brussels and dinner at home for the Italians, Ruffini, Zamberletti, Plaja on their side: better than on the previous occasion, but Ruffini still far from scintillating.

TUESDAY, 18 MARCH. *Brussels.*

Foreign Affairs Council, at which there was some short but relatively important discussion on the preparation for the European Council. I had to be there for that, even though it meant my very reluctantly missing Michael Astor's memorial service in London. Bernard-Reymond suddenly announced at the end of the morning that the position of the French Government was that the Commission must come forward with its proposals now, and then should do nothing in the way of suggesting last-minute compromises. This was an obvious attempt to neutralize me and was fortunately badly received by the others. My rather pompous assertion that we would take our responsibilities and do what we thought right at the time in the interests of Europe as a whole was very well received by nearly all the rest. Bernard-Reymond afterwards came up and apologized to me for having to say this under instructions, adding that he did not himself agree with it.

Dinner with the Natalis in a large, mostly Italian party. A long talk with Lorenzo (Natali) after dinner, who told me that he and the Italians were much in favour of my staying on as President and that he would stay on if I did.‡

---

*Tom Ellis, b. 1924, was Labour and then SDP MP for Wrexham 1970–83, MEP 1975–9.
†George Foulkes, b. 1942, worked for the European Movement in Scotland before he became a Labour MP for Ayrshire in 1979.
‡I did not, but he did.

WEDNESDAY, 19 MARCH. *Brussels.*

Long Commission meetings interspersed with Shirley Williams to lunch, rue de Praetère. She was friendly and bright and agreeable as she always is, though I think that her political position has receded a little, although not dramatically, since I last saw her. She had had a talk with Denis Healey who had said that he had to be pretty equivocal in order to get elected leader (of the Labour Party) but once elected he would be an absolutely ruthless social democratic leader, wanting a social democratic Cabinet and would indeed try to promote a split in the party from within as opposed to without. She was also charged to bear some sort of message to me suggesting my return to British politics with a view to becoming Foreign Secretary in a future Labour Government. The prospect does not appeal to me, because apart from my having burnt too many Labour Party boats, I really could not stand being Foreign Secretary under Denis. He would lecture one every day on every subject under the sun. This does not mean that I would not serve under anyone – I could serve under David Steel or under Shirley herself, I think, but not with somebody quite as pedagogic and know-all as Denis invariably is – with me at any rate.

I had Ortoli, Gundelach and Davignon, plus Emile Noël, plus Crispin for a 'Four Horsemen' dinner, rue de Praetère. They had asked for it rather urgently, Davignon in particular, but as we had got through most of the immediately tricky business in the Commission it was mainly a fence-repairing rather than a serious discussion occasion.

Just before they left Shirley arrived back to stay. As soon as they were gone she settled down for what was intended to be an hour or so's talk, but, unbelievably, went on until 4 o'clock in the morning. She talked extremely well and could not have been more personally agreeable. I told her why I did not think the Healey scenario was convincing, and to some extent she was re-unconvinced by me, although, fairly, retaining her position fully open for the autumn. She also appeared to understand perfectly well why I was unattracted by being Foreign Secretary under Denis. A great part of the conversation, however, was not concerned with politics as such but lapped around, with my describing how the Commission operated, with a lot of talk about Tony Crosland as a young man, a whole range of easy friendly gossipy conversation.

I suggested to her the possibility that she might be interested in coming as a Commissioner to Brussels. She did not totally reject it, but I think was not very attracted by it, and would in my belief, if she were to be shunted from politics for a few years – in which she saw certain advantage – prefer to do something like the chairmanship of the BBC. She also has somewhat in mind the idea of a Harvard professorship, which has no doubt been dangled before her. However, on balance I think she will probably stick to politics. It was a worthwhile, though a strange evening, and made particular nonsense of a malicious little story, originating no doubt from Château Palmer, which appeared in the *Guardian* next morning, though happily unseen until later by either Shirley or me, when it irritated me and upset her, that she had come to Brussels to give me the brush-off so far as any idea of political collaboration was concerned. If so, it was a jolly long brush-off!

FRIDAY, 21 MARCH. *Brussels*.

I went to see the King at Laeken from 9.45 to 10.30. He was looking much better after great back trouble all winter, with an operation and two months out of action. Today he seemed restored, although looking alone and isolated in the vast and rather dismal Palace of Laeken – redeemed only by its view. My state of health was not very good either, and a good third of the conversation was valetudinarian.

We also and inevitably talked about Europe. He was very keen to promote a budgetary solution acceptable to the British and made some very sensible remarks about how important it was to a country like Belgium that the basic European power matrix should be triangular rather than bipolar. We also discussed both British and Belgian internal politics a little and he claimed, though not in a dismissive or aggressive way, that the communal linguistic question was very much a matter of politicians rather than people. Whether he is right or not I do not know, but he is in a good position to judge.

SATURDAY, 22 MARCH. *Brussels and Nancy.*

Drove to Luxembourg, unfortunately in misty weather over the Ardennes and therefore missed the views. Did a brief tour of the city and then down to Ehnen for lunch alongside the Mosel. Then to Metz and to the cathedral, which I do not recollect ever having seen before. It is quite magnificent, high slightly gaunt nave and spectacular glass, from a whole variety of periods: some medieval, some seventeenth-century, some Chagall. The town is better than I thought, a good medium-large *chef-lieu*. Then to Nancy and stayed in the Grand Hôtel Concorde in the Place Stanislas, which is a sort of very little Crillon. Also, happily, very *petit Crillon* from the point of view of price: only 170 francs for a room, which for a view over one of the three best squares in Europe is not bad.

MONDAY, 24 MARCH. *Brussels.*

Plaja came to see me with the fairly amazing news that Cossiga had decided to postpone the European Council (due on the following Monday, 31 March) because his Government crisis meant that he did not have enough time to do the necessary pre-Council diplomacy. At first I was uncertain and thought the decision was unwise, as we seemed to me to be moving up to a satisfactory crisis culmination. On reflection I became a little more open to Cossiga's idea and made no public and very little private criticism of him. What was a mistake, however, was to announce the postponement before agreement to another date had been secured.

Lunch with COREPER in the Charlemagne, where conversation was almost entirely about this. COREPER becomes an increasingly hopeless body, almost guaranteed to seize the wrong end of any stick. Eugenio (Plaja) tries to be a good chairman and is about as good as they could get, but the continual bad exhibition tennis match, as I described it to them, between Butler and Nanteuil, is becoming a great bore for everybody and effectively destroying the institution. An afternoon telephone conversation with Werner, the Prime Minister of Luxembourg, where the postponed Council will, I suppose, have to be, owing to April being a month when the Community institutions meet there.

TUESDAY, 25 MARCH. *Brussels, Strasbourg and Brussels.*

8.40 plane to Strasbourg. The Parliament was grinding through the agricultural debate introduced by Gundelach the previous evening. I made a rather sharp fifteen-minute speech saying that, apart from the merits of the issue, if the Parliament wanted to be taken seriously it must stick on the course which it had beckoned us down in December. This went down rather well, though some of the French, including *Le Monde*, got agitated against it, but they do that about so many things that one cannot take it too seriously. I gave Klepsch (leader of the Christian Democrat Group) lunch at La Wantzenau. I had intended to go into the town but we were warned that there were such a lot of agricultural demonstrators about that it was arguably unsafe (which I doubted) and certainly a recipe for unpunctuality.

After lunch I tried to have a look at the demonstrators who, it was reported, had burnt the Union Jack. So I think they had, but then for good measure they burnt the Tricolor and seven other flags as well, so it seemed fairly even-handed. Then heard Gundelach's winding up, the quality of which was difficult to judge as it was, exceptionally, in Danish. Avion taxi back to Brussels.

THURSDAY, 27 MARCH. *Brussels and Copenhagen.*

Evening plane to Copenhagen. To the Hôtel d'Angleterre, of which Grand Metropolitan seem to be making a great mess. They are changing the terrace, changing the entrance, changing the furniture, and changing it a great deal for the worse. This was previously one of the more attractive hotels in Europe. Changes in ownership rarely do anything to hotels except make them worse.

FRIDAY, 28 MARCH. *Copenhagen and Brussels.*

At 11 o'clock to the Christiansborg for a meeting and lunch with the Prime Minister, Anker Jørgensen. When we got there, there was no sign of the little man, and it was a good forty-five minutes before he could be eventually extracted from some party caucus. His private secretaries said that he had just disappeared in the Parliament. However, when he turned up he was agreeable enough, although I think in some ways the BBQ has turned him into the most difficult of all the nine heads of government with whom I deal. This is partly linguistic, as we talk English, without an interpreter, and he is not wholly at home in it. Lunch started as soon as he arrived. It was a vast smørgasbord, accompanied – I would have thought rather tactlessly as we have various cases pending with the Danes about their discriminating against other Community drinks – by nothing but the most chauvinistic Danish combination of aquavit and Tuborg. However, we survived on that, and with the help of his *Chef de Cabinet* and Crispin managed to make some reasonable progress over lunch and certainly got Jørgensen to accept, which he had not done at Dublin, that something well above the financial mechanism would have to be done for the British, and that a figure of 1000 or 1100 million, while possibly high, was not out of the question.

Back to Brussels in the afternoon and to a special showing in the *salle de presse* of the Granada Television film called *Mrs Thatcher's Billion* on the Dublin Summit, which was remarkably good. Sarah Hogg played Mrs Thatcher in a way almost worthy of Sarah Bernhardt, and although not looking like their principals when not speaking, Schmidt (Martin Schulz) and Giscard (Paul Fabra) were also in different ways brilliantly played. By these three at any rate, it was a very convincing performance. Stephen Milligan played me, accurately in substance, but I thought without style. What, however, was noticeable was that the highly informed, blasé audience of about 150 assembled in the *salle de presse* broke into spontaneous applause when the film was over. It was a remarkable *tour de force*.

TUESDAY, 1 APRIL. *Brussels*.

A fifteen-minute speech to the Political Committee of the Parliament. The Political Committee is *sur place* a perfectly tolerable body with which to deal, but it seems to produce objectively explosive speeches from me. I made a reference on this occasion to the gap between the British and the others not being in effect more than two weeks' cost of the CAP. Two weeks' cost of the CAP equals a little more than 400 million units of account, therefore my sum was based on the unspoken premise that there was hardly anybody who was not willing to go to 700 million, and I believe the British would settle at 1100 million if not a little less. This was a perfectly accurate statement of the position. What effect it will have I do not quite know.

WEDNESDAY, 2 APRIL. *Brussels and London.*

To London after a Commission meeting, and to George Weiden-feld's big and long-planned dinner party for us. A great roll call of the great and good, of the liberal and central at any rate: Annans, Donaldsons, Mosers, Bonham Carters, Rodgers', David Steel, Nigel Ryan,* Edna O'Brien, John Gross',† Garry Runcimans,‡ George Thomsons, Clarissa Avon (Eden) as a wild card. I can't remember who else, but a large and enjoyable party.

SATURDAY, 5 APRIL. *East Hendred.*

No papers, so into Wantage, perhaps mistakenly as it turned out, to buy them. Discovered that the French Government, the Quai in particular, had launched a great onslaught on my Political Commit-tee speech on the previous Tuesday. Quite why was not clear. I suppose all part of their ploy to try and neutralize me in advance of the European Council, feeling that I had opened up the possibility of special measures for Britain last time and believing, because they are incapable, I think, of believing anything else in view of the way they behave themselves, that I am a British agent, which is hardly the case. However, their reaction, though ridiculous and unwarranted, was mildly depressing.

MONDAY, 7 APRIL. *East Hendred.*

Gilmours to lunch. It didn't rain, as it usually does when Ian is here. Ian did not have a great deal to say about budgetary questions, though obviously developing a certain optimism. No reaction from him, and therefore presumably no mutterings in the Foreign Office, about my Political Committee speech. On the centre party he was quite interesting and more favourable, I would judge, than when I last talked to him. At one stage he said firmly he thought I would (from my point of view) be right to go ahead, though

*Nigel Ryan, b. 1929, was editor of Independent Television News 1969–77, Vice-President of NBC News (New York) 1977–80, and Director of Programmes Thames Television 1980–2.

†John Gross, b. 1935, was then the editor of the *Times Literary Supplement* and is now the book critic of the *New York Times*. Miriam Gross was then the assistant literary editor of the *Observer* and is now the arts editor of the *Daily Telegraph*.

‡ Garrison Runciman, b. 1934, sociologist and Fellow of Trinity College, Cambridge, has also been chairman of his family shipping business since 1972.

obviously there were risks. I think he would probably like to see Heath involved, and said: 'You and Ted would be a formidable combination.'

TUESDAY, 8 APRIL. *East Hendred.*

A large lunch party for the Clive Wilkinsons,* Bradleys, Rodgers' and Oakeshotts.† It all lasted with a lot of conversation until 6.15, which was rather too late, but it was, I think, worthwhile. Tom (Bradley) and Matthew (Oakeshott) absolutely firm and hard in favour of a new party, Bill more forthcoming than I expected, Clive Wilkinson much the least. He clearly won't move and my judgement is that to a greater extent than I had thought the half-cock Colin Phipps publicity has done harm in the West Midlands.

WEDNESDAY, 9 APRIL. *East Hendred.*

In the evening I had two hours with a young man called Pimlott, who is writing a life of Hugh Dalton, and found him very good. He is a lecturer or research fellow at LSE and seems to understand Dalton very well, and I think should produce a serious, but also penetrating book about him.‡

SUNDAY, 13 APRIL. *Dorset and East Hendred.*

Returned from Dorset (where we had stayed two nights with Fred and Simone Warner) on a perfect morning via Salisbury, where we made a brief visit to the cathedral, and found it as usual cold, detached, perfect, but too much of a ship and too little of a shrine.

David Steel to dine and stay. Again, a satisfactory talk. I like him very much personally, found him as good and firm and committed as ever, no complaints on either side. He said that he had quite a difficult hurdle to clear in the shape of a Liberal gathering at Worcester in May, which would be less favourable to him than the Assembly in some way or other, but was fairly confident that he could get over it. Considerable commitment on both sides.

*Clive Wilkinson, b. 1935, was Labour leader on the Birmingham City Council 1973–84.
†Matthew Oakeshott, b. 1947, had worked for me in opposition and at the Home Office, 1972–6. SDP candidate for Cambridge 1983.
‡This was one of my better prophecies. *Hugh Dalton* by Ben Pimlott (1985) was a great biography.

MONDAY, 14 APRIL. *East Hendred and Brussels.*

Returned to Brussels by a plane which was two and a half hours late, by far the worst delay I have had for months. Arrived rue de Praetère slightly disorganized and more than slightly bad-tempered nearly an hour late for a lunch which I was giving for the Portuguese Ambassador, plus six others.

In the afternoon I had a request from the Israeli Ambassador for a visit, no doubt intended to balance the fact that he had heard I had seen some Arab ambassador. He is a disagreeable man, quite apart from my disapproval of Begin's policy, and it was not a rewarding conversation from either of our points of view. Then I saw Nanteuil at his request for him to present the French position in relation to the European Council, which although hard in some ways did not seem to me quite as impossible as I had expected. I rather disconcerted him by thanking him at the end, whereas he obviously expected me to be more shocked by what he had said, and consequently seemed rather thrown.

TUESDAY, 15 APRIL. *Brussels and Strasbourg.*

Strasbourg by the early train for a Commission meeting at noon to discuss preparations for the Foreign Affairs Council next week, which is rather tortuously to prepare for the European Council. Found them as usual before a difficult European Council in a rather bad, edgy, disorganized frame of mind, and therefore decided I had to set about having a series of bilateral meetings.

Stevy Davignon to dinner. I found him less inspiriting, less ingenious, more downbeat than usual. I got from him the information that he had decided to stay on in the next Commission even though he clearly had moved to a position of assuming that I was not staying on, which was different from what he had last urged on me in Strasbourg a few months ago. He was full of hesitations and doubts about what we should do on the BBQ, and falling back on asseverations that the Commission must take its responsibilities and act firmly or it would lose its reputation: must show nerve, coherence, delicacy, a whole series of phrases to which in the context I found it difficult to attach much meaning. Altogether it was Stevy far from his best, and I returned slightly dispirited, particularly as he was urging me to have a whole series of other dinners in order to bring into line the other 'Horsemen' who he said were rather disaffected by not having been consulted.

WEDNESDAY, 16 APRIL. *Strasbourg.*

I made a speech in the institutional debate in the morning, and lunched with Colombo, who, thank God, has replaced Ruffini as Italian Foreign Minister.

I decided that I ought to cancel my dinner with the Seligmans and the Warners in order to massage Ortoli, and took him to a restaurant. Happily I found him on extremely agreeable form, but with nothing to say about any issue of business before us. However, two hours of literary, reminiscent, personal conversation in French was not unamusing, and no doubt the occasion was vaguely useful.

THURSDAY, 17 APRIL. *Strasbourg and Hanover.*

Pointless Commission from 11 to 11.30, which the others had been very keen on on the Tuesday, but at which it turned out there was nothing to discuss, and then 1.30–3.00 luncheon with the other three 'horsemen' at Zimmer at La Wantzenau, which I deliberately chose because, with a *prix-fixe* menu, it is the cheapest of the 'good' restaurants and I am fairly tired of paying for them! Perfectly agreeable again, a certain amount of business discussed reasonably and amicably, but again no tremendous point.

Then by avion taxi to Hanover for a twenty-four-hour visit to the Nieder-Sachsen *land* government. Albrecht,* the Minister-President, I found young, quick and agreeable, without quite seeing him as a Christian Democrat Chancellor of Germany, which is what he much wants to be. Walther-Leisler Kiep, attractive and intelligent, was by far the best of his ministers.

SATURDAY, 19 APRIL. *East Hendred.*

At 12.15 the Ian Chapmans† arrived from Bristol, where they were attending the Booksellers' Conference, for Ian wanted to talk to me

*Ernst Albrecht, b. 1930, European Commission official 1958–70, Minister-President of Lower Saxony since 1976.
†Ian Chapman, b. 1925, has been Chairman of Collins since 1979, having been Managing Director since 1968. He was President of the Publishers Association 1979–81.

about several things. I like him very much and find him a most remarkable combination of the agreeable and the effective.

SUNDAY, 20 APRIL. *East Hendred.*

Had my gang of 'conspirators', Lindley, Phipps, Taverne, Barnes, Daly, John Harris, John Morgan and one or two others – Marquand unfortunately absent – for a meeting with lunch from 11.30 to 4.45. They were not bad at all, quite businesslike. Phipps was the least good. Lindley, of the ones I did not know well, was the best.

TUESDAY, 22 APRIL. *Luxembourg and Brussels.*

Foreign Affairs Council in Luxembourg from 10.30 until 3, the Italians believing in their own ministerial luncheon hours rather than anybody else's, and then from 4.30 until 10.15 p.m. The discussion was partly, although not very usefully, about preparations for the European Council the following weekend, but mainly about sanctions against Iran, with the British taking a tougher line in favour of breaking existing contracts than anybody else. Indeed Peter Carrington, who was next to me at our belated lunch, said bitterly, and as things turned out ironically, 'I do not believe anybody except us has the slightest intention of breaking existing contracts.'*

WEDNESDAY, 23 APRIL. *Brussels and Bonn.*

Michael Young,† now Lord Young of Dartington, David Watt and Crispin to lunch rue de Praetère. Mainly centre party conversation. Michael Young, whom I had not seen for a long time, was firm, constructive and sensible. David Watt was rather defeatist, in a sense conservative, believing nothing could ever happen. However, he had been very nice before lunch. It was only when he was confronted with the possibility of something that he much wanted that he became a wet blanket.

---

* In the outcome the British turned round like squirrels in a cage and became even more addicted to existing contracts than the Italians, who had many more of them with Iran.
† Michael Young, b. 1915, cr. Lord Young of Dartington 1978. Director of the Institute of Community Studies since 1953 from where he has started many organizations including the Consumers' Association. Joined the SDP in 1981.

Crispin and I then motored to Bonn for the dinner which Carstens (the Federal President) had decided to offer to the whole Commission. A curious but agreeable occasion, the purpose of which was not entirely clear to me.

FRIDAY, 25 APRIL. *Brussels.*

Breakfast meeting with Martens, the Belgian Prime Minister, plus about five of his officials, on the inevitable and perennial subject. Like most Martens meetings it was reasonably helpful and constructive. Simonet was also there. What was remarkable about it was that it was immediately after (but before any of us had heard of) the ill-fated American rescue attempt for the Iranian hostages. Although it had probably been on the news from 7.30, none of us had a hint of it, not Martens, not me, not most surprisingly Simonet, who had returned from Washington overnight and had been seeing the State Department literally twelve hours before. Consultation with allies did not seem to have been strong.

I spent most of the day on European Council preparations, although I also had a full hour with Gundelach, going through a great range of agricultural issues. At 8.15 to the Italian Embassy, where we were supposed to have a pre-dinner meeting with Cossiga. It was half an hour late starting and although still nominally pre-dinner, went on until 11.15. Cossiga certainly treated it as pre-dinner (i) by not offering us dinner, which was untypically Italian and particularly untypical of Cossiga, and (ii) by keeping about thirty guests, all the heads of the Brussels Italian colony, both their Commissioners, their three ambassadors, journalists, etc. waiting for dinner in the next room.

He expounded to us almost breathlessly the entirely fresh approach which Giscard had expounded to him that morning at breakfast in the Elysée before Cossiga had gone on to London. It was that the BBQ should be looked at the other way round and considered from the point of view of holding the deficit steady rather than putting in a fixed sum of money. At first I thought this was a destructive proposal, but I became convinced as Cossiga had been, and indeed the British Government had been, that it was possibly constructive. Giscard is an odd man and one can never tell quite how he will operate. A great deal of time in the course of the meeting was wasted by Marcora (Minister of Agriculture) who was also present, and who has a great capacity to talk irrelevantly and incomprehensibly. I returned to rue de Praetère rather exhausted but interested and excited by the new development.

SUNDAY, 27 APRIL. *Brussels and Luxembourg.*

The long-awaited European Council began in the Kirchberg at 3.45 and went on until 7.00. The BBQ was not dealt with at all during this session, and Mrs Thatcher, no doubt learning, perhaps over-learning from Dublin, avoided pressing it. When we assembled for dinner at the Villa Vauban discussion of it was once more avoided. General conversation at dinner, and then we were joined by the Foreign Ministers and went on until 12.30, dealing almost entirely with Political Cooperation questions. Mrs Thatcher was frustrated by this, but reluctant, despite my mild urging, to insist on opening the (BBQ) discussion. I think this was a mistake, both on Cossiga's part and on hers. A first round, which could be slept on, would have been desirable.

MONDAY, 28 APRIL. *Luxembourg and Brussels.*

Awakened about 5.30 on a dismal morning by a silver band which, perhaps in honour of the European Council, was parading round the Place de la Gare. To the Kirchberg at 9.15, but no session until 12.20, as there were a great number of bilaterals going on. I had a talk with Haughey at 9.45, then Cossiga from 10.00 to 10.30, then Mrs Thatcher about 11.00. It was difficult to know what the prospect was, but it was not looking particularly good.

When the Council eventually assembled, we met from 12.20 to 3.40. To sit this long was again I think a mistake, although well-intentioned, on Cossiga's part. We got down to the BBQ straight-away and Mrs Thatcher was certainly being much quieter, less strident, less abrasive, than at Dublin. Early on Schmidt brought forward a proposal which was very good for 1980: the British deficit should not be allowed to grow in that year beyond the average for 1978 and 1979. This opened up in my view a great opportunity for Mrs Thatcher, though it obviously still left the 1981 position open. But later in the discussion Giscard made the proposal that in 1981 the payment to offset the British deficit should be the same as the 1980 figure. This, on top of Schmidt's proposal, had the effect of giving the British a complete guarantee for 1980 against uncovenanted increases. For 1981 there would be no such guarantee but equally the amount paid to the British should be the same as in 1980, in other words an offer for the two years of about 2400 million units of account which might indeed, according to what the exact sum would be in 1980, have been somewhat higher.

I suggested at this stage that we might have an adjournment, which I thought would have been useful, and one or two people took it up, but Mrs Thatcher unwisely did not press for it, and Cossiga did not push it through. Had she been able to sit back and consider this — talk to her advisers, to Carrington and perhaps to me — we might have made some progress, but instead Cossiga went on too long.

I lunched with the others, Giscard asking me directly and semi-publicly across the table what I thought of the offer and my saying it seemed to me a pretty good offer, and one which should be accepted. Mrs Thatcher did not appear, being closeted with British ministers and officials, but then came back at 5.00 and refused it. One or two attempts at *nettoyage* were made but she remained adamant. I had told her before that I thought she was making a great mistake by not accepting, and she good-temperedly but firmly said, 'Don't try persuading me, you know I find persuasion very counterproductive.' So when she had spoken I said in the Council I thought she was making a major error, that it was a substantial offer, and that we were splitting Europe for a difference which was very small compared with the original gap.

We then ground on until 9.15 p.m. dealing with a variety of other subjects. Then we had a press conference from 10.50 to 11.30, in which I expressed the view that we had been tantalizingly close to agreement and made it fairly clear where I thought the fault lay. It really was amazing that she did not accept this offer. Carrington was clearly in favour of doing so, so I think were Armstrong and Palliser, but Carrington in my view did not put as much pressure upon her as he should have done, though I believe that this was made more difficult for him by the fact that Peter Walker, who was also present for the Agriculture Council, was putting strong pressure the other way.

After the press conference we decided to drive back to Brussels, and arrived, tired and deeply disappointed, at 1.30 in the morning. It was an extremely exhausting and madly irritating European Council. The only benefit from my point of view was a slight improvement of relations with the French, who have been waging a minor press campaign against me for playing too much of a British hand.

TUESDAY, 29 APRIL. *Brussels.*

Office only at 11.30. A series of meetings, including a farewell lunch, rue de Praetère, for the Lubbers (the Dutch Permanent Representative), who is going to Washington as Ambassador.

Home early in the evening to prepare for departure to India the next morning. There was some feeling that in view of the state of crisis in the Community I ought not to go, but my view was that this twice-postponed visit ought not to be interfered with again. I thought some time was needed for the dust to settle before anything could be done, and I must confess also to a certain desire, temporarily at least, to get that dust of Europe off my feet and to move into a different atmosphere.

WEDNESDAY, 30 APRIL. *Brussels and Delhi.*

Commission early. 11.20 plane to Frankfurt, and Air India 747 from there. Comfortable flight to Delhi, arriving at 1.30 in the morning, which was 10 p.m. Brussels time. Only protocol people at the airport, which was a relief at that time in the morning, and drove to Rashtrapati Bhawan, the old Vice-Regal Lodge, where we were installed at 2.15 a.m. in magnificent apartments. Apparently some Viceroys, not Mountbatten – but I think all the previous four of the post-Lutyens era – had themselves lived in the quarters we were in, but Mountbatten for some reason or other had moved to the other side of the vast house. Temperature very high, probably about 95°F when we landed, but dry and therefore not intolerable.

THURSDAY, 1 MAY. *Delhi.*

A rest day for acclimatization. Very sensible, although unusual. To lunch accompanied by Crispin and Jennifer with John

Thomson* (British High Commissioner) alone (his wife was away). Rather a good talk with him, whom I thought a sharp, intelligent, agreeable man. Between 6 and 7 p.m. in the fierce red sunset over the red city we did a drive to the Red Fort and the Great Mosque. Back and received K. B. Lall plus wife, the former (twice) Indian Ambassador to Brussels who had played such a role in Community/ Indian relations over twenty years. Then to a *son et lumière* performance at the Red Fort. Surprised at how much in the final part – it was a history of three hundred years – emphasis was put on the Indian National Liberation Army – the Chandra Bose/Japanese flirtation towards the end of the war.

FRIDAY, 2 MAY. *Delhi.*

Two wreath-laying ceremonies at the Gandhi and Nehru memorials from 8.30 to 9.15. Extremely hot, the Nehru shrine for some reason seeming hotter than the Gandhi shrine, but tolerable and brief ceremonies.

Then a seventy-five-minute meeting with Mrs Gandhi, with Crispin and one on her side. Moderately interesting talk with her. I found her rather easier, less forbidding, in a way less wrapped up in herself than I had nine years before. Mainly about world affairs, although she was bitterly critical of Desai for having released too many of the dangerous men she had locked up during the Emergency, and of almost everybody in Assam for their misrepresentation of herself and their disruptive attitude towards the Indian state. On Afghanistan she was mildly critical of the Soviet occupation, but spoke with more vehemence against the American response to it and the danger of the Soviet reaction to American bases, growing Sino-American friendship and the Russian belief (this was surprising to me) that the United States encouraged Islamic fundamentalists.

Mrs Gandhi obviously hoped (and almost assumed) that a world Summit would follow the publication of the Brandt Report, but had no plans for an Indian initiative to this end, apparently looking to either Mexico or the European Community to take the lead.

She made no concessions to blandness in making clear that India

* Sir John Thomson, b. 1927, was High Commissioner to India 1977–86, and Permanent Representative to the United Nations 1982–7.

wanted all the Community help she could get. She raised the privileged arrangements which others (i.e. the Lomé countries) already had with the Community. I said that the Lomé Convention which associated the Community with a large number of small and very poor countries (with one or two exceptions such as Nigeria) should not worry India. India was far too big and important to be a member of it. There had to be a more individual and equal relationship between the Community and India. If India had to share in the aid we gave under the Lomé Convention it would be for her no more than a drop in the ocean. Mrs Gandhi said she was not sure she agreed. With the strong Indian social and economic infrastructure, India could make use of whatever was provided. She thought President Giscard had grasped this point when he had visited India recently (a nice piece of gamesmanship). A strong India was well able to assist others. She would prefer to speak of Community aid not as a drop in the ocean but as a rung on the ladder of development.

Then a series of engagements, including a 'discussion' lunch with the Speaker and forty members of the Parliament, a call on the head of state and a lecture to the Indian Institute of International Affairs, until the Prime Minister's dinner in the ceremonial rooms of Rashtrapati Bhawan, which was fortunately brief, 8.15 to 10.15. Ten-minute speeches at the end of this, one from Mrs Gandhi, one from me. She was agreeable at dinner, and got on particularly well with Jennifer, who was on the other side of her. Dinner I suppose for about a hundred people, impressive surroundings, no alcohol, but rather good food.

SATURDAY, 3 MAY. *Delhi.*

At 10.30 saw Bahadur Singh,* the now retired Indian diplomat who had beaten me on my second time round for the presidency of the Oxford Union. Agreeable talk with him, although he was healthily free of Oxford *schwärmerei.* At 12.15 a meeting with the Minister of Commerce, followed by a lunch with him and perhaps forty others in the Taj Mahal Hotel. Press conference at 5.30 and then a long television interview. Provocatively anti-EEC inter-

---

*Bahadur Singh, 1915–87, was Indian Ambassador to Egypt and then to Italy.

viewer to whom I replied with some animation and firmness. Then at 7.30 a briefing of the ambassadors of the Nine followed by dinner at the Italian Embassy – their ambassador seemed an ass, which is most unusual in the Italian diplomatic service, but the others were not too bad.

Jennifer had been that day for an expedition to Agra, and had survived remarkably well in a temperature of 118°F in the shade. Temperature in Delhi was about 110°F. No humidity.

SUNDAY, 4 MAY. *Delhi and Udaipur.*

Flew to Udaipur (very high-class sight-seeing) in a comfortable but non-jet Indian Air Force plane. By boat to the Lake Palace Hotel on an island. The hotel is a very splendid place. In the evening we sat for two hours on a sort of rampart having a drink and watching one of the most memorable sunsets I have ever seen.

MONDAY, 5 MAY. *Udaipur and Bangalore.*

Flew for four and a quarter hours in the same slow plane to Bangalore, which despite its reputation as a much-favoured, healthy British garrison town, failed to enthuse me.

TUESDAY, 6 MAY. *Bangalore and Mysore.*

Helicopted to Mysore. To the Mahal Palace Hotel – a vast 1920s mansion – about three miles from the town, at which hardly anybody except us seemed to be staying, and were installed there in huge vice-regal-style rooms with a splendid view. Left fairly soon afterwards to drive to the Samanthapur Temple about twenty miles away, accompanied by the Curator of Monuments for Karnatica, an erudite and enjoyable man. This early temple has extraordinary carvings done in the special stone of the locality which is very soft when quarried and therefore can be most intricately and delicately worked, but then becomes very hard and therefore preserves itself over the centuries.

Afternoon visit to the main palace of the last Maharaja of Mysore, fairly modern, vast ironwork structure inside, all cast in Glasgow at the end of the nineteenth century, the ensemble bearing a considerable resemblance to the Winter Gardens at Blackpool. There is a striking similarity between English late Victorian and Edwardian pier architecture and the style favoured by Indian maharajas a little later. The Mysore buildings, which are on a very grand scale, were all built in the last decades of princely power.

WEDNESDAY, 7 MAY. *Mysore and Bombay.*

Helicopted for about twenty-five minutes to the Bandipur game sanctuary where we drove in jeeps through the bush or forest. (It was not tropical rain forest, but it was more than scrub.) We did relatively well for animals: no tiger – but it is now almost impossible to see a tiger anywhere – but two herd of wild elephants, one very close, and the other moving fast with a great trumpeting from the leader; a lot of rather beautiful gazelles, a lot of fine birds; and some other relatively rare creatures. Returned to Mysore for lunch and then left for Bangalore, again by helicopter, at 4.15, and on to Bombay by commercial flight on a clear, hot night. Drove the long distance into this immense city, which has a curious Manhattan-like appearance after dark, to the Taj Mahal Hotel where Mrs Sawhny, rich Bombay widow, Tata sister, gave us a dinner party which was very much an Indian version of a smart but enlightened New York occasion. A Tata brother (not the head of the firm), the leader of the local Liberal Party, several ladies much interested in the preservation of old Bombay, and nearly anybody involved in some form of good works.

THURSDAY, 8 MAY. *Bombay and East Hendred.*

London at 6.15 a.m. (9.45 Bombay time) and East Hendred at 7.15. It has been an interesting, worthwhile and not at all exhausting Indian trip.

FRIDAY, 9 MAY. *East Hendred, Paris and East Hendred.*

This, alas, was not a day of relaxation, for I set off for the 8.30 plane to Paris, which got me into the Schuman celebrations* in the

* For the thirtieth anniversary of the unveiling of the Schuman Plan, which led to the setting up of the Coal and Steel Community and the beginning of modern European unity.

Grande Salle of the Sorbonne by about 11 o'clock. There I made a fifteen-minute speech, wholly prepared text, in the midst of other dignitaries like Barre, Mme Veil, Colombo, etc. Lunch with Marie-Alice. East Hendred at 6.40 in good time for an expedition to the Downs in magical light.

MONDAY, 12 MAY. *East Hendred, London and Brussels.*

Lunch with the British Biological Research Institute at the Savoy. Solly Zuckerman was the great panjandrum of this, and present, though not in the chair. Large audience of four or five hundred, mainly from firms concerned in these matters, some scientists. I had quite a good Crispin speech of substance which I embroidered with a joke about Solly and Mysore monkeys. (Our room in Mysore had been invaded by monkeys one afternoon, and my story, which owed a certain amount to fantasy but not everything, was that one of them came and sat close, looking at me, and that such is the obvious intelligence of a monkey – unlike any other animal – that you feel in order to be polite you have to make an attempt at conversation. I could not at first think on what subject to address it, but after a bit I decided, so ubiquitous a presence is Solly in the world, and so close had been his contact with primates, that the best I could do was to ask him whether he knew my friend Lord Zuckerman, whereupon the creature nodded gravely, appreciatively and affirmatively. Politeness had been observed, and I was able to return to my book.)

To Brussels for one of my regular dinners for Ortoli and Gundelach – Davignon was away. Hard pounding on BBQ as is now usual.

TUESDAY, 13 MAY. *Brussels.*

Briefly to dine with the Tickells to meet for the first time Michel Rocard.* He is not a dominating personality. Indeed it is a little difficult to imagine him as President of the French Republic, but then it is always difficult to imagine such things before they occur, if they do. But he was both highly intelligent and highly agreeable. He

---

*Michel Rocard, b. 1930, Prime Minister of France since May 1988, became French Minister of Planning and Regional Development 1981–3, and of Agriculture 1983–5. In 1980, as more recently, he was the man wanting to be presidential candidate if Mitterrand was not.

made a particularly good impression because, when I asked him if he remembered Jean Loudon (formerly Jean Norman, Wantage doctor's wife with whose family she had told me he had stayed as a very young man immediately after the war), his face lit up and he said, 'Jean Norman, not possible, how is she? Vous la connaissez? I remember that summer vividly. J'avais dix-huit ans, et elle en avait deux de plus. J'étais tellement amoureux d'elle. She was the first love of my life. Comment va-t-elle maintenant?' It would be difficult to imagine Giscard reacting with similar naïve nostalgic enthusiasm.

WEDNESDAY, 14 MAY. *Brussels.*

Commission meeting with a fortunately light agenda. Then I had to greet the Grand Duke of Luxembourg who, accompanied by the Grand Duchess, had come for a head of state visit which took the normal form of a short talk with me alone first, then an hour's session with the Commission, then a lunch. He was agreeable and interested, and all went well.

An early evening visit from Muskie, the new US Secretary of State. I have known him for ten years, I suppose, and fortunately we had him to dinner at rue de Praetère about a year ago. So we started, certainly on his side, on terms of almost exaggerated friendly intimacy. He is a man with an agreeable, impressive manner. How much he knows about foreign affairs, I don't know, but he seems self-confident, perhaps a little over-so, making clear that he was going to be a more political Secretary of State than Vance.

I asked him whether he had not hesitated over taking the job. After all he had been in the Senate for twenty years, and a Senate seat was a big thing to give up for what, while I did not wish to predict the result of the election, might turn out to be no more than an eight-month spell of office. He said no, he had not hesitated for a moment, he was thoroughly fed up with the Senate. He had had to fix one or two personal affairs before he had given an affirmative answer to the President, but on the substance of the issue he had not had a moment's doubt.

Then rather late to a dinner given for Muskie by Tapley Bennett, US Ambassador to NATO. The dinner was far too large and therefore pointless. There were about forty people present, four tables, and I had some rather dull diplomatic neighbours. After dinner, Muskie made a longish, homespun, moralistic speech which was not too bad, not too good either. Then after he had sat down at the end of it, he proceeded to try and hold the whole room for about a quarter of an hour by telling some less than riveting self-centred anecdotes. I thought they were not greatly to the point and began to feel rather impatient with the amiable ex-Senator.

The main interest for me of the evening was that Simonet had come up to me before dinner and said that the Belgians, who had previously been strongly pushing my continuation in office, now thought the gap between Britain and the rest of the Community was so great that the time had not arrived when any Englishman could be President of the Commission almost indefinitely, which eight years would amount to. I was insistent that it did not affect me, because, as he knew, I did not want another term. I had decided four years was the right time, but it was nonetheless interesting and significant that he should have said it, and the reason that he gave. It made a pattern with my Strasbourg dinner with Davignon a month ago.

THURSDAY, 15 MAY. *Brussels, London and Sheffield.*

To Sheffield for a university-sponsored lecture on the Community and International Trade. Formidable audience of nearly a thousand, I cannot think where they got them from, who nonetheless seemed interested in a not very exciting but quite sensible lecture.

FRIDAY, 16 MAY. *Sheffield, London and East Hendred.*

7.55 train to London through spectacular May sunshine, which gave even the flat and dull East Midlands countryside an unusual iridescence. George Thomson to lunch at Brooks's. He expressed great enthusiasm about the prospect of a party realignment, and said that if he had known I was going to do anything like this, he might not have taken on the chairmanship of IBA, as it would inhibit him in what he could do; a pity. Motored to East Hendred, where so brilliant was the evening that we went up to the Downs twice, once before dinner and once in the twilight.

SATURDAY, 17 MAY. *East Hendred and Naples.*

Avion taxi to Naples for a Foreign Ministers' meeting, and to the Villa Rosebery on the sea to the north of Naples. It is curious that it should have so firmly maintained its Rosebery name, as he only owned it for twelve years. Lunch at 2 o'clock and then a fairly informal session from 3.30 to 6.45. The session was frustrating in that attempts by Peter Carrington, and to some extent by me, to get some serious discussion on the overhanging issue of the day, the BBQ, got nowhere. Colombo did not force it, and Genscher, who was inevitably the main potential *interlocuteur* as the representative of the country which would have to pay the most, was obviously not anxious to get involved.

SUNDAY, 18 MAY. *Naples and Brussels.*

Discussion over a general breakfast from 8.30 to 10.45, when we stopped. Then a calming walk (I hope) on the terrace with a very frustrated Peter Carrington. Then a brief visit to the Capodimonte Museum, which I had been to only once before. Ran into a whole posse of French diplomats, Nanteuil and his Hedwige (COREPER, thinking that the BBQ was being discussed, had insisted on being at hand in Naples, which meant they had an entirely free – in both senses – cultural weekend), Jacques Tiné, who was passing through, the French Ambassador to Rome (Puaux) and, I think, maybe yet another. Then to Brussels.

FRIDAY, 23 MAY. *Brussels and Lucca.*

A special Commission meeting, again on BBQ, which went doubtfully well. 1.10 plane to Milan. Spent about three hours working in the VIP room at the airport there and then plane to Pisa, and to La Pianella (Gilmours) by taxi only at 8.30. Arrived, typically, in rain. Coming from Northern Europe and India, it was the first rain we had seen for three weeks past.

TUESDAY, 27 MAY. *Lucca and Brussels.*

Ian and I, called by the rigours of the BBQ, had to leave at 4.00, so the visit was very truncated and the weather, as so often at this season in Italy, very shaky. We flew off in a British Government plane from Pisa to Bonn, Ian going to see Dohnanyi. I motored from Wahn to Brussels, then took a special late Commission meeting from 9.30 to 11.45 trying to get our budget paper into shape. Only moderate success. Late-night meetings are always difficult to move to a decision.

WEDNESDAY, 28 MAY. *Brussels.*

Saw Cheysson at 10.15, Davignon at 11.15 and then had a Commission meeting, perhaps if anything more difficult than the night before, all on the BBQ. Then gave Henri Simonet a late and brief lunch, my mind very much on budgetary problems as we were returning for a meeting in the afternoon.

Commission again from 4.00. A bit of progress but not all that much, and then a bilateral meeting with Ortoli, very hard-pounding, and then home to pick up Charles (my elder son), who had arrived unexpectedly to stay, and drove him to La Hulpe and Waterloo for about an hour. Enjoyable talk with him. Home and a dinner party for Ian (Gilmour), Michael Jenkins', Tickells, Hannay (Soames's old *Chef de Cabinet* now back in the Foreign Office), and Ian's nice Private Secretary, Michael Richardson. Hannay ground on tiresomely about the new draft of the Commission paper, which he was aware of, and which we had hammered out with difficulty during the day, saying that on one vital point it gave away far too much. Therefore rather a disputatious start to dinner. But everybody else thought Hannay had gone on boorishly for too long and eventually we managed (Ian being very helpful and nice) to get on to some general conversation and cheer up a bit.

THURSDAY, 29 MAY. *Brussels.*

Meeting with Colombo in my office from 10.30 to 11.45. Then the Commission again at noon. I tried to catch back a bit of what Hannay had complained about the previous evening: very partial success. In a minority of two with Tugendhat, which I had never been near in the Commission before.

The fateful Foreign Affairs Council started at 3.30 and went on, with a break in the middle during which we got our paper ready and presented it, to 8.30 p.m. The gap appeared wide in early exchanges (the Council was entirely devoted to the BBQ, apart from purely routine items). Then we adjourned and dined from 9.15 to 11.15. Neither François-Poncet nor Genscher was there. In the latter case, this did not matter at all as Dohnanyi was active, less inhibited, keen on a solution, and knew the *dossier* much better than Genscher. In the former case it may or may not have been an advantage. François-Poncet, I assumed, would be harder and sharper than Bernard-Reymond, who had not been particularly difficult in the early session. But at dinner Bernard-Reymond became very awkward and prickly, saying that he could not possibly stay the next day, giving a series of unconvincing excuses about what he had to do in Paris – something to do with the Pope's visit – but nothing seemed to hold together very well, and Peter Carrington became extremely irritated with him. The atmosphere for an hour or so at dinner deteriorated to such an extent that Carrington was on the point of breaking off the negotiations before they had even started. Fortunately, Ian Gilmour, with great nerve and firmness, got him off that. Even so, it still appeared that, the gap being still wide, though possibly not unbridgeable, the only thing to do was to adjourn and meet again, possibly on the Saturday, which Bernard-Reymond again said he could not do, possibly the Sunday, which was not attractive, or the Monday. However, Colombo, with very good judgement, gently rejected this and said no, no, what he thought we should do was to proceed by a series of individual discussions with the heads of delegations, which he and I would conduct, and see how far we could get.

Therefore we settled down at 11.30 at night, Colombo and I, Crispin, Renato Ruggiero and Plaja also in the room most of the time, and proceeded to see everybody. The exact order I cannot remember. I think we began with Bernard-Reymond and Carrington, or vice versa, but without getting particularly far, though Peter by this time had recovered his equanimity and was agreeable and quite skilful.

Then we saw Dohnanyi, who came in with a great scheme. He thought he could see a way through and he presented his solution with confidence and lucidity, and indeed it seemed to me a perfectly possible basis for settlement. Then we saw Carrington again and I presented it to him. He was not as enthusiastic as I expected, but thought there might be something in it, so we went on with further discussions. We saw the Benelux ministers together, and they did not make too much difficulty, though this was quite late in the night and they were a bit discontented at not having been brought in earlier: the Luxembourgeois in particular, for some reason or other, but the Dutch too, the new Belgian Minister (Nothomb) being rather easier. The Irish were remarkably amenable, the Danes a bit sticky as usual, but not impossible.

Then we saw the three main ones again several times; this process went on until about 6.30 in the morning, when we seemed to be getting near to a settlement. We then broke up for some time: there had been other intervals during the night during which I had to sustain myself with Irish whiskey, which I do not much like, for the bar for some curious reason had run out of all other supplies. By the morning the only real difficulty remaining, provided the French would accept – it was by no means clear either that they would or that they would not – was the question of a linkage between the 1981 agricultural payments and the supplementary payments to the British for that year. In other words, the French – or anyone else if they so wished – would have an opportunity to block if they did not like the view the British took about the agricultural price settlement. This, rather against my will, was in our paper, and it had been made semi-explicit at the insistence of nearly all the other members of the Commission who took part during the night, Davignon, Ortoli, Gundelach – a powerful trio.

The British said they could not possibly accept this. If it was explicit they could not defend it in the House of Commons. I tried hard to get them to do so, and indeed Ian Gilmour was in favour of taking the risk. Peter Carrington was not. We then had a series of agitated comings and goings, in the course of which Ortoli and I had our second row of the Council. The first had been after my statement in the pre-dinner session when he said I had presented the issue in an unbalanced way – he was in a very agitated state all the time – no doubt under great Paris pressure. But as is mostly the case with Francis, as soon as we had had that row he apologized and more or less made it up. But on this early morning occasion he was huffing and puffing and walking around looking even more like Brezhnev than usual, and was clearly very tense. So was I, for that matter. This row remained unresolved.

FRIDAY, 30 MAY. *Brussels and East Hendred.*

There was great pressure from the Benelux ministers in particular to get back to a plenary session, so we resumed at 7.15 a.m. and went on until 10.10, though we were suspended from 8.00 to 9.45. First, we had the problem of getting round the linkage problem. We set up a drafting committee of officials under Stevy (Davignon) in the chair (the British complaining he would be a very partial chairman). This committee curiously and surprisingly produced a satisfactory formula: it was extremely, almost excessively, simple, but ingenious. Emile Noël, typically and with a sudden shaft of subtle brilliance, was the author. It seemed to say nothing and might, I suppose, mean different things to different people. However, it had been accepted by Michael Butler and Hannay who had been in the committee for the British.

The French were a little reluctant to accept it, but there was then a considerable effort to persuade them on Davignon's part, who seemed to have swung round, and on Emile's, who naturally had the pride of authorship. They both argued with the French in a huddle behind their places at the table for some time, after which the French asked for a suspension for a quarter of an hour. This lasted not fifteen but ninety-five minutes.

When the French eventually trooped back into the room, my heart was almost literally in my mouth because I thought that after all this interminable work, and being so near to a result, it was going to be a repetition of Luxembourg, with the whole thing coming apart at the end. But miraculously and mysteriously the French announced quite simply that they would accept, but that they wanted a bit of the original British draft put in as well! Then I thought for a moment that the British were going to be sticky, but no, they accepted too, and the whole thing was over by just after 10 o'clock, eighteen and a half hours after we had begun. It was a prodigious achievement, leaving me exhausted but with a sense that something I did not believe could have come off had really been achieved and achieved very effectively. For the moment I even forgot the bitter thought that all the effort on the part of Colombo, Carrington, Gilmour and others, and all the strain on my relations with my Commission colleagues, was made necessary only by a foolish woman's stubborn whim a month before. The new settlement was only cosmetically different from that which Mrs Thatcher had turned down at Luxembourg.

We got back into my Berlaymont room at 10.20, had a glass or two of champagne to celebrate and then after an hour or so I went home to rue de Praetère, had a large breakfast there at noon, caught the 12.45 and got to East Hendred by 2 o'clock. I slept fairly contentedly all the afternoon. Still good weather.

SATURDAY, 31 MAY. *East Hendred.*

Up at 9.15, did a certain amount of telephoning in the morning to try to find out what was happening within the British Government, and then went to meet Marie-Alice (de Beaumarchais) at Didcot. Brought her back for lunch, to which the Gilmours also came. I had discovered on the telephone beforehand that the picture was that Ian and Peter Carrington had an extremely frosty reception from Mrs Thatcher at Chequers where they had gone straight from the airport and had had altogether three and a half hours with her, not apparently being offered even a drink, let alone lunch, until 2.30 Brussels time. Then a drink, produced rather reluctantly on a direct request from Peter Carrington, followed by a late and apparently not very adequate lunch. But it was not so much the refreshment as the atmosphere which depressed them, for there was no sense of welcoming them back as heroes from the battlefront, but of being extremely reluctant to accept what they had so unexpectedly and successfully negotiated. They left her feeling that she was going to see how things developed over the weekend and by no means necessarily going to recommend the settlement to the Cabinet. However, the press on Saturday morning had been quite satisfactory.*

SUNDAY, 1 JUNE. *East Hendred.*

Lunch at home for Marie-Alice, Ann Fleming, Wyatts and Charles. Croquet in the afternoon. Gordon Richardsons to a drink at 6.30. Drove to the Monument after dinner for the view in the twilight. An agreeable weekend, a sense of achievement, and a major weight lifted.

* And indeed proved to be more so on the Sunday and Monday, so that the Cabinet, even in the absence of a lead from the top, apparently accepted the settlement without dissent.

TUESDAY, 3 JUNE. *East Hendred and Brussels.*

9.45 plane to Brussels. Relatively calm morning except for the *Daily Mail* having a front-page story announcing that I was resigning from Brussels immediately to launch a new party. I did not take it too seriously, but it obviously caused a certain amount of agitation and excitement. We issued a firm denial during the morning saying that I was definitely staying until the end of the year. Nevertheless, with the BBQ temporarily out of the way, British politics were beginning to loom. My speech at the Press Gallery on the following Monday and the form it should take was already weighing on my mind.

FRIDAY, 6 JUNE. *Brussels and East Hendred.*

East Hendred by 8.00, where Bonham Carters and Hayden and Laura had all arrived to stay just before me (Jennifer in Edinburgh). After dinner gave them an outline for my speech for Monday. Mark rather sensibly was inclined to take the view that if he were me he would say as little as possible, but this was not the view of the others nor at that stage mine.

SUNDAY, 8 JUNE. *East Hendred.*

Half-way through lunch Shirley Williams rang up to ask if I had heard her on *The World at One* and I said alas, not. She said she hoped I would agree with what she had said and was very friendly. As in fact what she had said, which was much quoted subsequently, was that a centre party was out because it would have no roots, no conscience, no principles, no God knows what else, this was rather a curious telephone call, particularly as I, not knowing what she had said, nonetheless thought it a good idea to run through my speech with her, which I did, and she said it was more or less all right. (It did not of course actually mention a centre party as such.) She merely asked for a change at the end where I referred to a possible revival of Liberal and Social Democratic Britain. She said, 'Couldn't you use small letters and leave out the "and" – "liberal social democratic Britain"?' Thinking that if Paris was worth a Mass, Shirley was certainly worth an 'and' (and a lower case) I decided to do so, after which we rang off on terms of great amity. She said she was sure we would all be together in six months or so.

MONDAY, 9 JUNE. *East Hendred and London.*

Motored to London. Poisoned finger (which had developed on Saturday) worse. To Kensington Park Gardens for a short time, where there were a lot of photographers. Then to the House of Commons for the Parliamentary Press Gallery speech. Large, packed audience. The speech took just under half an hour, and I answered, not particularly well or particularly badly, three or four questions afterwards. Reception more or less all right, but not wildly enthusiastic. You could hardly expect that with an audience of hard-boiled journalists seasoned by a few parliamentary guests like Neil Kinnock.* However, Tom Bradley and one or two other friends who were there seemed quite tolerably pleased. I went off feeling rather like Guy Fawkes having set fire to a fuse and wondering what on earth was going to happen.

A meeting with Lindley, Phipps etc., from 7.00 to 8.30, by which time the speech was all over the evening papers and dominating the news bulletins. They were obviously pleased with the impact and so was I, at the time at any rate.

John Harris came to dine and we watched the various news bulletins, including hearing Denis Healey describe it as 'all bunkum'. This was done aggressively rather than skilfully by Denis, though he was able to use Shirley's words of Sunday with considerable effect.

TUESDAY, 10 JUNE. *London and Brussels.*

The speech was dominant in the newspapers, with a good deal of fairly adverse comment. The *Guardian* had a definitely unfriendly leader. So did one or two other papers, but the *Financial Times* was much more friendly than it had been after the Dimbleby Lecture. *The Times* was not bad, the populars mixed, but all giving it a great deal of space. Had barely time to take them in before leaving for the 9.45 plane to Brussels.

The President of Costa Rica for a brief meeting at 7.30, followed

*Neil Kinnock, b. 1942, who was to be elected leader of the Labour Party three years later, was then Opposition spokesman on education.

by a Berlaymont dinner for him. An agreeable and interesting Central American, but my mind somewhat on other things.

WEDNESDAY, 11 JUNE. *Brussels.*

Home at 4.15 p.m. and tried to sleep off exhaustion for a bit but in fact by this time I had got into a thorough gloom about the speech, which I was beginning increasingly to think had been a major tactical error. It took me to a ledge on the cliff-face from which it was going to be very difficult to get up or down. Had a mildly reassuring telephone conversation with David Steel.

THURSDAY, 12 JUNE. *Brussels and Venice.*

Venice by avion taxi just before 11 o'clock. In by motor launch through vast security precautions with frogmen all over the place and soldiers standing with their rifles at the ready on the banks of the canal along from the airport, and then lots of security boats and security helicopters around and above us as we crossed the back part of the lagoon and then past the Arsenale and into the Danieli. The Danieli was like an armed camp with the bit of the Riva outside it for 100 yards or more cordoned off. Installed there, in what was no doubt a grand but rather a disagreeable suite. It had two large sitting rooms and a moderate-sized bedroom. It was nominally on the first floor, but when I opened the window of the bedroom I looked straight out at soldiers with machine guns standing about ten feet from me on the top of the little bridge.

Lunched on the Danieli roof garden with a splendid view and splendid weather. Half enjoyed lunch. Then the opening session of the European Council in the old monastery on the Isolo San Giorgio, which ran for four hours from 3.50 and was, as one might have expected, not particularly notable. The mood was one of post-BBQ exhaustion. There were a number of routine items which I introduced, but there was no issue we particularly came to grips with. We signally failed to do so with energy.

Then back to the hotel and on for the heads of government dinner at the Ca' Orsini on the Grand Canal between the Accademia and the Rialto, where I stayed from 9.15 till about 11.15, and then tactfully left as they had to get down to the question of appointing my successor, which is purely inter-government business.

FRIDAY, 13 JUNE. *Venice and Brussels.*

Over to the Isolo San Giorgio for the session which was due to start at 10.30. However, owing to the fact that they had completely failed to reach agreement on a new President the night before, it did not begin until 12.30. There were hurried consultations and comings and goings about this. Thorn was pressing himself very hard, and had the support of Genscher but not of Schmidt, who kept on confusing issues by throwing in the names of one or two Dutchmen – 'that Dutch ex-Finance Minister whose name I cannot remember', he had suggested at one stage. In fact it was Duisenberg. Zijlstra I think he also had in mind. The French were at this stage adamantly opposed to Thorn. The British were willing to go for Thorn, but Carrington much preferred Davignon, who had in fact been offered the job by Barre about two weeks before, and believed he had it sewn up, and would have made a very good President. Mrs Thatcher felt committed to Thorn. Benelux was split all over the place and as a result the scene was generally disorderly. Little Thorn was pacing up and down and looking gloomy and agitated. When I asked him how he was feeling, he said awful. Very disagreeable for him. I think he ought to have removed himself from the scene, which would have been more sensible, but maybe he found it difficult. I returned to Brussels between 5.00 and 7.00.

TUESDAY, 17 JUNE. *Strasbourg.*

At 11.30 saw Glinne and Caborn of the Socialist Group about the case of Adams, whom it was alleged had been victimized in connection with the Hoffmann-La Roche exposure many years before, and to whom we had made an *ex gratia* payment, which alas did not entirely satisfy him or them. But we had gone as far as we could without trouble with the *Cour des Comptes*. Jennifer and I took Harry Walston and his new wife (ex Mrs Nicholas Scott) to lunch at La Wantzenau. Some discussion about my speech without a great deal of support from Harry. 'I agree with your objectives but not with your tactics' was the best I could get from him.

At 3.30 I had a meeting with Madame Chou En-lai and her delegation, very friendly and courteous, but without a great deal of interest to say.

SATURDAY, 21 JUNE. *Brussels and Venice.*

I left after lunch to proceed once more by avion taxi to Venice, this time for the Western Economic Summit. Arrived in horrible weather: cloudy, windy, with a tendency to rain. Moreover, it got steadily worse. Installed again in the Danieli, this time on the third floor as I had complained about the noise in the previous room. A great storm then came on.

I had a drink with Trudeau and found him much as when I had last seen him nearly two years before. Agreeable, not much idea as to what was going on, pleased to have won, sharp but not very constructive comments. Then in pouring rain went by motor launch to the Gritti, picked up the Carringtons and took them out to an enjoyable dinner, and my spirits temporarily rose.

SUNDAY, 22 JUNE. *Venice.*

Across to the San Giorgio, with the lagoon pretty rough, for photographs and a session from 10.30 till 1.00. *Tour de table*, nobody making any particularly bad or particularly impressive statements. I spoke for ten minutes at the end. Schmidt was probably the best, but too long as usual. Carter looked on better form than at Tokyo and spoke as he generally does on these occasions in a controlled but hardly inspired way. Mrs Thatcher was slightly peripheral, as indeed were Trudeau and the Japanese (owing to Ohira's death, the Japanese were represented at Foreign Minister not Prime Minister level). Cossiga was a fairly good but somewhat long-winded chairman.

Lunched with the Foreign Ministers from 1.30 to 3.00, during which we were trying to draft an Afghanistan and Middle East communiqué. Then, there being a purely political meeting of heads of government in the afternoon, I met with the Finance and Energy Ministers from 3.30 to 6.10. Then a general reception in the courtyard of the Palazzo Ducale, followed by a dinner upstairs with the Finance Ministers. I think we were the first people to dine in that room, or indeed in the building, for three hundred years and everything was visually spectacular, but not conversationally memorable.

MONDAY, 23 JUNE. *Venice.*

Three-hour session in the morning, which was almost entirely on the communiqué. Then I had a quite good bilateral meeting with Carter, who was accompanied by the Secretary of the Treasury, Miller, and three or four others, on the anti-dumping suit brought by US Steel which was liable to wreck about 2 billion dollars' worth of our trade unless something could be done. Carter sounded reasonably forthcoming.*

Everything was over by 5.00. It was a filthy evening. Warmish, low mist, driving wind, the lagoon the colour of milky coffee. I went for an hour's walk with Crispin: into the Piazza, indeed into St Mark's, through the doors of which the lagoon also was lapping strongly, on to the Rialto, then got rather lost on the other side of the bridge and eventually returned by vaporetto. The walk was not all that agreeable, partly because of the weather and partly because the intensive security – the Venetians by this stage must have been demented – meant that our own security men walked behind us, but the Italian security men, of whom we had about six, insisted on clearing a path in advance and jostling people out of the way. The Italian police, mostly from Naples, were fairly shocked by our idea of returning by vaporetto, but as they were even more lost than we were, there was nothing they could do about it.

FRIDAY, 27 JUNE. *East Hendred.*

Ted Heath to lunch on his way to a sailing expedition in the Solent. He talked without ceasing: sailing for the first course; music for the second; and the Brandt Report† for the third. But, particularly on the last, he talked very well. He showed a certain but not a vast interest in what I might or might not be doing in British politics. We agreed to keep in touch.

---

*Temporarily at least this meeting worked brilliantly; Carter consequently decided the issue in our favour.
†The Brandt Committee, of which Edward Heath was a prominent member, had proceeded fairly quickly from taking shape in Brandt's mind in 1977 (see p. 103 *supra*) to the publication of its first report (*North-South: A Programme for Survival*) in 1980.

SATURDAY, 28 JUNE. *East Hendred.*

A filthy day which became worse. The weather recently has been indescribably awful, a real monsoon season having set in. The Arthur Schlesingers and the Rodgers' came to lunch. Then had a long talk with Bill from 6.00 to 8.30. Friendly, inconclusive. But he seemed to take no objection to my Press Gallery speech.

MONDAY, 30 JUNE. *East Hendred.*

Weather a bit better, but I felt more exhausted than ever. Dick Taverne to lunch and found him satisfactorily self-confident and inspiriting and also more or less willing to go along with what I wanted, which was not to rush things too much. I slept most of the afternoon and early evening, a dismal end to a dismal month, most other things as bad as the weather. Let us hope July will be better.

THURSDAY, 3 JULY. *Brussels and Oslo.*

Drove to Amsterdam with Jennifer for a plane to Oslo. A dismal drive through a dank countryside. Arrived in Oslo in the wake of a great thunderstorm but with the temperature quite a bit over 70°F, far higher than anything we had known in Brussels or London during the preceding month. Drove to the rather attractive guest house where the Norwegians were putting us up and were given lunch there by Frydenlund,* the Foreign Minister. I liked both him and his wife very much.

No one had drawn my attention to the fact that the State Dinner that evening involved a black tie. I made vague suggestions to the Norwegians that perhaps they would not mind if I were unchanged, but it was quite clear that as they were proposing to give a very grand dinner they did rather mind. Oslo is a surprising place for a black tie to be obligatory. So I was forced to hire a dinner jacket, shirt, tie, even cufflinks, all of which were absolutely ghastly.

Then off to the Asheroos Castle, a splendid medieval building with a magnificent site and commanding through its windows great views over the fjord in a variety of directions under the long Norwegian twilight which was far from over when we left at 11.30. Substantial speeches of about twenty minutes by the Prime

* Knut Frydenlund, 1927–87, was Norwegian Minister of Foreign Affairs 1973–81 and 1986–7.

Minister (Nordli)* and by me, each announced by a fanfare of trumpets. Afterwards a slightly exhausting session with nearly all the Norwegian notabilities introduced to me.

FRIDAY, 4 JULY. *Oslo and Sundvolden.*

Early meeting with the Prime Minister in a modern building, chiefly notable for the fact that its roof, to which we ascended for a brief look-out, commands one of the best views of Oslo, a city whose site is so good that even the fact that it has hardly a single distinguished building, and that those few which have some pretence in this direction are mostly being destroyed, does not greatly matter. Nordli talked to me about the economy. He is preoccupied by unemployment, despite the fact that it appears to be only 1 per cent, though a little unevenly spread throughout the country, but preoccupied by it as an international rather than a Norwegian phenomenon.

Then I had an hour's fairly intimate talk with Frydenlund, about the world strategic position, the Schmidt mission to Brezhnev, how the changing balance of the North Atlantic Alliance affected the Norwegians – they are particularly worried about this, feeling that it was easier for them outside the European Community so long as America was the unchallenged captain of the boat and more difficult for them as the leadership becomes less clear.

At noon I had an audience with King Olaf in the large palace which, like so many royal palaces, seems to have been built about 1840. We had Balliol (both honorary fellows) and his attendance at the Armistice Day ceremonies when I was Home Secretary to talk about, but we also had a certain amount of conversation about Norwegian history. I found him agreeable and in remarkably good shape for his seventy-seven years. He was dressed rather like Harold Nicolson used to be, in worn brown shoes and an old blue pin-striped London suit. He had just been presiding over a King's Council, and was about to set off back to his house on the sea for some more sailing, being almost as keen an ocean racer as Heath.

Left Oslo at 5.30 and drove out about twenty-five miles to the Sundvolden Hotel on a land fjord, which had a curious but definite charm.

*Odvar Nordli, b. 1927, was Prime Minister of Norway 1976–87.

SATURDAY, 5 JULY. *Sundvolden*.

I was struck by how much the village, with its two general stores, its clapboard houses and its general feeling of looking for a simple life on a high income, reminded me of parts of New England. An enjoyable picnic lunch on an island and a swim in the fjord which was remarkably warm on the surface but cold underneath.

THURSDAY, 10 JULY. *Brussels, Bristol and East Hendred*.

8.45 plane to London on my way to Bristol for my twenty-first honorary degree.* Not one of the more exciting ceremonies, despite the distinction of the university. I was one of two honorands in the morning, the other being an internal university one. Fortunately no speech required from me at the ceremony but a brief one at the subsequent luncheon, where I enjoyed sitting next to the Chancellor, Dorothy Hodgkin.† Motored back to East Hendred. Another thoroughly nasty day of weather.

FRIDAY, 11 JULY. *East Hendred, London and East Hendred*.

With Jennifer to a meeting at Colin Phipps's flat in Draycott Avenue with him, the Social Democratic Association people (Haseler and Eden‡), Dick Taverne, Mickey Barnes, Clive Lindley, John Harris, Jim Daly – I think that was all. David Marquand unfortunately was not there. Had a moderately satisfactory discussion with them for about an hour and a half. Lindley quiet but sensible. Daly also sensible; John Harris spoke very well; Phipps in the chair; and the SDA people, though Haseler better than Eden, looking like hard-faced men who had done badly out of the Labour Party. The difficulty is that they are interested in spoiling tactics, which I am not. Mickey is interested in a charge of the light brigade and so in a more serious sense is Dick. However, eventually, with some sensible talking, not only on John Harris's part (despite his pre-

---

*But, until 1988, my last!
†Professor Dorothy Hodgkin, OM, b. 1910, crystallographer, Chancellor of Bristol University since 1970, one of my Oxford honorands in 1987.
‡Stephen Haseler, b. 1942, former Labour Chairman of the General Purposes Committee of the Greater London Council, is Professor of Government at the City of London Polytechnic. Douglas Eden is an associate of his of similar views and background. They had jointly set up the small, hardline anti-left Social Democratic Association in the late 1970s.

occupation with Westward Television which was about to blow up) and also on Jennifer's part, we managed to get them to agree that there was nothing that I should do, at any rate until after the Labour Party Conference. We should have a meeting in late October and see where we went from then. In the meantime, the SDA could do what they liked provided they did not implicate me, and those who are longing for action, like Mickey Barnes and Colin Phipps and maybe Dick, could associate themselves with them to the extent that they liked.

After lunch to Battersea Old Church for Hayden and Laura's wedding. Very pretty church and attractive service with good music. Vast Grenfell and Bonham Carter clans. A day of strong wind and scudding cloud, but bursts of sunshine, and the talk and riverside semi-party outside the church highly enjoyable.

SATURDAY, 12 JULY. *East Hendred.*

Ian Wrigglesworths to lunch. He was engaging, buoyant, friendly, attracted by some new development, but inevitably and naturally non-committal about what he would do. Another dismal day's weather.

THURSDAY, 17 JULY. *Brussels.*

Lunched with COREPER and had a not very satisfactory discussion with them as to whether the brake should be off the financial mechanism for three years or two (BBQ again). The French firmly in favour of only two, Germans inclining that way. I think this will prove quite a difficult issue at the Council next week.

FRIDAY, 18 JULY. *Brussels.*

Saw Dondelinger as chairman of COREPER, and in three-quarters of an hour's talk got him rather back on to the lines of the three-year option, saying that this was my view of what had been intended on 30 May and, I believed, equally firmly that of Colombo.

MONDAY, 21 JULY. *Brussels.*

Dohnanyi to lunch with Jennifer and me, rue de Praetère. Found him engaging as usual, although very sticky on the financial mechanism point, and possibly on the non-quota section of the Regional Fund too. But I think he is prepared to give on the latter issue. He told me that he was so difficult on the first issue not because his nerve was damaged by his reception by Schmidt after the British settlement, but because he knew Schmidt was not willing to move an inch further, because he (Schmidt) felt very strongly that Mrs Thatcher had got away with too much already.

Also Schmidt was further miffed because about three days before the Brussels Council at the end of May, he had assured Dohnanyi, who told him that he thought he could see his way through, that he (Dohnanyi) was quite wrong, he was deceiving himself, there was no chance of a success, because the gap between the British and French position was too wide to be bridged, and that was why he (Schmidt) was not going to try. Therefore when Dohnanyi brought it off, Schmidt, to say the least, had mixed feelings.

Council from 5.45 to 7.30, which was concerned with enlargement points, and then an hour's meeting with the Spaniards, Calvo Sotelo taking a fairly hard line, before going home to give Gaston Thorn* dinner. He is keen to stay on as President of the Council as long as he can, certainly until November, which I think is pushing it a bit, though his position is different from mine in 1976. He knows the Community much better and his Government responsibilities involve him in Community business which mine did not.

In general, he seemed keen enough to be informed and I told him I would give him my opinion on issues and people frankly, provided he did not pass it on, but that if he did pass it, I would know pretty quickly, and then could not continue to do so. I hope this bargain sticks. He seemed disinclined to assert a role in the choice of other Commissioners. He showed great interest in the house on the way out, how had we found it, did it belong to us, costs etc. I later discovered that this was because he was making a big bid with the Belgian Government to get them to do up and put at his disposal an official residence. As they have one spare – a very grand one in the rue Ducale – I think he may get away with it, but somewhat cynical comments about his intending to live in great pomp are floating around the Belgian Government.

---

*He had eventually secured his appointment as my successor in early July.

TUESDAY, 22 JULY. *Brussels.*

Council, and during the morning we satisfactorily disposed of the non-quota Regional Fund issue. The BBQ went less well, rather as I had feared, with the Germans taking an even harder-line position than the French, and Carrington – I think wisely – made little effort to make a great issue of it, and accepted a compromise which was two-thirds of the way towards the Franco-German position.

WEDNESDAY, 23 JULY. *Brussels and London.*

Commission for a total of six and a half hours – much the longest Commission day for three or four months. Much of the afternoon was taken up with dealing with the difficult question of the necessary altering of the Commission's contract with ICL for our own computers. We also had Gundelach for a good deal of the time on a packet of agricultural measures, including various settlements he had made with New Zealand and his negotiations with Australia. Then a tricky discussion at the end, everyone being very defensive and even suspicious, about the setting up of a small working group to do preliminary work under this Commission on the mandate for reform of Community finances given us by the Council, but which we will not be able to complete. However, we ended up in quite good temper at 7.15.

Back to my office for some signing and an end-of-term drink with the *cabinet* before the 8.45 plane to London. The last six weeks have been very wearing, not because I have been tremendously hard-worked – no long-distance travel since India, no major issue since the BBQ – but because of long-term exhaustion. I do not feel the normal sense of satisfaction at the end of a summer term and am even beginning to have, partly because of the formidable prospect at home, slight doubts as to how much I am now looking forward to the end of the four years. That may be just natural perverseness.

THURSDAY, 24 JULY. *London.*

Shirley Williams came to see me for an hour at Kensington Park Gardens on the most lovely evening. She was as engaging but elusive as ever, on the whole taking a pessimistic view, thought the

(Labour Party) conference would go wrong, certainly on policy issues, very likely on some of the institutional issues as well, and then most surprisingly, and in contradiction to what she had been telling me in the spring, said that she was far from certain that, even if Callaghan went, Healey would be elected leader of the party in the autumn. She thought Shore was catching up on him fast, and there was always the possibility of Foot being persuaded to run. So, she regarded everything as being very open, including what she is going to do.

It was nice of her to have come and I wished, as I think she did, that she could have come to our dinner for Crispin's fiftieth birthday which then followed. We had a party of thirty in the River Room of the Savoy: four members of his family, Robert Armstrongs and Michael Pallisers, Plaja, both Davignons and Emile Noël from Brussels, Henri Simonet, who had told me he was in London, Ted Heath, Caroline but not Ian Gilmour as he was attending Seretse Khama's funeral, Ann Fleming, Evangeline Bruce, Janet Morgan (the editor of the Crossman diaries, now in the Cabinet Office), Arthur Schlesingers, Nicholas Gordon Lennox's,* Thea Elliott, Harlechs and George Weidenfeld. I think that was about the lot. Good food, beautiful evening, nice view from the River Room, adequate speech from me but a better one, well phrased and turned, by Crispin.

FRIDAY, 25 JULY. *London and East Hendred.*

Neville Sandelson† to see me at his request to tell me that he wanted to give up his seat and concentrate on the Bar because the wearingness of his local dispute had become too great for him. Therefore at any time I wanted it he would resign Hayes and Harlington, which he was sure could be won on a Social Democratic ticket.

To the Rodgers' party in Kentish Town at 9.00, mainly in the garden on a baking hot night. About a hundred people, most of whom I had not seen for four years. Very enjoyable; the natives seemed thoroughly friendly! I suppose there were about fifteen

* Lord Nicholas Gordon Lennox, b. 1931, has been Ambassador to Spain since 1984.
† Neville Sandelson, b. 1923, Labour and then SDP MP for Hayes and Harlington 1971–83.

MPs, and the rest academic or journalist figures. Drove to East Hendred, where we arrived with rain beginning (typical end of July weather pattern in a bad summer: a couple of days of great heat dissolving into a great thunderstorm).

TUESDAY, 29 JULY. *East Hendred.*

The Marquands came late to lunch. However, as it appeared they had driven the whole way from Derbyshire, whereas we thought they were coming from London, and had indeed to drive back to Derbyshire in the afternoon, they had done very well to come at all. Sat out for two hours or so in the afternoon having a long political discussion, David and I being very much of the same, not over-sanguine, mind. David's judgement I think is now more sensible, and his tactical approach closer to mine, than that of almost any other member of the group.

WEDNESDAY, 30 JULY. *East Hendred.*

Robert Maclennan to lunch. His position was totally sympathetic, and interesting in his reports on a number of other people, though he tends to operate in a lonely way. He would like to break, he thinks he could carry Caithness and Sutherland as an independent or Social Democratic candidate or almost anything. But he does not want to do it as the only MP, though he would do it with a very small group of two, three or four, and thought that if we had Bill Rodgers we could get many more than this. But there was a possibility even without Bill.

FRIDAY, 1 AUGUST. *East Hendred, Rome and Bussento.*

8.50 plane to Rome. 1.30 train (late) to Sapri (to where the Italian police insisted on accompanying us). Bussento at 8.15.

The house looked much as I remembered it, with the trees grown up somewhat. The new apartment blocks at the back do not make as much difference as had been feared. The house was full of people (twenty-two); Jane and Virginia Bonham Carter* there with lots of friends.

* Eldest and second Bonham Carter daughters, then aged c. twenty-one.

TUESDAY, 5 AUGUST. *Bussento*.

After dinner got Mark (Bonham Carter) to describe in detail the story of his capture in Tunis in 1943, subsequent escape from the prison camp at Modena, and five-hundred-mile month's walk down the spine of Italy before he crossed the Allied lines near Bari. Although I had known the vague outline before, I had never known a lot of the details and had never got him to tell it, which he was reluctant to do, but then did fascinatingly well.

WEDNESDAY, 6 AUGUST. *Bussento*.

Slightly racked by conscience that I ought to have gone to the state funeral which the Italians had organized for the seventy-nine victims of the previous Saturday's bomb outrage at Bologna station. However, tormented myself quite unnecessarily as no foreigners were present, and the Italians clearly would not have welcomed them for it was an extremely awkward occasion politically, with only the Communist Mayor of Bologna, Berlinguer and Pertini, the old Socialist President of the Republic, being well received.

Weather continuing absolutely perfect. I have never known it so good in Italy.

MONDAY, 11 AUGUST. *Bussento*.

Claus and Mary Moser and the David Fosters* had arrived to stay in the early evening. Claus very bouncy – almost too bouncy, I thought, to begin with – but after dinner I found him extremely agreeable, talking very sensibly and interestingly about a lot of things: partly about music because David Foster is a great expert on its organization, Covent Garden, the Met, Salzburg, etc., but partly also about English politics, and partly about his life at N. M. Rothschilds'. A nice infusion and I am sorry that we are with them for such a short time.

TUESDAY, 12 AUGUST. *Bussento, Naples and East Hendred*.

10.38 train from Sapri to Naples. This Italian holiday was marked (i) by most exceptional weather – it never faltered throughout the

*David Foster, b. 1946, now Vice-President of Columbia Artist's Management, New York.

eleven days we were there; (ii) by varying health, but a significant improvement on what had been the case before; (iii) by a phenomenal amount of reading – partly because I was not trying to do any other work I got through nine or ten books, including some semi-serious Roosevelt reading – the last half of James MacGregor Burns's second volume, *Roosevelt the Soldier of Freedom*; a hostile book by John T. Flynn called *The Roosevelt Myth*; and Francis Perkins's *The Roosevelt I Knew*. In addition to that I read several novels – some of them in proof brought out by John or Miriam Gross: Iris Murdoch's *Nuns and Soldiers*, which I did not think nearly as good as *The Sea, the Sea*, although it has a certain attraction. I was easily able to get through it, long though it is; Barbara Pym's *A Few Green Leaves*, which I thought a little pale and lacking in substance despite its elegant writing; Graham Greene's *Ways of Escape*, which is a fragment of autobiography, not very long, built around the writing of a number of his books and rather good. Also Angus Wilson's new novel *Setting the World on Fire*, which I did not think good at all but nonetheless got through. Also a book by Leslie Benson's friend Jane Dick entitled *Volunteers in Politics*, which was an interesting, well-written description of the Stevenson campaign in 1952, about which she knew a great deal by direct experience, the Wilkie campaign in 1940, about which she also knew a certain amount from direct experience, and the Eisenhower campaign of 1952, which was based only on research but well done even so.

In addition I read *Misia*, a high-class *schmalz* biography by two American pianists of Misia Sert, who was painted by Vuillard, Bonnard, Toulouse-Lautrec and Renoir, who was generally a fairly tiresome woman but who made quite an interesting subject. The last night I read three Lytton Strachey essays, on Gibbon, Macaulay and Froude. We were lucky to have stayed at Bussento and not to have moved up and down the peninsula as we had originally intended. The Bonham Carters were extremely welcoming and the Gross' agreeable companions.

Brief lunch in Naples on the roof terrace of the Vesuvio Hotel, with a very good view of the bay. East Hendred in pouring rain at 8.30.

THURSDAY, 14 AUGUST. *East Hendred, London and East Hendred.*

George Brown to lunch at Brooks's. He was on remarkably good form, drinking a moderate quantity of wine, which seemed to me rather better than the absolute abstention of our last previous encounter. He was extremely keen to play a role (in a new party) and I believe on the whole he could be effective as I think he still has a hold on people's affections, though quite how much influence I find difficult to judge. I arranged to have some discussions which he would set up with trade union leaders and possibly to appear on a joint platform in the New Year.

Then my dreaded visit to the Harley Street gastroenterologist. I had discovered at the end of lunch that he was George Brown's doctor; not sure whether I find this reassuring. Saw him for three-quarters of an hour. Really rather an anti-climax. One of these visits which are very satisfactory at the time, but a little less so subsequently. At first you are suffused with the relief of a negative diagnosis, but after a bit realize that you have not been cured.

FRIDAY, 15 AUGUST. *East Hendred.*

Hendersons to lunch. Nicko not vastly informed about American politics, and in a sense I think not terribly interested in them, though interested in America as a place.

SUNDAY, 17 AUGUST. *East Hendred.*

Rodgers' to lunch from 1.15 to 4.30. Not a great deal of political conversation with Bill, and not very easy to get a grip on his position even when we did. He described the operations of the Gang of Three* and expressed himself very pleased with the result. He was perfectly amiable but I did not feel as close to him as I have on most occasions in the past.

---

* A term which came into brief currency that summer (it was soon to be superseded by a more famous number) following the publication in the *Guardian* of 1 August of a manifesto of warning to the Labour Party from Bill Rodgers, Shirley Williams and David Owen. The separation between them and me at this stage was that they were still operating within the Labour Party (indeed within the Shadow Cabinet), whereas I was not.

TUESDAY, 19 AUGUST. *East Hendred.*

Bradleys to lunch (the garden was just possible) from 1.10 to 6.30(!). I like them both immensely. Tom very resolute and I really feel closer to him than to any other of my old political friends. Despite Tom's professional pessimism, they cheered me up.

FRIDAY, 22 AUGUST. *East Hendred.*

Worked on the *Baldwin* manuscript getting it into a shape in which it could be retyped, the top copy having been lost. Had a satisfactory talk with David Steel on the telephone about 7.00. He is a remarkably buoyant young man.

MONDAY, 25 AUGUST. *Talsarnau.*

On a most beautiful morning I drove the three miles into Harlech at 8.00 to get the newspapers and then drove down to the beach near Glyn and sat looking across the estuary towards Portmeirion and reading them for an hour. Two sets of tennis with David and Pamela (Harlech). Walked along the beach on the south side of the estuary for an hour in the early evening. Perfect day.

TUESDAY, 26 AUGUST. *Talsarnau.*

An equally good day. Tennis for an hour at noon but only one, very long, satisfactory set. At about 5.30 we drove down to the sea and half walked and half waded across to the island of Ynys where there is a small deserted cottage. Then down once again, the evening being so perfect, with Jennifer to see the sun set over the Lleyn peninsula.

SUNDAY, 31 AUGUST. *East Hendred.*

The last day of the holidays. The David Owens to lunch in weather just good enough to be able to eat in the garden. A remarkable change in him since the last time I had talked to him, almost exactly a year ago, at East Hendred. Then it had been a slightly stiff occasion, he very much the ex-Foreign Secretary, a little defensive about his position and certainly not very open to me. In the intervening twelve months he had disapproved strongly of the Dimbleby Lecture although much less, curiously, of the Press Gallery speech in June. I suppose this was partly because he had begun to move. However, the events of this summer, particularly perhaps the Labour Party Special Conference, at which he had been booed for a multilateralist speech, had clearly left a deep impression on him and he had stiffened and toughened a lot, and also become in my view a great deal more agreeable than he had been since before he became Foreign Secretary. Very anxious to keep in touch for the future, and by no means certain what he was going to do if the Labour Party Conference went wrong, about which he was definitely pessimistic.

A good holiday on the whole, with my health considerably improving towards the end, although not yet perfect. The weather for us remarkably good in what was generally a bad summer in Northern Europe. I read a lot, mainly about Roosevelt, whom I was endeavouring to see whether I could write something about to match with my long Baldwin essay. Apart from the books I read in Italy, I read Grace Tully's *Roosevelt, My Boss*, Jim Farley's *The Roosevelt Years* and, slightly more peripherally, reread Arthur Schlesinger's *The Imperial Presidency*. Reluctantly, however, I decided that there was nothing very new to say about this tremendously written-about man, and therefore turned to considering Eisenhower as an alternative and started to read his *Mandate for Change, 1953–6*. I also reread Irwin Ross's *The Loneliest Campaign*, again with a thought of writing something about Truman. Rather deliberately I did much less Brussels work than in previous summers.

MONDAY, 1 SEPTEMBER. *East Hendred and London.*

Motored to London and lunched in the City with the senior partner of Deloittes (John Rae Smith) and one or two others. They wished me to consider joining them (after Brussels) in roughly the capacity of a non-executive director of a joint stock bank.

Later to Whitehall Court, where I had a meeting with Tom Taylor (Lord Taylor of Gryfe) and Christopher Reeves, the chief executive, of Morgan Grenfell. They were anxious for me to come to them on a much more substantial basis than Deloittes. I said I would consider this and arranged to have another meeting in a few months' time.

Then to St John's Wood where we dined with the Annans for the first time in their new (to us) house, together with the Gross' and the Bonham Carters. Very good evening, Noël giving us his best wine.

TUESDAY, 2 SEPTEMBER. *London and Brussels.*

I walked on a beautiful morning to buy the newspapers at the lower end of Ladbroke Grove. Met T. Benn in the shop. I thought I had seen him going in but was not quite sure because he looked surprisingly older and slightly puffy. However, when I came in, it clearly was him, so I seized the initiative and said, 'Tony, how are you?' Then about three minutes of rather agreeable conversation. Tony always has good manners, and we expressed dismay at our not having seen each other for so long and almost, though not quite firmly, arranged to dine *à quatre* as soon as I got back.

3.45 plane to Brussels and into the office: the old Berlaymont looking much as usual, although with an air of late summer calm still over it.

THURSDAY, 4 SEPTEMBER. *Brussels.*

Gundelach to lunch rue de Praetère. He is not at all well, poor man, his bronchitis of the summer having developed into some more or less serious heart trouble which is not altogether surprising in view of the way in which he totally exhausts himself.

Saw Ortoli briefly at 5.30, found him on good and friendly form, equivocal about whether he is going to stay on into the next Commission, perhaps for a year or so he is inclined to say, which in my guess means that he will certainly but mistakenly agree to be reappointed. Cheysson at 5.45, he in very bouncy form as usual. Had a substantial talk at a dinner of Léon Lambert's with Simonet, who is clearly drifting more and more away from Belgian politics.

SUNDAY, 7 SEPTEMBER. *East Hendred.*

George and Hilda Canning to lunch. George on extremely friendly and agreeable form. He thinks I should not get myself into too isolated a position and is above all extremely anxious that I should not be too close with Colin Phipps, who he said had done a lot of harm in the West Midlands. He spoke in tems curiously reminiscent of Woodrow (Wyatt), from a different point of view, more or less saying, 'Don't mess up a great career at its end.'

MONDAY, 8 SEPTEMBER. *East Hendred and London.*

To a luncheon meeting of the Jewish Board of Deputies in Tavistock Square. A most curious occasion. Out of a total audience of perhaps 120, there were about six MPs, mostly but not exclusively Jewish, and five ambassadors, the French, the German, the Irish, the Luxembourgeois, the Canadian – but not the Israeli. Presided over by Greville Janner,* self-confidently rather than professionally. A fair speech by me, certainly not better than that. However, I managed to avoid any of the deep pitfalls of Middle Eastern politics.

Read and worked in the early evening in Kensington Park Gardens until we had the Gilmours to dinner at a Notting Hill restaurant. Ian very depressed about the balance of power in the Government and its economic policy.

THURSDAY, 11 SEPTEMBER. *Brussels.*

William Rees-Mogg to dine alone rue de Praetère. William on very smoggish form, in a sense I suppose deeply worried about *The Times*, but at the same time bland, almost complacent. He certainly seemed to have no awareness of the fact that, as Louis Heren† had told me at the Jewish lunch on Monday, he had done very badly at the staff meeting which he had addressed following the strike. He said that he would like to stay as editor for, maybe, another two or three years, but thought that that would be long enough: certainly no thought of immediate retirement.

On politics he did not have a great deal to say. He was reasonably friendly to my position, though still slightly sceptical, mainly I think on the ground that he did not believe that the Liberals offered anything to build upon or even alongside, because he is convinced there are only two hard resolute reservoirs of opinion in British politics – one the left centre of the Conservative Party, and the other

---

*Greville Janner, QC, b. 1928, succeeded his father who had also presided over the Jewish Board of Deputies as Labour MP for Leicester in 1970.
†Louis Heren, b. 1919, was deputy editor of *The Times* 1978–81.

the right wing, the working-class right wing to a substantial extent, of the Labour Party. The Liberals had none of the bottom of either of these groups and would therefore, whatever Steel's personal qualities, be a particularly ineffective support for decision-making in a Government. Maybe there is something in this.

Saturday, 13 September. *Brussels.*

Rue de Praetère dinner party of the Tom Enders' (American Ambassador to the Community), Tugendhats and the Michael Jenkins', etc. Enders, as usual, interesting in his intelligent, detached, and perhaps slightly self-seeking way. Said that he thought he would not stay very much longer in Brussels, nor indeed in the US foreign service. What he really wanted to do was to become a Cabinet officer, which he thought he could manage in some future administration. The question he had to consider was what was the best route to that. He was rather tempted by business, but I said I thought that would not have great attraction for him except that of making money and giving complete financial independence. 'Oh, I can assure you I have that already,' he said, so I said that in that case I did not see a great deal of point in business. Perhaps he would go into politics in Connecticut, he then suggested. Maybe it would be a little difficult to become a Senator, but perhaps he could at least become a Congressman. Perhaps he wished he had gone into politics earlier, etc.

Sunday, 14 September. *Brussels.*

I had spent a good deal of the weekend rereading Evelyn Waugh's *Brideshead* in a remarkable first edition. Crispin had brought it on the Friday evening, it being a privately printed pre-publication edition which Waugh had sent 'with the compliments of Captain Evelyn Waugh' to his (Crispin's) uncle, E. S. P. Haynes, a literary gent of the period. I found it rather better than I remembered.

Tuesday, 16 September. *Brussels and Strasbourg.*

A rather bad session of the Foreign Affairs Council from 12.00 to 2.30, which got bogged down on what we thought was *une chose acquise* about the financial mechanism running on for the third year in relation to the BBQ. This however was opposed by the French and Germans, and the British gave way with almost too good a grace. I hope these tactics are right, but I have a little doubt. Then lunch with the Council late and back for a resumed session from 4.30 to 6.30, mainly on the BBQ once again. Then an avion taxi to Strasbourg.

WEDNESDAY, 17 SEPTEMBER. *Strasbourg.*

Took David Wood of *The Times* to lunch at La Wantzenau. Nice day and agreeable lunch with him, mainly about British politics and arguing round his various bits of friendly opposition to my views on realignment. He was a passionate supporter of Hugh Gaitskell, almost dazzled by him, to an extent which I had not previously realized.

SATURDAY, 20 SEPTEMBER. *Garderen (Holland).*

A curious buffet Dutch breakfast in the large dining room of the Hotel Spielenboss in the middle of Holland, to which we had driven the evening before with Michael and Maxine Jenkins for a touristic weekend, full of elderly, nonetheless boisterous Dutch (two of them were singing, but quietly). Took enough ham and cheese for our luncheon picnic and drove north to Geithorn, very much a sort of Bourton-on-the-Water of Holland. I think it actually describes itself as the Venice of the Netherlands, built along a series of canals all very neatly and elegantly kept up and with a certain dolls'-house charm. Picnic in very warm weather on the pebbles of the Zuider Zee near Urk.

SUNDAY, 21 SEPTEMBER. *Garderen and Brussels.*

Morning visit to the Krøller-Mueller Museum which is in a small national park, looks slightly like part of a crematorium, but has a most remarkable collection, particularly of Van Goghs but of other French impressionists and other schools too. Successful and enjoyable weekend.

MONDAY, 22 SEPTEMBER. *Brussels.*

A meeting with Calvo Sotelo at noon, mostly devoted to discussing my visit in ten days' time to Madrid. He has become deputy Prime Minister and brought with him his replacement as Minister for European Affairs, Punset.* Punset very anglophone having spent a lot of time working for the BBC and the *Economist*, and is a bright little LSE-type Catalan in contrast with Calvo Sotelo's Madrileno dignity.

WEDNESDAY, 24 SEPTEMBER. *Brussels.*

Lunch with Davignon, Ortoli and Haferkamp at the Fondation Universitaire, which is an agreeable old Belgian club in the Quartier Léopold. The reason it was Haferkamp and not Gundelach on this occasion was that the discussion was supposed to be about steel, and the lunch had been urgently requested by Stevy Davignon for this reason. The reason why it was at the Fondation Universitaire was that I had told Crispin rather to insist that Davignon gave us lunch for once and he had floored him by asking his *Chef de Cabinet*, 'And where does Monsieur Davignon propose to invite his guests?' First Stevy said he would take us out to the Royal Golf Club, but then the weather having deteriorated he switched to this perhaps more economical but thoroughly agreeable club!

THURSDAY, 25 SEPTEMBER. *Brussels.*

The group of Brussels British journalists to lunch rue de Praetère. About half the conversation was on British political affairs. I tried to play for time by saying they should not think in terms of the launch of a political party on 6 January,† but rather in terms of some intellectual groundwork leading, I hoped, to my making a number of significant speeches. This line was subsequently reported – remarkably fairly – by John Palmer in the *Guardian*. Nobody else took it in, or perhaps did not believe it.

*Eduardo Punset Casals, b. 1936, has been an MEP since 1987.
†The day on which I would finally return from Brussels.

FRIDAY, 26 SEPTEMBER. *Brussels, London and East Hendred.*

Plane to London and Frank Chapple* to lunch at Brooks's. He had recently been excluded from key committees of the TUC, but was nonetheless in a cocky, aggressive, agreeable mood. He agrees with me on absolutely every aspect of policy, but still does not want to contemplate a break, not out of weakness, but rather out of ill-informed confidence in the strength of his case. He believes that everything can be won by a tough battle from within, including committing the Labour Party almost to a nuclear missile in everybody's back garden. Curious that he should have this element of political unrealism. It was nonetheless well worth seeing him, probably a pity I did not do so earlier.

MONDAY, 29 SEPTEMBER. *East Hendred and London.*

An hour's meeting with Michael Palliser at Brooks's from 5.30 to 6.30, partly about the new British Commissioner, mainly about the future of Crispin. Mexico looks increasingly settled for him which is, I think, satisfactory. His knighthood rather less settled. Also discussed the future of Michael Jenkins. In addition, I put to Palliser my dilemma about the grand honour the Spanish Government were proposing to bestow upon me at the end of the week. He sensibly more or less invited me to accept it on the run, as it were.†

Dined at home and watched a lot of television, first *Panorama*, a programme on the state of the Labour Party, and then reports from Blackpool which showed Benn madder than ever, the conference in an ugly mood, Shirley in great fighting spirit, orating very successfully even if occasionally a little incoherently at I think a Campaign for Labour Victory meeting. Altogether well worth seeing – a full evening's conference television. No great tugs upon the heart strings, but great interest. The conference looks as though it is going worse even than I thought it would.

---

*Frank Chapple, b. 1921, cr. Lord Chapple 1985, was a former Communist who became the outspoken and moderate General Secretary of the electricians' union, EETPU, 1966–84.
†Foreign honours are much complicated by British Government rules; see entry for 15 December 1980 *infra*.

TUESDAY, 30 SEPTEMBER. *London and Brussels.*

In the afternoon a series of meetings, first with Ian MacGregor,* the new Chairman of British Steel, who has been hired at such vast cost, not so much in salary as in compensation to Lazard Frères. Thought him quite a tough Scotsman, no doubt very shrewd, but he did not seem to me the most dominant personality in the world, or the most dominant brain. He must be better than he looks.

Later saw Vredeling on his paper for increased worker consultation etc., which is causing a lot of trouble with UNICE and the employers generally. But I think that he has now concerted it well with Davignon. It has gone through the various processes of consultation and should be supported. I told him that I would do so in the Commission the next day.†

THURSDAY, 2 OCTOBER. *Brussels and Madrid.*

Early plane to Madrid. Met by Punset, the new Minister described earlier, and drove in with him to the Ritz Hotel, finding him very bright indeed. He raised two serious points of discussion, of exactly the right level, on the way in. It was a beautiful day in Madrid, quite different from when we were last there, clear sunshine and very hot for October, I think 85° during the afternoon, though cool at night. A 2 o'clock lunch (specially early in our honour) with Calvo Sotelo and Punset at the Palacia de la Trinidad.

Then an hour with Punset alone. Back at the hotel, I had a visit from Simonet, who had rung up saying he was there learning Spanish. I said, 'Even for you, Henri, the Ritz Hotel, Madrid, strikes me as a rather grand educational *pension.*'

I had a one-and-a-quarter-hour meeting at the Moncloa Palace with Suárez, the Prime Minister. Curiously, most of the conversation was about what we would call devolution, what the Spaniards call decentralization, the Basque and Catalan problems and their impact on the structure of the Government. He had been meeting the Basques all day and was obviously greatly preoccupied by that, Suárez still seems to me an impressive personality, and an

* (Sir) Ian MacGregor, b. 1912, was Chairman of the British Steel Corporation 1980–3 and of the National Coal Board 1983–7.
† It went through, by a rather narrow majority, and became the so-called Vredeling Directive.

agreeable one too. He remains very determined on European membership, even though his mind is much on internal Spanish questions.

At 9.30 in the same building he gave me a dinner, and also the Grand Cross of the Order of Charles III. Spanish political conversation with Suarez – through an interpreter even at dinner because he is absolutely monolingual. Very good food.

FRIDAY, 3 OCTOBER. *Madrid and East Hendred.*

Crispin and I went to the Prado for half an hour, concentrating on the Goyas which are an extraordinary mixture (I had seen them once before) of styles and approach, but seen in sum are quite remarkable. Then the Community ambassadors for half an hour, they perfectly agreeable, particularly Bobbie de Margerie, the Frenchman who clearly hopes to come to London.

Then a slow drive to Zarazuela, interrupted by a brief walk in a hot, sun-baked countryside looking as though we were still at the height of summer, for an audience with the King at noon. I saw him alone. He expressed strong continuing commitment to Europe, some dismay at the fact that decentralization was dismantling the state to the extent even that it might not be possible to hold it together, but at the same time fair confidence about what had been achieved politically. He has come to look older in the past two years; I still much like him.

We parted very friendlily, I presenting all my party to him and he asking me to propose myself for lunch or dinner with him whenever I was in Spain in the future. I thanked him warmly and also for the Grand Cross of Charles III, which is visually a splendid decoration with an enormous blue and white sash (much worn by those in Velazquez and Goya portraits in the Prado). It is, alas, difficult to think of many occasions when I might wear it.

Then back to Madrid for a glimpse of the Plaza Major, which is always worth revisiting, and a fairly grand Ministry of Foreign Affairs lunch given by Pérez-Llorca (who is thirty-nine but looks fifty-five, like my last Home Office Minister of State, Brynmor John) but without significant speeches – the significant speech had been at dinner the night before, which had been very well received by the Spaniards – Bassols (their Ambassador in Brussels) was said to have tears in his eyes. From there direct to the press conference at 4.30, which was perfectly easy, mainly on the timetable for Spanish entry, but I had worked out quite carefully what I could say on this. Also one or two routine questions about my position in British politics and some other matters about the Community. 6.15 plane to London. East Hendred at 9.30.

SUNDAY, 5 OCTOBER. *East Hendred.*

I spent almost the whole morning on the telephone, picking up impressions of the Labour Party Conference. I had spoken to Shirley the previous day, but I then spoke to Tom Bradley, to Clive Lindley, to Bill Rodgers, who said he was coming to lunch, to David Marquand for a long time, and to various other people. The Rodgers' arrived at 1.20, which was relatively punctual for them, and stayed till 4.30 with a good political talk. It was a much better meeting with them than the August one, which somehow had not gone right. Bill's broad view was that while they (the Gang of Three, etc.) were going to see what happened over the leadership, they were very dissatisfied with Healey.

I just cannot decide whether or not Bill is willing to break with the Labour Party. I suppose the odds probably remain that he is not. But he is certainly much nearer to it than nine months ago, and I think opening up the issue of a split, as I did in Dimbleby and subsequently in June, has been right. Certainly my analysis of the state of the Labour Party has been right. So I think have been my tactics of waiting for the autumn rather than rushing in further in the summer. I now feel much easier about the political situation and whatever it may hold. I do not feel myself boxed in, in the way that I did in June, July and August.

MONDAY, 6 OCTOBER. *East Hendred, Brussels and Luxembourg.*

To Brussels and saw Heseltine,* the Queen's deputy Private Secretary, for half an hour to tie up the plans for the Queen's visit in November. He was rather hesitant about the idea of the Queen participating in a Commission meeting, obviously being rather

---

* (Sir) William Heseltine, b. 1930 in Fremantle, Western Australia. Now (since 1986) Private Secretary to the Queen and Keeper of the Queen's Archives.

doubtful whether the Queen would like it, or would want to ask questions, and was distinctly unreassured when I said that in the case of the Dutch visit Prince Bernhard had in fact asked quite a lot of questions and no doubt Prince Philip could do the same. Then to Luxembourg by train.

TUESDAY, 7 OCTOBER. *Luxembourg and Brussels.*

A meeting with Thorn at 9 o'clock, nominally about the agenda for the Council. The main point which emerged was that he had been to see Giscard the day before and had found him *'impitoyable'* towards the Commission. Giscard had clearly frightened Thorn out of his life by telling him that the independence which had been shown previously was not acceptable and must stop. The Commission must represent the interests of the member states rather than having an independent role, Giscard apparently said, presumably equating member states with one member state. Thorn was visibly shaken.

Council immediately after that. The early part of the morning was taken up with a foolish argument over the preparation for a Community/Israeli Council. Then came the Association Council itself attended by their Foreign Minister (Shamir)* which went particularly badly, he being ungracious, boorish, hectoring, everything one can think of. As a result, the second leg of the BBQ – the supplementary measures and the timing of payments – did not start until about 12.45 which put Peter Carrington, who had arrived specially for a 10.45 start, in a very bad temper which persisted throughout lunch.

But mysteriously it all came out easily in the wash in the afternoon, the French being much less difficult than had been expected, and the Germans not difficult at all. 7.30 train to Brussels.

MONDAY, 13 OCTOBER. *Brussels and Strasbourg.*

Lunch in the Berlaymont for a group of British lobby correspondents. Fred Emery was the most notable. I tried to keep them off British politics, but inevitably only half-succeeded. As

---

*Yitzhak Shamir, b. 1915, was Foreign Minister of Israel 1980–3 and 1984–6, and Prime Minister 1983–4 and from October 1986.

a result Emery wrote a prominent front-page *Times* piece developing what Palmer had said previously. Quite satisfactorily put from
my point of view.

Avion taxi to Strasbourg. Question time at 6.30. Only one
question for me, about bloodstock of all things, which I had to take
over from Burke, who, although responsible, runs away from it
because the Irish are behaving so badly on the issue. I managed to
have mild fun with the supplementaries. Then back to the hotel to
finish Mrs Castle's 1974–6 *Diaries*. They are too sprawling and
self-obsessed, but nonetheless I have found them compulsive reading. She is neither particularly friendly nor particularly disagreeable about me. However, I agree with quite a number of her
judgements on others but rarely with her judgements on herself,
though occasionally even with those. On Wilson, curiously, I agree
with her to a very substantial extent.

TUESDAY, 14 OCTOBER. *Strasbourg.*

Extremely nice weather. To the Parliament at 10 o'clock, and hung
about as is habitual there waiting to deliver a quite important steel
statement which eventually came on at about 12 o'clock. It was a
rather good, firm statement and Stevy was very pleased with it.

In the evening, rather amazingly, I took Barbara Castle to dinner
for three hours. She was very talkative, as self-obsessed as ever, and
I think probably rather pleased to have been asked and to gossip
about old times. She is half sensible and half incorrigible. I enjoyed
the evening.

WEDNESDAY, 15 OCTOBER. *Strasbourg.*

I decided I could not go to Brussels that afternoon, as I wanted.
There was a *grève sauvage* at Zaventem and in addition it was
thought I ought to stay for (and perhaps intervene in) the institutional debate which was really the Parliament beagling Thorn
for not resigning as Foreign Minister of Luxembourg (and
hence President of the Council) in time to prepare for his presidency of the Commission. As it turned out there was no need to
intervene in the debate. But it was worth being there. It was quite a
full house. And it was interesting to see how Thorn handled it. At

one stage he said surely the Parliament did not wish him to add himself to the number of unemployed in Europe, and who was going to pay him if he resigned, which was not the most persuasive way of putting things. I think he will have to go pretty soon, or he will be in quite serious trouble.

FRIDAY, 17 OCTOBER. *London and Belfast.*

12.30 plane to Belfast. I opened the new Commission office in a semi-skyscraper, looking down on the splendidly flamboyant City Hall. I then did three television interviews, one for each Northern Ireland channel and one for RTE, the Dublin channel. These fortunately were not as dull as might have been expected, because I had to sort out the question of a possible £100 million Community grant for 'concerted action' in Belfast, about which Burke had gone too far in a speech in Ulster the week before, and which had led to a controversy between him, the City Council and the British Government. However, we had a tenable line on it, and in fact the whole incident, by dominating the press, focused attention on the Community and added considerably to the interest in my visit.

Called on the Lord Mayor, an ex-Unionist member of the Westminster Parliament who has now moved to a fairly centre position. Then out to Hillsborough. I was particularly struck, not so much by the house as by the small town at the gates, which is a beautiful early nineteenth-century ensemble with a town hall and another public building, good shop-fronts and houses, remarkably attractive, all in good stone. Then to Queen's University for a dinner which Geoffrey Martin, our new Commission representative in Belfast, had organized very well indeed. A great representative turn-up with about 120 people, including the Lord Mayor, all the other Ulster mayors, Humphrey Atkins* (Secretary of State) who spoke, Paisley and Taylor (two of the three MEPs – Hume was ill), the Vice-Chancellor, and various other notabilities.

SATURDAY, 18 OCTOBER. *Belfast and East Hendred.*

Drove through a rather attractive Northern Ireland dawn for the 7.30 plane to London Airport. We had Gordon Richardsons,

---

*Humphrey Atkins, b. 1922, cr. Lord Colnbrook 1987, was Secretary of State for Northern Ireland 1979–81.

Harlechs, Ann Fleming and John Harris to lunch. In addition, the Ginsburgs arrived unexpectedly. High confusion between them and Jennifer and me, but eventually we fitted them in. The lunch then went very well. Afterwards I played good croquet with both Richardsons and David Harlech.

SUNDAY, 19 OCTOBER. *East Hendred.*

Lunch with the Owens at Buttermere, the first time we had been there for four or five years. They were on agreeable form, David tough, and in some ways extreme. He definitely is not very enthusiastic about Healey winning; it would not amaze me if he abstained. He foresees a danger of Healey being in substance if not in manner a rather weak right-wing leader, particularly while he has his eye over his shoulder on the electoral college. Owen would now I think in many ways like a split, though he still firmly wants a Socialist International-affiliated new party. But how much he will do about it – he is certainly inhibited from saying some of these things in public – I do not know. He would also quite like to see a position in which the left brought forward and carried a motion that the leadership election should be postponed until the new electoral mechanism is in place in January, in order to avoid what he regards as a dangerous hiatus of weakness for a new, allegedly right-wing leader. In the course of a half-hour walk after lunch I had some serious talk about what the future policy of a new grouping might be.

MONDAY, 20 OCTOBER. *East Hendred and London.*

Crispin and I went to visit the National Radiation Protection Board at Harwell, where we were received by the Director and by Sir Fred Dainton,* the Chairman. Quite an interesting talk with them for about an hour and a half, Fred Dainton on the way out expressing strong and sympathetic political interest. We then had Tom and Joy Bradley to lunch at East Hendred. Tom again very tough and firm, but, perhaps because he likes to be in a fight, slightly more inclined to support Healey than is Owen, but at the same time saying

* Sir Fred Dainton, b. 1914, cr. Lord Dainton 1986, was Vice-Chancellor of Nottingham 1965–70, and has been Chancellor of Sheffield since 1978.

absolutely firmly that what he really wanted to do was to go with me.

At 6.30 I had a meeting with Clive Lindley, Dick Taverne and David Marquand at Kensington Park Gardens to discuss the setting up, as a sort of half-way house to a new party, of an enlarged Radical Centre Institute, possibly under a new name, and with trustees. We thought we would try to get some politicians as well as some academic figures; Bullock,* Dainton were agreed as obvious names here, Shirley if she would do it, and indeed Bill (Rodgers) or David (Owen), David Marquand himself, Dick Taverne, with me I suppose as President, funded to the extent of about £50–£100,000 a year, and producing policy statements.

Then to the Jim Cattermole retirement[†] dinner at St Ermin's Hotel. Very good attendance of about 130, a lot of MPs, all very friendly.

WEDNESDAY, 22 OCTOBER. *Brussels.*

Lunch with the Nanteuils for Olivier Wormser, *Directeur Economique* at the Quai d'Orsay when I had first known him in the late fifties, then Ambassador to Moscow, Ambassador to Bonn, Governor of the Bank of France. I was pleased to see him as always. He is a man of such exquisite refinement, though not at all bogus, that he always makes me feel slightly gross and vulgar. I feel I must not eat or drink much in his presence! However, I had a good talk with him for twenty minutes or so after lunch – he had come to Brussels to find out what was happening to the Common Agricultural Policy, he said, but on whose behalf or for what reason was not clear.

After the Commission meeting I had Enders, the US Ambassador, for forty minutes. He had nominally come to deliver a *démarche*, which the Americans were also sending to all the Community countries, in effect telling us to keep off the grass in the Middle East. In fact he did not deliver it, and merely asked what I thought about it, to which I said not much. It would have the effect, undesirable from the American point of view, of pushing the item on to the agenda for next weekend, whereas it had not been intended to

---

*Alan Bullock, b. 1914, cr. Lord Bullock 1976, was Master of St Catherine's College, Oxford, 1960–80, and Vice-Chancellor of Oxford 1969–73.
†As Director of the Labour Committee for Europe.

discuss it until the Political Cooperation meeting on (American) election day, 4 November, and therefore effectively after the American elections. He then raised the more general issue of how best the US could deal with the strengthening reality of Political Cooperation. It was not easy to tell him exactly what to do. The strengthening is to some considerable extent a reaction to the weakness of American leadership, and is bound to create some additional problems for them.

FRIDAY, 24 OCTOBER. *Brussels, Rome and Brussels.*

Rome by avion taxi. Twenty-five-minute speech of substance on the present state of the EMS, which was well-reported, to the Association of European Journalists at 11.30. After lunch we drove round the Campidoglio, looking at the statue of Marcus Aurelius for the last time, as it is crumbling gravely and is to be put in a museum and replaced by a copy. Back in the Berlaymont by 6.15.

SATURDAY, 25 OCTOBER. *Brussels and Luxembourg.*

Motored with Crispin through pouring rain to Luxembourg from 7.00 to 9.00. Council on steel from 9.30 to 2.15, which cleared a lot of points, but Lambsdorff stuck, after telephone calls to Bonn, on special steels. We did not wish to push him too much into a corner and run the risk of the Germans, for the first time, invoking the Luxembourg Compromise, and we were not sure whether they would or not. I was inclined to the view that they would. We agreed to have another Council next week.

At dinner I decided, perhaps because of the afternoon silence, that I would give them all several farewell pieces of my mind, which I did about a variety of issues from the seat of the European Parliament, to general relations with the Parliament, to the fact that the presidents of the European Council (i.e. heads of government

Drove to the Hotel Bel-Air at Echternach for the Foreign Ministers' informal 'Schloss Gymnich' weekend. All the others had nearly finished lunch, but at least I was there before Thorn, who was the host. Lunch from 3.00 to 4.00 and session from 4.00 to 7.15. This was quite good, but not riveting, mainly Political Co-operation, and I did not say much.

and, more relevantly, of state, for it is particularly Giscard who resists going) certainly ought to go and address the Parliament, which François-Poncet tried to wriggle around rather ineffectively: altogether a rather enjoyable bashing about for a few hours.

I had half an hour with Peter Carrington afterwards, which was also quite enjoyable. The only thing on which he was disappointing was Crispin's knighthood, which he says the lady is against, as she for some reason or another is not very pro-Crispin.*

TUESDAY, 30 OCTOBER. *Brussels and East Hendred.*

12.45 plane to London. Motored to East Hendred with Jennifer. An evening of television: first an enjoyable programme by Ludo Kennedy about American transcontinental trains, and then had the pleasure of seeing both Foot and Healey on different channels. Foot in a way not bad on ITN, Denis on a programme on which I cannot help feeling it was a deep mistake for him to appear, which was the Robin Day television version of *Any Questions* and is certainly not a 'prime ministerial' forum.† He was good on defence, not very good on anything else.

SATURDAY, 1 NOVEMBER. *East Hendred.*

To Sevenhampton on my own, where Ann had the Levers, and two Marks (Boxer and Amory), Joe Alsop, my old Washington friend, and Aline Berlin without Isaiah. Curious lunch – I actually enjoyed it very much, though Lever and Alsop do take a long time to tell their stories. However, I found it rather encouraging on the threshold of sixty to seem much faster than some other people!

A little serious talk with Lever after lunch about future political developments, particularly the projected (Radical Centre) Institute to which he was favourable. Basically his view is not too unsensible: yes, he would like to have a great political initiative in the direction I want, but he thinks we have not got enough obsessive

---

* He became Sir Crispin Tickell only when he was invested as a KCVO by the Queen (i.e. a specifically royal honour) on the occasion of her visit to Mexico in 1983. He was dubbed at Acapulco in a beach shirt.

† What a stuffy out-of-date 1960s and 1970s ministerial view this proved. Everyone (except perhaps for the actual Prime Minister), and certainly including me, is now very glad to appear on *Question Time.*

people. I think what he really means is what Woodrow (Wyatt) and one or two other people have said, that I have not got the obsessive political interest to be able to stump round the country, fight bye-elections, and create something out of nothing. Alas, he may be right.

SUNDAY, 2 NOVEMBER. *East Hendred.*

Tavernes, who had organized James Meade* to come over from Cambridge, to lunch. Meade is a slightly other-worldly, very nice, distinguished man, who is extremely anxious to be helpful to some new radical party, particularly in the formation of economic policy. He is also very keen on electoral reform and pretty close to the Liberals, saying that if the new party did not come off he would almost certainly join them.

MONDAY, 3 NOVEMBER. *East Hendred and London.*

With Crispin to what was, in effect, the first of my farewell visits: to Mrs Thatcher. An hour and a half's conversation – not I think of particular note. She showed little desire to look forward and discuss the European future beyond the end of my term. Justin Cartwright, a television producer who wants to do a dialogue between David Steel and me for *Panorama*, to see me in the early evening. I am not too keen to commit myself to do this early on my return. David Steel himself to dinner. I found him very good and sound, not unduly discouraged by continuing hesitancy, and understanding of my desire to wait some time, but not indefinitely, for the Gang of Three.

TUESDAY, 4 NOVEMBER. *London and Brussels.*

Home to rue de Praetère at 7.00 to hear the result of the Labour Party first ballot. A remarkable result: Healey in the lead but not at all strongly so, and a real possibility of his being beaten by Foot on the second ballot. A rather exciting prospect. A bitterly cold day.

*James Meade, b. 1907, Nobel Prizewinner, was Professor of Political Economy in the University of Cambridge 1957–69.

WEDNESDAY, 5 NOVEMBER. *Brussels.*

Listened to the news of Reagan's landslide victory as we drove to the Bois (for my run). No newspapers, however, for some reason or other. Dined with Jennifer with the Dick Leonards: an agreeable conversation with them, mainly reminiscence about Tony Crosland, on which subject Leonard is easy to talk to, because, although he was so close to Tony, and therefore very well informed, he is also objective without being at all cold either towards Tony, or towards me. He is a very nice man.

FRIDAY, 7 NOVEMBER. *Brussels.*

Ivor Richard,* newly appointed to be the next British junior Commissioner, to lunch rue de Praetère. Found him intelligent and agreeable but somehow slightly detached and complacent, and rather misconceiving his job I think, seeing it as far too much a propaganda job to be done in England with the object of reconciling the Labour movement and the trade unions to Europe. This admittedly would be a wonderful objective, but not I think achievable, and certainly not by a Brussels-based Commissioner.

SATURDAY, 8 NOVEMBER. *Brussels.*

Hayden, Laura and John Harris arrived for the weekend about noon. Crispin came in to settle the *placement* for his great party – or our joint great party – in the evening. We lunched at Ohain, and then walked on a beautifully fine clear cold day in the grounds of the Château de la Hulpe on the way back. At just after 8 p.m. we went to Crispin's for his dinner and dance for sixty-four people, which went on until about 3 a.m. I enjoyed it a lot. It was certainly a success, and as good a way as any of celebrating (?) one's sixtieth birthday.

MONDAY, 10 NOVEMBER. *Brussels.*

An official visit from Nordli, the Prime Minister of Norway, for nearly four hours from 11.45. I liked him, as I had in Oslo in July. I

---

*Ivor Richard, b. 1932, a Labour MP 1964–74, was British Permanent Representative at the UN 1974–9, and a European Commissioner 1981–5.

went home at 6.40, eager to hear the Labour Party election news, which came through at 7.00. Sensational result: Foot elected by ten votes. I cannot pretend that I was other than elated, as it clearly opened up a much greater prospect of political realignment. Dined with Jennifer at home, discussing this urgently and excitedly.

TUESDAY, 11 NOVEMBER. *Brussels.*

My sixtieth birthday has arrived at last; like so many things discounted in advance it did not therefore seem as bad as it might have done. Went into the office, not intending to do too much work, at 10.30. Saw Roland de Kergorlay (head of our mission in Washington) at 12.00; a brief drink with the immediate staff at 12.45 or so. Then with Jennifer to lunch at the Villa Lorraine. Excellent lunch and enjoyable occasion. Office from 3.30 to 4.45. Tickells and Michael Jenkins' to dinner.

WEDNESDAY, 12 NOVEMBER. *Brussels.*

At 4 o'clock I addressed a meeting of about 120 senior staff (A1s and A2s) on the Spierenburg Report – what he had done, what we intended to do, and what they had to do if they were to improve management, etc. A good speech, written by Nick, which I delivered firmly and forcefully, and they took with a mixture of enthusiasm (fairly limited), resignation, and some complaint; but worth doing, although a lot of them (not all) hate doing anything which in any way shakes them out of their ruts.

FRIDAY, 14 NOVEMBER. *Brussels and near Amsterdam.*

Bob McNamara to lunch rue de Praetère. Crispin and Caroline were the only others there. Very enjoyable conversation with him; I find him rather a spectacular man, and it was well worth having changed my plans and stayed in Brussels in order to see him. I don't know what we talked about exactly – but all a great pleasure. Drove to Holland in the afternoon for an Amsterdam visit the next morning. Stayed at the Waterland Hotel, which was in fact only about twenty-five kilometres from Amsterdam Airport, but they took us about two hours. We got constantly lost in drenching rain, had a drink at some extremely sunken café, which looked as though it was in Tennessee. We were then stopped by the police for going too *slowly* on to a motorway. They began extremely aggressively – very odd for the Dutch police – as though they thought we were smuggling drugs, but then quietened down a good deal. However, eventually we arrived at the hotel, a tiny and extremely elegantly furnished château in a little park at Velsen; roaring fires in all the rooms.

SUNDAY, 16 NOVEMBER. *Brussels and Stockholm.*

Jennifer and I by avion taxi to Stockholm, where we arrived at 7.30. We were met by the Prime Minister, Thorbjörn Fälldin, who seemed a nice man, though talking far from perfect English. Being a Conservative Prime Minister (the first for decades) certainly did not mean he was a good linguist. Installed at the royal guest house called Haga Palace, about five miles from the centre of the city.

MONDAY, 17 NOVEMBER. *Stockholm.*

One of my last days of official visits with a typical programme. At 10 o'clock we had a morning-long meeting of ministers, presided over by the Prime Minister. Then a working lunch in the Operakällaren, presided over again by the Prime Minister. Then quite a good meeting with Ullsten, the Foreign Minister. Then Feldt, who is the Social Democratic economic expert, Palme being away in the Middle East. Then Bohman, the Minister of the Economy. Then I briefed the Community ambassadors and then, after an interval, had the Prime Minister's dinner in the Foreign Office. Unfortunately it was unattractive weather in Stockholm. It had been very cold as with us but in the last few days has become mild and wet with a lot of dirty piles of half-melted snow all over the city.

TUESDAY, 18 NOVEMBER. *Stockholm and Strasbourg.*

The Speaker of the Parliament at 9.00. Then some sight-seeing, first a famous ship which sank in the harbour in about 1600 on its way to Poland, and then the Armoury Museum. At 11.00 I did a press conference and at 12.00 we lunched with the King and Queen in the Royal Palace. He is small and boyish-looking, slightly nervous but very agreeable. The Queen is mainly Brazilian and not at all German as I foolishly thought. I found her slightly difficult at first, but once one got going conversationally easy and interesting. After lunch we talked to them for about half an hour, standing in a group of four, they and Jennifer and me. The Swedish Court is a curious mixture of informality shot through with occasional strands of high formality. Lunch was in the slightly gloomy old castle (well suited to my *Ballo in Maschera* impression of what the Swedish Court should be like) looking out over the harbour across to the Grand Hotel. The family are about to move out of it very soon, not into a villa, but into another castle, apparently more suitable for children and some way out.

Arrived in Strasbourg for the last time at 4.30. To the Parliament for two hours, then to dinner (everything beginning to be for the last time now) at La Vieille Enseigne.

WEDNESDAY, 19 NOVEMBER. *Strasbourg.*

Lunch for four of the five pro-Market Labour MEPs at La Want-zenau. From 5.30 to 6.30 I gave a long interview to Tad Szulc for a *New Yorker* article which he was doing on the work of the European institutions. At 6.30 I went to see Mme Veil in order to complain (disinterestedly) about the Commission's Strasbourg accommo-dation, and got her to come and see my room, which, having moved from the splendour of hers, was a salutary experience, and she was duly shocked by it.

THURSDAY, 20 NOVEMBER. *Strasbourg and Luxembourg.*

Paid a sort of symbolic farewell visit to the *hémicycle* of the Palais de l'Europe – and then Jennifer and I motored to Nancy. Walked around the Place Stanislas and down the Allée before lunch. Drove to Luxembourg, where we installed ourselves in the Embassy. I then paid an hour's farewell visit to Werner, who gave me a nice picture. Then saw Thorn from 5.00 to 6.15 and talked about his future problems. Then back for speech titillation at the Embassy, where Crispin had arrived. The Jeremy Thomas's* have recently replaced the Patrick Wrights. I liked both the Thomas's. Then gave the Churchill Memorial Lecture.

MONDAY, 24 NOVEMBER. *Brussels.*

Downstairs at 11.30 to receive the Queen and Prince Philip. Took them up to my room, with two or three other people, for twenty minutes. Easy conversation. Then Commission meeting for an hour. Good presentations by Cheysson, Gundelach, Davignon and Tugendhat. I couldn't get the Queen to ask any questions but the Duke of Edinburgh butted in a good deal, and kept the thing going rather well. He started a great argument with Tugendhat about how ridiculous it was to want to spend more money and increase own resources. At that stage I came in and explained firmly to him why this was not extravagant but necessary if the Community was to do much outside agriculture, which was very much in Britain's long-term interest. However, as the Queen was rather silent, although not looking at all bored, he was on balance a help.

Then from 1.00 to 1.30 we had the reception for the Directors-General of all nationalities, and British staff selected by ballot, in the 'cathedral'. Then out in a great hurry to Val Duchesse to receive the Queen there at 1.40. Luncheon went on until 3.30, with only a formal toast – no speeches. But the Queen was then definitely on good form, agreeable, and apparently amused by some of the incongruities of Community life. For once Val Duchesse produced quite good food. Saw them all off with a certain sense of relief but thinking it had gone well and been worthwhile. It was fairly well covered by British television, and I hope will have some mildly beneficial effect on British public opinion *vis-à-vis* the Community. It was very good of her to have come.

Council and Political Cooperation from 4.30 until 10.00

TUESDAY, 25 NOVEMBER. *Brussels.*

Council for nearly four hours from 10.15, at which we mainly discussed, without getting very far, the social aspects of the steel

*Jeremy Thomas, b. 1931, Britain's Ambassador to Luxembourg 1979–82, has been Ambassador to Greece since 1985.

volet. The Germans and the French were both being fairly difficult. Before lunch there was a thoroughly nasty argument on New Zealand butter – getting absolutely nowhere – the French being unpleasantly difficult.

WEDNESDAY, 26 NOVEMBER. *Brussels and Paris.*

11.43 TEE to Paris after an early Commission meeting. Lunch on the train and arrived in rain at the Ritz at 2.45. Installed not as we had asked in a small suite on the garden side, but in an immense suite rather badly furnished in the *style arab* overlooking the Place Vendôme. Discovered to my horror that it was incredibly expensive – over 4000 francs for the night – and told Crispin that we could not possibly pay this and must either change rooms or move hotels. He went down to negotiate and had a rather good encounter with the management saying, 'Il faut que vous sachiez que Monsieur Jenkins n'est pas un sheik arab ni même un roi nègre.' The net effect of this, though we were not informed of this until afterwards, was that he got them to look up how much I had last paid and discovered that it was about 1500 francs. As a result they offered to reduce the bill to about 1800 francs, which was a considerable triumph.

Then we went to a meeting with Giscard, which lasted exactly an hour, from 4.20 to 5.20. He was alone, though I had Crispin. It was polite and courteous, even had bits of interest, and without being either fascinating or warm was not notably unfriendly either. We parted in good order, with honours tolerably even. Then at 6.00 we went to see Barre in Matignon and had just over an hour with him. The meeting was quite different: he was warm but at his most pedagogic and went on and on, giving me an only mildly interesting lecture on the state of the French economy in which, according to him, everything was about as good as it possibly could be.

THURSDAY, 27 NOVEMBER. *Paris and Dublin.*

Dublin at 2.30 for a fairly intensive series of Dublin farewell visits, beginning with President Hillery, who would not let me go, partly because he likes talking and partly I think because he wanted to make me late for the Taoiseach. In any case we went on long after the scheduled time, and I got to Haughey half an hour late. I had a reasonably constructive talk with him and more or less cut, at his suggestion, my meeting with Lenihan (the Foreign Minister) who is a very nice man, and when I rushed in to apologize to him, said that he was giving me dinner and it did not in the least matter.

Then to a press conference at the new Commission office, followed by a reception. A very good attendance at the reception – a lot of ambassadors, members of the Government, etc. – and quite a good speech by me. Then to Iveagh House, where I dined with Lenihan and various other ministers. A thoroughly agreeable occasion – I like Lenihan very much indeed – and there was a lot of warmth in his speech and a very good atmosphere. I have attached great importance to my Irish relations – as I should have done as a British President – and I think they have been good. Stayed at the Hibernian Hotel.

SATURDAY, 29 NOVEMBER. *East Hendred.*

David Owens with their children came to a long lunch from 1.20 to 5 o'clock. He told me firmly, for the first time, that he was prepared to join a new party, and that he thought that Shirley would come too, though he was curiously less sure about Bill. He was also, although agreeable in other ways, very firmly geared up to tell me that he thought that Shirley should be leader; they very much wanted me to play a full part in it, but that it was his view that Shirley should be leader because of her great popularity, etc. And it was made clear that it was in his view to be not a centre party but a 'Socialist International' party, and I was joining them rather than vice versa.

We will see how that works out, but at any rate it is a great advance which no one would have thought possible some time ago. There will now be a real break in the parliamentary party, and I may well get, at the end of the day, much more the sort of party I want than the sort of ex-Labour Party that for the moment he wants. But we will see. At 6.30 I had a telephone call with David Steel and informed him I thought things were going well without telling him the full details. To bed early feeling reasonably content with the movement of affairs. It is an incomparably better position than looked likely last July.

MONDAY, 1 DECEMBER. *Brussels and Luxembourg.*

Motored to Luxembourg for the European Council and arrived at the Holiday Inn, in which non-Ruritanian surroundings we were installed by the Luxembourg Government. Lunch with the Grand Duke in his palace. Sat between Schmidt and Nothomb (the new Belgian Foreign Minister). Schmidt not on very good form – looking tired, seeming tired, saying he was tired (he always does that), but whereas previously he seemed to enjoy being tired and enjoyed complaining that he was tired, he has now got to the state where he gets no enjoyment out of the complaint. There were beautiful views out on to a sunlit Luxembourg through the narrow fortified windows of the palace dining room. The European Council met from 3.20 until just after 7.00: economic and social situation, EMS, industrial innovation (a rather good discussion following a Commission paper), Thorn report on the Middle East. Then dinner for heads of government at the Palais Vauban, where we had been the previous spring, with no riveting conversation.

TUESDAY, 2 DECEMBER. *Luxembourg and Brussels.*

Final session of the European Council for three hours. I made a wind-up 'report on the four years' speech, thoughts for the future, etc. for twenty minutes, which was surprisingly well received, and started quite a vigorous and sensible discussion. Giscard began the discussion, was very gracious for him, and said the best compliment was to take some of the things I had said seriously and discuss them. It was an agreeable hour and a good wind-up to a series of wearing (and sometimes wearying) European Councils.

WEDNESDAY, 3 DECEMBER. *Brussels.*

Commission for two hours only as we all had to go and lunch with the King and Queen at Laeken. The great excitement of the morning was before the Commission began. When I walked in Crispin took me over urgently and rather secretly to Christopher Tugendhat. Christopher then told me how he had been shot at by an assassin an hour before and narrowly missed. It was all rather dramatic. At that stage he did not seem unduly upset but became manifestly more shaken as the morning went on; this was particularly noticeable at lunch.

Lunch at Laeken was very agreeably done by the King and Queen, who do seem to have a genuine friendship for us and spoke very warmly, so that the whole occasion was enjoyable, except for poor Christopher. For almost the first time I felt guilty for the benefits of 'protection'. There was absolutely no reason why terrorists (presumably Irish) should have assaulted him rather than me, and plenty of reasons for the reverse. But I am protected and he is not. Back for a resumed and I hope the last long meeting of the Commission from 3.40 to 7.15.

THURSDAY, 4 DECEMBER. *Brussels and Nuremberg.*

Avion taxi to Nuremberg, where we arrived just after 5.00. It was enveloped in snow. I felt we had moved not merely into Central Europe, but almost into Russian steppe land. Driving was quite difficult. We edged along to Nuremberg's twin ciy of Fürth, where we stayed in a new, rather overelaborate hotel called the Forst Haus. Much too early dinner there with the Chamber of Commerce at 6.30, and then motored with some difficulty into Nuremberg, the centre of which was muffled and silent but looking rather dramatic, for a two-hour meeting in the Rathaus. I made a moderately interesting speech on the budget, and there was a surprisingly good question and answer period afterwards, mainly about the adaptability or otherwise of European society to modern technology.

SATURDAY, 6 DECEMBER. *Brussels.*

Marie-Alice de Beaumarchais from Paris and Bonham Carters from London for almost our final Brussels weekend. Malines in the afternoon, the weather having become cold and clear again. Dined at the Enders'.

SUNDAY, 7 DECEMBER. *Brussels.*

Lunch at Ohain at 2.00, and then a long walk in sun and snow around the park of Château de la Hulpe.

MONDAY, 8 DECEMBER. *Brussels, Copenhagen and The Hague.*

Early plane to Copenhagen for my farewell visit to Denmark. To the Prime Minister just before noon, who took me to see the Queen. She had arrived back that morning from a week's private visit to England. Whether she had bicycled from the station was not clear, but she had certainly come by train the whole way from Ostend in an ordinary sleeping car, saying that this was a method of travel which she liked very much. Then a lunch given by Jørgensen in the Naval Officers' club, most agreeably done, with a surprisingly warm speech from him. Plane to Amsterdam and to the Hôtel des Indes at The Hague.

TUESDAY, 9 DECEMBER. *The Hague and Brussels.*

An hour's noon meeting with the new Queen Beatrix of the Netherlands. It was the first time that I had talked to her. She had a bottle of white wine in an ice bucket, which we consumed, and chatted away agreeably about Holland, and England, and Europe, and the world, and her life. She was, if anything, easier than the Queen of Denmark in spite of the latter's Cambridge degree. She has a mildly left-wing reputation but was at pains to deny this. She was very interested in what might happen in English politics. She looked a bit like Kitty Giles fifteen or twenty years ago. After that to lunch with van Agt and half the Government at the Catshuis, and again a very agreeable atmosphere, with warm speeches of farewell.

WEDNESDAY, 10 DECEMBER. *Brussels.*

My last COREPER lunch. Rather less warm farewells from ambassadors than from governments, I thought. At 7.45 we had the Commission's farewell reception at the Palais du Congrès, with a concert by the European Youth Orchestra, conducted partly by Heath. Princess Paola came as the representative of the Belgian Royal Family, and the reception lasted not too long afterwards.

THURSDAY, 11 DECEMBER. *Brussels, London and Brussels.*

10.45 plane to London and to Chatham House where, after a buffet lunch, I delivered a carefully prepared speech to a rather good assembled company. It was my case for Britain staying in the Community. Then to Brooks's, where Sir A. Tuke asked me to become a director of Barclay's Bank. I said I thought not owing (i) to Lloyds's prior suggestion, and (ii) to the South African connection, which he very fairly raised himself. Then to the Thames TV studio where I recorded a half-hour's interview with Lew Gardner, mainly about Europe and the case for staying in, but about seven minutes at the end on my political intentions. Inevitably this part of the interview attracted all the press attention.

Then to Sister Agnes's to see Ann Fleming, who had been critically ill in Swindon for some time, and found her better than I expected.

Next back to Brooks's where I had David Marquand and Clive Lindley on 'new party' matters from 6.00. Bill Rodgers arrived just before 7.30. A very friendly talk with him until I left in a great hurry at 8.05 for the 8.45 plane, which I just caught. Quite a day.

FRIDAY, 12 DECEMBER. *Brussels.*

To lunch with Léon Lambert, who provided a good occasion, but inevitably also one of his farewell speeches which meant a reply from me. Dined at home with Jennifer and the Bradleys, who had arrived to stay for the very last weekend.

SUNDAY, 14 DECEMBER. *Brussels.*

Began with the last of my many Brussels runs in the Bois de la Cambre. The Bradleys left mid-morning because the house was already somewhat dismantled. Jennifer and I lunched with the Michael Jenkins'. It poured with rain all day, only half right for weather symbolism – two of the autumns had been spectacular. At 7 o'clock Christopher Audland came for his last pre-Council briefing. Dined with Jennifer and bed at 11.45. So, effectively, ends our rue de Praetère existence.

MONDAY, 15 DECEMBER. *Brussels, Rome and Brussels.*

Early plane to Rome, and called on Pertini, the President of the Republic, in the Quirinale at 10.45. He was less talkative than on previous occasions, mainly because he received some bad piece of news just as I was arriving, but he quickly regained his animation. Then to the Palazzo Chigi to see Forlani (who has become Prime Minister in the endless Italian excuse-me waltz). Then to the Villa Madama for a ninety-minute meeting with Emilio Colombo, and then a large luncheon party of between sixty and seventy including all the Community ambassadors. A warm, substantial farewell speech from Colombo.

I was slightly irritated that I had had to decline the grandest Italian decoration, as indeed those of Belgium, Luxembourg and Holland, owing to the ridiculous British Government rules – a mixture of Court and Foreign Office protocol – about not accepting foreign decorations. I think it might have been more sensible to cut through it as in Spain, but Crispin for the best of motives was firm against.

We then drove – in a great hurry and with my last motorcycle escort – to Ciampino, where I took my last avion taxi back to Brussels. That evening the Foreign Ministers gave me a dinner at Val Duchesse. Not a bad but somehow not a terribly good occasion either. Home for a last night in the dismantled rue de Praetère.

TUESDAY, 16 DECEMBER. *Brussels and Luxembourg.*

I attended the Foreign Ministers' working lunch and unburdened myself to them on a number of subjects. Motored straight from there to Luxembourg for my final visit to the Parliament.

WEDNESDAY, 17 DECEMBER. *Luxembourg.*

To the Parliament at 9.00, ready for my farewell speech. However, typically, it was delayed until 10.20. It was quite well received. Lunch given by Mme Veil at the Golf Club. She kept saying that she had to rush off, and therefore we made our speeches before lunch began. Afterwards she seemed to eat a fairly hearty meal before leaving. Although I like her increasingly, she is hardly a calm hostess. Resumed Commission from 3.00 to 4.30. Then a twenty-minute farewell call upon the Grand Duke, agreeable as usual.

THURSDAY, 18 DECEMBER. *Luxembourg and Brussels.*

Woke up to more snow and the realization which had come on me during the night that I ought to have been doing something more about the yearly budget crisis which was proceeding in the Parliament. Therefore summoned a breakfast 'crisis meeting', people getting through the snow with some difficulty. Vredeling, Cheysson, Natali and Tugendhat came. As a result of this, it was agreed that I would go with Tugendhat to see Mme Veil at 9.30 a.m., put our position clearly, and try to get things back on the rails.

This I think worked tolerably well. It was my last visit to Luxembourg, my last day with the Parliament, and this encounter with Mme Veil my last meeting that could directly influence what went on in the Community. It was 9.50 a.m. when I drove off half-sentimentally in the snow, which was quite difficult as so frequently on that stretch of road to Brussels. Berlaymont at 12.30, and a substantial though slightly late appearance at the party in the *'cathédrale'* which the Commission was giving for the *huissiers*, interpreters, drivers, and all those who had worked fairly closely to us.

Office after lunch until nearly 8.00, interrupted by a dismal drinks party for the press. To the Amigo Hotel, where I was staying, and then went to dine with the Michael Jenkins' and a large party.

FRIDAY, 19 DECEMBER. *Brussels and East Hendred.*

Office at 9.15. A little signing before inner office Christmas drinks at 11.45, and then to London by the 12.45 plane, and on to East Hendred. The effective end of Brussels and the beginning of Christmas and, more significantly, of the return to British politics.

Epilogue

On Sunday evening, 4 January 1981, I returned to Brussels for forty-eight hours. I stayed with Michael and Maxine Jenkins in their house in the drève des Gendarmes. I held a final press conference in the Berlaymont, reviewing with modified rapture the previous four years. I received my old friend the French Permanent Representative who had been sent in by the Quai d'Orsay, true to the last to its habit of never missing a trick, to tell me that some speech of Christopher Tugendhat's was *inacceptable*. I gave a lunch for the Commission and a dinner for my *cabinet*. I signed a few last-minute documents. I formally handed over to my successor, Gaston Thorn, who was late and flustered. Within three hours, pausing only for my last farewell visit – to Comme Chez Soi – I was in the air for London. It was to be two years and nine months before I again saw Brussels.

Back in England, I was at once remarkably free and remarkably encumbered by political 'promises to keep'. I had no office, no job (for I did not think I should take up my part-time City commitment until a few months had gone by), and for the first time in London for thirty-three years, no Parliament on which to base myself. On the other hand, the new party, soon to be christened the SDP, was achieving a much quicker but by no means entirely painless birth than I had thought possible. As a 'Gang of Four' (a name which, as an import from China, was then barely out of the customs sheds) we had a slightly disputacious weekend on 17–18 January. I then went to America for five days, thinking that a brief detachment would do no harm, and returned on the morning of Saturday, 24 January, to watch on television an immensely helpful special Labour Party Conference. It is amazing, looking back, how dedicated a large section of that party was to forcing a predictably damaging partition. Although perhaps, in view of the 1987–8 behaviour of the SDP, political self-immolation should not occasion surprise.

On the Sunday morning we went to Limehouse and before the early January dusk had produced and launched the Declaration of that name. It did not set up a new party, merely a Council for Social Democracy. But what was crucial was that it put us wholly into the public domain. Thereafter popular response took over. After Limehouse the Gang of Four or any individual member of it could no more have stopped launching a new party than logs could prevent themselves being swept down a mountain torrent. The Council became the Social Democratic Party on 25 March, a month or so ahead of our original timetable, but not, we judged, early enough for us to be ready to fight the May local elections.

We could not however for long pretend that we were a popular movement but refrain from putting ourselves to the test of popular suffrage. The first bye-election vacancy was created at Warrington, an old industrial borough on the borders of Cheshire and Lancashire, in the last week of May. It was traditionally a safe Labour seat, and we rated it, on the basis of some calculus I have now forgotten, about 550th (out of 630) in order of favourability for us. However, I thought I had better fight it.

I had never much enjoyed electioneering, regarding it as a disagreeable cure which one had to endure every four years or so in order to have the indulgence of sitting in the House of Commons for the rest of the time. Such an approach was possible in traditional politics, but it was no way in which to found a new party, particularly as Brussels had inevitably given me a somewhat remote image. I therefore decided that I had better reconcile myself to a life of campaigning, and to my amazement found that I quickly came to enjoy it. During the five Warrington weeks my heart was rather in my mouth, because I had no idea whether the result was going to be an humiliation or a respectable defeat, but in retrospect at least the streets and landmarks of that somewhat sombre town have come to glow in my memory. This was as well, for the next two years were taken up with almost continuous electioneering. Apart from my own second bye-election at Hillhead and the General Election of 1983, there was Croydon and Crosby and Gower and Bermondsey and Darlington, as well as a number of less needle encounters. By a curious irony it was the House of Commons, when I re-entered it in March 1982, which I came to regard as providing the disagreeable interludes between the stimulating election campaigns.

All this preoccupation accounted for my failure to find any time to go back to Brussels before October 1983. But it did not mean that my mind had turned away from European issues. I followed them closely, maintained a good number of personal contacts, and spoke frequently on the subject. Britain to my dismay continued to find an infinite series of unconvincing excuses for remaining outside the European Monetary System. If the mark was too high, the dollar was too low, or vice versa, or the moon was in the wrong quarter. Every conceivable set of circumstances was surveyed and rejected, not overtly on principle, but on the ground that a more favourable combination must be awaited. Even deprived of British adherence, the System achieved a distinct practical success and reduced the fluctuations between the seven participating currencies by a substantial and measurable margin. Governments did not however push on with the further phases of development of the EMS which had been envisaged at Copenhagen and Bremen. The main monetary advance of the mid-1980s came through the spontaneous increasing use of the *écu* in private transactions and not through Government action.

With the disappearance of the Giscard-Schmidt partnership in 1981–2 the political leadership of the Community became temporarily weaker and its energies were diverted for too long and too obsessively into the British budgetary dispute. Most of the years of the Thorn Commission were therefore disappointing, although they brought the negotiations with Spain and Portugal to fruition (these countries entered on 1 January 1986) and prepared the way for the Single European Act of December 1985. Partly as a result of this institutional reform, Iberian enlargement, unlike the admission of Britain, Denmark and Ireland in 1973, has led to no weakening of Community purpose. On the contrary, the plans for 1992 and associated developments amount to the greatest resurgence of dynamism since the great days of the early 1960s.

Throughout these fluctuating fortunes for the Community the old SDP and its Alliance partner maintained a wholly committed European position. I therefore experienced no ideological break on my return from Brussels. It was merely a very sharp change of gear.

APPENDIX 1

Allocation of Portfolios, 4–7 January 1977

TUESDAY, 4 JANUARY. *Brussels.*

After lunch I went briefly to my temporary unattractive office in the rue de la Loi and then back to the house to begin a series of 'portfolio' interviews. The first two on the list, Haferkamp and Ortoli, were both late, as all the members of the old Commission had been off on an excursion to Paris, where Ortoli had assembled them for a farewell lunch at Lasserre. There was fog on the road and they therefore all arrived back behind time and disordered.

Haferkamp made it clear that his mind had become more and more fixed on the suggestion that I had thrown out to him at Ditchley, that he should do External Affairs. I said the principal difficulty about this was the question of how the German Government, and perhaps Genscher in particular, was going to take the switch from expectations between him and Brunner, and that I must see Brunner but that he (Haferkamp) also must try to help handle this in Bonn. There was also the question of whether he was prepared to work hard at this job and at his English, which, although it had already improved a good deal since I had first seen him in the autumn, clearly needed to be better for relations with the Americans. On all points he was sensible except for a great and unconvincing protestation that he always worked immensely hard at all jobs. However, a reasonably satisfactory interview.

Ortoli came next and, given the fact that it was my view that he was bound to have Economic and Monetary Affairs (this, indeed, was one reason why it was essential to get Haferkamp out of them) and that he greatly wanted this, there was not much problem with him either. He was, as usual, a mixture of the warm and the prickly and talked a little too much about his dignity as an ex-President rather than about his qualifications, which were great, for the Economic and Monetary job.

We then had Gundelach to dinner, together with Hayden and Crispin, and had a productive talk. He confirmed that he was willing to do Agriculture, was insistent, but reasonably so, that he must keep Fisheries for the time being, as the subject was so very much on the boil and he was the only person who really knew about it, but equally willing to hand it over in perhaps four to six months.* He also talked rather usefully about other aspects of the disposition of portfolios, sticking to the view which he had accepted when I put it to him at Ditchley that Haferkamp was the bigger man and would be better than Brunner in External Affairs. After dinner he talked a bit about agricultural policy, saying we would have to get an interim price settlement, which he would try and keep as low as possible, before we could embrace any question of structural reform, but that he hoped to be ready for structural reform by May or June.

WEDNESDAY, 5 JANUARY. *Brussels*.

Vredeling at noon. No great difficulty with him on this occasion. Having rejected so contumaciously at Ditchley the 'human face' portfolio of Environment, Consumer Affairs, Nuclear Safety and Transport, he expressed considerable pleasure and gratitude when I proposed to him Employment and Social Affairs together with the Tripartite Conferences.† As usual with Henk Vredeling there was a good deal of talk and it took me nearly an hour to deal with him.

After lunch I came straight up against what was likely to be one of the most difficult interviews: that with Brunner. And difficult indeed it proved to be. As I had never got near to promising him External Affairs he was not in any great position to complain. But complain he did and very hard indeed, and attempted to put a veto on Haferkamp's appointment. I said that I couldn't accept that and he then went off into, for him, some extremely rough talk indeed, talking at one stage, so Crispin avers, of 'loosing the dogs of Bonn' upon me, and at another stage of becoming part of the 'loyal opposition' in the Commission, and being about as threatening as he could.

* He never did.
† Periodic meetings of Commission, management and unions to discuss Community economic strategy.

We then boxed around a bit as to what alternative I could offer him, but I took the firm view that so long as he was talking in these terms there was no question of my making him any offer at all. He was threatening to resign; he was threatening all sorts of outside pressure and I thought it would be a great mistake to put forward any proposition even though I had a fairly firm one in my mind. When he had gone I decided I would have to re-summon Haferkamp to try and make sure that he was holding firm, as well as going through with the other interviews which I had lined up.

Giolitti was relatively easy. He was happy with Regional Policy, and the oversight of financial interventions generally. I also saw Vouël, the Luxembourger, and had a brief but I thought satisfactory interview with him, reiterating broadly what I had said to him at Ditchley: that if he wanted to he could keep Competition, but that, particularly as he had indicated to me at Ditchley that he might be slightly bored with Competition, I would also like him to consider the possibilities of Environment, Consumer Affairs etc. on the one hand, or the Budget on the other; but that he always had the fall-back of Competition. This, I learnt subsequently, raised great doubts about the security of his position in Vouël's suspicious and unsubtle mind.

Another difficult interview that afternoon was with Natali, who as a Christian Democrat and therefore the senior Italian automatically became a Commission Vice-President. Natali is an exceptionally nice man and one of considerable weight and solidity. Communication with him is difficult because his English is non-existent and his French rudimentary, but this is outbalanced by the fact that he is naturally helpful and friendly, with a proper sense of his own position, but this not taking a prickly form. However, the difficulty on this occasion was that I had practically nothing to offer him, except to talk rather vaguely in terms of special responsibilities, of which the main would be Enlargement. He wanted to get hold of Mediterranean agriculture and of Community relations with the countries on all sides of the Mediterranean, propositions which would have been impossible so far both as Gundelach as the Agriculture Commissoner and Cheysson as the Development Aid Commissioner were concerned, as well as being broadly unacceptable outside. So he had to go away with very little on his plate, though I made clear that this was not intended to be a final interview and I hoped to have a more substantial one on the following day. But this clearly left a sizeable loose end.

Davignon also came that evening, but caused no trouble. Despite all the rumours in the press that he would resign if not given External Affairs, he was perfectly happy, as I had known to be the case since Ditchley, to accept the new portfolio of Internal Market and Industrial Affairs. The interview with him was brief and amicable.

Then I re-summoned Haferkamp. The important point here, following on the Brunner interview, was how far he was prepared to hold firm. If he was going to weaken, my position *vis-à-vis* the German Government could be extremely difficult, and if I was going to be forced back into putting Brunner into External Affairs and finding it difficult to get Haferkamp out of Economic and Monetary Affairs, there were obviously going to be great repercussive difficulties about the disposition of other major portfolios affecting Ortoli and Cheysson and Vredeling, as well as the humiliation of having to appear to change under Brunner's threats.

Haferkamp at this meeting was fairly firm. I do not think I could put it above that. He wanted External Affairs, he thought it right that he should have it, but he was obviously a bit worried as to what the Bonn reaction would be, and I therefore could do little more than stiffen him and tell him we would talk again next morning. This interview did not encourage me, though I was nonetheless quite clear that I ought to hold firm on this major disposition. By this time Emile Noël, the Secretary-General, had been waiting for an hour and a half or so, and I could not do a great deal more than go down and have a scratch dinner with him and Hayden and Crispin and talk over the difficulties and bruises of the day and see what solutions we could find to them.

THURSDAY, 6 JANUARY/FRIDAY, 7 JANUARY. *Brussels.*

Immediately after my 9.45 arrival at the Berlaymont I had to take Ortoli aside and tell him that I had leaned very much in favour of his being reappointed, while Giscard had at times positively invited me to ask for the reverse to be the case, and that I now needed some help from him. In particular there must be no question of his adding to Directorate-General 2 (Economic and Monetary Affairs), DG15

(Financial Institutions and Taxation), nor I hoped of DG18 (Coal and Steel Funds), and that I also hoped that he would be generous in dealing with the frontier with Giolitti and would arrive at an amicable settlement with him. Ortoli freezes up, not so much in manner as in substance, as soon as anything touching his prerogatives is raised, and he said that he would have to think about these matters and let me know, but implying that it would all be very difficult.

I had several other interviews in the course of the morning: a useful one with Cheysson. There are no problems except marginal frontier ones about his portfolio (Development Aid – Relations with the Third World), although he obviously has some territorial ambitions in the Arab world, and like the clever busy little bee which he is he was very anxious to be consulted and get involved with other dispositions.

I also saw Haferkamp that morning. He was stronger than the previous evening: very firm on the fact that the German package as a whole was perfectly adequate (Brunner to have Energy as well as Science and Research). But I urged him very strongly to make his own soundings in Germany. Brunner was on the telephone the whole time; he (Haferkamp) really ought to talk to people, to Schmidt himself if possible, to Genscher, and also to Brandt, to whom he attached great importance. He left me shortly before lunch saying he would do this.

In the meantime, mixed messages had come in from Ortoli. He was clearly willing to be reasonably accommodating about DG15, totally unwilling to be accommodating about DG18, and inclined to be pretty difficult in dealings with Giolitti, certainly so far as the European Investment Bank was concerned. We then adjourned for lunch in my dining room. Haferkamp came in with the news, just before we started, that he had spoken to Brandt, he had spoken to Vetter (the head of the German trade unions), he had spoken to Wischnewski (Schmidt's aide and a member of the German Cabinet), who had spoken to Schmidt who was in Spain (I suspect Haferkamp has a slight fear of talking to Schmidt direct himself), and had got very good and positive reactions from them and was therefore totally stiff on External Affairs and was going forward to it with confidence and thought that Brunner would undoubtedly in due course accept Energy, etc. He had not, however, spoken to

Genscher, saying, not unreasonably, that he hadn't done badly in the twenty minutes since he had seen me previously.

After lunch there were the formal proceedings in the Commission room and I did not get back to bilateral interviews until about 5.30 p.m. The exact subsequent series of interviews is difficult to recall. They were in any event supplemented by Crispin's activities on the *Chefs de Cabinet* net. I think I saw at least once all the Commissioners except Cheysson and Davignon, whose positions were already fixed without difficulty, most of them twice, and some of them three times. The essential development of events was as follows. First we got news that Brunner had cracked. The German Government declined to intervene, leaving it to be settled in the Commission, and that left him no effective position. Later that evening I firmly offered him Energy, which he already knew was in the wind, and which he accepted.

The Natali position began to sort itself out. He saw me during the early evening and put in a strong bid for a mixed bag of Enlargement, plus Direct Elections, plus the Budget. Crispin, however, did some negotiations with him later in the evening, with the outcome that provided Environment was added to his list he would be prepared to forgo the Budget. The Natali settlement had the effect of unlocking the difficulty into which I was getting with Tugendhat. I had an interview with him before dinner, in which I told him firmly that it was his duty to accept Personnel, which he did not want, but which was important, and, secondly, the group of 'human face' portfolios. This interview led to a long argument and he went away from it unhappy. But once the Budget had been clawed back from Natali the difficulty became much less because the Budget, DG15 (Financial Institutions) and Personnel made a reasonably satisfactory though rather mixed portfolio for him. I sent for him immediately after dinner, told him this, and made him reasonably satisfied.

It therefore looked by about 10.30 p.m. as though we had a fairly complete solution before us, subject only to the fact that there was very little except a ragbag left for Burke, the Irish Commissioner. I saw him a couple of times in the late evening and offered him Transport plus Consumer Affairs, with a possibility of something else. He was clearly unhappy, but since I am afraid I thought that as he was not very good and as somebody was bound to be the loser (there just are not enough proper jobs for thirteen Commissioners), I did not see that there was a great deal more I could do.

However, between 10.30 p.m. and 1.30 a.m., when we eventually resumed, several other last-minute difficulties came up: a frontier dispute between Ortoli and Giolitti which took more resolving than I had hoped; and long procrastination from Vouël about the exact definition of his portfolio. In addition, Crispin was constantly reporting that Burke was in a black mood, was going round full of gloom and stirring up a certain amount of trouble; I should no doubt have reacted to this more quickly. However, with a list of thirteen portfolios, twelve of which at least had been agreed, I was able to re-summon the Commission at 1.30, to read out the list of twelve, and to get them accepted without undue difficulties, though certain minor frontier disputes were left unresolved. By 2.15 or 2.30 a.m. at the very latest we had all that agreed and were nearly ready to meet the press and announce our decisions. But we then had the great Burke saga, which lasted with a number of adjournments until 5.30 in the morning. He announced himself unable to accept the decision, conducting himself, in very difficult circumstances, with a certain rigid dignity, but also being slow and suspicious. His complaint that he was short of adequate responsibilities had some justification and for that reason attracted some sympathy.

In a series of adjournments we endeavoured to find whether there were some assuagements which we could give him, and several other Commissioners were forthcoming. Natali, Davignon, Tugendhat and Brunner were all persuaded to accept minor incursions to try to help him. I suggested that he should have special responsibility for relations with the Parliament. I had been against devolving this, but it seemed to me a reasonable price to pay to avoid having decisions taken by vote with no unanimity. As a result, after about the third adjournment, all of these taking place within the room, I was able to say that we were offering him a choice between nine different responsibilities. I was not suggesting he should take them all, but he could take any combination of three or four of them, which I thought was a wholly reasonable offer.

At that stage sympathy had swung strongly to the side of the majority position and against him. Nonetheless there was a great reluctance to go to a voted decision. Therefore, at about 4.40, I decided as a last attempt to say that we would have a further and last adjournment and on this occasion we would leave the room. My motive was partly that I wanted a drink; but secondly and more importantly it would get Burke out of the room and give him an opportunity to consult with his *cabinet* and perhaps escape from the *contra mundem* mood into which he had fallen. By a great good chance this worked; he came back and said that he would accept Transport, Consumer Affairs, Relations with Parliament, and Taxation. As a result of all this we were able to reach an agreed, unanimous, though painfully arrived at, solution by just before 5.30 in the morning.

Although the process had taken a long time – a somewhat longer time than four years previously when the Ortoli Commission was set up – it was not at all bad by earlier standards. At the beginning of the Malfatti Commission in 1971, the process had been accomplished only after about twenty votes, and at the beginning of the Jean Rey Commission, in 1967, the whole process had taken two weeks – and an extremely wearing and unproductive two weeks it had been.

APPENDIX 2

Presidents, Ambassadors, Governments

The Presidents of the European Parliament

Georges Spénale (French Socialist) *until July 1977, then*
Emilio Colombo (Italian Christian Democrat) *until July 1979, then*
Simone Veil (French Liberal, or UDF, i.e. Giscardian)

The Presidents of the European Court

Hans Kutscher (German) *until October 1980, then*
Josse Mertens de Wilmars (Belgian)

Ambassadors or Permanent Representatives of the Member States
who collectively formed COREPER (Comité des Représentants
Permanents)

Belgium	Josef Van der Meulen *until 1979, then*
	Paul Noterdaeme
Denmark	Gunnar Riberholdt
Germany	Ulrich Lebsanft *until 1977, then*
	Helmut Sigrist *until 1979, then*
	Gisbert Poensgen
France	Le Vicomte Luc de La Barre de Nanteuil
Ireland	Brendan Dillon
Italy	Eugenio Plaja *until 1980, then*
	Renato Ruggiero
Luxembourg	Jean Dondelinger
Netherlands	Jan Lubbers *until 1980, then*
	Charles Rutten
United Kingdom	Sir Donald Maitland *until 1979, then*
	Sir Michael Butler

*The Other Ambassadors to the Community
most frequently dealt with*

United States	Deane Hinton *until 1979, then* Thomas Enders
Spain	Raimundo Bassols y Jacas
Portugal	Antonio de Siquiera Freire
Greece	Stephane Stathatos
Australia	Sir James Plimsoll
India	K. B. Lall *until 1977, then* P. K. Dave
Japan	Masahiro Nishibori *until 1979, then* Takaaki Kajawa
China	Huan Hsiang *until 1978, then* Mao Chao Kang
Canada	Marcel Cadieux *until 1979, then* Richard M. Tait

Most Western countries had three ambassadors in Brussels: one to the European Community, one to NATO, and one to the Kingdom of Belgium. This may explain occasional apparent confusion.

Governments of the Member States

BELGIUM
Head of state	His Majesty King Baudouin
Prime Minister	Leo Tindemans *until October 1978, then* Paul Vanden Boeynants *until April 1979, then* Wilfried Martens
Foreign Minister	Renaat Van Elslande *until June 1977, then* Henri Simonet *until May 1980, then* Charles-Ferdinand Nothomb

DENMARK
Head of state	Her Majesty Queen Margrethe
Prime Minister	Anker Jørgensen
Foreign Minister	K. B. Andersen *until August 1978, then* Henning Christophersen *until October 1979, then* Kjeld Olesen

FEDERAL REPUBLIC OF GERMANY

Head of state	Walter Scheel *until July 1979, then* Karl Carstens
Chancellor	Helmut Schmidt
Foreign Minister	Hans-Dietrich Genscher
Economic Affairs	Hans Friderichs *until October 1977, then* Graf Otto Lambsdorff
Finance	Hans Apel *until February 1978, then* Hans Matthöfer
Agriculture	Josef Ertl

FRANCE

Head of state	Valéry Giscard d'Estaing (also head of government)
Prime Minister	Raymond Barre
Foreign Minister	Louis de Guiringaud *until November 1978, then* Jean François-Poncet
Economics	Raymond Barre *until September 1978, then* René Monory
Agriculture	Christian Bonnet *until March 1977, then* Pierre Méhaignerie

IRELAND

Head of state	Patrick Hillery
Prime Minister (Taoiseach)	Liam Cosgrave *until June 1977, then* Jack Lynch *until December 1979, then* Charles Haughey
Foreign Minister	Garret Fitzgerald *until June 1977, then* Michael O'Kennedy *until December 1979, then* Brian Lenihan

ITALY

Head of state	Giovanni Leone *until June 1978, then* Alessandro Pertini
Prime Minister (President of the Council)	Giulio Andreotti *until June 1979, then* Francesco Cossiga *until September 1980, then* Arnaldo Forlani

Foreign Minister	Arnaldo Forlani *until June 1979, then*
	Franco Malfatti *until January 1980, then*
	Attilio Ruffini *until April 1980, then*
	Emilio Colombo
Treasury	Gaetano Stammati *until March 1978, then*
	Filippo Pandolfi
Agriculture	Giovanni Marcora

LUXEMBOURG

Head of state	HRH Grand Duke Jean
Prime Minister	Gaston Thorn *until June 1979, then*
	Pierre Werner
Foreign Minister	Gaston Thorn *until November 1980, then*
	Colette Flesch

NETHERLANDS

Head of state	Her Majesty Queen Juliana
	until she abdicated in April 1980, then
	Her Majesty Queen Beatrix
Prime Minister	Joop den Uyl *until December 1977, then*
	Andries van Agt
Foreign Minister	Max van der Stoel *until December 1977, then*
	Christoph van der Klaauw

UNITED KINGDOM

Head of state	Her Majesty Queen Elizabeth II
Prime Minister	James Callaghan *until May 1979, then*
	Margaret Thatcher
Foreign Minister	Anthony Crosland *until February 1977, then*
	David Owen *until May 1979, then*
	Lord Carrington
Chancellor of the Exchequer	Denis Healey *until May 1979, then*
	Sir Geoffrey Howe
Agriculture	John Silkin *until May 1979, then*
	Peter Walker

The presidency of the Council of Ministers (and hence of the European Council, Committee of Permanent Representatives or

Ambassadors, and any other meeting or representatives of Community governments) rotated on a six-monthly basis. During my presidency of the Commission the Council presidencies were as follows:

January–June 1977:	United Kingdom
July–December 1977:	Belgium
January–June 1978:	Denmark
July–December 1978:	Germany
January–June 1979:	France
July–December 1979:	Ireland
January–June 1980:	Italy
July–December 1980:	Luxembourg

Governments of the Applicant Countries

GREECE

Head of state	Konstantinos Tsatsos *until May 1980, then* Konstantinos Karamanlis
Prime Minister	Konstantinos Karamanlis *until May 1980, then* George Rallis
Foreign Minister	Dimitrios Bitsios *until November 1977, then* Panayotis Papaligouras *until May 1978, then* George Rallis *until May 1980, then* Konstantinos Mitsotakis
Minister for EEC	Giorgios Koutogeorgis

PORTUGAL

Head of state	General António Eanes
Prime Minister	Mário Soares *until August 1978, then* Alfredo Nobre da Costa *until October 1978, then* Carlos Mota Pinto *until July 1979, then* Maria Pintasilgo *until December 1979, then* Francisco Sá Carneiro
Foreign Minister	José Medeiros Ferraira *until February 1978,* Victor Sá Machado *until August 1978, then* Carlos Correia Gago *until October 1978, then* João de Freitas-Cruz *until December 1979, then* Diogo Freitas do Amaral

SPAIN

Head of state	King Juan Carlos
Prime Minister	Adolfo Suárez Gonzales
Foreign Minister	Marcelino Oreja Aguirre *until September 1980, then* José Pedro Pérez-Llorca
Minister for EEC	Leopoldo Calvo Sotelo y Bustelo *until September 1980, then* Eduardo Punset Casals

INDEX

Compiled by Douglas Matthews

502; dines with RJ, 487; lunch with RJ,
533; at Weidenfeld dinner, 586; at East
Hendred, 608; wartime experiences,
622; at Annans', 627; visits Brussels, 652
Bonham Carter, Virginia, 621 & n
Bonino, Emma, 483
Bonn: RJ visits, 67, 168–9, 223–4, 226,
285, 331, 345, 419–20, 556, 564–5;
Western Economic Summit in, 115, 200,
212, 225, 279, 292–5
Bonnet, Christian, 58 & n
Bordu, Gerard, 72 & n, 163
Boulin, Robert, 238 & n
Bouteflika, Abdul Aziz, 111
Boutos, Ioannis, 318
Boutros-Ghali, Boutros, 211, 397, 513–14
Boxer, Mark, 475 & n, 642
Braden, Tom and Joan, 361 & n
Bradlee, Ben, 86, 273
Bradley, Joy, 639, 654
Bradley, Tom, 192 & n, 299, 526–7, 541,
587, 609, 625, 635, 639, 654
Braithwaite, (Sir) Roderic, 341
Brandon, Henry, 361 & n
Brandt, Willy, 54n, 103 & n; RJ dines with,
54–5; as possible successor to Schmidt,
68; meets Carter, 69; RJ visits, 103; and
Committee (and Report) on Third
World, 103, 595, 613 & n; at Federation
of Socialist Parties, 280; visits RJ in
Brussels, 295, 481; speeches at European
Parliament, 483, 563; and Kreisky, 508;
and Haferkamp, 665
Bremen: European Council meeting, 279,
283–4, 286–90, 659
Bretton Woods agreement, 23
Brewster, Kingman, 201-2, 300, 419, 445,
541
Brezhnev, Leonid, 123, 564, 571, 615
Briggs, Lord (Asa Briggs), 113 & n, 333,
419, 445, 533, 575n
Brinkhorst, Laurens, 342 & n, 349, 436
Bristol University, 616
Britain: 1979 election, 374; budgetary
contributions (BBQ), 375, 450, 464,
529–30, 542, 545–8, 551n, 565, 570,
575–6, 584–5, 588, 599, 602, 617, 619,
659; discussed at Luxembourg European
Council, 592–3; discussed at Foreign
Affairs Council, 504, 630; settlement,
606–7
Britain in Europe organization, 2
British Biological Research Institute, 599
British Conservative Group (Strasbourg), 501
British Institute of Management, 162
British Labour Group (Strasbourg), 141,
218, 505
Brittan, Samuel, 320 & n
Broussé, Max, 165
Brown, George (later Lord
George-Brown), 130, 174 & n, 222,
480, 624
Broxbourne, Lord (Sir Derek
Walker-Smith), 315 & n

Bruce, David, 86 & n, 221, 552
Bruce, Evangeline, 86n, 133, 234, 298,
361, 552n, 562, 620
Bruce, Neil, 393 & n, 394
Bruce of Donnington, Lord (Donald
Bruce), 326 & n, 338, 399
Brunner, Guido: languages, xv, xviii; as
Commissioner, xviii, 14; and press, 27;
advises RJ on Programme speech, 38;
proposals on Euratom, 101; RJ dines
with, 108, 421; in INFCEP, 132;
conversation, 143, 292; and monetary
union, 143; discussions with, 292; at Lee
Kuan Yew dinner, 316; entertains
Heath to dinner, 398; at Monnet Mass,
435; and British/Australian uranium
agreement, 464; and Spierenburg's
report, 509; and allocation of
portfolios, 661–2, 664–7
Brunner, Mrs Guido (née Speidel), 108
Brzezinski, Zbigniew, 83 & n, 84, 204, 561
Budget Control Sub-Committee, 399
Budget Council, 536
Bühl, Dieter, 219
Bullock, Lord (Sir Alan Bullock), 640 & n
Bumbry, Grace, 298
Bundy, McGeorge, 88 & n
Burger, Warren, 312, 562
Burke, Richard: as Commissioner, xviii;
and press, 27; inaugural speech, 28;
portfolio, 31–2, 460–1, 666–8; and
Parliamentary vote of censure, 61;
opposes monetary union, 143; attends
Commission, 262; Simonet on
understanding, 272; at hurling final,
306; at European Parliament, 637; and
Belfast, 638
Butler, Ann (Lady), 520
Butler, (Sir) Michael, 519 & n, 520, 564,
583, 606
Butler, Mollie, Lady, 297
Butler of Saffron Walden, Lord (Richard
Austen Butler), 297 & n
Butt, Ronald, 272
butter: sales of, 54, 58, 60, 63, 148, 563,
566, 579; New Zealand, 649

Caborn, Richard, 611
Cahors (France), 447
Cairo, 211, 513–15
Caldera Rodriguez, Rafael, 393
Callaghan, James (later Lord Callaghan of
Cardiff), 2n; appoints Tugendhat, xix;
foreign policy, 4; elected Labour leader,
5; offers RJ Chancellorship of
Exchequer, 12–13, 166; attitude to
Europe, 22; and representation of
European Commission at Summits, 40,
61, 76, 81; entertains Foreign
Ministers, 60–1; Schmidt and, 67–8;
Rodgers supports, 69; at Rome European
Council, 73, 75, 76–8; RJ visits in
Downing Street, 80–1; at London
Summit, 96–100; RJ's resentment

Deng Xiaoping, 407 & n, 408–9, 410–11
Deniau, Jean-François, 54 & n, 190; at
  Bonn Summit, 295; and MTNs, 342,
  421, 434; proposed Washington visit,
  358–9; Poniatowski on, 569
Denman, Sir Roy: on Haferkamp, xiv;
  attends first meeting, 126; in Moscow,
  159; meets Chinese Ambassador, 223;
  meets Whitlams, 264; at Bonn Summit,
  294; and Mme van Hoof, 314–15;
  dinner party for, 327; visits China, 402,
  409; lunch with, 443; on relations with
  Japan, 444
Desai, Morarji, 270 & n, 271, 295
Devlin, Lord (Patrick Devlin), 305 & n
Devonshire, Deborah, Duchess of, 283
DGB (German trade union) Conference,
  Hamburg, 266
Dilke, Sir Charles, 105, 182, 246, 452
Dillon, Brendan, 226, 519, 522, 563–4,
  566
Dimbleby Lecture: preparations for, 377,
  453, 462, 509, 517–18, 520, 523;
  delivered, 524; reception and reactions
  to, 525–8, 533, 535, 542, 548, 626
Diout, Abdou, 380n
Directors-General: appointment of, 19
Ditchley Park (Oxfordshire): December
  1976 Conference, 14–15, 19, 661, 662
Djuranovic, Veselin, 573
Dohnanyi, Klaus von, 45 & n; dines with
  RJ, 48–9, 241, 364; RJ meets, 102, 104;
  at Marshall Fund Lecture, 113; on
  Summitry, 152; and Regional Fund,
  190; in Foreign Affairs Council, 241; and
  Investment Bank funds, 262; lunches
  with RJ, 272, 617–18; invited to dine
  with Belgian royals, 291; discussions with
  RJ, 298; entertains RJ, 325; and EMS,
  326; and RJ's defence of Denman on
  Japan, 444; as possible SPD leader, 481;
  on British budget question, 503, 539, 547,
  576, 603–4; shocked at
  Bernard-Reymond, 515; Gilmour meets,
  603
Doko, Toshiwo, 158, 253
dollar: devaluation of, 197
Donaldson, Frances, Lady, 60n, 138, 204,
  298, 324, 518, 580, 586
Donaldson of Kingsbridge, Lord (Jack
  Donaldson), 60 & n, 138, 204, 298, 324,
  518, 570, 586
Donat-Cattin, Carlo, 295
Dondelinger, Albert-Marie, 519, 617
Douglas-Home, Charles, 281 & n, 431, 478
Douglas-Home, Jessica (née Gwynne),
  281n, 282, 478
Dreyfus, Pierre, 310
Drogheda, Garrett Moore, 11th Earl of, 133
  & n, 168, 272, 487
Du Fu, 413
Dublin, 105–6; European Councils in, 377,
  456, 492, 510, 512, 517, 528–32, 545; see
  also Trinity College

Ducci, Roberto, 494 & n
Duckham, Penelope (later Mrs Matthew
  Hill), xxi
Duisenberg, Wilhelm, 65 & n, 70, 611
Duncan-Sandys, Lord (Duncan Sandys),
  49 & n
Dunrossil, Viscount (John Morrison), 168
  & n
Dunwoody, Gwyneth, 218 & n

Eanes, General António, 171 & n, 172,
  577–9
Ebermann, Klaus, xxi, 206
Ecevit, Bülent, 269 & n, 271
Economic and European Monetary Union
  (EMU), 175–6, 178, 181, 185, 187, 191,
  194, 202–3, 214, 223
Economic and Finance Council (Ecofin),
  29n, 65; meetings, 160, 238, 313, 324,
  340; and monetary union, 174; RJ
  addresses, 187; lunch with, 297
Economic and Social Committee
  (European Council), 194, 255, 508
Economic Club of New York, 560
Economist, 165, 223, 252, 373, 400, 458,
  552, 631
Eden, (Sir) Anthony (1st Earl of Avon),
  134
Eden, Douglas, 616 & n
Eden of Winton, Lord (Sir John Eden), 429
  & n
Edwards, Nicholas, 478
EFTA (European Free Trade Association),
  149
Egypt, 200, 207, 210–11, 215, 376,
  513–15
Ehmke, Horst, 103
Eisenhower, Dwight D., 626
Elizabeth II, Queen, 97–8, 124, 130; visits
  Brussels, 635–6, 648
Elliott, Anthony, 80n, 303
Elliott, Thea, 80 & n, 443, 520, 552, 620
Ellis, Tom, 580 & n
Elslande, Renaat Van, 42 & n, 62
Elwyn-Jones, Lord (Frederick Elwyn
  Jones), 263, 299, 339
Emerson, Michael, xx, 66, 135, 173–4, 242
Emery, Fred, 624, 636–7
Emminger, Otmar, 198, 324–5, 337
Enders, Thomas, 557, 629, 640
enlargement, 149–51, 160–1, 170, 199,
  237, 266, 376, 618, 659; see also Greece;
  Portugal; Spain
Environment Council, 186
Erasmus, Desiderius, 278
Ersbøll, Niels, 108, 280, 536
Ertl, Josef, 334 & n, 345
Essex University, 296–7
ETUC, 217, 242, 448
Euratom (European Atomic Energy
  Community), 101 & n, 394 & n, 424,
  457, 475, 488
European Cooperative Savings Institute,
  253